Introduction
to Criminal Justice

Second Edition

Robert D. Pursley
University of Arkansas at Little Rock

GLENCOE PUBLISHING CO., INC.
Encino, California
Collier Macmillan Publishers
London

Robert D. Pursley has a Doctor of Public Administration degree from the University of Georgia. He is a former municipal police officer and U.S. Treasury agent. Presently an Associate Professor in the Department of Political Science and Criminal Justice at the University of Arkansas at Little Rock, Dr. Pursley has held teaching positions at the University of Georgia and Michigan State University. He will be the National Chairperson of the American Society for Public Administration's Section on Criminal Justice Administration in 1980–1981.

To my dearest son, Michael

Acquila non capit muscas

Glencoe Publishing Co., Inc.
17337 Ventura Boulevard
Encino, California 91316
Collier Macmillan Canada, Ltd.

Library of Congress Catalog Card Number: 78-71743

ISBN 02-470700-7

1 2 3 4 5 6 7 8 9 10   83 82 81 80 79

CONTENTS

Glencoe Criminal Justice Texts

*Glencoe Criminal Justice Series
G. Douglas Gourley, General Editor
Former Professor Emeritus and
Former Chairman
Department of Criminal Justice
California State University, Los Angeles

PREFACE

The second edition of *Introduction to Criminal Justice* reinforces the primary purpose of the first edition; that is, to explain the agencies, processes, and administration of the criminal justice system to the student taking the introductory course at the college level.

The goals of this text are three. The first is to provide a comprehensive survey of the criminal justice field for students majoring in this subject. The second is to give nonmajors a basic understanding of the role and functions of the criminal justice system in our society. Lastly, it is meant to fulfill the need for a thorough yet balanced explanation of the criminal justice system to all interested individuals.

FEATURES

The second edition has been thoroughly reorganized and restructured. The changes include:

- A new introductory chapter that concisely describes the purpose and components of the criminal justice system. This chapter also explains the process by which a criminal case moves through that system.

- A new section on crime causation theory and the major theorists who have written on the causes of crime in society.

- Chapter review questions that test the student's grasp of the content of each chapter.

- Chapter discussion questions on current issues affecting the criminal justice system and those within it.

- Synopses of important recent legal cases and court decisions that have had impact on the criminal justice system.

- Updated tables and statistical data on crime, crime rates, characteristics of prisoners, and other information.

- Appendices including the entire text of the U.S. Constitution, a guide to major court cases, lists of journals and other publications for research, and a glossary of key terms.

- A revised Instructor's Manual consisting of chapter outlines, answers to review and discussion questions, and an extensive test bank.

ORGANIZATION

Introduction to Criminal Justice is divided into six parts and seventeen chapters. Part One consists of a single chapter titled "An Introduction." Its purpose is to describe the goals and functions of the criminal justice system in a way comprehensible to readers who are not familiar with the complexities of the system.

Part Two, "Crime and Criminal Laws," focuses on crime as a social problem. The elements of crime, modern causal theory, crime classifications, and basic legal terms and documents are discussed in Chapter 2. Chapter 3, "Crime in America," looks at trends in crime in the United States, the Uniform Crime Reports and why they are criticized, new methods of collecting crime statistics, and victim compensation. The last chapter in this part examines "victimless" crimes, their social and economic costs, and the arguments for and against retaining their criminal status.

Part Three, "Law Enforcement," explores the role of the police in American society. The major functions of the police, influences on modern law enforcement methods, and the various local, state, and federal police agencies are discussed at length. Chapter 6 explains the role of the police in crime detection and investigation, the rules governing search and seizure operations, the factors affecting the legality of an arrest, police operational styles, and departmental organization. Current issues and trends including job enlargement, affirmative action, crime prevention methods, police corruption, and consolidation versus decentralization are discussed in Chapter 7.

The courts play a vital role in the criminal justice system. Part Four examines that role. Chapter 8 describes the characteristics of the American judicial system, the history, growth, and structure of state court systems, and the components of the federal judiciary. Pretrial, trial, and post-trial processes in criminal cases are explained in Chapter 9. Chapter 10 summarizes the roles of the principal "actors" in the trial process—the judge, the prosecutor, and the defense attorney—and the importance of plea bargaining in relieving court congestion. Part Four concludes with a review of current court-related issues and trends, such as bail reform, jury size, and jury unanimity.

Part Five, "Corrections," provides the student with historical background in corrections as well as giving an account of present forms of corrections. Over centuries, the purpose of corrections has evolved from the concept of punishing offenders to the concept of rehabilitating and reintegrating them into the community. In addition to these topics, Chapter 12 looks at landmarks in American correctional history such as the Pennsylvania system, the Auburn plan, and the reformatory movement. Chapter 13 examines the role and purpose of the jail, or temporary detention facility. Today's jail systems are beset by numerous serious problems, all of which are described. Chapter 14 is concerned with common types of prisons (from maximum security to camps), prison administration, the makeup of institutional staffs, prison programs for inmates, the composite picture of the typical male and female offender, and obstacles to correctional reform.

Two of the more important topics in corrections, parole and probation, are jointly described in Chapter 15. Beginning with the predecessors of parole, the chapter goes on to examine the functions of parole, guidelines in granting parole, the salient-factor score, the parole officer's role, and new trends in parole such as parole teams. The second half of this chapter looks at the origins of probation, state probation agencies, and probation as a career. Chapter 16 examines in detail community-based corrections, including its rationale, multiple programs, facilities, and future. The chapter concludes with a review of other trends and issues in corrections.

Part Six, "The Juvenile Justice System," consists of one chapter entirely devoted to the subject of juvenile justice. Among the topics discussed in this chapter are the growth of delinquency, the origins of the juvenile court, the juvenile justice process, and juvenile institutions and diversion programs.

ACKNOWLEDGMENTS

In the first edition I expressed my gratitude to my colleagues. For this second edition I feel I am indebted to my students. Through their use of the text, many helpful suggestions and observations were forthcoming. I have tried to incorporate them in this edition. I would be remiss, however, in not acknowledging two important colleagues who have always been a source of encouragement and inspiration. To Professors Kevin L. Parsons and Frank S. Horvath, I acknowledge a deep sense of gratitude. A special note of thanks goes to the following teachers who contributed valuable criticisms and advice for the new edition:

John Kragie, Indiana Purdue University

Bonnie Bondavalli, Illinois State University

William Conour, Indiana Purdue University

Nancy Schafer, Indiana Purdue University

And to Ms. Brigitte I. Rice for her help in proofreading the manuscript and preparing the index.

Finally, I wish to express my appreciation to Peter O'Brien, Glencoe's development editor, who worked very hard and made many insightful suggestions concerning this second edition.

PART 1

The Criminal Justice System

Law enforcement agencies such as the police are the first major component of the criminal justice system. Their role is to enforce the law and to maintain social order.

The courts, the second major component, are charged with determining the guilt or innocence of those accused of committing crime. In the trial process, the prosecutor and defense attorney, in adversary roles, argue the case and try to persuade the jury to return the verdict that each is seeking. The judge acts as an arbiter.

Corrections is the third component of criminal justice. Prisons and jails are used to house offenders for the term of their sentence or until they are released on parole. While correctional facilities are a means to remove offenders from society, they are also supposed to reform and rehabilitate criminals who will eventually return to the community.

1
AN INTRODUCTION

1. What are the primary and secondary goals of the criminal justice system?
2. What are the major agencies of the criminal justice system and what are their functions?
3. What are the auxiliary agencies of the criminal justice system and what are their functions?
4. How does a criminal case move through the criminal justice system?

These are some of the questions this chapter will answer.

Our criminal justice system is composed of a series of interrelated parts. These parts constitute a social system of cause and effect and interaction. Let's use the idea of an atomlike structure to try and explain this. The atom consists of a nucleus surrounded by electrons, the arrangement and behavior of which determine the nature and interaction of the whole. The nucleus is society and the agencies of criminal justice are the electrons. In this analogy, the nucleus exerts a controlling influence on the properties of the electrons. Likewise, a free society determines and defines the roles and performance standards that become the guidelines in the administration of criminal justice. Yet the relationship is not merely one-sided. The component parts of the criminal justice system are themselves highly interactive. Thus, the operational principles of one component, such as the police, affect other components, such as the courts, as well as society in general. These complex interactions make criminal justice administration an extremely important new branch of the social sciences.

In fact, these relationships are so intricate that the student of criminal justice must be prepared to learn a great deal about society if he or she is to understand the criminal justice process. The beginning student should be cautioned that the criminal justice system can never be understood as an isolated entity; nor can it be understood merely by studying legal texts and court decisions or by memorizing theories of crime causation, juvenile delinquency, or the principles of police or correctional management. The

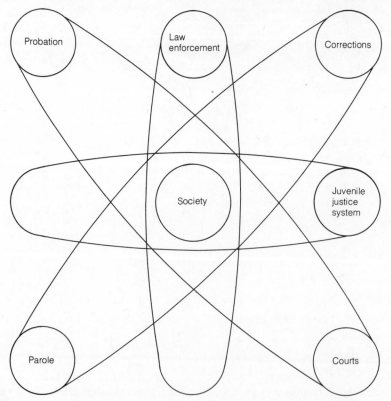

FIGURE 1-1 Relationship of the Agencies of Criminal Justice and Society

challenge—and most certainly the reward—lies in applying our knowledge of human behavior, social development, political philosophy, and similar interrelated concerns into the operations of our criminal justice system.

GOALS OF THE CRIMINAL JUSTICE SYSTEM

In a free society, the primary goal of a criminal justice system is to *protect the members of that society.* In this respect, it is a formal instrumentality authorized by the people of a nation to protect both their collective and individual well-being. Another major goal of any system of criminal justice is the *maintenance of order.* Although we in the United States subscribe to the first goal as our primary reason for a criminal justice system, totalitarian regimes such as that of the Soviet Union are more likely to see the maintenance of order and the protection of the ruling body as their primary objectives. However, Americans also recognize the need for political and institutional stability as a goal of an organized society. Since crime and disorder disrupt stability in society, we have vested the criminal justice system with the authority to act as the means by which the existing order is maintained.

In addition, within these two major goals, there are a number of important subgoals:

- The prevention of crime
- The suppression of criminal conduct by apprehending offenders for whom prevention is ineffective
- The review of the legality of our preventive and suppressive measures
- The judicial determination of guilt or innocence of those apprehended
- The proper disposition of those who have been legally found guilty
- The correction by socially approved means of the behavior of those who violate the criminal law

COMPONENTS OF THE CRIMINAL JUSTICE SYSTEM

To accomplish these primary and subgoals, a system of criminal justice has been established. Figure 1-2 depicts the formal agencies of justice that constitute the system, and the usual sequence in the overall process.

The criminal justice system consists of three major components—law enforcement, courts, and corrections—and the specialized auxiliary services of probation, parole, and the juvenile justice system. In many cases, probation and parole are grouped under the corrections component because, as alternatives to incarceration, these programs seek to "correct" the offender. The juvenile justice system has been established to deal with offenders below a prescribed statutory age.

Each one of the components of the criminal justice system shares certain common goals. For example, they collectively exist to protect society, to maintain order, and to prevent crime. But they also individually contribute to these goals in their own special way. In the discussion of component functions that follows, you should pay careful attention to the system's overall goals as well as the individual contributions of each component.

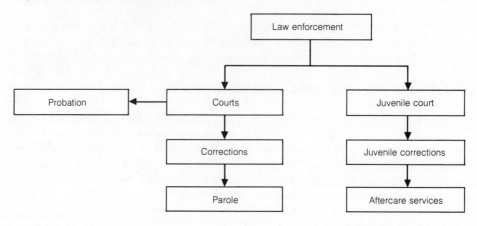

FIGURE 1-2 Agencies of Criminal Justice in the United States

FUNCTIONS OF THE MAJOR COMPONENTS

There are three major components of the criminal justice system: law enforcement, the courts, and corrections.

Law Enforcement

Law enforcement is the first component. It consists of all police agencies at the federal, state, county, and municipal levels. These agencies fulfill the following functions:

1. *To prevent criminal behavior.* Prevention involves all the efforts directed toward eliminating the causes of crimes. Among these efforts are delinquency prevention programs and citizen education programs . The purpose of the first is to reduce the likelihood of youths engaging in criminal activities. The second counsels citizens on ways to avoid being victims of crime and what to do should they be victims of crime.

2. *To reduce crime.* Crime reduction essentially means eliminating and reducing opportunities for criminal behavior. Such police programs as preventive and conspicuous patrol activity; intelligence and information gathering on crime-producing situations and known criminals; and target-hardening strategies that attempt to make certain physical sites less vulnerable to criminals are examples of police crime reduction efforts.

3. *To apprehend and arrest offenders.* The police engage in criminal investigations; the gathering of evidence; presenting this evidence in the courtroom; and testifying before the courts against those who violate the criminal law.

4. *To protect life and property.* This includes the full range of police services in such areas as crime prevention, crime reduction, and investigation and apprehension strategies designed to protect society. It also includes the provision of specialized services that are designed to assure public safety.

5. *To regulate noncriminal conduct.* Every day the police are involved in efforts to ensure compliance by regulatory means with laws of public safety and security. This function includes activities such as traffic regulation and crowd control.

Courts

The courts include those judicial agencies at all levels of government that perform the following functions in the administration of criminal justice:

1. *To protect the rights of the accused.* The courts are responsible for reviewing the actions of law enforcement agencies to ensure that the police have not violated the legal rights of the accused. Similarly, the courts are given the authority and responsibility to review the actions of other agencies of criminal justice to ensure that their actions do not violate the rights of the convicted offender.

2. *To determine by all available legal means whether a person is guilty of a crime.* Review of all evidence presented by the police or private citizens to determine its relevance and admissibility according to established guidelines of acceptability. The court also examines the circumstances that surround the crime as it relates to the issues it must adjudicate.

3. *To dispose properly of those convicted of crimes.* The courts have the responsibility to examine the background of the accused and the circumstances of the crime. From this information and according to existing and applicable laws, the court considers possible sentencing alternatives and then selects the most proper form of disposition for the convicted offender.

4. *To protect society.* After the accused has been found guilty and after a consideration of all factors, the court must determine whether the offender should be removed from society and incarcerated in order to protect the safety of life and property.

5. *To prevent and reduce criminal behavior.* This is the task of imposing proper penalties and sanctions that will serve to deter future criminal acts by the offender and also serve as an example and a deterrent to others who would commit criminal acts or threaten public safety.

Corrections

Corrections consist of those executive agencies at all levels of government that are responsible both directly and indirectly for the following functions:

1. *To maintain institutions.* The correctional component is responsible for maintaining prisons, jails, halfway houses, and other institutional facilities to receive convicted offenders sentenced to a period of incarceration by the courts.

2. *To protect law-abiding members of society.* Corrections is responsible for providing custody and security in order to keep sentenced offenders from preying on other members of society through the further commission of crimes.

3. *To reform offenders.* During their period of incarceration in a correctional institution, corrections is given the function of developing and providing services to assist incarcerated offenders to reform. Additionally, corrections is responsible for developing programs that will assist the offender in returning to society upon his or her release and to lead a noncriminal life.

4. *To deter crime.* Corrections is responsible for encouraging incarcerated and potential offenders to lead law-abiding lives through the experience of prison and the denial of liberty.

FUNCTIONS OF THE AUXILIARY COMPONENTS

The auxiliary components of the criminal justice system are probation, parole, and the juvenile justice system.

Probation

Probation is a court-related component. It encompasses those services at all levels of government that supervise an offender who has been found guilty of a crime. It is responsible for the following:

1. *To provide a sentencing alternative other than commitment to a correctional institution.* Probation provides an alternative to the court other than having to sentence the convicted offender to a period of imprisonment. It accomplishes this by providing a system whereby the offender can remain in the community under the supervisory authority of probation officials and the sentencing court.

2. *To deter and regulate potential criminal conduct.* Through direct community supervision and assistance, probation attempts to help the offender adjust to the strains of everyday life and to avoid situations that potentially might lead to criminal behavior.

3. *To provide reports and guidance for judicial decision making.* Probation personnel often conduct court-directed investigations of the convicted offender's background and circumstances of the crime. Such information is then used by the court in determining the proper disposition of an offender. Probation officers also keep the court advised of the probationer's progress during the period of probation and of any failure of the probationer to live up to the conditions of the probation agreement.

Parole

Parole is an executive agency function that is responsible for providing community supervision and assistance to an offender who has been conditionally released from a correctional facility prior to the statutory expiration of his or her sentence. The purpose of parole is:

1. *To provide an alternative to maintaining an offender in custody.* Parole provides a means to release an offender to the community under the su-

pervision of a parole agency at a time during the offender's period of incarceration when it is determined that the inmate is ready for release.

2. *To provide needed services to an ex-offender.* Like probation, parole efforts are directed toward assisting the ex-offender to readjust to the strains of life in a free society. Such services might include obtaining employment, help in abstaining from drugs or alcohol, and providing general counseling.

3. *To deter and regulate potential criminal conduct.* Parole attempts to assist in the prevention of criminal conduct by regulating the parolee's behavior and conduct.

4. *To prepare reports and guidelines for decision making.* Parole personnel are often responsible for preparole investigations of the circumstances into which a potential parolee might be released. Such considerations would include the community and law enforcement attitudes toward having the individual released back to the community under parole supervision, the attitude of the parolee's family, and the availability of a legitimate job. These factors are then transmitted to an independent parole board as an aid in determining whether the inmate should be paroled. Parole personnel are also responsible for advising the parole board of the satisfactory or unsatisfactory progress of parolees under their supervision and to initiate or request parole revocation proceedings if warranted.

Juvenile Justice System

The juvenile justice system consists of a broad range of specialized juvenile agencies of an adjudicatory treatment and incarceration nature. These agencies handle cases of delinquency and other matters involving minors and, in some cases, adults who have committed crimes against minors. This component of the criminal justice system also includes agencies and services that provide predelinquency (prevention), delinquency, and postdelinquency (treatment) services to youth. Its major functions are:

1. *To deter delinquent behavior.* By employing a wide range of programs that involve the juvenile court, the police, community agencies, and other sources, the juvenile justice system attempts to deter those youths who would commit delinquent acts. This is accomplished by both the provision of appropriate services and the use of specific sanctions.

2. *To provide needed care to the child.* The juvenile justice system is responsible for examining and determining the needs of youth who become involved with the system and providing appropriate services to deal with these needs.

3. *To determine whether the child is to be adjudicated a delinquent.* The juvenile court as a component of the juvenile justice system is responsible for examining the facts that surround the offense and examining admissible evidence.

4. *To provide for the proper disposition of the adjudicated delinquent.* If available evidence and circumstances indicate that the child is delinquent, the

juvenile court must determine the proper disposition of the youthful offender.

5. *To maintain institutions.* The juvenile justice system is typically responsible for maintaining a broad range of institutions for handling those children who come in contact with the system. These institutions can range from foster or group homes to more penal-like institutions for the dangerous and hardened youthful offender.

6. *To protect public safety.* The juvenile justice system is also responsible for institutionalizing the adjudicated delinquent if this is warranted by the need to protect society.

CONFLICT OVER THE ROLE OF THE CRIMINAL JUSTICE SYSTEM

Although there is generally broad agreement over the goals of the criminal justice system, there is far less agreement over how best to attain these goals. Based on the American governmental principle of checks and balances, the enforcement, judicial, and correctional aspects of the system are not vested within the authority of one agency. For example, giving the police the authority to arrest and to prosecute and to reform individuals would be an unacceptable practice. Such a system would obviously pose a dangerous threat to individual liberty in a free society.

However, although society provides the criminal justice system with certain guidelines as to how it is to operate, these guidelines are often expressed as contradictory values. For example, choices must be made among such competing values as the rights of the accused and the protection of society. This means that the administration of criminal justice must rest on some implicit idea of what justice is and what society requires. This is a difficult task, because people often interpret the meaning of justice and how it is to be accomplished very differently and inconsistently. As a consequence, the machinery of criminal justice has no all-encompassing consensual guidelines on how to operate in each case.

CRIMINAL JUSTICE MODELS

Although no one will argue that the primary purpose of the system is to protect society, differing opinions on how to do this often subject individual agencies and the entire administrative process to criticism by one group or another. This problem has been placed in perspective by Herbert Packer. He suggests that the administration of criminal justice is complicated by the competition between two opposing value systems that underlie the process. These values he refers to as the *crime control* and *due process* models of criminal justice.[1]

Crime Control Model

Packer's *crime control model* is based on the idea that the most important function of the criminal justice system is the repression of criminal conduct. This model is justified by pointing out that the failure of the police and other agencies of criminal justice to bring criminal conduct under control leads to the breakdown of public order and, as a result, the disappearance of social tranquility, which is an important condition of human freedom. In order to guarantee the maintenance of the existing social order, the administration of criminal justice must stress "efficiency"—that is, the increased capacity to apprehend, try, convict, and dispose of a high proportion of criminal offenders, with an emphasis placed on speed and finality in dealing with them.

Underlying the assumption of this model is the feeling that the offender is guilty—an assumption that contradicts the basic presumption of innocence that is supposed to surround the accused under our system of criminal jurisprudence. However, it should be pointed out that the crime control model sees this presumption of guilt as occurring only after extensive fact-finding procedures are employed by the police and prosecutors. In this way, all cases that probably would not result in a successful conviction are screened out at a preliminary stage, leaving only those where the offender is almost certainly guilty. Thus, all fact-finding is accomplished before the trial rather than through the trial process itself. Consequently, the trial and disposition process might resemble an assembly line.

Although such a system might appeal to many Americans, it suffers from the fact that it shifts the fact-finding responsibilities from an independent source (the court) and an independent review body (the jury or the judge) to the police and the prosecution element of the system. Although it might improve expediency, it is also fraught with serious dangers for possible abuse. It is not hard to imagine the inherent dangers in our time and age for the misuse of such a system.

Due Process Model

Whereas the crime control model resembles an assembly line at the judicial stage, the *due process model* has the features of an obstacle course. Under this model, each stage of the criminal justice process from arrest through the court's disposition of the accused is designed to present formidable impediments to carrying the accused any further along in the process. It rejects the police and prosecutorial role under the crime control model, and places the screening burden on the court.

Interestingly, some aspects of the crime control model are similar to the criminal justice process that exists in Great Britain and some European countries where the presumption of innocence must be demonstrated by the accused. The American ideal of criminal jurisprudence requires that the accused be considered innocent until proved guilty. Packer views both systems as striving for quality control, but in very different ways. He suggests that the due process model emphasizes "reliability" (i.e., society must be willing to live with the fact that some guilty offenders will be found innocent in order to ensure that innocent persons are not unjustly convicted), while the crime control model emphasizes "efficiency" and "productivity" (i.e., society must be willing to accept the fact that some innocent people will be incorrectly found guilty, but that the overall improvement in the administration of justice would more than compensate for such mistakes).

There are many Americans who unthinkingly criticize the due process model because it can permit some offenders to escape justice by having their cases dismissed on the grounds of a legal technicality rather than on the facts of their guilt. However, the question remains, what is the alternative? There are also those who would like to see greater expediency in arresting, trying, and convicting the offender. Others are concerned that an increase in such "efficiency" would necessarily diminish freedom and raise the specter of an oppressive state apparatus of criminal justice.

As the power of government grows, these issues seem to become more and more important. There is a redeeming factor, however, in that both groups seek to achieve the elusive concept of "justice." The methods may differ but the objective is the same. In any event, this fundamental philosophical difference besets the administration of criminal justice and injects the entire administrative process into the very social fabric of our nation.

THE OPERATION OF THE CRIMINAL JUSTICE SYSTEM

Now that the goals, agencies, and value systems that underlie the administration of criminal justice in America have been discussed, let's examine an overview of the operation of the system itself.

The layperson usually perceives the system as operating in this manner: The police investigate a violation of the law, and if sufficient evidence exists, arrest the violator and bring the accused before the courts. After a trial and the determination of the defendant's guilt, the court sentences the convicted offender to a form of community supervision such as probation or to an institution for incarceration. After serving a portion of the sentence, the offender might be released on parole, or released completely without parole supervision upon completing the full sentence. In this way, the system of criminal justice can be thought of as a massive machine that proceeds in a linear manner as it moves the offender from arrest to final disposition. This linear flow is represented in Figure 1-3.

Although, in a sense, this procedure shown in Figure 1-3 is technically what occurs, there is a great deal of "slippage" within the system at various decision points in the process. A major characteristic of the administration of criminal justice is the discretion that exists at each critical decision stage in the system. This leads to a situation where *relatively few of those charged with serious crimes are processed completely through all of the stages from arrest to a prison sentence.*

This is because of, in part, the due process model of criminal justice to which we subscribe. This model is analogous to an obstacle course for the state in its prosecution of criminal cases. However, due process procedures alone do not explain the "slippage" within the system. The criminal justice system operates like a complex filter, screening out offenders at various points. Consider Figure 1-4 for a moment. This figure represents the findings of the President's Commission on Law Enforcement and Administration of Justice, which related serious crimes committed in the United States to the numbers of arrests made and the disposition of offenders through the system. More recent research has generally verified the accuracy of the commission's findings.

Several points should come to mind. First, of all *serious crimes committed*, only about one-half are even reported to the police. Of the half that are reported, the police make arrests in only about one-fourth of the cases. Thus, out of every 100 serious crimes committed, the police make about 13 arrests. Of these 13 arrests, five are typically juveniles who are then referred to the juvenile justice system; this leaves approximately eight adults arrested for the commission of the original 100 serious offenses. Finally, less than one is sentenced to prison! Of course, it must be recognized that some of those arrested and convicted were sentenced to alternative dispositions such as probation or to institutions such as jails that are used for short-term periods of incarceration. Yet, the fact remains that the linear processing of offenders accused of serious crimes drastically breaks down in the actual operations of the system.

As increasing numbers of research projects have uncovered the existence of such circumstances, growing criticism has been leveled at the criminal justice system in recent years. This awareness of the facts has refueled the due process–crime control dispute.

However, as already stated—and it is worth repeating—our general insistence that due process rights must be afforded to a person charged with a crime is *not* the major underlying reason for the "filter effect." It is important to understand this.

What are the factors, then, that cause the filtering of cases as they are processed through the criminal justice system? This question and related issues will be explained in the following chapters.

Low Percentage of Arrests Made for Serious Crimes

Why are law enforcement agencies able to make arrests in only 25 percent of all reported crimes? Even if the arrest of one criminal results in his being convicted of two or more crimes which makes the statistical comparison between crimes and arrests appear worse than it really is, this is still a terribly low success rate. Although it is not known how much of a role such statistical differences actually play in the overall crime picture, the fact remains that the police arrest only a small percentage of offenders who commit serious crimes in this country.

In part, the answer to this low crime–arrest ratio almost certainly lies in the traditional inefficiency of the police in solving crimes. However, this inefficiency cannot be considered simply as ineptness. Our criminal justice processes and the powers of the police are severely curtailed by society's concern for the rights of the individual and our unwillingness to permit the police a great deal of autonomous authority. Consequently, it would seem that a free society must be willing to forego greater police efficiency for the assurance that police powers will not be used to curtail individual rights. A very precarious balance exists between police power and a free society—one that requires constant vigilance, as history has repeatedly demonstrated.

Another part of the answer lies in the very nature of most crimes. Much criminal behavior is covert, with the odds drastically in favor of the offender. The police, because of limitations in resources, personnel, and operating

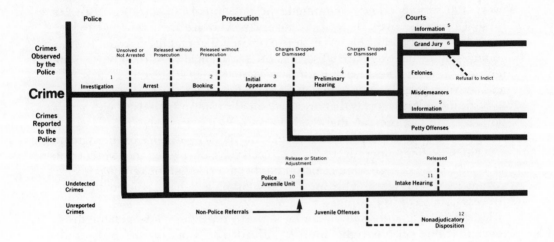

1 May continue until trial.

2 Administrative record of arrest. First step at which temporary release on bail may be available.

3 Before magistrate, commissioner, or justice of peace. Formal notice of charge, advice of rights. Bail set. Summary trials for petty offenses usually conducted here without further processing.

4 Preliminary testing of evidence against defendant. Charge may be reduced. No separate preliminary hearing for misdemeanors in some systems.

5 Charge filed by prosecutor on basis of information submitted by police or citizens. Alternative to grand jury indictment; often used in felonies, almost always in misdemeanors.

6 Reviews whether government evidence sufficient to justify trial. Some states have no grand jury system; others seldom use it.

Source: President's Commission on Law Enforcement and the Administration of Justice, *The Challenge of Crime in a Free Society* (Washington, D.C.: U.S. Government Printing Office, 1967).

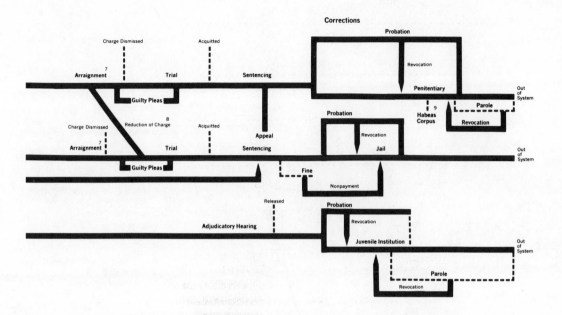

7 Appearance for plea; defendant elects trial by judge or jury (if available); counsel for indigent usually appointed here in felonies. Often not at all in other cases.

8 Charge may be reduced at any time prior to trial in return for plea of guilty or for other reasons.

9 Challenge on constitutional grounds to legality of detention. May be sought at any point in process.

10 Police often hold informal hearings, dismiss or adjust many cases without further processing.

11 Probation officer decides desirability of further court action.

12 Welfare agency, social services, counselling, medical care, etc., for cases where adjudicatory handling not needed.

FIGURE 1-3   An Overview of the Criminal Justice System

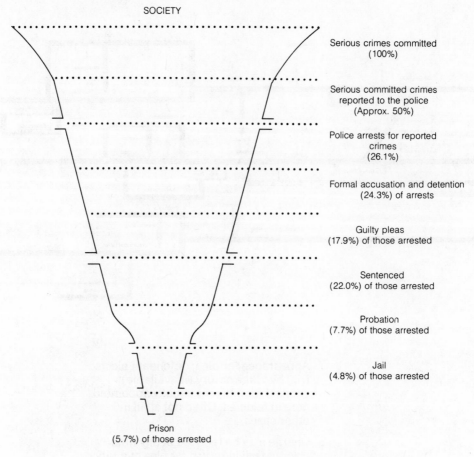

Sources: Adapted from the President's Commission on Law Enforcement and Administration of Justice, *The Challenge of Crime in a Free Society* (Washington, D.C.: U.S. Government Printing Office, 1967), pp. 262–263; and U.S. Department of Justice, *Offender-based Transaction Statistics* (Washington, D.C.: U.S. Government Printing Office, 1975), p. 20.

FIGURE 1-4   Flow of Offenders through the Criminal Justice System

strategies, play a defensive role in trying to curtail crime. They usually must wait until a crime occurs before they can take action. This gives the criminal the tremendous advantage of choosing the time, place, and method of the crime. Even a police agency with the most qualified police personnel and the most sophisticated crime-solving technology would probably be only slightly more efficient than one that has only mediocre personnel and resources. Although many people place stock in the ability of "more qualified" police personnel to make an appreciable difference in crime levels, this relationship has never been demonstrated (and probably never will be).

High Percentage of Juveniles Arrested

A second question raised by the statistics shown in Figure 1-4 is, why is there such a high arrest rate of juveniles for serious offenses? One may simply assume it is because juveniles commit such a high proportion of all serious crimes. However, several points could be raised to rebut such an assumption.

First, the arrest in itself does not necessarily mean that the person arrested committed the crime. In order to make such an assumption conclusively, one would need to know the total number of crimes committed (including those not reported to the authorities) what percentage of these were committed by juveniles, and what percentage of the total population are juveniles. Of course, the total number of serious crimes committed will never be known, and even if such information was available, in many cases it could not be known whether the crime was committed by a juvenile or an adult because the offender will never be arrested.

Another problem is that states have set age limits within which an individual can be considered as a juvenile for the purpose of criminal prosecution. A person over these statutory ages (usually 17 or 18) is considered an adult.[2] Thus, the period of time when a child is perhaps psychologically and physically most capable of committing crimes is limited to four or five years. If the arrest statistics are interpreted literally, juveniles would have to be extremely active in their preadolescent and adolescent years in the commission of serious offenses. Although juveniles from the ages of 12 to 17 may, in fact, be committing more serious crimes in proportion to their numbers than say those in the age bracket of 25 to 32, we should not be willing on the basis of what little we know to say that they are committing over one-third of all serious crime!

The most likely reason that juveniles are so overrepresented in the arrest statistics is that they are more likely to be caught. Their crimes are less sophisticated and covert than those committed by adults. Juveniles are more likely to engage in street crimes, which are precisely the types of crimes that police departments are most capable of dealing with.

High Percentage of Charges Dismissed or Reduced

A third question raised by the data concerns the large percentage of arrests in which either no complaint is filed or the charges are reduced. Why is it that so many offenders do not complete the preliminary steps in the judicial process and even fewer ultimately are sent to prison for their crimes?

There are several reasons why so many arrestees do not go beyond the pretrial screening stage. The first obvious reason is that the police arrest suspects without obtaining enough evidence to warrant prosecution. Thus the charges are dismissed. Another factor to be considered is that victims may refuse to file charges—for example, in crimes committed by one spouse against the other. Along this line the Vera Institute recently conducted a study of the reasons for various felony dispositions in New York City courts.[3] In these courts, judges, prosecutors, and defense attorneys cited the prior relationship of the defendant and the victim as one of the two most significant factors in determining the outcome of cases. For example, prior relationships existed in over half of all felonies that involved victims. These relationships included husbands and wives, lovers, prostitutes and their pimps or customers, neighbors, in-laws, junkies and dealers, even landlords and tenants. These prior relationship factors often lead to dismissals, reduced charges, and light sentences in return for a plea of guilty. The most frequently cited reason for dismissal in these cases was lack of cooperation by the complaining victim.[4]

A related factor is that witnesses and even victims may be unwilling to testify for a variety of reasons—for example, the fear of retaliation by the accused, because of inconvenience, or because they have moved from the jurisdiction. Without the witnesses' testimony, the state often has no case and the charges must be dropped.

Plea bargaining is another probable reason why so many charges are reduced at this stage. This is a form of negotiation between the defendant's attorney, the prosecutor, and the court, whereby the accused agrees to plead guilty in exchange for a reduction in the original charge, probation, or a reduced sentence. A New York City study found that of the 101,748 felony cases that came before the city's courts in 1974, over 80 percent were settled by the plea bargaining process.[5] A similar study conducted in New York three years later found the rate to be 74 percent.[6] The fact that nearly three-fourths of those who go beyond the formal accusation and detention stage (as shown in Figure 1-4) entered guilty pleas suggests that many of these pleas were a result of plea bargaining when one considers how few of the offenders who pleaded guilty to serious crimes were then imprisoned. But because of the complexity of the criminal justice system itself, there are still other reasons that bear on the poor arrest–detention statistic.

PRINCIPLES OF CRIMINAL LAW

Our system of justice operates on two key principles of criminal law. The first is the presumption of innocence. This means that those accused of crimes are considered innocent until proved guilty. The second principle is the burden of proof, which in criminal cases means that guilt must be proved beyond a reasonable doubt.

Theoretically, determining guilt is a process involving arguing the issues of fact or law in the particular case; in actual practice, however, this seldom happens. In many cases, the existence of guilt is supported by sufficient evidence; in others, where the issues of fact are such that the accused may or may not be found guilty beyond a reasonable doubt, concessions are worked out that may result in a reduced charge if the accused agrees to plead guilty.[7] In many criminal prosecutions, the main question becomes: Is there enough evidence to convict? Obviously, if there is ample evidence to convict, the prosecution is not interested in bargaining; by the same token, if there is not enough evidence to convict, there is no need for the accused to risk the prospects for a definite acquittal. It is in the gray area between certain guilt and probable innocence that plea bargaining takes place.

THE STUDY OF CRIMINAL JUSTICE: A FASCINATING SUBJECT

By now we can see that the process of administering criminal justice is a very broad, complex area of study. More than that, it is a fascinating area of academic inquiry touched by the mystique of crime and criminals. It is also one of the most important social issues of our time or any time in history.

In fact, it may well be the most important mirror of society. With the possible exception of how a society chooses its leaders, no other human activity demonstrates more clearly the values, attitudes, civility, and character of a nation than how it administers its criminal justice process. In recent years, this relationship has increasingly been recognized by a broad range of disciplines and scholars who have turned their attention to examining the criminal justice system of the United States and other nations. Many specialists have contributed and are continuing to contribute to a better understanding of crime and how we respond to it: sociologists, political scientists, legal scholars, psychologists, anthropologists, and economists are busily engaged in examining the system. Their findings will add to the already growing and dynamic character of this field of inquiry.

AN INTRODUCTION TO CRIMINAL JUSTICE

This introduction is intended to serve as a frame of reference for the chapters that follow. From this general overview, the material that follows will fill in this conceptual foundation in a series of gradual steps, each designed to further build upon the preceding step. We will examine such basic concerns as the theory and development of law, the nature of crime, and the special problems in the administration of today's system of criminal justice. This will lead to a detailed discussion of each individual component of the criminal justice process and how each developed, presently operates, and what changes are occurring in each—from the police, through the courts, into corrections, and concluding with the juvenile justice system.

SUMMARY

The study of the administration of criminal justice borrows heavily from disciplines such as law, sociology, political science, psychology, anthropology, and history. The criminal justice system and its component agencies are guided by the standards imposed on them by a free society. Because of its interrelationship with other social institutions, both past and present, the criminal justice process cannot be studied as an isolated entity.

The primary purpose of the criminal justice system is to protect the collective and individual members of a society. The system also functions to maintain the existing order which is crucial to the stability of an organized society. Within these two major goals are several subgoals such as the prevention and suppression of crime, the review of the legality of these efforts, the adjudicatory determination of those accused of crimes, and the correction by socially approved means of those who violate the criminal laws.

The criminal justice system consists of three major components—law enforcement, courts, and corrections—and the specialized auxiliary services of probation, parole, and the juvenile justice system. Each performs specific functions, yet all contribute in their own ways to the major goals of the overall system.

The criminal justice process is beset with growing conflict, particularly in the past several years, over philosophical differences in how best to attain the goals of the system. This conflict centers around the so-called arguments over the due process versus crime control models. This argument is of particular significance today as the specter of large government grows and the concerns this might raise for the rights of the individual.

Those who criticize the due process model of criminal justice administration often point to the so-called funnel effect of the process as an example of justice denied. Although our insistence that due process rights be afforded those charged with crimes might be partially the reason for the effect, it is not solely the cause. The criminal justice system operates with a great deal of necessary discretion and choices are made at critical decision points which result in those accused of crimes being filtered-out at such critical stages. Yet the alternatives to the due process model may, in the long-run, be even worse for society's well being than the present system. This is one of the most vexatious problems that must be considered as we work to reform the overall process in the years ahead.

REVIEW QUESTIONS

1. What are the primary goals of the criminal justice system?
2. What are the secondary goals of the system?
3. Name the major components of the criminal justice system and briefly describe the function of each component.
4. Name the auxiliary functions of the criminal justice system and briefly describe their functions.
5. Trace the major steps of a criminal case through the criminal justice system.

DISCUSSION QUESTIONS

1. What obstacles stand in the way of attaining the goals of the criminal justice system?
2. Is the criminal justice system a true system or a collection of unrelated parts?
3. Which of the two criminal justice models—crime control or due process—more accurately fits our system of criminal justice?

SUGGESTED ADDITIONAL READINGS

Advisory Committee on Intergovernmental Relations. *State-Local Relations in the Criminal Justice System.* Washington, D.C.: U.S. Government Printing Office, 1971.

Bent, Allen E. *The Politics of Law Enforcement.* Lexington, Mass.: Lexington Books, 1974.

Cole, George F. *Politics and the Administration of Justice.* Beverly Hills, Calif.: Sage, 1973.

———, ed. *Criminal Justice: Law and Politics.* North Scituate, Mass.: Duxbury Press, 1972.

Committee for Economic Development. *Reducing Crime and Assuring Justice.* New York: CED, June 1972.

Klonoski, James, and Robert Mendelsohn, eds. *The Politics of Local Justice.* Boston: Little, Brown, 1970.

Neubauer, David. *Criminal Justice in Middle America.* Morristown, N.J.: General Learning Press, 1974.

Oaks, Dallin, and Warren Lehman. *A Criminal Justice System and the Indigent.* Chicago: University of Chicago Press, 1967.

Parsons, Talcott. "The Law and Social Control." In William Evan, ed., *Law and Sociology.* New York: Free Press, 1962, pp. 56–72.

Quinney, Richard. *Class, State and Crime.* New York: David McKay, 1977.

Sanders, William B., and Howard C. Daudistel, eds. *The Criminal Justice Process.* New York: Praeger, 1976.

Viano, Emilio, and Alvin W. Cohn. *Social Problems and Criminal Justice.* Chicago: Nelson-Hall, 1977.

Vines, Kenneth. "Courts as Political and Governmental Agencies," in Herbert Jacob and Kenneth Vines, eds., *Politics in the American States.* Boston: Little, Brown, 1965, pp. 239–287.

Watson, Richard, and Ronald Downing. *The Politics of the Bench and Bar.* New York: Wiley, 1969.

Wilson, James Q. *Thinking About Crime.* New York: Basic Books, 1975.

NOTES

1. Herbert L. Packer, *The Limits of the Criminal Sanctions* (Stanford, Calif.: Stanford University Press, 1968).

2. There are some exceptions. For example, some states have youthful offender statutes which, in some cases, may extend the jurisdiction of the juvenile court over a youth beyond the statutorily prescribed age of 17 or 18.

3. Vera Institute of Justice, *Felony Arrests: Their Prosecution and Disposition in New York City's Courts* (New York: The Vera Institute, 1977).

4. Ibid., pp. 19–20; see also U.S. Department of Justice, *Offender-Based Transaction Statistics* (Washington, D.C.: U.S. Government Printing Office, 1975).

5. Aryeh Neier, *Crime and Punishment: A Radical Solution* (New York: Stein and Day, 1976), p. 156.

6. Vera Institute, *Felony Arrests,* p. 134.

7. Frank W. Miller, *Prosecution: The Decision to Charge a Suspect with a Crime* (Boston: Little, Brown, 1969).

PART 2

Crime and Criminal Law

From 1968 to 1977, robbery increased by 54 percent, according to the
Uniform Crime Reports. UCR also indicate that the Pacific Coast and the far
western states have the highest incidence of robbery in the United States.

During times of disaster or disorder, looting is a serious problem. Its victims
are the store owners, who stand little chance of recovering stolen goods.

Arson incidents have increased dramatically in recent years, to the point where they are now a serious problem. Both police and fire service personnel investigate cases in which arson is suspected.

The FBI compiles statistics on crimes such as robbery, arson, and possessing stolen property. These statistics are published annually in the Uniform Crime Reports. Data is supplied to the FBI voluntarily by more than 13,000 local, state, and federal law enforcement agencies.

2

CRIME, LAW, AND LEGAL TERMINOLOGY

1. What are the five elements of every crime and the various types of intent?
2. How have crime and criminal behavior been examined throughout history?
3. What are the major types of crimes and how are they defined?
4. What are the origins of criminal law in the United States?
5. How is criminal responsibility determined?
6. What are some common legal terminology and documents and how are they defined?

These are some of the questions this chapter will answer.

This chapter looks at the definition of crime and the origins of criminal law. It then briefly examines some major theories that have attempted to explain the causes of crime. In the remainder of the chapter specific crimes are classified and described, and a few of the major legal documents commonly used in the administration of justice are illustrated.

ELEMENTS OF CRIME

A crime has been defined as a voluntary and intentional violation by a legally competent person of a legal duty that commands or prohibits an act for the protection of society. A crime is punishable by judicial proceedings in the name of the state.[1] From this legal definition, a number of things are apparent. First, the act must be voluntary. Thus, if the particular criminal act can be shown to be involuntary, such as when an individual is forced to commit a criminal act against his or her will, the person cannot be found guilty of the crime. The questions that must be answered in such circumstances are: Did the offender actually act involuntarily, and what circumstances brought about this involuntary act? If, for example, a person was forced to participate in a crime at gunpoint, he or she committed the crime involuntarily and cannot be found guilty. In such cases, it must be demonstrated that the persons fear was justified and resulted in the individual's committing the crime.

For an act to be a crime, it must also be intentional. Thus otherwise criminal acts that occur by accident generally are not considered crimes.

An act, in order to be considered a crime, must also be committed by a legally competent person. By law, certain categories of people are considered incompetent to commit crimes, for example, someone who was "insane" at the time of the act or someone very young. The law views the acts committed by such persons as not being voluntary and intentional because they are mentally incapable of comprehending the nature of their behavior.

The definition of a crime also indicates that behavior that constitutes a crime can be either an act of commission or an act of omission. One is guilty of committing a crime by doing something that the law says one should *not* do, as well as not doing what the law says one *must* do. At this point, a fundamental requirement of criminal law should be explained. Any act of commission or omission, before it can constitute a crime, must be considered unlawful by statute *at the time that the act is committed.* For example, if you committed an act, which at the time of its commission was not illegal, you could not be later charged with a crime if the act, at a later date, was made a crime by law. Such laws are called *ex post facto* (after the fact) laws, and are forbidden by the U.S. Constitution.[2] Thus, the criminal law cannot be applied retroactively to charge persons for criminal acts that at the time of commission were not prohibited by law.

Finally, a crime is an act that threatens the welfare of society and that is punishable by judicial proceedings in the name of the state. Crime is therefore considered to be an act against the collective well-being of society. In a theoretical and legal sense, a crime is more than merely the act of an offender directed against an innocent victim; the victim represents society itself. This is one of the major distinctions in the law between criminal law and civil law. In civil law, in which someone brings a lawsuit against another for damages, both parties in the case are viewed as private citizens. The party alleging damages and bringing suit is called the *plaintiff,* and the one from whom the damages are sought is called the *defendant.* The case is referred to by the names of the plaintiff and defendant, respectively, as in *Smith* v. *Brown.* In criminal cases, the government is referred to as the *prosecution* and the accused as the *defendant.* In criminal cases, the prosecution represents the people, and the case name reflects this, as in *United States* v. *Brown, People* v. *Smith,* or *Colorado* v. *Green.*

By law, every crime contains what are called *elements* of the offense. These elements are inherent in the specific legal definition of the crime. Before a person can be convicted of a crime, each of the following elements must be proved by the state:

1. The act;
2. The intent;
3. The concurrence of act and intent;
4. The causation;
5. The result.[3]

For example, looking at the legal definition of a crime given earlier, it is evident that before the government convicts someone of a crime, it must show: (1) that an act was committed which, at the time of its commission, was prohibited, or that the accused failed to do something commanded by the law (the act); (2) that the accused did the act voluntarily and with full knowledge of what he or she was doing (the intent); (3) that the act resulted from the intent (the concurrence of act and intent); (4) that the act and the intent caused something to occur that was offensive to the law (causation); and (5) that it resulted in some harm to society (result).

Criminal Intent

Most of these elements of the law are fairly straightforward. For example, since every crime involves the commission or omission of an act, before the defendant in a criminal case can be found guilty of theft, there must be the actual taking of an object. In proving intent as an essential element of a crime, however, one enters into the gray area of criminal law. In criminal law proving intent is more complicated because it demands an evaluation of the psychological motives of the offender. The concept of intent is expressed in the Latin phrase *mens rea,* which means roughly that the law considers that the offender possessed the necessary intent as shown by his actions and by the common human experience.[4] For example, if a man commits a crime, it is assumed that he did so voluntarily, and since he did so voluntarily, he must also have intended to do so. The law then goes even one step further. Since it is presumed by the criminal's actions and our common experience that the crime was committed voluntarily, and thus intentionally and of free will, it is assumed that the act was committed *knowingly.* Figure 2-1 shows the legal reasoning behind showing intent as a necessary element of each crime.

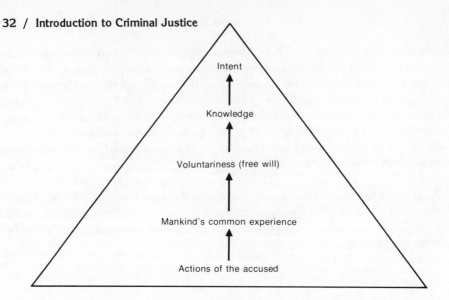

FIGURE 2-1 The Concept of *Mens Rea* in Proving Intent

Of course, the defendant in a criminal case can put into question this natural presumption of intent in various ways. The state may be able to show, for example, that the accused participated in a criminal act, but the accused may argue that by virtue of decreased mental reasoning capacity (e.g., insanity), he or she had no knowledge of the act. In some states, the defendant may be able to show that because of insanity he or she was the victim of an "irresistible impulse" which destroyed the ability to exercise free will (voluntariness) in the commission of the act. In these cases, intent might not be proved as a necessary element of the crime and the defendant might not be found guilty of the crime charged.

Two types of intent, *general intent* and *specific intent,* exist in our system of law.

General Intent General intent is considered to be present in the criminal's decision to commit an offense or deviate from standard conduct when that offense or deviation may expose members of the society at large to harm even without specific intent as to the object or consequences of such conduct.[5] In other words, behavior that does not conform to legal conduct is assumed to intend harmful consequences, whether the person actually intends harmful consequences or not. The most common example is drunk driving. Let us say a woman operating an automobile while intoxicated strikes and kills a pedestrian or another motorist. Certainly, she did not "intend" the consequences of her act. However, under the principle of general intent, she would be charged with manslaughter or vehicular homicide. Her general criminal intent is based on the legal assumption that, *first,* she voluntarily became intoxicated, and operated her car, which exposed others to harm. Second, there was foreseeable knowledge based upon experience that the voluntary state of intoxication and the subsequent driving of an automobile in such a physical condition could conceivably result in injury or death to others. Thus, there exists general criminal intent, and the state does not have to prove that the individual had an actual intent to kill.

Specific Intent Specific intent forms the basis for most crimes. Specific intent indicates that *before* the individual committed the act, he or she planned to carry out the offense. This specific intent exists as an element of all crimes except those that require only a showing of general intent. In rape, for example, the specific intent is to have carnal knowledge of a female, who is not one's wife, against her will (this definition of rape is presently being reassessed); in the case of theft, it is to take something of value from the true owner in order to permanently deprive the owner of his or her possession.

SEARCHING FOR THE CAUSES OF CRIME

Of course, there is no simple answer to the question of what causes crime. Attempts to explain the causative factors associated with crime, the characteristics of criminals, and society's response to crime and delinquency comprise the field of *criminology*.

Experts in criminology have studied the causes of crime from a number of different perspectives—sociology, law, psychology, psychiatry, anthropology, economics, political science, biology, and history. Traditionally, the study of crime causation focused on the fields of sociology, psychology, and psychiatry. In recent years, political scientists, political sociologists, and economists have become more active in this area. For instance the so-called *new* or *critical criminology* focuses on a Marxist perspective of society in which laws and the instruments of the administration of justice (the police, courts, corrections, etc.) are used by those in power for self-serving interests to maintain the status quo and to protect their interests from the have-nots.[6]

Although it is not possible for an introductory text to discuss all of the theories that have tried to explain crime, we can trace some of the major approaches and theories that have been identified as milestones in the development of approaches to crime and criminological thought.

HISTORICAL APPROACHES TO THE PROBLEM OF CRIME

In primitive societies, crime was attributed to the offender's "bad nature," and revenge was the motivation in seeking redress. If someone was attacked, the victim, either alone or aided by family members or friends, would get even with the attacker.[7] Although this was a simple and expeditious solution, it led to lawlessness and blood-letting feuds.

The spread of religious ideas modified and extended the idea of revenge. In medieval times, criminal behavior was interpreted as an attack against the diety, which unless placated would bring great misfortunes such as flood, pestilence, and plague upon the individual and the community.[8] These feelings were further strengthened by beliefs that crime and the offender were manifestations of the devil. Thus, so "possessed," the individual had to pay not only a debt to society, but also had to be reconciled with God. This, too, led to bloody examples of righteous retribution against the criminal.

By the late Middle Ages, the state possessed unlimited power. Crime then came to be viewed as an attack upon the ruler, and severe punishments were imposed upon those who would offend the "King's Law."

In the eighteenth-century Period of Enlightenment, the horrors of the bloody revenge that characterized the earlier periods began to give way somewhat. By the end of the century, instead of severe physical punishment, more moderate means of correction were widely advocated. This was also accompanied by a shift in dealing with crime and offenders in a legalistic manner. By this time, all crime was held to be an act against the public interest, and the administration of criminal justice had become a matter to be dealt with solely by the state.[9] Throughout Western Europe and the New World, reformers began calling for changes in the administration of criminal law. Of special concern was the protection of the rights of the individual against the arbitrary actions of the courts. Such reforms were widely implemented.

Although these reforms changed perceptions about the role of the state, procedural law, and the administration of justice, they had little impact upon how the law viewed human behavior as it related to crime. Crime was conceived in purely legal terms: punishment was regarded as a just response to guilt, not as a corrective or rehabilitative measure. The law (and the courts) operated entirely on the interpretation of the written law. The courts handed out punishment under the "free will" doctrine—that is, the assumption that the offender chooses to commit crime by his own free will. Now generally in disrepute this idea failed to recognize that human behavior is often the result of complex interactions, social problems, group characteristics, and a host of factors all of which destroy the concept of the offender acting on the basis of his or her own free will.

The Origins of Modern Criminology

During the nineteenth century, the origins of modern criminological thought began. This was a period when certain notable figures attempted to discover specific causes of crime.

The first of these was a physician, Cesare Lombroso (1836–1909). During his service with the Italian army, he became interested in the anatomical characteristics of criminals. After examining hundreds of convicts, Lombroso concluded that particular biophysical characteristics were often found among criminals. He proposed that criminals bore certain atavistic physical characteristics—for example, low foreheads, receding chins, an abundance of wrinkles, and protruding ears—that suggested that they were throwbacks to a primitive human.[10] Although Lombroso's ideas have no credibility today, they did mark a major attempt to study the factors associated with criminal behavior.

The next major contributor was Raffaele Garofalo (1852–1934). He contributed to the development of criminology through a discussion of many problems that are still applicable today, such as restitution to victims of crimes and the need for international efforts to combat crime. He rejected the idea that people commit crime by virtue of "free will"—at least as it was commonly defined by law. Criminals, he believed, lacked pity and probity, which he saw as a reflection of the moral sense of the community; they thus possessed a moral freedom to commit crime which, to Garofalo, denied the efficacy of the law in deterring potential offenders.

A disciple of Lombroso, Enrico Ferri (1856–1928), was the most modern of the three. Ferri saw crime as the product of geographical, anthropological, psychological, and economic forces. The core of Ferri's thought involved the replacement of moral responsibility with "social accountability."[11] His recommendations were consistent with his political belief in using the state as an instrument of social reform. Ferri maintained that free trade and abolition of monopolies would reduce food prices and therefore the crime of smuggling. Similarly, he felt that lowering taxes and building public works projects would do more to improve the quality of life and to reduce crime than harsh criminal penalties. He espoused a sociological criminology and recommended that judges be trained in psychology and psychiatry to enable them to recognize criminal types.

During the late eighteenth to early nineteenth centuries, other important developments took place. John Casper Lavater (1741–1801) proposed that biological factors *caused* individuals to behave differently. This was the so-called science of physiognomy which purported to be able to judge a person's character solely by observing one's outward appearance. Phrenology, or the determination of one's characteristics by the shape of the skull and by the nature and location of "bumps" on the skull, also became popular as an explanation for behavior. During this period, the science of statistics also began. Several noted statisticians suggested that this science be used to measure and classify crimes not unlike the use to which we put statistics and crime analysis today.

MODERN THEORIES OF CRIME

Four major orientations have emerged in the last hundred years from attempts to explain crime. The *biological school* looks for the causes of crime in the criminal's physical characteristics. The *psychological school* seeks an answer to the problem of crime by studying the mental processes. The *sociological school* attempts to find the roots of criminality in the environment rather than in the individual. Finally, there is the *multifactor school* which relates the causes of crime to a wide range of complex and multiple factors.

The Biological School

The biological approach focuses on biological or anthropological explanations for crime. The idea underlying this approach is that the criminal is biologically different from normal human beings. Researchers Richard Dugdale and Henry Goddard studied family trees and concluded that criminal tendencies are often transmitted through the genes to successive generations.[12]

Major contributions to this school of criminological thought are theories that relate criminality to particular physical types. These theorists contend that biological structure is of prime importance in determining behavior and that certain physical qualities denote the criminal. From his studies of criminals and law-abiding citizens, anthropologist Ernest Hooten concluded that such physical characteristics as low and sloping foreheads, straight hair, thick head hair, red-brown hair, blue-gray and mixed eyes, long thin necks, and sloping shoulders were more common among criminals than noncriminals.[13]

Theorist William H. Sheldon concluded from his research that people could be classified into three categories based on their physical characteristics. In addition, physical characteristics were related to personality and temperament. He concluded that the mesomorphic individual who was described as muscular, with a large trunk, heavy chest, large wrist and hands, was most likely to possess criminal characteristics. These individuals tended to possess the personality characteristics of assertiveness, compulsiveness, and ruthlessness.[14] Sheldon Glueck and Eleanor Glueck agreed with Sheldon. In their later studies of juvenile delinquents they also found that mesomorphs apparently had a higher delinquency potential than other body types.[15]

For various reasons, today little credibility is attached to these biological explanations for crime. There was a brief resurrection of biologically linked factors during the 1960s when the XYY chromosome theory gained some attention. This theory purported that male criminals were more likely than male noncriminals to have an extra Y or male sex chromosome.[16]

The Psychological School

The psychological and psychiatric theories seek answers to the causes of crime by a study of the mental processes. In this approach, psychoses, defects of the central nervous system, neurasthenia, and inadequate mental ability have all, at varying times, been blamed for crime. Members of the psychological school are contributors such as Sigmund Freud whose epoch-making theories opened the way to an understanding of psychodynamics in the development of criminal conduct. Other noted contributors to this school are Carl Jung, Alfred Adler, August Aichorn, Kate Friedlander, and Kurt R. Eissler.[17]

The Sociological School

The sociological school, which contends that the criminal is a product of society, focuses on the interrelationships among people and calls attention to the fact that persistent deviance typically requires and receives group support and that most deviant behavior is culturally patterned. Advocates of the sociological approach to crime causation reject the idea that crime can be fully understood by the analysis of offenders as individuals. In this approach, the analysis is extended to include the community, social institutions, and group relationships which shape both criminal and noncriminal behavior. Instead of regarding offenders generally as biologically and psychologically abnormal, criminality is explained as a product of learned behavior in the course of social interaction. Sociologists regard criminals as "normal" in that their personalities were developed through the same processes by which noncriminal personalities were developed.[18]

The Multi-Factor School

The multi-factor approach to explaining criminal behavior is a synthesis of the biological, psychological, and sociological schools. Adherents of this approach attempt to reconcile the differing disciplines with the goal of developing an integrated theoretical understanding of crime.[19]

The pioneers of the modern multi-factor approach were such notables as Adolphe Prins, Franz von Liszt, and G. A. von Hamel. Together they held to the idea of multiple causation and made efforts to rationalize the discrepancies among the three major groups of single-factor theories. This school recognizes the complexity of crime-producing factors and their interrelatedness. In addition, the multi-factor school attempts to develop general theories that integrate the various efforts of other theorists who have tried to explain the causes for crime.

Although concern with the factors that produce crime is not new, a great deal more research is needed before we can fully understand the complex nature of crime. Such work in criminology is now being undertaken throughout the world.

CLASSIFICATION OF CRIMES

Crimes are classified according to their seriousness and the type of penalty that they carry. This modern distinction among classes of crimes developed in early England and was incorporated into the common law. It was brought to the Colonies and exists relatively unchanged today.

According to common law, crimes fell into three categories:

- Treason
- Felonies
- Misdemeanors

Treason

In the early common law, treason was the most serious crime. At one time, it was more a crime of a personal nature directed toward the sovereign; later it was viewed to be an act that threatened the institutions of government and the nation's security.[20] Today, some legal scholars consider treason as the most serious type of felony rather than giving it a separate classification.

Felonies and Misdemeanors

For students of criminal justice, the distinction between felony and misdemeanor crimes is the most important in modern law. Generally, the various state penal codes distinguish between the two by the nature and extent of the punishment that can be imposed. A *felony* is usually defined as a criminal act that may be punishable by imprisonment in a penitentiary for more than one year or by death. A *misdemeanor,* on the other hand, is usually an offense that is punishable by fine or imprisonment for one year or less. In those few states that do not differentiate between felonies and misdemeanors according to the period of incarceration, the distinction between the two is the place of incarceration. If the crime carries the possibility of confinement in a penitentiary, it is considered a felony; if not, it is considered a misdemeanor. A few states classify certain offenses as *high misdemeanors*. In terms of seriousness, these offenses fall between felonies and misdemeanors. Although still technically misdemeanors, they often provide for penalties in excess of one year in a penitentiary.

Specific Criminal Offenses

Typically, state criminal codes list crimes by specific categories or types of offenses. Although state codes generally use the same categories to classify crimes, the elements or definitions of crimes may vary somewhat from state to state, and you should be aware of the particular differences in your own state. In spite of this limitation, there is enough similarity between state penal codes to warrant an examination of specific offenses. The categorization of crime in most penal codes is usually as follows:

- Inchoate offenses
- Crimes against the person
- Crimes against property
- Crimes against public morality and decency
- Crimes against the public order and administration of justice

Inchoate Offenses

Inchoate offenses are those criminal acts that are only partially completed—that is, circumstances intervene that prevent them from being carried out to their conclusion. They are, nonetheless, considered crimes because their design and purpose is criminal in nature and, except for intervening factors, they would constitute a completed crime. The major inchoate offenses are *attempts, conspiracy,* and crimes relating to what are called *principals* and *accessories.* The reason for making these inchoate offenses crimes is to protect society by deterring those who, without laws prohibiting these acts, might undertake the commission of a crime.

Attempt An *attempt* is the committing of an act that is a substantial step toward the commission of a specific crime. However, the complete criminal act is not actually carried through. Merely preparing to commit a criminal act is usually not enough to be charged with attempt.[21] For example, a man enters a supermarket and at gunpoint demands the cash receipts, but at that moment he is surprised and arrested. This constitutes an *attempted robbery*.

Conspiracy *Conspiracy* is the crime of unlawfully entering into an agreement with one or more persons to commit a specific offense. According to common law, the state had only to show that two or more persons merely entered into an agreement to commit a crime. Today, modern statutes require additional proof beyond the agreement—now there must be some overt act toward the completion of the crime itself.[22] Under conspiracy statutes, once the agreement is entered into, each member of the conspiracy is equally liable for the acts of all other conspirators regardless of whether the person was part of the subsequent acts or not. The members are all guilty as long as the acts were committed to further the agreed-upon illegal enterprise.[23]

Principals and Accessories Common law established the idea that parties to the commission of a felony should be considered either principals or accessories to the crime, depending upon their involvement. Today, many states do not distinguish between the two, but consider all accessories as principals in the crime. These states, however, usually cite two categories of principals. A *principal in the first degree* is one who is actually or constructively present during the commission of a crime. A person is considered actually present if he or she participates in the perpetration of the crime; a person is considered constructively present if he or she engineered the crime, but it was committed through an innocent agent. A *principal in the second degree* is one who might be actually or constructively present, but is involved only in aiding or encouraging the commission of the crime.

States that have retained the distinction between principals and accessories consider the principal to be someone who, in some way, participates in the actual commission of the crime. Someone who, in some way, has helped the principals is known as an *accessory*. An *accessory before the fact* is someone who, before the crime's actual commission, has procured, counseled, commanded, or encouraged someone else to commit the criminal act. An *accessory after the fact* is one who knowingly receives, hides, shelters, or in some way assists, either personally or through the agency of others, someone who has committed a felony. The law views the accessory after the fact as someone whose purpose and intent is to assist the felon in escaping justice. The elements of proof that the state must demonstrate before someone can be convicted of this crime are that: (1) a felony was committed and completed; (2) the individual who was helped committed the felony; (3) the one who helped the felon must reasonably believe that a felony was committed and that the person who was helped committed it; and (4) the accessory must personally or through the agency of another, have harbored, concealed, or otherwise helped the felon to escape.[24]

Crimes Against the Person

There are six major crimes against the person that you should become familiar with. Although there are other crimes against the person, these are considered the most serious felonies: *homicide, manslaughter, assault, rape, kidnapping,* and *robbery.* The subdivisions within these categories are outlined next.

Homicide and Manslaughter Homicides fall into two major categories: *criminal* and *noncriminal homicide.* The crime of *homicide* is defined as the killing of one human being by another human being who can be shown to be mentally competent. According to common law, there were only two distinctions of criminal homicide—murder and manslaughter. Murder under the common law was considered to be any homicide that was committed with "malice aforethought."[25] The penalty for murder was death. Many states over the years have modified the common law classification of homicide because the two categories were too restrictive. Experience has suggested that certain forms of murder did not warrant the death penalty because of mitigating circumstances that surrounded the commission of the crime. Thus, many states by statute have divided the crime of murder into degrees, requiring different penalties and elements depending upon the particular degree of murder committed.

Criminal homicide includes the following:

1. *First-degree murder* requires that the act be committed by willful, deliberate, and premeditated means with malice aforethought. Murder in the first degree must entail sufficient premeditation to characterize it as a cold-blooded and calculated killing. In some states, first-degree murders are also murders that fall into the category of *felony-murder*, or murders that are committed during the commission of such serious crimes as rape, robbery, kidnapping, arson, or burglary. Even though there is not a strict element of premeditation involved, the courts have held that participation in these types of criminal acts creates "a foreseeable risk of death."[26] Other states also consider the killing of a law enforcement officer or a prison guard as first-degree murder.

2. *Second-degree murder* is usually defined as any murder that is not murder in the first degree as determined by a jury. Usually, the element of premeditation and deliberation is not present to the point that must be demonstrated in first-degree murder. The death of a student who was beaten in a fight is an instance when the survivor might be charged with murder in the second degree.

3. *Manslaughter* differs from murder in that there is no malice aforethought, but there is still an unjustifiable and inexcusable taking of a human life. In manslaughter, the degree of malice is less and there is no premeditated design to kill. In some states, the crime of manslaughter is broken down into two subcategories—*voluntary* and *involuntary manslaughter*. In states that make this distinction, voluntary manslaughter is the intentional killing of another due to adequate provocation, but in the sudden heat of passion. The important feature of this crime is the question of the rage or sudden heat of passion which must be of "an intensity sufficient to obscure the reason of the actor."[27] Involuntary manslaughter is an unintentional homicide in which the death of the victim is not intended nor contemplated by the one performing the act. However, the act itself was done in such a reckless manner that it cannot be considered an innocent act or accidental. Closely related to this is the crime of *negligent homicide*, which applies primarily to death as a result of the reckless operation of a motor vehicle. The vehicle must be operated in a careless or negligent manner and the death must not be willful or deliberate. Negligent homicide can also be charged, however, in other types of cases. The killing of a friend with a gun that the accused "didn't know was loaded" is a rather common example.[28]

Noncriminal homicide stems from the common-law concept that under certain circumstances, homicide was not a crime. There are two types of noncriminal homicide: *justifiable homicide* and *excusable homicide*.

1. *Justifiable homicide* exonerates the one who commits the homicide because the act itself was justified and sometimes even ordered by the law. Some examples of justifiable homicide are the execution of a death sentence, lawful acts of war, prevention of the commission of a felony or atrocious crime, and the killing of a dangerous and known felon who was in the act of escaping.

2. *Excusable homicide* is an act that causes death, but is tolerated because of its nature or because of the circumstances. This includes self-defense and homicide where the killing is accidental or is simply a negligent and unintentional killing. In this instance, negligence is to be distinguished from "recklessness," which is an element of involuntary manslaughter.[29]

Assault and Battery   The felony of assault and battery also includes two categories: *aggravated* and *simple assault.*

1. The crime of deliberately attacking someone for the purpose of doing severe bodily injury to the victim is called *aggravated assault.* Before the charge of aggravated assault can be made, there must be apparent or present ability to carry out the threat, such as a weapon or superior physical strength, and the threat and possibility of rendering physical violence must be immediate and not in the future.

Mere threats do not usually constitute aggravated assault, but it is not necessary that there be actual physical contact. For example, raising a fist in anger as if to strike another person is sufficient in some jurisdictions to constitute an aggravated assault. This is based on the idea that as long as physical force is set in motion and the victim has reasonable apprehension of being personally injured, aggravated assault has occurred. Closely associated with aggravated assault are what some states call *felonious assaults.* These are specific types of aggravated assault which are classified according to intent. For example, assault with intent to commit murder; assault with intent to commit great bodily harm less than murder; assault with intent to commit rape or ravish; and assault with attempt to rob.

2. In most states, *simple assault* is defined as an assault committed without a weapon and without intent to commit great bodily harm or to commit a felony. In almost all instances, this crime is only a misdemeanor.

3. *Battery* is the actual completed assault.[30] Whereas a threatening gesture may be enough to constitute an assault, the actual unlawful touching of another person with intent to inflict injury constitutes battery. This points up the fact that serious offenses often include other and less serious crimes which are separate offenses. For example, assault is included in battery, and assault and battery are naturally included in violent crimes against the person such as murder, manslaughter, robbery, and rape. Usually, however, most jurisdictions merge the assault and battery with the higher offense and charge the accused only with the more serious crime.

Rape   The two categories of rape are *forcible* and *statutory rape.*

1. *Forcible rape* is generally defined as the carnal knowledge of a female above a certain age by a male who is not her husband. The crime of forcible

rape includes the following elements: (1) it must be an act of carnal knowledge and sexual intercourse with even the slightest degree of penetration by the male organ; (2) the victim must be female; (3) the use of force must be actual or implied, and the victim must perceive herself in danger of great bodily harm; (4) the act of willing consent must be absent.

In many states forcible rape has undergone some statutory revisions in the last few years. Until recently, a number of states required that before a man could be convicted of forcible rape it had to be shown as a condition of nonconsent that the victim "resisted to her utmost" the advances of her attacker. This degree of proof has been made more reasonable in most states. In the past, a favorite tactic of many lawyers for the accused has been to attack the credibility of the victim by trying to show the court that she is an unchaste or sexually promiscuous woman. In many cases, it became the victim who was on trial rather than the accused. Because of the rape victim's vulnerability to such questionable tactics by the defense counsel, it was not unusual for forcible rape victims to fail to report the crime to the police or to refuse to go through with the trial. Now, a number of states have set limits on the employment of such strategy by the defense.

The last few years have also seen other changes in rape laws by some states. Where, at one time, rape was considered as an offense that could be committed only against a female, some states now recognize that males can also be raped.

2. *Statutory rape* involves all the usual elements of rape with the exception that it is not necessary to show that force was used or that it was accomplished without the willing consent of the female. In fact, statutory rape is the act of engaging in *voluntary* sexual intercourse with a female under the statutory age of consent. This crime exists to protect the virtue and chastity of young females who are considered to be more vulnerable to the sexual advances of adult males.

Kidnapping By current statutes, kidnapping is the unlawful taking of a person against his or her will. Many states have separate statutes to prohibit the unlawful taking of a person and the unlawful taking of a person against his or her will for ransom. States generally attach greater penalties if the kidnapping includes the element of ransom.[31]

1. Whoever knowingly transports in interstate commerce, any person who has been unlawfully seized, confined, inveigled, decoyed, kidnapped, abducted or carried away and held for ransom or reward or otherwise, except in the case of a minor by a parent, therefore, shall be punished:
    A. By death if the kidnapped person has not been liberated unharmed and if the verdict of the jury shall so recommend, or
    B. By imprisonment for any term of years or for life, if the death penalty is not imposed.

2. The failure to release the victim within 24 hours after having been unlawfully seized, confined, inveigled, decoyed, kidnapped, abducted or carried away shall create a rebuttable presumption that such person has been transported in interstate or foreign commerce. [Author's note: This makes the offense a federal crime. When a citizen of a state is kidnapped, it is strictly a state crime until 24 hours have elapsed. After the 24-hour period, the victim is assumed to have

been transported in interstate commerce and the Lindbergh Act is invoked to give the FBI the jurisdiction to enter the case.]

3. If two or more persons conspire to violate this section and one or more such persons do not avert or act to affect the object of conspiracy, each shall be punished as provided in subsection A.[32]

Robbery and Extortion   Robbery usually falls into the categories of *armed* and *unarmed robbery*. Extortion, while similar to robbery, is a separate category.

Robbery is defined as the taking of personal property or things of value from another in his or her presence and against his or her will, by force or fear, violence or threat. The key element of robbery is the use of force or fear directed toward the victim that causes the victim to give up the property. To merely steal the property of another without confronting the owner and without the use of force or fear is *not* robbery. Even in such crimes as purse snatching or pocket-picking, this force or fear is not present, and as a result these crimes are generally considered larcenies (thefts).

A number of states categorize robbery into *armed* and *unarmed*, with the latter being a less serious offense. In these states, armed robbery usually entails the use of a dangerous weapon or an instrument that could lead the victim to believe that it is, in fact, a dangerous weapon. Unarmed robbery involves the use of physical force with no weapon.

The difference between *extortion* and robbery is that although extortion is an attempt to obtain property or money by means of actual or implied threat, the threat is less defined and is more of a threat to use force in the future. Thus, extortion does not quite contain the element of force or its immediate application that is required by robbery statutes. At the same time, however, extortion is more than a larceny since the element of force is still present.

Crimes Against Property

Although crimes against property are also crimes against the victim because he or she suffers a loss, a distinction between the two is made primarily for purposes of classification. Since in certain crimes against property there is no direct confrontation between the offender and the victim which theoretically would place the victim in greater personal peril, these crimes are often considered by the law as less serious than those committed against the person. Even so, the more serious of these property crimes are still felonies. The major crimes against property are *burglary, larceny, auto theft, embezzlement, receiving stolen goods, arson,* and *malicious destruction of property.*

Burglary   At the common law, burglary consisted of the following elements: (1) breaking and entering with the specific intent to do so (2) into the dwelling of another (3) at nighttime (4) with the intent to commit a felony therein.

Because these elements were rather restrictive, many states have enacted various degrees of burglary. The degree of seriousness is determined by the presence or absence of certain of the elements. For example, if the structure is not a dwelling, the crime may be considered a less serious offense; if the crime is committed during the daylight hours, it is considered less serious, and so on.

Other states, rather than specifying degrees of burglary, have retained the common law doctrine of burglary, but have added the additional crime of *breaking and entering* as a form of burglary. In these states, breaking and entering does not have to occur in a dwelling, during the night, or with the intent to commit a felony within; thus the burglary of a building in the daylight hours would constitute breaking and entering. Although a lesser offense than burglary or burglary in the first degree, breaking and entering is nonetheless almost invariably a felony.

Larceny   Larceny, the legal term for theft, is the taking and removal of the personal property of another with the intent to permanently deprive the true owner and to convert the property to one's own use. It is usually necessary that all these elements be present before the crime can be larceny. However, the courts have some latitude in determining whether their requirements have been met. For example, the necessary element of carrying away the property has been interpreted to mean any removal regardless of how short a distance the object was moved as long as the thief has successfully taken the property into his or her control.[33]

States have divided the crime of larceny into *grand larceny* and *petit larceny* on the basis of the value of the property taken. In Michigan, for example, if the value of the property stolen exceeds $100, the crime is grand larceny; below that amount, the crime is petit larceny. Grand larceny is a felony, and petit larceny is, in most instances, a misdemeanor. If over a period of time someone stole a number of items whose total value constituted grand larceny, that person could be prosecuted accordingly. The test the courts apply in such cases is "whether the entire taking was governed by a single intent and a general illegal design."[34]

Larceny usually involves the concept of stealth and not of force, and as such it is considered a "crime of opportunity."[35] There are different forms of larceny, which may be separate crimes. An example is *larceny by deception* (or false pretenses), where the accused obtains the personal property of the true owner by trickery, fraud, or some form of misrepresentation. In this case, if the owner had known the real identity or purpose of the taker, he or she would not have parted voluntarily with the property. Another form of larceny is *conversion,* where there is no fraud or misrepresentation involved. Rather, the taker knowingly and with intent to permanently deprive converts to his or her own use property that has come into the taker's possession legally.

A separate form of larceny is the crime of *pocket-picking.* It may be prosecuted under the existing larceny laws or as a separate offense. Either way, the elements are basically the same, with perhaps the additional requirement of actually taking from the concealed person of another. The crime of *shoplifting* is also a form of larceny. It also may be prosecuted under the general larceny statute of the state or it may exist as a separate offense. It may constitute grand or petit larceny, depending on the value of the merchandise stolen, and it may therefore be a felony or misdemeanor.

Auto Theft   Auto theft, while a form of larceny, is not held to the same requirements of proof as most larcenies. For example, it is often defined as the willful taking of a motor vehicle that belongs to another without the true owner's permission. The requirement of showing intent to permanently deprive is absent since many automobile thefts are committed by adolescents who take the vehicle for a "joy ride" and then abandon it.

Embezzlement   Another crime closely associated with larceny is the offense of embezzlement. Unlike the crime of larceny, which is a trespassory invasion of the property of another in which the criminal has no right to the property, a person who has the lawful possession of someone else's property cannot be guilty of the crime of larceny if he or she wrongfully converts the property to his or her own use.[36] Therefore, to deal with such matters as the theft of the master's property by the servant, the specific crime of embezzlement was enacted. Under embezzlement statutes, the following elements exist: (1) the fraudulent appropriation or conversion (2) of personal property of another (3) by a person having lawful possession by virtue of a relationship of trust and confidence (4) with intent to feloniously convert or use in a manner that was not intended by the nature of the possession. The important feature of this offense is the nature of the confidence and trust that exists between the offender and the victim. It usually applies when an employee entrusted with the lawful possession of an employer's property steals it and converts it to his or her own use. The relationship and degree of trust involved determines whether the crime is embezzlement or not. If, for example, you were to steal and convert to your own use a friend's property which was entrusted to your care, you would more likely be guilty of *larceny by conversion* rather than embezzlement.

Receiving Stolen Goods   A final larceny-related offense is the crime of receiving stolen goods. In some jurisdictions, this exists as a separate and specific offense. In other states, the one who receives or conceals stolen goods with the knowledge of their nature and with the intent to permanently deprive is considered as either an accessory after the fact or as a principal in the original crime in which the stolen goods were obtained.

Arson   Under the common law, arson was the "malicious burning of the house or outhouse of another man,"[37] and it applied to dwellings that were inhabited. Under modern arson statutes, this requirement has been dropped or degrees of arson have been added depending upon whether or not the structure was used for habitation. Committing arson to a dwelling is still considered the most serious violation of the arson law because of the obvious danger to the inhabitants. Nonetheless, arson now generally applies to the destruction of any permanent building or structure. In some instances, it also applies to personal property such as automobiles.

Malicious Destruction of Real and Personal Property   This crime involves the deliberate, willful, and malicious destruction of land, structures, and other forms of real property. In the offense of malicious destruction of personal property, the same elements exist, but the target is personal property. In both cases, whether the crime is considered a felony or a misdemeanor is determined by the value of the property that is damaged or destroyed.

Crimes Against Public Morality

Certain acts are offensive to the public morality and must be regulated by law. Many of our so-called vice laws fall into this category. Crimes of this nature are often called *malum prohibitum* offenses—that is, acts that are considered wrong because society prohibits them rather than *malum in se* crimes, such as murder, rape, or robbery, which are wrong in and of themselves. Because crimes against public morality are discussed more fully in Chapter 4, only brief attention is given to them here. Some of the more common of these crimes are *incest, seduction, indecent liberties with a child, adultery, bigamy, prostitution, homosexuality, obscenity,* and *pornography.*

Incest The crime of *incest* is committed when someone has sexual intercourse or performs an act of deviant sexual conduct with a person who is too closely related to marry legally. Realistically, this crime is seldom prosecuted because of the familial relationship involved and the obvious reluctance of the victim to testify. In most instances when it is prosecuted, it is because of certain aggravating circumstances such as a father having intercourse with his minor child.

Seduction *Seduction* is still considered a crime in a few states according to the common law. It is defined as an act of sexual intercourse with a chaste woman under the false pretext of marriage. Even where this crime remains in the criminal code, its enforcement is rare because of today's liberal views toward premarital or extramarital sex.

Indecent Liberties with a Child Taking *indecent liberties with a child* is the act of lewdly fondling or touching the body of a child. In recent years, some states have incorporated this offense into general sexual abuse laws which are defined in terms of degrees depending upon the nature and voluntariness of the act.

Adultery *Adultery* is the crime of having sexual intercourse with either an unmarried person or a married person who is not one's spouse. An unmarried person who has sexual intercourse with a married person, knowing that person to be married, is also guilty of adultery. Like so many other crimes of a private sexual nature, this offense today has little standing in the criminal courts. However, in certain civil cases such as divorce proceedings it still serves a function, but even this is rapidly changing because of the adoption of uncontested divorce proceedings in which grounds such as adultery are no longer required.

Prostitution *Prostitution* is the crime of performing or agreeing to perform for money an act of sexual intercourse or an act of deviant sexual conduct. In most cases, it is a crime in which females are charged with the offense, but it applies to males as well. The offense of prostitution also involves other related crimes. *Solicitation* is the offense of soliciting for a prostitute by encouraging, arranging, or offering to get people together for the purpose of prostitution.

The crime of compelling a female to become a prostitute or offering or arranging a situation in which a female can practice prostitution is known as *pandering*. The crime of *pimping* is the act of receiving money or property from a prostitute, knowing that it was earned by engaging in prostitution. *Patronizing a prostitute* is committed when a male engages in sex or deviant sexual conduct with a prostitute or enters and remains in a place of prostitution with the intent to engage in a sexual act.

Homosexuality *Homosexuality* is the crime of performing an "unnatural" sex act that involves only males. When a sex act is performed which involves only females, it is called *lesbianism*. Many states have now removed these as offenses, or at least have not encouraged the prosecution of these acts as long as they are done in private and involve consenting adults. In the case of an adult and a child, the offender is usually charged with contributing to the sexual delinquency of a minor.

Obscenity and Pornography Chapter 4 examines recent changes that deal with the crimes of *obscenity and pornography*. At this point, it is sufficient to note that one commits the crimes of obscenity and pornography when, with knowledge of the content, one sells, delivers, provides, or agrees to sell, offer for sale, or deliver any obscene writing, picture, record, or other representation of obscene material.[38]

Crimes Against the Public Order and the Administration of Justice

These offenses are prohibited because by their nature they are considered to subvert and destroy the institutions of government that contribute to the safety and well-being of its citizens. Some of the offenses in this category are *treason, sedition, espionage, forgery, bribery of a public official, perjury, contempt of a duly prescribed governmental function,* and *embracery*.

Treason The crime of *treason* is considered the most serious offense against the public order and is viewed as an attack against a nation and its government. Because it threatens the very existence of the nation, it goes beyond the mere act of rebellion against authority.

In the United States, the crime of treason is a constitutional offense and is proscribed in the U.S. Constitution. Most state constitutions also make treason against the state government a crime.

The U.S. Constitution provides that treason is the commission of any of the following acts: (1) levying war against the United States; or (2) aiding, comforting, and supporting an enemy of the United States.[39] The courts have held that an overt act beyond conspiracy must occur in order to constitute treason, which employs force, violence, or some violent means through or with an assembly of people.[40]

The U.S. Constitution is quite specific regarding necessary proof to convict someone for the crime of treason. It provides that no person shall be convicted of treason unless upon the testimony of two witnesses to the same overt act, or a confession [by the accused] in open court."[41]

Other treason-related crimes, proscribed by Congress, cover treasonous conduct not specified in the Constitution. One of these is the crime of *the attempted overthrow of the United States government.* This offense applies to attempted acts of treason or conspiracy to commit treason that do not satisfy the elements of treason as defined by the Constitution. Congress has also passed *misprision of treason* laws, which make it a crime if a U.S. citizen fails to report an instance of treason when the citizen knows or has reasonable grounds to believe that treason or treasonable acts have occurred.

Sedition, Espionage, and Forgery   *Sedition* involves the intent to subvert the Constitution and government by means of open violence. It is not considered as serious as treason because it involves only the subversion of the government rather than acts that would be considered as attacks upon the nation. *Espionage* is the crime of gathering or transmitting information with the intent, knowledge, or forseeability that such information might be used against the United States or to the military advantage of any foreign government.[42]

Although it may seem strange that *forgery* is classified as a crime against the public order, it is considered as such because of its potential effects on the economic well-being of society. In fact, as Loewy says, "Forgery is generally punished more severely than other nonviolent theft crimes. The rationale for this appears to be the impact that a forged instrument has on the entire commercial system as well as the impact on the person whose name is forged."[43]

Specifically, forgery is the crime of intending to defraud by falsely making or materially altering a document which, if genuine, would have legal efficacy or be the basis for legal liability.[44] According to common law, forgery was considered a misdemeanor. Under modern statutes, it is often a felony, and only in certain instances a misdemeanor, depending upon the type of instrument that was forged and the value of the property involved.

If the forgery is accompanied by words or actions that suggest that the forged document is valid, a separate offense called *uttering* is involved. It is not necessary that someone believe the forged document to be valid; the mere offering of the forged document constitutes the offense.[45] This fact, together with the fact that there is no petit forgery (that is, no distinction made between a felony and a misdemeanor by the amount of the check) in some jurisdictions, means that a person who forges and cashes five $10 checks can be convicted of ten separate felonies.[46]

Bribery of a Public Official   Among the crimes against the administration of justice is *bribery of a public official,* which is the offering, promising, giving, or soliciting of something of value with the corrupt intent to influence the actions of a public official. The key elements of this offense are the corrupt intent and the attempt to influence a public official to perform his or her duties in an improper manner.[47]

Perjury   *Perjury* is making an intentional statement under oath in a judicial or nonjudicial proceeding with the knowledge that the statement is false. *Subornation of perjury* occurs when someone procures a person to commit perjury with the preconceived knowledge and intent that perjury be committed. The witness does not have to perjure himself or herself on the witness stand for this crime to be completed. The crime is considered complete when there is a false taking of the oath by the procured witness.[48]

Contempt   The crime of contempt falls into two categories. The first of these is *civil contempt,* which is the refusal to obey the lawful decision of a competent court. This is considered contempt because it has the affect of hindering the process of justice. *Criminal contempt,* on the other hand, is disrespectful conduct toward the court which damages the court's dignity and authority. Although the offender can be fined and imprisoned after being found guilty of civil contempt, the punishment is not meant to be punitive, but rather, executive—that is, necessary for the court to carry out its proper functions. In the case of criminal contempt, the punishment is considered punitive because it punishes the offender for impugning the power of the court.

Refusal to testify before a legislative body may be regarded as *contempt of a legislative body.* This offense is based on the idea that legislative bodies must be informed if they are to effectively carry out their objectives.[49] State legislatures rarely cite an individual for refusal to testify, but the U.S. Congress has done so on occasion. Congress, however, cannot punish someone for contempt who rightfully exercises his or her constitutional rights against self-incrimination.

Finally, a crime that strikes at the center of the administration of justice is the offense of *embracery.* This is the crime of attempting to corrupt or influence a juror with respect to a verdict. To those concerned with the equitable administration of criminal justice in the United States, this is a base offense because, in the words of the Supreme Court, it "saps the very foundation of the jury system."[50]

ORIGINS OF CRIMINAL LAW

In the United States, we can trace our criminal law to four basic sources: (1) the English common law; (2) federal and state constitutions; (3) laws passed by Congress and state legislatures; and (4) decisions of the courts in criminal prosecutions. Each of these sources has had an impact upon our system of criminal law.

Our criminal law is founded in English common law. Records indicate that laws began to develop in England as far back as 600 A.D. These laws reflected a strange and usually inconsistent mixture of Roman law and the tribal rules and customs of invaders from Scandinavia, northern France, and what was to become the modern state of Germany. After the Norman Conquest in 1066, William the Conqueror and his successors attempted to bring a uniformity to the applications of the criminal law. They were able to accomplish this by suggesting the development of a court system that would apply "equal" or "common" application of the law with some degree of uniformity throughout the land. However, the ruling monarchs were quick to sense that they should not interfere too much with the operations of the courts; they merely provided the means for more uniform application and development—the courts and the judges still enjoyed relative independence.

In the strictest sense, the common law developed by common understanding or by public consent. In deciding which acts should be classified as criminal, the judges drew from common experience and attitudes. Certain crimes were considered inherently and historically offensive, and in this way the common law crimes of treason, murder, battery, kidnapping, burglary, arson, rape, and robbery were established. Although the common law is normally considered "unwritten law," this is not necessarily so. A major part of the common law did develop but without benefit of written statutes. Parliamentary legislation over the years has added numerous offenses that were not covered by the original common law. These, too, are considered part of England's common law tradition.

It was this common law tradition that the English colonists brought to America. As a practical matter, after independence, the states continued to use the basic English system. In parts of the United States, the new state governments automatically retained the common law. In others, the states confirmed this continuance with a statement of ratification. Some states did not adopt the common law as such, but rather, incorporated into writing, as new statutes of the state, practically all the basic principles of the common law.[51]

The federal and state constitutions are a second source of the criminal law. As fundamental laws of the nation and the respective states, these constitutions are sources of criminal law in that they provide the skeletal framework for the entire system of law. In this respect, all other sources of law—the common law, laws passed by Congress and the state legislatures, and the decisions of the courts—must conform to the basic guidelines established by these sources.

The third source of law is laws passed by Congress or the state legislative bodies. This power is affirmed by the respective federal and state constitutions as well as by numerous court decisions. This type of legislative law is referred to as *statutes*. When Congress passes legislation that defines certain behavior as a "crime," is referred to as a *federal statute;* when a state legislature passes such a law it is called a *state statute*. A law passed by the city council or other legislative bodies of a municipality is called an *ordinance*.

These various criminal statutes and ordinances are compiled into *codes*. For example, the state of Ohio compiles its criminal laws into the Ohio Revised Code. The federal equivalent is known as the *Federal Criminal Code,* or the *United States Criminal Code,* usually abbreviated as USC.

The last source of our criminal law is found in the decisions of our courts. This is an increasingly important area of modern criminal law. Through both their express and implied powers, the courts can interpret common law doctrines, constitutional law, and statutory law. Much of the courts' work is in the interpretation of the federal and state constitutions and existing statutory law. For example, the United States Supreme Court has broad powers to modify or redefine existing law.

However, the courts cannot indiscreetly set aside prior court decisions. A fundamental doctrine in judicial decision making is the concept of *stare decisis* which states that once a court reaches a decision, that decision sets a precedent for all subsequent and similar cases. Without this important principle, there would be no existing legal stability in our judicial system. On the other hand, it does not rule out the need for flexibility in our laws. This relationship is well expressed by Gammage and Hemphill when they say:

> Still, the principle of stare decisis does not always mean blind adherence to a previously decided case. It prevents capricious change, but it does not forbid a review of a case in view of a clear showing of error or injustice at the time of a later case. Also, in some instances conditions on which the earlier decision was based may have changed, so that the precedent is no longer desirable or just. Therefore, the doctrine of stare decisis provides for stability, but it is not so binding as to forbid change in the law when this is desirable to keep pace with changing social and economic forces that are an outgrowth of the times.[52]

CRIMINAL RESPONSIBILITY

A discussion of criminal law would not be complete without a brief look at the concept of criminal responsibility. When a crime is committed, certain conditions in the mental or legal state of the accused might exist that could relieve the accused of criminal responsibility. If these conditions do exist, they can diminish or completely negate criminal responsibility. These conditions are *insanity, intoxication, infancy, mistake of fact, duress, entrapment, self-defense,* and *the statute of limitations.* The latter means that there is a time limitation in which to prosecute a case.

There isn't space to discuss each of these conditions, but because it is frequently pleaded in criminal cases, *criminal insanity* should be explained further. In the law, criminal insanity is a legal defense that applies in two instances: first, if the accused is insane at the time of the commission of the act; and, second, if at the time of the trial he is found to be insane although he may have been sane at the time he committed the act, he cannot be compelled to stand trial. In the first case, insanity is said to have diminished the person's ability to form the necessary intent. In the latter case, the accused is considered incapable of understanding the charges against him or her and of assisting in the defense.

Over the years, the rules governing insanity as a defense have often changed. Today, there are four basic tests for criminal responsibility involving insanity permitted in American courts. These are: (1) the M'Naghten Rule; (2) the Irresistible Impulse test; (3) the Durham Rule; and (4) the Substantial Capacity test proposed by the Modern Penal Code.

M'Naghten Rule

In 1843, Daniel M'Naghten killed English prime minister Robert Peel's private secretary, thinking the secretary was Peel. It was declared that "at the time of the committing of the act, the party accused was laboring under such a defect of reason, from disease of the mind, as not to know the nature and quality of the act he was doing, or if he did know it that he did not know what he was doing was wrong."[53] This case established the M'Naghten Rule, which is also called the "right–wrong test."

Irresistible Impulse

The M'Naghten Rule led to many problems because terms such as "disease of the mind" and "know" could not be precisely defined. As a result many jurisdictions supplemented the M'Naghten Rule with the irresistible impulse test. Under this doctrine the defendant could successfully plead insanity when disease of the mind prevented the person from controlling his or her conduct.

Durham Rule

Seeking to further clarify the issue, in 1954 Circuit Court of Appeals for the District of Columbia adopted a test for insanity called the Durham Rule. This rule states that "an accused is not criminally responsible if his unlawful act was the product of mental disease or defect."[54] A major problem with the Durham Rule has been defining "mental disease or defect." Although the M'Naghten Rule is worded similarly, it does at least state that one important trait must be evident in the accused's behavior. That trait is an inability to distinguish right from wrong. Under the Durham Rule, however, only mental disease or mental defect need be present.[55]

Substantial Capacity Test

Another test for criminal insanity, one that many courts are increasingly turning to, is the substantial capacity test. This test is advocated by the American Law Institute in its Model Penal Code. The test states:

> A person is not responsible for criminal conduct if at the time of such conduct as a result of mental disease or defect he lacks substantial capacity whether to appreciate his criminality (wrongfulness) of his conduct or to conform his conduct to the requirements of the law.[56]

The rule is basically a broader statement of the M'Naghten–irresistible impulse test. It rejects the Durham Rule because that rule lacks a standard for reference and because it does not define the term "product" [of mental disease]. The test's most significant feature is that the accused show only a lack of "substantial capacity" in being able to distinguish right and wrong.[57]

In recent years a movement to abolish the insanity defense has gained popularity. Two arguments are usually advanced. The first is that the insanity defense permits society to incarcerate an innocent but dangerous person; that is, a person who has committed a dangerous act, but who lacks sufficient capacity to be criminally responsible. This is accomplished by a civil process of committing a person who is found not guilty by reason of insanity. The other argument is that the insanity defense tries to draw a line that is essentially illusory. Most criminals are mentally unbalanced to some degree and the concept of mental disease is not nearly so clear as that of a physical disease.[58] However, it is not likely that such efforts to abolish the insanity defense would be acceptable to the courts and our legislative bodies.

BASIC LEGAL TERMINOLOGY

Criminal justice students and citizens in general should have some familiarity with basic legal terms and documents. The terms *arrest, arrest warrant, search warrant, subpoena, writ of habeas corpus, bail,* and *extradition* are commonly heard, but few people really know the legal definitions and requirements of each. The remainder of this chapter explains these common legal terms and shows the reader examples of these documents.

Arrest

An arrest is taking a person into custody in the manner authorized by law. Just as a specific offense has elements, so does the act of arrest. First, there must be an intention to arrest; second, the intention to arrest must be communicated to the person arrested; third, the one arresting must have the one being arrested under his or her control; last, there must be an understanding by the person arrested that he or she is being arrested.[59] However, if one or more elements are missing, the arrest *may* not be *in*valid. For example, if an intoxicated person is arrested while unconscious, the arrest is not invalid.

In most states, a police officer can make an arrest without a warrant under the following conditions: (1) if a felony has been committed in the officer's presence; (2) if there is probable cause (reasonable grounds) to believe a felony has been committed and the person being arrested committed the felony; or (3) if a misdemeanor has been committed in the officer's presence. An arrest by a citizen, normally called a "citizen's arrest," is restricted in most states to instances where felonies have been committed in the citizen's presence or where the citizen has probable cause to believe a felony has been committed and the person being arrested committed the felony. Citizens are normally prohibited from making arrests for misdemeanors.

Arrest Warrant

An arrest warrant is an order signed by a magistrate or judge that commands the person addressed or anyone authorized to execute the warrant to take a named person into custody and to bring that person before the court to answer for the crime specified in the warrant. In the event that the name of the offender is not known and therefore cannot be entered on the face of the warrant, a "John Doe" warrant can be issued which does not name the individual.

There are several ways in which an arrest warrant is issued. The victim of the crime or complaining witness may go directly to the prosecutor (district attorney) with the information about the crime. The prosecutor then prepares a supporting affidavit (a form of a sworn statement) which the complainant swears to and signs. The prosecutor and the complainant then go before a magistrate who is authorized to issue an arrest warrant for the particular offense. (In some states, complaints for minor misdemeanors may be sworn to before the prosecutor or the clerk of courts.) The magistrate questions the complainant thoroughly to determine if there is probable cause to believe a crime has been committed and if the one named in the complaint is the probable offender.[60] If the magistrate is satisfied that the facts are correct, the warrant will be signed and turned over to the police to serve.

Police officers may also initiate complaints. The police officer goes before the magistrate or in some cases the prosecutor to file the complaint. In these circumstances, the police officer becomes the complainant and has to swear to the facts. Figure 2-2 is an arrest warrant issued by a federal magistrate.

Search Warrant

A search warrant, like an arrest warrant, is an order issued by a magistrate that commands and authorizes a law enforcement officer to search the premises described on the warrant for articles listed on the warrant. The procedure and substance of search warrants are defined by the Fourth Amendment of the U.S. Constitution, which reads:

> The right of the people to be secure in their persons, houses, papers and effects, against unreasonable searches and seizures, shall not be violated and no Warrants shall issue, but upon probable cause, supported by oath or affirmation, and particularly describing the place to be searched and the persons or things to be seized.

To obtain a search warrant, a police officer must go before a magistrate and file a sworn affidavit that indicates the *particular place* to be searched and the *particular things* to be seized (see Figure 2-3). Police officers are forbidden from searching any other place than that described in the warrant. However, police officers can seize items that are not listed in the warrant as long as they are offensive to the law and the search did not exceed the scope of the warrant.[61] The magistrate must examine the officer's affidavit to determine whether probable cause exists to believe that illegal objects or persons are present on the premises. If the magistrate is satisfied that there is probable cause, the warrant will be issued (see Figure 2-4).

When the search warrant is executed, the law enforcement officer must leave a copy of the warrant with the person who occupies the searched premises. If the premises are unoccupied at the time of the search, a copy of the warrant must still be left in plain view. In addition, the police must leave an itemized inventory of all property seized and return a copy of the inventory and notice that the warrant has been served to the authorizing magistrate. Figure 2-5 shows the return and inventory portion of a search warrant. Once the search warrant has been issued, it is common for statutes or courts to require that it must be executed within a fixed period of time, such as ten days.[62]

Warrant for Arrest of Defendant (Rev. 7-52)   Cr. Form No. 12

United States District Court
FOR THE

EASTERN DISTRICT OF PENNSYLVANIA

UNITED STATES OF AMERICA

v.

JAMES ADAM TROJANOWICZ

No. P-76-226 Cr.5

To ¹ any Special Agent of the Federal Bureau of Investigation

You are hereby commanded to arrest James Adam Trojanowicz **and bring him**

forthwith before the United States District Court for the Eastern **District of** Pennsylvania

in the city of Philadelphia **to answer to an** Indictment **charging h**im **with**

Bank robbery and bank robbery with assault by use of a dangerous weapon.

in violation of

18 USC 2113(a) and 18 USC 2113(d)

Dated at Philadelphia, Pennsylvania .... Rupert A. Lorinskas ....,

                                                                                              Clerk.

on October 24 1976

                                                            By ...... J. P. Thelen ......,

Bail fixed at $ 50,000.00 cash or approved surety.   *Deputy Clerk.*

RETURN

District of   ss

Received the within warrant the 10 th **day of** November 1976 **and executed same.**

.... Special Agent, FBI ....,

By Corneal A. Veltema ,

¹ Insert designation of officer to whom the warrant is issued, e. g., "any United States Marshal or any other authorized officer"; or "United States Marshal for .... District of ...."; or "any United States Marshal"; or "any Special Agent of the Federal Bureau of Investigation"; or "any United States Marshal or any Special Agent of the Federal Bureau of Investigation"; or "any agent of the Alcohol Tax Unit."

FIGURE 2-2 Warrant for Arrest of Defendant

Subpoena

A subpoena is a court order that compels someone to appear and provide testimony concerning a particular matter that he or she is supposed to have knowledge of (see Figure 2-6). One form of subpoena is a *subpoena deuces tecum,* which directs the person named to appear with certain specified documents (see Figure 2-7). In this manner, the court can compel the subpoenaed person to produce certain records and documents. The federal and all state

Form A. O. 106 (Rev. Nov. 1972)

Affidavit for
Search Warrant

United States District Court

FOR THE

WESTERN DISTRICT OF TENNESSEE

UNITED STATES OF AMERICA

vs.

A HOUSE LOCATED AT
646 CROSBY STREET
MEMPHIS, TENNESSEE

Docket No.

Case No. 724(p)

**AFFIDAVIT FOR
SEARCH WARRANT**

BEFORE HONORABLE NORMAN A. SPENCER, Chief Judge, United States District Court
Memphis, Tennessee
Name of Magistrate or Judge _Address of Magistrate or Judge_
The undersigned being duly sworn deposes and says:

That he has reason to believe that XXXXXXXXXXXXXX
(on the premises known as)

646 Crosby Street
Memphis, Tennessee

which is a one-story, ranch style, yellow brick house, with black shutters, and
a detached garage

in the Western District of Tennessee

there is now being concealed certain property, namely two (2) red ceramic plaques which contain
a white powdered substance believed to be cocaine.
here describe property

which are in violation of Title 21, United States Code, Sections 841 (a) (1) and
952(a) (1).
more fully alleged grounds for search and seizure

And that the facts tending to establish the foregoing grounds for issuance of a Search Warrant
are as follows: On April 18, 1976, Inspectors T.O. Bryan and R. Jones, U.S. Customs
Service, while inspecting incoming merchandise from Mexico at Metro Airport routinely inspected
two plaques shipped from Mexico to a Memphis address. In the plaques a white powdered substance
was discovered. Inspector Bryan conducted a field test which indicated the white powdered
substance was cocaine. On April 19, 1976 at approximately 1:30 P.M., a white male described
as 6'0", medium build, 175 lbs., identified himself as Tony Carano and claimed the plaques. He
was observed placing the plaques into a 1975 tan Chrysler (Ohio LC-197). He then was followed
by U.S. Customs Agents and Drug Enforcement Administration Agents to 646 Crosby Street, Memphis,
Tennessee where he entered the house with the plaques.

Material witnesses will be Inspectors T.O. Bryan and R. Jones, United
States Customs Service Agents; Michael Wornica and William Foster, Special Agents of Drug
Enforcement Administration.

Michael Wornica
Signature of Affiant.

Special Agent, DEA

Official Title, if any.

Sworn to before me, and subscribed in my presence, April 19 , 19 76

Norman A. Spencer
Judge or Federal Magistrate.

* If the warrant is to authorize execution pursuant to 21 U.S.C. § 879 without prior notice of authority or purpose, indicate the circumstances
creating the need for such a warrant.

FPI LC 3-73-90M-6990

FIGURE 2-3 Affidavit for Search Warrant

Form A. O. 93 (Rev. Nov. 1972)   Search Warrant

United States District Court
FOR THE

WESTERN DISTRICT OF TENNESSEE

UNITED STATES OF AMERICA	Docket No.
vs.	Case No. 724(p)
A HOUSE LOCATED AT 646 CROSBY STREET MEMPHIS, TENNESSEE	**SEARCH WARRANT**

To   UNITED STATES MARSHAL OR ANY DULY AUTHORIZED OFFICER

Affidavit(s) having been made before me by   Michael Wornica, Special Agent, Drug Enforcement Administration

that he has reason to believe that { ~~on the person of~~ on the premises known as }   646 Crosby Street, Memphis, Tennessee,   which is a one-story, ranch style, yellow brick house, with black shutters, and a detached garage

in the   Western   District of   Tennessee

there is now being concealed certain property, namely   two (2) red ceramic plaques which

here describe property

contain a white powdered substance believed to be cocaine.

and as I am satisfied that there is probable cause to believe that the property so described is being concealed on the person or premises above described and that the foregoing grounds for application for issuance of the search warrant exist.

You are hereby commanded to search within a period of __two days__ (not to exceed 10 days) the person or place named for the property specified, serving this warrant and making the search { ~~in the daytime-6:00 A.M. to 10:00 P.M.~~ at anytime in the day or night[1] } and if the property be found there to seize it, leaving a copy of this warrant and a receipt for the property taken, and prepare a written inventory of the property seized and promptly return this warrant and bring the property before me as required by law.

Dated this 19th day of   April,   , 19 76

Norman O Spence,
Judge or Federal Magistrate.

[1] The Federal Rules of Criminal Procedure provide: "The warrant shall be served in the daytime, unless the issuing authority, by appropriate provision in the warrant, and for reasonable cause shown, authorizes its execution at times other than daytime." (Rule 41(C))

FIGURE 2-4   Search Warrant

RETURN

I received the attached search warrant   April 19,   , 1976   , and have executed it as follows:

On April 20,   , 1976 at 11:30 o'clock   P   M, I searched the person or premises described in the warrant and

I left a copy of the warrant with ____ ANTHONY MARTIN CARANO _____
name of person searched or owner or "at the place of search"

together with a receipt for the items seized.

The following is an inventory of property taken pursuant to the warrant:

Two red ceramic plaques depicting oriental scenes of a pagoda.

This inventory was made in the presence of   Special Agent James Moore, Drug Enforcement Administration   and

I swear that this Inventory is a true and detailed account of all the property taken by me on the warrant.

Michael Warnica

Subscribed and sworn to and returned before me this 21st   day of   April   , 19 76 .

Norman A. Spenor ,
Judge or Federal Magistrate.

FPI-LC-60M-3-73 6989

FIGURE 2-5   Search Warrant Return

Subpoena to Testify   Cr. Form No. 20 (Rev. 5-68)

United States District Court

FOR THE

Southern District of Louisiana

UNITED STATES OF AMERICA

v.

Paul J. Clifton

No. N75-251 Cr.

To   Eugene A. McCoy,   1121 Sunshine Lane,   Wadsworth, Mississippi

You are hereby commanded to appear in the United States District Court for the Southern

District of Louisiana   at 544 Federal Building   in the city of

New Orleans   on the 20th day of January   1976 at 11:00 o'clock   A.M.   to

testify in the above-entitled case.

This subpoena is issued on application of the[1]   United States of America

_January 12_____, 19 76__.

_Kenneth A. Selby_____
    Attorney for United States
_544 Federal Building_____
    Address New Orleans, LA 63217
Phone 492-412-8040

Bernard A. Toman
                                                    Clerk.
By __Parker J. Meredith_____
                                                    Deputy Clerk.

RETURN

Received this subpoena at   on
and on   at   I served it on the
within named
by delivering a copy to   and tendering[2] to   the fee for one day's attendance and the mileage
allowed by law.

                              ----------------------------------,
                     By ----------------------------------,

Service Fees

Travel_____ $
Services _____
    Total_____ _____ $

[1] Insert "United States," or "defendant" as the case may be.
[2] Fees and mileage need not be tendered to the witness upon service of a subpoena issued in behalf of the United States
or an officer or agency thereof. 28 USC 1825, or on behalf of a defendant who is financially unable to pay such costs
(Rule 17(b), Federal Rules Criminal Procedure).

FPI MI—4-18-72-2400 PADS-7544

FIGURE 2-6   Subpoena to Testify

Subpoena to Produce Document or Object   Cr. Form No. 21 (Rev. 10-51)

United States District Court
FOR THE

EASTERN DISTRICT OF MICHIGAN

UNITED STATES OF AMERICA

v.

GUY WILLIAM FOSTER, and

To   KENNETH A. BERISKO

No.

Mr. Frank S. Horvath, 22 Elm Lane, Napoleon, Ohio

You are hereby commanded to appear in the United States District Court for the   Eastern
                                         Clerk's Office

District of   Michigan   at   Federal Building   in the city of
                                          410 W. Cass Avenue

Detroit   on the   7th   day of   January   1976 at   1:30   o'clock P M.

to testify in the case of United States v. G.W. Foster and K.A. Berisko   and bring with you
all proof of ownership of the following: Case Backhoe, Serial Number 5198756;
Case Loader, Serial Number 5432670; Case Tractor, Model T460A, Serial Number
5674397; and a Case Bulldozer, Model 210AE, Serial Number 245673, all stolen
on or about September 3, 1975.

This subpoena is issued upon application of the[1]   United States of America

December 28   , 19 75 .

Frank K. Gibson
    Attorney for   the United States
544 Federal Building
    Address Detroit, Michigan   By

                                                           Clerk.

                                                           Deputy Clerk.

[1] Insert "United States" or "defendant" as the case may be.

RETURN

    Received this subpoena at   Detroit, Michigan   on January 2, 1976
and on January 3, 1976   at Napoleon, Ohio
served it on the within named   Frank S. Horvath
by delivering a copy to h im   and tendering to h im   the fee for one day's attendance and the mileage
allowed by law.[2]

Dated: January 3, 1976

                         , 19

Service Fees
      Travel $
      Services

         Total $

                                         , U.S. Marshal   ,

                    By

[2] Fees and mileage need not be tendered to the witness upon service of a subpoena issued in behalf of the United States
or an officer or agency thereof. 28 USC 1825.

FPI—LK—6-28-66—800 Pads—6390

FIGURE 2-7   Subpoena to Produce Document or Object

governments provide by law that anyone who is issued a subpoena and fails to appear or testify (in the absence of self-incrimination) will be charged with contempt of court.[63]

Writ of Habeas Corpus

Another important legal document is the writ of habeas corpus, which may be used when a person is held in restraint by the state. It is a court order that directs the police or penal authorities who have a particular person in custody to "produce the body" at a time and place specified in the writ and to show why the person is held in custody or restraint.[64] After the court hears the facts, the person may be placed back into custody, may be released on bail, or may be discharged. This is accomplished by a written order of the court that must be obeyed. Figure 2-8 illustrates a federal habeas corpus writ.

HABEAS CORPUS   D. C. FORM 10
_____

United States District Court
FOR THE

Southern District of Florida
_____

To   Warden, Talegda State Prison
       or Any United States Marshal

YOU ARE HEREBY COMMANDED, to have the body   of G. William Foster

by you restrained of his liberty, as it is said,

by whatsoever names detained, together with the day and cause of   being taken and detained,

before the Honorable THOMAS P. WINSTON   , Judge of the United States

District Court for the Southern   District of Florida   , at the court room of said

Court, in the City of Miami   subject to call April 22 thru May 22, 1976,
                                   at   xxxxxx   xxxxxxxx

xxxxxx   xxxx   , then and there to do, submit to and receive whatsoever the said

Judge shall then and there determine in that behalf; and have you then and there this writ.

WITNESS the Honorable LEON H. WEAVER, CHIEF JUDGE

United States District Judge   at Miami, Florida

this   19th   day of   April   , A. D. 1976 ,

David B. Kalinich
....
                                        Clerk.

By Janet J. Purely
                                        Deputy Clerk.

FIGURE 2-8   Writ of Habeas Corpus

The courts have called the writ of habeas corpus the "great writ of liberty."[65] The first Habeas Corpus Act was enacted in the reign of Caroline II of England (1689) and was regarded as a great constitutional guarantee of personal liberty. The writ of habeas corpus was provided for in the U.S. Constitution and in the constitutions of all the states. Among the powers denied Congress in Article I of the Constitution is the right to suspend the privilege of the writ except in cases of rebellion and invasion.[66]

Other Writs

There are other writs that students of criminal justice should be familiar with. A *writ of mandamus* is an order from a higher court to an inferior court or other agency such as the police or prosecutor that compels the performance of a certain act as required by law. A *writ of injunction* is an order from a higher court to a lower court or to some other governmental agency or private citizen to "cease and desist" from performing a certain act. Finally, a *writ of coram nobis* is a writ of review directed to the trial court by the accused. This writ petitions the court to set aside its judgment against the accused because certain facts existed that, through no negligence on the part of the accused, were not brought out at the trial and which, if presented, would likely have changed the court's ruling in the case.

Other Terms

Venue is the geographical location of the crime and the jurisdiction of the court to try a particular case.

Bail is a procedure for obtaining temporary liberty after arrest or conviction by means of a written promise to appear in court as required. To obtain bail, it may be necessary to deposit cash, a surety bond, (to guarantee their return to court), or evidence of ownership or equity in real property. In recent years, the practice of releasing on one's *own recognizance* has developed. In these cases, the individual is released without having to post any form of financial security.

Extradition is the legal process of initiating and requesting another state (or nation) to surrender persons who have committed crimes and are fugitives from justice in the requesting jurisdiction. The procedure by which one sovereign state yields or returns the individual to the state initiating the request is called *rendition*.

SUMMARY

The basic elements of a crime are the act, the intent, the concurrence of act and intent, the causation, and the result. Each crime has specific elements that must be proved before the accused can be convicted.

The origins of criminal law are found in the common law. Other sources of law are the federal and state constitutions and the codified statutes and interpretation of law by the courts.

Historically, the problem of crime has been dealt with by revenge, retribution, and punishment. Beginning in the late eighteenth century a more scientific analysis of crime began through the pioneering efforts of such researchers as Lombroso, Garofalo, and Ferri. Modern theories of crime causation can be grouped into several schools of thought: the biological approach; the psychological approach; the sociological approach; and the newest, the multi-factor school.

Crimes are classified into misdemeanors, felonies, and treasonous acts. These three broad categories are further divided into crimes against the public order and the administration of justice.

The student of criminal justice must become familiar with certain basic legal principles and documents, as discussed in the last part of the chapter, before embarking on a more detailed study of the administration of justice.

REVIEW QUESTIONS

1. List and define the various elements of a crime and the various categories of intent.
2. List the four major modern schools of thought that attempt to explain the causes of crime and the characteristics of each.
3. Define the following types of criminal offenses:
   a. Felonies and misdemeanors
   b. Inchoate offenses
   c. Crimes against the person
   d. Crimes against property
   e. Crimes against public morality
   f. Crimes against the public order and the administration of justice
4. Describe the origin of our criminal law. What has contributed to its development?
5. How is criminal responsibility determined?
6. Define the following:
   a. Arrest
   b. Search warrant
   c. Subpoena
   d. Writ of habeas corpus
   e. Venue
   f. Bail
   g. Extradition

DISCUSSION QUESTIONS

1. In your opinion, which of the four schools of criminology—biological, psychological, sociological, or multi-factor—comes closest to explaining correctly the causes of criminal behavior? Explain why you think so.
2. Is the legal distinction between principals and accessories in committing a crime a valid one? Why or why not?
3. Should the insanity defense be abolished in criminal cases? Why or why not?

SUGGESTED ADDITIONAL READINGS

American Bar Association. *Tentative Drafts on ABA Project on Standards for Criminal Justice.* New York: Institute of Judicial Administration, 1968.

Bureau of National Affairs. *The Criminal Law Revolution and Its Aftermath, 1960–72.* Washington, D.C.: Bureau of National Affairs, 1973.

Chamelin, Neil C., and Kenneth R. Evans. *Criminal Law for Policemen.* Englewood Cliffs, N.J.: Prentice-Hall, 1971.

Hall, Jerome. *Theft, Law and Society,* 2d ed. Indianapolis, Ind.: Bobbs-Merrill, 1952.

Leonard, V. A. *The Police, the Judiciary and the Criminal.* Springfield, Ill.: Charles C. Thomas, 1969.

Nelson, William E. "Emergency Notions of Modern Criminal Law in the Revolutionary Era: A Historical Perspective." *New York University Law Review* 42 (May 1967): 453–468.

Rich, Vernon. *Law and the Administration of Justice.* New York: Wiley, 1975.

Wells, Paul W. *Basic Law for the Law Enforcement Officer.* Philadelphia: Saunders, 1976.

NOTES

1. M. Cherif Bassiouni, *Criminal Law and Its Processes* (Springfield, Ill.: Thomas, 1969), p. 50.

2. U.S. Constitution, Art. 1, sec. 9.

3. Bassiouni, *Criminal Law and Its Processes,* p. 50.

4. See Arnold H. Loewy, *Criminal Law* (St. Paul, Minn.: West, 1975), pp. 115–118.

5. Bassiouni, *Criminal Law and Its Processes,* p. 66.

6. For example, see Gresham M. Sykes, "The Rise of Critical Criminology," *Journal of Criminal Law and Criminology* 65 (June 1974): 206–213; and Berry Krisberg, *Crime and Privilege: Toward a New Criminology* (Englewood Cliffs, N.J.: Prentice-Hall, 1975).

7. See Stephen Schafer, *Theories in Criminology: Past and Present Philosophies of the Crime Problem* (New York: Random House, 1969), especially pp. 97–110.

8. Stephen Schafer and Richard D. Knudten, *Criminological Theory* (Lexington, Mass.: Lexington Books, 1977), p. xiii.

9. Donald R. Taft, *Criminology,* 3rd ed. (New York: McGraw-Hill, 1956), p. 357.

10. Elmer H. Johnson, *Crime, Correction, and Society,* rev. ed. (Homewood, Ill.: Dorsey, 1968), p. 154.

11. Enrico Ferri, *Criminal Sociology,* trans. J. I. Kelly and John Lisle (Boston, Mass.: Little, Brown, 1917), pp. 502–520.

12. See Richard L. Dugdale, *The Jukes: A Study in Crime, Pauperism, and Heredity,* 4th ed. (New York: Putnam, 1942); and Henry H. Goddard, *The Kallikak Family* (New York: Macmillan, 1912).

13. Ernest A. Hooten, *Crime and Man* (Cambridge, Mass.: Harvard University Press, 1939).

14. William H. Sheldon, *Varieties of Delinquent Youth* (New York: Harper & Row, 1949).

15. Sheldon Glueck and Eleanor Glueck, *Physique and Delinquency* (New York: Harper & Row, 1950).

16. See Nicholas N. Kittire, "Will the XYY Syndrome Abolish Guilt?" *Federal Probation* 35 (June 1971): 26–31; National Institute of Mental Health, *Report on the XYY Chromosomal Abnormality* (Washington, D.C.: U.S. Government Printing Office, October 1970).

17. Schafer and Knudten, *Criminological Theory,* p. xx.

18. Johnson, *Crime, Correction, and Society,* p. 188.

19. Schafer and Knudten, *Criminological Theory,* p. 200.

20. R. T. Prudhoe, *England's Great Common Law* (London: Cambridge University Press, 1922), p. 49.

21. H. Sayre, "Criminal Attempts," *Harvard Law Review* 41 (1928).

22. *State v. Carbone,* 10 N.J., 329, 91 A. 2d 571 (1961).

23. Bassiouni, *Criminal Law and Its Processes,* p. 168.

24. Ibid., pp. 170–171.

25. Loewy, *Criminal Law,* p. 25.

26. *State v. Jenkins,* 230 A.2d, 262 (Del. 1967).

27. *Lang v. State,* 6 Md. App. 128, 250 A.2d, 276 (1969).

28. A. F. Bradstatter and Alan A. Hyman, *Fundamentals of Law Enforcement* (Encino, Calif.: Glencoe, 1971), p. 103.

29. Bassiouni, *Criminal Law and Its Processes,* p. 178.

30. See Rollin M. Perkins, *Criminal Law and Procedure* (Brooklyn, N.Y.: Foundation Press, 1966), p. 345.

31. Neil C. Chamelin and Kenneth R. Evans, *Criminal Law for Policemen,* 2nd ed. (Englewood Cliffs, N.J.: Prentice-Hall, 1976), p. 184.

32. 18 U.S.C.A.. 1201.

33. *People v. Lardner,* 300 Ill. 264, 133 N.E. 375 (1921); *People v. Bakerm,* 365 Ill., 328, 6 N.E. 2d 667 (1937).

34. *People v. Cox,* N.Y. 137, 36 N.E. 2d 84 (1941).

35. Brandstatter and Hyman, *Fundamentals of Law Enforcement,* p. 109.

36. Bassiouni, *Criminal Law and Its Processes,* p. 259.

37. Blackstone, *Commentaries,* p. 254.

38. Bassiouni, *Criminal Law and Its Processes,* p. 245.

39. U.S. Constitution, Art. 3, sec. 3; see also *Kawakita v. United States,* 342 U.S. 717, 72 S. Ct. 950 (1952).

40. See *Cramer v. United States,* 355 U.S. 1, 65 S. Ct. 918 (1945); and Bassiouni, *Criminal Law and Its Processes,* p. 287.

41. U.S. Constitution, Art. 3, sec. 3.

42. See 18 U.S.C.A.

43. Loewy, *Criminal Law,* p. 102.

44. *People v. Adams,* 300 Ill. 20 132 N.E. 765 (1921).

45. *Murphy v. State,* 17 R.I. 698 24 Atl. 473 (1892).

46. See *Barker v. Ohio,* 328 F.2d 582 (6th Cir. 1964).

47. *Randall v. Evening News Association,* 97 Mich. 136, 56 N.W. 361.

48. Bassiouni, *Criminal Law and Its Processes,* p. 300.

49. *Giancana v. United States,* 352 F.3d 921.

50. *Hoffa v. United States,* 385 U.S. 293, 87 S. Ct. 408 (1966).

51. Allen C. Gammage and Charles F. Hemphill, Jr., *Basic Criminal Law* (New York: McGraw-Hill, 1974), p. 14.

52. Ibid., p. 22.

53. M'Naghten Case, 8 Eng. Rep. 718 (H.L. 1843), p. 722.

54. *Durham v. United States*, 214 F.2d 862, 874–875 (D.C. Cir. 1954).

55. Lowey, *Criminal Law*, pp. 222–223.

56. American Law Institute, Model Penal Code, 401 (1962).

57. Joseph J. Senna and Larry J. Siegel, *Introduction to Criminal Justice* (St. Paul, Minn.: West, 1978), p. 83.

58. Loewy, *Criminal Law*, p. 228.

59. Although it is commonly believed that certain words and actual physical contact with the arrestee are required, this is not the case.

60. See Lloyd L. Weinreb, *Criminal Process* (Mineola, N.Y.: Foundation Press, 1969), pp. 17–22.

61. See *Bostwick v. State*, 124 Ga. App. 113, 182 S.E.2d 925 (1971).

62. See *Federal Rules of Criminal Procedure* 41 (d); and Yale Kamisar, Wayne R. La Fave, and Jerold H. Israel, *Basic Criminal Procedure* (St. Paul, Minn.: West, 1974).

63. For example, see *Mich. Stats. Ann.* 8 279 23 C.L. (1948).

64. Hazel B. Kerper, *Introduction to the Criminal Justice System* (St. Paul, Minn.: West, 1972), p. 404.

65. *Ex Parte Kelly*, 123 N.J. EQ 489, 198 A. 203 (1938).

66. Kerper, *Introduction to the Criminal Justice System*, p. 403.

3

CRIME IN AMERICA

1. What is the nature of the so-called crime problem in America?
2. What is the Uniform Crime Reporting Program and what offenses constitute Part 1 (index crimes)?
3. What are some of the characteristics of crime and the trends in crime as reported by official statistics and studies?
4. What are some of the criticisms of the Uniform Crime Reports?
5. What is the National Crime Panel and how does it function?
6. How will the proposed new Bureau of Criminal Justice Statistics function?
7. How can the use of computers aid crime reporting and recording?
8. How do victim restitution programs operate?

These are some of the questions this chapter will answer.

Crime, which has always been a problem, became a major public issue in the United States during the 1960s. By 1970, several public opinion polls indicated that crime was viewed as the most serious social problem—surpassing race conflicts, inflation, and even the Vietnam war.[1] The media have dramatized the problem with examples of criminal acts that confirm official statistics indicating rising crime rates. *Life* magazine described a six-story building in New York in which 17 of 24 apartments had been burglarized. One resident even purchased a German shepherd watchdog to protect himself, but it too was stolen.[2] *Life* followed up this story with a questionnaire exploring individual experiences with crime. The 43,000 responses, which were not necessarily representative of the general population of the United States, indicated that at least 70 percent of those responding were afraid to go out on the streets after dark, were occasionally afraid of crime even while at home, and were prepared to pay more for improved protection.[3]

Perhaps because crime is so well publicized by our media, it is often perceived that of all the industrialized and urban societies in the world the United States has one of the highest crime rates, if not the highest.[4] The average American usually thinks of crime in terms of violent offenses such as homicide, forcible rape, and robbery. However, the serious student of criminal justice must approach the inflammatory rhetoric that surrounds crime with due caution. When we closely examine the actual facts behind the reports on crime—such as the methods of calculating crime statistics and the frequently inadequate research supporting those figures—we must be extremely careful about accepting such statements as fact.

First, there is no solid evidence that crime is any greater in the United States than in other industrialized nations because there is no precise way to measure crime rates. We do know that serious crime is certainly not confined to the United States. In Britain, for example, crimes of violence increased from 26,716 to 41,088 between 1966 and 1970, with London experiencing more violent crimes in the first half of 1971 than in the whole of 1970. Similar trends are observable in continental Europe and Latin America.[5] In Africa, a serious wave of violence, accompanied by demands for public execution, struck Nigeria following its civil war. When such so-called crime waves are added to the violence in Northern Ireland and the recent surge of international terrorism, the crime situation in America can be put into perspective and tends to appear less imposing a problem. For example, data gathered by the World Health Organization in 1972 on homicide rates per 100,000 population showed the following results for the countries listed.[6]

COUNTRY	RATE
El Salvador	29.5
Guatemala	20.4
Mexico	14.3
Thailand	12.7
United States	9.1
Venezuela	7.8
Cuba	3.7
Canada	2.3
Hungary	2.1
Hong Kong	1.8

TABLE 3-1
Eight Most Frequent Crimes for Which Arrests Were Made by the Police (1976)

RANK	OFFENSE	NUMBER	PERCENTAGE OF ALL CRIME ARRESTS
1	Drunkenness	1,071,131	13.5
2	Larceny (theft)	928,078	11.7
3	Driving under the influence	837,910	10.6
4	Disorderly conduct	545,639	6.9
5	Narcotic drug laws	500,540	6.3
6	Burglary—breaking or entering	406,821	5.1
7	Simple assaults	354,010	4.5
8	Liquor laws	302,943	3.8
	Total		62.4

Source: Based on FBI, *Uniform Crime Reports, 1976* (Washington, D.C.: U.S. Government Printing Office, 1977), p. 184.

To obtain a realistic picture of crime in this country, we must know what types of behavior constitute the reported crimes. According to the *Uniform Crime Reports,* an estimated 11,304,800 so-called serious crimes were reported to the police during 1976. However, this represents only a small percentage of crimes committed and an equally small percentage of crimes for which arrests were made. The majority of crimes committed and handled by the criminal justice system are much less serious offenses. Such crimes as drunkenness, larceny (theft), driving under the influence, disorderly conduct, and crimes related to drug laws (particularly marijuana) are disproportionately represented in official crime statistics. Add to this the vast number of traffic cases and other misdemeanors that are processed by the police, courts, and jails, and a different picture of crime emerges. For example, Table 3-1 summarizes the types of crimes for which arrests were made in 1976.

This is not to say that the United States does not have a serious crime problem; however, a closer look would tend to call into question certain popular assumptions about crime and the ability of the criminal justice system to deal with it. Although the typical image of crime centers on the more serious offenses of murder, forcible rape, and robbery, these particular offenses actually constitute slightly more than 4 percent of the crimes *reported* to the police. If we considered just the crimes of homicide and forcible rape, this figure would diminish to six tenths of one percent. If, in fact, we knew the true total extent of crime in America (reported and unreported crimes), the relative percentage of these crimes would shrink even further.

The remainder of this chapter will examine the question of crime and how very misleading crime statistics can be. As will be seen, we need to analyze crime and crime data much more rationally if we are to understand this particular social problem.

THE UNIFORM CRIME REPORTING PROGRAM

During the 1920s, the International Association of Chiefs of Police (IACP) saw the need to develop a national system for gathering and publishing crime statistics. As a result, in 1930 Congress authorized a national and uniform

TABLE 3-2
Uniform Crime Report Offenses

PART I (Index Offenses)	PART II (Other Offenses)	
1. Criminal homicide	8. Simple assaults	19. Gambling
2. Forcible rape	9. Arson	20. Offenses against the
3. Robbery	10. Forgery and counter-	family and children
4. Aggravated assault	feiting	21. Driving under the
5. Burglary	11. Fraud	influence
6. Larceny-theft	12. Embezzlement	22. Violation of liquor
7. Auto theft	13. Buying, receiving, or	laws
	possessing stolen	23. Drunkenness
	property	24. Disorderly conduct
	14. Vandalism	25. Vagrancy
	15. Weapons (carrying,	26. All other offenses
	possession, etc.)	(excluding traffic)
	16. Prostitution and com-	27. Suspicion
	mercialized vice	28. Curfew and loitering
	17. Other sex offenses	(juveniles)
	18. Violation of narcotic	29. Runaway (juveniles)
	drug laws	

system of compiling crime statistics known as the Uniform Crime Reporting Program. Congress vested the Federal Bureau of Investigation with responsibility for developing the program and authorized that agency to be the national clearinghouse for statistical information on crime. Under this program, crime reports were to be voluntarily submitted to the FBI by city, county, state, and other federal law enforcement agencies throughout the country. To provide for uniformity in reporting crimes by various jurisdictions, national standardized definitions of crimes and the method of reporting them were adopted. Although there still remain a few police agencies that do not routinely report crimes to the FBI, by 1976 over 13,000 law enforcement agencies voluntarily supplied crime data to the FBI. From these data, the FBI publishes annual *Uniform Crime Reports* (UCR), which are statistical summaries of all reported crimes. In the past few years, forty-three states have developed central agencies (sometimes the state police) that collect the data from all local governmental jurisdictions and then forward the statistics for the state to the FBI.

Offenses in the Uniform Crime Reporting Program are broken down into two categories. Part I of the UCR consists of seven major crimes or "index offenses," that the FBI views as indicators of national and regional crime trends. The data on these index offenses are further broken down into specific areas such as age and sex, population groups, suburban and non-suburban counties, arrest rates, and clearances. Part II consists of 22 other offense categories for which data are not as complete. Table 3-2 indicates the 29 offenses covered in the UCR.

CRIME AS A SOCIAL PROBLEM

Because of the nature of the factors that seem to be associated with crime, many authorities doubt that crime can ever be brought under control. Wilson, for example, sees crime as the result of three social factors: (1) the numbers of youth in society at a given time; (2) the disruptive nature of our society on the family unit; and (3) the opportunities for crime in our urbanized society.[7] Whether or not we fully accept his ideas, these forces probably do, in some way, influence the potential for crime. What is certain is that crime is not a problem that can be left entirely to the criminal justice system to solve. Clearly the issues that underlie crime transcend the ability of the police and the courts to deal with this complex problem in any meaningful way.

Historical Background

Crime is not only a recent experience in America. Every generation has been threatened by crime and violence. In San Francisco in the 1860s, accounts told of extensive areas of the city where "no decent man was in safety to walk the street after dark; while at all hours, both night and day, his property was jeopardized by incendiarism and burglary."[8] In New York, roving teenage street gangs who "preyed upon innocent victims" gave rise to the word "hoodlum" in 1877.[9] Even before the American Revolution, increases in robbery and violent crimes reported in New York, Boston, and Philadelphia, led some citizens to complain that municipal governance was a failure and that citizens should revert to self-action if individual safety was to be preserved.[10]

Many instances of crime and violence occurred in our early history. During the great railway strike of 1877, hundreds were killed in outbreaks of violence and terrorism that swept the country and culminated in a massive confrontation between strikers and company police and militia; scores were killed or injured, and almost 2 miles of buildings and railway property were destroyed.[11] During the 1863 draft riots, the looting and takeover of New York for three days by mobs equaled the disorders that racked our cities in the 1960s. Racial disturbances have long plagued our major cities, as seen by the race riots that took place in Atlanta in 1907, in Chicago, Washington, and East St. Louis in 1919, and Detroit in 1943.[12] Al Capone, "Pretty Boy" Floyd, and the Barkers are all examples of our heritage of crime.

Neither the specific variables that produce crime nor the interaction of those variables are fully understood. But some important factors are known. They are as follows:

Social Characteristics

- Density and size of the community
- Social composition of the community in terms of age, sex, and race
- Existing cultural mores that control social behavior
- Economic conditions
- Relative stability of the population
- Educational, religious, and recreational characteristics

Individual Characteristics

- Attitudes conducive to criminal behavior
- Perceived value and meaningfulness of legitimate behavior
- Self-esteem; perceived abilities to compete in the legitimate world

Specific Characteristics of the Criminal Justice System

- Effective strength of the police force
- Quality of police personnel
- Policies of the prosecuting officials and courts
- Attitude of the public toward the police and other criminal justice agencies
- Administration and investigative efficiency of the local police

How accurately crime and its effects on society can be measured depend on the quality of the tools used to make the analysis. We are handicapped in understanding crime because we do not have adequate measuring instruments, nor do we have the knowledge to account properly for the multitude of factors that might have some relationship to criminal behavior. As a result of these limitations, any analysis of our existing crime statistics, and therefore any conclusions that might be drawn from them, must always be suspect. These limitations also present significant problems in measuring the impact and results of many of the programs that have been designed to reduce crime in this country.

CRIME TRENDS AND CHARACTERISTICS

At this point, let us examine some of the data provided by the Uniform Crime Reports. Although the UCR is not an accurate reflection of crime in America, as we shall see later, let us analyze the trends and characteristics of crime that it purports to show. First, the UCR indicates that crimes seem to be increasing at an alarming rate in the United States. Table 3-3 shows the national crime rate and the percentage change in the reported seven index crimes from 1968 to 1977.

What is particularly disturbing about these trends is their apparent disproportionate increase in just a few years. At the current rate, some offenses can be expected to double each decade. Particularly disturbing to many observers

TABLE 3-3
National Crime Rate and Percent Change for Index Offenses from 1968 to 1977

OFFENSE	PERCENT CHANGE FROM 1968
Murder	+ 38.6
Forcible rape	+ 99.0
Robbery	+ 54.0
Aggravated assault	+ 82.2
Burglary	+ 64.2
Larceny (theft)	+ 69.6
Motor vehicle theft	+ 23.6
Total average increase	+ 50.0
Violent crimes	+ 69.7
Property crimes	+ 62.1

Source: FBI, *Uniform Crime Reports, 1977* (Washington, D.C.: U.S. Government Printing Office, 1977), p. 35.

are the spiraling rates of such violent crimes as forcible rape, robbery, and aggravated assault. Although a leveling-off has been evident in the last few years—even a decline has been noted in some categories—there are many observers who feel that the increased occurrence of these crimes is proof of the malaise that underlies American society today.[13] Certainly the publicity given these offenses contributes to a growing fear and concern among Americans.

In recent years, the threat of violence has been the political campaign rhetoric of "law and order" by "safe streets" advocates, who call for repressive measures to deal with this situation—a cure that may be more damaging to individual freedom in the United States than the cause.

Crime Cycles

Statistics indicate that there are seasonal, weekly, and even daily cycles both in the rate of crime and in the types of crime committed.

Seasonal Variations in Crime   The relationship between the seasons of the year and the occurrence of crime has fascinated criminologists for many years. A number of nineteenth-century studies concluded that sexual crimes occurred more frequently in the summer months and that crimes against property were more likely to be committed in winter.[14] In 1912, Cesare Lombroso wrote the first important study of seasonal crime rates.[15] By examining statistical data on sexual crimes, murders, and political crimes of rebellion, he concluded that these types of crimes are most frequent during the hottest months.[16] Von Mayr also arrived at a similar conclusion. From an analysis of criminal statistics in Germany from 1883 to 1892, he concluded that a correlation existed between the seasons of the year and certain types of crime; that is, offenses against the person reached their maximum in August and their minimum in December, whereas offenses against property reached their maximum in December and their minimum in April.[17]

Cohen, analyzing the UCR over a 5-year period, also found some seasonal crime trends in the United States. Murder was generally more frequent in the summer than in the winter, but there were variations in the relative frequencies of these offenses by month in different geographical regions. The crimes of aggravated assault and forcible rape were generally lowest in January and then began to rise until they reached their peak in midsummer. Robbery generally tended to decline until July, after which it continued on an upswing that peaked in the month of December. The property offenses of burglary, larceny-theft, and automobile theft were less uniform than robbery in their patterns of occurrence. Nonetheless, Cohen believes that these property crimes also reflect seasonal influences, with a slight rise from January through March, a lower but relatively constant level to August, and a general upswing to a peak in either November or December. Overall, he concluded that crimes against persons increase in the summer months, while property crimes are most frequent during the winter.[18] The reason given by criminologists for these seasonal differences is that the warm summer months find more people in daily contact with each other, while the winter months provide shorter days and the cover of darkness for the commission of property crimes that require stealth.[19]

Daily Variations in Crime Most data indicate that major crimes are most likely to be committed on weekends, with the trend peaking on Saturday and then declining from Sunday through Tuesday, after which crime begins to climb toward the Saturday peak.[20] Table 3-4 provides data that indicate that in Kansas City, at least, such is the case.

Hourly Variations in Crime Analyses by the Kansas City Police Department, which has an excellent research unit, indicate that the incidence of index crimes is highest during the hours from 8:00 P.M. to midnight; on the average a little over 28 percent of the crimes committed during any 24-hour period occur during those 4 hours. This phenomenon is documented by similar studies done by other law enforcement agencies.[21]

The Geography of Crime

In addition to seasonal and time differences, there are regional and community differences in rates of crime and types of crimes.

Crime by Regions Data indicate that regional differences in the United States for both total crimes and the relative frequency of certain index offenses exist. However, these statistics should not be interpreted to imply that physical geography by itself is a major factor—at most, the data may suggest that there is a relationship between geographical areas and their sociological characteristics. For example, geographical areas of the country differ in the distribution and characteristics of their population. Although these differences are not as great as they were in the past, they still exist. Regions differ in the relative distributions of their populations according to such characteristics as age, sex, race, life styles (urban versus rural), educational attainment, customs, residential mobility, occupation, and other factors. These characteristics determine which crimes are likely to be committed, the opportunities for certain types of offenses that exist, the likelihood that crimes will be reported to authorities, and which crimes are most likely to be handled by official intervention by the criminal justice system.

Table 3-5 indicates some striking geographical differences in the distribution of index crimes. For each index offense in the table, the regions with the highest and lowest number of the specific offenses are indicated in the boxes. The total indicates the average number of these offenses per 100,000 population for the entire nation. Converting the rates of occurrence for each 100,000 population compensates for the differences in population size by geographic region. The data reflect that, overall, the west north central states have the lowest rate of index offenses. On the other hand, the Pacific states generally reflect the highest index crime rates. A comparison of earlier UCR reports seems to suggest that these same regional trends have existed for a number of years.

Another interesting characteristic of the data is that the southern states rank first in the numbers of homicides, a pattern that seems to have existed

TABLE 3-4

Percentage Distribution of Index Crimes by Day of Week and Hour of Day—Kansas City, Mo., 1972

DAY OF WEEK	PERCENTAGE OF WEEKLY CRIMES	MIDNIGHT TO 4 A.M.	4 A.M. TO 8 A.M.	8 A.M. TO NOON	NOON TO 4 P.M.	4 P.M. TO 8 P.M.	8 P.M. TO MIDNIGHT
Monday	13.8	12.9	5.8	12.4	20.8	22.3	25.8
Tuesday	12.1	11.6	4.3	13.4	22.5	23.1	25.1
Wednesday	13.4	11.9	4.0	13.3	21.9	21.3	27.4
Thursday	13.9	12.5	5.9	12.8	20.4	22.8	25.9
Friday	15.1	10.7	4.3	10.7	19.7	21.5	33.1
Saturday	17.6	18.3	6.5	7.3	15.6	20.0	32.3
Sunday	14.1	21.5	7.3	7.1	14.3	21.8	28.0

Source: *Comprehensive Law Enforcement Plan, Missouri Law Enforcement Assistance Council, 1972.*

TABLE 3-5

UCR Index Crimes per 100,000 Population by Geographic Regions, 1976

REGIONS	MURDER, NONNEGLIGENT MANSLAUGHTER	FORCIBLE RAPE	ROBBERY	AGGRAVATED ASSAULT	BURGLARY	LARCENY-THEFT	AUTO THEFT
Northeast	7.0	20.4	288.1	208.1	1,446.7	2,541.9	645.5
Middle Atlantic	8.2	22.2	340.1	222.5	1,439.7	2,542.8	569.4
North Central	7.4	23.4	175.8	175.1	1,195.2	2,944.0	402.1
W. North Central	4.6	19.6	103.2	136.3	1,094.0	2,684.5	292.9
South	11.3	26.3	139.9	251.7	1,346.2	2,716.6	291.3
E. South Central	12.2	20.9	107.1	202.1	1,094.4	1,897.3	253.9
W. South Central	11.4	28.1	121.2	202.2	1,383.3	2,869.1	316.4
West	8.5	38.9	206.8	294.1	1,962.1	3,740.0	532.4
Pacific	8.9	42.0	238.0	312.6	2,047.5	3,705.5	585.9
Total U.S.	8.9	26.4	195.8	228.7	1,439.4	2,921.3	446.1

Source: FBI, *Uniform Crime Report, 1976* (Washington, D.C.: U.S. Government Printing Office, 1977).

over the years. Other studies have corroborated these long-standing high rates of homicide,[22] a fact that has led a number of criminologists to attempt to explain this phenomenon in terms of the cultural and social stratification that has existed in the South.[23] Similarly, the high rate of index offenses that occur in the Pacific states seem to be well established. Keith Harries found in his 1968 and 1971 examinations of the geographical occurrence of crime that the Pacific states were in the forefront in the number of robberies, aggravated assaults, forcible rapes, and burglaries and second only to the South in the number of homicides.[24]

A recent and excellent analysis of crime in the United States done by Harries indicated that the larger the metropolitan area, the higher the relative crime rate; that the larger the black population, the higher the rates of homicide and assault; that major violent crimes except rape are much more likely to occur on the street than in an inside location; and that there was a correlation between the number of aggravated assaults in a community and the number of the other six index crimes.[25]

Crime by Type of Community Another established trend shows that cities have a much higher crime rate than rural areas. However, some trends seem to be developing that indicate a possible narrowing of this gap. Since the early 1970s, the UCR has indicated that index crimes in towns of less than 50,000 and in suburban communities have been increasing rapidly. Although, since that time, increases in these crimes have slowed, the question still remains, what are the reasons for the drastic increases in reported crimes in areas that had previously been thought of as havens of security? Probably part of the answer is simply that more of these offenses are being committed in small towns and suburban communities than in the past. The movement of large shopping centers and commercial establishments to the suburbs has increased opportunities for crime and the vulnerability of these establishments to criminal attack. Suburban and rural banks are an excellent example. Minimum security and the proximity of arterial routes make them a favorite target for robbery. For example, a study done by the DeKalb County Police Department, which is adjacent to the city of Atlanta, Georgia, indicated that a high percentage of crimes committed in that county were by individuals residing in Atlanta. Criminals in Atlanta selected sites to commit burglaries, robberies, larceny, and auto theft in the county and then, with the help of the freeway and interstate highway system, returned to the city of Atlanta and disappeared.[26]

Another factor that may contribute to the increases of reported crimes in small towns and suburban communities are the actions of the local police. Police agencies in these areas are becoming more sophisticated in crime detection, recording techniques, and crime reporting. Just a few years ago, only a handful of the larger local police departments employed advanced techniques in these areas. Now some of the smaller cities have even surpassed metropolitan police departments in levels of service and the use of advanced techniques which, because of better reporting methods, send more complete data to the FBI.

THE CONTROVERSY OVER THE UNIFORM CRIME REPORTS AND CRIME RATES

Because most of the published information on crime in the United States is based on the UCR, it is appropriate at this point for us to analyze how meaningful an indicator of crime the report actually is. The Center for Studies of Crime and Delinquency of the National Institute of Mental Health has indicated that if criminal statistics are to be meaningful, they must fulfill the following requirements:

1. Provide information about the types of crimes committed.

2. Indicate something of the circumstances that surround the crime.

3. Provide some information about the kinds of persons involved.

4. Indicate the forms of disposal decided on by the courts or other authorities.

5. Separate first offenders (or first convictions) according to age, sex, and other social and psychological data.

6. Provide data on the cost of maintaining the services connected with the detection and prevention of crime and the treatment of offenders, and relate these to some measures of effectiveness.[27]

The fact that the UCR does not meet any of these requirements satisfactorily has led to its widespread repudiation by most knowledgeable people who have studied problems of crime in this country. The noted criminologist Lloyd Ohlin has said that the UCR index, which is often cited as the official summary of crime, is *almost worthless* (emphasis added).[28] Sellin, another eminent scholar in the study of crime, has said that the United States "has the worst crime statistics of any major country in the western world."[29] Even Attorneys General Edward H. Levi and Griffin B. Bell, whose agency is responsible for collecting and disseminating the statistics, stated that crime statistics shown in the UCR were of questionable validity.[30] Why does the Uniform Crime Report receive so much criticism?

Reasons for Criticism of the UCR

The following nine points are the major criticisms generally given as reasons why the UCR cannot be considered a valid indicator of the extent of crime in the United States:

- *Unreported crimes are not included:* The UCR reflects only crimes reported to the police. This presents several problems: First, not all police agencies in America report crimes to the police. As of 1977, the police agencies' reporting covered 95 percent of the nation's population. Second, surveys indicate that many people do not report to the police[31] that they were victims of crimes and, therefore, these crimes remain unknown.[32]

- *Reliance on voluntary submission of data:* Since the UCR relies on the reporting police agencies to voluntarily submit data, the opportunities for the police to falsify crime records are always present. There have been several notorious instances of police departments under reporting crime to the FBI for political reasons.[33] However, now that federal monies have become available to local police agencies, there may be an incentive to over report crimes in order to obtain more federal funds.[34]

• *Number of reported crimes influenced by numerous factors:* It is a demonstrated fact that police agencies with more sophisticated and accurate records systems may contribute to "paper" increases in crime.[35] Also, the fact that theft insurance is widely available may increase the number of crimes reported to the police. Since insurance companies require a police report for any claims payments, the insured must report the crime. Similarly, theft insurance may induce fraud. The insured may report nonexisting crimes and losses to the police to obtain an insurance settlement.

An increasing willingness by minority group members to report crimes may be another factor. In the past, the police may have overlooked and failed to report crimes in certain areas of the city. Minority groups, in particular, are far less inhibited today in reporting crimes to the police.[36] For example, new attitudes toward rape may be encouraging higher rates of victim reporting for this crime. In fact, this crime has risen drastically in the last few years in the UCR, a fact which is certainly in part explained by increased reporting of rape incidents.

Finally, changes in classification also affect reporting. Since 1973, the UCR has listed all larcenies regardless of value of the property stolen as a Part I crime. Before 1973, only larceny over $50 was a Part I crime. This change has resulted in the Part I crimes jumping dramatically.

• *Data not meaningful:* For the most part, the UCR is only a tabular summary of crime and, as such, does not provide crime analysts with much meaningful information. For instance, the police particularly, could improve their efficiency if they had more data upon which they could rely such as crime data related to age, sex, race, economic status;[37] the rate of population mobility as a basis for the measurement of crime rates;[38] occurrence data that indicate the extent to which different kinds of neighborhoods are subjected to different kinds of index crimes;[39] data on unreported offenses; and victim surveys to supplement the UCR.[40]

• *Data based on inconsistent definitions of crime:* Although the UCR and the FBI try to define crimes and classifications uniformly, the President's Commission on Law Enforcement and Administration of Justice found that jurisdictional differences in crime definitions exist and even the best police departments make mistakes in classifying crimes.

• *Poor classification:* The UCR does not properly classify "serious" offenses in its Part I index. For example, larceny and auto theft are included, but more serious crimes such as kidnapping, arson, or the sale of hard narcotics are not.

• *Overemphasis on crime control as a measure of police effectiveness:* The UCR may force the police to place too great an emphasis upon crime statistics as an effective measure of their accomplishments. Increases in reported crime rates seem to imply that the police are ineffective when in fact the opposite might be true. A police department may report a high crime rate because it is efficiently managed, has developed an accurate records system, is administered with integrity, and has the confidence of citizens who are then more likely to report crimes to the police.

Also, the use of published UCR data as an indicator of police effectiveness may force the police, for political reasons, to commit resources to crime-related activities that are out of proportion to the strictly crime-related activities they are engaged in.

• *Lack of baseline data:* There is no accurate baseline data for analysis. For example, if we want to compare crime rates of time A with crime rates of time C, we must know the exact extent of crime at time A. This then becomes the baseline against which all subsequent comparisons will be made.

Although the UCR does make comparisons with preceding years, the comparison is faulty because the year that is used as the baseline is itself inaccurate. For example, if we compare the crime rates in 1979 with those in 1969, we know from the preceding discussion the many factors that can affect the crime rate: how can we say, with any degree of validity, that crime is *really* increasing, decreasing, or remaining constant? To do so, we would need an accurate baseline period and an accurate subsequent period to measure against.

• *Total exclusion of certain crimes:* The last widely criticized failure of the UCR is the general omission of many forms of white-collar crime. For instance, the UCR does not include such criminal acts as a politician taking a bribe, a merchant cheating a customer, a lawyer swindling a client, or a physician injuring a patient while intoxicated. The police simply do not learn about many white-collar crimes. It has been estimated, for example, that 90 percent of crimes that involve computer manipulation are never reported.[41]

By now, it should be apparent that the question of whether crime in the United States is increasing, decreasing, or remaining stable cannot be answered with any degree of certainty. The next section examines a major step that has been taken to better measure the incidence of crime in the United States today.

New Efforts to Improve the Measurement and Recording of Crime

In 1977, the UCR indicated that nearly 11 million Index offenses were recorded by the police. However, as we have seen from our discussion of the UCR, this underrepresents the actual amount because many crimes are not reported. In an attempt to develop a more accurate picture of unreported crime in the nation, a new crime analysis program has been created and is beginning to compile data. The new program was implemented in 1973 by the Law Enforcement Assistance Administration (LEAA) of the U.S. Department of Justice, which has initiated a $12 million annual survey to obtain statistical data concerning the incidence of crime, its cost, and the characteristics of its victims and of various criminal events. The program is called the National Crime Panel. To conduct the surveys, LEAA has contracted with the U.S. Bureau of Census which is also compiling the data. In the words of LEAA:

> [The National Crime Panel] is one of the most ambitious efforts yet undertaken for filling some of the gaps in crime data; victimization surveys are expected to supply criminal justice officials with new insights into crime and its victims, complementing data resources already on hand (i.e., the UCR) for purposes of planning, evaluation and analysis. The surveys subsume many of the so-called hidden crimes that, for a variety of reasons, are never brought to police attention. They also furnish a means for developing victim typologies and, for identifiable sectors of society, yield information necessary to compute the relative risk of being victimized.[42]

Using scientific sampling procedures, the panel began to survey crime victimization among individuals, households, and commercial establishments, concentrating on the crimes of forcible rape, robbery, assault, larceny, burglary, and auto theft.[43] The idea behind the project is to randomly select citizens who are representative of a city's residents. Researchers interview the citizens in the sample to see whether they have been victims of crimes, and if so, what types of crimes, how the crimes were committed, and whether they reported their victimization to the police. These studies are often referred to as *victimization studies*. From the sample, researchers project data for the city's entire population. The initial surveys were conducted in New York, Chicago, Los Angeles, Philadelphia, and Detroit. Another similar study is also being conducted in 13 other large cities in the nation.

The preliminary data gathered during the first half of 1973 indicated broad discrepancies between the number of serious offenses committed and the number reported in the UCR. It appeared that the problem was not only the failure of citizens to report their victimization to the police, but also the fact that many reported incidents were not listed by the police in their official statistics. It should be recognized, however, that in some instances the police do not record crimes when reported because the reports prove to be unfounded. In any event, the data from this first survey of serious crime added fuel to the controversy surrounding the validity of the UCR. Table 3-6 examines the preliminary findings of the victimization survey.

TABLE 3-6
Incidents from the National Crime Panel Preliminary Report

TYPE OF CRIME	TOTAL INCIDENTS	INCIDENTS REPORTED TO THE POLICE	INCIDENTS FROM THE UNIFORM CRIME REPORTS
Rape	81,600	35,900	23,409
Robbery	600,600	318,100	179,478
Aggravated assault	637,200	314,500	198,560
Burglary	3,691,300	1,863,300	1,171,358
Larceny	11,085,800	2,406,500	1,980,007
Motor vehicle theft	586,100	381,700	429,492
Total	16,682,600	5,320,000	3,982,304

Source: Law Enforcement Assistance Administration, *Newsletter* 4, No. 6 (December, 1974), p. 5.

Since these preliminary findings were made, the surveys have been expanded. In 1977, LEAA released additional figures for the year 1975. These subsequent surveys indicate that the UCR discrepancies are not quite as large as the preliminary surveys indicated. Nevertheless, the 1977 report found that serious discrepancies still exist between the numbers of crimes reported to the police and those discovered through the victimization studies. Figure 3-1 shows the average percentage of crimes reported to the police in the cities surveyed.

Among the crimes examined, those against commercial establishments were most frequently reported. Of the crimes not directed at businesses, auto theft was most frequently reported, while personal and household larceny were reported about only one-fourth of the time they occurred.

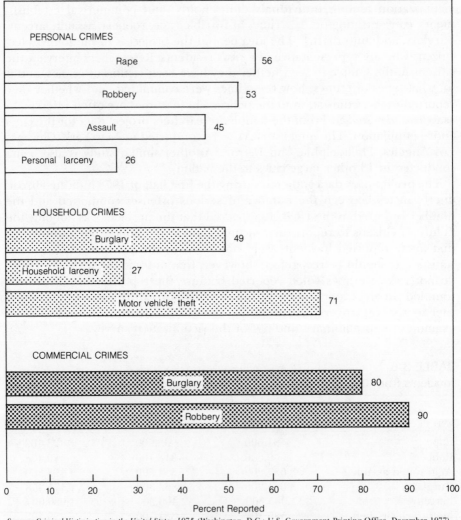

PERSONAL CRIMES

Rape	56
Robbery	53
Assault	45
Personal larceny	26

HOUSEHOLD CRIMES

Burglary	49
Household larceny	27
Motor vehicle theft	71

COMMERCIAL CRIMES

Burglary	80
Robbery	90

Percent Reported

Source: *Criminal Victimization in the United States, 1975* (Washington, D.C.: U.S. Government Printing Office, December 1977), p. 14.

FIGURE 3-1 Percent of Victimizations Reported to the Police, 1975

Interestingly, the Crime Panel studies have produced some unexpected findings. In the first place, serious crime is reported to the police more frequently than had been thought. Where the earlier victimization studies indicated that the total amount of unreported crime was nearly three times that reported to the police, the Crime Panel data indicates that the amount of unreported serious crime is slightly less than one-half of the offenses that are committed.[44] Even in the case of forcible rape, nearly one-half of the victims notified the police, a figure much higher than had been expected. The surveys also reported that in at least three-fourths of the personal incidents involving violence or the threat of violence, the confrontation was between strangers—that is, between the victim or victims and one or more unknown assailants. This finding conflicts with the often expressed belief that a large percentage of such crime involves people who are in some way acquainted.[45]

The Crime Panel surveys found that victimization rates produced common patterns in each of the 18 major cities studied.[46] Males were much more likely to be victims of crimes than females, and persons under age 35 were much more likely to be victims of crimes than older persons. It was also found that members of minority races had significantly higher rates of victimization throughout all comparable age levels than whites, particularly for the offenses of robbery and aggravated assault. Single people were much more likely to be assaulted than were persons who were married, widowed, divorced, or separated. Persons with family incomes of less than $3,000 were much more frequently victims of the violent crimes of rape, robbery, and aggravated assault. Those with higher incomes were more likely to be the victims of larceny without contact than were people with lower incomes. From these data, it is obvious that the more serious crimes particularly affect members of minority groups and persons with low incomes. This was especially true of crimes against the person and crimes of a violent nature.

An effort was also made to determine which crimes were more likely to be reported to the police and which were not. Generally, nonviolent crimes against the person were most likely not to be reported; and those involving violence against the victim were more likely to be reported. Crimes against the household including auto theft were more often reported than were crimes against the person.

In order to shed some light on the question of why people do not report to the police the fact that they have been victimized, Crime Panel researchers attempted to determine why those who indicated they had been the victims of crimes did not notify the authorities. The most frequent reason given was that the victims felt "nothing could be done." About one-third of the victims felt that it "wasn't important enough."[47] There was no direct indication that they did not trust the police.

Although we cannot know why the victims felt so strongly that nothing could be done, we, must wonder what is behind such an attitude. It may demonstrate a significant lack of confidence by victims in the ability of the police to bring the offender to justice. It may, in fact, be a general lack of confidence in the entire criminal justice system to perform its role in society.

TABLE 3-7

National Crime Panel Victimization Rates and Percentage Change for Crime Occurrences, 1973–1976

OFFENSE	PERCENT CHANGE
Rape	−12.0
Robbery	−2.5[a]
Assault	+2.0
Burglary	+4.0[b]
Larceny	+5.4[c]
Auto theft	−14.0

[a] Consists of personal and commercial robbery.
[b] Consists of household and commercial burglary.
[c] Consists of personal larceny with and without contact and household larceny.
Source: Department of Justice, *Criminal Victimization in the United States, A Comparison of 1975 and 1976 Findings* (Washington, D.C.: Government Printing Office, November 1977), p. 11.

A last important finding of the Crime Panel surveys shows a discrepancy over a period of time between the panel's actual findings and what is published in the UCR. Table 3-7 shows the change in victimization rates according to the Crime Panel surveys for the years 1973–1976. The reader should compare these figures with similar UCR figures that are shown in Table 3-3.

However, it should also be noted that the victimization surveys themselves suffer from several important methodological weaknesses that affect their accuracy.[48] The researchers who conduct these surveys find that their biggest problem is the tendency of those interviewed to incorrectly remember when the crime occurred. Another problem is panel bias or the tendency of some of those who are repeatedly sampled in the same household over a period of time to become less willing to cooperate in the long and complex interviewing process. This decreasing cooperation could be expressed in a decreasing willingness to report victimizations to the interviewer. Although the Census Bureau is working to control and minimize such problems, they do exist.

BUREAU OF CRIMINAL JUSTICE STATISTICS

Since 1931 there has been a recognized need for the creation of a national clearing house for criminal justice statistics.[49] In 1977, a step toward this goal was undertaken by the Attorney General Griffin B. Bell who proposed that a *Bureau of Criminal Justice Statistics* (BCJS) be created in the Department of Justice.

Behind this effort is the realization that present day crime-related statistics are incomplete, inaccurate, and lack credibility. In the words of a special staff charged with the responsibility of determining the feasibility of the BCJS:

It is impossible to know on a national scale how many crimes are committed . . . how many crimes committed result in reports to the police, how many reported crimes result in arrests, how many arrests result in prosecutions, and how many prosecutions result in convictions. It is impossible to know on a national scale how many convictions result in probation, in fines, and in prison sentences, and, of the prison sentences imposed, what proportion of each sentence is served. It is impossible to know on a national scale who among those who serve sentences are likely to return to prison. In brief, it is impossible to follow on a national scale criminal offenders through the criminal justice process and know what happens to them and what, in turn, happens to the system.[50]

If approved by Congress, the proposed Bureau of Criminal Justice Statistics would have several important responsibilities, including: to compile, collate, analyze, publish, and disseminate national statistics concerning all aspects of crime, criminal justice, and criminal offenders; to develop and maintain compatible crime gathering and recording systems among state and local governments; to establish national definitions and standards for justice statistics; and to centralize the statistical records of the 54 federal agencies who now gather specialized crime statistics.[51]

Although it is not possible to list all of the presently existing statistical crime gathering information systems that the proposed BCJS would consolidate, some of the more important inclusions would be: National Prisoner Statistics, Expenditure and Employment Data for the Criminal Justice System, U.S. Attorneys Docket and Reporting System, Narcotics and Dangerous Drugs Information, National Crime Information Center (NCIC), and the Federal Prosecutor's Management Information System (PROMIS).

Although it is not known at this time whether such an agency will be authorized, the need for better and more complete crime-related statistics is unquestioned.

APPLICATION OF COMPUTERS

In the past few years, a great deal of attention has focused on the application of computers to the study of crime. Criminal justice agencies, particularly the police, see the storage and retrieval capabilities of the modern computer as a means to classify known criminals, store information on stolen property, and maintain and cross-index *modus operandi* (method of operation) files of particular crimes and criminals. For example, some police agencies feed the computer characteristics of certain crimes, including the method of commission, the description of the suspect(s), property stolen, and any other available clues. When a new crime is committed, they crosscheck all the characteristics of the offense to see whether these characteristics match up with prior unsolved crimes. In this way, they try to develop a composite work-up of similar offenses, that is, a composite set of clues from a number of crimes having similar characteristics. Thus the investigating officer can have a great deal more information than would otherwise be available. Without the computer to compile and store the information, each investigating officer would have only the information from one crime to work with and might not know that similar crimes were being investigated by other police personnel.

Researchers also see the computer as a tremendous aid in the study of crime and criminals. First, the computer could help to classify criminals according to specific individual characteristics that can be analyzed. For example, by feeding computers enough information on the background and psychological and other characteristics of types of offenders, a profile of offenders who commit certain types of crimes might be developed. Such a profile would be an important aid in identifying such persons and bringing them to justice or developing programs to treat them once they are institutionalized.

Researchers also envision the computer as an important tool to study the effects of different treatment and rehabilitation programs. For example, case histories and personal characteristics of the offenders could be examined in relation to the particular treatment programs that the offenders were exposed to. In this way, researchers hope to discover what specific types of programs seem to work best given the identified characteristics of an offender. This matching of the offender with the appropriate treatment has long been a goal of rehabilitative programs.

SEARCH Program

Although such uses of the computer are not yet a reality, there have been some prototype demonstration projects of more meaningful application of computer technology to criminal justice. One of the most highly publicized endeavors was the development of the System for Electronic Analysis and Retrieval of Criminal Histories (SEARCH). This was a federally funded effort to gather crime data and related information in a 15-state network. A master computer system was set up to gather the crime data of all the participating states. Such important data as information on offenders and their criminal histories were to be included. A unique feature of SEARCH was that it would provide a means to examine the relationship between characteristics of offenders and the types of crimes they committed, as well as the type of treatment they had been exposed to if they had been previously imprisoned.[52]

SEARCH was never made fully operational because of congressional concern and the withdrawal of appropriations needed to develop it. A few states have continued efforts to develop state systems based upon the SEARCH model, such as Michigan's Criminal Case History (CCH) computer system.

PROMIS Program

A recent effort to link computer technology to the study of crime has been the development of offender-based transaction statistics (OBTS) as discussed in Chapter 1. The most extensive use of an OBTS system is now being adopted in several jurisdictions throughout the United States. This special adoption, which is called PROMIS,[53] stands for Prosecutor's Management Information System. Although PROMIS was initially established to help manage and schedule the processing of criminal cases through the courts, a major effort is now underway to expand the capabilities of the system and to develop its potential for research applications.[54] Eventually, it is envisioned that PROMIS-type applications to the administration of justice will help answer such questions as:

- What is the relationship between police charges and those pressed by the prosecutor? In what way is plea bargaining reflected in the charges? In what types of cases are the reduction of charges most significant?

- What is the relative frequency of guilty pleas, jury trials, and bench trials, and how do they relate to offense and offender characteristics?

- What are the conviction rates by offense type, by trial type, and by defendant characteristics? What is the gap between original and final charges, and what are the most typical forms of reduction in charges?

- What is the relationship between sentences imposed and offense and offender characteristics? What is the relationship between sentences and plea or trial convictions, and between sentences and offenders freed on bail or detained?

- What are the practices of correctional agencies in granting parole, training or treatment programs, types of probation, work release, and admission to halfway houses?

- How does recidivism (defined as rearrest or reconviction) relate to actions taken against an individual as recorded in previous OBTS cycles? For example, was the individual convicted in his or her previous case(s)? incarcerated? treated?

- What is the average (median) time lapse between steps in the process for all cases—misdemeanors or felonies, violent offenses or property offenses, etc.? What parts of the system are more time consuming than others?

- How does the total number of cases for a given period—and the resulting caseload—affect the quantity of cases prosecuted, pled, and convicted? How does this number affect the type of dispositions made?

- What is the attrition rate of cases at each phase? What types of crimes are most likely to drop out? How are these factors related to caseloads at each agency?

- Is there a clear and consistent interagency policy to apply more resources in certain types of cases? For example, is more police work, special prosecution, or a speedier trial obtained for violent crimes, recidivists, major misdemeanors, etc.?[55]

The Effects of Computers on Privacy

Although the value of the computer is unquestioned, its use has certain other implications that should be mentioned. Of great concern is the question of individual freedom and the right of privacy. The centralization and availability of criminal case histories may pose a grave threat to the right of privacy and the dignity of the individual which, in the long run, may be more threatening to our society than the problem of crime. It was because of this fear that Congress withdrew funding for SEARCH. In recent years, there has been a growing concern that the government, and particularly law enforcement agencies, now have the technology to gather significant files on persons they view as a threat to society. Although it may seem warranted when dealing with organized crime figures and others involved in the commission of serious crime, there is always the danger that this technology could be employed to gather information on those who express views that are merely not in line with the existing political ideology. Such use would strike at the very precepts of democracy.

Because of the public sensitivity to the potential threat that computer systems represent, it is doubtful that such systems will ever be fully used in criminal justice. This is particularly unfortunate for science, but it is a price that must be paid. In the final analysis, the development and use of computer systems in criminal justice will probably be limited to the gathering of specific data that can be used in such limited ways as helping to identify suspects, to suggest ways to reduce court delays, and to make decisions on whether to grant or deny probation and parole; such systems will be of little help in explaining crime or criminal behavior.

CRIME AND VICTIM COMPENSATION

Increasing attention is now being focused on the victim of crime. As a result, we are seeing the development of victim-centered programs in ever larger numbers throughout the United States. The thrust for the development of these programs revolves around two issues: (1) the recognition that being a victim of a crime often produces psychological trauma and economic loss; and (2) the growing feeling that there is an imbalance in our system of criminal justice that focuses almost exclusively on the offender while ignoring the innocent victim.[56]

One means of assisting victims of crime and focusing on their plight is through victim compensation programs. Such programs are usually based on the concept that the state has the responsibility to ensure the safety of its citizens and when it fails to fulfill this responsibility, it is liable for the harm suffered by the crime victim. As a result, compensation is paid by the state for losses that result from a criminal attack.[57]

The first jurisdiction in modern times to establish a special program for compensating crime victims was adopted in 1963 by New Zealand. A year later, Great Britain established a similar program and by 1976, Great Britain's Criminal Injuries Compensation Board was receiving 10,000 applications a year.[58] The idea soon spread across the Atlantic to the United States. By 1978, 13 states had adopted some form of victim compensation legislation. Although the states differ somewhat in their authorizing legislation and in the administration of their programs, they all provide compensation for bodily injury or death suffered by innocent victims of crime. The new federal criminal code now under consideration by Congress also calls for the establishment of a Victim Compensation Fund and a United States Victim Compensation Board to administer the program.

In spite of some important differences in the way these programs operate, there are certain general similarities. First, they compensate only for personal injuries; property losses are excluded. Losses for death entitles the surviving spouse, children, or parents to receive the compensation. Generally, the amount of compensation covers such things as medical expenses and loss of support or earnings. With the exception of Delaware and Hawaii there is no compensation for such things as "pain and suffering" associated with the victimization. Also, many of the states have adopted a $10,000 ceiling on the total amount of compensation that can be awarded.

Usually, the victim is required to file a claim before the administrative hearing board within a prescribed period of time after being injured. Except in the state of Washington, the victim must have reported the crime to the police, and, usually, within a particular period of time prescribed by statute. For example, under the proposed new federal criminal code the victim must have reported the crime to the police within 72 hours from its occurrence. In addition, the claimant is required to cooperate with all government agencies involved in the investigation or prosecution of the offense.

In Alaska, Hawaii, Florida, and Minnesota, law enforcement officials are required to inform victims of their rights under the program. This has led to some innovative developments in certain jurisdictions. For instance, the Fort Lauderdale, Florida, program of victim assistance has been sponsored by that city's police department since its inception in 1974. Specially trained civilian personnel are assigned to the police department and, as victim advocates, provide services to victims of violent (as well as property) crimes. The program has demonstrated that police department sponsorship aids advocates in contacting victims. Anne Newton describes the operations of the program in Fort Lauderdale:

> In its early stages, a major effort of the Victim Assistance Project was to develop a community resource bank from which victim services could be drawn. There are now more than 55 community service agencies with whom victim advocates maintain constant contact. Advocates also work closely with the media in protecting victims from adverse publicity or sensationalism.
>
> Victim advocates work regular duty hours and are on call at all other times, providing interagency liaison, transportation, and referral to responsible agencies. In an emergency, advocates are called to the scene by the police. If immediate assistance is not necessary, advocates are informed of the case by police on the following day. Advocates may identify victims themselves by scanning police operations reports and then contact the victim directly. Many victims come directly to the victim advocate office.[59]

To determine how extensive these victim compensation programs are, a study was conducted for the 1974–75 year among the 11 states that had such programs. In terms of both claims filed and awards made, the state of New York led the group. During the 12-month period, New York's Crime Victims Compensation Board had 2341 claims filed; of those, 910 awards were made which totaled slightly over $3 million. States such as California, Maryland, and New Jersey also handled relatively high numbers of claims and awards.[60]

SUMMARY

Although it is often claimed that the United States has the highest crime rate in the world, there is really no way to prove or disprove this statement. What little facts are known about crime in America come mostly from official accounts published annually in the Uniform Crime Reports. The UCR indicates that certain characteristics appear to be associated with crime in this country; for example, some geographical areas have a higher relative incidence of certain types of offenses than other areas.

The UCR is widely criticized for its inaccuracy in reflecting the types and numbers of crimes in the United States, and it is recognized as being woefully inadequate. In an effort to better measure the nature and extent of crime, the federal government has established the National Crime Panel. This effort surveys citizens and commercial establishments to ascertain the amount of unreported crime that occurs. It would appear that of the crimes surveyed, only about one-half of all crimes are reported to the police.

Because of the concern over crime statistics, the Attorney General has recommended that a new Bureau of Criminal Justice Statistics be created. The purpose of this new agency would be to compile, collate, analyze, publish, and disseminate national statistics concerning all aspects of crime, criminal justice, and criminal offenders on a national basis.

The potential for the use of sophisticated computer systems for crime data gathering and analysis has been widely discussed. The major concern, however, of such a system is the possibility for potential misuse. Many civil libertarians are opposed to such systems.

A recent interest in the victim of the crime has led to the development of a number of victim compensation programs throughout the United States. A number of states now have such programs, and the federal government is considering establishing such a program for victims of federal crimes.

REVIEW QUESTIONS

1. Name the seven index offenses in the FBI's Uniform Crime Report.

2. What regional area of the United States has the highest rate of robbery (in 1976)? Of aggravated assault? Of burglary? Of larceny? Of auto theft?

3. The Center for Studies of Crime and Delinquency has identified six requirements that are necessary for an accurate criminal statistics report. What are these requirements?

4. Uniform Crime Reports have been criticized for several reasons. Select and describe the four that you think are most important.

5. What is victim compensation? In your opinion is the federal or state government obliged to compensate victims of crime?

DISCUSSION QUESTIONS

1. Is there a crime problem in America? Discuss.

2. How can information-gathering methods on crime in the United States be improved?

3. The weaknesses of the Uniform Crime Reports render them useless in giving an accurate picture of crime in the United States. Discuss.

4. What are the benefits and problems that will result from using computers to analyze and keep records on crime and criminals?

SUGGESTED ADDITIONAL READINGS

Ferdinand, Theodore N. "Demographic Shifts and Criminality: An Inquiry." *British Journal of Criminology* 10 (1970): 165–178.

Friedman, Lee S. *Economics of Crime and Justice*. Morristown, N.J.: General Learning Press, 1976.

Gibbons, Don C., Joseph F. Jones, and Peter G. Garabedian: "Gauging Public Opinion about the Crime Problem." *Crime and Delinquency* 18 (April 1973): 134–146.

Graham, Fred P. "A Contemporary History of American Crime." In H. D. Graham and Ted R. Gurr, eds., *Violence in America*. New York: Bantam, 1970, pp. 485–504.

Hawkins, E. R., and Willard Waller: "Critical Notes on the Cost of Crime." *Journal of Criminal Law, Criminology and Police Science* 46 (January-February 1956): 657–672.

Kitsuse, John T., and Aaron V. Cicourel: "A Note on the Uses of Official Statistics." *Social Problems* 11 (Fall 1963): 131–139.

Lottier, Stuart: "Distribution of Criminal Offenses in Sectional Regions," *Journal of Criminal Law, Criminology and Police Science* 29 (1938): 1038–1045.

National Academy of Sciences. *Understanding Crime*. Washington, D.C.: U.S. Government Printing Office, 1977.

Nettler, Gwynn. *Explaining Crime*. 2nd ed. New York: McGraw-Hill, 1978.

President's Commission on Law Enforcement and Administration of Justice: *Task Force Report: Crime and Its Impact—An Assessment*. Washington, D.C.: U.S. Government Printing Office, 1967.

Robison, Sophia M. "A Critical Review of the Uniform Crime Report." *Michigan Law Review* 64 (April 1966): 1031–1054.

Sellin, Thorsten, and Marvin E. Wolfgang: *The Measurement of Delinquency*. New York: Wiley, 1964.

Turk, Austin F. "The Mythology of Crime in America." *Criminology* 8 (February 1971): 397–411.

U.S. Department of Justice: *National Crime Panel Survey of Chicago, Detroit, Los Angeles, New York and Philadelphia*. Washington, D.C.: U.S. Government Printing Office, April 1975.

Winslow, Robert W. *Crime in a Free Society*. Belmont, Calif.: Dickenson, 1968.

Wolfgang, Marvin E. "Urban Crime." In James Q. Wilson, ed., *The Metropolitan Enigma*. Cambridge, Mass.: Harvard University Press, 1968, pp. 246–251.

NOTES

1. Frank F. Furstenberg, Jr., "Public Reaction to Crime in the Streets," *American Scholar* 40 (1971): 601.

2. "Fortress on 78th Street," *Life*, November 19, 1971, pp. 26–36.

3. "Are You Personally Afraid of Crime?" *Life*, January 14, 1972, p. 28.

4. National Commission on the Causes and Prevention of Violence, *To Establish Justice, To Ensure Domestic Tranquility* (New York: Bantam, 1970), p. xxv.

5. David Lawrence, "Why Is Crime Now a Worldwide Epidemic?" *U.S. News and World Report,* September 6, 1971, p. 84.

6. World Health Organization, *World Health Statistics Annual, 1972,* (Geneva, Switzerland, 1975), p. 234.

7. James Q. Wilson, "A Long Look at Crime," *FBI Law Enforcement Bulletin* 44 (Feb. 1, 1975): 1–6.

8. Daniel Bell, *The End of Ideology* (New York: Collier Books, 1962), p. 172.

9. Robert V. Bruce, *1877: The Year of Violence* (New York: Bobbs-Merrill, 1969), p. 13.

10. Bell, *The End of Ideology,* p. 165.

11. Bruce, *The Year of Violence,* pp. 138–158.

12. Robert M. Fogelson, "The 1960s Riots: Interpretations and Recommendations," a report to the President's Commission on Law Enforcement and Administration of Justice, 1966 (mimeo).

13. For example, see Marvin E. Wolfgang, ed., *Annals of American Academy of Political and Social Science,* 364 (March 1966).

14. Hugo Herz, *Verbrechen and Verbrechertum in Osterreich* (Tubingen: Laupp, 1908).

15. Cesare Lombroso, *Crime, Its Causes and Remedies* (Boston: Little, Brown, 1912).

16. Ibid., p. 7.

17. Georg Von Mayr, *Statistik and Gesellschaftslehere* (Tubingen: Mohr, 1917), p. 608.

18. Joseph Cohen, "The Geography of Crime," *Annals of the American Academy of Political and Social Science* 217 (September 1941): 30.

19. Elmer H. Johnson, *Crime, Correction and Society* (Homewood, Ill.: Dorsey, 1968), p. 45.

20. Ibid.

21. See "Crime Distribution in Los Angeles," research report, Los Angeles Police Department, 1972.

22. For example, see Stuart Lottier, "Distribution of Criminal Offenses in Sectional Regions," *Journal of Criminal Law, Criminology and Police Science* 29 (1938): 336; Lyle W. Shannon, "The Spatial Distribution of Criminal Offenses by States," *Journal of Criminal Law, Criminology and Police Science* 45 (1954): 270; and Keith D. Harries, "The Geography of American Crime, 1968," *Journal of Geography* 70 (1971): 204–213.

23. Raymond D. Gastil, "Homicide and a Regional Culture of Violence," *American Sociological Review* 36 (1971): 414.

24. Keith D. Harries, *The Geography of Crime and Justice* (New York: McGraw-Hill, 1974), pp. 16–36.

25. Ibid.

26. Discussion with the chief of the DeKalb County Police Department, December 1972.

27. National Institute of Mental Health, *Criminal Statistics* (Washington, D.C.: U.S. Government Printing Office, 1972), p. 1.

28. "Crime Statistics Often Numbers Game," *The New York Times,* February 4, 1968, p. 58.

29. National Commission on the Causes and Prevention of Violence, *Violence in America: Historical and Comparative Perspectives* (Washington, D.C.: U.S. Government Printing Office, 1969), p. 372.

30. See Richard Lyons, "Fuzzy Crime Statistics," *The New York Times,* September 18, 1977, p. 14e., col. 3.

31. President's Commission on Law Enforcement and Administration of Justice, *Criminal Victimization in the United States: A Report of a National Survey,* (Washington, D.C.: U.S. Government Printing Office, 1967), pp. 36–44.

32. President's Commission on Law Enforcement and Administration of Justice, *Report on a Pilot Study in the District of Columbia on Victimization and Attitudes Toward Law Enforcement* (Washington, D.C.: U.S. Government Printing Office, 1967).

33. For example, see Will Sparks "Terror in the Streets," *Commonweal* 82 (11): 345–348; and U.S. National Commission on the Causes and Prevention of Violence, *To Establish Justice, To Ensure Domestic Tranquility* (Washington, D.C.: U.S. Government Printing Office, 1969).

34. See Michael E. Milakovich and Kurt Weis, "Politics and Measures of Success in the War on Crime," *Crime and Delinquency* 21 (January 1975): 1–10.

35. President's Commission, *Criminal Victimization in the United States,* p. 33.

36. Johnson, *Crime, Correction and Society,* p. 47.

37. David Pittman and William F. Handy, "Uniform Crime Reporting: Suggested Improvements," in Alvin Gouldner and S. M. Miller, eds., *Applied Sociology* (New York: Free Press, 1965), pp. 180–188.

38. Hugo O. Englemann and Kirby Throckmorton, "Interaction Frequency and Crime Rates," *Wisconsin Sociologist* 5 (1967): 33–36.

39. Sara Lee Boggs, "The Ecology of Crime Occurrence in St. Louis: A Reconceptualization of Crime Rates and Patterns," unpublished Ph.D. dissertation, St. Louis: Washington University, 1964.

40. Philip H. Ennis, "Crime, Victims and the Police," *Transaction* 4 (1967): 36–44.

41. Lyons, "Fuzzy Crime Statistics."

42. Law Enforcement Assistance Administration, *Criminal Victimization Surveys in the Nation's Five Largest Cities* (Washington, D.C.: U.S. Government Printing Office, April 1975), p. 1.

43. Law Enforcement Assistance Administration, *Crime in the Nation's Five Largest Cities—Advance Report* (Washington, D.C.: U.S. Government Printing Office, April 1974).

44. President's Commission, *Criminal Victimization in the United States.*

45. Johnson, *Crime, Correction and Society,* pp. 31–32.

46. President's Commission, *Criminal Victimization in the United States.*

47. Law Enforcement Assistance Administration, *Criminal Victimization Surveys.*

48. See James Garofalo, *An Introduction to the National Crime Survey* (Washington, D.C.: U.S. Government Printing Office, 1977), p. 5.

49. See The National Commission on Law Observance and Enforcement (The Wickersham Commission), Report No. 3. *Report on Criminal Statistics* (Washington, D.C.: 1931), p. 1.

50. Statistical Systems Policy Review Group Staff, "A Plan for a Bureau of Criminal Justice Statistics," Memorandum. (Washington, D.C.: U.S. Department of Justice, January 6, 1977), p. 2.

51. Ibid., p. 3.

52. Paul K. Worneli, "Project SEARCH: System for Electronic Analysis and Retrieval of Criminal Histories," *National Symposium on Criminal Justice Information and Statistics System* (Washington, D.C.: U.S. Government Printing Office, 1970), p. 17.

53. See Institute for Law and Social Research, *PROMIS: Briefing Series,* Vols. 1–20. (Washington, D.C.: U.S. Government Printing Office, November 1975).

54. Carl E. Pope, "Offender-Based Transaction Statistics," *New Directions in Data Collection and Reporting* (Washington, D.C.: U.S. Government Printing Office, 1975), p. 12.

55. Susan Katzenelson, "Analysis of the Criminal Justice System with Offender-Based Transaction Statistics," in Leonard Oberlander, ed., *Quantitative Tool for Criminal Justice Planning* (Washington, D.C.: U.S. Government Printing Office, 1975): 86–87.

56. See Stephen Schafer, "Victim Compensation and Responsibility," *Southern California Law Review* 43, no. 1 (1970): 55–67; Joe Hudson, Bert Galaway, and Steve Chesney, "When Criminals Repay their Victims," *Judicature* 60 (February 1977): 312–321); Laura Nader and Elaine Combs-Schilling, "Restitution in Cross Cultural Perspective," in Joe Hudson, ed., *Restitution in Criminal Justice* (St. Paul, Minn.: Minnesota Department of Corrections, 1975), pp. 23–41; Gilbert Geis, "Compensation to Victims of Violent Crimes," in Rudolph J. Gerber, ed., *Contemporary Issues in Criminal Justice: Some Problems and Suggested Reforms* (Port Washington, N.Y.: Kennikat, 1976), pp. 94–115.

57. Stephen Schafer, "Compensation to Victims of Criminal Offenses," *Criminal Law Bulletin* 10 (1977): 605–636.

58. Law Enforcement Assistance Administration, *Victim Compensation and Restitution Programs* (Washington, D.C.: U.S. Government Printing Office, March 1978).

59. Anne Newton, "Aid to the Victim. Part II: Victim Aid Programs," *Crime and Delinquency Literature* 8 (December 1976): 511–512.

60. ———, "Aid to the Victim. Part I: Compensation and Restitution," *Crime and Delinquency Literature* 8 (September 1976): 368–390.

4
VICTIMLESS CRIMES: LAW AND MORAL VALUES

United Press International

1. What are so-called victimless crimes?
2. What are some problems associated with trying to compare victimless crimes with more traditional types of crimes?
3. What are the costs of trying to enforce victimless crime laws?
4. What are the arguments for and against the retention of victimless crime laws?
5. What are some of the issues associated with gambling, drunkenness, narcotics and drug use, obscenity and pornography, prostitution, and homosexual behavior?

These are some of the questions this chapter will answer.

No subject in the administration of justice has been debated more than the question of the enforcement or nonenforcement of victimless crimes. Noted authorities, such as Kadish, see the enforcement of laws against victimless crimes as an attempt to enforce morals. This can result in the "crisis of over-criminalization" that threatens the very administration of criminal justice.[1] On the other hand, there are those who strongly defend not only government's right to enforce these laws, but its duty to do so. Lord Devlin, a great English jurist, has urged the legitimacy of the enforcement of victimless crime statutes on the ground that "society cannot ignore the morality of the individual any more than it can his loyalty; it flourishes on both and without either it dies."[2]

In recent years, most scholars of criminal justice have sided with those opposed to enforcing such laws. To a large extent, public opinion seems to reflect the "new morality" of the last few decades. Society seems to be accepting and tolerating behavior and conduct that used to be considered deviant—and along with this, more libertarian attitudes toward certain forms of moral behavior.

This chapter examines these controversial areas of the law and explores the issues from both viewpoints whenever possible. Because those who oppose the enforcement of laws against victimless crimes have been more active in gathering data to support their argument, the reader may be led to believe that since more information has been provided in support of the antienforcement stance, that the author shares this view. This is not the author's intention but rather reflects the relative amount of data developed by both sides. To date, those in support of such laws continue to base their arguments on moral sentiment alone. Any discussion of this subject must include all the available facts; the reader can then make his or her own judgment on the issue.

THE CONCEPT OF VICTIMLESS CRIMES

To consider homosexuality, prostitution, fornication, adultery, drunkenness, obscenity and pornography, narcotics use, and gambling as crimes is to imply that those who participate in such acts offend the whole of society. To many, this form of reasoning presents the problem of reconciling the traditional definition of crime with the true nature of these particular offenses—of connecting the prohibited behavior with actual harm done to society. Critics of the statutory criminalization of these acts point to the fact that many of these offenses are private acts among consenting adults and, in some cases, involve only the individual and are not harmful to others not directly engaged. They contend that if the acts are harmful, the harm is inflicted only on the participants themselves.[3]

The traditional relationship between perpetrator and victim is also absent. There is no unwilling victim because for the most part the acts are *voluntarily* and *mutually* entered into by *both* parties, neither of whom views himself or herself as a "victim" in the traditional sense.

Those who advocate the decriminalization of such acts offer some rather convincing evidence that the laws against them have had little effect upon preventing their occurrence.[4] As a matter of public policy or official disregard by the authorities (which are often synonymous), the laws on homosexuality, prostitution, drunkenness, obscenity, and pornography are, in many communities, disregarded openly. When these laws are enforced, it is often not done with uniformity and fairness. This serves to destroy the concept of equal application of the criminal law, which further undermines citizen respect for the administration of justice.[5]

If the criminal justice system is also to be held responsible for the reformation of offenders, it fails miserably in dealing with individuals who violate these victimless crime statutes. Such cases clog our lower courts and place special burdens on our already crowded and understaffed prisons and jails. Rehabilitative personnel, in particular, are further taxed in trying to deal with these offenders. This points out a major paradox of the entire system of justice: The arrest and incarceration of these individuals often results in their leaving the institution more embittered than when they entered. For the first time they view themselves as "victims"—not of the crime for which they were found guilty, but of a hypocritical and unjust system of justice which, in a discriminatory manner, penalizes them for their deviant behavior. What they may correctly perceive is that similar behavior by others is often overlooked and sometimes even engaged in by their accusers. The question must be asked whether the system of criminal justice may unwittingly be guilty of encouraging procriminal attitudes among these individuals and whether present enforcement practices will result in future diminishment of these behaviors.

COSTS OF ENFORCING VICTIMLESS CRIME LAWS

There are other considerations as well. The most frequent charge leveled at the enforcement of victimless crime laws is that it places an inordinate strain upon the resources of the criminal justice system—resources that many feel could better be devoted to dealing with more serious offenses and offenders.[6] When these costs are examined in relation to the ineffectiveness that such enforcement has on the reduction of these "anti-social" acts, the value of straining our financial and personnel resources in this regard must be questioned.

Direct Costs

The costs to the criminal justice system of enforcing these laws are not known. In recent years, some states have begun dealing with these offenders in special programs that fall outside of the criminal justice process, but as late as 1970 nearly 50 percent of all arrests fell into the victimless crime category. By 1975, the proportion had dropped to 38 percent. But even with this decline, we can conservatively place the cost of prosecuting these crimes in terms of billions of dollars. Not figured in this calculation is the category of "all other offenses" (a large miscellany of 987,320 arrests in 1976), many of which would fall into the victimless crimes category, but are excluded from our calculations because they cannot be specifically identified from the published FBI data.

Indirect Costs

There is another associated "cost" to society that never appears in the ledger sheets of any governmental agency. One very serious consequence of the laws relating to victimless crimes is that they have often provided the basis for a network of organized crime operations. Organized crime is an excellent study in economic market strategy — it exists and flourishes because it provides the goods and services people want and cannot obtain legally. Such commodities and services as narcotics, gambling, and prostitution provide crime syndicates with operating and investment capital. Ironically, the state, in effect, gives organized crime a virtual monopoly on the provision of these illicit goods and services. In turn, crime syndicates often invest their huge profits in legitimate businesses which allows them to continue to provide their services to the consuming public.

The Eighteenth Amendment provides an excellent example of how this process occurs and how difficult it is to legislate morals. This amendment, which prohibited the manufacture, sale, or transportation of intoxicating liquors, ushered in prohibition. In the 14 years that passed before this amendment was repealed, it provided the foundation for many of the criminal cartels that exist today. It also indicated to many criminologists how futile it was to try to legislate social behavior, and how damaging such legislation could be on the administration of criminal justice.

Furthermore, victimless crime laws often serve as the basis for official corruption. Because the offender wants what is illegal, those who provide it must continually bribe the police, courts, and other officials to permit their profitable enterprise to continue with a minimum of interruption. According to authorities on organized crime, gambling and large-scale distribution of drugs could not exist unless public officials were bribed. One estimate puts the graft at more than $2 billion a year.[7]

The police appear to be particularly vulnerable to organized crime's efforts to assure that their supply of vice services will continue uninterrupted, especially in the areas of organized narcotic trafficking, gambling, and prostitution. This fact was first documented thoroughly in 1931, when the federal government released a 14-volume study of crime in America known as the *Wickersham Commission Reports*. Commenting on the problem of organized crime and police and judicial corruption, the reports said:

> Those criminal octopus organizations have now grown so audacious, owing to their long immunity from prosecutions for their crimes, that they seek to make bargains with law enforcing officers and even with judges of our courts to be allowed for a price to continue their criminal activities unmolested by the law.[8]

Today, the problem seems to be just as prevalent in some of the larger municipal police departments in this country. Scandals that involve police and judicial corruption in enforcing victimless crime laws have occurred periodically throughout the country. During the 1950s and 1960s, Chicago's police department suffered scandals involving narcotics payoffs; in the 1960s, Buffalo, New York, was rocked with scandals of police and judicial involvement in organized gambling and prostitution. The latest and perhaps most extensive documentation of police corruption occurred in New York City in 1972, when the Knapp Commission released a devastating report of widespread police involvement in narcotics, gambling, and prostitution which had been going on for many years. It should be noted, however, that the majority of police agencies uphold their integrity in spite of the corruption around them and in spite of organized crime's efforts to influence them.

The crimes relating to narcotics use contribute heavily to the total crime picture. In the United States, the heroin addict cannot obtain the drug legally but must pay a high price to obtain it illegally. Patrick Murphy, former police commissioner of New York, contends that half the crimes committed in that city are by addicts who steal and rob to obtain money to support their addiction. Although Murphy's statement cannot be confirmed or denied, it is an established fact that narcotic addicts are involved in a great deal of crime. For example, addicts polled in a New Jersey study averaged nearly six previous arrests. Although a number of arrests were for narcotics-related charges such as the sale and abuse of drugs, the vast majority were for other types of crime, such as burglary or robbery.[9]

Finally, there is one last unanticipated consequence of the enforcement of victimless crime laws that also bears on the indirect costs of this type of legislation. Since these laws are by their very nature discriminatory—in theory, enforcement, and application—they have alienated large segments of the population not only from the criminal justice system, but from the institutions of government that are represented by the agencies of justice. This is particularly true among young people in all socioeconomic strata. The youth of today see instances of official corruption where the police and courts invoke sanctions against the more vulnerable poor and young, yet tolerate flagrant abuses among the rich and powerful. The issue, it would seem, is not the inherent wrongness of these types of offenses as much as it is the inherent wrong brought about by the seemingly selective enforcement of laws against these crimes. At a time when popular opinion is already indicating that many Americans no longer trust public officials and governmental agencies, this may well be the most serious charge leveled at the continued efforts to enforce these laws. The agencies of criminal justice, because they are the most highly visible extension of governmental authority, must be symbols of public respect and confidence and serve as an example of the precepts of equity and justice. As long as they are required to handle the problems associated with the enforcement of victimless crime laws, it would seem that these agencies cannot gain public respect and confidence.

Under these circumstances, it is not difficult to understand why many noted criminal justice authorities have called for the revocation of most statutes pertaining to victimless crimes. Among them are James Vorenberg, director of the President's Commission on Law Enforcement and Administration of Justice; Dr. Norval Morris, director of the University of Chicago's Criminal Justice Center; Patrick Murphy, now director of the Police Foundation; and Arlen Spector, former district attorney of Philadelphia. Such prestigious organizations as the National Council on Crime and Delinquency and the American Bar Association have also recommended the repeal of many of these statutes.

Most of these efforts at repeal have developed around efforts to reclassify crimes based upon their actual threat to the well-being of society. Among the suggested new legislation to deal with these offenses are the provisions contained in the Model Penal Code proposed by the American Law Institute, the suggestions contained in the Sentencing Alternatives of the American Bar Association, and the Model Sentencing Act of the National Council on Crime and Delinquency. Each of these proposals calls for either the abolishment of these victimless crimes as offenses or a significant reduction in the penalties attached. A number of states and the federal government have already revised, or are in the process of revising, their criminal codes to reflect these suggestions.

ARGUMENTS FOR KEEPING VICTIMLESS CRIME LAWS

Many groups and individuals actively oppose the decriminalization of these acts or the reduction of the penalties for these crimes. Much of their argument centers on the theme of the moral well-being of society, and they reject the idea that these acts are "victimless." For example, they maintain that harm is indeed done to the individuals participating in such acts regardless of the fact that it is voluntarily inflicted harm. Physical harm is associated with the use of marijuana or the opiates, and venereal disease and perhaps even involvement of children in prostitution would grow if such behavior were legally tolerated by society.

However, proponents for maintaining these laws are even more concerned about what the tolerance of these forms of behavior portends for society in general. Many people in the United States would be offended by the tolerated presence of these activities. The question then becomes whether or not people who do not participate in these acts should be subjected to what they perceive as the offensive behavior of others. These citizens could certainly be considered as "victims."

Some of the opposition to eliminating these acts as crimes are found within the criminal justice system itself. Law enforcement agencies are particularly opposed to the decriminalization of narcotics use, gambling, prostitution, and to a lesser extent, pornography and obscenity.[10] Their concerns are usually expressed in terms of the moral implications, the disruptiveness of such acts to general law and order, and the attraction that their abolition as crimes would have to other forms of crime. Although this response might be faulted for its emotionalism, it should not be discounted, because it is the police who are often nearest the problem and who may have developed a better insight into the problem than the rest of us.

At this time, the verdict is not in. The fact remains that there is little evidence to conclusively support either side in the argument. What all the polemics that surround this issue do prove is that the criminal law serves as an important indicator of basic human behavior. That humanity has progressed at all is often displayed in the different attitudes towards what constitutes "crime" and what is "good" or "bad" by changing standards of judgment.

At this point, let us examine each of these victimless crimes in an effort to see how they mirror social and legal trends.

GAMBLING

It is generally agreed that gambling is the greatest source of revenue for organized crime.[11] The major concern of most law enforcement officials in the United States today centers on five kinds of gambling operations: (1) the numbers, sometimes known as "policy," "bolita," "the figures," or "the digits" (one bets on a combination of numbers that are determined by various means); (2) casino-style gambling; (3) lotteries; (4) parimutuel betting at race tracks and off-track betting; and (5) large dice and card games. Most independent gambling operations that become successful are to be approached by an organized crime group that convinces the independent operator, by means of fear or the promise of greater profit and protection, to share his revenue with the organization.[12] In just the Northeastern United States alone, estimates are that organized crime syndicates control over one-half of all illegal gambling activities.[13]

The President's Task Force on Organized Crime estimated that illegal gambling in the United States runs between $7 billion to $50 billion annually, with the amount probably closer to the larger sum.[14] Gambling is a natural target of organized crime activities. It is necessary to develop large-scale organizations in order to prevent severe losses, since a small operator may take more bets on one horse or one number than the operator could pay off if that horse or number were to win. The operator has to cover these sums by laying off bets. Layoff betting is accomplished through a network of local, regional, and national layoff men who take bets from gambling operations.[15]

Illicit gambling also encourages other offenses, such as loan sharking, which is the lending of money at usurious interest rates. Money is loaned to pay for the incurred gambling debts with interest rates varying from 1 to 150 percent a week depending on the relationship between the lender and borrower, the intended use of the money, the size of the loan, and the repayment potential.[16] A 6-for-5 loan—that is, interest at 20 percent a week—is common with small borrowers. Understandably, the lender is more interested in continuing the exorbitant interest payments than in collecting the principal. This leads to a second area of criminal activity associated with gambling, that of extortion by use of threats of force or force of the most brutal kind. Interest rates are paid, protests are eliminated, and the borrower is coerced by fear into not reporting the activity to enforcement officials.[17] Although no reliable estimates exist of the gross revenue from organized loan sharking, it is known that profit margins are even higher than for gambling operations, and many officials consider the profits to be in the billions.[18]

Decriminalizing Gambling

The point has often been made that assigning criminal status to gambling poses no deterrent to gambling activities. Because people apparently will continue to gamble regardless of whether it is considered a crime or not, many feel that gambling should be sanctioned by governmental regulation and that the monies gained through regulation of gambling enterprises be used to support governmental projects, thereby relieving the burden on the taxpayer. They contend that Nevada, where casino gambling is legal, has been able to accomplish just that. In recent years, a number of states have, in fact, begun state lotteries, and New York City, in 1971, approved off-track betting. In 1978 New Jersey residents approved legislation authorizing casino gambling in Atlantic City. Although these arguments seem logical enough, there is, unfortunately, little research to substantiate the claim that government-sponsored gambling has appreciably curtailed organized and illicit gambling activities in these areas. In fact, there are a number of observers who feel that legalized forms of gambling such as state lotteries have had no effect on organized crime, and have even created greater disrespect for the antigambling laws.[19] The argument that the present statutes that prohibit gambling are a corruptive influence on public officials is based on our nation's past experience with the relationship between organized gambling and official corruption and is much more plausible because of adequate documentation of the relationship.

On the other hand, there are those who feel just as strongly that not only should the gambling laws remain on the books, but that the law should be more vigorously enforced. They reason that by means of strict and persistent enforcement, those who are susceptible to gambling will not find gambling activities and, therefore, will be saved from themselves. Whenever proposals are made to legalize gambling opposition groups invariably arise such as the antigambling league that formed in New York a few years ago. This particular group ran ads depicting a woman and four small children, with the caption, "Who will feed the children when my husband gambles his paycheck away?" Viewed in light of the widespread availability of existing illegal gambling operations, this campaign points up the fact that the public is either misinformed or unaware of the complexities of the problem.

In recent years some behavioral scientists have added to the confusion surrounding the argument. They have maintained, at least tacitly, that gambling provides certain psychic benefits beyond the financial rewards of winning. Zola, for example, has pointed out that among the lower classes gambling allows people to achieve recognition for their accomplishments.[20] Others contend that such gambling activities as playing the numbers satisfy the emotional needs of ghetto dwellers as well as give them the feeling that if they "win big," they will increase their chances for upward social mobility.[21] Other researchers have found that many residents consider numbers as an integral part of neighborhood life and that its existence is crucial to the economic security of the community because of the jobs it provides.[22]

Regardless of the arguments for and against the decriminalization of gambling, it is apparent that a reappraisal of the past attempts and repeated failure to deal with this problem is in order. One of the first priorities seems to be to determine whether stricter and more uniform enforcement of the law is warranted or whether gambling should be openly sanctioned, thereby destroying the corruptive influences of covert operations on the justice system while minimizing the psychic and financial costs to individuals and society as a whole.

DRUNKENNESS

In 1976, over 1 million arrests were made for public drunkenness. This figure does not include the more serious related offenses such as driving under the influence or the often related offense of disorderly conduct or vagrancy. The great volume of these arrests places an extremely heavy burden on the criminal justice system. In the words of the President's Commission, "It burdens police, clogs lower criminal courts and crowds penal institutions throughout the United States."[23]

Drunkenness is punishable under a wide variety of laws which usually describe the offense as being drunk in a public place. The failure of many of these laws is that they do not provide a precise definition of what constitutes the act of being intoxicated. Consequently, the police may use such pretexts as the smell of liquor on a person's breath or a "glassy-eyed" appearance to arrest someone because they felt the individual was not cooperative or did not display the proper respect.

Although public intoxication is considered a crime in almost every jurisdiction, there have been some recent changes in dealing with the public inebriate. Approximately 20 states have abolished their drunkenness statutes and are rewriting their legislation to reflect some significant changes in dealing with public inebriates. Michigan's new statute is indicative of legislation being adapted by other states. Under the Michigan law, a local government is prohibited from adopting or enforcing a law, ordinance, resolution, or rule that imposes a civil or criminal penalty for public intoxication, being a common drunkard, or being incapacitated by alcohol. This prohibition does not apply to laws concerning drunken driving and similar offenses or the sale, purchase, or possession of alcoholic beverages at stated times. Minnesota not only revoked its laws pertaining to public intoxication, but went one step further by ordering that 25 health districts set up special facilities to handle persons who have problems with alcohol who come to the attention of the authorities.

This deemphasis on drunkenness as a crime seems to be reflected in the Uniform Crime Reports. For example, in 1965 there were over 2 million arrests for this offense. The number would be expected to be quite high during this period, however, because several cities experienced urban disorders in which a particularly high rate of arrests for this offense were made. To clean up and control an area, the police were often likely to arrest many persons found on the streets for being intoxicated. By 1971, the number of arrests had dropped to 1.8 million, by 1973 it was down to 1.2 million and by 1976 it had fallen to slightly over 1 million. However, arrest data for the last few years seem to indicate that a new phenomenon is developing. Many of the states that passed legislation to deemphasize drunkenness as a crime are experiencing increased arrests for the offense of disorderly conduct. It may be that some police are now using this offense to deal with the public inebriate.

Costs to the Taxpayer

The costs to the taxpayer of dealing with drunkenness are unknown, but conservative estimates put the sum at over $4 billion annually. The costs involved in the arrest of the public inebriate alone are staggering. For example, the St. Louis Detoxification and Diagnostic Evaluation Center made a rather exhaustive study of the handling of drunkenness arrests by the St. Louis Police Department. It found that the arrest of an individual on the charge of intoxication required the arresting officer(s) to spend an average of 95.8 minutes in arresting, transporting, and processing the arrestee.[24] This drain on law enforcement resources indicates that more efficient methods need to be developed to deal not only with personnel resources, but also with the costs of prosecution, courts, and incarceration as they relate to the problem of drunkenness. Costs will further increase if the courts hold that these offenders are entitled to representation by court-appointed counsel, which may be likely if present trends continue. For example, in 1972 in *Argersinger* v. *Hamlin*, the U.S. Supreme Court held that no person could be imprisoned as the result of a criminal prosecution in which the defendant was not accorded the right to public representation.[25] The language of this decision implies that indigent drunks who are arrested for this offense are entitled to taxpayer-supported legal representation at their trials. Indeed, some local and state courts have moved in this direction.

Costs to Society and the Process of Justice

In addition to the economic costs involved in enforcing drunkenness laws, there are other important considerations. A large percentage of those arrested, convicted, and incarcerated or fined for public intoxication are later rearrested and the cycle begins anew. Anyone who has witnessed the trials of these offenders cannot but be aware that the concept of due process for these individuals is being blatantly disregarded. At best, the "trial" consists of a few minutes spent before the magistrate prior to sentencing. It is almost an assembly-line operation as the defendants are paraded through the courtroom, found guilty, and fined or incarcerated. The only thing absent is the clang of the cash register as "justice" is dispensed.

In addition, the process has absolutely no deterrent effect on the vast majority of individuals arrested for this offense. The criminal justice system has neither the resources nor the ability to deal with this problem. The irony of the situation, however, is that dealing with the problem is precisely what society expects. The police, courts, and corrections are supposed to solve the problem of the public nuisance whose presence is offensive to other members of society. The emphasis then, is not on helping people, but on merely removing a social eyesore from view.

The enforcement of laws against drunkenness is particularly discriminatory in application. Although the National Institute on Alcohol Abuse and Alcoholism of the National Institute of Mental Health has repeatedly pointed out that alcoholics or persons with serious drinking problems number in the millions in the United States and come from all socioeconomic strata, lower-class persons account for a disproportionate number of all arrests. The more affluent citizens may be just as publicly intoxicated as the poor wino in the ghetto, but because of the social circles in which they move as well as the greater reluctance of the police to arrest them, they are less likely to appear in court on a charge of drunkenness unless more serious behavior is involved.

It must be mentioned, however, that the arrest of certain chronic alcoholics can, in a strange way, perform a humanitarian role: As pitiful as some jails are, they may provide a better home for many derelict alcoholics than they would find on the street. At least jails provide shelter from the weather and some security from criminals who would prey upon the alcoholics in their helpless condition.

CURRENT NEEDS AND NEW DIRECTIONS

As has been pointed out, the laws are changing. People are beginning to realize that chronic alcoholism is a disease that requires treatment that cannot be provided by the criminal justice system. Following the release of the 1967 President's Crime Commission recommendations on public intoxication, alternative solutions were sought. As a result, the American Bar Association and the American Medical Association Joint Committee on Alcoholism began to study this problem. In August 1971, they published a model act, which they encouraged the states to adopt. Under the ABA-AMA model act, the laws against public intoxication would be repealed except in cases where the individual could be considered a disorderly intoxicant. All intoxicated persons who were not actually disorderly would be handled under civil detoxification inpatient and outpatient procedures in hospitals and clinics.[26]

The most significant development in the area of model legislation occurred in 1971. In August of that year, the National Conference of Commissioners, representing the governors of all fifty states, adopted a Uniform Alcoholism and Intoxification Treatment Act. As a result of this meeting, the representatives of the various states agreed to work with their respective state legislative bodies in getting the Uniform Act adopted in their states.

Section 1 of the Uniform Act enunciates the following policy:

> It is the policy of this state that alcoholics and intoxicated persons may not be subjected to criminal prosecution because of their consumption of alcoholic beverages, but rather should be afforded a continuum of treatment in order that they may lead normal lives as productive members of society.[27]

The Uniform Act requires, among other things, that:

1. The states establish programs for the treatment of intoxicated persons and alcoholics.

2. Intoxicated persons and those incapacitated by alcohol be assisted to their homes or to treatment facilities by the police or emergency service patrols in protective custody under civil law.

3. Political subdivisions of any state be prohibited from adopting any law that makes public intoxication or any related behavior or conditions (except drunken driving) an offense or the subject of any sanction of any kind.

The Easter and Driver Cases

The courts are also taking a more active role in the decriminalization of public intoxication. On September 23, 1964, Dewitt Easter, a homeless derelict alcoholic, was arrested for public intoxication. At his trial, it was brought out that he had been arrested approximately 70 times since 1937 for public intoxication and other minor offenses related to his alcoholism. This aroused the curiosity of the media, and Easter's plight received a great deal of publicity. In the Easter case, the argument of the defense was unique. It was contended that since Easter was an alcoholic, his drinking was an illness, and because of this, his actions were involuntary, and he, therefore, could not be held criminally responsible for his actions.

Following the national publicity that surrounded the Easter case, another test case was started by one Joe Driver, who filed a habeas corpus petition in the U.S. District Court for the Eastern District of North Carolina. Driver was appealing a 2-year jail sentence for public intoxication which had been upheld by the North Carolina Supreme Court.[28] Driver's record showed over 200 arrests for public intoxication and other minor offenses related to his alcoholism. As a result, he had spent at least two-thirds of his adult life in jail for nothing more than being drunk in public. Like Easter, Driver challenged his conviction on the fundamental principle of criminal responsibility—that criminal sanctions may be applied only to voluntary action—and a chronic alcoholic does not drink voluntarily. It was also argued that since Driver was a homeless derelict alcoholic, his appearance in public was not of his own choice.

After adverse decisions from the lower courts in both cases, the federal courts returned unanimous favorable decisions. In the Easter case, the District of Columbia Court of Appeals agreed that a chronic alcoholic's public intoxication is involuntary and, therefore, not punishable.[29] In Driver's case, the court held that the Eighth Amendment, which prohibits cruel and unusual punishment, prevents the conviction of a chronic alcoholic for public intoxication.[30]

Since these two important decisions, numerous state and federal courts have wrestled with the problem. In 1968, a similar case went before the U.S. Supreme Court. In the case of *Powell* v. *Texas,* the Supreme Court upheld the Texas trial court conviction of Powell for the crime of public intoxication, but expressed agreement with the principles and philosophy enunciated by the lower federal courts in the Easter and Driver cases.[31] This has created some confusion in the lower courts. A number of states, however, have tried to comply with the rulings in the Easter and Driver cases and have struck down their public intoxication statutes and ordinances. The issue is, unfortunately, still not clear, and there are certain to be more court tests of the constitutionality of public intoxication laws in future years.

Detoxification Programs

Detoxification centers to treat public alcoholism and drunkenness have grown in recent years. These special centers, which may be publicly or privately supported, are shelters for the initial placement of public inebriates. In lieu of being placed into jail, the individual is brought by the police or a special service unit to a center where he or she remains until sober. Many of these units have established a network of coordinated facilities to treat the individual. Both inpatient and outpatient services are provided as well as hospital referral programs. Alcoholics Anonymous programs, mental health agency services, counseling services, and assistance in obtaining employment. Special provisions are also being established in the more progressive programs for self-referral programs and residential treatment facilities so that the alcoholic does not have to return to the streets upon release.

The future will probably witness the growth of such centers throughout the country. The major problem seems to be obtaining adequate financial support for such programs.

NARCOTICS AND DRUG USE

There is probably no area of the criminal law that is more involved in public controversy than the laws concerned with the voluntary *use* of illegal drugs, ranging from the opiates such as heroin to cocaine to hallucinogens such as LSD to milder forms of narcotics such as marijuana, amphetamines, and barbiturates. The *sale* of illegal drugs falls outside our consideration and is not included in the category of victimless crimes.

Opiates and Other Narcotics

The history of our current drug laws dates from 1914, when Congress passed the Harrison Narcotic Control Act, which regulated the sale and distribution of narcotics and provided the legislation for criminal enforcement at the federal level. In recent years, the problems associated with drug addiction have led to increased efforts by the criminal justice system to deal with the problem of narcotics use and related offenses. Public opinion in this area varies widely. Some people favor tougher penalties against both users and sellers of opiates, particularly against the latter. Responding to this, a number of states in recent years have introduced legislation that carry the penalty of life imprisonment for those convicted of the sale of "hard" drugs. Other people favor incarcerating drug users under existing criminal penalties and requiring them to submit to treatment during their incarceration. There are also those who believe that the only acceptable national policy is to follow the example of Great Britain. Under the system adopted in Britain, which began as a result of the *Rolliston Committee Report* in 1926, it is possible for addicts to receive drugs legally as long as they are registered as addicts. However, recent years have seen some problems develop with this approach. Because of a large increase in the number of addicts in that country, the Dangerous Drugs Act of 1967 was passed. This act established treatment centers where only specially authorized physicians were permitted to dispense drugs to addicts. Efforts are thus being made to reduce the supply of drugs that were being diverted by some unscrupulous physicians to a growing black market in drugs in that country.[32]

Drug Maintenance Programs   The idea of supplying the known addict with heroin has frequently been discussed in the United States. One experimental project was proposed by the Vera Institute of Justice in New York City. Under this proposed plan, 300 adult addicts, who had demonstrated resistance to other forms of treatment for narcotics addiction, would be maintained on heroin for 6 months. They would also be offered a full range of medical, psychological, and social services. The Vera Institute believes that many questions about heroin maintenance could be answered through such an approach. One question they hope to answer is whether a program could be developed that would attract heroin addicts with physical and psychological dependencies who could not shake their addiction, yet wanted to function satisfactorily in a job and as socially adjusted individuals.[33]

Although such heroin maintenance programs have been discussed, critics are quick to point out that such distribution programs are not likely to work.

Their reasoning is based on the fact that heroin effects last only 4 to 6 hours and narcotic addicts with well-established habits must take the drug 6 times a day to avoid withdrawal symptoms. Under these circumstances, it is not likely that many addicts would be effectively served by such distribution programs. It is more likely that it would be necessary to give them supplies that they could take home, and as a result, the dispersal of the drugs to unregistered users would surely occur.[34]

Methadone Treatment Centers　Another recommendation calls for the establishment of methadone treatment centers. Methadone, itself a drug, is an inexpensive substitute for heroin. It can be given orally and its effects last up to 36 hours. Addicts maintained on this drug do not experience the severe symptoms associated with withdrawal from heroin or other addictive narcotics. The use of methadone also has the advantage of preventing addicts from becoming involved in the illegal traffic in drugs or crimes to support their habits. They simply stop by the treatment center whenever they feel the need for the drug. Periodic tests are made to ensure that they have not reverted to heroin use.

The results of methadone treatment are mixed. Some programs have been quite successful, while others have enjoyed only marginal success.[35] As might be imagined, the problem often has been one of trying to keep the addict from reverting to the use of illegal drugs. In addition, the methadone programs have come under attack from various critics who contend that the program simply substitutes one dependence-forming drug for another.[36]

Alternative Legal Approaches　In 1972, Massachusetts adopted a statute pertaining to the pretrial diversion of drug offenders as a possible alternative to the use of the criminal justice system in dealing with these individuals.[37] Under the provisions of its Comprehensive Drug Abuse Rehabilitation and Treatment Act, any person charged with a drug offense is notified at his or her first court appearance of the right to an examination to determine if he or she is a drug-dependent person who would benefit by treatment. A person who elects to be examined and is found to be drug-dependent, may request commitment to a treatment facility in lieu of prosecution. If it is a first drug offense not involving sale, the judge must commit the accused to the drug treatment facility. If the defendant is charged with the sale of drugs or has previously been found guilty of the use of drugs, the judge has complete discretion to refuse a treatment commitment. A defendant is treated at either inpatient or outpatient facilities, with a minimum treatment period of 2 years for addicts and 1 year for drug-dependent nonaddicts. Compliance with the treatment order, whether or not the individual is in fact "cured," leads to dismissal of the charges. The consent of the defendant is required for both examination and commitment.[38] California has also passed similar diversion legislation for first-time drug users.[39]

Solutions to this most vexing problem are still unclear. Somehow, the United States must address the problem in ways other than the traditional method of trying to legislate and enforce the problem out of existence. No one at this time can say with any degree of validity that enforcement is the solution. All that enforcement seems to have accomplished is to drive up the cost of narcotics, and as a result, addicts commit other crimes to support their habits. On the other hand, to legalize the use and distribution of these drugs might encourage more widespread addiction.

Marijuana

Most states have had laws prohibiting the use of marijuana for 50 years, but the widespread use of this drug is a relatively recent phenomenon. The National Commission on Marijuana and Drug Abuse estimates that at least 24 million Americans have used marijuana at one time or another.[40] One of the most comprehensive surveys of marijuana use in the United States was conducted in the junior and senior high schools of San Mateo, California, from 1967 to 1970. It was found that 50.9 percent of the senior high school students had used marijuana at least once during the previous 12 months.[41] A follow-up study conducted in 1976 showed that the figure had increased to 55.3 percent.[42]

Marijuana arrests as a percentage of all arrests for the use of narcotics has grown rapidly in recent years. For example, in 1965 of the total drug arrests only 31.1 percent were for marijuana.[43] By 1970 the percentage had increased to 45.4 percent, and by 1975 this figure jumped to 69.2 percent—with 93 percent of these arrests for the possession of small amounts.[44] Not only has the incidence of marijuana use increased substantially, its users have been found in new demographic sectors identified by age, sex, region, education, and occupation.

These facts have generated considerable critical comment about the deterrent value of statutes that prohibit its use as well as concern with the operation of the criminal justice system. Whether marijuana statutes can be enforced by the present law enforcement system in a manner consistent with constitutional definitions of fairness and legitimacy raises serious issues. As an example, concern has been expressed about the extent to which current marijuana statutes encourage police misconduct, particularly in the area of search-and-seizure procedure.[45] Another question concerns the selective enforcement of marijuana statutes and the consequence of law bearing unequally on age, racial, and occupational groups.[46] Finally, questions have been raised about whether the criminal processing of marijuana offenses is an appropriate way of handling the population involved. It has been argued that both the stigma and the severe penalties associated with marijuana offenses are not only undesirable, but damage the credibility, integrity, and effectiveness of the criminal law and its enforcement system.[47]

Arguments Against Legalizing Marijuana The major argument against legalizing marijuana use or reducing the penalty for marijuana offenses centers on the claim that marijuana use leads to the use of hard drugs and addiction. There is some conflicting evidence in this area. Some studies show that a large percentage of addicts also used marijuana early in their lives, while other studies show that there appears to be no relationship between marijuana usage and criminality and eventual addiction.[48]

The argument has also been raised that the frequent use of marijuana leads to serious psychological disturbance, a fact that has been substantiated by various studies, although the evidence appears inconclusive.[49] The research studies that have indicated this relationship have been refuted by many other scientists on grounds of faulty research procedures or similar studies that drew different conclusions.

Another frequent argument is that marijuana use can impair the sensory functions and cause the user to jeopardize other members of society by the operation of an automobile, etc. This argument is usually repudiated on the grounds that the use of alcohol is well documented to cause similar effects, yet it is readily available. Many reputable medical groups consider that the consumption of alcohol has more negative consequences for the individual and society than does the use of marijuana.[50]

Whatever results from the heated debates surrounding the decriminalization of marijuana use, certain facts are quite clear. Punitive policies toward the use of marijuana have resulted in a number of consequences, as follows:

1. The penal code automatically brands as criminals at least one-third of the younger generation who have used marijuana.

2. Hostility and disrespect for the criminal justice system and particularly the police have increased in relation to the growing use of marijuana.

3. Many people see in the enforcement of the marijuana laws and the statements issued by some governmental agencies a great deal of hypocrisy and outright lies. This further alienates individuals from their government and decreases the government's credibility.

4. Tremendous expense is associated with the futile attempts to enforce the marijuana laws and to control marijuana distribution. In California alone, the 1972 estimated cost of enforcing marijuana laws was over $577 million.[51]

5. Enforcement efforts have resulted in a flourishing and lucrative traffic in marijuana. This has encouraged the drug culture and organized crime to further exploit this market.

6. Enforcement has further widened the generation gap between adult members of society and youth.[52]

Society must now arrive at some clear idea of what must be done. Certainly, use of marijuana should be no more encouraged than is the use of alcohol or tobacco. Perhaps out of frustration in trying to deal with the problem, recent public opinion surveys indicate that an increasing percentage of Americans favor either decriminalization or the reduction in penalties associated with its use, and even its sale.[53] These changing attitudes have been expressed in the laws dealing with marijuana. As of early 1978, nine states have made the possession of 1 ounce or less of marijuana a simple civil infraction. Oregon was the first state to act, in 1973, and Alaska, California, Maine, Colorado, Minnesota, Mississippi, New York, and North Carolina have all followed. As a result, one-third of the American people can now smoke marijuana without fear of anything more serious than a $100 fine,which is issued like a traffic citation.

The federal government is also considering changing its law. President Carter, acting on a campaign promise, asked Congress in 1977 to reduce the federal penalty for possession of an ounce of marijuana from $5,000, a year in jail, or both, to a civil fine—probably $100. However, Congress is still reluctant to change and there are those who feel that conservatives who oppose marijuana law liberalization may gain strength through an informal alliance with the increasingly powerful groups that favor capital punishment, oppose abortions, homosexual rights, gun control, and the equal rights amendment for women.[54]

OBSCENITY AND PORNOGRAPHY

The terms *obscenity* and *pornography* are used synonymously. In the most general sense, obscenity simply means that which is offensive to chastity.[55] Pornography is the depiction in some way of offensive, obscene materials. In the discussion that follows, these two terms are used interchangeably, as they normally are in the law.

The creation and enforcement of obscenity and pornography laws raises the question of whether the state should have the power to prohibit personal conduct solely on the grounds that it is considered by society to be harmful to the morality of the actor. Those opposed to relaxation of obscenity and pornography laws claim that permissiveness in this area will undermine the moral fabric of our nation and will make its impact felt most notably on the vulnerable members of society, such as the young or those with deviant sexual desires. Although the research efforts of Kinsey and the Commission on Obscenity and Pornography and the experience of the Scandinavian countries would tend to discount this argument, further research is needed before a definitive conclusion can be drawn.

Those who advocate the legalization of obscene material argue that adults should have the right to choose the books they read, the movies they see, and the plays they attend. They claim along with other civil libertarians that this right is granted them under the First Amendment's guarantees of freedom of speech, press, and assembly.

The merits of both these positions have been frequently argued before the courts. Unfortunately, the criminal justice system has been no more able to resolve this question than any similar victimless crime issues, and the immediate future shows very little promise of improvement.

The History of Obscenity Laws

The offense of obscenity as it is known today did not exist in either England or the United States until the nineteenth century. Although "obscenity" was made a crime in England in the sixteenth century, only seditious or heretical writings or plays that attacked the state or the church were considered obscene. In 1727, a man named Curl was prosecuted for "obscene libel" for publishing the book *Venus in the Cloister or the Nun in Her Smock*. This case developed the common law crime of obscenity.[56] The court was not as concerned with the explicitness of the book as with the fact that it discredited established religion.[57]

Most historians are of the opinion that there was little concern over obscenity in colonial New England because the colonists felt little need for legal prohibitions. By the early nineteenth century, a number of books were banned in England and America. One of these books, *Fanny Hill,* brought the first obscenity case dealing with a book to the attention of the courts in 1821. The publisher was found guilty under the Hicklin (or Cockburn) test which maintained that obscenity was to be judged by "whether the tendency of the matter charged as obscenity is to deprave and corrupt those whose minds are open to such immoral influences, and into whose hands a publication of this sort may fall."[58] Thus obscene materials were those that had a special corruptive influence on youth. That same year, Vermont passed the first state statute to prohibit obscenity. The Hicklin test of obscenity first appeared as a law in the State of Massachusetts in 1835 which held that the test should be whether the work was "manifestly tending to the corruption of the morals of youth."[59] It was the state legislatures that took the most active role in dealing with obscenity during this period, and it would be many years before the courts would become the prime forces in dealing with this offense, as they are today.

Early Federal Legislation Although antiobscenity laws appeared on the books during the first half of the nineteenth century, they were not often enforced. It was only after the Civil War that citizen groups began to agitate for stronger enforcement. In 1868, the New York legislature passed a bill to suppress obscene literature.[60] At this time, a grocery store clerk in New York, named Anthony Comstock, took it upon himself to track down, on his own time and at his own expense, the sellers of obscene publications and to have them prosecuted under the 1868 act. Comstock, however, felt limited because of the lack of a federal obscenity statute. So, Comstock joined efforts with the YMCA to work for national antiobscenity legislation that would make possible prosecution of publishers as well as local dealers. Together, they formed the Committee for the Suppression of Vice, and with Comstock leading them, the committee set about lobbying Congress to pass laws prohibiting the sale and distribution of obscene matter. In response to this lobbying, Congress in 1873 passed an act governing the passage of obscene material through the mail.[61]

In 1933, the first major modification of early statutes and court decisions was made by the federal courts. Until this time, material was considered obscene if it could be judged corruptive to the morals of youth or corruptive to those whose minds might be open to such immoral influences. In that year, the federal courts were called upon to examine James Joyce's famous novel *Ulysses*. The U.S. Court of Appeals ruled that the novel was not obscene. In this case, the court established a new test that maintained that obscenity was to be judged by "its effect on the average person."[62] In addition, the work had to be considered as a whole and could not be judged obscene because of certain isolated passages.

Major Early Supreme Court Rulings In 1957, the Supreme Court was first called upon to examine the relationship between obscenity and the guarantees of the freedom of expression granted by the First Amendment and the due process provision of the Fourteenth Amendment. In the case of *Roth* v. *United States*, the court ruled that obscenity was not protected by the First Amendment, as not every form of speech or protection is guaranteed by the Constitution. It reaffirmed the decision handed down by the court in the *Ulysses* case that the "average person" standard should apply, and added two additional tests. These were "whether the dominant theme as a whole appeals to prurient interests; and whether it is without redeeming social importance."[63] The *Roth* test brought with it the problems of defining the "average person," "contemporary community standards," "prurient interest," and "redeeming social importance."

In 1961, another test standard was added. In the case of *Manual Enterprises* v. *Day*, the court expanded the already existing tests under the Roth case to include the concept of "patent offensiveness" of the material.[64] Three years later, in *Jocobellis* v. *Ohio*, the court faced the question of whether local standards were to prevail in applying the existing tests. The court replied that the constitutional status of an allegedly obscene work must be determined on the basis of a national standard.[65] In 1966, the Supreme Court decided the cases of *Ginzberg* v. *United States* and *Mishkin* v. *New York*. In these cases, the test of whether the work was without redeeming social value was employed as well as a modification of the "average person" test in that "when the material in question is designed and primarily disseminated to a clearly defined group, it is to be judged by the standards of that group."[66]

As a result of these rulings, obscenity was determined by the following criteria: (1) the appeal of the dominant theme of the material to prurient interest; (2) the "patent offensiveness" of the material in its description or representation of sexual matters; and (3) the material's utter lack of redeeming social value. The standard for determining the prurient appeal and the offensiveness to the community in sexual description is that of the national contemporary community as applied to the average person. The exception is where deviant groups are involved.[67]

In trying to formulate vague tests and have these tests apply nationwide, the Supreme Court found itself enmeshed in a web of confusion. Beginning in the late 1960s, the Court began reassessing its role in trying to determine what is or is not obscene or pornographic. This reassessment has had some far-reaching effects on obscenity and pornography laws in this country. In 1971, the National Commission on Obscenity and Pornography released its much-publicized report.[68] After considerable research, the commission found no significant relation between exposure to erotic materials and antisocial behavior. Twelve of the 18 members of the commission recommended repeal of all state and federal statutes prohibiting the sale, exhibition, or distribution of sexual materials to consenting adults.[69]

Important Recent Decisions

Two recent Court decisions have had a significant impact on obscenity laws. In 1969, in the case of *Stanley* v. *Georgia*, the Supreme Court overturned the ruling of the Georgia Supreme Court which upheld the conviction of Stanley for possession in his home of three pornographic films. The Court ruled that the First and Fourteenth Amendments prohibit making private possession of obscene material a crime. Under this ruling, an individual has the right to read or observe what he or she pleases in the privacy of his or her own home.[70] In 1971, the Court also upheld lower court decisions that set limits on the power of the postal authorities to prohibit the mailing of obscene materials on the basis that consenting adults should have the right to choose their own moral standards as long as they do not directly offend others.

The most recent decision of the Supreme Court in the 1973 case of *Miller* v. *California* seems to be another landmark decision. The Court in this notable case determined that it was unable to formulate a meaningful definition of obscenity that could be applied nationwide. Instead, it decided to formulate guidelines and leave the ultimate decision of what is obscene or pornographic to local communities. It has now become the responsibility of local governments to make that determination.[71]

However, although the Supreme Court did establish the "community standards" doctrine, its guidelines are equally as vague and confusing. The Court said:

> "The basic guidelines for the trier of fact must be (a) whether 'the average person, applying contemporary community standards' would find the work taken as a whole, appeals to the prurient interest . . . (b) whether the work depicts or describes, in a patently offensive way, sexual conduct specifically defined by the applicable state law, and (c) whether the work, taken as a whole, lacks serious artistic, political, or scientific value . . ."[72]

Experience has shown that states and local communities are finding that they are no more effective in reaching a solution than was the Supreme Court. Numerous state legislatures are wrestling with the problem of defining obscenity and pornography in light of the Supreme Court guidelines. Communities are unable to define their contemporary standards. As a result, local police, prosecutors, and court officials are increasingly reluctant to take official action against adult bookstores, movie theaters, and other pornographic enterprises. Those who have tried enforcement action often find that their ordinances are unenforceable in state courts. It would appear that a solution is still to be found.

SEX OFFENSES

The sex offenses of prostitution, homosexuality, fornication, and adultery are classified as victimless crimes. The original purpose of laws against these offenses was to deter acts considered morally harmful to the basic fabric of society. However, these laws have had no demonstrated deterrent effect except perhaps to drive such behavior underground.

In recent years, society has become much more tolerant of these acts. This is particularly true with the crimes of fornication and adultery and, in some instances, certain forms of homosexual behavior and prostitution. The offenses of fornication and adultery, for instance, are widely tolerated in our society, and the laws against them are most certainly unenforceable by today's moral standards. Florida, for example, has prosecuted only one case of adultery in the last 100 years.

Prostitution

While some states, such as Nevada, permit counties to license and regulate houses of prostitution, the laws against prostitution are still zealously enforced by many local police agencies. Perhaps because prostitution is more directly offensive to certain members of the community than the more covert forms of "deviant" sexual behavior, the police are forced to take periodic steps to remove prostitutes—at least those who openly solicit customers.

What can we say about the enforcement of prostitution laws? In the first place, in spite of the enforcement efforts of the police, it is a very large business. Winick and Kinsie, in their comprehensive study of prostitution, suggest that it is nationwide in scope and involves over a billion dollars annually. They estimate that this "oldest profession" involves between 100,000 and 500,000 women in the United States alone.[73]

Arguments for Prosecuting Prostitution as a Crime Those who favor the strict enforcement of laws against prostitution present a number of arguments. First, the existence of prostitution in a community encourages the growth of other criminal activities such as drug abuse, assaults, and homicides—crimes that often involve the customer, the prostitute, and her pimp. It also leads to a greater incidence of venereal disease, and to the corruption and demoralization of law enforcement. The existence of prostitution in a community also corrupts the morals of youth and leads young girls into this form of behavior as a livelihood. Finally, by sanctioning prostitution, the community encourages moral decay and sexual promiscuity among its members which destroys familial relationships and the sanctity of marriage.

Arguments for Legalizing Prostitution Others who feel that it would be far more prudent to legalize and regulate such behavior argue that prostitution cannot be enforced out of existence—instead, the best that we can hope to accomplish is to control it through regulation. Even this, however, often becomes a travesty of justice. In many communities there are few attempts to interfere with the higher-class call girls, the massage parlors, or, in some areas, the "houses" that can afford protection. The energy that law enforcement can devote to the matter is concentrated on streetwalkers. For them, prostitution is a revolving-door crime, somewhat like gambling in which those arrested are typically given minimal sentences and are soon back on the streets. Often there is a great deal of hypocrisy in the enforcement of prostitution laws. For instance, the prostitute's customers are virtually never prosecuted because of opposition by the hotel and convention interests who maintain that such actions would be "bad for business." In addition, the police often have to engage in perjury to avoid the charge of entrapment and to obtain sufficient evidence to convict.

Finally, the laws against prostitution make it even more necessary for the exploitive pimp to "protect" his girl and to arrange for bail and police protection. Those who could decriminalize this offense often suggest that cities with perennial problems of prostitution establish licensed brothels in designated areas where they would be least offensive to the citizenry. Such a policy is thought to have certain advantages: (1) it would better contain this behavior within certain locations in the community instead of having such operations widely dispersed; (2) through careful licensing and periodic medical examinations of prostitutes, the rates of venereal disease associated with prostitution could be reduced; and (3) it is also felt that close police supervision of regulated brothels would reduce many of the problems associated with illegal prostitution. Such problems as the activities of pimps whom the women must turn to for protection and the violence that surrounds this arrangement would be eliminated, and narcotics trafficking, blackmail, robberies, assaults, and other forms of criminal activity could be curtailed. Finally, there are those who look upon the regulation of prostitution as a method for communities to obtain additional revenues through licensing fees and taxes.

It would seem that countries that have tried to legalize prostitution have found it to be a mixed blessing.[74] The fact that the activity is licensed and regulated has not eliminated many of the traditional problems associated with prostitution. Nevada, on the other hand, in which prostitution is legal in 15 of the 17 counties, claims that it has been able to control the dispersion of prostitution in that state as well as the other criminal problems associated with it by means of licensed brothels regulated by the police or the local district attorney's office.[75]

Some local communities have recently adopted new strategies to deal with problems of prostitution. One is to arrest the prostitute's customer as well as the prostitute. Another is to have female police officers operate in areas frequented by streetwalkers; when a male approaches the policewoman and propositions her, he is arrested. Both of these enforcement strategies rely upon the fact that it is a crime to participate in a sexual act with a prostitute or to solicit a woman's services for prostitution.

Homosexual Behavior

Another problem area in the law is the crime of homosexual behavior. As of 1975, 43 states and the District of Columbia imposed criminal penalties on consenting adults who engage in private homosexual conduct. Most of these laws are sodomy statutes which also prohibit oral and anal intercourse between humans, as well as sexual acts with animals.[76] It is necessary to make a distinction at this point between homosexual activities that involve consenting adults and similar activities directed at children or other nonconsenting individuals. It is only the statutes prohibiting this sort of behavior between consenting adults that many people are advocating be removed from the statute books.

The existence of such laws has had a significant impact upon homosexuals in at least three ways. First, laws prohibiting homosexual contact may inhibit persons who seek sexual satisfaction in this manner. Second, such laws may encourage blackmail by providing a means whereby homosexuals can be threatened with exposure or prosecution, and this may discourage employers from hiring homosexuals for fear that their vulnerability to blackmail might pose security risks.[77] Finally, such laws indirectly sanction discrimination against homosexuals in employment, housing, and public accommodations.[78] In addition to these problems, enforcement of the criminal statutes that prohibit homosexual conduct has often been the subject of abuse. While working with the police in a number of cities, the author witnessed numerous instances when police personnel engaged in the harassment and intimidation of known "gays."

The most reliable and most often quoted figures on the extent of homosexuality in the United States are those reported in the studies by Alfred Kinsey and his research associates. Their studies found that 4 percent of the American white males are "exclusively homosexual throughout their lives after the onset of adolescence."[79] They further found that over 37 percent of the total male population had sometimes during their lives engaged in homosexual activity.[80]

Some nations are more enlightened in their approach to dealing with homosexuality. In 1957, the Wolfenden Committee in Great Britain, after exhaustive study, concluded that it found no evidence to support the view that homosexuality is "a cause of the demoralization and decay of civilizations."[81] In short, the committee considered that private, adult consensual homosexuality was "not the law's business."[82] In 1966, Parliament approved recommendations made by the Wolfenden Committee, agreeing that consensual homosexuality in private would no longer be a criminal offense provided that someone under age 16 was not involved.[83]

In the United States in the past few years, there has been a growing trend among the states to liberalize laws regarding certain forms of homosexual behavior. In 1969, a Task Force on Homosexuality sponsored by the National Institute of Mental Health released a report which urged that the United States follow the example of Great Britain and abolish laws prohibiting private homosexual conduct among consenting adults. The report put the issue in perspective when it said: "Homosexuality presents a major problem for society largely because of the amount of injustice and suffering in it, not only for the homosexual, but also for those concerned about him."[84]

In the past few years, admitted homosexuals have been taking an active and public role in the repeal of such statutes. Organizations such as the Gay Liberation Front and others are openly challenging the constitutionality of laws that prohibit such acts among consenting adults. As a result, the police and the courts have grown reluctant to enforce these laws. However, there is a pernicious side to these more liberal attitudes as well. There is evidence that greater toleration by the police and courts may indirectly, at least, be responsible for the increasing incidence of homosexual exploitation of children. Although it is hard to document any causal relationship, this growing problem must be watched very carefully.

SUMMARY

Gambling, drunkenness, narcotics use, obscenity and pornography, fornication, adultery, prostitution, and homosexuality are often referred to as victimless crimes because the usual relationship between the offender and the victim is absent. In fact, it would be more appropriate to refer to them as "consensual crimes." Increasingly, large segments of our society are calling for new methods of dealing with those who engage in such behaviors, and the laws governing these crimes have undergone major changes in recent years. These changes are reflected in new institutions and processes and increased efforts to divert offenders from the criminal justice system.

Victimless crimes are of particular interest to students of criminal justice because they demonstrate graphically how institutions and groups such as the courts, other agencies of criminal justice, professional associations, interest groups, and others affect our system of law and government.

REVIEW QUESTIONS

1. What are the so-called victimless crimes? Why are these "crimes" different from other criminal acts?
2. Outline briefly the arguments for abolishing the criminal status of victimless crimes.
3. Outline briefly the arguments for keeping the criminal status of victimless crimes.
4. What are the dangers in decriminalizing gambling?
5. What steps would be taken in handling public drunkenness cases if the Uniform Alcoholism and Intoxification Treatment Act is adopted?
6. Name and discuss three rehabilitative methods that are being tried to treat drug addicted offenders in lieu of imprisonment.
7. Should marijuana use be decriminalized? Why or why not?
8. What is the current ruling of the Supreme Court in regard to what is or is not obscene? What difficulties have resulted from this ruling?
9. What are the arguments for and against decriminalizing prostitution?

DISCUSSION QUESTIONS

1. Do you think the criminal status of victimless crimes should be kept or abolished? Why or why not?
2. What are some of the difficulties for the criminal justice system in enforcing victimless crimes?

SUGGESTED ADDITIONAL READINGS

Basmajian, Haig A. *Obscenity and Freedom of Expression.* New York: Burt Franklin, 1976.

Callahan, Daniel. *Abortion: Law, Choice, and Morality.* New York: Macmillan, 1970.

Cressey, Donald R. *Criminal Organization.* New York: Harper & Row, 1972.

——— *Theft of the Nation: The Structure and Operations of Organized Crime in America.* New York: Harper & Row, 1969.

Duster, Troy. *The Legislation of Morality: Laws, Drugs and Moral Judgement.* New York: Free Press, 1970.

Esselstyn, T. C. "Prostitution in the United States." *The Annals* 376 (March 1968): 123–135.

National Council on Crime and Delinquency. *The Alcoholic Offender*. New York: NCCD, August 1964.

National Institute of Law Enforcement and Criminal Justice. *The Development of the Law of Gambling: 1776–1976*. Washington, D.C.: U.S. Government Printing Office, 1977.

Pittman, David J., and C. Wayne Gordon. *Revolving Door*. New York: Free Press, 1958.

Plascowe, Morris. "Sex Offenses: The American Legal Context." *Law and Contemporary Problems* 25 (Spring 1960): 217–225.

President's Commission on Law Enforcement and Administration of Justice. *Task Force Report: Drunkenness*. Washington, D.C.: U.S. Government Printing Office, 1967.

Regush, Nicholas M. *The Drug Addiction Business*. New York: Dial Press, 1971.

Rubington, Earl. "The Chronic Drunkenness Offender." *Annals of the American Academy of Political and Social Science* 315 (January 1958): 65–72.

Schur, Edwin M. *Crimes without Victims*. Englewood Cliffs, N.J.: Prentice-Hall, 1965.

NOTES

1. Sanford B. Kadish, "The Crisis of Overcriminalization," *The Annals of the American Academy of Political and Social Science* 374 (November 1967): 157–170.

2. Lord Devlin, *The Enforcement of Morals* (London: Oxford University Press, 1965), p. 23.

3. For example, see Herbert L. Parker, *The Limits of the Criminal Sanction* (Stanford, Calif: Stanford University Press, 1968), p. 266.

4. Gilbert Geis, *Not the Law's Business?* (Washington, D.C.: U.S. Government Printing Office, 1969), pp. III–IV.

5. See Eugene Doleschal, "Victimless Crime," *Crime and Delinquency Literature Abstracts,* June 1971, pp. 254–269.

6. Kadish, "The Crisis of Overcriminalization."

7. Milton G. Rector, "Victimless Crime: Whose Responsibility?" *Trends* (July-August 1972): 6–9.

8. National Commission on Law Observance and Enforcement, *Wickersham Commission Reports,* vol. 1, p. 149.

9. George Nash, *The Impact of Drug Abuse Treatment upon Criminality: A Look at 19 Programs* (Montclair, N.J.: Drug Abuse Treatment Information Project, December 1973), pp. 1–2.

10. See Edward M. Davis, "Victimless Crime: The Case for Continued Enforcement," *Journal of Police Science and Administration* 1 (March 1973): 11–20.

11. See Kefauver Commission, *Second Interim Report,* no. 141, 82d Cong., 1st Sess., 11 (1951).

12. Statement by former inspector, Arthur C. Grubert, New York City Police Department, April 19, 1965, New York.

13. Task Force on Legalized Gambling, *Easy Money* (Washington, D.C.: U.S. Government Printing Office, 1974), p. 17.

14. President's Commission on Law Enforcement and Administration of Justice,

Task Force Report: Organized Crime (Washington, D.C.: U.S. Government Printing Office, 1967), p. 3.

15. Donald R. Cressey, "The Functions and Structure of Criminal Syndicates," in ibid., pp. 35–36.

16. See MacClellan Committee, *Final Report,* S. Rep. No. 1139, 86th Cong., 2d Sess., pt. 4 at 722 (1960).

17. President's Commission on Law Enforcement and Administration of Justice, *Task Force Report: Organized Crime,* p. 3.

18. New York Commission of Investigation, *The Loan Shark Report,* 17 (1965).

19. See Ernest T. Bird, "State Lotteries–A Good Bet," *State Government,* Winter 1972, pp. 23–29; and Task Force on Legalized Gambling, *Easy Money,* p. 9.

20. Irving K. Zola, "Observations on Gambling in a Lower-Class Setting," *Social Problems* 10 (Spring 1963): 360.

21. Thomas J. Johnson, "Numbers Called Harlem's Balm," *The New York Times,* March 1, 1971.

22. St. Clair Drake and Horace R. Clayton, *Black Metropolis: A Study of Negro Life in a Northern City* (New York: Harcourt Brace, 1945), pp. 493–494.

23. President's Commission on Law Enforcement and Administration of Justice, *The Challenge of Crime in a Free Society* (Washington, D.C.: U.S. Government Printing Office, 1967), p. 233.

24. The St. Louis Detoxification and Diagnostic Evaluation Center, "Alternative Disposition of the Public Inebriate" (Washington, D.C.: U.S. Government Printing Office, 1969), p. 16.

25. *Argersinger* v. *Hamlin,* 407 U.S. 25 (1972).

26. U.S. Department of Health, Education, and Welfare, *First Special Report to the U.S. Congress on Alcohol and Health,* (Washington, D.C.: U.S. Government Printing Office, 1972), p. 92.

27. National Institute of Mental Health, *Alcoholism and the Law* (Rockville, Md.: January 1973), p. 14.

28. *State* v. *Driver,* 262 N.C. 92, 136 S.E. 2d 208 (1964).

29. *Easter* v. *District of Columbia,* 361 F. 2d (D.C. Cir. 1966).

30. *Driver* v. *Hinnant,* 356 F. 2d 761 (4th Cir. 1966).

31. *Powell* v. *Texas,* 392 U.S. 514 (1968).

32. Carl M. Liebemann and Jack D. Blaine, "The British System of Drug Control," *Drug Dependence* (Washington, D.C.: U.S. Government Printing Office, 1970), pp. 12–16.

33. Vera Institute of Justice, *Heroin Research and Rehabilitation Program* (New York: Vera Institute, May 1971).

34. National Advisory Commission on Criminal Justice Standards and Goals, *Community Crime Prevention* (Washington, D.C.: U.S. Government Printing Office, 1973), p. 101.

35. For example, see V.P. Dole and M. E. Nyswander, *New York State Journal of Medicine* 66 (1965): 645; Methadone Maintenance Evaluation Committee, *First National Conference on Methadone Treatment* (New York: The Rockefeller University, 1968); Vernon D. Patch, A. E. Raynes, and Alan Fisch, "Methadone Maintenance and Crime Reduction in Boston—Variables Compounded," paper presented at the annual meeting of the American Psychiatric Association, May 1973; and S. B. Sells, ed., *The Effectiveness of Drug Abuse Treatment, Volume I: Evaluation of Treatments* (Cambridge, Mass.: Ballinger, 1974).

36. *Governor's Report on Narcotic Addiction Programs in New York* (Albany, 1969).

37. Mass. Gen. Laws Ann., ch. 123, §38–55 (supp. 1972).

38. John A. Robertson and Phyllis Teitelbaun, "Pre-Trial Diversion of Drug Of-fenders: A Statutory Approach," *Boston University Law Review* 52, no. 2 (Spring 1972).

39. See Robert Berke and Michael I. Dillard, *Drug Offender Diversion in California: The First Year of Penal Code 1000,* a report of the State Drug Abuse Prevention Advisory Council, January 1974.

40. National Commission on Marijuana and Drug Abuse, *Marijuana: A Signal of Misunderstanding,* vol. II (Washington, D.C.: U.S. Government Printing Office).

41. Department of Public Health, Research and Statistics Section, *Five Mind-Altering Drugs (Plus One),* San Mateo County, Calif. 1970, p. 5.

42. Summary Report, *Surveys of Student Drug Use,* San Mateo County, Calif., 1976, p. 2.

43. National Commission on Marijuana and Drug Abuse, *Marijuana,* p. 612.

44. National Institute for Law Enforcement and Criminal Justice, *Marijuana: A Study of State Policies and Penalties* (Washington, D.C.: U.S. Government Printing Office, November 1977), p. 27.

45. R. Bonnie and C. Whisenand, "The Forbidden Fruit and the Tree of Knowl-edge: History of American Marijuana Prohibition," *Virginia Law Review* 56 (1970): 971–1003.

46. Department of Public Health, San Mateo County, *Five Mind-Altering Drugs.*

47. J. Kaplan, *Marijuana: The New Prohibition* (New York: World, 1970).

48. National Commission on Marijuana and Drug Abuse, *Marijuana,* p. 620.

49. For example, see Harold Kolansky and William T. Moore, "Effect of Marijuana on Adolescents and Young Adults," *Journal of the American Medical Association* 216 (April 19, 1971): 486–492.

50. R. S. Weingarter, "Fact and Fiction Surrounding Marijuana," *Journal of Mental Health* 5 (June 1973): 61–78.

51. National Institute for Law Enforcement, *Marijuana,* p. 153.

52. Geis, *Not the Law's Business?,* p. 169.

53. See National Commission on Marijuana and Drug Abuse, *Marijuana,* pp. 916–917; Drug Abuse Council, *National Survey of Marijuana Use and Attitudes,* 1974; National Institute of Drug Abuse, *Nonmedical Use of Psychoactive Substances* (Washington, D.C.: U.S. Government Printing Office, 1976), p. 114.; Lloyd Johnston, "Monitoring the Future," statement to the press, November 23, 1976, as reported in National Institute of Law Enforcement, *Marijuana,* p. 36.

54. Neal Pierce, "Campaign for Decriminalization of 'Pot' Advancing," *Arkansas Democrat,* September 11, 1977, p. 23, col. 1.

55. Rollin M. Perkins, *Criminal Law and Procedure* (Brooklyn, N. Y.: Foundation Press, 1966), p. 206.

56. A. Schroeder, "Obscene Literature at Common Law," *Albany Law Journal* 69 (1907): 146.

57. *Technical Report of the Commission on Obscenity and Pornography,* vol. II (Washington, D.C.: U.S. Government Printing Office, 1971), p. 69.

58. *Regina* v. *Hicklin,* L.R. 3Q.B.360 (1868).

59. Ibid., p. 76.

60. New York State, 309.

61. L. Broun and E. P. Leech, *Anthony Comstock: Roundsman of the Lord* (New York: Boni & Liveright, 1925).

62. *United States* v. *One Book Called "Ulysses,"* 5F, Supp. 182 (1933).

63. 354, U.S. 476 (1956).

64. 370, U.S. 478 (1962).

65. 378, U.S. 184 (1964).

66. 383, U.S. 412 (1965).

67. M. Cherif Bassiouni, *Criminal Law and Its Process* (Springfield, Ill.: Thomas, 1969), p. 247.

68. *The Report of the Commission on Obscenity and Pornography* (Washington, D.C.: U.S. Government Printing Office, 1971).

69. Ibid., pp. 51–52.

70. 394, U.S. 557 (1969).

71. 413, U.S. 15 (1973).

72. Ibid.

73. Charles Winick and Paul M. Kinsie, *The Lively Commerce: Prostitution in the United States* (Chicago: Quadrangle, 1971).

74. Geis, *Not the Law's Business?*, pp. 172–221.

75. *The New York Times*, January 13, 1974, p. 9, col. 3.

76. "The Constitutionality of Laws Forbidding Private Homosexual Conduct," *Michigan Law Review* 72 (August 1974): 1613.

77. "Security Clearances for Homosexuals," *Stanford Law Review* 25 (June 1973): 409–411.

78. *The New York Times*, December 23, 1973, p. 5, col. 1.

79. Alfred C. Kinsey, Wardell B. Pomeroy, and Clyde E. Martin, *Sexual Behavior in the Human Male* (Philadelphia: Saunders, 1948), pp. 650–651.

80. Ibid, p. 651.

81. Great Britain Committee on Homosexual Offenses and Prostitution (CMND 247, 1957), p. 22.

82. Ibid., p. 24.

83. The Sexual Offenses Act, 1967 (1967, c. 60), Halsbury, 3d ed., vol. VIII, pp. 577–582.

84. National Institute of Mental Health, Task Force on Homosexuality, *Final Report* (Washington, D.C.: U.S. Government Printing Office, Oct. 10, 1969), p. 4.

Law Enforcement

The patrol officer on the local beat is the only contact with law enforcement that the average citizen will likely ever have. The patrol force is the largest operating unit in a police department.

For their protection, patrol officers often cover high-crime areas in pairs. They maintain constant radio communication with their precinct.

Aerial surveillance has proven to be a valuable tool in police work. It is both flexible and effective in preventing crime and capturing criminals.

At the heart of police operations is the communications center. This is Chicago's. It has computer inquiry terminals for eight of the city's thirteen zones to handle calls for police assistance and traffic control.

In criminal investigations, specially trained dogs are used to detect the presence of narcotics and other drugs.

Not all law enforcement officers work for local agencies. The Departments of Justice and Treasury employ numerous personnel for various jobs. At Nogales, Arizona, for example, a U.S. Customs Service Inspector weighs crates of produce at a commercial inspection facility before allowing the shipment to be taken into the United States.

5

LOCAL, STATE, AND FEDERAL LAW ENFORCEMENT AGENCIES

1. What are the two major functions of the police?
2. How have police agencies evolved through history, particularly in England, and who were the most notable police reformers?
3. What are the special characteristics of police agencies as they developed in America?
4. What are the major federal law enforcement agencies and their respective jurisdictions?
5. What functions, operations, and problems are associated with the Law Enforcement Assistance Administration?

These are some of the questions this chapter will answer.

In a free society, the police are both an anomaly and a necessity because they are granted more authority than other members of society—for example, their right to search, to use deadly force, to arrest—is awesome to the degree that it can deprive individuals of their personal freedoms. The anomaly of this police power is that it is given under a system of government that grants authority reluctantly and, when granted, is sharply curtailed by a system of checks and balances. What is also awesome is the fact that this authority is delegated to individuals at the lowest level of the police bureaucracy.[1]

Yet, as Goldstein points out, a democracy heavily depends on its police, despite their anomalous position, to maintain the order that permits a free society to exist. The police, therefore, become *our agents* to prevent people from preying on one another; to provide a sense of security; to facilitate movement; to resolve conflicts; and to protect the very processes and rights on which a free society exists. The strength of our democratic processes and the quality of life in America is determined to a large degree by the methods our police employ in discharging their functions.[2]

POLICE FUNCTIONS

Within the framework of our Constitution and system of laws, the police play two important roles: they maintain order and enforce the law.[3] All of their activities from directing traffic to conducting investigations and making arrests are found in these two basic roles. The maintenance of the social order is their prime responsibility and only when they cannot accomplish this duty must they employ the more extreme measure of enforcement. Because the police must have the powers to enforce compliance with the law, they have been given the powers of inquiry and arrest. However, implicit in our criminal justice system is the precept that the police through their programs should be able to induce voluntary compliance, and only when this fails, are they justified in using their arrest powers.

This relationship is apparent when examining police functions. The most obvious example is the basic level of police activity—the officer patroling his beat. Such officers are primarily concerned with behavior that either disturbs or threatens the peace—from the neighbor who plays his stereo too loudly to a bank robbery. In each instance, the order in society is disturbed, albeit more so in the case of the bank robbery.

The order maintenance activities of the police involve far more time than the law enforcement aspects of their role. For instance, one study of a metropolitan police department indicated that more than half the calls the police received were for help or support in connection with personal and interpersonal problems that were not directly of a law enforcement nature.[4] In Detroit, one researcher found that only 16 percent of the calls to the police were crime-related that directly called upon their law enforcement powers.[5]

To understand how these roles developed, one has to understand the historical relationship between society, law, and police powers, and how these factors became interrelated to produce the present conception of the role of the police. This chapter explores this historical relationship and also examines the growth, development, and organization of police agencies at all levels of government. Next, the chapter deals with how specific law enforcement functions such as arrest and investigation must meet these role criteria. Finally, in this section on law enforcement, there is a discussion of some of the reform efforts now being directed at the police to improve their ability to fulfill these roles.

EARLY DEVELOPMENT OF LAW ENFORCEMENT

Historians have not provided us with much insight into the development of law enforcement. For the most part, early law enforcement duties in the ancient empires were performed by existing military forces. Around 500 B.C., Rome created the first specialized investigative unit called *quaestors* or "trackers of murder." Later, during the reign of Augustus Caesar (27 B.C. to 14 A.D.), principles of police administration developed that are similar to some modern methods. For example, special detachments of quasi-military personnel operated out of designated districts in the city of Rome. They were responsible for maintaining patrols and searching out criminals. This same principle of organization was also established throughout the provinces conquered by Rome.

With the fall of the Roman empire, the kind of centralized government that was needed to maintain law and order came to an end. Western Europe then became enveloped in what historians often refer to as the "Dark Ages." Gradually, the feudal system evolved as a means to bring some social order out of the chaos that followed the collapse of Rome. By the eleventh century, the feudal system had become established. This was a period when power—including the powers of law enforcement—was vested in the hands of feudal lords. Although the church had some influence in defining certain forms of conduct as "criminal," it was a period of "might makes right." Those laws that were observed and enforced were based more on the interests and rights of those in power—the feudal lords—than on any concept of state, justice, or the public good.[6] Since the feudal lords had broad powers to define what was "criminal" depending upon their station in life, they could act with relative impunity.[7] There is no indication that there were specific police officials empowered to enforce laws during this time. Instead, what police powers existed were vested in the lord's men-at-arms who acted under his direction.

DEVELOPMENT OF THE POLICE IN GREAT BRITAIN

It is important to understand the development of law enforcement in Great Britain for two reasons. First, because it serves as the model for our own system of criminal justice. Many of the institutions, processes, and foundations of criminal justice developed in England and were adopted in America when the colonies were founded. Second, and perhaps more importantly, many of the attitudes now held by Americans about legal principles and the police are a result of the centuries of experience Englishmen had under their existing system of criminal justice. For example, the distrust of strong centralized government and the fear of oppressive police systems under such government have long been a historical fact and characteristic of the English experience. With such a historical perspective, it is easier to understand the foundation for such continuing concerns today.

BEGINNINGS OF THE MODERN ERA OF LAW ENFORCEMENT

The British police system and the influence it has had in America were not because of the British people, but in spite of them. In the words of Reith, a noted historian on the development of the police, "It is almost solely the product of personalities; those of five individuals whose single-mindedness in vision, ideals and purposes was eventually brought by the last of them to practical adaptation in the shape of the police as we know them today."[8]

The first of the five creators of modern police concepts was the novelist Henry Fielding. Although he is most widely remembered for his novels, his achievements as a magistrate who worked to achieve social and police reform are certainly no less significant in terms of their lasting value to humanity. He conceived of the idea that police action should be directed at the *prevention* of crime instead of seeking to control it, as was the custom at the time, simply by waiting for its occurrence and then attempting to repress it by means of violence or brutal punishments.

Fielding was a perceptive observer of the nature and causes of crime in London. He saw that crime and criminals had become so open in the city that the constables of the time were powerless to intervene and completely at the mercy of the criminal elements. The situation had become so bad that the constables would not dare to arrest the majority of the criminals. Fielding also observed that the law-abiding citizens of London did not grasp the possibilities of collective security against the criminal. Fielding alone conceived the idea that there was another method of dealing with crime and disorder besides that of waiting helplessly for its manifestations and then attempting to meet violence with violence. He proposed that people could collectively go into the streets, trace the criminals to their haunts, and arrest them. To test this theory, he selected six citizens of integrity and physical prowess and under his leadership they swept the criminal elements from the Bow Street area of London. Many criminals were arrested; others fled. The work of these men and the simplicity of their results caused a sensation. So astonishing were the results of his Bow Street Amateur Volunteer Force that the government provided Fielding with a salary and asked him to extend the idea into other areas of London. Before he could accomplish this, he died in 1754, and for a few years his efforts were carried on by his brother. Soon, however, his original group degenerated into a motley band known as the Bow Street Runners, and it took another 30 years before Henry Fielding's values and ideas received the recognition they justly deserved.

The next reformer was Patrick Colquhoun, a prosperous Glasgow businessman who expressed a deep interest in social and criminal reform. He was appointed as a magistrate in London and began to study the significant social problems of the day and their relationship to crime. He worked diligently to help bring about needed social reforms for the poor. Intrigued by Fielding's earlier work, he crystallized the novelist's ideas into the "new science of preventive police."[9] He proposed that a large police force should be organized for London under the direction of a board of control. Although his plan was ultimately rejected, in 1789 he formed a special river police force patterned after Fielding's idea that proved to be a success and pointed to a solution to a citywide and nationwide problem. Unfortunately, his ideas were still too advanced for the times, for the English people still harbored a great deal of mistrust toward any form of organized police that could be entrusted with enforcement authority.

The next significant reformer was Sir Robert Peel, the home secretary of England. Although many writers give Peel credit as the most instrumental of police reformers, some historians who have thoroughly researched the history of the English police credit him only with the handling of the bill that created the Metropolitan Constabulary, and the foresight to choose wisely the first two commissioners of the new agency who actually planned, organized, and directed the establishment.[10]

Whatever Peel's contribution, the Metropolitan Constabulary for the city of London was created in 1829. Among its principles still considered to be an integral part of professional police service today are:

1. The police must be under governmental control.

2. The police must be stable, efficient, and organized along military lines.

3. The efficiency of the police will be determined by the absence of crime.

4. The deployment of police strength both by time and area is essential.

5. Applicants for the police force should be judged on their own merits.

6. A perfect command of temper is an indispensable trait of a policeman.

7. Policemen should be hired on a probationary basis.

8. Police records are necessary to the proper distribution of police strength.

9. Training of police officers assures greater efficiency.

Although these were the enunciated principles of the new London Metropolitan Constabulary, they were nothing more than ideas when the first two police commissioners, Charles Rowan and Richard Moyne, were appointed in 1849. The combined efforts of these two men established the concepts of modern policing and left an indelible mark on the functions of the British police, even today. The Metropolitan Constabulary was almost disbanded before the principles could be tested. Parliament was being widely criticized by angry groups of citizens calling for the repeal of the act. Members of Parliament were engaged in acrimonious debate, and the fate of the new department hung in the balance. While denunciations swirled about them and Parliament was locked in prolonged debate, these two dedicated and capable administrators began to assemble the agency. The first task was to screen personnel for positions in the new department. Rowan and Moyne realized that this was perhaps the most critical concern, for public approval would depend a great deal on the type of personnel they obtained. The applicants were offered a career for life if they satisfied the standards and could produce accordingly. Out of 12,000 initial applicants, 1,000 were chosen and placed into six divisions. They first concentrated their efforts in the high-crime areas of the city. During their probationary period, the new constables were supervised extensively. During the first 3 years of the department's operation, there were 5,000 dismissals and 6,000 required resignations. This use of the probationary period was a forceful indication of the commissioners' serious intentions.[11]

The success of the new department was almost phenomenal. Crime and disorder sharply declined, yet without the loss of individual freedom to the law-abiding. The commissioners were so successful in their efforts to organize, recruit, and train a professional police agency that within 10 years the people considered Peel a sort of folk hero, and the constables of the London Metropolitan Constabulary became known as "Bobbies" out of respect for Sir Robert Peel. With this success, the idea of a centralized, trained, and well-organized permanent group of police constables soon spread throughout England.

DEVELOPMENT OF LAW ENFORCEMENT IN AMERICA

If the history of law enforcement up to the nineteenth century in England can be considered shameful, the American experience must be considered a disgrace. America seems to be uniquely adept at ignoring the lessons of history. During the 200 years of our existence, we have overlooked the repeated lesson that laws are meaningless in the absence of the authority to secure the *observance* of those laws. During the early years of our nation's growth, the country was involved in the making of laws and the structuring of elaborate procedural machinery, while ignoring the need to provide effective means by which the laws could be enforced.

Although we patterned our police forces after the British model, we often adopted only those features that had already proved to be ineffective at best. We adopted the weak and defective constable system of rural England and transplanted it to America. The elected constables of England became the elected sheriffs and deputy sheriffs of the counties within our states and the elected marshals of our towns and cities. The lack of concern displayed by Americans for the necessity of law enforcement must, in part, be attributed to our heritage of disdain for strong central government and the Jeffersonian ideal of the "little republics." Jefferson believed very strongly in the idea of local self-government, by which each citizen was afforded the opportunity to be actively involved in the conduct of government. It was Jefferson's belief, adopted from the writings of John Locke and later supported by Alexis de Tocqueville in his celebrated work *Democracy in America,* that local government should have "preeminent authority over such responsibilities as the care of the poor, roads, police, administration of justice in minor cases, and elementary exercises for the militia."[12] These ideas received strong support from the American people and remain an ideological legacy today.

This conception of the locus, authority, and rights of local government has had a significant impact on the development and patterning of law enforcement services throughout the United States. Past estimates have placed the number of law enforcement agencies between 32,000 and 40,000.[13] A more recent survey places the figure at over 39,785, but only slightly over 20,000 of these agencies can be considered primarily law enforcement agencies; the remainder are various public agencies that have quasi-law enforcement roles in very specialized areas.[14] These figures indicate that law enforcement in this nation is extremely fragmented and decentralized. Table 5-1 indicates the number and types of police or quasi-police agencies that exist.

Many of these police agencies today still consist of one person or a few persons in villages or small towns. Yet the ideological roots of such modern-day arrangements go back in history to a system similar to the early Germanic kin police. That is, the police are viewed as representatives of the people or, in this case, the local community, from which they receive their authority. According to Reith, this has presented almost insuperable problems for the development of police organizations in the United States. Reith goes on to say:

> The weakness of law enforcement machinery in the United States is because of the fact that, as the people's choice, the police were allowed to become corruptly the instruments and servants not of the law, but of policy and of local and corrupt controllers of policy. By her solution of the problem of the breakdown of the Constable system, England was able to abolish the old system entirely, and under the new system which she created in 1829, her police were made, entirely and exclusively, instruments of law and not of policy and servants of the public. By the fact of having secured independence, the United States lost the benefit of this conception, and the development of the American police has suffered ever since.[15]

The development of local law enforcement in the United States was often conditioned by predisposing factors and local conditions. For example, in the North the primary unit of local government was the town. At first, settlers in these areas banded together in small communities for mutual protection from Indian attacks. Later, as the Industrial Revolution made its impact, these towns grew, and so did the need for law enforcement. Since these were primarily urban settlements, the English urban police model of the town

TABLE 5-1
Publicly Funded Law Enforcement Agencies in the United States (1974)

TYPES OF LAW ENFORCEMENT AGENCIES	NUMBER
State police and patrol agencies	49
State law enforcement agencies	355[a]
Sheriff's departments	3,033
County law enforcement agencies	3,333[b]
Municipal police departments	14,301
District, municipal, and local agencies	15,983[c]
Campus police organizations	406
Federal law enforcement organizations	37
Miscellaneous and quasi-law enforcement agencies	2,288[d]
Total	39,785

[a] Includes various boards and agencies with limited law enforcement responsibilities (alcoholic beverage control boards, state game and fish departments, state fire marshals, state dock authorities, etc.).
[b] Includes agencies with limited and specific law enforcement authority (county coroners, county detectives, county attorneys, probation and parole officers, etc.).
[c] Includes constable and borough police, transit district agencies, harbor police, regional crime squads in Connecticut, etc.
[d] Miscellaneous agencies not falling into the other categories.

Excerpted from article by John P. Granfield published in the July 1975 issue of *The Police Chief* with permission from the International Association of Chiefs of Police.

constable or watchman developed. As some of the cities grew even larger, more elaborate systems were developed in which groups of night watchmen were given the responsibility to maintain law and order and to suppress crime.

In the South, the agrarian nature of this region led to the adoption of strong county government as the primary unit of local government. Just as the sheriff was the primary law enforcement official in rural areas in England so did this office become one of the most, if not the most, influential in county government throughout the Southern states. Even today, although the authority has diminished somewhat over time, the office of the county sheriff is one of considerable importance and power in the South.

Law enforcement services in the West are an amalgam of organizational arrangements that predominated in the North and South. Settlers who migrated westward tended to adopt police organizations like those in the areas from which they came. Many of the same factors that led to the creation of towns in the Northeast were also experienced in the westward movement. For example, the necessity to form protective communities against hostile Indian attacks resulted in the establishment of towns and the adoption of constables or town marshals. At the same time, the vastness of the area encouraged an agrarian and livestock economy more suited to the adoption of the county sheriff form of law enforcement. As a result of these patterns, law enforcement services in the various regions of the country still have a somewhat distinctive difference today. In the Northern states, municipal police are more prevalent, while the South retains a great deal of authority in the county sheriff. In the Western states, more of a balance is struck between the jurisdictional authority of municipal police and the sheriff.

Municipal Police

The development of city police in the United States is inextricably a part of the changing social, economic, and political forces that left their imprint upon the history of municipal governance. In the early seventeenth century, major reliance was placed upon the use of military forces, perhaps assisted by a constable or night watchman. Later, the constable system replaced the military in this role. Still later, a separate day watch was established, and finally the day and night watches were combined into a single police organization.

The first night watch was established by Boston in 1636. In 1658, the city of New York added a similar unit, followed by Philadelphia in 1700. New York's night watch was referred to at the time of its creation as the "Shiver and Shakers" or the rattle watch, because the night watchmen used rattles to announce their presence and to communicate with each other as they made their rounds. Like their counterparts in England at the time, these watchmen were often lazy, inept, and not entirely reputable. In a number of cases, minor offenders were sentenced to serve on the watch as punishment for their crimes. Just as in England, citizens called to serve on the watch could hire substitutes.

For the next 100 years, there were no major changes in providing law enforcement services. When cities grew large enough to warrant a form of law enforcement, they adopted the night watch system of Boston, New York, and Philadelphia and incorporated all their negative features.

In 1833, Philadelphia passed a city ordinance that was a major innovation. It established the first daytime police force consisting of salaried men who worked under the direction of a captain appointed by the mayor. In 1854, the day police were consolidated with the night watch into one department, under the leadership of a marshal who was elected for a 2-year term. During this period, the city of New York also developed a daytime police service, when the New York State legislature, in 1844, authorized communities to organize police forces and appropriated special funds that could be given to cities to provide around-the-clock police protection. By the outbreak of the Civil War, a number of other cities, such as Chicago, New Orleans, Cincinnati, Baltimore, and Newark, had adopted similar police operations, and the foundation of today's municipal police departments had been laid.

The following years were very difficult ones for the establishment of law enforcement, as the police were dominated by political interests and corruption. Departmental reports of the time indicate instances of utter lawlessness on the part of the police themselves. For example, in 1852, documents of the New York Board of Aldermen reported such acts as assaulting superior officers, refusing to go on patrol, forcibly releasing prisoners from the custody of other policemen, drunkenness, theft, pimping, and extorting money from prisoners. These acts were daily occurrences that the police committed under the protection of their political overlords.[16] In Baltimore, Cincinnati, Boston, St. Louis, and other major cities, control of the police was vested in a patronage system which was controlled by the dominant political party. In many documented cases, such as in Baltimore, the police were employed principally as an instrument of the political faction in power to control elections.[17] Nowhere was the undisciplined attitude of the police more clearly shown than in their refusal to wear uniforms, which they considered to be a symbol of servitude. Gradually, they began to wear distinctive apparel, but this was brought about more by their identification with a particular precinct or group of politicians than by anything else. For example, in Philadelphia the police in one ward would wear felt hats to identify their source of patronage while those in another ward would wear white duck suits as their badge of political identification.[18]

Spurred by reform groups, a number of cities and states tried to bring about change. A few states tried to take the control of local police forces in certain large cities out of the hands of the local politicians by putting the departments under state control. This attempt met with great hostility and, except in a few cities, proved to be unworkable. In other cities, special supposedly nonpartisan police boards or commissions were established, and some cities still retain this arrangement.

Today, for various reasons, significant reform has occurred among most municipal police departments. The major reason, however, is that municipal government itself has come under the influence of reform, and changes in police departments are part of an overall change. In the late nineteenth and early twentieth centuries, such reform groups as the National Municipal League and the League of Women Voters began developing programs of municipal reform with the goal of eliminating corruption, increasing efficiency of city government, and making local government more responsive to the will of the public. Although it is not possible to examine all the features of municipal reform and their interrelationships, such characteristics as the adoption of civil service systems; nomination by petition; the initiative, recall, and referendum; the short ballot; the council-manager form of government; nonpartisan elections; and certain sociological and demographic phenomena have brought significant changes to city governance and, as a direct consequence, to the municipal police services.[19]

The State Police

In comparison with municipal police, state police agencies are relatively new. The impetus for the development of state police agencies came from a number of circumstances. One was the realization that inefficient and corrupt municipal law enforcement agencies and sheriff's departments were unable to provide adequate law enforcement services in their respective jurisdictions. With the failure of state governments to impose state governing boards over the operations of local law enforcement services, some states chose to create special police agencies that would have the power to enforce all state laws.

Another factor was the introduction of the automobile, which provided criminal offenders with mobility. It became increasingly difficult for local and county police agencies to apprehend criminals who could easily flee their jurisdiction. In addition, the automobile provided unique enforcement problems of its own. As the number of automobiles increased, so did state highway systems. As a consequence, increasing attention had to be devoted to traffic regulation on these highways—control that had to be multijurisdictional and one that could not be handled satisfactorily by the local police and sheriff's departments.

Finally, state governments came to the realization that there was no agency that could enforce the criminal code of the state nor was there adequate regulatory legislation. If a particular law or regulation was not being enforced for whatever reason by the political subdivisions in the state, the state was powerless to compel local compliance or to force local police officials to take enforcement action.

Prototypes of State Agencies The first state police-type agency was the Texas Rangers. This agency was established by the Texas Provisional Government in 1835 when Texas was still a republic.[20] It was originally established as a purely military unit for use on the Texas borders. Later, it began work in the area of criminal investigation and gradually developed into a state police force that effectively controlled sporadic outbreaks of anarchy caused by the absence of any law enforcement machinery in the new state. Today it is primarily concerned with the conduct of criminal investigations and rendering technical assistance to other law enforcement agencies in Texas.

Massachusetts was the next state to recognize the need for a statewide enforcement agency. In 1865, responding to the problem of uncontrolled vice in certain communities, the state legislature gave the governor authority to create a small group of state constables whose primary purpose was to investigate organized vice activities. In 1879, because of official corruption in this unit, it was reorganized into a new state investigative unit called the Massachusetts District Police, which ultimately became the Massachusetts State Police in 1920.

In 1903, Connecticut established a state investigative unit patterned after the Massachusetts District Police. Like the earlier Massachusetts constables, this unit was set up primarily to investigate vice, which had become rampant in certain communities and which local police agencies were powerless to take enforcement action against because of police corruption and political collusion. This unit also proved to be incapable of solving the problem and later was absorbed into a more effective organization known as the Connecticut State Police.

The credit for establishing the first truly professional and modern state police organization belongs to Pennsylvania. In 1905, the Pennsylvania State Constabulary was formed. It is considered the first true state police organization because the state law enforcement agencies that preceded it were created in response to limited needs, such as frontier problems or the enforcement of vice laws. This agency was established largely because local police forces were unable to control the riots that had become a feature of the coal mining regions. Armies of coal miners fought bloody labor disputes with mercenary forces hired by mine owners and management. It was also hoped that the new agency would improve law enforcement services in the rural areas of the state where county officials were unable to provide adequate protection. A last reason for the agency's creation, and one which is invariably cited by many who oppose the creation of state police forces today, was that Governor Pennypacker realized that he needed some assistance in carrying out the responsibilities and mandates of his office. Pennypacker issued the following statement when he created the agency:

> In the year 1903 when I assumed the office of chief executive of the state, I found myself thereby invested with supreme executive authority. I found that no power existed to interfere with me in my duty to enforce the laws of the state, and that by the same token, no condition could release me from my duty to do so. I then looked about me to see what instruments I possessed wherewith to accomplish this bounded obligation—what instruments on whose loyalty and obedience I could truly rely. I perceived three such instruments—my private secretary, a very small man; my woman stenographer; and the janitor. So, I made the state police.[21]

Organizational and jurisdictional characteristics also entitle the Pennsylvania State Police to be considered the first such agency. In terms of organization, this agency was under the administrative control of a superintendent appointed by the governor. Troop detachments and substations were situated throughout the state so that even the most remote areas were protected.[22] This organizational arrangement and deployment of personnel served as the model for other state police agencies. In terms of jurisdiction, this agency was empowered to enforce all state laws throughout Pennsylvania.

Today's State Agencies Today, some states have bona fide state police departments and others have primarily traffic enforcement agencies, commonly referred to as *highway patrols*. There are some basic distinctions between the two. State police agencies have full jurisdiction and authority to enforce all state laws anywhere in the state. Their responsibilities are quite broad. For example, state police agencies in Pennsylvania, New York, and Arkansas provide a full range of police services and support activities. In addition to performing routine patrol and traffic enforcement activities, they have investigative units that investigate major crimes, intelligence units that investigate organized crime activities, juvenile units, crime lab services, statewide computer facilities that compile crime data for the state, and other related functions.

Highway patrol organizations, on the other hand, such as those in Florida, Georgia, Ohio, and California, are mainly specialists in traffic regulation and enforcement. For the most part, their responsibilities are to enforce traffic laws on state and interstate highway systems. In some cases, they have the responsibility to investigate crimes that occur in specific locations or under specific circumstances, such as on state highways or state property or crimes that involve the use of public carriers. For the most part, their investigative resources and functions are quite limited, and their support and technical services relate specifically to traffic. States having such units usually have separate small investigative agencies that assist the highway patrol organizations and other local and county police agencies, but operate under very limited jurisdictional authority. For example, Georgia has a state investigative bureau under its department of public safety, but the bureau is not permitted to conduct investigations in the political subdivisions of that state without the approval of the local county sheriff.

Many state legislative bodies, faced with the growing volume of automobile traffic on state highways, recognized the need for a statewide regulatory police agency but were reluctant to create anything but a traffic control agency. As a consequence, the legislation that created highway patrol agencies was purposely designed to ensure that these bodies would be little more than traffic enforcement units. The reluctance to give these agencies full state police authority was the result of several factors. First, America has traditionally mistrusted executive authority. Many legislators were afraid that a state police under the authority of the governor would become an instrument of oppression led by the governor and easily used against his political opposition. The early use of organizations such as the Pennsylvania State Police in strike-breaking activities engendered a great deal of hostility among supporters of organized labor, who campaigned vigorously in a number of states against the establishment of state police forces. This opposition, combined with the legislator's traditional hostility towards increasing the power of the chief executive, proved to be decisive.

Finally, the strong political connections of local law enforcement officials, particularly the county sheriffs, were brought to bear. These officials perceived the creation of a state police system as a direct threat to their own authority. Today, strong sheriff associations exist in almost every state and at the national level. Suggestions that highway patrol agencies be expanded into state police organizations are met with furious opposition from these organizations, which have become quite adept and powerful in local political circles and in state capitals. The fact that these fears have never materialized in those states that have given their state police full police authority seems to be of no concern to those interests opposed to the concept of a state police.[23] Similarly, the fact that the state police have reached, in many states, a level of professionalism and detachment from control of political interests far beyond those of county and municipal police agencies seems to also have had little bearing. In many ways, the lack of a state police organization is an unfortunate and costly disservice to the citizenry of these states, who deserve and pay for better law enforcement than they often receive from their local departments.

County Law Enforcement

In most areas, the law enforcement services in rural and unincorporated portions of a county are handled by the sheriff's department.

The office of the sheriff dates back to eighth-century England. Under the tithing system, a reeve was given the responsibility for coordinating and directing the activities of the tithing members throughout the shire (county). Appointed by the local earl, the shire reeve was the earl's chief ministerial representative in the shire. These shire reeves were very powerful and influential local officials. Among their responsibilities were to protect and oversee the earl's property and the property of the king which the earl was obligated to protect. In addition, they were responsible for the collection of taxes, overseeing the conduct of local tribunals while serving as chief magistrate of these courts, the apprehension and prosecution of those who violated the king's law, and other minor administrative tasks. Thus, unlike today's sheriffs, these early shire reeves were not only responsible for the law enforcement or executive tasks of governance, but the judicial responsibilities as well—a combination of responsibilities that often resulted in a crude and perverse form of justice.[24] The early colonists adopted the idea of sheriff as an important county office, but by the time the Colonies were settled, the sheriff had become primarily a law enforcement and custodial officer with no direct judicial powers.

Because of a combination of historical and political reasons, the sheriffs in many states have broad authority and power. In 33 states, the sheriff is a constitutional officer and is regarded as the chief law enforcement officer in the county. This authority stems from early English law which invested the sheriff with the power of *posse comitatus*—that is, authority to coordinate the activities of all other local police agencies. The sheriff's political power is derived from the fact that the office is part of the county's executive. The sheriff's political status and the visibility of the police function make the sheriff a key political figure. Historically, the argument for retaining the sheriff's constitutional powers has been based on the need to protect the independence of the office. Politically, the office has retained this status because of its pivotal place in local party politics.

Today, the office of the sheriff has three primary responsibilities. The first is to provide law enforcement services in the county. Whether the sheriff provides law enforcement services to municipalities in the county is contingent upon a number of factors. Some states, by virtue of home rule and other statutory provisions, have given cities the authority to provide their own police departments. In some states, when this grant of authority is given, the city police department has primary jurisdiction over all offenses committed therein, and the sheriff's department has authority and jurisdiction only outside the municipality, except in a few instances. Often an agreement is reached between cities and the sheriff's department whereby the sheriff will not enforce the criminal laws within the community except to take specific action in cases such as official police corruption, civil strife, or other conditions that might warrant his department's intervention.

The other two responsibilities of this office are to maintain the county jail and to serve as an officer of the county courts. The sheriff often receives many of the prisoners who have been arrested in the county. In some cases, particularly where there are larger cities within the county, the city police retain arrestees in city jails, pending their trial. Even where cities have their own jail facilities, however, more serious offenders are often transferred to the county jail before trial because of the existence of greater security measures and other facilities that city jails do not provide. Even a serious felon who has been retained in city jail will usually be transferred to the county jail after the trial to await transportation to a state institution.

As an officer of the county courts, the sheriff has numerous responsibilities. Often, this office provides personnel to serve as court bailiffs, transports prisoners to and from the courts, transports juveniles that have been adjudicated as delinquents and sentenced to institutions, and transports mental patients who have been remanded to state mental health facilities. The sheriff's department is also responsible for certain civil process matters such as court-ordered liens, service of forfeiture and eviction notices, divorce papers, the sale of confiscated property, administration and sale of foreclosed property, and related civil judgments as directed by the courts. Figure 5-1 shows the typical organizational arrangement of a medium-sized sheriff's department.

In recent years, the enforcement responsibilities of the sheriff's department have come under a great deal of attack from such prestigious groups as the

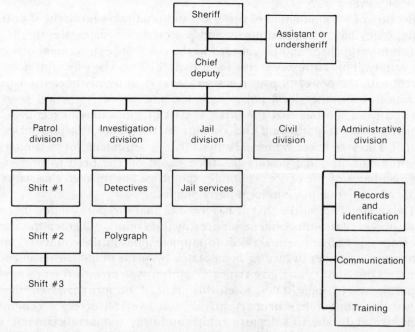

FIGURE 5-1 Administrative Organization of a Medium-Size Sheriff's Department

Committee for Economic Development and the Advisory Commission on Intergovernmental Relations.[25] These and other groups argue that too many sheriff's departments are infused with self-serving political interests that detract from their professional law enforcement role. On balance, many of these criticisms are probably justified when one examines the characteristics of these agencies on a national scale. In too many documented cases, these agencies become patronage empires for the sheriff and other elected county officials who use this office to reward their political followers. As a consequence, because the personnel are not covered by civil service protection, there is a constant turnover in staff. Modern law enforcement requires extensive training and knowledge that personnel in these agencies do not have when hired and do not acquire on the job. In many instances, the sheriff is more a politician than a professional in law enforcement.

Although sheriff's departments are often susceptible to criticism because of their selection standards, lack of training, and quality of service, there are certainly exceptions. In fact, a number of these departments, particularly in California, are among the finest law enforcement organizations in the United States. The Los Angeles County Sheriff's Department is one of the most professionally well-equipped and trained police agencies in the nation. The Multnomah County (Oregon) Sheriff's Department was one of the first agencies to require a 4-year college degree as a condition of employment. Unfortunately, such standards among sheriff's departments are too often the exception rather than the rule.

County Agencies Today In recent years, a number of recommendations have been made to improve county law enforcement. One suggestion has been to abolish the constitutional authority of the sheriff and invest the office only with statutory powers. This idea is in line with county reform efforts designed to replace the plural executive organization of county government with a centralized county administration represented by a county chief executive or a county board of commissioners. County reorganizations along these lines would tend to increase the accountability of county agencies. As long as the sheriff retains constitutional status, however, it is nearly impossible for county officials to maintain meaningful control and accountability over the actions of the sheriff's department.

Another recommendation is that states, through appropriate legislation, provide the option of assigning the responsibility for countywide police services to an independent county police force under the control of the county chief executive or county board of commissioners. Today, there are about 60 such county police departments throughout the United States. Many counties that have adopted the county police department have given this agency full authority and responsibility to perform all law enforcement functions. In many cases, the sheriff's department has been retained, but its responsibilities have been limited to maintenance of the jail and providing the usual services to the county courts.

Unfortunately, these reorganizations have created problems for some communities, many of which stem from the legal and political traditions inherent in the sheriff's office. Georgia, for example, recognizes the sheriff as a constitutional officer, yet permits counties to establish independent police agencies. As a consequence, a few counties in that state to show their dissatisfaction with the quality of service provided by the sheriff have created county police departments; however, they are forced to retain the sheriff, who still has the same full responsibilities. This duplication is costly, and people do not know whether to call the sheriff's department or the county police. A great deal of political acrimony has also been apparent between the heads of these two agencies as well as among political supporters and elected officials who side with either the sheriff or the county police. This results in charges and countercharges of incompetence, poor service, corruption, and a host of other claims being leveled at one agency by supporters of the other.

A Need for Reappraisal There would seem to be an immediate need to reappraise the office of the sheriff and its enforcement responsibilities. The Advisory Commission on Intergovernmental Relations recommended that states give metropolitan counties the option of assigning basic responsibility for countywide police services to an independent county police force under the control of the county chief executives or county board of commissioners. As part of this arrangement, the sheriff's department would turn over all court and jail duties to the appropriate court and correctional agencies.[26] Although this recommendation might have some merit, it is impractical. Perhaps a more valid solution is for the states to begin enacting legislation to force sheriff's agencies to become more professional. Such legislation would place sheriff's department personnel under civil service, require them to be compensated solely on a salary basis, provide them with adequate retirement benefits, and require them to undergo a specified period of training. In the years to come, many states will probably begin to require that sheriff's departments measure up to the challenges facing modern law enforcement.

FEDERAL LAW ENFORCEMENT AGENCIES

Law enforcement at the federal level is characterized by certain distinctive features. In the first place, most federal enforcement agencies are highly specialized units that enforce specific offenses as contained in the U.S. Criminal Code. Therefore, the jurisdictional authority of most of these agencies is quite limited. Since Congress has been reluctant to expand the enforcement responsibilities of existing agencies, the number of separate agencies scattered throughout the executive branch has proliferated. For example, the Departments of Agriculture, Labor, Justice, Defense, Treasury, Interior, and others have developed law enforcement or quasi-enforcement agencies to deal with criminal and regulatory functions within their jurisdictions. In addition, a number of independent regulatory bodies, such as the Interstate Commerce Commission, the Securities and Exchange Commission, and the Federal Trade Commission, perform certain regulatory and compliance functions that require enforcement and quasi-enforcement units.

In many instances, the enforcement problems of local and state governments are mirrored in the operations of federal law enforcement agencies. Jurisdictional disputes, lack of coordination among different agencies, agency rivalries, lack of communication, and failure to share intelligence information and other resources have created some very serious problems in the effective enforcement of federal laws. And, given the nature of the federal bureaucracy, the problems seem even more difficult to solve than similar problems among the political subdivision in our states.

As a result, in 1977 President Carter instituted a plan to streamline and consolidate the approximately 141 federal agencies that now have law enforcement or quasi-enforcement powers. Prompted by his campaign promise to restructure the federal government along lines of greater efficiency and lower costs, he made the law enforcement agencies of the federal government a special target of what he and the Office of Management and Budget saw as examples of grossly inefficient and costly service duplication. As might be imagined, an immediate outcry was heard particularly from some Treasury Department agencies against such a proposal. At this time, the proposed consolidation study is still only being considered. Whether such a major reorganization will ever be enacted by Congress is a subject for wide speculation and doubt.

In 1789, when the Constitution was ratified, the police provisions of the federal government were quite specific and narrow. The framers of the Constitution wanted to form a stronger central government than had existed under the Articles of Confederation, but they were aware that the new states would not accept too strong a national government. As a consequence, they vested only certain powers in the national government and reserved the rest for the states.[27] Among the important specific police powers originally vested in the federal government were those given to Congress to "lay and collect taxes," "to regulate commerce," "to establish post offices and post roads," and "to provide for the punishment of counterfeiting."[28] These powers have played a very important role in the creation of federal police agencies because much of the enforcement authority of federal agencies hinges on the power of taxation and the regulation of interstate commerce. With the growth of taxation legislation and the expanded interpretation by Congress and the federal courts of what constitutes interstate commerce, the law enforcement authority of the federal government has grown substantially. Federal law enforcement authority has also derived from the power of Congress to enact all "necessary and proper" laws and the federal judiciary's interpretation of the Fourteenth Amendment, and from the immediate need of the federal government to enforce new laws and court rulings.

Although the beginning student of criminal justice should be aware that there are many law enforcement agencies of the federal government, only the major agencies can be examined in any meaningful way. Since a large share of enforcement activities of the federal government are centered in the Department of Justice and the Treasury Department, each of these are examined closely.

DEPARTMENT OF JUSTICE

The Department of Justice is responsible for the major enforcement functions of the federal government. To accomplish its broad enforcement responsibilities, it incorporates such agencies as the Federal Bureau of Investigation, the Immigration and Naturalization Service, the Drug Enforcement Administration, the U.S. Marshal Service, and the Organized Crime and

Racketeering Section. It also includes the Law Enforcement Assistance Administration, which (although not an enforcement agency) has in recent years played a significant national role in the administration of criminal justice.

The Federal Bureau of Investigation

The FBI is the chief investigative arm of the Department of Justice. Although the office of attorney general was established in 1789, the Department of Justice was not created until 1870, when the problems of post-Civil War reconstruction and the need to centralize and coordinate the federal government's legal activities led to its formation. Before that time, the prosecution of federal violators was handled separately by the various governmental departments.

It soon became apparent that a special group of investigators would be needed to enforce the laws that would come under the jurisdiction of the newly created Department of Justice. However, opposition from Congress, private citizens, and the nation's leading newspapers was immediate. Again, the fear of a centralized police agency was expressed. Successive attempts to create a small law enforcement unit as a permanent subdivision of the Department of Justice was rebuffed by Congress at every turn.

At the incessant urging of President Theodore Roosevelt, Congress agreed to compromise. In 1909, Congress authorized the establishment of the Bureau of Investigation, but gave it very limited enforcement powers. In 1910, Congress passed the Mann Act, which prohibited the interstate transportation of females for purposes of prostitution and other crimes that involve interstate commerce. Enforcement of this law was turned over to the Bureau of Investigation. During World War I, espionage and selective service violations were added to its jurisdiction, and in 1919 Congress passed the National Motor Vehicle Theft Act, which increased the scope of its authority.

Although the Bureau of Investigation can be credited with some noteworthy achievements during this time, especially with recovering large areas of public lands that had been illegally taken over by private citizens, these accomplishments were clouded over by serious defects. The agency was poorly managed and organized and was itself often engaged in extralegal activities for corrupt politicians. Men with criminal records were sometimes appointed to positions of authority, and the bureau conducted brutal raids, illegal searches, and massive dragnet operations aimed at locating draft dodgers or aliens accused of sabotage. Innocent citizens were frequently arrested during these operations. As a result, there was serious talk about disbanding the bureau and transferring its jurisdiction to other federal agencies.[29]

In 1924, a young government attorney by the name of J. Edgar Hoover was given the task of restructuring the agency and weeding out the corruption. Hoover agreed to accept the directorship only if the attorney general would assure him that the bureau would be free of politics, and that all appointments and promotions would be based on merit. These conditions were accepted, and he was appointed director. He immediately set to work reorganizing the bureau, establishing new administrative procedures, and initiating a general clean-up campaign. He removed incompetent and unreliable personnel, and the character and ability of all applicants were thoroughly investigated before their appointment. In 1935, Congress changed the name of the Bureau of Investigation to the Federal Bureau of Investigation.[30]

The FBI Today   Over the years, the legal jurisdiction of the FBI has been extended to cover all federal crimes that are not the specific responsibility of any other federal law enforcement agency. At the present time, this numbers about 185 offenses. Among the more significant crimes that come under the FBI jurisdiction are kidnapping; robbery, burglary, or embezzlement of funds from any member bank of the Federal Reserve System or any bank insured by the Federal Deposit Insurance Corporation; theft, embezzlement, or robbery of federal property; piracy of aircraft and other crimes aboard aircraft; interstate flight of a person to avoid prosecution, custody, or confinement; violation of the Civil Rights Act; and interstate gambling and organized crime.

Divisions of the FBI   The FBI is organized into ten operating divisions. The Identification Division was created in 1924 to provide a national depository and clearing house for fingerprints. It now contains in excess of 2 million fingerprints which are classified into civil and criminal categories. Access to these records is strictly limited to appropriate governmental agencies.

The Training Division at Quantico, Virginia, operates the FBI training program for its personnel. At this site, it also conducts the National Academy Program which is an 11-week course for selected state and local law enforcement officers throughout the United States. This division also develops training programs that FBI agents teach to police personnel throughout the country.

The Crime Records Division gathers, compiles, and studies the great volume of information on crime that is published in the Uniform Crime Reports (UCR). In 1967, this division implemented a computerized crime information gathering and dissemination service known as the National Crime Information Center (NCIC). Under this arrangement, each state has a number of computer terminals that interface with the FBI master computer in Washington. Records of stolen property and persons wanted for major crimes are supplied by police agencies throughout the country; these records are then filed in the computer in Washington. The police officer in the field has direct on-line connection to the master computer. The system works this way: A police officer in Colorado who is following a car with Tennessee plates that is believed to be stolen contacts a police radio dispatcher who, in turn, relays the inquiry to Washington through the on-line state terminal. In a matter of seconds, the field officer is notified whether the automobile bearing the Tennessee plates is listed with NCIC as stolen.

Another important unit is the Laboratory Division. This division provides a wide range of scientific skills to aid in the investigation of crimes. The services of the laboratory are available without charge to local and state law enforcement agencies. The Laboratory Division maintains a questioned document section for the examination of handwriting, typewriting, forgeries, fraudulent checks, papers, inks, tire treads and related matters; a physics and chemistry section which conducts scientific examinations through chemistry, toxicology, metallurgy, spectrography, etc., on evidence such as firearms, fibers, glass, blood, hairs, and many others; and a cryptanalysis section which is primarily responsible for examining cipher messages and codes.

Some of the other important operating Divisions are organized according to the types of investigations that the FBI conducts. For example, the General Investigation Division supervises the investigation of most of the federal crimes that fall under this agency's jurisdiction such as bank robbery, interstate transportation of stolen vehicles, organized crime, civil rights violations, and burglary, robbery, and theft. The Domestic Intelligence Division investigates matters that involve espionage, sabotage, and subversive activities.

Immigration and Naturalization Service

This agency, created in 1891, is responsible for administering the immigration and naturalization laws, which relate to the admission, exclusion, deportation, and naturalization of aliens. Under the Immigration and Nationality Act, the INS screens applicants for admission to this country in an effort to exclude 31 categories of persons deemed to be "undesirable aliens" because of criminal histories, moral turpitude, or other related reasons. The agency also investigates aliens in order to identify those engaged in various types of criminal activity and is responsible for the detention and deportation of those who illegally enter the United States. The service maintains records of all persons granted or denied admission. Its Border Patrol works to prevent the illegal entry of aliens and the smuggling of illegal goods or contraband.

The Border Patrol was created in 1924, when Congress allocated funds for the establishment of a border patrol unit within the then existing Bureau of Immigration; a group of 450 officers were assigned to the unit.[31] Today, the Border Patrol is divided into 22 sectors, each headed by a chief Border Patrol agent. In each sector there are usually two assistant chief Border Patrol agents, one intelligence officer, a Border Patrol pilot, and any number of Border Patrol stations. The Border Patrol is most active on our borders with Canada and Mexico. Its primary responsibility is to deter entry of illegal aliens and goods. In recent years, a great deal of its efforts have centered on our common border with Mexico in an attempt to intercept and arrest those involved in smuggling narcotics. In many instances, the Border Patrol is involved in joint investigations with other federal and local police agencies in these areas as well as with the Mexican police. Since the traffic in drugs along our borders has become such a serious problem, investigation and efforts to stem this flow have required massive and cooperative efforts by various federal and local agencies as well as international cooperation.

Drug Enforcement Administration

The Drug Enforcement Administration was created in 1973, when Congress approved the consolidation of the former Bureau of Narcotics and Dangerous Drugs, the Office of National Narcotics Intelligence, the Office for Drug Abuse Law Enforcement, and the drug investigation and drug intelligence operation of the U.S. Customs Service into one major federal agency with overall responsibility to enforce the federal narcotics and dangerous drug laws. This major reorganization occurred after previous attempts to stem the problem of narcotics had failed, owing partly to the fragmentation among various federal agencies of jurisdictional authority relating to illegal narcotics.[32] Ever since the Hoover Commission's Report on Governmental Reorganization in 1949, various commissions had recommended the consolidation of federal enforcement agencies. Finally, the seriousness of the narcotics problem forced Congress to act and create a consolidated federal agency to deal with this specific problem.

The basic responsibility of the DEA is the control of the distribution and use of narcotics and dangerous drugs. Its major targets are organized groups that deal in the growth, distribution, and marketing of these drugs. Its enforcement efforts are therefore directed at national and international cartels that control the manufacturing and distribution networks. It operates its own network of enforcement personnel and regional laboratories throughout the United States and in 31 foreign countries. Often, this agency conducts investigations in cooperation with local and state police in which major drug traffickers are involved.

To assist state and local governments throughout the country to combat illicit drugs, it has developed specialized training programs. It also conducts specialized narcotics training programs for police personnel of foreign countries in such diverse places as Mexico, Peru, Australia, and the Philippines. As does the FBI, the DEA makes available to other police agencies the scientific expertise of its crime laboratories and provides expert scientific testimony on evidence these labs receive and analyze for local and state police agencies. This agency is also authorized to regulate and inspect nearly 5,000 licensed drug manufacturing and distribution firms to prevent possible diversion of legally manufactured drugs to illicit sources.

U.S. Marshal Service

The office of marshal appeared in England shortly after the Norman conquest. As this office developed, the marshal became the court officer who escorted into the courts the offender, the victim, and the witnesses to the crime. Today, there are two types of marshals in the United States. Some small communities that are not large enough to require a municipal police department have a town marshal who is the equivalent of a chief of police. In some instances, the town marshal may hire deputies to assist in providing law enforcement services in these communities, but usually the position is a part-time one. Town marshals are also usually responsible for serving the local municipal or mayor's court. In this capacity, they may be called upon to serve subpoenas and arrest warrants and escort prisoners to trial.

The other type of marshal is the U.S. marshal, a federal law enforcement officer who serves the federal courts under the jurisdiction of the U.S. attorney general. Although the Colonies had marshals who performed law enforcement services, it was not until the passage of the Judiciary Act of 1789 that this office became a federal one. This act prescribed the judicial structure of the federal government and authorized the appointment of a U.S. marshal for each state and territory to serve these newly created federal courts.

The first U.S. marshals were appointed by President Washington for 4-year terms. In 1801, this appointive power of the president was recognized by law. These early U.S. marshals performed a wide variety of assignments for the federal government. They were directed by Congress to take the census, hire and supervise jails for federal prisoners, take into custody all vessels and goods seized by revenue officers, sell lands possessed by the United States, serve as fiscal agents of the courts, and perform other miscellaneous tasks as directed.[33]

The role played by U.S. marshals in the enforcement of the laws in the Old West has been well publicized. In many instances, they were the only federal law enforcement personnel in the Western states and territories.[34] Although the federal government had Post Office inspectors and later Secret Service agents in these areas, these groups were too small and had too limited a jurisdiction to be very effective in maintaining law and order. As a result, the responsibility of enforcing most federal laws fell to the U.S. marshals.[35]

The modern office of U.S. marshal has undergone two major reorganizations in recent years. The last major reorganization occurred in 1969, when the United States Marshal Service was created. The service was placed under the authority of a director who is supervised by the deputy attorney general, the second in command in the Department of Justice. The director of the U.S. Marshal Service supervises 95 U.S. marshals in districts covering the 50 states, the District of Columbia, the Canal Zone, Guam, the Virgin Islands, and Puerto Rico. All U.S. marshals (except the U.S. marshal for the Virgin Islands) are appointed by the President with the consent of the Senate for 4-year terms.

At the present time, in each of the federal judicial districts, there is a U.S. marshal, who is authorized by the attorney general to appoint the necessary number of deputy marshals and clerical assistants. These deputies are appointed on the basis of competitive examination and must possess certain minimum qualifications which indicate that they can perform general law enforcement functions and deal with the public. However, their appointments can be canceled at any time by the U.S. marshal as the "public interest" may require.[36]

The authority of U.S. marshals and their deputies is fairly broad. In most cases, their authority at the federal level is very similar to that of the sheriff within the states. Generally, a U.S. marshal has the power to enforce all federal laws except those that have been specifically delegated by law to other federal agencies; the marshal is also responsible for serving legal documents issued by the federal courts, congressional committees, and governmental agencies. Although the Marshal Service has law enforcement authority, its work today lies mainly in assisting the courts. Basically, the responsibilities of this office fall into four major categories:

1. The U.S. marshal or a deputy marshal is required to attend the sessions of the federal courts and to maintain the decorum of the courtroom, to handle juries, to protect witnesses and judges, and to perform duties in the courtroom as the judge may direct.

2. The U.S. marshal is responsible for seizing, guarding, selling, or otherwise disposing of personal or real property according to federal court orders. He or she is responsible for making arrests and placing federal prisoners in jail, transporting federal prisoners between jails and courtrooms during the course of trials, and transporting convicted prisoners to a penitentiary or similar institution.

3. The U.S. marshal performs service of process for the federal courts. This includes handling of subpoenas or summons, seizure of goods and chattels, storage of seized articles, publication of notices, and sale of property.

4. The U.S. marshal is a disbursing officer for the Department of Justice and the federal courts; he or she is responsible for disbursing the salaries of Department of Justice and federal court personnel, disbursing witness and juror fees, and making associated court payments.[37]

Organized Crime and Racketeering Section

In 1951, the Kefauver committee, a congressional committee investigating organized crime, concluded after an exhaustive study: "There is a sinister criminal organization known as the Mafia operating throughout the country."[38] In the intervening years, the existence of organized crime has become generally acknowledged.[39] Numerous congressional committees have examined the problem, but organized crime continues to thrive.[40]

One of the major problems of dealing with organized crime is that the activities of large criminal cartels encompass geographically and statutorily the entire spectrum of enforcement and prosecutorial jurisdiction.[41] American law enforcement is too decentralized to handle the problem at the local and state level. The Organized Crime and Racketeering Section (OCR) of the Department of Justice was established in 1954 to spearhead and coordinate investigations of organized crime. Its specified functions were to:

> Coordinate, generally, enforcement activities directed against organized crime and racketeering and to accumulate and correlate data related to organized crime and racketeering, . . . initiate and supervise investigations, formulate general prosecutive policies and assist U.S. Attorneys in preparing indictments and conducting trials in the field.[42]

By 1957, there were only ten attorneys in OCR. Its inability to grow and become effective during this period has been attributed to a "lack of coordination and interest by some Federal investigative agencies."[43] In 1958, following the famous meeting of leading organized crime figures in Apalachin, New York, the Special Group on Organized Crime was established within the Justice Department. The function of this office was to establish regional offices from which intelligence could be gathered and federal grand jury proceedings conducted regarding the activities of the organized crime figures who met at Apalachin. Spurred on by congressional investigations of organized crime moving into labor unions, the FBI and Treasury enforcement agencies began supplying OCR with regular intelligence reports on leading Cosa Nostra figures. However, efforts were still on a small scale, and only minimal criminal intelligence information from other law enforcement agencies was available.

In 1961, Attorney General Robert Kennedy took an active interest in the Department of Justice's investigations and prosecution of organized crime figures. Under his leadership, the number of attorneys and federal investigators assigned to OCR grew dramatically, as did efforts to coordinate intelligence activities. Whereas in 1961 only 49 organized crime figures were convicted, by the time Kennedy left the Department of Justice in 1965, convictions had increased to 468.[44]

Strike Forces After Robert Kennedy left office, the momentum of the organized crime efforts slowed due to a number of organizational problems. In an attempt to reinvigorate the organized crime drive, President Johnson in 1966 issued a memorandum that called for increased federal efforts.[45] Johnson followed this in 1968 with a special executive order which provided that the attorney general was to coordinate the criminal law enforcement activities of all federal agencies against organized crime. This executive order was the basis for the creation of organized crime strike forces within the Organized Crime and Racketeering Section. Today, the OCR coordinates its strike force efforts through three groups: (1) the Administrative Unit; (2) the Intelligence and Special Service Unit; and (3) the Special Operations Unit.[46]

The Administrative Unit consists of the chief of the OCR and four deputy chiefs. This group manages the efforts of OCR, coordinating field activities and investigations among the various federal agencies involved. Each deputy chief is responsible for the operation of strike forces in a particular geographical area. There is almost daily contact between each local strike force and the OCR in Washington with respect to the status of pending investigations.

Before the strike force takes any prosecutive action, it submits to the OCR a prosecution memorandum setting forth the evidence obtained as a result of field investigation. The memorandum contains the strike force attorney's recommendations on whether or not a prosecution should be initiated. Unless the OCR approves, no criminal prosecution is begun.

The Intelligence and Special Services Unit provides a comprehensive, centralized intelligence file devoted exclusively to organized crime. Over the years, this unit has compiled a computer-based index with the names of thousands of individuals who have some association with organized crime. It also maintains a special "racketeer profile" on about 30,000 individuals who are in some way importantly involved in organized crime. The bulk of the intelligence contained in this special file has been supplied by federal investigative agencies and includes such items as the names of known racketeers, their criminal activities, associates, place of employment or legitimate business activities, residence, telephone numbers, and automobile license numbers.[47]

The files are utilized in a number of ways. The unit handles an average of 50 information requests daily from strike force personnel, federal investigative and regulatory agencies, and local and state law enforcement agencies.[48] An additional function of the system is to provide a data source for the preparation of comprehensive surveys of particular problems. One such use is to determine if a strike force should be established in a given area. The files are constantly reviewed to ascertain the activities of organized crime figures around the country. In addition, in order to keep the files as current as possible, a list of 3,700 principal organized crime leaders is periodically circulated to various federal agencies for updating.[49]

The Special Operations Unit performs four major functions: (1) the review of applications for electronic surveillance under federal statutes;[50] (2) the preparation of recommendations with regard to granting immunity from prosecution for witnesses; (3) the analysis of correspondence; and (4) legal research in the conduct of investigations and case preparation.

In recent years, there have generally been anywhere from 15 to 20 strike forces operating throughout the country, usually in metropolitan areas where there are particular organized crime problems. The OCR designates the areas in which these strike forces will operate. In addition, strike force teams can be pulled in or out of a geographical area, depending upon the need. Each strike force has an attorney-in-charge who is directly responsible for the work of other U.S. Department of Justice attorneys assigned to the strike force. The attorney-in-charge supervises the work of the strike force attorneys and investigators; he or she coordinates the efforts of the team with the U.S. attorney in the jurisdiction where the strike force is working and with the OCR in Washington.

A strike force usually consists of eight to ten federal investigators who receive special training in this type of investigation. Most investigators are assigned from the Justice and the Treasury Departments and represent the FBI; Drug Enforcement Administration; Secret Service; IRS Intelligence; Customs; and the Bureau of Alcohol, Tobacco and Firearms. However, in certain cases, the Postal Service or the Securities and Exchange Commission will also provide investigative personnel.

An important component of the strike force concept is the utilization of special federal grand juries. In jurisdictions where strike forces operate, a special federal grand jury is empaneled to deal with organized crime activities in that area. The grand jury deliberates on the evidence gathered by the strike force to determine whether prosecution is warranted.

Law Enforcement Assistance Administration (LEAA)

Although the Law Enforcement Assistance Administration (LEAA) is not a federal law enforcement agency, it deserves attention because it may be the single most important development that has affected criminal justice in the United States. This agency grew out of the Office of Law Enforcement Assistance (OLEA), which was created in 1965 to make federal funds available to states, localities, and private organizations to improve methods of law enforcement, court administration, and prison operation.[51] The act creating this agency was the first federal law that made money available to local government for the purpose of improving their administration of criminal justice.

In 1968, the Omnibus Crime Control and Safe Streets Act became effective. This act repealed the Law Enforcement Act of 1965 and replaced the Office of the Law Enforcement Assistance with the LEAA. The Safe Streets Act was a milestone in that it expressed a fundamental philosophy about crime in the United States—namely, that although it is a problem of national dimensions, it is most appropriately addressed at the state and local levels through the support of federal monies. This was a drastic departure from the past. Traditionally, state and local law enforcement and other criminal justice activities did not seek federal involvement. Like public assistance activities in general, this area had not been regarded as belonging to the federal government's natural sphere of interest, but rather was seen as the responsibility of state and local governments.[52]

Block Grants   Under the provisions of the act, as administered by LEAA, block grants based on population were made available to all 50 states, Guam, Puerto Rico, American Samoa, the Virgin Islands, and the District of Columbia. The grants are to be used to develop crime-related programs and to assist and improve local and state agencies in their enforcement of criminal justice. In addition, LEAA awards action and discretionary grants to foster the development of state and local planning capabilities that would further improve the administration of justice.

LEAA requires states to develop centralized state planning agencies (SPAs) as well as local planning units. These SPAs are responsible for allocating to local units of government much of the money that the states receive from LEAA. Overseeing the operations of these SPAs, as well as the local planning units in the states, are supervisory boards whose members represent state and local criminal justice agencies, other public agencies, and citizen groups.[53] New legislation was written in 1973 requiring a state to develop a comprehensive master plan that is multiyear in nature in order to be eligible for federal funds from LEAA. Thus, each SPA was required to coordinate the activities of local planning agencies into a single master plan of how the problem of crime was to be handled in the particular state.

In its early years, the programs that LEAA funded as well as its priorities were heavily criticized by members of Congress and many large city mayors. Much of the money earmarked for local governments and distributed to the states went to regional planning councils instead of the major cities where the problems of crime are most acute.[54] As a consequence, the act was amended in 1971 to provide for direct assistance to local units of government consisting of a population of 250,000 or more.[55] Other criticisms have been leveled at LEAA's past emphasis on funding law enforcement agencies at the expense of other components of the criminal justice system, and its funding of "hardware" items such as riot equipment, radios, and automobiles.

And the criticisms do not end there. In 1976, the Twentieth Century Fund, which is a private research foundation engaged in policy-oriented studies of economic, political, and social issues, published a report on the first 7 years of LEAA's operations entitled, *Law Enforcement: The Federal Role*.[56] Much of the report was very critical of the federal grant assistance programs to state and local governments.

In the first place, the legislation that created the agency was passed in an atmosphere of fear and retribution. When Congress passed the Omnibus Crime Control and Safe Streets Act in 1968 it did so in the wake of the successive assassinations of John F. Kennedy, Malcolm X, Martin Luther King, Jr., and Robert F. Kennedy. The legislation was enacted against the background of the rise of black power, an increasingly militant anti-Vietnam War movement, and a growing national polarization epitomized in the presidential election of 1968, when Richard Nixon ran as a law-and-order candidate.[57] The broad mandate to "stop crime" without giving any thought to the limited capacity of federal dollars to accomplish this goal has plagued the agency ever since.

The operations of the agency and its grant programs have also been accused of being over politicized. There are documented cases, for instance, when the Nixon administration overruled the agency and awarded sizable grants to jurisdictions based on what must be understood as purely political considerations.[58] Then later, in 1972, LEAA established its most expensive and ambitious effort—the high-impact–anticrime program. The goal of the program was to reduce the incidence of certain street crimes in eight selected cities at an overall cost of $160 million. It soon became apparent that almost all the cities involved viewed the massive federal aid as a "windfall." Rather than developing overall programs, cities like Atlanta, Baltimore, and Newark used their first monies—prior to any planning or analysis—to put hundreds of new policemen on the payroll. In Newark, the Impact Cities director was active in the mayor's election campaign. Thus an aura of politics and patronage began early.[59]

Although the high impact anticrime program was originally scheduled to run for 5 years, its failure became so obvious that LEAA finally terminated the plan in just slightly over 3 years at a cost in excess of $100 million.

National Institute of Law Enforcement and Criminal Justice   Nevertheless, it is hard to judge the relative success of LEAA. Some of the over $7 billion it has cost the American taxpayer to date has had a positive effect. For instance, it has created the National Institute of Law Enforcement and Criminal Justice that serves as the research and evaluation arm of the agency. Its purpose is to monitor the major grant programs LEAA engages in and to conduct empirical and applied research in the criminal justice area. This unit contracts with individuals, universities, and private technical firms to develop new approaches and to conduct independent evaluation of projects. One of the most significant undertakings by this unit is its Exemplary Projects Program. The specific goal of the Exemplary Projects Program is to encourage widespread use of advanced criminal justice practices by systematically identifying outstanding criminal justice programs throughout the country, verifying their achievements, and publicizing them so that other communities and agencies of criminal justice can adopt similar programs.[60] A few of the Exemplary Project Programs to date are the volunteer Probation Counselor Program, Lincoln, Nebraska; Prosecutor Management Information Center, Washington, D.C.; Street Crime Unit, New York City Police; and the Neighborhood Youth Resources Center, Philadelphia.

The National Institute of Law Enforcement and Criminal Justice has also developed the National Criminal Justice Reference Service and the National Criminal Justice Statistics Center. The reference service compiles and disseminates information on current research and publications in the field of criminal justice. Persons engaged in activities related to criminal justice are provided annotated bibliographies of publications that may be of interest to them. In addition, the service maintains a reference library of selected publications available to all its users through a document interlibrary loan program as well as a microfiche distribution source in which certain materials not readily available through other sources are distributed free of charge to users of the service. Recently, a loan and referral program for films and other media materials was developed.

The National Criminal Justice Statistics Center gathers criminal justice statistics to promote a better understanding of the processes of justice and renders technical assistance to states that are also engaged in developing statistical centers. The center publishes and distributes a number of reference sources and monographs dealing with national statistics such as the *Annual Expenditure and Employment Data for the Criminal Justice System, Directory of Criminal Justice Agencies, National Prisoner Statistics,* and *National Jail Census.* The primary interest of the systems analysis unit of the center is to identify the application of systems analysis techniques that might be useful in improving the administration of criminal justice. The center also maintains various information systems at the national level which are used to support the administration of LEAA programs and extends technical assistance to state and local governments in applying computer technology to automated records systems.

Law Enforcement Education Program   Another major effort has been the Law Enforcement Education Program (LEEP) which from 1969 to 1974 spent over $158 million. Under this program, LEAA makes payments to institutions of higher learning so that, in turn, they can make loans and grants to persons "employed in or preparing for employment in criminal justice agencies." In practice, some 90 percent of all LEEP participants have been "in-service criminal justice personnel." As the Twentieth Century Fund report says: "although LEEP funds might have been used to train a generation of criminal justice planners, 80 percent of the LEEP participants have been police officers."[61]

LEEP has also been criticized for funding too many fly-by-night institutions and programs that literally survive by and cater to the LEEP program. Many such institutions throughout the country hastily established "police science" or "criminal justice" programs when the federal dollars became available. These programs were built without adequate faculty resources and often emphasized police training rather than a curriculum, which is more properly associated with higher education.

But the program has its successes as well. If nothing else, it has provided thousands of individuals with an opportunity to receive a college education. Were it not for the LEEP program, many in-service criminal justice practitioners would never have had the opportunity to obtain advanced education.

The Need for Reappraisal   In spite of this agency's many contributions to the improvement of criminal justice, its continued existence is questionable. The complaint of Congress is that in spite of all the monies made available, LEAA has failed to demonstrate that it has been instrumental in reducing crime. However, LEAA has demonstrated that federal assistance to state and local agencies of criminal justice is needed if the necessary improvements are to be made. State and local units of government simply do not have the financial resources necessary to support improvement programs nor do they have the human resources with the necessary knowledge and skills to plan, develop, and evaluate crime control programs.

Recognizing the importance of continuing the federal role in this area, President Carter has approved a legislative package to Congress that would create the Justice System Improvement Act. This would be the first step in reauthorizing and restructuring the programs now administered by LEAA. The act is specifically designed to correct the major criticisms directed at the LEAA programs including excessive red tape, poor targeting of grant funds, wasted funds, insufficient local control over expenditures, and ineffective research and evaluation efforts.

What effect this will have on the operations of LEAA and the federal role is not yet clear. However, it can be said that the experiences of LEAA and of federal involvement in the attempt to improve the administration of justice and reduce crime have demonstrated that money alone cannot solve the problem. The agencies of criminal justice cannot be expected to remedy the crime problem without society's directing associated efforts toward the elimination of the crime-producing factors.

TREASURY DEPARTMENT

Another very important department with law enforcement responsibilities at the federal level is the Treasury Department. The law enforcement agencies of this department are specialists in certain types of federal crimes that fall under the authority of the secretary of the treasury. The primary law enforcement agencies of the Treasury Department are the Secret Service; the Bureau of Alcohol, Tobacco and Firearms; the Customs Service; and the Intelligence and Inspection and Internal Security units of the Internal Revenue Service. In addition, the Treasury Department enforcement agencies are assisted by various support systems and serve as the United States liaison with Interpol.

Secret Service

The counterfeiting of currency has been a problem in the United States since the country's inception. During the Revolutionary War, Britain tried to destroy the economic base of the Colonies by printing vast quantities of currency that appeared to be issued by the Continental Congress. The English felt that if it could destroy the Colonies' economic foundation it could destroy their ability to wage war. The effort nearly succeeded. Owing to the presence of vast quantities of spurious currency, the country was hard pressed to purchase needed war materials from European nations, and because of this came closer to losing the War of Independence than most people realize.[62]

After the Revolutionary War, the problem of dealing with counterfeiting continued. This was a period when the greater part of American currency was issued by private banks that were licensed by states to print money. Operating without adequate regulation, they designed their own currency and validated it with signatures of their own officials.[63] "Wildcat banks," having nothing more than a charter and a printing shop, became common in many states. The tactic of these banks was to print and sell a huge amount of currency as quickly as possible and then leave town. A book published in 1839 maintained that there were 97 such banks whose currency, though legal, was worthless. It also listed 254 more banks whose currency had become the object of successful and widespread counterfeiting.[64]

In response to this situation and because it became necessary to raise large sums of money during the Civil War, Congress passed the National Currency Act of 1863, which established a national banking system and a uniform national currency, called "greenbacks." The market value of these greenbacks, which were not backed by gold reserves, began to depreciate almost as soon as they were issued, and a sharp inflation affected the entire economy. Counterfeiters had a heyday circulating imitation greenbacks extensively. The local police were the only enforcement authority against counterfeiters, and they were practically helpless. The Secretary of the Treasury then set up a system of rewards for the detection of counterfeit currency, but the situation was so bad that the counterfeiters themselves were collecting the rewards. Finally, in 1865, the Secret Service was created as a federal investigative agency with authority to enforce the laws against counterfeiting.

When this agency was created, it was estimated that nearly one-third of all paper money in circulation was counterfeit. The agency immediately began the task of curtailing the problem. In its first year of existence alone, it arrested over 200 counterfeiters.[65] In 1977, special agents of the Secret Service seized over 39 million in counterfeit bills.[66]

In addition to its investigative responsibilities in the area of counterfeiting, it has another major investigative responsibility—the suppression of the forgery and fraudulent negotiation of government checks and bonds. In 1977 alone, the agency received more than 121,000 checks and over 12,000 bonds for investigation.[67]

Today, the Secret Service is best known for protecting the president and his family. Originally, there had been little concern for the safety of United States presidents. The attempted assassination of President Jackson and the successful assassinations of Presidents Lincoln in 1865 and Garfield in 1881 failed to prompt Congress to pass legislation to assign special bodyguards for presidents of the United States. In 1901, President McKinley was assassinated in spite of the security provided by local police and soldiers. Informed of the assassination, the Secretary of the Treasury promptly assigned the Secret Service the duty of protecting presidents, and in 1906 Congress appropriated the funds and officially assigned the Secret Service its protective role.

After the tragic assassination of John F. Kennedy in 1963, Congress increased the scope and responsibilities of the Secret Service as a result of recommendations by the Warren Commission. Among the recommendations implemented were an increase in the amount of training and number of

Secret Service agents assigned to presidential protection, enlargement of the protective intelligence function, increased liaison with other law enforcement agencies, and acquisition of sophisticated technical security equipment, computer systems, and communications.

Following President Kennedy's assassination, Congress passed legislation that authorized the Secret Service to protect the widow and minor children of a former President; it also made the assassination of the president a federal crime. In 1965, the Secret Service was authorized to protect a former president and his wife during his lifetime, and minor children of a former president. This responsibility was extended in 1968 to provide protection for the widow of a former president until her death or remarriage, and protection of minor children of a former president until the age of 16.

After the assassination of Senator Robert F. Kennedy in 1968, Congress authorized the Secret Service to protect major presidential and vice-presidential candidates and nominees. Since that time, the Secret Service has also been given the responsibility to protect foreign dignitaries visiting the United States.

Today, the Secret Service is organized into five main divisions. The Administrative Division deals with such concerns as administrative operations, management, finance, personnel, and training. The Inspection Division is responsible for inspection of field offices located throughout the United States and its possessions and for rendering advice on special problems. The Division of Investigation, which investigates violations of laws relating to the Treasury Department, has four sections:

- An investigation unit, which coordinates and directs the organized crime activities of the agency.

- A counterfeit unit, which directs the investigations against counterfeiting, develops technical aids, and provides training to bank and commercial personnel in the detection of counterfeiting.

- A forgery unit, which investigates forgeries of U.S. checks, bonds, and federal food stamps.

- A special unit to supervise the uniformed guards who provide security for the Treasury and Treasury Annex buildings.

The fourth division of the Secret Service is the Office of Protective Services. The units in this division provide permanent protective security for government officials. Included are the Executive Protection Service, Presidential Protection Division, Vice-Presidential Protection Division, special units for any residences that the president might maintain and a unit to protect visiting heads of state. The Executive Protective Service consists of the uniformed police personnel who guard the White House and any other buildings that might house a presidential office. Agents of the Presidential Protection Division accompany the president and protect him wherever he resides or travels; this division also coordinates the various field offices of the Secret Service during the course of the president's travel.

The fifth division is the Office of Protective Intelligence. This unit compiles intelligence information on individuals who might try to harm any of the officials who are protected by the Secret Service. In addition, it is responsible for developing and installing technical security devices, communication and computer systems, and other scientific equipment needed to provide protection.

The Bureau of Alcohol, Tobacco, and Firearms

The Bureau of Alcohol, Tobacco, and Firearms (ATF) has undergone a number of important alterations since its inception. This agency was created in 1862 when a tax was imposed on liquors and tobacco. The act that imposed this tax also created the office of the commissioner of internal revenue, who was authorized to hire three detectives to suppress the illegal manufacturing of distilled spirits. A few years later, an additional 22 agents were hired, and the agency continued to grow at a slow pace until 1919.

In 1919, the Eighteenth Amendment to the Constitution was ratified and prohibition was ushered in. Under the provisions of the National Prohibition Act, the manufacture, sale, transportation, and importation of intoxicating liquors became a federal crime. The responsibility for the enforcement of this act came under the authority of the commissioner of the Bureau of Internal Revenue (now the Internal Revenue Service). Operating under the commissioner was a prohibition commissioner whose authority included the direct enforcement of the National Prohibition Act and the imposition of taxes on alcohol produced legally for medicinal and industrial purposes.

The prohibition commissioner established 18 districts throughout the United States. Each district had a director who supervised prohibition agents. The prohibition agents were authorized to investigate all violations of the Prohibition Act and report these violations to the U.S. attorneys for prosecution. During the next 15 years, more reorganizations came about as attempts were made to streamline the organization and to lessen some problems of enforcement and graft that periodically shook the agency with scandal.

In 1934, the Alcohol Tax Unit (ATU) was created under the authority of the Secretary of the Treasury. The idea was to centralize the enforcement efforts of all federal agencies engaged in the enforcement of Internal Revenue laws dealing with alcoholic beverages. In 1951, the Alcohol Tax Unit was replaced by a new agency with expanded duties, the Alcohol and Tobacco Tax Division.

During the mid and late 1960s, increasing congressional and citizen concern was focused on the relationship between guns and rising crime in the United States. It began with the assassination of President Kennedy in 1963 and was renewed with the killing of Martin Luther King in 1968. After King's assassination, a gun bill was passed in Congress as part of the Omnibus Crime Control and Safe Streets Act. However, before the Omnibus Crime Bill was signed into law, Senator Robert Kennedy was killed in Los Angeles in June 1968. The assassination aroused so much antigun sentiment in Congress that a flurry of bills was introduced in both the House and Senate to control guns, ammunition, and explosives. These efforts resulted in the passage of the Gun Control Act of 1968.

Responsibility for enforcing the Gun Control Act was given to the Alcohol and Tobacco Tax Division of the Internal Revenue Service. With this responsibility, the name of this agency was changed to the Alcohol, Tobacco, and Firearms Division. In 1972, the Secretary of the Treasury removed the Alcohol, Tobacco, and Firearms Division from the authority of the Internal Revenue Service and made it a separate bureau. Since then, the laws relating to alcohol, tobacco, firearms, and explosives have been withdrawn from the Internal Revenue Service.[68]

Since ATF's enforcement responsibilities in the area of distilled spirits and tobacco have changed very little, we need not concentrate on their enforcement powers in these areas. It is in the area of gun control and explosives that much of their current investigative efforts are concentrated. Among other responsibilities, ATF regulates businesses that deal in the importing or selling of firearms and prohibits the possession of certain firearms such as machine guns or sawed-off rifles and shotguns, silencers, and destructive devices. It is responsible for the control and investigation of interstate commerce that transports firearms and explosives. It conducts investigations of the possession and use of firearms and explosives by certain categories of people such as aliens, convicted felons, those who have been discharged from the armed forces under dishonorable conditions, and mental incompetents. It also investigates all thefts of firearms and explosives and all criminal detonations of explosives and bomb threats or the use of explosives during the commission of a felony. Because of its jurisdiction in these areas, it is also involved in extensive intelligence-gathering activities involving militant extremist groups that might resort to the illegal use of firearms and explosives.

The ATF works very closely with state and local police in dealing with firearms and explosives. It has established a National Firearms Tracing Center which traces firearms ownership from manufacturer to retailer to purchaser. It is also currently involved in a gun violence profile program in 17 major metropolitan areas in conjunction with local police in an effort to determine the types and sources of guns used in street crimes. In addition, the ATF helps other police agencies investigate actual or attempted bombings and conducts extensive training programs under a 1974 LEAA grant for local and state police personnel in an effort to familiarize them with federal gun control legislation, bomb scene investigative techniques, and organized crime operations.

Customs Service

The Customs Service assesses and collects duties, internal revenue taxes, fines, penalties, and other fees associated with the importation of merchandise. It examines persons, carriers, cargo, and mail that enters the United States and carriers and cargo that leave the country. The Customs Service is also responsible for detecting and preventing all forms of smuggling designed to defraud the government of revenues or gain illicit entry of prohibited articles and contraband. It uses such means as high-speed aircraft with infrared scanning devices to intercept the flow of illicit contraband entering our borders. When narcotics or dangerous drugs are found, Customs contacts the

DEA, which handles the investigation if warranted or turns it over to a local law enforcement agency for disposition. Customs officers made some 14,300 drug seizures and arrested 10,000 persons during 1973. The value of these drug seizures, which included over 1,200 pounds of hard narcotics, was more than $1 billion.[69]

The Customs Service is made up of two groups of personnel. The majority are inspectors, who are usually uniformed and are likely to be stationed at the various ports of entry to search for smuggled goods. There are also investigators, whose primary responsibilities are to conduct on-going investigations in which the service is involved. To assist its inspectors and investigative personnel, the Customs Service maintains eight regional laboratories in major cities across the nation. Their broad mission is to supply scientific knowledge to customs import specialists, particularly in identifying and classifying commercial imports. They also help local police agencies with testing unidentified substances such as narcotics.

Internal Revenue Service

The Internal Revenue Service performs a number of law enforcement functions through its Intelligence, Audit, and Inspection and Internal Security Divisions.

Its primary criminal investigative unit is the Intelligence Division which investigates possible criminal violations of federal tax laws, particularly those that deal with personal and corporate income tax and excise, estate, and gift taxes. The offenses that this division deals with most frequently are willful nonfiling of returns and attempts to evade full payment of taxes. The Intelligence Division works very closely with the Audit Division. This latter unit seeks to promote the highest possible level of voluntary compliance with tax laws. To accomplish this, it conducts an extensive audit of tax returns. Issues may arise in the conduct of these tax audits which are civil concerns, or the audits may turn up deliberate attempts to defraud the federal government of tax revenues. When criminal violations are uncovered, the case is turned over to the Intelligence Division for investigation and possible prosecution.

Today, the Intelligence Division conducts two major enforcement operations: (1) the General Enforcement Program, which is directed at cases that involve legitimate persons and businesses; and (2) the Special Enforcement Program, which focuses on those who obtain unreported income from illegal activities, including bribery, extortion, and the sale of narcotics. In recent years, agents of the Special Enforcement Program have played a significant role in the investigation of organized crime activities in the United States because much of the income from such activities is not reported.

The Inspection and Internal Security Division was created in 1952 to serve as a watchdog over IRS activities after a serious scandal indicated that alarming numbers of IRS employees were involved in accepting bribes for not reporting income tax violators. The primary function of this unit is to investigate all allegations of bribery and serious misconduct by IRS employees and to arrest employees who accept bribes as well as citizens who through such actions attempt to corrupt the integrity of the IRS. This unit also conducts extensive background investigations of persons applying for sensitive positions within the IRS and certain other federal agencies.

The Intelligence Division operates a few limited training programs for state and local police personnel. These training programs are designed to instruct in methods of financial investigative techniques, such as rules of evidence as they apply to financial documents, tracing and records examination, and indirect methods of proving personal and corporate income.

Interpol

The International Criminal Police Organization (Interpol), although not an agency of the United States, nonetheless has a very close working relationship with the enforcement units of the U.S. Treasury Department. Its American liaison office is staffed by federal law enforcement personnel in the U.S. National Central Bureau, located in the Treasury Department. Any federal, state, or local law enforcement agencies seeking information from any of Interpol's 120 member nations must forward their requests through the National Central Bureau of the Treasury Department, which since 1958 has been designated as our representative to this international organization.

There are a great many misconceptions about the role of Interpol. This organization, which has its headquarters in St. Cloud, France, is not an investigative unit; its sole purpose is to coordinate investigative efforts among member nations by serving as a clearing house and depository for intelligence information. Its massive computer banks contain data on wanted criminals, stolen items, and other related information supplied by user nations. Other Interpol services include transferring requests from one nation to another to conduct investigations leading to arrest or extradition, conducting criminal history and license plate or operator's license checks, issuing an international wanted circular and all points bulletin in any or all of the member nations, and tracing weapons and motor vehicles.[70]

SUMMARY

The police are the overseers of the criminal justice system. Although they are usually thought of in their role as law enforcers, the police spend more of their time in providing nonenforcement related services than in enforcing laws.

The organization of police service as we know it today is less than 150 years old. During the history of Western civilization, various organizational arrangements were devised to enforce laws. As society became more complex, methods for providing police services were modified and improved. There has been a historical fear that a centralized and full-time police service could be employed to restrict individual liberties. This fear was particularly pronounced as a result of England's experience which was carried over into the American colonies.

The history of law enforcement in America, particularly in our cities, is not a proud one. Early city police departments were often corrupt organizations that served the interests of political factions more than they did the community. Gradually, as municipal reform became a reality in the late nineteenth and early twentieth centuries, law enforcement improvement began and continues to this day.

Federal law enforcement is generally a very specialized form of investigative authority. Unlike local and some state law enforcement agencies, the jurisdictional authority of most federal law enforcement units is quite narrow. In addition, federal law enforcement agencies tend to be investigative units, rather than providing more broad-based police services.

The major criminal investigative units within the federal government are found in the Department of Justice and the Treasury Department. In recent years, with the passage of additional crime-related legislation by Congress and the development of a larger federal role in law enforcement, important federal crime-related agencies such as the Law Enforcement Assistance Administration have come into existence. The future will probably see increasing federal involvement and assistance to state and local police forces.

REVIEW QUESTIONS

1. What are the two functions of the police? Give two examples of each of these functions.
2. What are the responsibilities of the following levels of law enforcement?
   a. Municipal police
   b. State police
   c. County sheriff
3. What specific police powers were vested in the federal government by the Constitution? In what ways have these powers been expanded by Congress and other sources?
4. Which department is responsible for the major law enforcement functions of the federal government? What are the major subdivisions of this department?
5. What is the present mandate of the FBI? What crimes does the FBI investigate?
6. Briefly describe the law enforcement responsibilities of the following federal agencies:
   a. Immigration and Naturalization Service
   b. Drug Enforcement Administration
   c. U.S. Marshal Service
   d. Organized Crime and Racketeering Section
   e. Law Enforcement Assistance Administration (LEAA)
7. What are the law enforcement duties of the following Treasury Department agencies?
   a. Secret Service
   b. Bureau of Alcohol, Tobacco, and Firearms
   c. Customs Service
   d. Internal Revenue Service

DISCUSSION QUESTIONS

1. How has the history of law enforcement had an impact on the American police today?
2. Discuss the operations and significance of the Law Enforcement Assistance Administration (LEAA).
3. President Carter has proposed consolidating federal law enforcement agencies. Is consolidation a good idea? Why or why not?

SUGGESTED ADDITIONAL READINGS

Ahern, James R. *Police in Trouble,* New York: Hawthorn, 1972.

Banton, Michael. *The Policeman in the Community,* New York: Basic Books, 1964.

Black, Algernon D. *The People and the Police,* New York: McGraw-Hill, 1968.

Broderick, John J. *Police in a Time of Change,* Morristown, N.J.: General Learning Press, 1977.

Chapman, Brian. *Police State,* New York: Praeger, 1970.

Dorman, Michael. *The Secret Service Story,* New York: Dekarte Press, 1967.

Folley, Vern L. *American Law Enforcement,* 2nd ed., Boston: Holbrook, 1976.

Goldstein, Herman. *Policing a Free Society,* Cambridge, Mass.: Ballinger, 1977.

Moore, Harry W., ed. *The American Police,* St. Paul, Minn.: West, 1976.

Niederhoffer, Arthur. *Behind the Shield: The Police in Urban Society,* Garden City, N.Y.: Doubleday, 1967.

Ottenberg, Miriam. *The Federal Investigator,* Englewood Cliffs, N.J.; Prentice-Hall, 1962.

Reiss, Albert J. *The Police and the Public,* New Haven, Conn.: Yale University Press, 1971.

Skolnick, Jerome. *Justice Without Trial: Law Enforcement in a Democratic Society,* New York: Wiley, 1966.

Turner, William W. *Hoover's FBI—The Men and the Myth,* Los Angeles: Sherbourne, 1970.

Westley, William A. *Violence and the Police,* Cambridge, Mass.: M.I.T. Press, 1971.

NOTES

1. Herman Goldstein, *Policing a Free Society* (Cambridge, Mass.: Ballinger, 1977), p. 1.

2. Ibid.

3. James Q. Wilson, *Varieties of Police Behavior* (Cambridge, Mass.: Harvard University Press, 1968), p. 16.

4. Elaine Cumming et al., "Policeman as Philosopher, Guide and Friend," *Social Problems* 12 (1965): 267–286.

5. Thomas E. Bercal, "Calls for Police Assistance: Consumer Demands for Governmental Service," *American Behavioral Scientist* 13 (1970): 681–691.

6. Zoe Oldenbourg, *The Crusades* (New York: Random House, 1966), p. 11.

7. Ibid., p. 16.

8. Charles Reith, *The Blind Eye of History: A Study of the Origins of the Present Police Era* (London: Faber, 1912), p. 31.

9. Ibid., p. 137.

10. For example, see Patrick Pringle, *Hue and Cry: The Birth of the British Police* (London: Museum Press, 1955); Charles Reith, *The Blind Eye of History*, pp. 148–149; and Albert Lieck, *Justice and Police in England* (London: Butterworth, 1936).

11. A. C. Germann, Frank Day, and Robert Gallati, *Introduction to Law Enforcement and Criminal Justice* (Springfield, Ill: Thomas, 1973), pp. 61–62.

12. Anwar Syed, *The Political Theory of American Local Government* (New York: Random House, 1966), p. 38.

13. See, for example, Bruce Smith, *Police Systems in the United States,* 2d rev. ed. (New York: Harper & Row 1960), p. 22; and Committee for Economic Development. *Reducing Crime and Assuring Justice* (New York: CED, 1972), p. 30.

14. John P. Granfield, "Publicly Funded Law Enforcement Agencies in the U.S.," *Police Chief* 42, no. 7 (July 1975): 26.

15. Reith, *The Blind Eye of History*, pp. 82–83.

16. Documents of the New York Board of Aldermen, Document No. 53, pp. 1047ff.

17. Raymond B. Fosdick, *American Police Systems* (New York: Century, 1920), p. 68.

18. James T. Allison and Robert T. Penrose, *Philadelphia, 1681–1887. A History of Municipal Development* (Baltimore: Johns Hopkins Studies in Historical and Political Science, vol. II, 1887), pp. 37–41.

19. For an excellent analysis of the reform movement in municipal government, see Edward C. Banfield and James Q. Wilson, *City Politics* (New York: Random House, 1966); Richard Hofstadter, *The Age of Reform* (New York: Knopf, 1955), especially chap. IV; Lorin Petersen, *The Day of the Mugwump* (New York: Random House, 1961); Frank M. Steward, *A Half Century of Municipal Reform: The History of the National Municipal League* (Berkeley: University of California Press, 1950); and T. R. Mason, "Reform Politics in Boston," unpublished dissertation (Department of Government, Harvard University, 1963).

20. Vern L. Folley, *American Law Enforcement* (Boston: Holbrook, 1973), p. 64.

21. Katherine Mayo, *Justice to All: The Story of the Pennsylvania State Police* (New York: Putnam, 1917), pp. 5–6.

22. Folley, *American Law Enforcement,* p. 67.

23. Committee for Economic Development, *Reducing Crime and Assuring Justice,* p. 31.

24. T. A. Tobias, *The History of English Law* (London: Westholver and Westholver, 1920), pp. 109–110.

25. See Advisory Commission on Intergovernmental Relations, *State-Local Relations in the Criminal Justice System* (Washington, D.C.: U.S. Government Printing Office, 1971); and Committee for Economic Development, *Reducing Crime and Assuring Justice.*

26. Advisory Commission on Intergovernmental Relations, *State-Local Relations in the Criminal Justice System,* p. 27.

27. James M. Burns and J. W. Peltason, *Government by the People* (Englewood Cliffs, N.J.: Prentice-Hall, 1966), p. 63.

28. Art. 1, sec. 8.

29. Donald F. Whitehead, *The FBI Story* (New York: Random House, 1956), pp. 66–68.

30. Bela Rektor, *Federal Law Enforcement Agencies* (Astor, Fla.: Danubian, 1975), p. 36.

31. U.S. Department of Justice, *The Border Patrol* (Washington, D.C.: U.S. Government Printing Office, 1972), p. 2.

32. Vernon D. Acree, "This Is Customs," *Drug Enforcement* 1, no. 3 (Spring 1974): 10.

33. Thomas F. Adams, *Law Enforcement* (Englewood Cliffs, N.J.: Prentice-Hall, 1968), p. 88.

34. Rektor, *Federal Law Enforcement Agencies,* p. 103.

35. Department of Justice, "Outline of the Office of the United States Marshal," (Washington, D.C.: Executive Office for United States Marshal, 1973), p. 2.

36. 28 U.S.C. §§ 541–542.

37. Rektor, *Federal Law Enforcement Agencies,* p. 113.

38. *Senate Special Committee to Investigate Organized Crime in Interstate Commerce, 3d Interim Report,* S. Rept. 307, 82d Cong., 1st Sess. 2 (1951).

39. See, for example, *Senate Select Committee on Improper Activities in the Labor or Management Field, 1st Interim Report,* S. Rept. 1417, 85th Cong., 2d Sess. (1958); *Permanent Subcommittee on Investigations of the Senate Committee on Government Operations, Organized Crime and Illicit Traffic in Narcotics,* S. Rept. 72, 87th Cong., 1st Sess. (1965); *House Committee on Government Operations, Federal Effort against Organized Crime,* House Rept. 1574, 90th Cong., 2d Sess. (1968).

40. Former Attorney General John Mitchell stated that $50 billion per year is a conservative estimate of gross profits of organized crime. *The New York Times,* March 9, 1969, p. 1, col. 2.

41. P. Johnson, "Organized Crime: Challenge to the American Legal System," part 1, *Journal of Criminal Law, Criminology and Police Science* 53 (1962): 418.

42. "The Strike Force: Organized Law Enforcement v. Organized Crime," *Columbia Journal of Law and Social Problems* 496 (1970): 502.

43. President's Commission on Law Enforcement and Administration of Justice: *Organized Crime* (Washington, D.C.: U.S. Government Printing Office, 1967), p. 11.

44. Ibid.

45. "The Strike Force," p. 504.

46. Interview with Edward T. Joyce, deputy chief, Organized Crime and Racketeering Section, July 17, 1975.

47. Ibid.

48. "The Strike Force."

49. Ibid.

50. Specifically, Title III of the Omnibus Crime Control and Safe Streets Act (1968).

51. Folley, *American Law Enforcement,* p. 83.

52. Eleanor Chelinsky, "A Primary-Source Examination of the Law Enforcement Assistance Administration (LEAA), and Some Reflections on Crime Control Policy," *Journal of Police Science and Administration* 3 (June 1975): 203–221.

53. National Advisory Commission on Criminal Justice Standards and Goals, *Criminal Justice System* (Washington, D.C.: U.S. Government Printing Office, 1973), p. 7.

54. National League of Cities and United States Conference of Mayors, *Criminal Justice Coordinating Council* (Washington, D.C.: National League of Cities, 1971), p. 3.

55. Pub. L. 91–644, Title I-4(2), Jan. 2, 1971.

56. Twentieth Century Fund, *Law Enforcement: The Federal Role* (New York: McGraw-Hill, 1976).

57. Ibid., p. 40.

58. Ibid., esp. Chapter 3.

59. Ibid., pp. 54–57.

60. National Institute of Law Enforcement and Criminal Justice, *Exemplary Program* (Monograph), April 1975, p. 3.

61. Twentieth Century Fund, *Law Enforcement*, p. 31.

62. James M. Thoreabeau, *The History of the American Revolution* (New York: Crittendon, 1912), p. 69.

63. Rektor, *Federal Law Enforcement Agencies*, p. 178.

64. Miriam Ottenburg, *The Federal Investigator* (Englewood Cliffs, N.J.: Prentice-Hall, 1962), p. 228.

65. Walter S. Bowen and Harry F. Neal, *The United States Secret Service* (Philadelphia: Clifton, 1960), p. 20.

66. Washington Crime News Service, "Secret Service—Tough on Counterfeiters," *Crime Control Digest* 12 (January 16, 1978): 9–10.

67. Ibid., p. 10.

68. Treasury Department order No. 221, *Federal Register,* June 10, 1972, 11696.

69. Vernon D. Acree, "U.S. Customs Assistance Programs," *Police Chief* 42, no. 7 (July 1975): 36.

70. David R. MacDonald "Treasury Department Assistance Programs to State and Local Law Enforcement Agencies," *Police Chief* 42, No. 7 (July 1975): 30.

71. James M. Thoreabeau, *The History of the American Revolution* (New York: Crittendon, 1912), p. 69.

72. Rektor, *Federal Law Enforcement Agencies*, p. 178.

73. Miriam Ottenburg, *The Federal Investigator* (Englewood Cliffs, N.J.: Prentice-Hall, 1962), p. 228.

74. Walter S. Bowen and Harry F. Neal, *The United States Secret Service* (Philadelphia: Clifton, 1960), p. 20.

6

THE ROLE OF
THE POLICE

1. What is the role of the police in our society?
2. What are the rules governing search and seizure operations?
3. What are the key issues involved in the legality of an arrest?
4. What is self-incrimination? What protections are guaranteed to an accused against self-incrimination?
5. How do police operational styles differ?
6. How are the components of a police department organized?

These are some of the questions this chapter will answer.

This chapter begins by examining some of the specific enforcement activities in which the police are engaged. These responsibilities are viewed in relation to established constitutional issues and cases that have effected these activities. This discussion is followed by an examination of the development of police roles and their attitudes toward those roles. Finally, the internal organization of police agencies is analyzed.

ROLE OF THE POLICE

Any discussion of the role of the police must take into consideration the police operational process because it establishes the framework for police behavior. In recent years, this operational process has come under increasing scrutiny by the courts through their interpretations of police behavior in some major cases. This section examines some of the more typical enforcement processes engaged in by the police and highlights significant court cases that bear on the conduct of police personnel in their enforcement role.

Crime Detection

The police are typically the first component of the criminal justice system to deal with the commission of a crime. This detection of the commissions of crime usually occurs in one of several ways. The most typical way that crimes come to the attention of the authorities is for the victim of the crime to report its occurrence to the police. A less typical way for the police to be advised of a crime is through the reporting of a crime by someone who has witnessed its commission or has come upon evidence indicating that a crime has been committed. A third way is for the police themselves through their routine operations to discover that a crime has been committed or to witness its commission. For example, while patrolling his beat a police officer might discover a building with a broken lock on a door indicating that a possible burglary has occurred or is occurring at the time he discovers it.

An important part of crime detection is often the result of aggressive police work. Experienced police officers and detectives often concentrate their surveillance and investigative efforts on persons, situations, or places in which past experience has taught them that criminal behavior is likely. For example, investigators may receive a "tip" that a particular individual is dealing in narcotics. They will then try to arrange a "buy" or at least keep the individual under surveillance in the hope that they can gather enough evidence and satisfy the particular elements required for an arrest and a successful prosecution under the existing statute.

Situations also lead to many instances of crime detection. The police may be having problems with "car stripping" in a particular locale. They may then detail a group of detectives or plainclothesmen to watch a particular parking lot in the vicinity in the hope that they will be able to arrest the perpetrators in the act. Sometimes the police even contrive the situation. This is called a *decoy operation*. For example, the Philadelphia police organized a so-called "Watermelon Detail." In this operation, two seamy appearing police officers in an old battered station wagon pull over to the curb and set up a watermelon selling operation. The purpose of the detail is that the proceeds from the sale will be an inviting target for armed robbery. Apparently, the operation proved to be quite successful. In this type of case, police provided an opportunity for the commission of a crime. Sometimes such police behavior invokes the defendant to claim that the situation is in effect entrapment. *Entrapment* is a defense to a criminal action when an individual is enticed by an officer of the law (or the officer's agent) to commit a crime that otherwise would not have been committed. Almost typically the court will refute this argument on the grounds that the action of the police "merely by affording opportunities or facilities for the commission of the crime does not constitute entrapment."[1]

However, the police are not always the first and only criminal justice agency to initiate the crime detection process. The Prosecutor's Office, for instance, is sometimes involved in certain types of criminal investigations such as fraud, organized crime, or forms of political corruption. The investigatory grand jury is another method of crime detection that is used by some communities under certain circumstances. Another means is the investigative powers vested in the Congress through its legislative committees. Through congressional hearings and investigations such facts can be turned over to law enforcement officials and the courts for appropriate action. Examples of this authority can be seen in the operations of the Senate Watergate Committee and the House Judiciary Committee in their investigation into the political operations of the Nixon administration.

Criminal Investigation

Once a crime has been detected, the police might conduct an investigation depending upon such factors as the seriousness of the offense, the availability of resources, and the probability of a successful investigation (which means an arrest and a successful prosecution). Often the victim may view the crime as having major importance, although the police will conduct nothing more than a preliminary or superficial investigation. For instance, if you live in a city where auto theft is quite prevalent, you could have your car stolen, only to be notified by the police a few hours later that it has been found abandoned and slightly damaged. The police will often conduct nothing more than a preliminary investigation and fill out a report of the incident. Given the situation and the lack of available evidence for an arrest and prosecution, the police often feel that such crimes are simply beyond their capability to solve.

Generally, the police investigative process revolves around certain objectives.[2] The first objective is simply to determine if a crime has been committed, and if so, what type of crime? This is usually accomplished by analyzing the available facts and evidence to see if the elements of a crime are present, and perhaps, whether the nature of the crime is civil or criminal in order to determine whether the police have jurisdiction over the matter. Second, the process attempts to identify the offender through the available evidence or resources. The third objective is to apprehend the offender. In addition to these objectives, the police are responsible for gathering and preserving evidence that will both justify their enforcement action in the particular case as well as enable the fact-finding process of the courts to successfully prosecute the case and obtain a conviction based upon the existing facts and circumstances. In this regard, the police investigative process becomes a crucial aid to the prosecution and conviction of the perpetrator.

The actions that govern the police investigative process revolve around certain procedural issues. These procedures are often governed by the U.S. Constitution and by case law interpretations of police behavior as they relate to these constitutional safeguards. Four major concerns in this area need to be briefly discussed. These are: (1) search and seizure; (2) arrest; (3) custodial interrogations and confessions; and (4) lineups.

Search and Seizure

MAPP v. OHIO (1961)

Application of the Exclusionary Rule Against Illegal Searches and Seizures to the States

FACTS:

On May 23, 1957, three Cleveland, Ohio, police officers arrived at the home of Mrs. Mapp. They had received information that a person was allegedly hiding out in the home who was wanted for questioning in relation to a recent bombing, and that there was a large amount of policy paraphernalia being hidden in the home. Mapp and her daughter lived on the top floor of the two-family dwelling. The officers knocked on the door and demanded entrance to the house, but Mrs. Mapp, after telephoning her attorney, refused to admit them without a search warrant. The officers then advised their headquarters of the situation and undertook a surveillance of the house.

Three hours later, four additional officers arrived and again sought entrance. When Mrs. Mapp did not immediately come to the door, at least one of the several doors was forcibly opened and the police gained admittance. Meanwhile Mapp's attorney arrived, but the officers would neither permit him to enter the house nor to see Mapp. It appears that Mrs. Mapp was halfway down the stairs when the officers broke into the hall. Mrs. Mapp demanded to see the search warrant, and a paper, claimed to be a warrant, was held up by one of the officers. She grabbed the "warrant" and placed it in her bosom. A rough struggle ensued in which the officers recovered the paper. As a result, Mrs. Mapp was handcuffed because she had been "belligerent" in resisting their attempts to retrieve the "warrant" from her bosom. While handcuffed she was forcibly taken upstairs where the dressers and closets throughout the house were thoroughly searched. The police then searched the basement and found some obscene materials in a trunk. Mrs. Mapp was arrested for having such materials in her possession.

At the trial, no search warrant was produced by the prosecution, nor was the failure to produce one explained or accounted for. The facts tended to support the belief that a search warrant never existed. Mrs. Mapp was convicted of the crime and sentenced to prison.

DECISION:

The U.S. Supreme Court decided that the police exercised wanton disregard for the constitutional rights of the accused.

SIGNIFICANCE OF THE CASE:

The Supreme Court indicated that the Fourth Amendment is contained by inference in the Fourteenth Amendment, and that from this date, any evidence that was illegally obtained by the police would be inadmissible in any courtroom in the country.

In their investigative process, the police are restricted as to what they can seize and under what circumstances by the Fourth Amendment, which states that no warrant will be issued except upon probable cause. Generally speaking, the police are required to produce a search warrant before they can search for and seize evidence. However, the law realizes that obtaining a search warrant might not be feasible under the circumstances of the moment. For this reason, the courts recognize and authorize the police to search and seize under two general exceptions to the requirements for a warrant: (1) The police may search by virtue of a lawful arrest; and (2) by the authority of a waiver of consent. However, this does not give the police carte blanche authority to conduct unreasonable searches, and the courts have examined closely the circumstances under which these two exceptions have been applied by the police.

The first exception to the warrant requirement recognizes that *based upon a lawful arrest,* the police officer may search the person arrested for self-protection and to prevent the destruction of evidence. However, the Supreme Court has limited the scope of the search in this instance. For example, a police officer may be advised over the car radio that a jewelry store robbery has just taken place. A description of the suspect is given. On the way to the scene, the officer sees an individual in front of a house who answers the general description. The officer stops and questions the person, and the individual's actions lead the officer to suspect the person of the crime. The officer is then authorized under the probable cause doctrine to arrest and then search the individual. As a result of the search, suppose that miscellaneous jewelry is found in the suspect's pockets, and suppose further that the arrestee admits to living in the house. The police officer cannot by virtue of this arrest then search the house for other incriminating evidence. A search made under circumstances such as these cannot legally go beyond the area where it is possible for the person to reach for a weapon or destroy evidence.

CHIMEL v. CALIFORNIA (1969)

The "Scope" of a Search Incident to a Lawful Arrest

FACTS:

On the afternoon of September 13, 1965, three police officers arrived at the Santa Ana, California, home of Chimel with an arrest warrant charging him with the burglary of a coin store. After the officers identified themselves to Chimel's wife, she admitted them into the house where they waited 10 to 15 minutes until Chimel returned home from work. When he entered the house, one of the officers handed him the arrest warrant and asked for permission to look around. Chimel objected, but was advised that the officers could conduct a search on the basis of the lawful arrest. However, no search warrant had been issued.

Accompanied by Chimel's wife, the officers then searched the entire three-bedroom house. The officers told Chimel's wife to open drawers in the master bedroom and sewing room and "to physically move contents of the drawers from side to side so that (they) might view any items that would have come from (the) burglary." After completing the search, the officers seized numerous items, including some coins.

At the defendant's subsequent state trial on two charges of burglary, the coins taken from his house were admitted into evidence against him over his objection that they had been unconstitutionally seized. He was convicted and the judgment was upheld by the California Supreme Court.

DECISION:

The U.S. Supreme Court decided that the search of Chimel's home went far beyond any area where he might conceivably have obtained a weapon or destroyed any evidence, and that no constitutional basis existed for extending the search to all areas of the house. The Court concluded that the scope of the search was unreasonable under the Fourth Amendment as applied through the Fourteenth Amendment, and Chimel's conviction was overturned.

SIGNIFICANCE OF THE CASE:

The Chimel case changed the policy with regard to the scope of a search made by an officer incident to a lawful arrest. In the past, a police officer was permitted to search all areas under the control of the defendant. The Court's ruling on the Chimel case allows the officer to search only the defendant and the immediate physical surroundings under the defendant's control, which is generally interpreted as an arm's length distance around the defendant.

By the same token, the police can search without warrant if the officer receives the permission from someone who has a right of privacy in the area to be searched.[3] However, the courts require that such consent must be voluntary and must be given knowingly and intelligently. Any element of coercion or intimidation invalidates the consent. The whole area of search and seizure under the Fourth Amendment including search warrants, search incident to a lawful arrest, and consent searches are governed by the general *exclusionary rule doctrine* which was first established in 1914 and finally made applicable to the states in the *Mapp v. Ohio* case. Through this application of the exclusionary rule by the U.S. Supreme Court, all police actions in searching for and seizing evidence must meet certain standards or the evidence will be excluded as constitutionally inadmissible.

SCHNECKLOTH v. BUSTAMONTE (1973)

The "Voluntariness" of Consent Searches and "Totality of Circumstances"

FACTS:

While on routine patrol at 2:40 a.m., a Sunnyvale, California, police officer stopped a car that had one headlight and the light above its license plate burned out. Six men were in the vehicle, including its owner, Bustamonte. When the driver who was not Bustamonte, couldn't produce a driver's license, the officer asked if any of the other five had any evidence of identification. Joe Alcala, a passenger in the front seat produced one. After the occupants got out of the car at the officer's request, and after two additional policemen had arrived, the officer who had originally stopped the car asked Alcala if he could search the car. After Alcala replied to go ahead, the officers found three stolen checks under the left rear seat.

The trial judge denied the motion to suppress the checks in question at Bustamonte's trial and he was convicted. The U.S. Court of Appeals overturned the conviction on the grounds that proof of knowledge of the right to refuse consent is a necessary prerequisite to demonstrating a "voluntary" consent.

DECISION:

The U.S. Supreme Court overturned the decision of the U.S. Court of Appeals and upheld the trial court's conviction.

SIGNIFICANCE OF THE CASE:

The Supreme Court held that when the subject of a search is not in custody and the state attempts to justify a search on the basis of his or her consent, the Fourth and Fourteenth Amendments require that the consent was voluntarily given and not the result of duress or coercion, either express or implied. Voluntariness must be determined on the bases of all the circumstances, and although the subject's knowledge of a right to refuse is a factor to be taken into account, the prosecution is not required to demonstrate such knowledge as a prerequisite to establishing a voluntary consent.

TERRY v. OHIO (1968)

"Stop and Frisk"

FACTS:

A Cleveland detective, Martin McFadden, was patrolling a downtown beat when he observed two strangers, Terry and Richard Chilton, on a street corner. He saw them proceed back and forth along an identical route about 24 times, pausing each time to stare in the same store window. Each completion of the route was followed by a conference between the two. During one conversation, they were joined by a third man, Katz, who left swiftly. Suspecting the two men of casing the store for a burglary, the officer followed them and saw them rejoin the third man a few blocks away in front of another store.

The officer approached the three, identified himself as a policeman, and asked their names. The men mumbled something, whereupon McFadden spun Terry around, patted down his outside clothing, and found a pistol in his overcoat pocket but was unable to remove it. The officer ordered the three into the store where he removed Terry's revolver and ordered the three to face the wall with their hands raised. He frisked Chilton and Katz and then seized a revolver from Chilton's outside overcoat pocket. McFadden did not put his hands under Katz's outer garments since he discovered nothing during the frisk that might have been a weapon, nor did he put his hands under Terry's or Chilton's garments until he felt the guns in their overcoats. The three were taken to the police station where Katz was later released.

Terry and Chilton were charged with carrying concealed weapons. The defense moved to suppress the evidence of the weapons. Although the trial court rejected the prosecution's theory that the guns had been seized during a search incident to a lawful arrest, the court denied the motion to suppress the illegally seized evidence and admitted the weapons into evidence. The court acted on the grounds that the officer had cause to believe that Terry and Chilton were acting suspiciously, that their interrogation was warranted, and that the officer for his own protection had the right to frisk their outer clothing because he had reasonable cause to believe that they might be armed. The court distinguished between an investigatory stop and an arrest, and between a frisk of the outer clothing for weapons and a thorough search for evidence of crime. Terry and Chilton were found guilty, and the case was subsequently appealed to the United States Supreme Court.

DECISION:

The Court affirmed the defendants' conviction stating that "where a reasonably prudent officer is warranted in the circumstances of a given case in believing that his safety or that of others is endangered, he may make a reasonable search for weapons of the person believed by him to be armed and dangerous regardless of whether he has probable cause to arrest that individual for crime or the absolute certainty that the individual is armed." Although it is important for the police to obtain a warrant whenever possible before undertaking a search and seizure, the warrant requirement obviously cannot be followed where immediate action based on street observations is required.

SIGNIFICANCE OF THE CASE:

The Court declared that the police officer's conduct was reasonable based on the circumstances. This established the constitutional rule that an officer who does not have the authority to arrest may stop a person and make an exterior search of the individual if the officer, based upon his experience, perceives suspicious circumstances and has reasonable fear for his safety. The Court indicated that the frisk or search must be reasonably limited in scope to the circumstances that justified the interference with the suspect in the first place.

Arrest   In effect, an arrest is the beginning of imprisonment, when an individual is first taken by government and restrained of his or her liberty.[4] The law of arrest, which is generally uniform in all the states as well as the federal code of criminal procedure, has not changed significantly in nearly 400 years. Our arrest laws have evolved from those that were firmly planted in our English common law heritage.

Let us briefly review the basic law of arrest (see Chapter 2), which states that a police officer can arrest without a warrant on the following conditions: (1) if a felony has been committed in the officer's presence; (2) if there is probable cause to believe that a felony has been committed and that the person being arrested committed the felony; or (3) if a misdemeanor has been committed in the officer's presence. The authority for these arrest powers is contained in the various state and federal statutes which, in turn, have been affirmed by various court decisions.

Although the police confront individuals in various circumstances each day, the mere stopping and questioning does not necessarily constitute an arrest. As Chapter 2 detailed, certain elements must be present in order for a valid arrest to occur. If these elements are questioned, the court has the sole responsibility to determine whether a legal arrest has taken place.[5]

When making a *legal* arrest the police officer has the authority to use whatever *reasonable* force is necessary. The key issues are the legality of the arrest and the reasonableness of the force used. If the arrest is not legal, the officer has no right to use force and criminal and civil charges can be brought against the officer for the arrest and the subsequent use of force. Reasonableness is also an issue. Suppose that a police officer stops a motorist for a minor misdemeanor. While the officer's back is turned the motorist starts to run away. The police officer cannot then shoot the fleeing misdemeanant because use of such force would be entirely inappropriate and unreasonable under the circumstances.

One of the most troublesome areas in the law concerning a warrantless arrest is the question of probable cause. For this reason, most legal experts recommend that, whenever possible, an arrest warrant be obtained before the actual physical arrest is made. This requires the police to exercise discretion in determining not only whether probable cause exists, but also whether an arrest should be made.

UNITED STATES v. WATSON (1976)

Warrantless Arrests and Probable Cause

FACTS:

A government informant received a stolen credit card from Watson and delivered it to a postal inspector. At the inspector's suggestion, the informant arranged a second meeting with Watson a few days later. This meeting took place in a restaurant. Believing that Watson had additional stolen credit cards, the informant gave the postal inspectors a prearranged signal and they entered and made a warrantless arrest of Watson. He was then taken outside the restaurant and a search of his person was conducted, but no cards were found. However, a search, based on his consent, of his nearby automobile produced two stolen credit cards.

He was convicted of possessing stolen mail. However, the Court of Appeals reversed the trial court's decision, finding that in spite of probable cause, the postal inspector had ample time to obtain an arrest warrant but did not do so.

DECISION:

The U.S. Supreme Court overturned the reversal of the conviction by the Court of Appeals.

SIGNIFICANCE OF THE CASE:

The statute was upheld that postal inspectors are authorized to make arrests for felonies without warrant if they have reasonable grounds to believe that the person arrested has committed or is committing such a felony. The Court concurred that in this case reasonable grounds (probable cause) for an arrest existed. Since these factors existed, there was no compelling reason to obtain an arrest warrant even though there might have been time to obtain one.

In-Custody Interrogation and Lineups   The police investigative process also includes custodial interrogation and the special investigative procedure referred to as a police lineup or showup. Like other police investigative procedures, these, too, have come under the scrutiny of the courts. Generally, such practices fall under the provisions of the Fifth Amendment which says that *"no person . . . shall be compelled in any criminal case to be a witness against himself."* Also applicable is the Sixth Amendment which states: *"In all criminal prosecutions, the accused shall enjoy the right to a speedy and public trial . . . and to be informed of the nature and cause of the accusation; to be confronted with the witnesses against him; to have compulsory process for obtaining witnesses in his favor, and to have the assistance of counsel for his defense."*

ESCOBEDO v. ILLINOIS (1966)

In-Custody Police Interrogation as a "Critical Stage" and the Right to Counsel

FACTS:

On the night of January 19, 1960, Danny Escobedo's brother-in-law was fatally shot. At 2:30 a.m. that morning, Escobedo was arrested without a warrant and interrogated for approximately 15 hours. During that time he made no statement and was released at 5 p.m., only after his attorney had obtained a writ of habeas corpus from the state courts.

On January 30, 1960, 11 days after the fatal shooting, Escobedo was arrested a second time at about 8:00 and taken into the police station for interrogation. Shortly after he arrived at police headquarters, his lawyer arrived, but the police did not permit the attorney to see his client. The attorney repeatedly requested to see his client and, at the same time, Escobedo requested to see his lawyer. The police told Escobedo that his lawyer didn't want to see him and that they would not allow him to see his attorney until they were finished interrogating him. It was during this second interrogation that Escobedo made certain incriminating statements that were used against him when he was convicted in the state courts for his involvement in his brother-in-law's murder.

The defense raised the issue at trial and before the Supreme Court of the United States that the interrogation stage was a "critical stage" in Escobedo's case and that he had been denied the right to counsel under the Sixth Amendment. The defense further argued that since Escobedo was denied his right to counsel under the Sixth Amendment, his incriminating statements should have been suppressed and should not have been used against him.

DECISION:

The Supreme Court agreed that Escobedo's right to counsel under the Sixth Amendment was denied and consequently suppressed his incriminating statements.

SIGNIFICANCE OF THE CASE:

The Supreme Court held that the interrogation was in fact the most "critical stage" of his criminal proceedings. Since Escobedo was in police custody, he should have been notified of his right of counsel and afforded this right if he had so requested by virtue of the Sixth Amendment. If the right to counsel is withheld, incriminating statements cannot be used against the accused.

MIRANDA v. ARIZONA (1966)

Confessions and Police Interrogations

FACTS:

On the evening of March 3, 1963, an 18-year-old girl was abducted and forcibly raped in Phoenix. Ten days later, Miranda was arrested at his home by Phoenix police and taken to police headquarters where he was put into a police lineup. There he was immediately identified by the victim and within a 2-hour period signed a confession, admitting that he had seized the girl and raped her.

At his trial, it was brought out in cross-examination by the defense counsel that Miranda had not been advised before his interrogation of his right to counsel and to have counsel present during the interrogation.

DECISION:

The U.S. Supreme Court reversed the conviction and the introduction of his confession on the grounds that Miranda's rights against self-incrimination were not protected.

SIGNIFICANCE OF THE CASE:

The Court ruled that the prosecution may not use statements that stem from custodial interrogation unless it demonstrates the use of certain procedural safeguards against self-incrimination by the accused. These safeguards include: (1) warning the accused of the right to remain silent; (2) explaining that all statements may be used in evidence against the accused; and (3) explaining that the accused has the right to the presence of an attorney, either retained or appointed, unless he or she voluntarily, knowingly and intelligently waives these rights. If at any time the accused indicates that he or she wants to exercise these rights, the opportunity to do so must be made available; similarly, if the accused indicates that he or she does not want to be interrogated, the police cannot proceed with the questioning.

The Fifth Amendment to the Constitution is one of our fundamental guarantees against the police powers of the state. This privilege against self-incrimination is also found in the constitutions of 48 states, by statute in New Jersey, and by statutory construction in Iowa. Until 1964, the Fifth Amendment was interpreted by the United States Supreme Court to apply only to federal proceedings. But in that year, two cases were decided in which the Supreme Court held that the Fifth Amendment may be invoked in both state and federal proceedings.[6] Its importance is well stated by former Supreme Court Justice Goldberg in the *Murphy* v. *Waterfront* Commission case, where he stated:

> The privilege against self-incrimination "registers an important advance in the development of our liberty—one of the great landmarks in man's struggle to make himself civilized." . . . It reflects many of our fundamental values and most noble aspirations: our unwillingness to subject those suspected of crime to the cruel dilemma of self-accusation; our preference for an accusatorial rather than an inquisitorial system of criminal justice; our fear that self-incriminating statements will be elicited by inhumane treatment and abuses; our sense of fair play which dictates "a fair state-individual balance by requiring the government to leave the individual alone until good cause is shown for disturbing him and by requiring the government in its contest with the individual to shoulder the entire load: ". . . our respect for the inviolability of the human personality and of the right of each individual "to a private enclave where he may lead a private life;" . . . our distrust of self-deprecatory statements; and our realization that the privilege, while sometimes "a shelter to the guilty," is often "a protection to the innocent . . ."

History, ancient and modern, is replete with examples of governments that established totalitarian rules by forcing citizens to incriminate themselves. One significant distinction of the Roman law was the right of a Roman citizen not to be tortured for incriminating purposes. The Bible contains an account of an incident that took place in Asia Minor where St. Paul was stretched out on the rack by Roman soldiers; when he finally convinced them that he was a Roman citizen, they were required, by law, to stop the torture.[7]

Although today's police may not use the rack to induce incriminating statements, some of their methods are no less violative of the constitutional rights of the accused. Given the history of governmental abuse of citizens in self-incrimination situations, it is ironic that the Fifth Amendment is held in such low esteem by the general public whom the privilege was designed to protect. Instead, they too often see it as a means to protect "criminals" by permitting them to invoke the Fifth Amendment and thereby avoid answering incriminating questions.

Many of the court-related problems that the police have had with the Fifth Amendment have been through in-custody induced confessions or admissions in which suspects incriminate themselves under very questionable circumstances or without being advised of their rights. These confessions or admissions are then used to convict them. In a number of instances, there is also violation of the accused's rights under the Sixth Amendment, specifically the right to have counsel. A fundamental interpretation of this right has been that in order to prevent the possibility of self-incrimination, the accused has the right to have the advice of counsel and to have counsel present during such in-custody police interrogations.

UNITED STATES v. WADE (1970)

Lineups, the Right to Counsel, and Physical Characteristics

FACTS:

On September 21, 1964, a federally insured bank in Eustace, Texas, was robbed by an armed bandit. The robber had small strips of tape on each side of his face as he held the cashier and vice president at gun point. After filling a pillow case with money, the bandit hurriedly left the bank.

On March 23, 1965, Billy Joe Wade was placed under a federal indictment for this bank robbery. On April 2, 1965, Wade was arrested, and on April 26, 1965, the Federal District Court appointed counsel to represent Wade in this prosecution. Approximately 15 days after Wade's lawyer had been appointed by the court, agents of the Federal Bureau of Investigation arranged a lineup for the purpose of having the bank personnel identify the defendant. There were five or six people in addition to Wade in the lineup. Each person wore strips of tape on each side of his face, and when ordered said, "Put the money in the bag."

At the trial, the two bank employees positively identified Wade as the robber. No mention was made about the lineup on direct examination by the prosecutor. Wade's lawyer cross-examined the identification witnesses and established that there had been a lineup as well as the facts that surrounded the lineup. Wade's lawyer charged that the FBI lineup violated Wade's Fifth Amendment right against self-incrimination, as well as his Sixth Amendment right to counsel. The defense particularly emphasized the fact that Wade was already under indictment and had a lawyer at the time of the lineup, and that the failure to notify the lawyer of the lineup, as well as the absence of Wade's lawyer at the lineup, violated Wade's constitutional rights.

Wade was convicted in the District Court, but the U.S. Court of Appeals reversed Wade's conviction and held that the lineup did not violate Wade's Fifth Amendment right but that there was a violation of Wade's Sixth Amendment right to counsel. The United States appealed this decision of the Fifth Circuit to the Supreme Court of the United States.

DECISION:

The U.S. Supreme Court held that a lineup is a "critical stage" of a criminal proceeding, and that an accused person at a lineup has the right to counsel under the Sixth Amendment.

SIGNIFICANCE OF THE CASE:

The accused has the right to have a lawyer present during any lineup or confrontation. In a footnote, the court also suggested that at least six persons in addition to the accused who are approximately the same height, weight, coloration of hair and skin, and bodily types as the suspect should participate in the lineup. They should also be similarly dressed.

The final investigative process to be examined is that of the police lineup. Although infrequently, this investigative tool has also come under review by the U.S. Supreme Court in the case of *United States* v. *Wade*. This investigative process has been interpreted by the Court as a "critical stage" of a criminal proceeding, and that an accused person at a lineup has the right to counsel under the Sixth Amendment. The Court further indicated that the lineup is a "critical stage" because, in effect, the accused is denied his right to a fair trial if he does not have a lawyer representing him at the lineup. The function of the lawyer at the lineup is to assure fairness in the viewing procedure and to obtain basic information by which the lawyer could meaningfully cross-examine identifying witnesses at trial.

From this review of police investigative procedures, it is clearly seen how legal guidelines, particularly through court interpretations, provide the framework for police enforcement actions. The next section examines how the police themselves define their role and how this role definition is expressed.

Concerns over the Police Role

To say that the police role involves order maintenance and law enforcement tells us everything, and at the same time, nothing. In the first place, such statements without additional explanation do not really provide a meaningful picture of how the police interrelate with the overall administration of criminal justice. Second, it doesn't explain how these objectives are achieved. Criticisms of the police do not center on the goals of law enforcement and order maintenance, but rather on the ways in which the police attain these goals. Thus, it is the methods that the police use to achieve these goals and the ways these programs and techniques interrelate with the criminal justice system that need further examination. The interrelated nature of the police function began to arouse curiosity at the beginning of the 1950s; before this period, studies of crime and the criminal justice system tended to be highly specific in nature. Because of this approach, the police, the courts, and corrections were treated as almost discreet and isolated entities. Examinations of the interrelationships among these component units were limited to statistical summaries of raw data. For example, reviews were made of statistical summaries of police arrests and successful prosecutions as indicated by guilty pleas or judgments of guilt. Such raw data were used to show that there was a high attrition rate between the numbers of arrests and the cases successfully prosecuted. However, no meaningful attempt was made to examine *why* this occurred. For example, no attempt was made to relate the relative contribution that police behavior and arrest policies had on this relationship.

In 1951, William Westley, a young sociologist, completed a remarkable doctoral thesis that explored the complexities and interactions of a police department. Although his pioneering research into the actual operations of a medium-sized midwestern police department was not to be recognized for its value until some years later, it did provide the most significant scholarly research into this hidden area of police behavior up until that time. In this way, it established a significant focus for the scholarly research that would come later.[8]

In 1955, the interactional policies of the police as they were related to the administration of justice became the subject of a significant research undertaken by the American Bar Foundation. This effort became the first major attempt to record and report actual observations of the daily activities of police officers, prosecutors, judges, and correctional personnel.[9]

The Westley study, and the summaries and observations from the American Bar Foundation study offered a sharp contrast to the general image of how the police functioned and how the criminal justice system operated. Most notably, the studies pointed out that these agencies were much more informally operated than what the public realized or what formal police policies would have us believe. In fact, the studies showed that the pressures of workload, citizen demands and expectations, and the interests and personal values of those working in the system were often more instrumental in how the system operated on a day-to-day basis than were such guidelines as established policies and procedures, the Constitution, laws, statutes and ordinances.[10] It also pointed out that the police were both affected by and affected the administration of justice in ways that were not anticipated before the research had begun. Among the most important conclusions of the American Bar Foundation's survey were such findings as:

1. The functioning of the criminal justice system was heavily dependent upon the police who in turn were very affected by the other components. Police policies and practices affected the operations of the entire system.

2. The police used their arrest powers to achieve a whole range of objectives in addition to that of prosecuting wrongdoers. For instance, they used this authority to harass, to investigate, to punish, and to provide safekeeping.

3. The volume of business handled by the police was much more than the volume processed through the rest of the criminal justice system.

4. The police often used informal methods to fulfill their formal responsibilities and to dispose of the endless array of situations they encountered.

5. The police felt that they are in a "no-win" situation in which public expectations exceed the police's capacity to fulfill these expectations.

6. Individual police officers were found to routinely exercise a great deal of discretion in how to handle the many diverse situations they encountered. Specifically, the police exercised a great deal of discretion in deciding when to arrest for a wide variety of offenses.[11]

Looking back at these pioneering efforts, it is obvious that they have had a significant impact upon subsequent studies of the entire criminal justice system. For example, when it was discovered that the police do not generally operate according to the popular conception, the following key questions arose: How do they operate? Why do they operate in this manner? What are the implications of this behavior? These questions not only opened up new areas for researchers to examine but also provided the basis for viewing the administration of criminal justice in an interrelated way. Accepting the premise that the police both affect and are, in turn, affected by the other agencies of criminal justice, then a more integrative approach is needed.

Such a viewpoint was given additional credibility a few years later when the President's Commission on Law Enforcement and Administration of Justice released its various reports in 1967. The commission urged the development of a systems-wide approach to the study of criminal justice. It was no longer considered feasible to study the police in isolation or to hold on to misconceptions about the actual functioning of the police. As a reflection of this new mode of thinking, college programs dropped such labels as "police science" or "police administration" programs and adopted the more inclusive title of "criminal justice studies." Similarly, textbooks that had been formerly devoted solely to the police broadened their focus to include other components of the criminal justice system. This integrated approach forms the basis for today's study of the administration of criminal justice.

Police Operational Styles

Because the police do not always share a common perception of their role—and, in fact, because their role does vary depending upon the circumstances and the individual characteristics of the police officers themselves—it is extremely difficult to define the full range of possible police roles. One way to deal with this problem of definition is to examine certain role categories into which most police officers can be grouped. Using this approach, it is possible to divide most police behavior into four general operational styles: the *enforcer,* the *social service agent,* the *zealot,* and the *watchman.*[12] Although these are not "pure" categories in that none of these are strictly inclusive—that is, no police officer totally conforms to one role style to the complete exclusion of the others—it does, however, provide a useful and convenient way of examining a very complex area of police role behavior.

The Enforcer   The *enforcer* is a police officer who places a relatively high value on social order and "keeping society safe," and a relatively low value on individual rights and legal due process. This type of officer is vehemently critical of such institutions as the Supreme Court, particularly as the Court expressed itself via its decisions during the 1960s. Often this type of officer is also very critical of politicians, police administrators, minority interest groups, and others whom he or she views as either corrupt, incompetent, weak, or simply naive. Overall, this individual is likely to view these groups as dangerous and a threat to the established order. These officers may rationalize their negative attitudes toward such individuals and groups by convincing themselves that their "street experience" has provided them with a grasp of reality that eludes others. The enforcer is often guilty of stereotyping. For example, this type of officer might contend that most blacks are either criminal, amoral, or a drain on the resources of white society, and that politicians are corrupt and potentially dangerous because of the sanctions they are willing to impose on the police for "political purposes." With such attitudes, the enforcers are likely to harbor deep hostility for such groups and feel that they likewise harbor deep-seated resentment toward them as police officers.[13]

This officer's primary preoccupation and interest lies in dealing with the more serious crimes. This is not to imply that he or she doesn't consider less serious crimes as unimportant—they are simply less important. As a member of "the thin blue line," the enforcer's first obligation is to come down hard on those engaged in such crimes as homicide, rape, robbery, and serious burglaries. Even in these instances, however, he or she selectively classifies crimes almost as much by the race and character of the perpetrator and victim as by the crime category itself. For example, if a Black, Puerto Rican, or Hispanic kills another, the enforcer's reaction is initially, "it's just another 'Nigger' (or whatever pejorative term applies in the case) just cuttin' on another Nigger."

Because this type of police officer is most concerned with serious offenses, he or she may feel that intervening in such enforcement practices as domestic disputes and minor traffic violations as being an undeserving use of time. If the enforcer does intervene in such situations, it is usually done with the preconceived idea that a domestic dispute constitutes an actual or potential felonious assault or that an erratic driver is, in fact, intoxicated and should be arrested. As the noted sociologists W.I. and Dorothy Thomas point out: "if men define situations as real, they are real in their consequences."[14] Such might also be said of the enforcer style of police officer.

The Social Service Agent The *social service agent* is another category. In many instances he or she may be more typical of the young, highly educated and somewhat idealistic police officers that have for the past several years been going into the police service. They have a diversity of perceptions about their role. They tacitly accept the idea that the police should be involved in a wide variety of activities. Furthermore, these activities do not have to be directly related to crime or police enforcement strategies. For example, the social service agent might go out of his or her way to assist a stranded motorist or to counsel youth. They perceive this role as an important function of their job. In this way, they define their overall role quite broadly. They often have perceptions of themselves similar to those of the enforcer category. That is to say, they feel somewhat superior and capable of making appropriate decisions but for different reasons. Whereas the enforcers are convinced of their superiority by virtue of their experience with the pathologies of human behavior, the social service agents feel superior because of their education and the "rightness" (if not righteousness) of their perceptions. These types of police officers also place a relatively high value on individual rights and due process. In many instances, they are better able to abstractly deal with such situations when they confront them. For example, if a case is lost because of police error in collecting evidence, they are perhaps less likely to blame the action on the courts. Since they both understand better and are more likely to subscribe to individual rights and the requirements for due process, they are more likely to consider the process as a costly learning experience and resolve more deeply that they must never make the same mistake again. In this way, they are less likely to externalize blame unto others.

However, because of this rather idealistic response, they might be less able than the enforcer to deal with the frustrations of police work and the administration of justice. After all, the enforcer can rationalize frustration by projecting blame. In this way, if the courts let a suspect go because of a legal technicality it can be viewed as an expected consequence given the enforcer's opinion of courts and judges. Such a situation may be harder to accept for one who has the characteristics of a social service agent. A few such experiences may, in fact, cause this type of individual to become quite cynical.

Like the enforcer, the social servant officer also places high value on social order and protecting society. Whereas the social service agent may be able to behave and think like an enforcer in certain situations, that behavior is usually situationally induced. When the situation changes, the social servant officer has the flexibility to adjust his or her behavior accordingly. On the other hand, the enforcer typically remains inflexible in both outlook and behavior regardless of the circumstance.

The Zealot The third category or style that can be used to define various police roles is that of the *zealot*. This type of role characteristic is an amalgam of both the enforcer and the social service agent styles. The correctness of the zealot's actions is based on the belief in the righteousness of the cause. Zealots tend to categorize their perceptions of behavior into black and white, or right and wrong. They see their role as one of enforcing all the laws and dealing with all offenders equally. Like the enforcer, the zealot emphasizes the detection and apprehension aspects of police work although the zealot is less likely to distinguish as much between major and minor crimes. A police officer of this type recognizes that serious crimes are more important and that their successful solution will provide the officer with greater prestige and status in the police organization. However, the zealot also importantly recognizes the fact that the solution of such crimes generally escapes the average police officer. Because of this zealots often become advocates for the full-service range of police activities, and particularly those that are directly related to the criminal enforcement activities of the job. This type of officer typically defines his or her role as a general law enforcement agent and is generally less critical than the enforcer. In fact, the zealots tend to accept the diverse groups of society for what they are.[15]

Zealots are also ambivalent about the enforcer type. Although they agree with some of the enforcer's attitudes and values particularly as they relate to concerns about enforcement, they disagree with the narrow concerns expressed by the enforcer in the types of crimes he concentrates on. The zealot may feel that as a police officer he or she is required to deal with a full-range of both serious and minor criminal infractions. This being the case, the zealot-type officer may resent the narrow viewpoints of the enforcer who tends to restrict the scope of enforcement activities.[16]

Although the zealots recognize concerns about individual rights and due process, they are not above bending them if they feel that the situation warrants it and that they can slightly bend the rules.

Finally, although they take a larger perspective of the police role than do the enforcer types, the zealots also tend to criticize the wide scope taken by the social service agent. They view the social worker role as unsuited to police work both because of its use of nonpunitive techniques and because of its demands upon police time and resources which detracts from their basic role of general law enforcement.

The Watchman   The fourth major role style of law enforcement is that of the *watchman*. This term is derived from James Q. Wilson's study of the styles of policing practiced by several cities.[17] In the cities that Wilson studied, he developed a typology of various police styles. He categorized one style as the *legalistic* which combines features of the enforcer and zealot. A second typology was that of the *service style* which is somewhat analogous to the social service agent style. A third orientation he referred to as the *watchman style*. This style is characterized by a set of values and attitudes that emphasize the maintenance of public order as the primary police goal rather than law enforcement or the broader ranging public service model. In this type of role the police officer ignores many common minor violations and general service situations. Wilson describes this model in this way:

> The police ignore many common minor violations, especially traffic and juvenile offenses, to tolerate, though gradually less so, a certain amount of vice and gambling, *to use the law more as a means of maintaining order than of regulating conduct, and to judge the requirements of order differently depending on the character of the group in which the infraction occurs* (emphasis added). Juveniles are "expected" to misbehave, and thus infractions among this group—unless they are serious or committed by a "wise guy"—are best ignored or treated informally. Negroes are thought to want, and to deserve, less law enforcement because to the police their conduct suggests a low level of public and private morality, an unwillingness to cooperate with the police or offer information, and widespread criminality. Serious crimes, of course, should be dealt with seriously . . .[18]

Although it is difficult and somewhat risky to generalize this role model to specific classes of police officers and situations, there are certain factors that might bear upon its relevancy to the workaday police occupation. Through some years of observation, this author has seen the adoption of this role model and the values and attitudes it conveys become somewhat characteristic of certain types of police personnel. Most often it seems to be found among older police officers nearing retirement who find themselves working general patrol operations. These type of officers generally take a nonchalant view of their role. Their guiding policy is "take it easy," "don't get involved," and "do what you have to do and no more." Their focus becomes one of keeping things as easy as possible which means overlooking certain forms of behavior that would more typically involve the zealot or the social service agent. Although they will take action in the case of major crimes, they differ from the enforcer in that they do not actively and aggressively seek to enforce these crimes or to become involved in their investigation. Because their attitude is one of, "if it happens, I'll do what is necessary," they are guided by the situation rather than by any preconceived plan.

This watchman role may also be situational in nature. The particular assignment of the police officer to a minority neighborhood particularly if it is a walking beat might induce this form of role behavior. For example, during the late 1960s when there were inflamed feelings between the police and ghetto residents in many of our major urban cities, the suggested role for police personnel assigned to these neighborhoods was to "play it cool," "don't get the residents upset by busting-up sidewalk crap games or giving out parking tickets." Police assigned to these neighborhoods, particularly if they were permanently assigned to them, would operate by overlooking many of the minor infractions in order not to bring about a confrontation or a possible riot. To some extent these same role models still exist in these type neighborhoods today.

In our discussion of the police role, two important dimensions have been examined: the police process itself and the psychological characteristics of the police officer. Both of these factors come into play in an interrelated manner when discussing the role of the police in our society and the various styles of policing that exist. Together these factors explain a great deal about what is referred to as police behavior. The remainder of the chapter examines the internal structure and characteristics of a municipal police agency.

THE ORGANIZATION OF POLICE DEPARTMENTS

Police departments typically follow the military model of organization which means that the various components are organized according to line, staff, and auxiliary services. The existence and number of these components are typically determined by the size of the particular police department. Obviously, very small cities will not have an extensive organizational arrangement. For the purposes of the discussion, let us assume that we are examining a fairly large police department in one of our major cities.

Line Services

Line services are the direct operational components of the police service. They are concerned with performing the basic overall police task. Depending upon the size of the police agency, the following line units might be set up: *patrol; traffic; criminal investigation; juvenile or youth bureau;* and *vice, organized crime,* and *intelligence* (see Figure 6-1).

Patrol   Every police agency has a patrol unit. The patrol force is the foundation of the police department and its largest operating unit. In large departments about 50 percent of all sworn personnel serve in this unit. In small departments the patrol force is, in effect, the department. Its personnel, who serve in uniform, are distributed throughout the city and most directly perform all the major functions required of modern law enforcement.

Traditionally, the prevention and suppression of crime has been regarded as the primary mission of the patrol force. For years this has been a commonly accepted idea by the police, public officials, and the average citizen. Today, there is a growing recognition that this function, in terms of its priority, might be misplaced.

In the first place, there is the question of whether police patrol has much value in preventing and suppressing crime. A very controversial study conducted in the Kansas City, Missouri, police department a few years ago, seriously calls into question the impact of police patrol activities on preventing crime.[19] Although for years police administrators have assumed that a properly deployed patrol force would have a deterrent effect on crime, there is now some doubt.

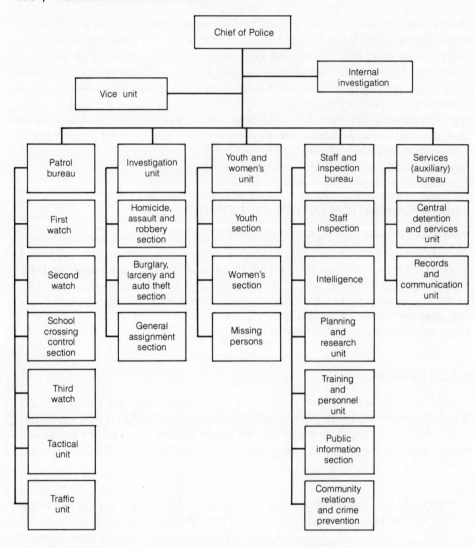

Adopted from: George Eastman, ed. *Municipal Police Administration* (Washington, D.C.: International City Management Association, 1969), p. 33.

FIGURE 6-1 Structural Organization of a Police Department Serving a Medium-Sized City

Of course, a major problem concerning the deterrent effect of preventive activities as engaged in by the patrol unit is the lack of measurable indicators of effectiveness. Since the primary objective of preventive patrol is the prevention and suppression of crime, the only true measure of effectiveness is the account of crime *not* committed. Obviously, there are no direct methods for determining how many crimes would be committed if it were not for preventive patrol efforts.[20]

Another responsibility of members of the patrol force is *crime investigation*. However, in many instances, this has been a largely superficial activity. Many times patrol officers merely conduct a preliminary investigation at the scene of the crime and then turn the investigation over to specialists such as detectives to do the follow-up work.

It is increasingly becoming obvious that the *maintenance of social order* is one of the most important functions that members of this unit perform. As noted in our discussion of the history of law enforcement, the desire for an orderly and peaceful society contributed greatly to the recognized need for the creation of police agencies. In fact, the term *peace officer* has been used synonymously with *police officer*.

The order maintenance role of the patrol officer is supplementary to the officer's role as law enforcer.[21] The order maintenance function usually arises when the patrol officer decides not to invoke his or her law enforcement powers and chooses instead some lesser form of control. Thus, order maintenance is often a direct result of the discretionary authority granted to the patrol officer.[22] As a noted authority in the field says:

> Patrol officers usually learn after many years of experience that effecting an arrest may not be the most satisfactory way of dealing with a troublesome situation. Instead, there are options open to the patrol officer which, in the long run, may produce more suitable results. As an example, an arrest in a situation involving a domestic (family) dispute, even though warranted under the immediate circumstances, rarely results in an effective solution to the fundamental problem and in most cases is never prosecuted. As a result, patrol officers have developed alternative strategies for handling such cases. The order maintenance function of the patrol officer includes the element of "peace keeping," which is a fundamental obligation of the police. Peace keeping, like order maintenance, differs from law enforcement in that patrol officers may choose to exercise their law enforcement authority in a very limited fashion and in a manner designed to produce more immediate and satisfactory results. For example, at the scene of a public disturbance, instead of arresting the combatants for disorderly conduct the patrol officer will order the participants to "break it up," or "go about their business." This course of action is taken for entirely pragmatic and understandable reasons. This method of dealing with the immediate problem is more expeditious and expedient than others, consumes less time . . . and usually produces a satisfactory conclusion to the incident.[23]

Concepts of how best to provide patrol services to citizens have been changing in recent years. Years ago, the officer walking the beat was the visible symbol of police authority. In more recent years and particularly since World War II, police officers have been pulled off walking beats and assigned to multifrequency radio-equipped cars. The reasoning behind this change was that the police would be able to cover more territory and react to crimes a lot more quickly—and do them both at far less cost. Police management thinking also underwent changes after the war. Departments were organized much more like the military. Police administrators emphasized centralized control, close supervision, instant communications, and motorization. Individual officers were not allowed to stay very long in one neighborhood. The emphasis was on internal mobility under the dual theories that a mobile department is a "clean" department and that the mobile policeman became a "well-rounded" officer. The whole concept was called "professionalism."[24]

Today, the trend is reversing itself. Cincinnati, Oakland, Los Angeles, and many other cities are bringing back the idea of the beat cop. Cincinnati, for example, under a program called Com-Sec, assigned the same police officers regularly to a specific neighborhood, where they were encouraged to develop local contacts and rapport with residents—an obvious return to the oldtime beat idea. The Com-Sec experimental area was a 4-mile square section that includes the downtown business complex, which embodied only 5 percent of the city's total area, but accounted for 25 percent of its crime. Com-Sec divided that area into six neighborhoods, each with its own particular social and criminal composition. The plan called for each neighborhood to have its own mini-police department, supervised by a lieutenant and three sergeants, who command a team of from eighteen to eighty personnel, depending upon the sector. The idea behind Com-Sec and similar programs is to make the small neighborhood patrol unit a part of the neighborhood and to develop community assistance and support for the police task.

Crime-Specific Enforcement Units   As mentioned in Chapter 5 on federal law enforcement, LEAA's Impact Program was designed to attack the problem of violent street crimes in eight large American cities. It also sought to encourage local law enforcement agencies to counteract the surge in these offenses by concentrating their efforts on certain major crimes.

The special police units that are assigned to concentrate on these specific offenses are known by a number of names. Detroit called its crime-specific unit STRESS. Chicago refers to its as the Tactical Unit; Oakland, California, created a special Burglary Prevention and Control Coordination Group. Other jurisdictions might refer to them as selective enforcement units or metropolitan squads. These units employ various techniques. Atlanta, for example, was particularly concerned with an increase of armed robberies in liquor stores and similar places of business. To counteract this, special teams of undercover stake-out officers were positioned in selected places of business that past experience indicated were most likely to be victimized. In other cases, decoy squads of police personnel dressed as civilians walk the streets to cut down on mugging or rape attempts.

Many of the more effective crime-specific enforcement programs incorporate similar features: first, police personnel chosen for these assignments are specially trained in combating specific offenses; second, as in the case of the crime of burglary, special efforts are made to make citizens aware of ways to help the police and lessen their own chances of victimization. Typically, antiburglary information is distributed through mass mailings and presentations before citizen's groups. In a special form of citizen education called target hardening, police personnel advise business people and homeowners how to make their businesses and residences less vulnerable to crime.

Another important component of crime-specific enforcement programs is evaluation. As is true of any study, careful attention must be given to the gathering and interpretation of data used to measure the program's effectiveness. The California Council on Criminal Justice, which is responsible for criminal justice planning and coordination throughout the state, developed one of the most comprehensive crime-specific plans involving the four largest cities and the two largest county police agencies in the state. One of the most crucial features of the plan was the built-in provision for evaluation that was developed before it was implemented.[25]

Traffic The traffic unit of a police department is responsible for developing and maintaining police-related traffic programs with responsibility for (1) enforcement, (2) citizen education, (3) investigation, (4) parking, and (5) engineering. A great deal of police effort is devoted to the general traffic safety, which involves: (1) gathering statistical facts about accidents so that preventive action can be taken; (2) assisting accident victims by appropriate first aid and the transportation of injured parties; (3) offering public education and awareness programs dealing with the safe operation of motor vehicles and inspecting vehicles to ensure compliance with established safety standards; (4) assisting the traffic engineer and traffic safety education agencies by providing them with information useful in their accident prevention work; (5) serving as the city government's inspection, investigative, and reporting unit to uncover problems and suggest improvements to expedite vehicular and pedestrian movement and parking; and (6) determining facts about accident occurrence as a basis for both accident prevention and service to involved citizens who need objective evidence to obtain justice in civil settlements of accident losses.[26]

Usually the traffic unit operates as a support and backup unit to the patrol force. It often handles major traffic accidents where there is serious bodily injury or extensive property damage, conducts preliminary investigations of hit-skip cases, prepares evidence in traffic-related cases for criminal or civil court cases, and compiles and disseminates all traffic-related data to other police units and municipal agencies such as the traffic engineer.

The job of a traffic specialist requires special skills in such areas as accident investigation, alcohol testing equipment, and traffic engineering support. A number of highly regarded and extensive training programs such as Northwestern University's Traffic Institute and various programs sponsored by the National Safety Council have been developed to increase the skills of police traffic specialists in all areas of traffic enforcement and services.

Criminal Investigation The criminal investigator (detective) is a police specialist who concentrates on the apprehension and conviction of adult criminal offenders. Unlike most other police units, this specialist group has as its primary goal the apprehension of the offender rather than the prevention of crime. The primary responsibilities of this unit are: (1) identification, location, and arrest of criminal offenders; (2) collection and preservation of physical evidence; (3) location of witnesses; and (4) recovery and return of stolen property.[27]

The criminal investigative unit is necessary because long-term continuing investigations cannot be accomplished by the patrol force without seriously depleting that unit's manpower. Often the patrol unit conducts preliminary investigations and even complete investigations when feasible. However, given the present operating characteristics of most municipal police departments, the detectives must take over most sustained investigations.

In smaller departments, a single investigative generalist handles most of the investigations; in larger departments, the detective unit is subdivided into specialized subunits. The administrative recommendation in recent years has been to divide the detective unit into three specialist groups; (1) the crimes-against-persons unit; (2) the crimes-against-property unit; and (3) the general assignment section.[28]

The crimes-against-persons unit conducts investigations where a person is the victim of a crime—for example, murder, forcible rape, robbery, or assault. The crimes-against-property unit conducts investigations that involve the loss of property. Such crimes as burglaries, larcenies, and auto theft fall in this category. The general assignment section conducts all other investigations such as fraud cases or general "con" games, embezzlement, and bad checks. Although this is the recommended organization for many of the medium to large city police departments in the United States, the very largest cities may need a greater degree of specialization. For example, New York City has special units that handle nothing but burglaries, homicides, and similar crimes. Even burglaries may be further broken down into business/commercial and residential. Detroit has a special homicide squad called "Squad Six" which handles only drug-related homicides.

In recent years many police departments have undertaken a number of organizational changes that have somewhat modified the traditional operations of the criminal investigation unit. In the first place, detectives are more often generalists who no longer are assigned to investigate only certain offenses, but are required to be proficient investigators in a wider range of crimes. Second, especially with the advent of team policing (which is discussed in the next chapter), patrol personnel and neighborhood team units are performing more and more of the investigative functions formerly assigned to the detective unit.

Juvenile or Youth Bureau Since a large percentage of police encounters involve juveniles, many police departments have created specialized juvenile units or youth bureaus to deal specifically with youth activities that directly affect the police.[29]

The responsibilities of the juvenile unit are quite broad and require special skills. The Children's Bureau of the U.S. Department of Health, Education, and Welfare sees the broad service role of this unit as consisting of the following:

1. Assisting the chief administrator in forming and implementing policies for dealing with juveniles.

2. Reviewing nonaction complaints and following up on action situations after initial contact by other police personnel.

3. Reviewing all reports that deal with contacts between police and juveniles.

4. Promoting liaison with other community agencies that deal with children, such as community welfare councils, juvenile courts, the school system voluntary social and welfare agencies, and other concerned institutions.

5. Completing follow-up investigations of specific types of complaints against children.

6. Adjusting cases when the best interest of the child and community can be served without resorting to court action.

7. Processing youths who are a danger to themselves or the community.

8. Working closely with the investigation's unit in the examination of major offenses committed by children.

9. Providing for prevention and repression of delinquent behavior by youth.[30]

In recent years, police juvenile units have begun to adopt policies that place them in line with the overall change in philosophy that characterizes all criminal justice agencies. This new philosophy is reflected in a concerted effort to divert youth away from the juvenile justice system so that their problems can be defined and handled outside the context of delinquency and official sanctions. Some far-sighted police departments are encouraging *proactive* rather than *reactive* strategies for dealing with youth. In other words, they seek to prevent and deter delinquent behavior rather than wait until a delinquent act has been committed and then arrest the child and process him or her through the courts.

Although this proactive approach has been criticized by many police personnel as "social work rather than police work" and a form of "coddling" the child, there are some very sound arguments for the adoption of this role by the police. Probably the best one is that the police and the schools are the first public agencies to come in contact with the delinquent or predelinquent child. If quick intervention is a partial solution to the problems of delinquency in this country, the police are in a position to intervene effectively. Unlike the schools, which have the primary function of education, the police already have a general preventive role to play, have a greater understanding of crime and its causes, and are available on a 24-hour basis.

Vice, Organized Crime, and Intelligence   In some larger agencies, the problems and responsibilities of enforcing vice laws, dealing with organized crime, and gathering intelligence in these areas is handled by specialized units. Vice is often the responsibility of a small group of investigative specialists, with organized crime and intelligence gathering the responsibility of another group. However, many police agencies now recognize that there is often a direct relationship between vice activities in a community and organized crime so that these formerly separate functions are typically made the responsibility of a single unit.

The effectiveness of any police department, particularly a small specialist subunit, in these areas is questionable. Local police must overcome formidable problems in dealing with these types of crime. The first problem is that local police departments simply do not have the trained personnel, investigative equipment, or jurisdictional authority to counteract organized crime efforts. The federal agencies have demonstrated that successful organized crime investigations require extensive manpower commitments, the availability and use of technical and legal investigative resources, and a sizeable operating budget.[31] In addition, organized crime efforts transcend local jurisdictional boundaries, and therefore local law enforcement is hampered in conducting the necessary multijurisdictional investigations.[32]

Another major problem area that must be addressed when considering the problems of local efforts against organized crime is corruption among police and other local public officials. This has long hampered effective local investigations and prosecutions of organized crimes.[33] A final impediment is the traditional organization of local police departments and a general police reluctance to exchange intelligence between departments or even share it among members of the same police agency. The President's Commission points this out when it says:

> The apparent versatility exhibited by professional criminals suggests that the traditional organization of police agencies into specialized squads such as robbery, burglary, auto theft, and bunco requires reconsideration. It suggests also the need for a much greater degree of communication between law enforcement agents with information on professional criminals. Detectives tend to be too reluctant to share their information sources with other detectives or to supply information to any centralized intelligence unit which may exist. Also the traditional complaint orientation of police departments is not appropriate for dealing with persons who are engaged continuously, rather than episodically in criminal activities.[34]

As a consequence, most vice, organized crime, and intelligence units in local police departments are relegated to making isolated and unimportant arrests of small-time narcotics dealers, prostitutes, and other low-level criminal operatives.

Staff Services

The staff units of a police department are support units whose primary function is to assist the line services in their task of carrying out the basic police responsibilities. With the demands placed on police agencies for more and better services, there has been an increased emphasis on upgrading staff services, which in turn has improved the operational capabilities of the line units. There are six basic staff units that may be found in municipal police departments: *training; personnel; planning and research; community relations; legal;* and *internal investigations.*

Training Until recently, most police agencies in cities of medium size and larger had a training unit. The recent trend has been to turn recruit training over to regional training academies operated by the state. There have been two reasons for this: first, it was recognized that unless recruit training was available to all newly hired police personnel from *all* communities in the state, the same problems would continue to exist—namely, the small cities could not offer any training for their personnel, and even the larger cities would provide only mediocre training because of their lack of resources and qualified personnel to conduct the necessary training.[35] Second, states have passed legislation that requires all newly appointed police personnel to undergo a stipulated minimum number of hours of training in approved police training programs before they can be certified as police officers anywhere in the state. Most states have such legislation and have established regional training centers.

However, a number of larger departments still maintain their own training programs. Whether given at the department or regional level, a typical recruit training program covers the following subjects:

1. Classroom notetaking
2. The role of law enforcement

3. Police-community relations
4. Police ethics
5. Racial and minority groups
6. Laws of arrest, search and seizure, constitutional guarantees
7. Code of criminal procedure, criminal law
8. Vehicle and traffic law
9. Traffic control
10. Traffic accident investigation
11. Laws of evidence
12. Evidence resources in a criminal case, including the crime scene search
13. Collection, care, identification, and preservation of evidence
14. Court organization and procedure
15. Courtroom demeanor and testifying
16. Basic criminal investigation
17. Notetaking and report writing
18. Interviews, interrogation, admissions, statements
19. The patrol function
20. Care and use of firearms
21. Defensive tactics
22. Techniques and mechanics of arrest
23. Emergency aid to persons
24. Recognition and handling of abnormal persons.[36]

In the past, police training programs traditionally emphasized firearms proficiency, physical training, and defensive tactics. However, recent emphasis has been more on subjects that examine the psychological and sociological environment in which a police officer must work so that he or she can better relate to citizens and to the job of a police officer.[37]

In addition to recruit training, police training personnel are responsible for developing special *in-service training programs,* which deal with specific subject areas. Some departments, as in New Haven, Connecticut, have introduced special taped spot lectures that are periodically broadcast over the police radio to all units in the field.[38] This innovative extension of the in-service training program covers such topics as interpersonal relations with members of the community, legal issues, and operational techniques, such as how to properly stop vehicles that are carrying possible suspects. Another method of in-service training used by a number of police training units is *roll-call training,* an idea that was originally developed in the Los Angeles Police Department. Under this system, training is presented for 15 to 20 minutes during the roll call period at the beginning of a shift and just before the officers go out on duty.

Police agencies that still operate their own training programs often use some of their best college-educated personnel as members of the training unit. This seems to be a logical choice of assignment because these individuals are often eager and bright men and women who consider keeping up with new developments in the field as part of their professional responsibility.

Personnel Typically found only in the largest police departments, police personnel functions are handled by the city's central personnel office.

Police personnel units are concerned with such matters as: (1) the selection, recruitment, assignment, and promotion of personnel; (2) performance evaluation so that individuals with certain talents can be used most advantageously for assignment and promotion; (3) coordinating functions with training personnel so that unsuitable performance is recognized and remedial programs are instituted to maintain a suitable level of service; (4) reviewing intradepartmental matters such as evaluating the effectiveness of supervision, investigating complaints against officers, and suggesting suitable disciplinary measures when needed; and (5) rendering attention to the welfare of police personnel. Also included are such duties as checking whether conditions of employment are satisfactory, whether provisions for pension plans and retirement are implemented, and whether there are good relations among supervisory and subordinate personnel in the department.

Planning and Research Every police agency is involved in planning activities. However, some departments have created special supporting units to assist police management in this endeavor. The planning and research unit of a police department is responsible for assisting management in the following areas:

1. The establishment of written policy that will determine specific agency goals and the means to measure the attainment of these goals.

2. The development and suggestion of plans that will improve police service.

3. The gathering and organizing of data needed for agency planning. This includes such areas as: (1) administrative plans; (2) tactical/operations plans; (3) fiscal and management plans; and (4) extradepartmental plans.

4. The conduct of research and development and the gathering of appropriate data that will be useful to police management in making decisions.[39]

The increased emphasis on planning has created the need for new skills among police personnel and has led to a greater use of civilians. Such areas as statistics and research methodology, systems analysis and computer technology, grant-writing skills and evaluative program techniques, and budget preparation are responsibilities of the planning unit. As a consequence of this new emphasis, many universities offering 4-year and graduate programs in criminal justice are emphasizing these skills in their academic course offerings. For example, the School of Criminal Justice at Michigan State University in addition to basic courses in police administration requires course work in systems development, fiscal administration, information systems, and quantitative methods at the master's level.

An important component of the overall planning and research activity is *operations analysis,* which looks at such things as reports of serious crime in order to determine the location, time, special characteristics, similarities to other criminal attacks, and various significant facts that may help to identify patterns of criminal behavior so that the department may take appropriate action through preventive and apprehension strategies, manpower deployment, etc. Similarly, traffic patterns and problems are analyzed so that corrective action may be taken. Research and development (R&D) activities are also undertaken to improve the capabilities and use of existing police equipment. These activities focus on examining the capabilities and limitations of existing equipment and making recommendations for improvement or the purchase of different equipment. These recommendations guide the administrator in developing the budget and making purchases for the agency.

Community Relations and Crime Prevention   The issue of police-community relations (PCR) has assumed particular importance for the police in recent years. Until the 1950s, the concept of a formal community relations unit was virtually unknown in police departments, but by the late 1960s some far-reaching changes had been made. During the tumultuous 1960s social unrest attracted the attention of four presidential and numerous local commissions; it was the subject of countless studies, articles, books, and speeches. As a result of this pressure, police departments began to adopt community relations programs.[40]

Although most police departments still consider the PCR unit to be a staff support unit, knowledgeable critics argue that it more appropriately should be a line unit that operates directly out of the office of the police chief or that it should not exist as a specialized unit—that the primary responsibility of PCR should rest with all line units and personnel.[41] The argument usually given is that the chief administrator should demonstrate total commitment to PCR programs and set the example for the department, and that the creation of a specialized unit will give the impression to line personnel that PCR is a function only of the special unit and that line personnel need not be concerned.

Although it is not possible to list all the activities that an effective PCR unit is engaged in, Table 6-1 indicates three general areas and the specific programs that might fall into each.

Unfortunately, the PCR programs that have been adopted in recent years have not reached their expected potential. There are a number of reasons for this: Many of these programs and units were created in an atmosphere of crisis, and commitment was maintained only as long as the crisis was remembered. Low budgets, a large proportion of token Black officers, training projects divorced from the rest of the police training curriculum, the employment of civilians, and other characteristics have communicated to the police department that community relations is not a serious activity.

As used by most police agencies, police-community relations programs have been criticized as being nothing more than a form of "public relations" gimmickry. As one noted observer says:

[A] good many of these divisions (police-community relations units) have been poorly organized, lack real constructive programs and guidelines for constructive improvement of police-community relations, and are merely "eye wash" to impress city officials and the public in general. . . . Many have jumped on the bandwagon of

TABLE 6-1
Areas of Concern for PCR Programs

PUBLIC RELATIONS

Personal cleanliness and good grooming
General politeness, courtesy, and good manners
Telephone etiquette
Car cleanliness
Modifications in the military-type uniform (redesigned blazers, jackets, etc.; incon-
   spicuous carrying of weapons)
Speaker's bureau activities, skill demonstrations, equipment exhibits, etc.
Open houses at police stations
Dog shows, water safety shows, etc.
Displays on bumper stickers, car cards, billboards
Awards and citations for outstanding police officers and citizens
Liaison for press personnel and facilities
Cooperation between the chief and media executives
Tidiness and good order in administrative facilities
American flag insignia worn

COMMUNITY SERVICE

Informational or interpretive newspaper or magazine features, newsletters, and door
   knob hangers; radio and television presentations (e.g., education on drugs, auto
   safety, auto theft, house burglaries)
Safety instruction for operating autos, bicycles, and other vehicles
Youth programs (e.g., Police Athletic League, summer camping)
Store-front centers in neighborhoods
Annual or periodic reports, *if* designed for public understanding
Complaint procedure
Public fund raising for tuition to help improve the education of police officers (by a
   citizens' organization)
Ride-in-a-patrol-car programs.
Sponsorship of scouting units (e.g., Explorers)
Police junior band or drum-and-bugle corps
Law enforcement career clinics in high schools
Policeman Bill and *Officer Friendly* types of programs in elementary schools
Police aid and advice for parades, demonstrations, etc.
Emergency facilities for demonstrations
Police assignments to job opportunity centers
Assistance to crisis-intervention agencies
Crime prevention literature
Helping Hand programs
Distribution of information to new residents
Tire-changing assistance
Checks on vacationers' residences
Ambulance service
Lost-and-found auctions (e.g., bicycles)
School counseling assistance
Social service referrals

COMMUNITY PARTICIPATION

Councils of social agencies (e.g., United Fund, Community Chest)
Family and neighborhood stabilization councils
Coordinating councils on community relations

TABLE 6-1 *(cont.)*

COMMUNITY PARTICIPATION
Councils on police-community relations
Precinct or district police-citizens committees or workshops
Councils on crime and delinquency
Interdenominational clergy-police councils
Police-community relations seminars
Community or neighborhood councils

Source: Louis A. Radelet, *The Police and the Community,* 2nd ed., © 1977, p. 28. Reprinted by permission of Glencoe Press.

police-community relations without knowing or preparing to handle the problems and obstacles that must be resolved in order to realize any of the potential benefits. This then seems to be the state of police-community relations at the present time.[42]

This points up a problem that has plagued many of these programs. The police were simply not sincerely interested in developing a real dialogue with the most dissatisfied segments of the community. The police often demonstrated that they felt comfortable with a one-way, "look what we're doing" process of communications, but they were unable to take the criticism that was often on the receiving end of the needed two-way system of joint communication. Generally, two-way communications with the community were limited to "safe" groups such as the merchants associations and fraternal organizations.

Most community relations programs have also been established as a function separate from patrol, crime prevention, investigations, and other traditional aspects of policing. Because the segregation of community relations has been emphasized, it has tended to be marginal to the operations of the police department. PCR programs have also suffered from unclear objectives and almost no meaningful evaluation. Often goals were defined in such broad generalities as "improving the relationship between the police department and citizens" or "giving citizens a greater appreciation of the police department and increasing their willingness to cooperate in attaining its objectives".[43]

Many authorities appear to be less than optimistic that PCR will continue even as a marginally viable special goal of police departments for the above reasons. What is more, the urban disorders that precipitated the development of these programs are no longer a major issue in the 1970s. In fact, this change away from PCR seems to have occurred already. Many police departments have already done away with their former PCR units and established crime prevention units in their place, as we shall see in the next chapter on crime prevention.

Internal Investigations   Since the 1960s, many persons outside law enforcement have urged the establishment of civilian review boards that would investigate complaints against police personnel. Undoubtedly, this demand has been prompted by feelings that the police have avoided making fair and vigorous investigations of wrongdoing within their ranks.

The function of an internal investigations unit is to investigate complaints against police personnel or other actions which may bring disrepute to the agency. This includes interviewing the complainant, any witnesses, and the police officer(s) involved, and presenting all the evidence to the police internal trial board or the prosecutor if the investigation reveals that the allegation of police misconduct is justified. Specifically, the responsibilities of such a unit include making appropriate inquiry of:

1. Any allegation or complaint of misconduct made by a citizen or other person against the department or any of its members.

2. Any alleged or suspected breach of integrity or case of moral turpitude from whatever source it may be reported or developed.

3. Any situation where an officer has been killed or injured by the deliberate or willful act of another person.

4. Any situation in which a person has been injured or killed by an officer either on or off duty.

5. Any situation involving the discharge of firearms by an officer.

6. In addition, other delegated responsibilities might include: (1) assisting in any disciplinary case when requested by police management personnel; (2) assisting any member of the department by investigating cases of harassment, threats, or false accusations against the officer; and (3) fully advising citizen complainants of the decisions and actions taken following receipt of complaints.[44]

In larger agencies, the internal investigations unit usually consists of a small group of carefully chosen and experienced personnel who possess the highest principles of professionalism and personal integrity. In smaller departments, the task of inquiry may be turned over to a trusted investigator; in some small agencies, the chief of police personally conducts such inquiries.

The organizational chart of a police department as shown in Figure 6-1 has this unit directly under the office of the police chief. The reason for this structure is quite obvious. Because of the importance of such activity to the department and the sensitive nature of this unit's work in terms of the attitudes and perceptions of both the private individual citizens and police personnel, the unit should have direct and frequent access to the chief. The full authority of the chief's office should stand behind the responsibilities of this unit.

Auxiliary Services

The auxiliary services are support units other than staff services which assist the line units in performing the police function. The following typical auxiliary services are briefly described here: *records and communications; data processing; temporary detention; laboratory;* and *supply and maintenance.*

Records and Communication   The central records and communication unit in a modern police agency is responsible for storing, indexing, retrieving, and disseminating to police operations personnel and management all pertinent information of a police nature. The records section, however, deals more with crime-related information than with management-related information.

For example, the records section gathers data on crimes committed, wanted persons, case histories of known offenders, stolen property, *modus operandi* (method of operation) information, and other similar items.

The functions of records and communication are, of necessity, integrated processes, and as agencies adopt on-line computer capabilities, data processing of crime-related information is also tied into this unit. Central records and communications systems provide the means by which law enforcement agencies can quickly and efficiently gather information about crimes, store this information, and instantly retrieve it when needed.

The records and communication unit often provides the following specific services to line units in the field: (1) receiving personal and telephone complaints; (2) receiving and dispatching radio messages to police mobile units in the field; (3) monitoring adjoining county and municipal police and fire departments, state law enforcement agencies, and other public safety radio systems; (4) receiving and transmitting teletype messages; (5) upon requests from field units, making inquiries from regional, state, and national computerized records systems; (6) controlling the movement of unauthorized personnel within the building; and (7) in some cases providing booking, personal identification, and jail security assistance.[45]

Data Processing   Only the largest police departments have data processing units. The very large agencies often have their own computer facilities and supporting software components. Medium-sized departments often use existing municipal computer facilities on a time-sharing basis. The data processing unit assists line and staff operation and police management personnel in a number of ways. It can be used for processing uniform crime-reporting information on a monthly basis; gathering intelligence and compiling budgeting information and other information of administrative value, such as fleet operating costs and personnel records. Many departments are using computer-assisted work force deployment programs; by gathering and analyzing data pertaining to crime patterns in terms of both geographical areas and hours of occurrence, police patrol personnel can be assigned to the areas and at the specific times when the data indicate that the majority of crimes occur or the workload is heaviest.

The data processing unit is also responsible for developing computer capabilities for the operations units that are designed so that information stored in the computer can be immediately retrieved for dissemination to requesting units. Such a system would normally contain the following information:

1. Wanted persons
   a. Persons with warrants outstanding
   b. Persons wanted for questioning
   c. Missing persons
   d. Persons under investigation or surveillance
   e. Revoked and suspended driver's license data

2. Criminal history information
   a. Arrest data
   b. Conviction data

    c. Parole and probation data
    d. Aliases and nicknames
    e. Personal and physical characteristics
    f. Method-of-operation (modus operandi) patterns

3. Vehicles
    a. Stolen vehicles
    b. Stolen license plates or tags
    c. Vehicles wanted in connection with crimes
    d. Other vehicle status, such as repossessed, impounded, or abandoned
    e. Vehicles under surveillance

4. Property
    a. Stolen property
    b. Lost property
    c. Recovered property

5. Miscellaneous
    a. Parking tickets
    b. Schedule of court cases

Temporary Detention   Police agencies that operate their own jail facilities have a temporary detention or jail unit. Unfortunately, many small police departments often turn this job over to the dispatcher or some other individual who usually is neither concerned nor qualified to handle the responsibilities of prisoner care.[46]

The jail unit is usually responsible for the following functions:

1. The search and control of prisoners during the booking process.

2. The booking of prisoners.

3. Fingerprinting and photographing of prisoners.

4. Compliance with legal requirements such as the right of the prisoner to counsel, etc.

5. The custody and return of the prisoner's property.

6. The inspection, supervision, and care of prisoners and jail facilities.

7. The transfer of prisoners to court or to some other jail or institution.[47]

In addition to these routine responsibilities, the jail unit may supervise prisoners engaged in work details or treatment programs. In some jurisdictions, the detention staff may also serve as court officers.

Laboratory   Only very large police departments maintain crime laboratory facilities. Staffing such a unit is too costly for all but a few large agencies that can justify it on the basis of a demonstrated need to conduct frequent scientific analyses. Typically, the laboratory equipment in a medium-sized agency is limited to such things as special cameras, photographic darkroom, latent fingerprint analysis capabilities, and perhaps some infrared equipment, such as night vision devices. Thus, most of it can be mastered by a police technical expert in a relatively short time.

In many states, a central laboratory provides the services for the local and county police agencies. For example, Michigan has established regional crime labs throughout that state under the auspices of the Michigan State Police. Often the state laboratories have mobile crime vans that can be dispatched to the scene of a crime or major disaster to make scientific analyses on the spot. These laboratories also provide various scientific experts from their staffs who work closely with local police agencies in field investigations and whose members are available as expert witnesses to testify at trials. Such federal agencies as the FBI, DEA, and others also provide laboratory services to local police agencies upon request.

The police laboratory typically performs scientific analyses in the following areas:*

- Chemical examinations:
  Narcotics
  Alcohol
  Explosives
  Incendiary materials
  Toxic substances
  Analysis of unknown specimens—for identification and tracing
  Analysis for comparison—the evidence specimen is compared with specimens of known origin

- Physical examinations:
  Automobile parts—broken ornaments, lenses, and other parts
  Broken windows—and other glass problems
  Electrical appliances
  Locks and keys
  Tool marks and other impressions
  Etching deleted numbers

- Personal markings for identification purposes:
  Fingerprints
  Foot and shoe impressions
  Laundry and dry-cleaning marks

- Documentary examinations:
  Questioned handwriting
  Typewriting
  Erasures and obliterations
  Paper, ink, and pencil problems

- Firearms problems:
  Identification of bullets and cartridges
  Firearms examination
  Trajectories

- Biological examinations:
  Blood

*Harry Sodermann and John J. O'Connell, *Modern Criminal Investigation,* 5th ed., Copyright © 1962; previous copyrights 1935, 1940, 1952 by Funk & Wagnalls Publishing Company, Inc. Used by permission of the publisher.

Semen
Hair and fibers

- Photography:
Contrast and filter photography
Infrared and ultraviolet photography
Photomicrography
Radiography

There are many opportunities today for criminalists—that is, specialists who apply the physical sciences to the solution of crimes. Preparation for a career in this field requires a strong background in such scientific areas as physics, chemistry, and biology together with an adequate foundation in criminal investigation, criminal law, and evidence and a knowledge of the criminal justice system. A number of universities offer specialized undergraduate and graduate degree programs in criminalistics.

Supply and Maintenance Found in only the very largest police departments, the supply and maintenance unit consists of such services as building and automotive maintenance, radio service, tailor shop, and the police armorer. More commonly, city maintenance personnel maintain the policy facility, although some cities use prisoners from the city jail to provide most of the routine maintenance. Responsibility for vehicle and radio maintenance is most often let out on bid to private contractors.

SUMMARY

The law enforcement role of the police involves such activities as crime detection, criminal investigation, search and seizure, arrest, and conducting in-custody interrogations and lineups. Each of these major areas have been defined by the courts in terms of certain constitutional issues. These definitions provide the framework for the operating strategies of the police.

However, the police role is a complicated issue and has come under increasing examinations in recent years. This research has indicated that the effect of the police on the other components of the justice system is substantial. Likewise, research has illustrated that the way in which the police perceive their own role will determine, in large measure, how the police process operates.

The internal characteristics of a large municipal police agency shows that the organizational structure is broken down into line, staff, and auxiliary components, each component playing an integral role in the overall organization.

REVIEW QUESTIONS

1. What are the three ways in which the police learn of the commission of a crime?

2. In their investigative process the police have three objectives. What are these objectives?

3. Under what circumstances can the police conduct a search without a warrant?

4. What have the following cases signified in police investigative procedures?
   a. *Mapp* v. *Ohio*
   b. *Chimel* v. *California*
   c. *Schneckloth* v. *Bustamonte*
   d. *Terry* v. *Ohio*

5. What has been the significance of the following cases in police interrogation?
   a. *Escobedo* v. *Illinois*
   b. *Miranda* v. *Arizona*

6. Briefly describe the following police operational styles.
   a. The enforcer
   b. The social service agent
   c. The zealot
   d. The watchman

7. Draw an organizational chart for a typical police department of a medium-sized city.

8. What are the five units in the line services of a police department? Briefly describe the duties of each unit.

9. What are the basic staff units usually found in a municipal police department? Briefly describe each.

10. What courses might be offered in a typical recruit training program for police officers?

11. What are the responsibilities of an internal investigations unit in looking into a complaint against police personnel?

12. Name and briefly describe the auxiliary support services of a police department.

DISCUSSION QUESTIONS

1. Do the operational styles described in this chapter seem valid to you? Why or why not?

2. Have court rulings such as *Miranda* v. *Arizona* and *Escobedo* v. *Illinois* made police investigation procedures impossible? Explain.

SUGGESTED ADDITIONAL READINGS

American Bar Association. *Standards Relating to the Urban Police Function* (Chicago: American Bar Association, 1972).

Bopp, William J. *Police Personnel Administration* (Boston: Holbrook Press, 1972).

Butler, Alan J. *The Law Enforcement Process* (Port Washington, N.Y.: Alfred, 1976).

Cohn, Alvin W., and Emilio C. Viano, eds. *Police-Community Relations: Images, Roles, Realities* (Philadelphia: Lippincott, 1976).

International City Management Association. *Municipal Police Administration* (Washington, D.C.: International City Management Association, 1969).

Munro, Jim L. *Administrative Behavior and Police Organization* (Cincinnati: W. H. Anderson, 1974).

Saunders, Charles B. *Upgrading the American Police* (Washington, D.C.: Brookings, 1970).

Shanahan, Donald T. *Patrol Administration—Management by Objectives* (Boston: Holbrook Press, 1975).

Stahl, O. Glenn, and Richard A. Staufenberger, eds. *Police Personnel Administration* (North Scituate, Mass.: Duxbury Press, 1974).

Weston, Paul B. *Police Organization and Management* (Pacific Palisades, Calif.: Goodyear, 1976).

Whisenand, Paul M., and Fred R. Ferguson. *The Managing of Police Organizations* 2nd ed. (Englewood Cliffs, N.J.: Prentice-Hall, 1978).

Wilson, O. W. *Police Administration* (New York: McGraw-Hill, 1963).

———— and Roy C. McLaren. *Police Administration* 3d ed. (New York: McGraw-Hill, 1972).

NOTES

1. *Sorrells* v. *United States,* 287 U.S. 435.

2. This list of objectives is generally taken from John J. Horgan, *Criminal Investigation* (New York: McGraw-Hill, 1974), especially pp. 6–8.

3. The question of legality in this instance often revolves around who has this right to give the consent.

4. J. Shane Creamer, *The Law of Arrest, Search and Seizure* (Philadelphia: Saunders, 1968), p. 48.

5. Ibid., p. 49.

6. *Molloy* v. *Hogan,* 378 U.S.I.: *Murphy* v. *Waterfront Commission,* 378 U.S. 52.

7. Creamer, *The Law of Arrest, Search and Seizure,* p. 213.

8. See William A. Westley, *Violence and the Police* (Cambridge, Mass.: M.I.T., 1970).

9. Herman Goldstein, *Policing a Free Society* (Cambridge, Mass.: Ballinger, 1977).

10. Ibid., p. 23.

11. See Kenneth Culp Davis, *Discretionary Justice: A Preliminary Inquiry* (Baton Rouge: Louisiana State University Press, 1969) and *Police Discretion* (St. Paul, Minn.: West, 1975); Donald M. McIntyre, Jr., ed., *Law Enforcement in the Metropolis* (Chicago: American Bar Foundation, 1967).

12. A similar typology has been developed by other observers of the police role. See John J. Broderick, *Police in a Time of Change* (Morristown, N.J.: General Learning Press, 1977).

13. See Seymour Martin Lipset, "Why Cops Hate Liberals and Vice-Versa," *The Atlantic* 223 (March 1969): 76–83.

14. W. I. Thomas and Dorothy S. Thomas, *The Child in America* (New York: Knopf, 1928), p. 51.

15. Broderick, *Police in a Time of Change,* p. 57.

16. Also see Joseph J. Senna and Larry J. Seigel, *Introduction to Criminal Justice* (St. Paul, Minn.: West, 1978), especially pp. 176–179.

17. James Q. Wilson, *Varieties of Police Behavior* (Cambridge, Mass.: Harvard University Press, 1968).

18. Ibid., pp. 140–141.

19. See George L. Kelling et al., *The Kansas City Preventive Patrol Experiment: A Summary Report* (Washington, D.C.: Police Foundation, 1974).

20. International City Management Association, *Local Government Police Management* (Washington, D.C.: International City Management Association, 1977), p. 164.

21. Ibid., p. 168.

22. For further reading on this often controversial subject of police discretion, see Herman Goldstein, *Policing a Free Society,* (Cambridge, Mass.: Ballinger, 1977), especially Chap. 5; Kenneth Culp Davis, *Police Discretion* (St. Paul, Minn: West, 1975).

23. International City Management Association, *Local Government Police Management,* p. 169.

24. Richard Baker, "Remember Your Friendly Neighborhood Cop?" *Sky Magazine* 3, no. 7 (July 1974): 21.

25. See JoAnne W. Rockwell, "Crime Specific . . . An Answer?" *Police Chief,* 39 (September 1972): 38–43.

26. George D. Eastman, ed., *Municipal Police Administration* (Washington, D.C.: International City Management Association, 1969), p. 106.

27. N. C. Chamelin et al., *Introduction to Criminal Justice* (Englewood Cliffs, N.J.: Prentice-Hall, 1975), p. 120.

28. For example, see International City Management Association, *Local Government Police Management,* pp. 130–133; and O. W. Wilson and Roy C. McLaren, *Police Administration,* 3rd ed. (New York: McGraw-Hill, 1972), p. 21.

29. For a good insight into the role of the police in problems involving juveniles, see Robert C. Trojanowicz, *Juvenile Delinquency: Concepts and Control* (Englewood Cliffs, N.J.: Prentice-Hall, 1973), especially Chap. 7.

30. U.S. Department of Health, Education, and Welfare, Children's Bureau, *Police Work with Children: Perspectives and Principles,* Children's Bureau Pub. No. 399 (Washington, D.C.: U.S. Government Printing Office, 1962), pp. 9–10, 44.

31. Hank Messick, *The Silent Syndicate* (New York: Macmillan, 1967), p. 43.

32. Gus Tyler, ed., "Combating Organized Crime," a special issue of *The Annals of the American Academy of Political and Social Science* 347 (May 1963).

33. For example, see Donald R. Cressey, "Corruption of the Law Enforcement and Political Systems," in John E. Conklin, ed., *The Crime Establishment* (Englewood Cliffs, N.J.: Prentice-Hall, 1973), pp. 131–145.

34. President's Commission on Law Enforcement and Administration of Justice, *Crime and Its Impact—An Assessment* (Washington, D.C.: U.S. Government Printing Office, 1967), p. 101.

35. For example, a 1965 survey of 4,000 police departments conducted by the International Association of Chiefs of Police revealed that 85 percent of the officers appointed were sent into the field prior to their recruit training. President's Commission on Law Enforcement and Administration of Justice, *Police* (Washington, D.C.: U.S. Government Printing Office, 1967), p. 138.

36. V. A. Leonard and Harry W. More, *Police Organization and Management,* 4th ed. (Mineola, N.Y.: Foundation Press, 1974), p. 40.

37. See James E. Cavanaugh, "A New Emphasis in Recruit Training," *Police,* January-February 1968, pp. 32–36, and statement by G. L. Kuchel, "Number One Problem," *Police Chief* 37 (August 1970): 17.

38. See Harold Berg, "Training on Patrol—A Top Program," *Police Chief* 41 (November 1974): 28.

39. National Advisory Commission on Criminal Justice Standards and Goals, *Police* (Washington, D.C.: U.S. Government Printing Office, 1973), p. 117.

40. Robert Wasserman, Michael P. Gardner, and Alana S. Cohen, *Improving Police Community Relations* (Washington, D.C.: U.S. Government Printing Office, June 1973), p. 1.

41. For example, see Louis A. Radelet, *The Police and the Community* (Encino, Calif.: Glencoe, 1973), p. 615, and *Improving Police Community Relations,* p. 9.

42. Bernard J. Clark, "Police-Community Relations," in Alvin W. Cohn and Emilo C. Viano, eds., *Police-Community Relations: Images, Roles, Realities* (Philadelphia: Lippincott, 1976), pp. 70–76.

43. Wasserman, Gardner, and Cohen, *Improving Police Community Relations,* pp. 3–4.

44. Eastman, *Municipal Police Administration,* pp. 203–204.

45. Ibid., p. 25.

46. See U.S. Bureau of Prisons, *The Jail: Its Operation and Management* (Washington, D.C.: U.S. Government Printing Office, n.d.).

47. Wilson and McLaren, *Police Administration,* p. 531.

7
CURRENT ISSUES
AND TRENDS

1. What organizational changes have been occurring in law enforcement?
2. How has affirmative action affected police agencies?
3. What are the reasons for police corruption?
4. To be more effective should police agencies be consolidated or decentralized?
5. Are college-based police training programs desirable?
6. How important is private security and what are the areas of specialization within private security?

These are some of the questions this chapter will answer.

The decade from 1966 to 1976 probably brought more fundamental and far-reaching changes for the police service in America than had occurred in the entire preceding century. The magnitude of the changes and the brief span of time in which they took place are particularly noteworthy. In the past, change in law enforcement operations and philosophy was very slow, so slow in fact that it was almost imperceptible, even to close observers.

In the past the police would point to such examples of innovation and change as the adoption of the automobile or two-way communications systems. These, however, were merely technological advances superimposed on old traditions, practices, and philosophies. Today it is these traditions, practices, and philosophies that are the immediate targets of change.

Traditionally, the police have been very slow to change. When change has occurred, it has usually been brought about by such *external* sources as the courts or reform groups, rather than by the police themselves. Although these outside influences have brought about many needed reforms in the police service, such changes, because they are externally rather than internally induced, have too often been temporary in nature. As a result, once external pressures relax, change has a tendency to decelerate rapidly.

At the present time, however, these pressures do not seem to be diminishing. Rather, they seem to be remaining constant. But they are being exerted in new areas. One area of change has been in the organizational structure of police departments. Another was the result of the demand during the 1960s for more effective police-community relations. A secondary effect of this demand was that affirmative action programs were started in order to bring about better representation of minorities and women in police work. Concern over the apparent inability of the police to cope with crime has resulted in more attention to crime prevention programs. Also, as the cost of law enforcement has increased, communities have demanded more cost-effective police operations. In this chapter, current issues such as police organization, affirmative action, crime prevention, and police corruption are reviewed. Trends such as conflict management strategies, consolidation and decentralization, and the increase in the use of police security forces are also examined.

Generally, an observer of the American police service would be pleased with the changes that have occurred in the past 20 years. Perhaps more than any other component of the criminal justice system, the police have demonstrated the capacity to change and to improve. Although this is certainly not true of all police operations, great strides have been made in upgrading police services and police personnel. Particularly, with the improvement in police management, new advances are being made in the use of police resources, and, as a result, a better understanding of their role in a democratic society is occurring.

ORGANIZATIONAL CHANGES

Traditionally, the police have relied upon a semimilitary model of organization. The military model, with its emphasis upon superior-subordinate relationships, rank structure, discipline, and defined areas of accountability, was supposed to provide the necessary control and supervision over police practices. It was felt that this organizational model was most appropriate for several reasons: (1) the police, like the military, have a practical monopoly on the legal use of force in our society; (2) our English heritage and the perennial fear that if the police were not closely controlled, they might threaten civil liberties; and (3) our experiences during the nineteenth century where in too many cases police personnel themselves operated with impunity in their relations with society and toward the commands of their superiors.

Whatever advantages the military model may have had in bringing some form of order and control to the police service, recent years and a growing body of evidence have increasingly demonstrated that the model has many major drawbacks. In the first place, it encouraged rigid bureaucratic behavior. It has been criticized for creating an authoritarianism in police agencies that is perhaps dysfunctional given the changing role of police today.[1] Rather than encouraging closer community-police interaction, the militaristic model has perpetuated a distance between the police and the public by the wearing of militaristic uniforms, visible rank and insignia of authority, and the use of technology (e.g., motorized patrol). It has certainly encouraged citizens to treat the average police officer more as a symbol than as an individual.[2]

It also seems that new officers are often "depersonalized" by being required to wear uniforms and to suppress individual opinion in favor of assuming what is essentially a uniform personality molded by the department. It does not end here. In fact, in many police agencies, new recruits soon learn that they are rewarded for conformity and for nonthinking compliance with departmental directives and may be severely reprimanded or punished for minor infractions.

In this environment, the "go-along to get along" people are rewarded. However, this blind adherence to traditional police dogma is becoming more irritating to the growing numbers of college-educated police officers. Although police agencies have been getting an increasing proportion of better educated young people into their ranks, they still tend to demand the same conformance. As a result, too many young, well-educated, and highly motivated men and women are leaving police departments.

Today, some police agencies are attempting to correct these organizational problems by making three basic changes: (1) reorganizing the department so that police officers are more involved with the community; (2) involving police personnel more with the policy-making process of the department; and (3) involving police officers in expanded areas of personal responsibility in an effort to increase their job satisfaction.[3]

Job Enlargement

The emphasis on increasing job satisfaction has often led to some interesting experiments in organizational change. Under job-enlargement opportunities such as exist in Baltimore, Cincinnati, and Kansas City, police officers in the patrol unit are given the chance to conduct criminal investigations and participate in the organization and development of community crime prevention and other programs that under traditional police organization would be the province of specialist units. Baltimore, for example, has a police agent program in which college-educated police personnel can expect to become police agents after a few years on routine patrol. The police agent is somewhat of a "supercop" who is expected to handle difficult investigations, perform operations research and planning, and be involved in the development of community programs and other more demanding (and rewarding) aspects of police work.

Neighborhood Team Policing

One of the most widely publicized forms of organizational change has been the development of *neighborhood team policing.* This concept developed in England and Scotland a few years after World War II but only recently has become widely accepted by American police administrators. Neighborhood team policing aims at the decentralization of police departments so that police personnel can become more responsive to neighborhood concerns.[4] Although the traditional precinct or district stations are also a form of police decentralization, they are significantly different from neighborhood team policing, which breaks up relatively large divisions or precincts into teams of 20 to 40 police officers and police command personnel. A team commander is responsible and accountable for the effectiveness of the team. Assigned to a specific neighborhood that contains from 12,000 to 35,000 residents, and business people, the team's duties are to control crime, improve community relations, and provide all routine police services on a 24-hour basis.

The neighborhood team is given a number of specific responsibilities and a unique method of organization to carry out its duties. The first emphasis is on indigenous planning—that is, the entire team and the community are encouraged to cooperate in planning. Team commanders are urged to be innovative in developing specific programs and police strategies for the neighborhood. This form of planning is far different from that found in traditional police organizations.

In developing its methods of operation, the team first surveys the area in order to become familiar with the neighborhood and its residents and to determine available neighborhood resources that may prove to be helpful. As greater rapport between the police and the community is established, traditional hostilities and suspicion are lessened. When this occurs, the residents become the "eyes and ears" of the police team. Without this community involvement, the police could not be nearly as effective in their crime prevention, crime control, and apprehension strategies.

Another feature of team policing is the idea of job enlargement and specialist integration. The team is responsible for carrying out most of the police tasks that traditionally have been given to specialized units. For example, the team performs all traffic functions within its neighborhood, and conducts and follows up on most crime investigations. This permits team members to gain experience in a full-range of police activities. Normally, when this program is implemented, former specialists (detectives, traffic investigators, analysts, etc.) are assigned as members of the team. By working within the team and interacting closely with other team members, the specialists can pass on their expertise. In most police agencies this exchange of skills among specialized units is almost nonexistent.

In the final analysis, team policing attempts to offer the usual advantages of small town law enforcement services while capitalizing on the available resources in a large police department. It is usually most applicable to larger cities or medium-sized communities which have identifiable ethnic and minority group neighborhoods. To date, this concept, or some version of it, has been or is being utilized in Albany, New York; St. Petersburg, Florida; the Venice division of the Los Angles Police Department; Oxnard, California; Cincinnati, Ohio; and other cities.

The Affirmative Action Issue

The issue of discrimination in the personnel policies of police departments and the affirmative action programs that have been used to attract minorities have created a great deal of concern in the past few years. Increasingly, police agencies are finding themselves involved in litigation over their traditional hiring, promotion, and dismissal policies. The basic issue is whether police agencies have practiced discrimination in their personnel policies of the past and are continuing to do so.

Background Information   A logical starting point in understanding the history of the affirmative action programs is the Civil Rights Act of 1964.[5] Title VII of this act prohibits discriminatory employment practices. On March 8, 1971, the U.S. Supreme Court issued a landmark decision in *Griggs* v. *Duke Power Company.*[6] This was a suit brought by a group of minority employees of Duke Power Company who alleged that the firm was in violation of the Civil Rights Act of 1964 because the company by requiring high school diplomas and the passing of a standard intelligence test for employment and promotion was discriminating against minorities. The court held that intelligence tests and requirements were discriminatory *unless they could be shown to measure the attributes needed to perform the specific job.*

The Equal Employment Opportunity Act of 1972 supersedes the 1964 Civil Rights Act, and this legislation has been extended to state and local governments.[7] The federal Equal Employment Opportunities Commission (EEOC) was created to oversee the enforcement of the act, and various states have created their own fair employment practices commissions.

In recent years, suits and countersuits involving the police have sprung up all over the country. In a number of court cases minority groups have been successful in having police employment examinations ruled discriminatory. In addition, such long-standing police requirements for employment as age, height, weight, sex, arrest record, and other factors have also been successfully challenged in the courts.[8] Unfortunately, the effects of personnel selection have sometimes been negative. For example, the EEOC ruled that the preemployment requirement of a college education by the Arlington, Virginia, police department was discriminatory.[9] The Connecticut State Police, along with many other police agencies, has been forced to lower the minimum age to 18, change the height and weight requirements, and eliminate the need for a high school diploma.

Discrimination in Hiring Practices   How discriminatory have police practices been in the past in regard to the hiring of minority males and all females? Some indication can be obtained from a 1973 study of police personnel practices conducted by the International Association of Chiefs of Police and the Police Foundation.[10] In this study, 493 of the largest state, county, and city police departments in the country were contacted about their personnel policies. Overall, minority males (Blacks, Spanish-surnames, Orientals, Indians, etc.) together with all women totaled about 4 percent of all sworn police personnel in these departments.[11] A later study conducted in 1975, indicated that about 7 percent of the nation's patrol officers were black and about 4 percent were women. Persons of Asian, Mexican, and Indian descent accounted for only a very small fraction of the total police personnel. No new nationwide compilation has been made since.[12]

The situation, however, is improving. Much of the argument against women, for example, has centered on the idea that they were incapable of performing the physical tasks that are required in police work. Studies conducted of female police officers in Washington, D.C., and in the New York City police department found some interesting facts. Generally, women performed as well as men even when dealing with citizens who were dangerous, angry, upset, drunk, or violent. Men were likely to be slightly more aggressive which resulted in more police-initiated contacts, arrests, and traffic citations. Women, as shown in the Washington, D.C. study were less likely to be involved in behavior that necessitated departmental disciplinary action. In New York, the public felt that the women officers were more competent, pleasant, and respectful than their male counterparts. In most of the other measures used to judge police performance, men and women officers performed similarly.[13]

Discrimination in Promotional Practices   Turning to the issue of promotional opportunities for minority males and all females, the picture is worse. Of the 493 agencies surveyed in the 1973 study, 243 indicated that they employed minority male police officers in command or supervisory positions. Table 7-1 shows the distribution of minority male command or supervisory personnel in these 243 large police agencies. Only 94 of the 493 agencies surveyed indicated that they employed females in command or supervisory positions. Table 7-2 indicates their distribution among the 94 police agencies. Minority males and all women seem to have enjoyed limited promotional opportunities in law enforcement in the past, particularly at the higher command levels.

The issue of the appropriate criteria for promotions is a troublesome one. Typically in the police service, written examinations, proficiency scores, oral interviews, and in some cases "politics" play a role in determining promotions. Particularly strong emphasis has been placed on the scores from written promotional examinations, yet too often this measures academic knowledge and test-taking abilities rather than applied supervisory or managerial talents.[14]

TABLE 7-1

Distribution of Minority Male Command or Supervisory Personnel in 243 Large State, County, and Local Police Agencies

RANK	TOTAL NUMBER	PER AGENCY
Corporal	131	.5
Sergeant	855	3.6
Detective	613	2.6
Lieutenant	230	1.0
Captain	92	.4
Major	20	.1
Deputy/Director	20	.1
Chief	7	.0
Other	18	.1
Total	1,986	8.4

Source: Terry Eisenberg, Deborah A. Kent and Charles R. Wall, *Police Personnel Practices in State and Local Governments* (Washington, D.C.: Police Foundation, December 1973):34 (adopted with permission).

TABLE 7-2

Distribution of Females in Command or Supervisory Personnel Among 94 Large State, County, and Local Police Agencies

RANK	TOTAL NUMBER	PER AGENCY AVERAGE
Corporal	7	.1
Sergeant	139	1.5
Detective	118	1.3
Lieutenant	28	.3
Captain	6	.1
Major	0	.0
Chief	0	.0
Other	6	.1
Total	304	3.4

Source: Terry Eisenberg, Deborah Kent, and Charles R. Wall, *Police Personnel in State and Local Governments,* © 1973, p. 36. Reprinted by permission of the International Association of Chiefs of Police and Police Foundation.

Recently, police departments in a number of cities such as New York City and Los Angeles have been attempting to develop alternative assessment programs modeled after promotional procedures developed by the Office of Strategic Services during World War II and used by a number of large private corporations in their search for managerial talent. These assessment programs rely on extensive analyses of the job to be performed, psychological tests to measure the qualities needed as a supervisor or manager, and situational tests. In situational tests, the applicant for promotion is given a number of hypothetical management problems related to police work and is judged by how well he or she handles the problems. These tests, which are conducted and evaluated by high-level police managerial personnel and management specialists, are structured to test such managerial requirements as decision-making skills, planning and organizing abilities, knowledge, initiative, and other important considerations.[15]

Future Personnel Practices The entire area of personnel practices, particularly in relation to employment, is far from settled. Many police agencies are making significant efforts to recruit minority personnel with varying degrees of success. Some of the major problems in these recruiting efforts are brought about by the general hostility of many minorities toward the police. Another problem faced by the state police and to a lesser degree some county police agencies is the reluctance of qualified minorities to leave their homes in urban areas to serve in rural state police or county posts. There is also the problem of attracting and retaining qualified minority personnel because they are now in demand by private firms offering higher salaries and other considerations as an inducement. Furthermore, these recruiting efforts are often opposed by existing police officers who do not feel that women are capable of becoming police personnel and who view affirmative action programs as operating under a dual standard that accepts less-qualified minorities at the exclusion of whites. How these issues will be settled, nobody knows. What is obvious is that women and racial minorities will almost certainly enjoy increasing opportunities for careers in law enforcement in the years ahead.

CRIME PREVENTION

In the preceding chapter, it was noted that more and more police agencies today are stressing general crime prevention programs in lieu of police-community relations efforts. The two are not necessarily at odds, however. Crime prevention programs are, in fact, a form of police-community relations. But problems often arise when the police view their crime prevention efforts as all that is required of them in police-community relations.

Today, crime prevention efforts and programs are quite popular in the criminal justice literature. Yet crime prevention is nothing new; what is new, is the recognition that in order for crime prevention programs to be effective they must involve both the police and the community, in a cooperative venture.

One of the positive by-products of the emphasis on crime prevention programs is the restructuring of police organizations so that there is greater interaction with the public. In turn, this interaction seems to foster better understanding by the police of the community and vice versa.[16]

Understanding the Concept of Crime Prevention

Both as a concept and as active programs, crime prevention rests on certain established premises. First, there is no single explanation for the causes of crime. Social scientists have cited such factors as economic instability, a history of family problems, limited opportunities for legitimate access to economic goods and services, deviant peer group influences, and personal susceptibility to narcotics addiction as a few of the factors that underlie crime in this country. Such factors demonstrate a few key points: first, it has not been possible to isolate and identify the specific factor(s) responsible for crime. Second, even if they could be identified, the correction of these "social ills" is far beyond the present ability of society to remedy. Third, the police themselves have very little impact on the broad social problems that may underlie crime.

What this suggests is that society is faced with certain conditions that are so broad and encompassing that they reject any meaningful solution short of drastic measures and repression that are intolerable to a free society. Instead, what must be done is for each member of society to assume a larger role which, through collective action, can remedy some of the crime-producing problems; this expanded responsibility should also serve to control the behaviors of those who without certain externally imposed controls would continue to prey on society. This latter idea is based on the concept that in many instances the act of committing a crime results from two things: (1) the *desire* to commit the crime; and (2) the *opportunity* to do so. Because it is often very difficult to remove the desire, through collective action it should be possible to limit the opportunity. Although it is not possible to list all the existing crime prevention programs, a few of the more popular and widespread programs are listed here:[17]

- Operation identification: the inscribing of items of personal property with identifiable markings.

- Residential, commercial, and industrial security inspection: the inspection of these structures with the goal of improving security devices (locks, lights, etc.).

- Neighborhood alert: the involvement of neighborhood groups in conducting security inspections, watching for suspicious persons and activities, etc.

- Block clubs and block groups: these are similar to the neighborhood alert program except that they are usually more organized and have regular activities. For example, the formation and use of members to patrol the neighborhood on a regular basis.

- Physical planning programs: the design or redesign of structures and architectural arrangements to provide better security.

- Various senior-citizen related programs: special programs to reduce victimization among these groups (e.g., escort services, programs on how to avoid fraud and confidence game activities, and so forth).

THE RISING CONCERN OVER POLICE PRODUCTIVITY

Increasingly, police departments are being held accountable for the costs of their services. The public is no longer willing to accept police excuses for not being more effective in controlling crime nor for demands for increased personnel and other resources as long as police are unable to demonstrate that the phenomenal increase in the cost of police services has had a substantial impact on the well-being of the community. At the municipal level of government alone, costs of police service have increased from $5.5 billion in 1972 to an estimated $10.3 billion in 1978.[18] It would seem that a day of public reckoning is fast arriving. For example, in August 1975, the mayor of San Francisco without the approval of the city council capitulated to police salary demands that would cost the city an additional $21 million. According to the *Washington Post*, "the police merely walked off the job, then violated a court order to return to work, allegedly performed acts of sabotage, and walked

TABLE 7-3

Some Recommended Measures of Police Productivity

POLICE FUNCTION BEING MEASURED	MEASURE EMPLOYED
Police patrol operations	1. Number of patrol officers assigned to street patrol in terms of total patrol officers.
	2. Work-hours of patrol time spent on activities contributing to patrol objectives in terms of total patrol work-hours.
	3. Number of calls of a given type and response time for answering these calls.
	4. Arrests resulting from patrol which survive the first judicial screening.
	5. Felony arrests from patrol surviving the first judicial screening.
	6. Arrests (felonies and misdemeanors) which result in convictions.
Provision of noncrime services	1. Number of noncrime calls for service which are satisfactorily responded to in terms of work-hours devoted to noncrime service calls.
	2. Medical emergency calls that emergency room personnel evaluate as having received appropriate first aid.
Human resource management	1. Number of disciplinary charges filed and number substantiated in terms of total departmental personnel.
	2. Number of work-hours lost during the year due to illness, injury, or disciplinary action.
Miscellaneous considerations	1. Population served per police employee and per dollar.
	2. Crime rates and changes in crime rates for reported crimes (relative to dollars or employees per capita).
	3. Clearance rates of reported crimes (relative to dollars or employees per capita).
	4. Arrests per police department employee and per dollar.
	5. Crime rates including estimates of unreported crimes based on victimization studies.
	6. Clearance rates including estimates of unreported crimes based on victimization studies.
	7. Percent of crimes solved in less than x days.
	8. Percent of population indicating a lack of feeling of security.
	9. Percent of population expressing dissatisfaction with police services.

Sources: The National Commission on Productivity, *Opportunities for Improving Productivity in Police Services* (Washington, D.C.: National Commission on Productivity, 1973), pp. 14–28, 49–52; and The Urban Institute, *The Challenge of Productivity Diversity: Improving Local Government Productivity Measurement and Evaluation, Part III, Measuring Police-Crime Control Productivity* (Washington, D.C.: The Urban Institute, June 1972).

picket lines armed with revolvers."[19] This same paper called it "a major skir-mish in the nationwide struggle by cities for financial survival." Often, the result of such police action leads to increased hostility on the part of citizens toward their police.

The problem is not whether there is a need to develop ways to measure police productivity, but how to measure police service in any meaningful and quantifiable way. Traditionally, the police have relied on official crime statis-tics as an indicator of their efficiency. Such statistics are unreliable and do not reflect other, more time-consuming tasks that the police perform. In spite of these limitations, it is reported that former President Nixon used to summon the chief of the Washington, D.C., police to the Oval Office to re-view the previous month's crime reports as an index of that department's performance.[20]

Special research institutes such as the Police Foundation and the Urban Institute are now studying ways that might be used to measure police pro-ductivity. They have identified certain "levels of concern," among which are:

- The productivity of an individual police officer.
- The productivity of police units (e.g., shifts, police districts, neighbor-hood team policing units, or precincts).
- The productivity of particular kinds of units, such as motorized police, foot patrols, investigative units, tactical forces, canine corps, etc.
- The productivity of the police department as a whole.
- The productivity of the crime control system, including both police ac-tivities and private activities to reduce crime.
- The productivity of the total community criminal justice system, includ-ing the police, the courts, the prosecutor's office, corrections and social service agencies, and private sector crime prevention activities (such as use of locks, watchdogs, etc.)[21]

Although it is not possible to examine all the measures developed to mea-sure police productivity, Table 7-3 indicates some that might be applied. The effective measurement of police services, however, will not occur overnight. Like other public service agencies, the police perform functions that almost defy quantitative measurement. This problem is compounded by the fact that where public safety is an issue, tolerances for misjudgments are very limited and the case for an insurance margin most compelling.

POLICE CORRUPTION

"Nothing undermines public confidence in the police and in the process of criminal justice more than the illegal acts of (police) officers." Such was the opinion of the President's Commission on Law Enforcement and Administra-tion of Justice in its 1967 report on the police.[22] In spite of law enforcement's improvements in the past decade, the police establishment in America is still troubled. During the past 25 years fundamental doubts concerning the credi-bility of police have arisen through a series of social, political, and judicial challenges.[23] Although they were only occasional subjects of concern in the past, police policy and practice are now under constant scrutiny. In fact, problems of police corruption and malfeasance are just now being studied seriously.[24]

Although police in such areas as New York, Chicago, Denver, Philadelphia, and Detroit receive the major publicity when police corruption is uncovered, the problems of corruption have infiltrated law enforcement agencies of all sizes, regions, and at all levels of government. Generally, police corruption falls into two categories: (1) corruption of authority; and (2) opportunistic corruption. In spite of an overlap, these two areas provide a general framework for categorizing forms of the problem.

Corruption of Authority

Corruption of authority emanates from the broad discretion police have in much of their work and the tension between efficiency standards versus the activities that must insure due process.[25] Corruption of authority can take many forms. It might be the receipt of unearned material gained by virtue of the position of police officer, such as free meals, liquor, police discounts on merchandise, commercial sex, and free admission to entertainment. Other examples of corruption of authority are discriminating practices in the enforcement of criminal laws; abuses in search and seizure, interrogation, and other due process requirements; illicit methods of gathering information; and the use of corporal punishment and deadly force.

Opportunistic Corruption

Opportunistic police corruption would include such police practices as kickbacks, opportunistic theft from arrestees, victims, crime scenes, and unprotected property; shakedowns; protection of illegal activities; the "fix" (e.g., quashing criminal prosecutions or taking care of traffic tickets) criminal activities; and, internal pay-offs.[26]

REASONS FOR CORRUPTION

Why do police personnel become corrupt? One might say, simply, greed and the opportunity to satisfy greed with little chance of being caught and punished. But such an answer, though true, does not explain everything about corruption. It fails to explain, for example, forms of police corruption such as acts of brutality or violations of due process in which no pay-off is received.

Nor does the old idea of a few corrupt individual police officers, so-called rotten apples, stand up under scrutiny. It is a partial answer but not a total one. A better explanation might be to see police misconduct as a form of group behavior in which police act the way they do because of a prevailing norm system within the police organization, or among their fellow officers, which permits (perhaps even condones) various degrees of corruption and deviance. In the 1972 Knapp Commission Report on police corruption in New York City, the commission said:

A fundamental conclusion at which the Commission has arrived is that the problem of police corruption cannot—as it is usually asserted—be met by seeking out the few "rotten apples" whose supposedly atypical conduct is claimed to sully the reputation of an otherwise innocent Department. The Commission is persuaded that the climate of the Department is inhospitable to attempts to uncover acts of corruption, and protective of those who are corrupt. The consequence is that the rookie who comes into the Department is faced with the situation where it is easier for him to become corrupt than to remain honest.[27]

Police cover-ups of such practices have been widely documented in recent years.[28] Why do such practices exist? In the first place, some police organizations are simply reluctant to expose and publicly punish their own members for violations that would sully the law-abiding members of the organization. Albert Deutsch found the use of cover-up tactics commonplace among law enforcement officers, particularly police chiefs, who are personally untainted by corruption.[29] Guilty officers may be secretly tried, warned, or punished, transferred to another department unit or assignment, permitted to resign in lieu of dismissal and/or prosecution.[30] The problem in handling such matters in this way is that it might even support corrupt behavior. For instance, an officer may weigh the risk of such light sanctions against the possible gain that the inappropriate behavior might offer.[31]

Corruption persists, too, to some degree because of the very nature of police organizations. The environment of many police departments tends to nurture a secretive and conforming subculture among its members. Those who do not conform are quickly and rigidly ostracized. Thus, this threat of being viewed as an outsider further reinforces organizational solidarity and a "me-against-them" attitude.

What can be done to combat police corruption and misbehavior? This subject has been widely discussed in the past several years. Special government study commissions, professional police associations, and other groups have provided insight into such factors as peer group influence, poor administration and supervision, inadequate salaries and working conditions, the vulnerability of the police to corrupting influences, and inadequate selection, training, and retention of police personnel as particularly troublesome areas that underlie much of the problems that lead to and perpetuate police corruption.

As police become more professional—as indeed they are—many of these factors will be ameliorated. This, together with a more vigilant public, gives every indication that, although the problem will not completely disappear, it probably will be drastically reduced in the years ahead.

CONFLICT MANAGEMENT STRATEGIES

By the very nature of their occupation, police personnel are called upon to intervene in situations of actual or potential violence. From the years 1967 to 1976, 20 percent of all police officers killed in the line of duty died while responding to such disturbance calls as family quarrels, individuals with a gun, or the handling of mentally deranged persons. These same type circumstances led to even higher rates of assaults on police officers.[32] The management of interpersonal conflict is not only one of the most hazardous assignments but also probably the most time-consuming aspect of the police function. For example, one study monitored telephone calls to the Syracuse, New York, Police Department and found that almost 20 percent of them concerned disputes in public and private places and among family members, neighbors, and total strangers.[33] The police departments of Kansas City, Missouri; Dallas, Texas; Cambridge, Massachusetts; and New York City report similarly high percentages of time allocated to situations involving interpersonal conflict.

In the last few years large numbers of police agencies have sought ways to alleviate this problem by training their personnel in techniques of *crisis intervention* to protect themselves and to prevent injury to others. Social scientists trained in techniques of behavior analysis and control have been conducting intensive programs for police personnel to help them handle potentially violent situations.[34]

Crisis-management services usually take two forms: (1) the *generalist-specialist* model; and (2) the *generalist* model.[35] In the generalist-specialist model, used by a number of very large municipal police agencies, a selected group of general patrol officers handle all family disturbance and related calls in a specified area. These officers operate in uniform and on all tours of duty on a 24-hour basis. When not engaged in the management of disturbances, they provide general patrol services in an assigned area. This model has some noted advantages. The special group of police officers who handle crisis calls can be trained extensively in conflict-management techniques, a practice that would not be feasible for all personnel in the department. The special group also can develop greater awareness of existing social agencies and their programs and thus can properly refer people in need of help to such agencies. Lastly, these specialists can be chosen because of their demonstrated abilities and willingness to handle conflict situations.

The generalist model is better suited to small police agencies that cannot support specialists in this area. In this model, all patrol personnel are given at least limited training in handling potentially dangerous encounters, and they all handle these situations along with their other responsibilities.

THE POLICE CONSOLIDATION/DECENTRALIZATION ISSUE

Since World War II, certain developments have taken place among local governments throughout the United States, particularly in metropolitan areas. First, urbanization has occurred at a phenomenal rate, creating unusual problems in governmental management, increased demand for urban services, and problems in social adjustment. Second, numerous communities have incorporated to avoid annexation to central cities, provide tax relief, or achieve other purposes, thus creating significant problems such as overlapping and fragmented jurisdictions. Third, many cities have found themselves unable to provide adequate urban services because of financial limitations. Finally, the antiquated governmental framework found in most counties does not allow for effective responses by counties to urban problems. For example, metropolitan areas in the Midwest and the Far West often contain more than 100 separate governments; in some of our largest metropolitan areas, the picture is even worse. The metropolitan area of Chicago has 1,113 governments, Philadelphia has 876, Pittsburgh has 704, and New York has 551.[36]

Many of these local units of government in metropolitan areas maintain their own police departments. For example, Figure 7-1 depicts the overlapping and fragmentation of police departments in metropolitan Detroit, where

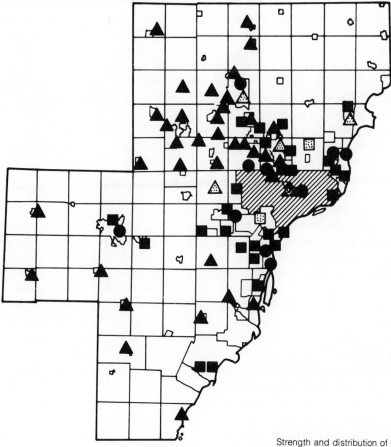

Strength and distribution of police agencies in the metropolitan Detroit region

Number of officers	Departments	Code
0-20	40	▲
21-50	27	■
51-100	10	●
101-150	5	◬
151-200	2	▨
201-5000	1	▨

Source: President's Commission on Law Enforcement and Administration of Justice, *Task Force Report: The Police* (Washington, D.C.: U.S. Government Printing Office, 1967), p. 69.

FIGURE 7-1 Fragmentation of Urban Police Departments in the Metropolitan Detroit Area

there are 85 police departments. Almost 78 percent of these local departments have less than 50 members, and nearly one-third have less than 20 members. The Detroit Police Department, which has 4,682 members, has more police personnel than all the rest of the 84 surrounding jurisdictions combined.

This fragmentation of police services has caused many study commissions, consultant groups, and scholars to recommend that police services in metropolitan areas be combined.[37] The President's Commission on Law Enforcement and the Administration of Justice states: "Each metropolitan area and each county should take action directed toward the pooling, or consolidation, of police services through the particular technique that will provide the most satisfactory law enforcement service and protection at the lowest cost."[38] Those who support consolidating police services in metropolitan areas point out that a large police department could provide better police service at a far lower cost than is required to maintain many small independent departments.

Since local governments are facing problems of financing police services, consolidation of police services will be a major proposed reform in the years ahead. But is total consolidation of police services the answer? There is evidence that it has not always lived up to the promises of the reformers. For example, research of consolidated government in Nashville-Davidson County, Tennessee, indicates that consolidation of Nashville with its contiguous suburbs actually increased drastically the costs of providing local governmental services.[39] When residents of the suburbs were also asked if they perceived any difference in police services after the consolidation, 58 percent said that services were the same and 8 percent thought that services were worse.[40] Others who have studied this question have concluded similarly. Citizens living in the suburbs of Cleveland and Detroit were very well satisfied with the services of their small, suburban police departments.[41]

In recent years, many community attempts to consolidate suburban police departments have been soundly defeated by the voters at the polls. A proposal to make the Erie County (Pennsylvania) Police Department the single law enforcement agency in the county was defeated by suburban residents in 24 out of 25 suburbs and all 16 villages in the surrounding area.[42] Several years ago, suburban voters in Dade County, Florida, recently voted against further consolidation of the police departments that serve the area. Suburban residents in Marion County, Indiana, strongly opposed merging their smaller police forces with the Indianapolis Police Department.[43]

Given these facts, it would seem that the consolidation of local police departments (and governments) in the forseeable future is not as likely to occur as some of its advocates indicate. As some researchers such as Ostrom and Canfield have shown, many communities want to maintain their own individual police departments.[44]

Consolidation of Support Services

A community's desire to maintain its own police agency probably will not preclude some forms of consolidation, such as the consolidation of staff and auxiliary services on a metropolitan or regional basis. For example, such services as centralized communication operations in a metropolitan area will continue to grow. In these types of operations, a central dispatcher receives all calls for police assistance in a particular geographical area and dispatches units from the various participating cities. This system has been demonstrated to be very effective in Genesee County, Michigan, where Flint and 20 surrounding cities participate in a centralized communication network.

Similarly, records, laboratories, training, and jail services lend themselves to consolidation efforts. For example, areawide records centers and communications centers are needed for effective and coordinated police operations in metropolitan areas where many police agencies serve essentially a common area. If certain basic police information is collected on an areawide basis according to common standards and forms and then integrated into an areawide records center, several advantages will result. First, inquiring jurisdictions need check only one source rather than several; this should eliminate duplication of effort and of physical facilities and greatly increase the speed with which an inquiry or search may be handled. Second, detailed crime analysis and planning studies could be conducted which may suggest, for example, more effective deployment of personnel in high-crime areas.[45]

Laboratory, training, and jail facilities might also be more appropriately handled on an areawide basis because of the prohibitive costs to individual units of government of providing and maintaining these services. Now that the states have enacted legislation requiring certain hours of training for police officers and have established legislation dealing with the maintenance and custody of jail facilities and prisoners, small cities must in many cases pool their resources to comply with these new standards.

Contract Law Enforcement

Another form of consolidation that has received a great deal of attention in recent years is contract law enforcement. Under this arrangement, small communities contract with the county or an adjacent city for police services. The most notable example of this kind of arrangement is the Lakewood Plan, in which the Los Angeles County Sheriff's Department provides police services to 29 incorporated cities within the county.[46] Under the Lakewood Plan, each city pays the L.A. Sheriff's Department an annual fee based on the police services wanted. Connecticut has also experimented with this idea through its Resident State Trooper Program. Under this arrangement, small towns can contract with the state police for a resident trooper to carry out all of the functions of police service.[47] However, like consolidation attempts in general, contract law enforcement has still not been widely adopted.

Special Squads

Another agreement that is becoming more common is one that provides for so-called metropolitan squads, major case squads, or metropolitan strike forces. Such agreements are made between police departments and, in many instances, are just informal agreements among police administrators to participate in a joint cooperative venture dealing with certain types of offenses. Since efforts to combat organized crime recognize no jurisdictional boundaries, many communities in a metropolitan area participate in an areawide investigative and intelligence-gathering group. Usually this special group is made up of representatives from each of the cooperating departments and it concentrates on certain crimes and offenders. In some cases, the county prosecutor's office is responsible for supervising and coordinating the activities of the group; in other cases, a command officer from one of the participating police departments is placed in charge. In many instances, this arrangement has worked quite well; in other areas, political problems concerning the designation of control over the group and accountability of its members have limited the effectiveness of such joint efforts.

COLLEGE-BASED POLICE TRAINING

A few states, notably California and Florida, have developed training programs for all police personnel in cooperation with their state junior college systems. Florida, for example, has turned over training responsibilities to certified community colleges; all police recruits must complete a stipulated period of training at one of these academic centers. Such cooperative undertakings permit the state to draw upon the resources available in community colleges. This approach also has the potential of alleviating a traditional police problem—isolation. In the past, the police trained their own personnel either formally or informally while on the job. Because of this, the police were neither exposed to new ideas nor were they inclined to examine their own thinking or the way they traditionally have operated. Even today, some old-time police officers question, "What can citizens who have no experience in police work tell me about policing?" The answer is: A great deal. In too many instances, the police officer sees situations only from his or her own viewpoint and does not understand how the public perceive police action. The police and the community need to discuss their attitudes about the police so that both groups have a better understanding of each others concerns and attitudes. Cooperative training ventures try to accomplish this goal.

There is another advantage in encouraging college-based police training programs. Many community colleges offer associate degree programs in police science or criminal justice, and faculty members in these programs often have extensive experience in law enforcement or other areas of the criminal justice system. These individuals can coordinate efforts of faculty specialists so that the educational experience can be more enriching for the student. In addition, they can develop contacts with resource people in the community who, as guest lecturers, can strengthen both the training program itself and the degree program offered by the college. Finally, it is hoped that these training programs will encourage participating police personnel to continue in their education and some day obtain a degree themselves.

This writer's discussions with training directors in Florida seem to indicate that many of the advantages discussed are being realized. Now, additional states are beginning to adopt such an approach. It would appear that the future will see increasing use of the college or university as an important component of recruit, in-service, supervisory, and managerial training programs for the police as well as for other agencies of the criminal justice system.

These are just some of the trends that point the way law enforcement agencies of the future are going. Other trends in such areas as collective bargaining, methods of recruitment and selection, career development, communication and information systems, lateral entry, and a host of other areas have potentially important consequences for the newly emerging police service in the United States.

PRIVATE SECURITY

Private security services fall into two general categories: (1) crime-related public and private security services; and (2) noncrime-related services such as privately sponsored fire and general safety programs and personnel-administration technology.[48] Fire and general safety programs provide preventive fire and safety services to private and public firms in light of such federal legislation as the Occupational Safety and Health Act, which requires that employers provide certain standards of health and safety for their employees. The area of personnel-administration security refers to programs designed to screen personnel to ensure their integrity and trustworthiness. The remainder of this section concentrates on both crime-related and noncrime-related public and private security services.

The Extent and Growth of Security Forces

Crime-related public and private security services absorb considerable resources. The most thorough examination of security forces in the United States arose from a five-volume study of the industry conducted by the Rand Corporation beginning in 1969 and sponsored by the National Institute of Law Enforcement and Criminal Justice of the Law Enforcement Assistance Administration. In 1969, over 800,000 people were security workers, and well over $8 billion was devoted to security services and equipment. One in every 100 persons in the civilian labor force was employed in security work, and over $40 per capita was spent on security.[49] About 36 percent of all security personnel were employed in the private sector and the remainder in governmental agencies at all levels of government. Between the years 1960 and 1969, it is estimated that expenditures for private security increased approximately 150 percent.[50] This is a phenomenal growth rate, and the past ten years have probably seen a similar increase.

One of the most common explanations for this tremendous growth in the growth of security forces is that the public increasingly feels that public law enforcement agencies are not capable of providing the kinds of services required. Although this may be part of the reason, most knowledgeable observers would include some or all of the following:

- Increasing business losses due to crime ($21.9 billion in 1977). (This U.S. Commerce estimate is based on estimates of loss from *conventional* crimes only—for example, robbery and burglary; it does not include such crimes as white-collar crime, shoplifting, and bad checks.)
- Insurers raising rates or refusing coverage so that security measures are used increasingly as a substitute for insurance.

- Insurers requiring the use of certain private security systems or granting premium discounts when certain private security measures are used.
- The federal government's need for security in its space and defense activities during the past decade, and more recently, the need for security against air hijackings, violent demonstrations, and bombings of government facilities.
- The basic business trend toward purchases of specialized services, which may contribute to the growth of the contract security forces.
- The nation's growth and advancing state of the art in electronics and other scientific areas, which has sparked new and distinct manufacturing branches of several protection companies, providing greatly improved security devices, especially for intrusion detection.
- The general increase in corporate and private income, which has resulted in more property to protect and, at the same time, more income to pay for protection.[51]

Areas of Specialization

There are basically six areas of security specialization, with, of course, some overlapping of functions and responsibilities.

Plant Protection Plant protection concerns the physical integrity of the property and the safety of employees in a particular industrial plant. It is concerned with such things as reducing operating costs of the firm by employing safety and theft-control measures, such as on-site inspection of company property, visible patrol and guardianship of property boundaries, inspection of employees as they leave the premises, and other similar activities.

It protects the safety of employees by programs of inspection of fire and safety equipment, lights, and fences, and by preventing access to the facility of persons or objects that are potentially hazardous from either a general safety or a crime-control viewpoint. Until World War II, this specialty constituted almost the entire security industry.

Security of Classified Information Safeguarding classified information developed as a specialty during World War II and has become of great concern in recent years. As technology has developed, the government has more and more turned to private firms for contract work in research and development. This has increased the need for security in these firms. For example, the development of atomic resources for use in nuclear reactors has tremendous implications. It is entirely conceivable that certain radical groups could obtain enough scientific data to construct crude yet effective atomic bombs which they could employ in terrorist activities against the U.S. government and the civilian populace.

Classified information security specialists are also increasingly being employed by firms concerned with protecting industrial intelligence. Firms wishing to protect their trade secrets have to be additionally concerned that their own employees or persons infiltrating their organization from the outside are not supplying their competitors with information that could seriously jeopardize their market position.

A very sensitive area of concern in industrial intelligence is computer security. As more and more firms employ data processing to store trade secrets, compile payroll information, and process credit accounts, the potential for theft, fraud, and sabotage of the computer system and all the firm's important records is very real.[52] One knowledgeable computer security specialist considers the threat so grievous "that if the facts were known how vulnerable business (and government) secrets are by virtue of the adoption and use of computers, corporation and government officials might even conceivably not employ their usage."[53]

Physical Security Physical security is concerned with certain technical and managerial questions. For example, physical security specialists survey and inspect facilities and make recommendations for ways to improve security measures. Is it more economical, for instance, to use electronic intrusion devices such as alarm systems, closed-circuit TV, and scanners to provide physical security rather than to employ a uniformed guard force? Because technical developments in the field of electronic intrusion devices are very rapid and the operation of such devices requires increasing technical knowledge, the physical security specialist is expected to have a broad knowledge of the applications and operations of these devices and how to operate them.

Personnel Security Personnel security deals with the question of quality control over personnel selections, promotions, and similar personnel matters. This is an extremely sensitive issue in today's society. The use of such standard techniques as lie-detector screening, background investigations, and similar inquiries creates concern. On the one hand, employers increasingly need to be assured that the people they employ are loyal and trustworthy—particularly those people in positions of trust who have access to sensitive information. On the other hand, individuals demand the right of privacy. Somehow, the rights of the individual must be judiciously balanced with the need to maintain appropriate security.

At the present time, there are no clear guidelines of appropriate safeguards in these areas. Although some states and the federal government have adopted legislation that prohibits the use of lie detectors for employment and the federal Fair Credit Reporting Act imposes standards of accuracy on private firms that regularly investigate and prepare preemployment, credit, and insurance reports, these provisions do not adequately cover the possible abuses of surreptitious electronic eavesdropping or questionable methods of investigating the backgrounds and habits of employees or candidates for positions of employment. In many cases, the aggrieved party has no recourse but to sue under the general tort law of the state.[54] Even these tort remedies are far from effective, and often the aggrieved party cannot afford the costs of such a suit.

Fire and Safety Security Fire and safety security is concerned with the inspection and engineering of fire and safety security measures. This, too, is a somewhat technical field that incorporates such areas as structural design and architecture, safety systems design, inspection, and testing. Fire and safety security specialists work closely with engineers, architects, and systems design personnel to develop, implement, and refine existing security devices. Since there are so few qualified individuals in this area, they often serve as consultants to private and governmental institutions concerned with fire and safety hazards.

Disaster Control and Defense Planning   Disaster control and defense planning specialists are responsible for developing disaster and defense plans for firms or governmental agencies. These specialists are concerned with both natural disasters and acts of war or sabotage directed at key industries or governmental complexes. World War II demonstrated that the destruction of military-related industrial concerns can severely hamper and even preclude the ability of a country to continue to wage war. As a consequence, contingency plans must be made to continue the production of necessary goods and services under the most extreme and adverse situations. Protection must extend not merely over the machinery and equipment, but also to the human beings upon whom the continued operations of industrial concerns and the government ultimately depend.

Education and Careers in Security

In 1974 the American Society for Industrial Security, a professional organization of security specialists, conducted a survey of institutions of higher education and found that 100 colleges and universities throughout the nation offered either a degree or course work in industrial security.[55] Some of the more typical courses in an industrial security program are:

- Introduction to security
- Protection of classified government information and business assets
- Civil disturbance and emergency planning
- Traffic and access control
- Security management
- Loss prevention in business, industry, and institutions
- Criminal evidence and procedure
- Issues and concerns in security law
- Investigative techniques

Students who major in security are also encouraged to take courses in business organization and management, accounting, data processing, and business and administrative law, as well as relevant courses in criminal justice.

SUMMARY

Until recently, police change has been quite slow. Under unremitting pressure, changes are now occurring in American law enforcement that will have meaningful future implications. Some of the more important changes are occurring in the traditional nature of the police organization itself. The old quasi-military model of police operations seems to be breaking down a bit. Faced with such changes as better-educated young officers seeking careers in law enforcement and the need to create more opportunities for job satisfaction, alternative police models are being considered. One of the most highly touted approaches is the team policing concept.

Another issue of current importance is affirmative action. Police personnel policies that have traditionally excluded females and minority group members are being changed. Increased opportunities for careers in the police service should open up for these groups in the future.

The police are also beginning to somewhat redefine their role. More and more emphasis is being placed on the preventive aspects of police work. This can be seen by the growing awareness of crime prevention strategies as an important aspect of police work.

Because of the financial problems that face many communities today, police productivity has also become an important issue. Increased emphasis is being placed on techniques to improve police productivity and to measure the effects of alternative police strategies.

The last issue—and one that has been around for many years—is the concern over police corruption. As more information is gained about police behavior and why corrupt practices flourish, better chances of combatting the problem exist.

There are also several other trends that should grow in importance in the years ahead. The first is the interest in developing effective conflict management capabilities for the police. It is also likely that greater efforts will be made to consolidate local police forces and to more fully develop college-based police training programs. The last trend discussed was the growing field of private security. Career opportunities and the need for private security personnel and programs are growing to augment public law enforcement efforts.

REVIEW QUESTIONS

1. What is the purpose of such programs as job enlargement and neighborhood team policing?

2. What is affirmative action? How are police agencies responding to it?

3. In attempting to improve the effectiveness of crime prevention, various programs have been initiated. Name six of these programs and explain their purpose.

4. What are two types of police corruption? Why is police corruption a continuing problem?

5. What is conflict management? What models are used in handling conflict situations?

6. What are the arguments for and against consolidation of metropolitan police services?

7. What advantages do college-based training programs offer for police personnel?

8. What are the two general categories of private security services?
9. Name the six areas of security specialization and briefly describe the functions of each.

DISCUSSION QUESTIONS

1. It is said in this chapter that police corruption will most likely never be totally eradicated. Do you agree with this statement?
2. Is consolidation of police services on a metropolitan or regional basis a good idea? Discuss the advantages and disadvantages.

SUGGESTED ADDITIONAL READINGS

Abrecht, M. E., and B. L. Stern. *Making of a Woman Cop.* New York: Morrow, 1976.

Bittner, Egon. *The Functions of the Police in Modern Society.* Washington, D.C., U.S. Government Printing Office, 1970.

International City Management Association, *Local Government Police Management* (Washington, D.C.: ICMA, 1977).

Ishak, S. T. *Consumer's Perception of Police Performance: Consolidation vs. Decentralization: The Case of Grand Rapids, Michigan Metropolitan Area.* Bloomington: Indiana University Press, 1972.

Jeffrey, C. Ray. *Crime Prevention through Environmental Design.* Beverly Hills, Calif: Sage, 1971.

Juris, Hervey A., and Peter Feville. *Police Unionism.* Lexington, Mass.: Lexington Books, 1973.

Kakalik, James, and S. Wildhorn. *The Private Police Industry,* Vols. 1–5. Washington, D.C.: U.S. Government Printing Office, February 1972.

Measuring Police-Crime Control Productivity. Part III of *The Challenge of Productivity Diversity—Improving Local Government Productivity Measurement and Evaluation,* prepared for the National Commission on Productivity by the Urban Institute. Washington, D.C.: National Technical Information Service, U.S. Department of Commerce (Document no. PB223117), 1972.

Ostrom, Elinor, and Roger B. Parks. "Suburban Police Departments: Too Many, To Small?" *Urban Affairs Annual Reviews,* Vol. 7. Beverly Hills, Calif.: Sage, 1973.

The Police Foundation, *Team Policing: Seven Case Studies.* Washington, D.C.: The Police Foundation, 1973.

U.S. Department of Justice: *Innovation in Law Enforcement.* Washington, D.C.: U.S. Government Printing Office, June 1973.

The Urban Institute: "Neighborhood Team Policing." Project report to LEAA. Washington, D.C.: The Urban Institute, 1973.

Washington, Brenda E. *Deployment of Female Police Officers in the United States.* Gaithersburg, Md.: International Association of Chiefs of Police, 1974.

Weisbord, Marvin R., Howard Lamb, and Allan Drexler. *Improving Police Department Management through Problem-Solving Task Forces*. Reading, Mass.: Addison-Wesley, 1974.

NOTES

1. For example, see Robert D. Pursley, "Traditional Police Organization: A Portent of Failure?" in William Bopp, ed., *Police Administration* (Boston: Holbrook, 1975), pp. 83–86; and Egon Bittner, *The Functions of the Police in Modern Society* (Washington, D.C.: U.S. Government Printing Office, 1970), especially Chap. VIII.

2. See Herman Goldstein, *Policing a Free Society* (Cambridge, Mass.: Ballinger, 1977), especially Chap. 10.

3. For example, see Tony Pate et al., *Kansas City Peer Review Panel: An Evaluation Report* (Washington, D.C.: Police Foundation, 1976).

4. This description of team policing was adapted from Peter B. Bloch and David Specht, *Neighborhood Team Policing* (Washington, D.C.: LEAA, December 1973).

5. 42 U.S.C.A. 2000, et seq.

6. *Griggs* v. *Duke Power Company*, 915 Sup. Ct. 849 (1971).

7. Pub. L. No. 92–261.

8. For example, see *Morrow* v. *Crisler*, Civil Action No. 4716, U.S. District Ct., S. Miss. (1971); *Smith* v. *East Cleveland*, 363 F. Supp. 1131 (1973); *Wilson* v. *City of Torrance*, Civil Action No. 74-963. U.S. District Ct., E. Ca. (1974).

9. Memo from the Washington Post, January 27, 1975.

10. Terry Eisenberg et al., *Police Personnel Practices in State and Local Government* (Washington, D.C.: Police Foundation, 1973).

11. Ibid., p. 35.

12. *U.S. News and World Report*, "Police Under Fire, Fighting Back," April 3, 1978, pp. 37–40.

13. See Peter B. Bloch and Deborah Anderson, *Policewoman on Patrol: Final Report* (Washington, D.C.: Police Foundation, 1974); and Joyce L. Sichel et al., *Women on Patrol: City* (Washington, D.C.: U.S. Government Printing Office, January 1978).

14. See Bejamin Shimberg and Robert DiGrazia, "Promotion" in O. Glenn Stahl and Richard A. Staufenberger, eds., *Police Personnel Administration* (Washington, D.C.: Police Foundation, 1974), pp. 101–124.

15. See Paul F. D'Arcy, "Assessment Center Program Helps Test Managerial Competence," *Police Chief* 41 (December 1974): 52–53.

16. See National League of Cities, *Community Crime Prevention and the Local Official* (Washington, D.C.: National League of Cities, 1974).

17. See California Council on Criminal Justice, *Selected Crime Prevention Programs in California* (Sacramento, Calif.: 1973).

18. U.S. Commerce Department, Economic Indicator in Government Services (mimeo) (Washington, D.C.: U.S. Department of Commerce, June 1978).

19. Leroy F. Aarons, "Police-Fire Strike Unnerves Other Cities" (Washington Post syndicated column), *The State Journal*, Lansing, Mich., August 26, 1976, A11.

20. Reported in Edward K. Hamilton, "Police Productivity: The View from City Hall," in Joan L. Wolfe and John F. Heaphy, eds., *Readings on Productivity in Policing* (Washington, D.C.: Police Foundation, 1975), p. 13.

21. Harry P. Hatry, "Wrestling with Police Crime Control Productivity Measurement," in ibid., p. 90.

22. The President's Commission on Law Enforcement and Administration of Justice, *Task Force Report: The Police* (Washington, D.C.: U.S. Government Printing Office, 1967), p. 208.

23. Allan N. Kornblum, *The Moral Hazards* (Lexington, Mass.: Lexington Books, 1976), p. 1.

24. See, for example, Douglas S. Drummond, *Police Culture* (Beverly Hills, Calif.: Sage, 1976); Herbert Biegel, *The Closed Fraternity of Police and the Development of the Corrupt Attitude* (New York: John Jay Press, 1978); Thomas Barker and Julian Roebuck, *An Empirical Typology of Police Corruption: A Study in Organizational Deviance* (Springfield, Ill.: Thomas, 1973); and Antony Simpson, *The Literature of Police Corruption,* vol. I (New York: John Jay Press, 1977).

25. Kornblum, *The Moral Hazards,* p. 2.

26. This "typology of corruption" is adopted from Barker and Roebuck, *An Impirical Typology of Police Corruption,* p. 21.

27. *The Knapp Commission Report on Police Corruption* (New York: Braziller, 1972).

28. For example, see Jerome H. Skonick, *Justice Without Trial: Law Enforcement in Democratic Society* (New York: Wiley, 1967); William W. Turner, *The Police Establishment* (New York: Putnam, 1968); William A. Westley, *Violence and the Police* (Cambridge, Mass.: MIT Press, 1970); and Albert Deutsch, *The Trouble with Cops* (Boston: Crown, 1955).

29. Deutsch, *The Trouble with Cops.*

30. Turner, *The Police Establishment,* p. 39.

31. Thomas Barker and Julian Roebuck, "Police Corruption as a Form of Organizational Deviance," Donal E. J. MacNamara and Marc Riedel, eds., *Police: Perspectives, Problems, Prospects* (New York: Praeger, 1974), pp. 5–12.

32. Federal Bureau of Investigation, *Uniform Crime Reports–1976* (Washington, D.C.: U.S. Government Printing Office), pp. 280–289.

33. E. Cummings, *Systems of Social Regulation* (New York: Atherton, 1968).

34. See Morton Bard, *Family Crisis Intervention: From Concept to Implementation* (Washington, D.C.: LEAA, December 1973).

35. Ibid., p. 9.

36. Advisory Commission on Intergovernmental Relations, *Urban America and the Federal System* (Washington, D.C.: U.S. Government Printing Office, 1969), pp. 75 and 117.

37. For example, see David L. Noorgard, *Regional Law Enforcement* (Chicago: Public Administration Service, 1969); Advisory Commission on Intergovernmental Relations, *State-Local Relations in the Criminal Justice System* (Washington, D.C.: U.S. Government Printing Office, 1971); Committee for Economic Development, *Reducing Crime and Assuring Justice* (New York: Committee for Economic Development, June 1972).

38. President's Commission on Law Enforcement and Administration of Justice, *Task Force Report: The Police* (Washington, D.C.: U.S. Government Printing Office, 1967), p. 308.

39. Elinor Ostrom and Roger B. Parks, "Suburban Police Departments: Too Many and Too Small?" in Louis H. Masotti and Jeffrey K. Hadden, eds., *The Urbanization of the Suburbs* (Beverly Hills, Calif.: Sage, 1973), Chap. XIV. An increase in the per capita costs of municipal services also occurred after the Ontario legislature created Toronto Metro; see H. Kaplan, *Urban Political Systems: A Functional Analysis of Metro Toronto* (New York: Columbia University Press, 1967).

40. Robert E. McArthur, *Impact of City-County Consolidation of the Rural-Urban Fringe: Nashville-Davidson County Tennessee* (Washington, D.C.: U.S. Government Printing Office, 1971), pp. 19–22.

41. See Adam Campbell and H. Schuman, "A Comparison of Black and White Attitudes and Experiences in the City," in C. H. Harr, ed., *The End of Innocence: A Suburban Reader* (Glenview, Ill.: Scott, Foresman, 1972), p. 109.

42. David L. Skoler and J. M. Hetler, "Government Restructuring and Criminal Administration: The Challenge of Consolidation," in *Crisis in Urban Government: A Symposium on Restructuring Metropolitan Urban Government* (Silver Spring, Md.: Thomas Jefferson Publishing, 1970), pp. 53–75.

43. Elinor R. Ostrom, Roger B. Parks, and Gordon P. Whitaker, "Do We Really Want to Consolidate Urban Police Forces? A Reappraisal of Some Old Assertions," *Public Administration Review,* October/November 1974, pp. 423–432.

44. For example, see Elinor R. Ostrom, "Community Public Services and Responsiveness: On the Design of Institutional Arrangements for the Provision of Police Services," paper presented at the American Political Science Association annual meeting, Chicago, August 29–September 2, 1974; and Roger B. Canfield, "Citizen Satisfaction and Police Effectiveness: Perspectives Beyond Productivity and Social Equity," paper presented at the 1974 National Conference of the American Society for Public Administration, Syracuse, N.Y., March 17–21, 1974.

45. Noorgard, *Regional Law Enforcement,* p. 24.

46. Letter from Gilbert E. Schollen, Los Angeles County Sheriff's Department, December 17, 1975.

47. James H. Ellis, "The Connecticut Resident State Police System," *Police* 5 (September-October 1960): 69–72.

48. The term *personnel-administration technology* is taken from Leon H. Weaver, "Security and Protection Systems," *Encyclopedia Brittanica,* 15th ed. (New York: Encylopedia Brittanica, 1974), p. 454.

49. James S. Kakalik and Sorrel Wildorn, *Private Police in the United States: Findings and Recommendations* (Washington, D.C.: U.S. Department of Justice, February 1972), p. 10.

50. Ibid., p. 13.

51. Ibid., p. 15.

52. For example, see Robert L. Taylor and Robert S. Fiengold, "Computer Data Protection," *Industrial Security,* August 1970; Leonard J. Krauss, "Safe Security Audit and Field Evaluation for Computer Facilities," *AMACON* 3, no. 1 (January 1972): 8–11; and William F. Brown, *AMR's Guide to Computer and Software Security* (New York: AMR International, 1972).

53. William E. Nye, "Computers: Our Achilles Heel?" *Business Automation,* August 1973, p. 23.

54. Tort law is the law that defines the general duties of citizens to each other and allows lawsuits to recover damages for the injury caused by one citizen's breach of such a duty.

55. Arthur A. Kingsbury, "Security Education," *Security Management,* September 1974.

PART 4

The Court

Trial by jury is the right of every citizen, guaranteed by Article 3 and the Sixth
Amendment of the U.S. Constitution. In a criminal trial, a jury usually
consists of twelve jurors who are randomly chosen from the local community.
The verdict of the jury must be unanimous.

As the arbiter of justice, the judge interprets the law, rules on motions, grants
or refuses bail, supervises the courtroom, advises the jury, and sentences
the guilty.

The prosecutor, or district attorney, charges the accused of a crime. In court the prosecutor's adversial role is to attempt to prove the guilt of the accused and to convince the jury of that guilt.

The chief duty of the defense attorney is to represent the client and win the case. The defense attorney attempts to refute the prosecutor's case through evidence, witnesses, or other means. Most important of all, the defense attorney must convince the jury of the defendant's innocence.

8
THE ROLE OF
THE COURT

Forsyth/Monkmeyer

1. What are the organizational characteristics of the U.S. courts?
2. How important have historical influences been on the U.S. court system?
3. What are the components of the state court system?
4. What are the components of the federal judiciary?

These are some of the questions this chapter will answer.

Situated between the police and the corrections component of the criminal justice system, the American system of courts plays perhaps the most important role in the administration of American justice—a role that has often been criticized for not being effectively fulfilled. An examination of the progress made in recent years by all the agencies of criminal justice would probably show that the courts have demonstrated the least progress and the least willingness to improve the ways in which they discharge their responsibilities.

This section first examines certain characteristics of the court system, its development, and present structure. Then the trial process, institutional arrangements, and court personnel are considered. Finally, an examination is made of the particular changes that courts are undergoing, and what recommendations are being made to improve the handling and disposition of criminal cases by our courts.

JUDICIAL ORGANIZATION

The organization of the American judicial system is characterized by the following features: (1) a dual system of courts; (2) an absence of supervisory control; (3) specialization; and (4) geographical organization.[1]

A Dual System of Courts

The court system in the United States is organized on the principle of political federalism. Although the first Congress, acting under the authority of the Constitution, established the federal court system, the states were permitted to establish their own court structures. In fact, most legal matters were left to the state courts. Only in recent years have the federal government and the federal courts begun to exercise increasing jurisdiction over crimes and civil matters. In this context, jurisdiction simply means the authority to enforce the laws and to try those who violate these laws. As a result of new federal legislation and broad interpretation of the power to regulate interstate commerce, the federal courts now have authority over 2,800 federal crimes.

Thus, a dual system of state and federal courts exists. In many instances, the state and federal courts have *concurrent jurisdiction* over specific crimes. For example, someone who robs a bank in California is in violation of the State of California Criminal Code as well as the U.S. Criminal Code, and could be brought to trial in either a state or federal court, or both.

Although being tried in both systems for the same crime can occur legally, it seldom does in reality. The local United States Attorney, following policies established by the U.S. Department of Justice, generally works out an agreement with local police and judicial authorities to decide on whether the federal government or the state will prosecute the case. In recent years, the Department of Justice has encouraged U.S. Attorneys to try the offender in the state courts and be sentenced to a state institution. If there is any confusion or disagreement over where the trial should be held, the determining factor is usually what jurisdiction made the arrest and maintains custody of the offender.

Federal Exclusionary Rule   Although in theory an individual could be tried in a state court, serve a sentence in a state institution, and then be subjected to the same process by the federal authorities, this situation rarely occurs. Normally, where concurrent jurisdiction exists, the federal authorities simply decline to prosecute. However, there have been notable exceptions. If the federal authorities feel that the state courts have rendered a serious miscarriage of justice (e.g., a major drug dealer receiving a 6-month sentence), the federal authorities may, with the approval of the U.S. Department of Justice, pursue an "independent interest" and prosecute the individual in federal court upon his or her release from the state authorities.

The implications of this dual legal system and court structure have had other significant implications for the administration of justice. For example, in 1914 in the case of *Weeks* v. *United States*,[2] the U.S. Supreme Court established the Federal Exclusionary Rule. Weeks was charged by federal agents with conducting a lottery in interstate commerce by use of the mails. He was arrested at his place of employment, and his residence was searched without the authority of a search warrant. During this search, incriminating evidence was found and was later introduced at his federal trial. On appeal to the U.S. Supreme Court, he alleged that this search was unlawful under the provisions of the Fourth Amendment. The Supreme Court agreed and established the Federal Exclusionary Rule, which held that evidence unlawfully obtained by federal agents in violation of an individual's constitutional rights could no longer be introduced into federal prosecutions. The Supreme Court, however, made it quite clear that this decision applied only to federal agents and federal courts and not to police officers or courts at the state level. This led to the famous "Silver Platter Doctrine." Since the Federal Exclusionary Rule prohibited only federal officers from illegally seizing evidence and introducing it into federal trials, nothing prevented state police officers from illegally searching for and seizing evidence and turning it over to the federal authorities on a "silver platter" for introduction into the federal courts. It was not until 1961 in the now famous *Mapp* v. *Ohio* case,[3] that the U.S. Supreme Court finally imposed the Federal Exclusionary Rule on state courts.

The jurisdiction of federal courts and the laws that guide their actions are often shaped by different political interests than are the laws and court actions of the states. For example, minority groups that have received no consideration from their state courts have frequently sought help from Congress in having the jurisdiction of the federal courts enlarged so that they may obtain redress for their grievances through the federal judiciary. A good example is the Civil Rights Act of 1964. This legislation and subsequent laws empowered federal law enforcement officials to investigate and bring to trial individuals who interfere with the exercise of civil rights. This legislation has frequently been used in cases where state agents such as law enforcement personnel have violated the civil rights of citizens within their states.

Absence of Supervisory Control

The second most notable characteristic of American courts is that they perform their function with little or no supervisory control. The U.S. Supreme Court and the state supreme courts are usually supreme courts only in the sense that they serve as appellate courts from the lower judiciary, and they establish certain procedures for the lower courts.

For instance, many people believe that there is an automatic right to appeal to the U.S. Supreme Court and that in this way the Supreme Court exercises authority over the lower federal courts and the state courts. In fact, the Supreme Court hears an extremely small proportion of cases heard by the lower courts. There are a number of reasons for this: First, before someone who is tried for a crime on a state level can appeal to the Supreme Court, that person must have exhausted every appellate process available in the particular state. Second, the case must involve a substantial federal question and/or constitutional issue. Third, the issue must be of significant social importance to warrant a Supreme Court hearing. And last, the process is extremely costly and time-consuming, which, in itself, is often a major inhibiting factor.

This absence of supervisory control over the courts is also manifest in other ways. Often no single authority has the power to control the assignment of court personnel, the formulation of the budget, or the distribution of supplies and facilities among the courts or the flow of cases through each court. Although some states are moving in the direction of giving supervisory authority over lower state courts to the state Supreme Court, this movement is not uniform throughout the nation. At the federal level this situation is somewhat remedied by the Administrative Office of the United States Courts and by the assistance now being provided this office by the newly created Judicial Center. In many states, the legislature is required by state constitutions or statutes to ensure the necessary operating budget for the judiciary. Since most of our state judges are elected, they are theoretically responsible only to the people, which makes it nearly impossible to supervise them or remove them from office except through the ballot box.

This absence of supervisory control is even extended to the court support personnel. Court bailiffs, probation officers, clerks, and other functionaries in many instances are appointed by the court; these positions are often patronage appointments for faithful political support in the state or local political arena.

Specialization

Another important feature of the court system, particularly at the state and local levels, is its arrangement according to specialized areas. For example, the lower courts at the local and municipal levels are often courts of limited jurisdiction that can try only misdemeanors. In felony cases, the trial is conducted by a court of original and general jurisdiction at the county, district, regional, or state level. In a similar vein, specialized juvenile courts have been established to handle crimes committed by youth, and in some larger municipalities, specialized branches of local courts handle traffic offenses or vice crimes. This same procedure is also carried over into civil law, where different courts have been established to handle claims, wills and estates, and civil suits, based upon the amount of money sought for damages.

Geographical Organization

Our courts are also organized by geographical boundaries. The states and the federal government are divided into judicial districts, with various levels of courts situated in each area.

This arrangement has important implications for the administration of criminal justice. The particular location of a court influences its responsiveness to political interests. Rural courts are less likely to be as understanding or concerned about certain criminal violations as are urban courts. For instance, the judges in rural areas often perceive that their constituents are less likely to sanction offenses against blue laws, which prohibit certain businessess from operating on Sundays, liquor and drug offenses, gambling, and other normative vice offenses. In Michigan, for example, the courts in the Upper Peninsula, a rather isolated rural area, are notoriously more stringent in the application of penalties against drug offenses than are similar courts in the Detroit area.

Numerous studies have been made of how courts and individual judges differ in terms of the sentences they impose in different locales. In one study of the federal system, the average prison sentence for narcotics violations was 83 months in the Tenth Circuit, but only 44 months in the Third Circuit.[4] Another study some years ago found that the average sentence for forgery ranged from a high of 68 months in the Northern District of Mississippi to a low of 7 months in the Southern District of that state; the highest average sentence for auto theft was 47 months in the Southern District of Iowa, and the lowest was 14 months in the Northern District of New York.[5]

This is not to imply that differences in sentences imposed by courts in different areas necessarily reflect different social values and attitudes. No research has ever conclusively established such a relationship, though the constituency of each local community clearly must have some impact on the operation of the courts in that region.

HISTORY AND DEVELOPMENT OF STATE COURT SYSTEMS

In their 300-year history, the state court systems have undergone a remarkable evolution. This section will examine notable changes from the colonial period to the present.

The Colonial Period

During the early years of the American colonies, courts were simple institutions with little authority or jurisdiction. Power rested in the hands of the colonial governors, who were appointed by the English king. For the most part, the few courts that did exist served in advisory capacities to the governors. Members of these courts were appointed by the governor and served at his pleasure. The judicial officials were given the limited authority to settle matters too trivial to warrant the time and effort of the governor.

This was a period when the tasks of governing were relatively simple and routine. Because the population was small and scattered throughout small settlements, there was no need for extensive political institutions. In the place of legislative bodies, an assembly of advisers advised the governor on matters pertaining to the administration of the colony. As the population of the colonies grew and social relations became more complex, town and county courts were formed to provide a local authority for settling conflicts. The establishment of courts in the county seats was an idea that first developed in the shires of England. Each county seat was situated so that a rider on horseback could reach the county seat and return home in one day. Town courts, which had developed in medieval England, were also adopted by the colonies as the population grew and the need for this type of court developed. In medieval England, the settlement of local, minor squabbles demanded a mode of judicial administration unhampered by the inconveniences of a highly centralized system. To meet this problem, the office of *justice of the peace* was developed which was an appointive official with authority to settle petty civil cases and try minor criminal offenses. The justice usually was a respected townsman without legal training, but blessed with common sense. The system of local justices became a permanent part of the English system and was transported virtually unchanged to American soil, where it has remained in use in some states for over 300 years.[6]

Appeals from these courts usually could be taken to the governor and the assembly and, ultimately, to the courts of England—although such appeals rarely occurred. Because these courts had such limited jurisdiction, the issues before them usually did not warrant the time and expense of an appeal.

Influences on the Court's Development   The early colonies were often settled by different groups—Maryland by Roman Catholics, Pennsylvania by Quakers—and thus the judicial and legal systems developed differently in each colony, depending upon local beliefs and customs. With only a few exceptions, the English common law tradition and English court structures were adopted. However, the individual colonies soon modified these somewhat to suit the requirements of local demands. The commercial development in each colony also contributed to different rulings and court arrangements.[7] In a number of ways, these early variations among the colonies are still reflected in the variety of court systems in the states.

Glick and Vines consider that the lack of legal experts in the colonies was an important feature in the early development of the colonial court systems.[8] There are a number of reasons why legal and judicial talent was not available to assist in the creation of colonial courts. In the first place, the king's law and those who administered to it were held in disrepute by many of the colonists. As a result, very few professionally trained lawyers and jurists were attracted to the colonies from England and Europe. In addition, lawyers and judges were not welcomed by the colonial merchant class and wealthy land-owners, who were concerned that the development of a professional class of attorneys would renew the persecution by the law they had experienced in the past as well as create competition for the general social, economic, and political control they enjoyed in the colonies.[9]

As a consequence, these early courts came under the domain of prestigious laymen in the towns and counties. The judges were usually wealthy merchants, planters, or landowners, who, without benefit of legal training, settled the local disputes that arose. As might be imagined, these courts often served the interests of the wealthy, and in terms of political control, judicial, economic, and financial interests became interlocked.

As the population grew, courts were added to the judicial system in order to respond to increased litigation. The major impetus behind the expansion of colonial courts, however, was the economic growth of the colonies. As commerce increased, so did the need for courts to settle differences between economic interests. As early as the late seventeenth century, the colonies of Massachusetts, Pennsylvania, and Connecticut began to divide cases between existing courts. In this way, specialized jurisdictions of courts began to be established, and the early development of a higher court for appeal began to appear. In 1698, Connecticut established a few special courts to deal with wills and estates, which until this time had been handled by the county courts. These new courts were called probate courts, and the idea of this type of specialized court spread to other colonies.[10] The spread of these specialized courts encouraged the development of legal experts and judges to service these courts. This, in turn, fostered the growth of rules and procedures to process the growing litigation.

State Court Development in the Postrevolutionary Period

After America gained its independence, the powers of the governors of the new states were drastically reduced, and the state legislatures became the focus of authoritative power. The courts that existed in the states at this time were purposely kept very weak. The legislative bodies, and indeed the citizens of the new nation, were quite content with this arrangement. The citizens still remembered the courts as extensions of the authority of the colonial governors, and they did not relish the possibility that the courts might serve the same function for the governors of the new states. This fear that the executive branch and the judiciary might wield too much power at the expense of the states' legislative bodies prevented the development of an independent state judiciary. The state legislatures scrutinized quite closely the actions of the state courts, and they freely appointed and removed judges and even abolished courts that did not agree with their policies.[11]

Beginning in the early 1800s, distrust of the judiciary became even more pronounced as some courts began to rule that the actions of legislative bodies were unconstitutional. This power of the courts to declare the actions of the legislature or executive branches to be in violation of constitutional provisions is known as the power of *judicial review*. In 1803, in the famous case of *Marbury v. Madison*,[12] the U.S. Supreme Court established this power for the nation's highest tribunal. This power of judicial review of legislative action is largely an American creation. Before the Revolution, it had been used on a few occasions to justify opposition to the crown's edicts, but it did not become an important instrument of authority until the early nineteenth century. Exercise of the power of judicial review often led to a struggle for political power between the judiciary and the legislative branches of the states. Despite the efforts of the state legislatures to curtail the power of the courts by removing judges and eliminating certain courts, the state courts became more assertive and openly declared, in a number of instances, that state legislative action, particularly in the area of economic interests, violated state constitutions.

These struggles were instrumental in developing state court organization because they nurtured the idea that an independent judiciary was necessary to maintain an equal and meaningful separation of powers between the branches of state government. Although certain state legislatures continued to perform an appellate function for a number of years, by the beginning of the Civil War the power of state legislatures to serve as an appellate body from judicial decisions had been abolished in all states.

The Development of the State Courts from 1850 to the Present

The rapid growth of our nation from 1850 to 1900 had pronounced effects on the growth of the state court systems. This was a period of rapid industrial expansion and massive immigrations from Southern and Eastern Europe. As America moved into its "golden age" of technology, the courts, like all institutions of that period, were affected by the fundamental changes that society was undergoing.

The growth of industry and commerce led to new conflicts that had to be resolved; rules had to be imposed, and legislative bodies had to enact new laws to regulate the changing character of American society. The advent of the automobile alone contributed enormously to the workload of the courts. As people clustered together in large cities, the incidence of crime increased, and the courts were called upon to adjudicate more and more criminal matters. While this was occurring at the state level, similar problems and developments were happening at the federal level. Congress, through its express powers to regulate commerce between the states, coin money, lay and collect taxes, and make all laws "which shall be necessary and proper," was passing increasing legislation and enacting criminal penalties for noncompliance. Thus, the criminal (and civil) workloads of the federal courts increased drastically as the need to enforce these laws grew apace.

As the existing courts found themselves inundated with litigation, specialized branches began to appear. For a time, existing city courts, primarily justices of the peace, dealt with much of the new litigation, but since most of these justices and lower level magistrates had little or no training in the law, they were unable to deal with the complex legal questions involved in many of the cases that came before them. As a result, new court systems were created. Small claims courts were added in a number of states to simplify legal procedures and to collect small debts at minimal cost. Juvenile and family relations courts were also developed to handle cases involving juvenile offenders and troubled families. Many communities created special courts to handle motor vehicle offenses. As these courts developed, so did the need for specialists such as social workers, psychiatrists, and other treatment personnel assigned to juvenile courts. The adult criminal courts expanded their staffs and added probation officers to supervise the offender after adjudication of guilt. Figure 8-1 depicts the growth of state court systems in America.

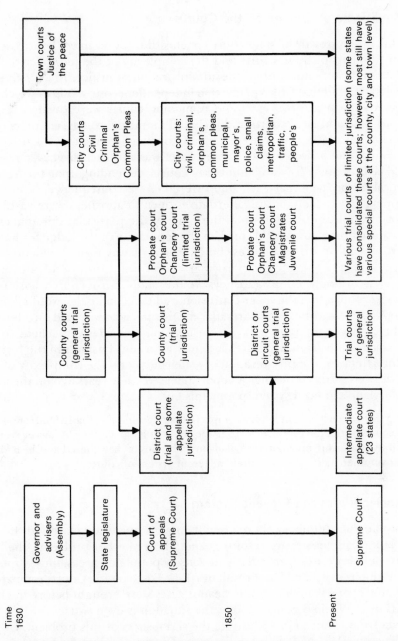

Source: Henry Robert Glick and Kenneth N. Vines, *State Court Systems,* © 1973, p. 20. Reproduced by permission of Prentice-Hall, Inc., Englewood Cliffs, N.J.

FIGURE 8-1   Historical Development of the State Court System

The Effects of Change on the Courts

This rapid growth of state court systems did not occur without cost. The sheer numbers of these courts and the complexity of the judicial system has had a significant impact upon the administration of justice. In a 1930s study, Lepawsky found that Chicago had 556 independent courts, 505 of which were justice of the peace courts.[13] The remaining courts were divided between various state and local courts and included municipal courts, circuit courts, a superior court, a county court, a probate court, a juvenile court, and a criminal court. The jurisdiction of these courts was not exclusive. A single case could be brought before any number of courts, depending upon the legal and political advantages that each one offered. As a consequence, "courtroom shopping" prevailed, and the alternatives open to attorneys were vast.[14]

For example, depending upon the value of the particular criminal case to the state, a prosecutor would consider the reputation of the judge for handing down lenient or stiff sentences, how difficult it was to get evidence introduced, and how quickly the particular courts could dispose of a case, and choose accordingly. Often attorneys would "shop" for a court whose procedures were such that the sheer confusion, red tape, and delay would frustrate the opposition or where the particular magistrate, who was paid on a fee basis, might be eager to trade a favorable decision for a lawyer's client for the assurance that he would get the particular attorney's business in the future.[15]

Unfortunately, the proliferation of state courts and the complexity of their jurisdictions is still confusing. A report released a few years ago on the nature of Maryland's judicial system points this out:

> Maryland's court system is very complex. There are no less than 16 different types of courts, with little uniformity from one community to another. A lawyer from one county venturing into another is likely to feel almost as bewildered as if he had gone into another state with an entirely different system of courts.[16]

Problems with the Present System

Despite their numbers, there are not enough courts to go around. Because of a lack of administrative resources and a host of other problems, the lower courts in many states, particularly in densely populated areas, must cope with an enormous caseload. The President's Task Force on the Courts estimated in 1965 that over 4½ million misdemeanor cases were brought before the lower courts of the United States. Today, the situation is even worse.

Data from various cities illustrate the seriousness of this problem. In 1972 Washington, D.C., had eight judges in the District of Columbia Court of General Sessions to process the preliminary stages of more than 2,400 felony cases and to hear and determine 9,300 serious misdemeanor cases, 41,000 petty offenses, and nearly 44,000 traffic offenses.[17] In 1969, the courts that handled the criminal cases in Milwaukee disposed of 11,078 cases; 30 judges handled most of these cases in addition to 95,000 civil cases. Jacob reports that if each judge in Milwaukee shared this workload equally and worked 255 days a year, he would have to dispose of 13 cases every day.[18] In Detroit, over 20,000 misdemeanor and nontraffic petty offenses must be handled each year by one judge in the Early Sessions Division.[19]

Unsystematic growth and poor administration have left the courts facing a critical situation. As litigation has increased the problems have been compounded. One of the major problems is the delay in processing cases. In analyzing Manhattan's criminal courts, Jennings says:

> Congestion and delays in courts throughout the country threaten to strangle our system of justice. For, as delays increase, the innocent who cannot afford to make bail suffer longer in jail, the guilty who are released pose greater threats to society, and the deterrent value of speedy justice is lost. The resulting pressures to dispose of cases more and more quickly lead to still other wrongs: less and less attention is given to each case, greater reliance is placed on the disposition of cases through "plea bargaining" and the likelihood of injustice increases.[20]

The National Center for State Courts analyzed state court structures throughout the country and concluded that the existing organizational methods of many state court systems resulted in a host of problems that worsened case delay. Court structure was only part of the problem. Other factors were inadequate court resources, workload differences, and the lack of systematic and uniform procedures.[21]

The Center identified several major consequences of delay in processing cases. Each of these have costs both to society and to the individual. The first is the *cost to the litigant*. In criminal cases the effect of delay upon the defendant varied in direct relation to pretrial custody status. For the defendant awaiting trial in jail, whatever good that delay might have produced was outweighed by the cost to the defendant in terms of confinement with all sorts of criminals and disillusionment with the judicial process.

A national study of bail practices indicated major differences among jurisdictions in pretrial release rates for felony defendants. Among the 20 cities studied, the percentage of defendants incarcerated varied from 16 percent in Minneapolis to 66 percent in Boston. The median for all the cities in the study was 36 percent.[22] Although jailed defendants are almost always brought to disposition more quickly than defendants who are released on bail, the average time spent in jail prior to disposition ranged from 13 days in Boston to 134 days in Denver with a median of 56 days.[23]

· Lengthy case-processing time has an impact on the outcome of the case. One such effect is the "deterioration of the evidence" problem. As time passes, witnesses forget what happened, move away, or die. Thus the state's case weakens over time. The defense is therefore more likely to receive a favorable verdict or dismissal of the charges.[24]

Another cost of case delays is the *social cost*. For example, excessive time to dispose of criminal cases is said to hinder all purposes of the penal law: deterrence, societal protection, and even rehabilitation. In the case of deterrence, delays reduce the so-called deterrent effect of "swift and sure" punishment.[25] Societal costs are obvious when defendants who are out of jail and awaiting trial commit new crimes during their period of release. One study in Washington, D.C., concluded that the "crime cost" of delay is directly linked to the length of time released defendants await disposition. Comparing crime statistics to data on the total number of days all felony defendants were released, it found that for every 1,000 days of defendant's release one crime is committed, and for every 2,000 days of release one felony is committed.[26]

THE COMPOSITION OF THE STATE COURT SYSTEMS TODAY

All 50 states have at least three levels of courts. The highest level consists of the appellate courts. At this level is the state court of last resort as well as intermediate appellate courts in the more densely populated states. The main function of these appellate courts is to review the decisions of the lower courts. The middle level is made up of those courts of general jurisdiction that usually handle felony criminal trials and major civil cases. The lowest level consists of courts of limited and special jurisdiction that have original jurisdiction to try misdemeanor cases, conduct preliminary hearings for felony offenses, try traffic cases, adjudicate civil matters that involve small amounts of money, and, in some cases, to handle wills and estates.

Although the basic structure of state court systems is similar, the specific number, names, and functions of state courts vary widely. Normally, court systems are divided into four levels as shown in Table 8-1 with the Supreme Courts and the Intermediate Appellate Courts grouped into one level. The major differences among the states are in the presence or absence of intermediate appellate courts and the great variation in the number of trial courts of limited or special jurisdiction. Most states have only one or two types of trial courts of general jurisdiction. State court systems vary from the very simple, with clearly defined jurisdictions, to highly complex systems that have numerous trial courts of limited jurisdiction whose functions frequently are unclear and may overlap.[27]

TABLE 8-1
Structure of State Court Systems

SUPREME COURT

All states have one supreme court. In Maryland and New York it is called the court of appeals.

INTERMEDIATE APPELLATE COURTS

Twenty-eight states have intermediate courts of appeal. Alabama, Oklahoma, Tennessee, and Texas have separate courts for criminal and civil appeals. These courts have various names: court of appeals, appellate division of supreme court, and superior court.

TRIAL COURTS OF GENERAL JURISDICTION

Forty states have one type of trial court of general jurisdiction; eight states have two; Indiana has three; and Tennessee has four. The names of these courts vary widely: circuit court, district court, court of common pleas, supreme court (New York), and superior court.

TRIAL COURTS OF LIMITED OR SPECIAL JURISDICTION

Eighteen states have only one or two of these kinds of trial courts; eleven states have five or more; New York has nine and Texas has ten such different courts. The names and functions of these courts vary widely. They include probate courts, police courts, small claims courts, justice of the peace courts, city courts, municipal courts, juvenile courts, and magistrate courts.

Source: Adopted from the Council of State Governments, *State Court Systems* (Lexington, Ky.: The Council of State Governments, 1978).

Justice of the Peace   The office of justice of the peace represents the lowest rung in the judicial organization in a number of states. Although it boasts an honorable tradition dating back to the fourteenth century, today this office is often the object of scorn. In the early days of our nation's history, this was an appointive office, but since the days of Andrew Jackson this post has usually been an elective one. With few exceptions, legal training is not required. A survey conducted in the late 1960s in Oregon and Pennsylvania indicated that less than 2 percent of the justices of the peace in those two states possessed a law degree.[28]

A more recent study showed the following educational backgrounds among 411 past and present members of the Association of Justices of the Peace of Virginia: four were lawyers; 71 percent had never gone to college, and 18 percent were not even high school graduates.[29] Compensation is usually in the form of fees collected from litigants, a system that has led to a great deal of abuse. The term of office is short, usually 2 years. While the office was at one time found in virtually all localities, it is fast disappearing in urban areas.

Although the jurisdiction of justice of the peace varies among the states, in all instances it is very limited. Typically, the jurisdiction of this court extends only to minor misdemeanors and traffic offenses. In a few states that retain crimes that constitute high misdemeanors, this court is empowered in some instances to hold preliminary hearings on these offenses. The justice sometimes has authority to settle civil disputes that involve very small sums of money—usually not over a few hundred dollars. Other duties might include providing notary services, performing marriage ceremonies, and issuing minor warrants. Decisions of the justice are commonly appealable to higher courts, where the case may be tried *de novo*—that is, a completely new trial will be held. In most instances, there are no provisions for jury trials in these courts.

Years ago, when travel was difficult and communications were slow, justices of the peace served a useful purpose. They were able to handle petty cases without the expense and loss of time involved in carrying grievances to higher courts. In modern society, these same conditions do not prevail, and many states have eliminated these particular courts. The major criticism of justice of the peace courts is that since legal training is generally not required, this office is frequently occupied by individuals totally unfit to administer the law. There have been instances when illiterates were elected to this post, and often the office is filled by small-time politicians more interested in the political opportunities of the office than in its legal responsibilities. In most instances, the justices also operate without a courtroom, with the result that proceedings may be, and usually are, conducted in any kind of setting. The justices are forced to keep their own records, since no clerical assistance is provided, and thus frequently no permanent records are maintained. Another major criticism is that this court generally operates completely unsupervised by any other judicial or court regulatory authority. In the words of one state's attorney general, "They are a form of justice unto themselves."

Because of these weaknesses, a number of states have adopted drastic reforms or abolished the office outright. States that have purposely set about to unify the structure of their state courts usually absorb the functions of these courts by transferring their jurisdiction to local courts of record. In other instances, their jurisdiction has been sharply curtailed. A few states have provided for their gradual elimination, and still others have undertaken various reforms, such as requiring the maintenance of records, abolishing the fee system, and requiring that justices have law degrees and be licensed to practice in that particular state or that they be certified and licensed by completing formal training programs. There are, of course, many justices of the peace who execute their duties honestly and efficiently, but there are still too many who contribute to an already bad system of justice at this level and who continue to perpetuate the fact that this particular court, overall, is the weakest link in the judicial claim.

Magistrate's Courts Magistrate's courts are the urban counterpart of rural justices of the peace. These courts are sometimes referred to as police, mayor's, and in some states, recorder's courts. Usually, their jurisdiction is similar to that of the justice of the peace. The major difference between the two is settings in which they are found. This is reflected in the types of cases that each handles. In large urban areas, magistrate's courts typically handle the bulk of all criminal matters that involve misdemeanors and the like. In some instances, depending upon whether the city maintains special courts for traffic violations, small claims, and minor civil matters, the magistrate's courts will also handle these.

Magistrate's courts are often criticized as having the same weaknesses as the justice of the peace courts. In fact, the situation may be even worse in these urban tribunals because of the pressures and influences exerted upon them by unscrupulous politicians and lawyers. In a notable public statement, former Philadelphia District Attorney Arlen Specter, long a foe of the magistrate system in that city, declared that "the only difference between Chief Magistrate Walsh and his 27 cohorts and Ali Baba and the 40 Thieves is that one group is somewhat larger.[30] The history of judicial corruption and venality in these courts has certainly contributed to this feeling and is indicative of the need for reform of many of these tribunals.

Municipal Courts Because of the volume of cases, many large cities have established municipal courts. The first municipal court was established in Chicago in 1906. The jurisdictions of these courts are sufficiently broad to include many cases that might be heard by magistrates or the general trial courts of the state. These courts are usually authorized to try misdemeanor cases and civil cases that involve amounts up to a few thousand dollars, to serve as initial-appearance and preliminary hearing tribunals in cases of felony offenses, and to hear appeals from magistrates' courts if such courts are retained after the creation of the municipal courts.

The municipal court is typically much better equipped and staffed than are the magistrate's and justice of the peace courts, and the decorum is more typical of what one expects to see in a courtroom. The judges must be trained in the law, are usually elected to longer terms of office, and are provided with clerical assistance.

Municipal courts are often part of a unified state court structure and must adhere to certain uniform policies and procedures imposed on them by law.

Still, in spite of the recommendations of many judicial reform groups, a number of states have retained a nonunified state judiciary and have imposed only minimal requirements on these courts. In large cities, the municipal court is often divided into specialized sections assigned to hear certain types of cases—for example, one section may hear traffic cases, another small claims, and a third domestic relations or civil matters. In this type of arrangement, a chief judge, either appointed or elected, has the responsibility for the overall administration of the court, which usually includes the authority to assign or transfer judges within the court as case dockets require or depending upon the particular talents or predilections of the judges.

Miscellaneous Local Courts   Some cities have created special courts to handle specific types of cases. Michigan, for example, has created special local courts on the county level in each of that state's 83 counties to handle probate matters and all juvenile delinquency cases as well as cases that involve neglected or dependent children.

Many states also have county courts which serve as the tribunals between justices of the peace and the general trial courts. The jurisdiction of these county courts varies widely from state to state. In some states, they exercise a great deal of authority, and in others they play a very limited role in the judicial process. Often, their jurisdiction overlaps with that of the justice of the peace courts and the general trial courts. Usually, these county courts are presided over by judges trained in the law, and they have many of the features of the municipal courts which are their urban counterparts.

General Trial Courts   All 50 states are divided into judicial districts, with each district usually composed of one or more counties, depending upon population. In each district, there is a general trial court. States use a variety of titles to identify this court—for example, in Michigan, general trial courts are called circuit courts; in California, superior courts; in Minnesota, district courts; and in Ohio, common pleas courts. General trial courts are usually presided over by a single judge or in more populated districts, a number of judges. The judge, who must be a member of the bar, presides over scheduled sessions held in courtrooms usually located in the county courthouses.

Persons accused of felonies are prosecuted in these general trial courts. The attorney who prosecutes in the name of the state is the locally elected prosecutor, known in different states as the district attorney, county prosecutor, solicitor, or county attorney. Trials, which are conducted before juries, are heard only after formal accusation is brought either by grand jury indictment or the filing of an information. Violations of state criminal laws are as a rule tried in these courts unless some other court is specifically directed or empowered to hear these cases.

General trial courts have what is referred to as *original jurisdiction* over felony cases—that is, felony trials are initiated and held in these courts. Most states specify that their lower courts of limited jurisdiction have original jurisdiction in misdemeanor cases (crimes punishable by sentences of up to one year in jail). Many states also authorize general trial courts to exercise *appellate jurisdiction* as well. Under these provisions, a misdemeanor tried under the original jurisdiction of the lower courts can be appealed to the general trial court in instances where there is some dissatisfaction with the legal rulings of a lower court. When an appeal is made to a general trial court, there will be a trial *de novo,* or completely new trial. This procedure differs significantly from that in intermediate courts of appeal or the state supreme court where only the particular legal points in question are reviewed.

Intermediate State Appellate Courts In order to reduce the number of cases that must be reviewed by the state supreme court, the 28 most heavily populated states have formed intermediate appellate courts. These courts are composed of three or more judges, who are usually elected to office. Usually, their terms of office are longer than the terms of office of lower court judges in the state system. In addition, many states employ a rotational system of electing these jurists. For example, if a state elects judges to eight-year terms of office on this bench and there are eight judges on the appellate court, every two years there would be new elections to fill two judgeships.

These courts, like the federal courts of appeal, have basically only appellate jurisdiction. Only in some states, in cases of disputed elections, do these courts have original jurisdiction in which they actually try cases. In both civil and criminal appeals, the usual procedure is for the attorneys for both sides to submit briefs to the court and present oral arguments before the judges. The judges examine these briefs, hear the arguments, and review the record of the case in the lower court. The judges then, in consultation with each other, reach a decision by means of majority vote. Ordinarily, an appeals court does not concern itself with the facts of a particular case, but bases its decisions upon whether the law has been correctly interpreted and applied by the lower court.

State Supreme Courts As is the case in the federal judiciary, every state court system has an appellate court of last resort, usually called the state supreme court. These courts are established by the respective constitutions of the states. In almost all states, judges are elected to this court. Usually they are elected for longer terms of office than those of judges in the lesser courts in the state. In most states, a candidate for the supreme court bench must have had a required number of years in the practice of law to become eligible to run for this position. Typically, the chief justice of this court is either the senior member, is chosen by the other justices, or is elected by the voters. A few states still follow the practice of having the chief justice appointed by the governor or the legislature.

The primary purpose of this court is to receive and adjudicate appeals on major questions that arise in the lower courts. Where a state has an intermediate court of appeals, the supreme court will receive most of its caseload from appeals from this court. The main purpose of the state supreme court is to interpret the law and apply it in the particular case. This court normally has the final word in the state on all issues that pertain to the state constitution. Its decisions are final and authoritative on state and local laws.[31]

Just as with the U.S. Supreme Court, decisions are written and published in an official series of volumes called a *reporter.* In most cases, decisions by a state supreme court marks the end of litigation. Review by the U.S. Supreme Court is restricted to those cases that involve a federal question—that is, an issue of federal law. When review is sought on the grounds that state action has resulted in a denial of due process of law as guaranteed by the Fourteenth Amendment, it becomes the Supreme Court's responsibility to decide whether the federal question is important enough to warrant a review of the case.

A special agreement or judicial courtesy known as *comity* has developed between the federal and state courts. This is an understanding that federal courts will accept and apply the interpretations of state law as it pertains to state statutes and state constitutions. If no significant federal question is involved or if there is no conflict between state and federal law, the decisions of the state courts will not be reviewed by the federal courts.

Comparative State Court Systems   All the courts discussed above might typically be found at the state level. The number of courts, their names, and their respective jurisdictions vary considerably from state to state. Table 8-2 indicates how the court organizations of three states differ. Although the most populous state in the nation, California has streamlined its system so that only

TABLE 8-2

A Comparison of the Judicial Structure in Three States

CALIFORNIA	INDIANA	TEXAS
	Appellate Courts	
Supreme court	Supreme court	Supreme court
Court of appeals	Court of appeals	Court of criminal appeals
		Court of civil appeals
	Courts of General Jurisdiction	
Superior court	Circuit courts	District courts
	Superior courts	
	Criminal courts	
	Courts of Limited and Special Jurisdiction	
Municipal court	County courts	Criminal district
Justice courts	Municipal courts	courts
	Probate courts	County courts at law
	Juvenile courts	County civil courts at law
	City and town courts	Probate courts
	Small claims courts	County criminal courts
		County criminal courts of appeal
		County courts
		Justice of the peace courts
		Municipal courts

Source: *State Court Systems* (Lexington, Ky.: The Council of State Governments, 1978)

five types of courts exist in the state. California has been one of the leaders in centralizing the state judiciary and making it more efficient. Indiana provides an example of a state that has an intermediate form of court consolidation which although not ideal is still far better than the fragmented structure that exists in Texas. The state of Texas is extremely decentralized as can be seen by its multitude of courts of limited and special jurisdiction. In spite of periodic efforts to abolish this system, Texas has, for various political reasons, been unable to restructure these lower courts and bring its judiciary in line with some of the more progressive court systems.

THE FEDERAL JUDICIARY

In many respects, the federal court system is far less diversified than the various state systems. However, even in the federal system, there are more courts than most people realize. Figure 8-2 diagrams the federal court system. There are two major types of courts at the federal level in terms of both their creation and their functions: the *legislative courts* and the *constitutional courts*. The power to establish legislative courts is vested in Congress by Article 1 of the Constitution, which gives Congress "the power to create tribunals inferior to the Supreme Court" and the power to make all laws "necessary and proper" for executing its powers.

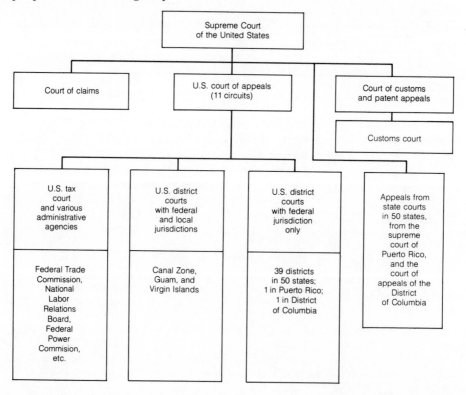

Source: *The United States Courts—Their Jurisdiction and Work* (Washington, D.C.: U.S. Government Printing Office, 1975), p. 3.

FIGURE 8-2 The Federal Court System

These legislative courts are courts of special jurisdiction, such as the tax court, which has jurisdiction over controversies that involve taxpayers and the Internal Revenue Service. Also included are some territorial courts in the Canal Zone, Guam, and the Virgin Islands. Finally, there are district and appellate courts in the District of Columbia which were created by Congress through its constitutional power to govern the nation's capital. Since legislative courts have only a limited relationship to the administration of criminal justice, they will not be examined here.

The Constitutional Courts

Although Article III of the Constitution provided for a Supreme Court, the creation of the entire organization of the lower federal judiciary has been left to Congress to create. With the exception of the specialized District of Columbia courts, four constitutional courts handle federal criminal cases and, in some instances, state criminal cases on appeal. These are the U.S. magistrate's courts, U.S. district courts, courts of appeal, and, of course, the U.S. Supreme Court. Table 8-3 shows the appellate and original jurisdiction of the federal courts.

U.S. Magistrate's Courts U.S. magistrate's courts are the lowest courts in the federal judicial structure. Presided over by U.S. magistrates (formerly called U.S. commissioners), they used to occupy a place in the federal system similar to that of the justice of the peace in the state judicial system. Since the passage of the Federal Magistrate's Act of 1968 and subsequent 1976 legislation, their authority has changed somewhat. They now have the authority to try criminal cases that involve minor offenses where the possible penalty is $1,000 or less and one year or less of incarceration. However, even in these instances, defendants must waive their rights to a jury trial and be tried in front of the U.S. district court before they can be tried by the U.S. magistrate. These judicial officers are empowered to hold bail hearings, issue search and arrest warrants, conduct initial and preliminary hearings, review habeas corpus petitions, review civil rights petitions, hold evidentiary hearings, and conduct pretrial conferences in both civil and criminal hearings. They are also responsible for handling any special assignments delegated by a federal district court judge that do not conflict with any constitutional questions of authority.

Until the 1968 legislation, U.S. magistrates were part-time judicial personnel who were paid on a fee basis and were not required to be attorneys. To qualify as a U.S. magistrate today, an individual must be an attorney with considerable practical experience. Most of the full-time appointees are former state and county judges, assistant U.S. attorneys, public defenders, or trial lawyers with many years of criminal and civil experience. The term of appointment for a full-time magistrate is eight years, and appointments are made by district court judges. Full-time magistrates earn an annual salary of $48,500, and are not permitted to engage in the private practice of law. Part-time magistrates receive up to $24,250 in salary and may practice law, but not in federal courts that handle federal criminal cases.

TABLE 8-3

Appellate and Original Jurisdiction of the Federal Courts

COURT	ORIGINAL JURISDICTION	APPELLATE JURISDICTION
U.S. Supreme Court (1)	Cases between the United States and a state	All lower federal constitutional courts and some legislative and territorial courts
	Cases between two or more states	The highest state court in cases of a substantial federal question
	Cases involving foreign ambassadors, ministers, and consuls	
	Cases between a state and a citizen of another state or country	
U.S. courts of appeals (11)		U.S. district courts
		U.S. territorial courts, Tax Court, and some District of Columbia courts
		U.S. regulatory commissions and certain administrative agencies
U.S. district courts (95)	All federal crimes	Limited appellate jurisdiction involving certain actions tried before U.S. magistrate's courts
	All civil actions under the constitution, laws, and treaties of the United States when the matter in controversy exceeds $10,000	
	Cases involving citizens of different states or aliens if the matter in controversy exceeds $10,000	
	Review and enforcement of orders and actions of certain administrative agencies and departments	
U.S. magistrate's courts	Very minor misdemeanors	
	Preliminary hearing	
	Setting bond	
	Issuance of warrants	

U.S. District Courts   At the present time, there are 95 districts courts, with at least one in each state. The more populous states, such as California, New York, and Illinois, are divided into districts with a U.S. district court in each. For example, Illinois has a northern, southern, and eastern district. A district may be divided into divisions and may have several locales where the court hears cases. Each district has from one to 27 judges, depending upon the caseload. By law, 398 district judgeships are authorized, and the salary of each is $54,500 per year. In districts with two or more judges, the judge who is senior in service and who has not reached 70 years of age is the chief judge.

These courts are the workhorses of the federal judiciary. In 1977, they had over 386,000 filings, including civil, criminal, and bankruptcy cases.[32] District courts in the Canal Zone, Guam, and the Virgin Islands have jurisdiction over local cases as well as those that arise under federal laws. Since the courts in these three places are not limited to the types of cases defined in the Constitution as part of the federal judicial power, they are legislative rather than constitutional courts.

U.S. district courts have original jurisdiction over almost all criminal cases that arise under federal criminal law. These courts are similar to the courts of general jurisdiction in the state systems. Although the district courts, for the most part, have original jurisdiction only, when necessary they do have the obligation and authority to review actions and orders tried before U.S. magistrates. The criminal workload of these district courts during the 1977 fiscal year was 41,464 cases. The most frequently prosecuted crime was fraud, followed by violations of narcotic laws, larceny, forgery and counterfeiting, embezzlement, and bank robbery.[33]

Each district has a number of important officers for the court. The first of these is the U.S. attorney, an officer comparable to the local prosecutor or district attorney in the state court. A U.S. marshal's office is also located in each district. Both of these officers are appointed by the President with the advice and consent of the Senate. The U.S. attorney is the criminal prosecutor for the federal government. He or she appoints a number of assistant U.S. attorneys, often in conjunction with the wishes of influential members of the president's political party. The U.S. attorney is not supervised by the federal district court judges, but functions under the authority of the U.S. attorney general and the U.S. Department of Justice.

In addition, in each district there are U.S. magistrates, probation officers, court reporters, and one or more bankruptcy judges. Each district court also has a plan under which lawyers are provided for poor defendants in criminal cases. To assure adequate service, full-time public defenders are appointed in courts where criminal cases are numerous.

Courts of Appeals Standing immediately above the U.S. district courts in the federal court system are the U.S. courts of appeals. There are 11 circuits where a court of appeals is located; each includes three or more states except the District of Columbia Circuit. U.S. courts of appeals are essentially what the name implies—appellate courts only. Criminal appeals may be taken from a U.S. district court to the court of appeals of the circuit where the trial is situated. For example, someone tried in Miami for a federal crime would have his or her case heard in the U.S. District Court for Miami (Southern Florida U.S. Judicial District). If the individual appealed, the case would go to the Court of Appeals for the Fifth Circuit, which is located in New Orleans, since the Fifth Circuit includes Florida.

The courts of appeals hear cases that are appealed from the lower federal courts. In only three instances can a case that has been tried in the lower federal courts bypass the particular court of appeals and go straight to the Supreme Court: (1) if the case has been decided by a special three-judge district court; (2) if it is a case where a federal statute has been held unconstitutional by a U.S. district court and the United States is a litigant in the case; or (3) it can be shown that the case is "of such imperative public importance . . . as to require immediate settlement."

Proceedings in the U.S. courts of appeals vary somewhat from court to court, and like the Supreme Court the impact of individual judicial personalities play a role. However, all appellate court proceedings, whether at the state or federal level, share certain features and differ markedly from those of the trial courts. Whereas trial judges are almost always passive participants, appellate court judges may be as active as they desire—for example, they often cross-examine counsel freely when a brief is rendered or an oral argument advanced. Juries are not used in appellate courts. Cases are decided on their merits after hearing or submission.[34]

The 11 U.S. courts of appeals currently receive about 19,000 cases every year. They hear cases *en banc*—that is, from three to nine judges hear one particular case. The appeals court may affirm the decision of the district court or reverse it and send it back for a new trial. Criminal appeals to the U.S. Supreme Court from the courts of appeals may be taken in certain cases that involve federal constitutional questions or where the constitutionality of a statute is being called into question. However, cases appealed from state supreme courts are not heard by the federal courts of appeals. Table 8-4 indicates the various circuits of the U.S. courts of appeals.

U.S. Supreme Court The U.S. Supreme Court stands at the apex of the federal judiciary. It consists of nine justices, appointed for life by the president with the advice and consent of the Senate. One justice is designated as the chief justice. The officers appointed by the Court include a clerk to keep the records, a marshal to maintain order and supervise the administrative affairs of the Court, a reporter to publish its opinions, and a librarian to serve the justices and the lawyers of the Supreme Court bar. The chief justice is also authorized to appoint an administrative assistant.

The Court meets annually on the first Monday of October of each year. It usually continues in session until June and receives and disposes of about 5,000 cases each year. Most of these cases are disposed of by the brief decision that the subject matter is either not proper or not of sufficient importance to warrant full court review. But each year between 200 and 250 cases of great importance and interest are decided on the merits; about one-half of these decisions are announced in full published opinions.

The Constitution does not spell out the Supreme Court's appellate jurisdiction, but leaves this question to Congress. In an effort to relieve the Court from an intolerable burden of cases, Congress passed a law in 1925 that permits the Court to exercise its own discretion in deciding what cases it will hear. This is called its *certiorari power* and comes from a special *writ of certiorari*, which is a writ of review issued by the Court. The writ of certiorari commands a lower court to "forward up the record" of a case which it has tried so that the Supreme Court can review it. For example, a defendant who has been

TABLE 8-4

Circuits of the U.S. Courts of Appeals

COURTS OF APPEALS	NUMBER OF AUTHORIZED JUDGESHIPS	LOCATION
First Circuit (Main, Massachusetts, New Hampshire, Rhode Island, Puerto Rico)	3	Boston
Second Circuit (Connecticut, New York, Vermont)	9	New York
Third Circuit (Delaware, New Jersey, Pennsylvania, Virgin Islands)	9	Philadelphia
Fourth Circuit (Maryland, North Carolina, South Carolina, Virginia, West Virginia)	7	Richmond
Fifth Circuit (Alabama, Florida, Georgia, Louisiana, Mississippi, Texas, Canal Zones)	15	New Orleans
Sixth Circuit (Kentucky, Michigan, Ohio, Tennessee)	9	Cincinnati
Seventh Circuit (Illinois, Indiana, Wisconsin)	8	Chicago
Eighth Circuit (Arkansas, Iowa, Minnesota, Missouri, Nebraska, North Dakota, South Dakota)	8	St. Louis
Ninth Circuit (Alaska, Arizona, California, Hawaii, Idaho, Montana Nevada, Oregon, Washington, Guam)	13	San Francisco
Tenth Circuit (Colorado, Kansas, New Mexico, Oklahoma, Utah, Wyoming)	7	Denver
Eleventh Circuit (District of Columbia)	9	Washington, D.C.

found guilty in a criminal trial in a state court and who has exhausted all judicial appellate remedies available in the particular state may petition the Supreme Court for a writ of certiorari. The Supreme Court may grant or deny the petition. If the Court decides to hear the case, it will request that the highest state court (or, when applicable, the particular court of appeals) send all proceedings in that case to the Supreme Court for review. The Supreme Court will not try the case de novo, but will decide upon the particular point of law involved and render its decision.

The U.S. Supreme Court does not have the right to review all decisions of state courts in criminal matters. It has the authority to review only those cases where a federal statute has been interpreted or a federal constitutional right of the defendant has allegedly been violated—that is, where there is a substantial federal question.

In a state trial for a criminal offense, before the defendant can have the case reviewed by the U.S. Supreme Court, he or she must invoke the rights to due process and dual citizenship under the Fourteenth Amendment as well as the particular constitutional right that has been violated. This amendment prohibits the states from depriving citizens of the due process of law and grants dual citizenship as citizens of both their respective state and the United States. These two clauses permit the Supreme Court to intervene in state criminal trials. The Fourteenth Amendment reads in part:

> All persons born or naturalized in the United States, and subject to the jurisdiction thereof, are citizens of the United States and of the State wherein they reside. No State shall make or enforce any law which shall abridge the privileges or immunities of citizens of the United States: nor shall any State deprive any person of life, liberty or property, without due process of law; nor deny to any person within its jurisdiction the equal protection of the laws. . . .

Getting back to our example, let us assume that an individual who was convicted in a state court alleges that his or her Fourth Amendment rights regarding search and seizure have been violated. The defendant cannot merely petition the Supreme Court to grant certiorari based upon the violation of the Fourth Amendment. Instead, the appeal would have to be framed in a manner similar to this: Since my Fourth Amendment rights have been violated, and since this is a violation of my right to due process, and since I am also a citizen of the United States (Fourteenth Amendment), I am petitioning the Supreme Court for review of my case. Thus, the Fourteenth Amendment acts as the "carrier" or incorporation amendment—that is, it must accompany the particular Bill of Rights violation (in this case, the Fourth Amendment) before it can come before the Supreme Court. The defendant on trial in a federal court for a federal crime would need merely to show that his or her Fourth Amendment rights were violated and would not have to invoke the Fourteenth Amendment to appeal the case.

Because of its vested constitutional power, the only federal court whose decisions are binding on state courts is the U.S. Supreme Court. This means that in criminal cases, the Supreme Court decides whether the accused in a case before it has been accorded all his or her due process rights. When the Supreme Court decides a case, the ruling is usually not retroactive. For example, if the Court overturns the conviction of a defendant on a legal technicality, all other persons convicted under the same set of circumstances prior to the decision in this particular case would not have their convictions set aside because of the present ruling. In most situations, the new rule would be applied only from the date of decision forward. Whether a decision will have a retroactice effect is determined by the Supreme Court, based upon the nature of the right, the extent to which the previous rule has been relied upon, the possible consequences that such a change in the rule would have upon the administration of justice, and other considerations.[35]

Over the years, the U.S. Supreme Court has been extending its supervisory authority over state courts by applying the due process clause of the Fourteenth Amendment to constitutional issues in state criminal trials. Table 8-5 depicts the major amendments that pertain to the administration of criminal justice and the particular cases that imposed these safeguards. It should be remembered, however, that not even the U.S. Supreme Court has absolute authority and jurisdiction over all litigative matters.

TABLE 8-5
Twelve Major Provisions in the Bill of Rights Applicable to the Criminal Process

AMENDMENT	PROVISION	APPLICABLE TO STATES	CASE
IV	Unreasonable searches and seizures	Yes	*Wolf* v. *Colorado*, 338 U.S. 25 (1949); *Mapp* v. *Ohio*, 367 U.S. 643 (1961)
V	Grand Jury presentment/indictment	No	*Hurtado* v. *California*, 110 U.S. 516 (1884)
	Double jeopardy	Yes	*Benton* v. *Maryland*, 395 U.S. 784 (1969)
	Privilege against self incrimination	Yes	*Malloy* v. *Hogan*, 378 U.S. 1 (1964)
VI	Speedy trial	Yes	*Klopfer* v. *North Carolina*, 386 U.S. 213 (1967)
	Public trial	Yes	*In re Oliver*, 330 U.S. 257 (1948)
	Jury trial	Yes	*Duncan* v. *Louisiana*, 391 U.S. 145 (1968)
	Confrontation of witnesses	Yes	*Pointer* v. *Texas*, 380 U.S. 400 (1965)
	Compulsory process	Yes	*Washington* v. *Texas*, 388 U.S. 14 (1967)
	Right to counsel	Yes	*Gideon* v. *Wainwright*, 372 U.S. 335 (1963); *Angersinger* v. *Hamlin*, 407 U.S. 25 (1972)
VIII	Excessive bail and fines	No	None
	Cruel and unusual punishment	Yes	*Robinson* v. *California*, 370 U.S. 660 (1962)

SUMMARY

The American judicial system has a dual system of courts—one system that operates at the state level and the other at the federal level. Both systems are organized geographically. Since external supervision is not imposed, the courts can, in many instances, operate more autonomously than the executive or legislative branches of government. Our courts are highly specialized. This specialization is usually determined by their limited jurisdiction.

The historical development of court systems reflects the general cultural, demographic, and political trends that have been a part of our history as a nation. As American society became more complex, the need increased for laws to regulate behavior and for courts to enforce these laws. The state court systems reflect the particular social forces within each state. In recent years, a number of states have attempted to streamline their judiciary and to consolidate the random proliferation of courts. While some states have been able to accomplish this, many others have not.

State and federal courts have similar organizational characteristics. Both systems maintain courts of special and limited jurisdiction at the lowest level in the judicial hierarchy. Next are the courts of general jurisdiction, which handle major criminal and civil cases, and above them are the appellate courts.

About one-half of the states and the federal government have a court of last resort at the pinnacle of the judiciary. In the federal system, this court is the Supreme Court.

REVIEW QUESTIONS

1. Name and briefly describe the main features of the American judicial system.
2. What is the Federal Exclusionary Rule?
3. Explain the role of each of the following components of the state court system.
   a. justice of the peace
   b. magistrate's court
   c. municipal court
   d. general trial court
   e. intermediate state appellate court
   f. state supreme court
4. What are the two major types of courts at the federal level? How do they differ?
5. Under what conditions will a case bypass the court of appeals and go directly to the U.S. Supreme Court?
6. Name 12 major provisions of the Bill of Rights that have been applied to the criminal process. To which constitutional amendments do these provisions apply?

DISCUSSION QUESTIONS

1. What are the features of judicial organization? How do these features influence the operations of our courts?
2. Discuss the structural characteristics of state court systems.
3. Discuss the structural characteristics of the federal court system.
4. Name some of the important officers found at the various state and federal court levels.

SUGGESTED ADDITIONAL READINGS

Abraham, Henry J. *The Judicial Process.* London: Oxford University Press, 1968.

American Judicature Society. *Intermediate Appellate Courts.* Report no. 20. Chicago: American Judicature Society, 1968.

Aumann, Francis R. *The Changing American Legal System.* Columbus: Ohio State University Press, 1940.

Becker, Theodore L. *Political Behavioralism and Modern Jurisprudence.* Chicago: Rand McNally, 1961.

Council of State Governments. *State Court Systems.* Lexington, Ky.: The Council of State Governments, 1978.

Jahnige, Thomas P., and Sheldon Goldman. *The Federal Judicial System.* New York: Holt, 1968.

Knob, Karen M. *Courts of Limited Jurisdiction: A National Survey.* Washington, D.C.: U.S. Government Printing Office, 1977.

President's Commission on Law Enforcement and Administration of Justice. *Task Force Report: The Courts.* Washington, D.C.: U.S. Government Printing Office, 1967.

Vanderbilt, Arthur T. *The Challenge of Law Reform.* Princeton, N.J.: Princeton University Press, 1956.

Vanlandingham, T. "The Decline of the Justice of the Peace." *Kansas Law Review* 389 (1964):380–397.

NOTES

1. Herbert Jacob, *Urban Justice: Law and Order in American Cities* (Englewood Cliffs, N.J.: Prentice-Hall, 1973), pp. 80–91.

2. 232 U.S. 383 (1914).

3. See *Mapp* v. *Ohio,* 367 U.S. 643 (1961).

4. Federal Bureau of Prisons, *Statistical Tables* (Washington, D.C.: U.S. Government Printing Office, 1965),pp. 26–27. At the time of the study, the Tenth Circuit consisted of Colorado, Kansas, New Mexico, Utah, Oklahoma, and Wyoming; the Third Circuit was made up of Delaware, New Jersey, Pennsylvania, and the Virgin Islands.

5. A. Youngdahl, "Sentencing Disparities in U.S. District Courts," *Report of the Institute for Judicial Administration* (Washington, 1965), pp. 33–41.

6. Russell W. Maddox and Robert F. Fuquay, *State and Local Government* (Princeton, N.J.: Van Nostrand, 1962), p. 208.

7. Francis R. Aumann, *The Changing American Legal System* (Columbus: Ohio State University Press, 1940), p. 6.

8. H. R. Glick and K. N. Vines, *State Court Systems* (Englewood Cliffs, N.J.: Prentice-Hall, 1973), p. 19.

9. Charles Warren, *A History of the American Bar* (Boston: Little, Brown, 1911), p. 8.

10. David Mars and Fred Kort, *Administration of Justice in Connecticut* (Storrs: Institute of Public Service, University of Connecticut, 1963), p. 22.

11. Herbert Jacob, "The Courts as Political Agencies," in Herbert Jacob and Kenneth N. Vines, eds., *Studies in Judicial Politics* (New Orleans: Tulane University Press, 1962), p. 17.

12. U.S. (1 Cranch) 137 (1803).

13. Albert Lepawsky, *The Judicial System of Metroplitan Chicago* (Chicago: University of Chicago Press, 1932), pp. 19–23.

14. Ibid., pp. 43–62.

15. Ibid., p. 61.

16. *Survey of the Judicial System of Maryland* (New York: Institute of Judicial Administration, 1967), pp. 11–12.

17. *Report on the District of Columbia Courts* (Washington, D.C.: U.S. Government Printing Office, 1973), p. 2.

18. Jacob, *Urban Justice,* p. 105.

19. President's Commission on Law Enforcement and Administration of Justice, *The Courts* (Washington, D.C.: U.S. Government Printing Office, 1967), p. 31.

20. J. B. Jennings, *Evaluation of the Manhattan Criminal Court's Master Calendar Report, Phase I* (New York: Rand, 1972), p. iii.

21. Lee Thomas W. Church, Jr., *Pretrial Delay: A Review and Bibliography* (Williamsburg, Va.: National Center for State Courts, 1978).

22. W. H. Thomas, Jr., *Bail Reform in America* (Berkeley: University of California Press, 1976), p. 54.

23. Ibid., p. iii.

24. L. R. Katz, L. P. Litwin, and R. H. Bamberger, *Justice Is the Crime: Pretrial Delay in Felony Cases* (Cleveland: Case Western Reserve University Press, 1972), pp. 52–53; L. Banfield and C. D. Anderson, "Continuances in Cook County Criminal Courts," *University of Chicago Law Review* 35 (1968): 262; M. A. Levin, *Urban Politics and the Criminal Courts* (Chicago: University of Chicago Press, 1977), p. 198; and T. C. Clark, "The Omnibus Hearing in State and Federal Courts," *Cornell Law Review* 59 (1974): 118–119.

25. President's Commission on Law Enforcement and Administration of Justice, *Task Force Report: The Courts* (Washington, D.C.: U.S. Government Printing Office, 1967), pp. 80–82.

26. National Bureau of Standards, *Compilation and Use of Criminal Court Data in Relation to Pretrial Release of Defendants: Pilot Study* (Washington, D.C.: U.S. Government Printing Office, 1970), p. 160.

27. Glick and Vines, *State Court Systems,* pp. 28–29.

28. *The Christian Science Monitor,* May 9, 1967, p. 5. Note: Pennsylvania now requires its justices of the peace either to be licensed attorneys or to complete a course of training and instruction in the duties of that office.

29. Weldon Cooper, "Justice of the Peace in Virginia: A Neglected Aspect of the Judiciary," *Virginia Law Review* 52, no. 151 (January 1966): 34–40.

30. Public statement, December 1, 1966.

31. Henry J. Abraham, *The Judicial Process,* 3rd ed. (New York: Oxford University Press, 1975), p. 143.

32. Annual Report of the Administrative Office of the United States Courts, *Reports of the Proceedings of the Judicial Conference of the United States* (Washington, D.C.: U.S. Government Printing Office, 1977).

33. Ibid., p. 253.

34. Stephen T. Early, Jr., *Constitutional Courts of the U.S.* (Totowa, N.J.: Littlefield, Adams, 1977), p. 103.

35. Hazel B. Kerper, *Introduction to the Criminal Justice System* (St. Paul, Minn.: West, 1972), p. 226.

9

THE CRIMINAL PRETRIAL, TRIAL, AND POST-TRIAL PROCESS

Heron/Monkmeyer

1. What are the steps in the conduct of a misdemeanor case?
2. What are the steps in the conduct of a felony case?
3. What is bail and how important is it in the judicial process.
4. What is the function of a grand jury?
5. What are the preliminary proceedings in the trial court?
6. What role does the jury play in trying a criminal case?

These are some of the questions this chapter will answer.

This chapter examines in detail the various steps in the conduct of a criminal trial. Before beginning this chapter, the student should become familiar with the basic criminal processes for a misdemeanor and a felony, as shown in Figures 9-1 and 9-2. It is also advisable to read the provisions of the Fifth and Sixth Amendments of the Constitution (see Appendix A).

PRELIMINARY TRIAL PROCEEDINGS

To begin the prosecution of an accused, a complaint is filed before a magistrate or judge, usually in a court of limited jurisdiction. Although these courts have original jurisdiction only in misdemeanor cases, they often conduct many of the pretrial processes in a felony case.

The purpose of filing a complaint is to determine whether an arrest warrant should be issued. The existing evidence and, in some cases, the testimony of the complainant is presented to demonstrate that there is probable cause to believe that the accused has committed a crime. If the judge or magistrate determines that probable cause exists, he or she issues the arrest warrant. If the accused is in custody, the warrant authorizes that individual's detention pending an initial appearance; if the accused is not in custody, the warrant directs the police to arrest the individual and bring him or her before a magistrate.

CONDUCT OF MISDEMEANOR CASES

The conduct of a misdemeanor trial and the steps in the process are much less elaborate than those for a felony. An accused arrested for a misdemeanor is brought before the particular court of limited jurisdiction that has the authority to try such cases. When the defendant appears before the court, the offense complaint is read and explained. Before the court can proceed, the

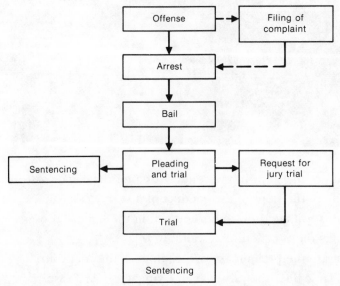

FIGURE 9-1   Basic Criminal Process for a Misdemeanor

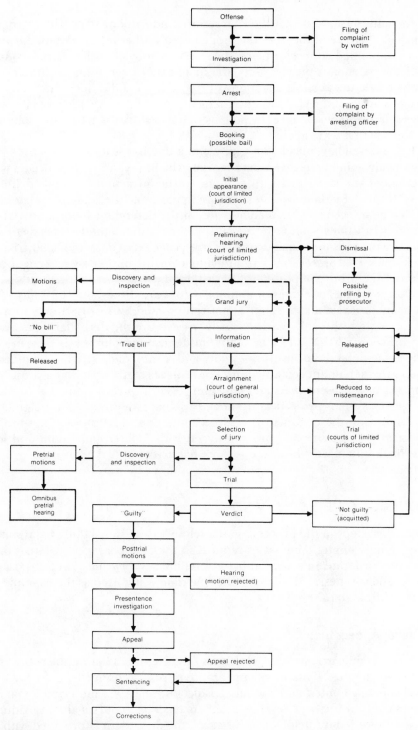

FIGURE 9-2 Basic Criminal Process for a Felony

defendant must attest that the charges are understood. Depending upon the particular nature of the case, the judge may ask whether the defendant wants court-appointed counsel if he or she cannot afford to retain private counsel.

If the defendant pleads guilty, the magistrate, after a limited inquiry that may include the possible testimony of the accused and others concerning the circumstances of the case and the characteristics of the offender, will impose a fine, a limited jail sentence, or both as prescribed by the particular statute or ordinance that was violated.

If the defendant pleads not guilty, the judge has several alternatives. The judge may immediately conduct the trial, which is typically what occurs when the defendant is charged with a minor traffic infraction or public drunkenness. If the defendant indicates a desire to postpone the trial until a later date so that he or she can obtain an attorney, if the defendant wants a jury trial in those jurisdictions where it is permissible,[1] or if the defendant needs time to prepare the case and obtain witnesses, the judge sets a date for a later trial and establishes bail or releases the individual on his or her own recognizance without requiring the posting of a cash bond.

Most misdemeanor cases of a minor nature are disposed of by guilty pleas. In many jurisdictions, the state is not represented by a prosecuting attorney. In these cases, the only parties usually present are the defendant, the arresting officer, and the judge. In many misdemeanor courts, it is only in cases where the defendant pleads not guilty and a subsequent trial is arranged or where the defendant retains counsel or requests a jury trial that a prosecutor appears to represent the state. However, even in jurisdictions that normally assign an assistant prosecutor to such cases, there are usually some significant differences in the conduct of misdemeanor trials. The proceedings are less adversarial in nature and are conducted with greater courtroom and legal informality than are the more serious felony cases in the courts of general jurisdiction.

CONDUCT OF FELONY CASES

The initial steps in the processing of a felony case differ slightly from state to state. For example, some states require an initial appearance; whereas other states incorporate this step into the preliminary hearing. For purposes of comprehensiveness, it is assumed that the state being used as the example has both of these steps.

Initial Appearance

An individual arrested for a felony is first presented before the court by an initial appearance. This initial appearance is usually conducted before a lower level court of limited and special jurisdiction, such as a municipal or magistrate's court at the state level or a U.S. magistrate's court if the individual is accused of a federal felony. At this stage, the defendant is provided with the notice of such rights as the right to counsel, the right to remain silent, and the right to a preliminary examination. The accused is also informed of the charges and, if an individual was arrested without an arrest warrant, sufficient evidence must be established so that an arrest warrant can be issued even though the accused is already in custody.

Since the U.S. Supreme Court has established the necessity that counsel be present during any "critical stage" of the criminal process, or when the criminal investigation has narrowed down from a general search to the investigation of a single individual, the court will generally postpone the initial appearance until the accused has obtained counsel.[2] If the defendant indicates that he or she cannot afford an attorney, an inquiry is made into the defendant's financial status which is often referred to as an "indigency hearing." If the accused claims indigency, the court requires that an indigency affidavit be signed in which the accused swears to financial impoverishment. Once this is done, the court appoints assigned counsel or refers the accused to the Office of the Public Defender.

Bail

The judge usually determines bail at this stage. Some states permit the arrested person to make bail at the time that he or she is booked for certain crimes. If the defendant has already done this and is not incarcerated at the time of the initial appearance, the judge can still modify the amount of bail bond required as long as it conforms to the maximum limit prescribed by statute. Likewise, the judge has the discretion in a number of crimes to release the individual on his or her own recognizance without requiring the posting of a form of cash bond. In more serious crimes and in some jurisdictions, the accused cannot be released on bail until he or she has undergone the initial appearance.

Under the Federal Rules of Criminal Procedure, the accused must be brought before the magistrate at this stage "without unnecessary delay." This emphasis on conducting a prompt inquiry arose from two U.S. Supreme Court rulings in which the Court held under the *McNabb-Mallory* rule and the *Upshaw* v. *United States* decision that an unjustified delay is unreasonable and sufficient to presume that all statements made by the arrestee between the arrest and the delayed hearing are inadmissable in evidence as the product of an unlawful detention.[3] So that clear guidelines can be imposed on such language, in 1975 Congress passed the "Speedy Trial Act."[4] Under the provisions of this act, the defendant must be processed through the various trial stages within certain stipulated times. Failure by the federal courts to comply with these times will result in the defendant's motion for a dismissal of the charges.[5]

Although many stages have similar provisions that call for an initial appearance without unnecessary delay, most state courts (unless they, too, have adopted specific time frames under a "Speedy Trial Act") consider delays simply to be a part of the overall judicial process. In reality, the problems of delay in processing the defendant through the initial appearance are usually not that serious. The more serious delays usually occur later in bringing the accused up for a preliminary hearing, arraignment, or the actual trial.

Preliminary Examination (Hearing)

After the initial appearance, the accused is scheduled for a preliminary examination at a later date. The U.S. Supreme Court ruled in 1975 that a preliminary hearing is required by the probable cause provision of the Fourth Amendment.[6] The defendant can waive this right and proceed to the next stage in the judicial process. Often, however, if the accused has retained an attorney, the lawyer will insist on the right to a preliminary examination. The preliminary hearing gives a tactical advantage to the defense because the defense attorney can use this forum to gain as much knowledge as possible about the strengths and weaknesses of the state's case.

At the hearing, the court will again inquire whether the defendant has counsel if his or her attorney is not present. If the accused can afford private counsel, he or she will be advised to retain the services of an attorney (unless the defendant clearly refuses the assistance of counsel at this stage), and the preliminary hearing will be postponed until a later date.

The state and the defendant have the right to produce witnesses who testify under oath. The state will attempt to introduce only enough evidence to make a *prima facie* case—that is, to show probable cause to believe that a crime has been committed and that the defendant committed it. The state need not (and most experienced prosecutors will not) introduce all its evidence at this time. The full range of witnesses and evidence are saved for the later trial. This tactic prevents the defense from knowing all the facts of the state's case and thus gaining too much insight at this time into its possible weaknesses. Both the prosecutor and the defense counsel have the right to cross-examine the witnesses introduced by the opposing side. The testimony of all witnesses is transcribed, and since the testimony is under oath, it can be used to impeach the credibility of a witness if it is inconsistent with later testimony given at the trial.

Release After Preliminary Hearing

Since preliminary hearings are conducted on an inquiry basis, they are not limited by the rules of evidence that apply to trials. If the state fails to show probable cause, the defendant is dismissed by the magistrate. The preliminary hearing only assures that the defendant will not be incarcerated without the existence of valid probable cause and gives the accused the opportunity to be released on bail. A release by a magistrate on a preliminary hearing or a dismissal of the charges is not, however, binding upon the state. Since the defendant has not stood trial and has not been placed in jeopardy, the prosecutor in most states can file another complaint on the same offense, having the individual arrested and brought again before the courts for another preliminary hearing. In recent years, some states have required that the prosecutor provide additional evidence which was not known to the state at the time of the first preliminary examination before the accused can be rearrested and brought back before the court for another preliminary hearing on the same charge.

Binding Over and Review of Bail   If the state satisfies the court that it has met its burden of proof, the judge issues an order binding over the defendant to the next step in the judicial process. The judge is also required to certify that a preliminary examination has been held and that the evidence presented has established probable cause to believe that a crime has been committed and that the accused committed it. This certification confers jurisdiction upon the grand jury or the trial court and authorizes the prosecutor to continue to the next step in the judicial process.

The defendant, at this time, is advised of the right to waive grand jury examination. This right exists only in federal courts and those states that still use the grand jury. If the defendant knowingly and intelligently waives these rights, the court will bypass the grand jury and transfer the case to the court that has jurisdiction over the conduct of felony cases.

Lastly, the court again reviews the bail which may be raised or lowered depending on the authority vested in the judge by virtue of existing statute, and the judge's discretion to exercise that authority. This practice of requiring a bond to obtain the release of an accused gives some assurance to the court that the accused will return for trial. During the period of release on bail, the accused is under the authority of the court and must comply with any conditions established by the judge who authorizes the bail. The terms "bail" and "bond" are often used interchangeably, but there is a distinction. Bail is the posting of a surety or some other valuable consideration such as money that will give the court some assurance that the accused will be available at the time of the trial. If the accused fails to appear, the surety is forfeited to the court. In some instances, a bond may be merely the accused's word that he or she will appear at the trial. This is usually referred to as a recognizance bond.

Generally, the court has discretion in setting the pretrial bail in all but the most serious capital offenses (e.g., murder). Although an offense may warrant bail, the judge in most jurisdictions can refuse to authorize bail and the posting of bond if the release of the accused would jeopardize his or her own safety or the safety of others. The basic premise that underlies the granting of bail is the fundamental principle that all persons accused of crime are presumed innocent until proved guilty. This concept became an implicit guarantee of the rights of a member of a free society and was reinforced by the Eighth Amendment to the U.S. Constitution which provides that "excessive bail shall not be required."

Discovery and Inspection   Once the preliminary hearing has been conducted and the accused has been bound over to the next stage in the judicial process, many jurisdictions provide that discovery and inspection procedures be instituted. In recent years, expanded rights of discovery and inspection have developed, particularly in the federal court system. States are now adopting similar procedures to guide the conduct of criminal trials in their courts. The idea behind discovery and inspection is to ensure that each party has the opportunity to test the evidence submitted by the other side. It is contended that advance knowledge of the evidence to be used is essential to prepare for the cross-examination of a witness or to gather evidence to refute testimony.[7]

As discussed under the preliminary examination, the prosecutor often does not disclose all the state's evidence; states that have expanded the scope of pretrial discovery and inspection have limited the ability of the prosecutor to withhold evidence. However, this right to discovery and inspection works two ways—just as the evidence of the state is made more readily available to the accused, so is the evidence that the defendant might have more readily accessible for examination by the prosecutor.

The possible extent of pretrial discovery and inspection rights for both sides is indicated by the following suggestions on this matter by the National Advisory Commission on Criminal Justice Standards and Goals:

> The prosecution should disclose to the defendant all available evidence that will be used against him at trial. Such disclosure should take place within five days of the preliminary hearing or apprehension or service of summons following indictment, whichever form the initiation of prosecution takes in the particular case. The evidence disclosed should include, but should not be limited to the following:
>
> 1. The names and addresses of persons whom the prosecutor intends to call as witnesses at the trial:
>
> 2. Written, recorded or oral statements made by witnesses whom the prosecutor intends to call at the trial of the accused or of any codefendant;
>
> 3. Results of physical or mental examinations, scientific tests and any analyses of physical evidence and any reports or statements of experts relating to such examinations, tests or analyses; and
>
> 4. Physical evidence belonging to the defendant or which the prosecutor intends to introduce at trial.[8]

The commission also recommends that the defense supply the prosecution with certain evidence. Similar recommendations have been made by the American Bar Association Project on Minimum Standards for Criminal Justice in its *Standards Relating to Discovery and Procedure before Trial*.[9] This defense-supplied evidence requires the disclosure of such facts as the intent to rely on an alibi or an insanity defense; any reports, results, or testimony that supports such defenses; physical or mental examinations or scientific tests, experiments, or comparisons, or any other reports or statements of experts that defense counsel intends to use at a hearing or trial.[10]

Of course, these standards exclude such information as statements made by the witness (which might be incriminating) or whether the defendant will testify at the trial.[11] Those who advocate the liberalization of discovery and inspection do so on the grounds that it will maximize the early resolution of issues regarding the admissibility of evidence and will encourage administrative disposition of cases with no significant increased danger of conviction of innocent defendants and no unjustifiable infringements upon the right of guilty defendants to be treated with dignity.[12]

THE GRAND JURY

As discussed earlier, the case may be bound over to the grand jury after the preliminary hearing. The beginnings of the grand jury can be traced back to 1166 when the Assize of Clarendon was established. An assize was a court session that had developed earlier in France and was brought to England by the Norman conquerors. The assize was to consist of 12 individuals who personally knew the accused. These jurors would then question witnesses in order to determine whether the accused appeared to be guilty of the alleged crime. Since they knew the accused and often the accusor as well, these "grand jurors" were supposed to be in a good position to screen out unfounded accusation and, theoretically at least, afford certain protections to the accused.

Legal historians, however, point out that this was not usually what happened.[13] Some historians indicate that this "grand jury" was not at all created to shield the citizen from false accusations or the powers of the state. In fact, it was created expressly by King Henry II to enable the king to wrest the administration of justice from the Church and the federal barons. The grand jury thus served primarily as a weapon for the monarch, enforcing his law, whether or not it was legal and proper. Because of its misuse, the grand jury was often cited as a condemnation of the monarch.[14] Some 500 years later during the religious strife in England in 1681, the grand jury finally threw off the yoke of the king and asserted its role as a shield for the innocent against malicious and oppressive prosecution.

The idea of the grand jury was incorporated in the U.S. Constitution and the constitutions of most states. The Fifth Amendment to the U.S. Constitution provides that "no person shall be held to answer for a capital, or otherwise infamous crime, unless on presentment or indictment of a grand jury." From this it would appear that the Constitution clearly requires that persons accused of major crimes be accused by a grand jury, yet less than half the states use the grand jury today. The reason is that the U.S. Supreme Court has not seen fit to require that the grand jury requirement be made applicable to the states through the due process clause of the Fourteenth Amendment.

Today, the grand jury is supposed to serve two important functions:

1. Determine whether an accused should stand trial by virtue of the fact that there is probable cause to believe that a felony has been committed.

2. Protect the innocent from false accusations and harassment by the state where there is no reason to believe a felony has been committed.

In recent years, the grand jury system has been widely criticized for failing to accomplish either task. Because of its inadequacies, it has come to be viewed by some observers as actually inhibiting justice and the rights of due process.

Filing an Information

The grand jury does not determine the guilt or innocence of the accused, but only whether the individual should be brought to trial. In states that do not routinely use the grand jury, an individual is usually brought to trial after the preliminary hearing by the filing of an *information* by the prosecutor. This information must state the charges, the statute that was violated, and the approximate time and place of the occurrence of the crime; subsequently, the accused must be served with the notice of these facts and specifications. In recent years, even states that still have the grand jury are increasingly bypassing it by using the information. In many other instances, the accused waives this right to grand jury and thereby also bypasses it.

Although the grand jury is an extension of the court, it has the authority to act independently of the court. Neither the court nor the state may limit the scope of grand jury investigations. It has the power to subpoena witnesses and documents, to grant immunity to witnesses who testify before it, and to proceed in independent criminal investigations. These investigations may be of public officials as well as of private citizens. The grand jury is charged by statute to inquire into matters relating to crime and corruption within its jurisdiction and to bring to trial those whom it feels the state has been derelict in not prosecuting. In addition, many jurisdictions require that the grand jury periodically investigate certain functions or governmental operations within the jurisdiction, such as jail facilities or law enforcement agencies, and publicly report its findings and recommendations. These particular functions are called its *investigatory responsibilities;* however, in most routine criminal cases most of the work of the grand jury falls under its *hearing responsibilities,* which is the focus for the remainder of the examination of the grand jury in this section.

Hearing Responsibilities

The grand jury is usually composed of 16 to 23 citizens of the judicial district who are chosen by a statutorily prescribed selection process and summoned by a court with general jurisdiction over criminal cases.[15] After the grand jurors are selected and before they commence their activities, the court selects a foreman from among them. The responsibility of the foreman is to verify that a quorum of grand jurors is always available when evidence is being presented and that there are a sufficient number of votes to return an indictment. In many jurisdictions, the foreman also administers the oath to witnesses who testify before this body and performs related administrative tasks required to handle the grand jury proceedings.

The decisions of the grand jury need not be unanimous. Most state statutes prescribe that a two-thirds or three-fourths majority is all that is necessary to return or refuse to return an indictment. An indictment is a formal accusation by the grand jury that is arrived at after consideration of the evidence against the accused. In order to indict someone, the foreman writes on the indictment "A True Bill" and attests to this with his or her signature (see Figure 9-3). For example, let us assume that in a particular state there are 18 grand jurors, of which 12 must concur for an indictment. After hearing all the evidence, 13 grand jurors believe that there is sufficient evidence to believe that a crime has been committed and that the accused committed it. Thus, the 13 would vote for indictment and a true bill would be signed. The accused would then be bound over for trial. If the required two-thirds majority could not be reached, the foreman would write "No Bill" on the indictment, and the accused would be released.

The Indictment

The indictment is a very important legal document that must carefully set forth a number of facts. It must:

1. State the type and nature of the offense.
2. Cite the specific statute alleged to have been violated.

3. Set forth the nature and elements of the offense charged.
4. State as definitely as possible the time and place of the occurrence of the crime.
5. State the name and address of the accused if known, and if not known, provide a description sufficient to identify the accused with reasonable certainty.
6. Bear the signature of the foreman showing that it has been returned as a true bill.

UNITED STATES OF AMERICA

IN THE UNITED STATES DISTRICT COURT FOR THE

WESTERN DISTRICT OF MICHIGAN, SOUTHERN DIVISION

- - - - - - - - - -

UNITED STATES OF AMERICA,	)	
	)	
Plaintiff,	)	No. 76-223 Cr.7
	)	
vs.	)	
	)	
EUGENE JOHN McCOY,	)	INDICTMENT
	)	
Defendant.	)	
	)	

The Grand Jury charges:

Timothy J. Ott

Timothy J. Ott
CHIEF JUDGE
UNITED STATES DISTRICT COURT

That on or about the 12th day of July, 1976, at Emmettsville, in Ingham County, in the Southern Division of the Western District of Michigan,

EUGENE JOHN McCOY

by force and violence and by intimidation did take from the person and presence of Carol Ann Drucker approximately Fourteen Thousand Five Hundred Twenty-two and no/100 ($14,522.00) Dollars in money belonging to and in the care, custody, control, management and possession of the Exchange National Bank, Emmettsville Branch, 279 East Robinson Avenue, Emmettsville, Michigan, the deposits of which were then insured by the Federal Deposit Insurance Corporation. 18 U.S.C. S 2113(a)

A TRUE BILL

Charles E. Eckenrode   *James T. Hardmann*

Charles E. Eckenrode   FOREMAN
United States Attorney

FIGURE 9-3 A True Bill of Indictment

7. Indicate the names of all co-defendants in the offense charged as well as the number of counts against them.[16]

Grand Jury Proceedings

Grand jury proceedings have some important characteristics. First, in the law they are referred to as *ex parte* (one-party) proceedings. This means that the accused and his or her attorney are not permitted to be present during the conduct of the grand jury hearing. Under these circumstances, the accused does not have the opportunity to cross-examine the witnesses, to object to their testimony, or to the introduction of evidence. Only the state or representatives of the state such as police officers and their witnesses are authorized to be present during the conduct of the hearing. The hearings are presided over by the prosecutor, who, in essence, runs the grand jury. He or she controls the introduction of witnesses and the presentation of evidence, and sets the general framework for the questioning by the members of the grand jury.

Witnesses are usually not permitted to be represented by counsel during the grand jury hearing. The conduct of these hearings is very informal in comparison to that of a trial. Usually, the witness is brought in, the oath is administered, and the witness relates what he or she knows in response to questions from the prosecutor or grand jurors. The rules of evidence do not apply. As an example, hearsay evidence is admissible. In a trial, a witness, except under a few limited circumstances, could not testify to what he or she heard someone say because the witness does not have direct knowledge of the facts and the truth of the matter; no such prohibition applies to witnesses before the grand jury.

The grand jury has the right to compel witnesses to testify except in cases where the witness is subject to the right against self-incrimination. However, the grand jury has the right to extend immunity to a witness. This is a guarantee that even though the testimony is self-incriminating, the witness will be immune from later prosecution for testifying.[17] Since the grand jury has this right, it also has the authority to jail for contempt those witnesses who will not cooperate unless they claim self-incrimination and immunity is not given.

The proceedings of grand juries are secret, as are the actual deliberations. Any testimony given by a witness to the grand jury is considered a privileged communication and cannot be revealed. Grand jurors are required to adhere to the strict rules of secrecy during their term of appointment. They are also told to disregard all information they hear outside of the grand jury room which may have a bearing on the case and to concentrate solely on the testimony and evidence presented to them in the conduct of the hearing.

PRELIMINARY PROCEEDINGS IN THE TRIAL COURT

Arraignment

After an indictment has been returned as a "true-bill" by the grand jury or an information has been filed by the prosecutor, the accused is arraigned before a court of general jurisdiction that has the authority to try the case. The arraignment is the procedure whereby the accused is called into court to answer the charge. It is not a trial, and the court does not at this time examine any matters that pertain to the accused's guilt or innocence. If the defendent has not previously been given a copy of the indictment or information, he or she is now given one. The contents of the indictment or information are also read to the defendent. In this way, the state informs the defendant that it is ready to proceed with the charges.

If the defendant still does not have counsel, the court must assure him or her of this right, and if indigent, the defendant will be given court-appointed legal assistance. The court will point out that counsel is advisable so that the accused knows and understands the nature of the charges and the implications of the plea that the accused might make. In the event that the accused does not have counsel, many courts will automatically enter a not guilty plea.

Pleas

During the arraignment, the accused is asked to enter a plea to the charge. Basically, depending upon the statutory provisions of the particular jurisdiction, the defendent may enter a plea of *not guilty, nolo contendere,* or *guilty* or may merely stand mute.

If the defendant pleads not guilty, he or she denies each allegation in the accusation, and in so doing requires the state to establish these allegations beyond a reasonable doubt. In states that permit the practice, the accused, after entering a plea of not guilty, will be advised of the right to trial by jury or before a judge without a jury. Once the defendant indicates this choice, the case is placed on the court calendar or docket and scheduled for future trial.

The plea of nolo contendere literally means "I will not contest it." This plea technically means that the individual does not wish to contest or argue the issue of guilt or innocence. Such a plea, in a number of jurisdictions, has to be approved by the prosecutor and the judge. In essence, it is a guilty plea and has the same effect. It authorizes the court to enter judgment and sentence upon the plea. This plea has some legal significance in that in subsequent criminal or civil proceedings, the admission of guilt is not present as it would be if the accused had entered a plea of guilty to the charge. Under these circumstances, the acknowledgment of guilt could not be introduced into a later trial. Since it serves no purpose other than to protect the individual from the consequences of his or her conviction, some states do not feel it serves the purpose of justice and have abolished it. Other states require that the court give its permission before such a plea can be entered.

If the defendant remains mute when asked how he pleads to the charge, an automatic plea of not guilty will be entered by the court. The major advantage of standing mute is that in some jurisdictions a plea is the same as saying that the defendant accepts the jurisdiction of the trial court and, as a result, waives the right to protest any irregularities or defects that may have occurred in the preliminary examination or grand jury.[18]

If the defendant pleads guilty, the judge immediately inquires whether the plea is made with the full understanding of its ramifications and whether it is voluntarily made. The courts have held that a guilty plea must be free from coercion or promises and must not be otherwise unfairly obtained or the result of ignorance or fear.[19] If the court is not thoroughly convinced that these requirements have been met, it cannot accept the plea. Nor should the court assume that these requirements are fully met simply because the defendant is represented by an attorney. Since a guilty plea is the same as a waiver of the defendant's right to require the prosecution to prove his or her guilt beyond a reasonable doubt, the judge is under a strict responsibility to be certain that such a plea is voluntary and knowingly given. If it should later be proved that this is not the case, grounds will exist for the reversal of the conviction.

If the plea is guilty, the court may immediately sentence the defendant. A number of states require that a presentence investigation be conducted of the defendant's background so that the judge can be guided in determining the appropriate sentence to impose.

Pretrial Motions

After the indictment or information has been filed, the defendent may, prior to the arraignment or before the trial, employ a number of motions in an effort to have the case dismissed or to gain a particular legal advantage in the preparation of the case or the introduction of evidence at the trial. A motion is a request that the court examine a particular legal point that the defense contends is an error in the state's case. In filing the motion, the defense hopes that the ruling will be in behalf of the accused. Although it is not possible to review all the motions that the defense might raise, some of the more frequently encountered and important motions are examined here briefly.

Motion to discharge or dismiss the case. This is probably the most important of the various pretrial motions. It is initiated upon written request of the defendant prior to the beginning of the trial, but usually after the plea has been entered. The defendant asks the court to dismiss the indictment, information, or complaint for any number of reasons, such as (1) the grand jury that returned the indictment was illegally selected and empaneled; (2) the grand jury permitted the presence of unauthorized individuals during their deliberations; (3) the charge brought against the defendant does not state an offense punishable under the laws of the state; or (4) there has been a fundamental denial of the defendant's constitutional rights, such as the denial of the right of defense counsel to have the opportunity to cross-examine witnesses at the preliminary hearing or failure to advise the defendant of his rights against self-incrimination.

Motions may also be directed at the indictment or information, contending that these documents are not technically correct in that they fail to specify clearly the charges, the elements of the offense, or the specific offense violated or that the foreman of the grand jury did not certify in writing a true bill. The defendant may also allege that the statute of limitations has run out on the particular offense of which he or she is accused. Many states require that in the case of felonies, prosecution must begin within 7 years after the commission of the offense, except in capital cases, which have no statute of limitations.[20] Lastly, the defendant may allege that he has been granted immunity from the courts for the offense for which he now stands charged.

In reality, many of these motions serve no useful purpose to the accused other than to delay the start of the trial. Often, the judge simply directs the prosecutor or the grand jury to correct the deficiencies in the documents that are found to be incorrect. Only in such cases as former grants of immunity or the expiration of the statute of limitations will the motions result in a dismissal of the charges.

Motion for a bill of particulars. This is a motion by the defense that requests the state to provide additional facts in the indictment or information so that the accused can develop a proper defense. This motion must be filed within a specified time after the arraignment but before the commencement of the trial. If this motion is upheld by the court, the prosecutor will be ordered to clarify the charges by adding the necessary facts to the original indictment or information in the form of an amendment. For example, if a bookstore owner was charged with the possession and sale of pornographic material, the defense would want to know which of the confiscated reading materials the prosecutor intends to use as the basis for the case.

Motion to suppress or quash evidence. This is an attempt to have evidence that the state has gathered excluded from consideration. This motion may be brought before or after the arraignment or during the trial when there is an objection to the admission into evidence of certain items or testimony.

This motion contends that the evidence that the state plans to use was illegally obtained by means of a violation of the defendant's rights and is, therefore, not admissible. Often, this motion is filed by the defense to exclude evidence that has been obtained as a result of an illegal search and seizure or wiretap or to challenge the validity of a confession.

In determining whether to grant this motion and thereby exclude the evidence, the judge will conduct a special hearing, at which witnesses who have relevant testimony are examined. If the evidence seized by the police was attained by means of a search warrant, the burden of proof is on the defense to show that it was illegally searched for and seized. If the evidence was taken without a warrant, the burden or proof is on the state. Under these circumstances, the prosecutor is permitted to cross-examine the defense witnesses as well as to introduce the state's witnesses. When the hearing is concluded, the judge, based upon all the testimony presented, rules whether or not the evidence can be used against the defendant. If the judge rules that it cannot, the state cannot use the evidence against the accused and may then be forced to ask the court to dismiss the case if it cannot possibly obtain a conviction without the evidence.

If the defense, during the conduct of the trial, objects to evidence that the state introduces and files a motion to suppress, the trial will immediately stop, and there will be a similar special hearing on the motion. However, in order for the defense to file this motion during the trial, it must show that it did not have the opportunity to do so before the trial began. The hearing on the motion is then conducted in a special session from which the jury is excluded.

Motion for change of venue. The defendant may also introduce a motion to move the trial to another jurisdiction. This motion is based on the defendant's contention that because of prejudice against him, he cannot obtain a fair trial in the particular locale of the court. Often, in cases of sensational crimes that have received considerable publicity in the local media, the defense will contend that an impartial trial is impossible. In most cases, the state will be permitted to file counterarguments against a change of venue. After hearing the evidence, the court decides whether, in the best interests of justice, the trial should be moved elsewhere.

Motion for continuance. States have enacted statutes that specify the various conditions under which a trial date can be postponed. Both the defense and the prosecution can apply for a continuance. Some of the more common reasons for a continuance to be granted are: (1) that counsel for the defense or the prosecution is ill, has died, or is engaged in the trial of another case; (2) that the defendant is ill; (3) that a material witness for the defense or the state is unavailable at the time; or (4) that the bill of particulars that amended the original indictment or information has introduced new facts or allegations which require more time to present an adequate defense.

Some of the other pretrial motions that might be introduced are motion for discontinuance, motion for a list of witnesses, motion for a joinder of related prosecutions, motion for a severance of joint prosecutions, and motion for a change of judge.

The Omnibus Pretrial Hearing

The omnibus pretrial hearing is among the recent innovations designed to enhance the efficiency of the criminal justice system. It may be defined as a procedural device where a single judicial hearing with a minimum of formalities and filings is conducted "to ensure that discovery has been properly conducted and that issues are simply and efficiently raised."[21]

Essentially, it is a hearing in which a judge (hearing the case) entertains any motions by either side and rules on them (e.g., challenges to the voluntariness of admissions or confessions, challenge to suppress evidence, motion for continuance, etc.) In addition, the hearing is used to satisfy the court that such things as standards regarding the provision of counsel have been complied with and to inquire whether the parties have completed the discovery process, and if not, to issue orders appropriate to expedite completion. The idea behind this process is to complete these matters in one comprehensive hearing before the trial. In this way, the omnibus pretrial hearing results in a sharpening and narrowing of issues for trial, an economizing of cost and time, and a reduced likelihood of appeal—all of which are particularly important in light of the ever-increasing litigation before our federal and state courts.[22]

Selection of the Jury

After hearing any motions, the judge rules on them. If the accused pleads not guilty or stands mute, the court asks whether the defendant wants a jury trial. If he indicates that he does, the case is placed on the general trial court's criminal docket, and the next step in the trial process is the selection of jurors.

The right to trial by jury has historically existed in the common law. In 1215 when the Magna Carta was signed, it contained a special provision that no freeholder would be deprived of life or property except by judgment of his or her peers. This right was incorporated into the U.S. Constitution, where Article III, Section 2 states: "The trial of all crimes, except in cases of impeachment, shall be by jury." Likewise, the Sixth Amendment provides that "in all criminal prosecutions, the accused shall enjoy the right to a speedy and public trial by an impartial jury of the State and district wherein the crime shall have been committed."

Although the right to a jury trial is a fundamental constitutional guarantee, until 1968, in the case of *Duncan* v. *Louisiana,* the U.S. Supreme Court did not guarantee this right to defendants in state courts.[23] In that case, the Supreme Court overruled one of its earlier decisions and applied the right to jury trial to defendants in state courts by virtue of the Fourteenth Amendment.

The trial jury in a felony case usually consists of 12 jurors. Why the courts have settled on the number 12 is not known for certain although some believe it is based on the fact that Christ had 12 disciples. The Constitution does not specify the number of jurors required, and many states use less than 12 jurors in misdemeanor cases. Under the early common law, jurors were witnesses who were summoned to testify for the state or the defense. Today jurors are impartial persons who will render a decision on the facts presented them during the trial.

The prospective jurors are chosen by means specified in the particular legislation of the state. Usually, names of prospective jurors are compiled by the designated official (jury commissioner, clerks of courts, sheriff, etc.) from voter registration lists of the jurisdiction. The names are placed on slips of paper and drawn at random by some means. These prospective jurors constitute what is known as the jury panel or *venire*. The number of individuals ultimately selected at the beginning of each term of court depends on the number and nature of the cases pending. If cases have received notoriety, more individuals may need to be selected in order to find unbiased jurors.

From one to four alternate jurors are also chosen, depending upon the particular state. These alternate jurors substitute for primary jurors who become ill during the trial or the deliberations of the jury. These alternate jurors sit in on the trial, but do not vote unless they have replaced one of the original twelve.

The selection of jurors must satisfy minimum standards of due process in that they must be a representative sample of the community, and there can be no discrimination based upon race, religion, or national origin. All states prescribe that certain characteristics will exclude an individual from jury service. Some of the more common are the inability to read, write, or understand the English language; mental deficiency or some disabling physical defect such as deafness or blindness; blood relationship to the defendant; prior conviction of a felony; and service on the grand jury that returned the indictment. Certain individuals are exempt from jury duty by virtue of their occupation or particular status. Some examples are physicians, dentists, attorneys, and, in some jurisdictions, military personnel on active service and mothers whose absence from the home would create a particular hardship.

WILLIAMS v. FLORIDA (1970)

Whether the use of trial juries of less than 12 persons violates a defendant's constitutional rights to a trial by jury.

FACTS:

Johnny Williams was tried and convicted of robbery by a 6-member jury in a Florida state court. During the proceedings, Williams objected to being tried by a 6-member jury, which, under Florida law, was permitted in all cases involving noncapital offenses. He asserted that a jury of less than 12 members violated his constitutional rights under the Sixth Amendment, as made applicable to the states by the Fourteenth Amendment. His argument was denied and he was sentenced to life imprisonment. The Florida Court of Appeals upheld the conviction, and the case was appealed to the Supreme Court.

DECISION:

The Sixth Amendment, as applied to the states through the Fourteenth Amendment, does not specifically require that a 12-member jury be used in criminal cases. As long as a criminal jury is a representative body, less than 12 jurors are permitted. The decision of the trial court and the Florida Court of Appeals was upheld.

SIGNIFICANCE OF THE CASE:

The Supreme Court left the respective states to decide how many jurors should hear a criminal trial as long as the number is large enough to assure a cross section of the community.

Voir Dire Examination   After these exclusions, the prospective jurors are drawn, and the process known as the *voir dire examination* begins. This is the process of examining and questioning each prospective juror under oath to see if he or she is acceptable to both the prosecution and the defense. In some states, the examination is conducted by the attorneys for the prosecution and defense; in other states, the judge does the questioning, with the counsel for the state and the accused indicating specific questions that they want the judge to ask. Both sides may challenge prospective jurors that they want removed from serving on the jury. When it can be shown that the juror is prejudiced or is otherwise unable to perform the duties of a juror fairly and impartially, the challenge is called a *challenge for cause*. Both the prosecution and defense can exclude an unlimited number of jurors for cause, and the voir dire examination will continue until a full panel of qualified jurors is found. In heavily publicized cases, this can be a very time-consuming process. For example, in December 1970, when Black Panthers Bobby Seale and Ericka Huggins were put on trial in New Haven in connection with the murder of another Black Panther, it took over four months to conduct the voir dire, and over 1,000 prospective jurors were excluded for cause.

Peremptory Challenge   Jurors can also be excluded through a *peremptory challenge*. A peremptory challenge, as its name implies, is a challenge that requires no reasons or explanation, and its use is wholly discretionary.[24] The number of peremptory challenges is strictly limited by statute and varies from state to state and according to the seriousness of the crime. Usually, the number is greater for felonies than for misdemeanors and even greater for capital offenses. For example, in offenses not punishable by death or life imprisonment, Michigan permits both the prosecution and the defense to exclude five jurors by means of peremptory challenges. In cases where the possible penalty is death or life imprisonment, that state provides that the defense can exercise 20 peremptory challenges and the prosecution 15. Attorneys use these peremptory challenges where there is something about the prospective juror that the attorney is unsure of or does not like.

THE TRIAL

Once the jury has been selected and sworn in, the trial process begins. The indictment or information is read, and the state makes its *opening statements*. In its opening statement, the prosecutor usually explains how the state plans to introduce witnesses and physical evidence that will show beyond a reasonable doubt that the defendant committed the crime for which he or she is being tried. In the opening statement, the prosecutor is required to stick to the facts of the charges and the manner in which the state plans to prove its case.

Next, the defense is permitted to make its opening statement, although it may waive this right if it desires. If the defense elects to make an opening statement, it will also explain to the jury how it plans to introduce and develop its own evidence to show that the defendant did not commit the alleged crime.

Once the opening statements have been concluded, the *state's case* is presented. At this point, the state calls its first witness who usually establishes the elements of the crime; subsequent witnesses then introduce any physical evidence that the state may have. The prosecutor begins with a *direct examination* of the witness. Usually this direct examination consists only of eliciting facts in some chronological order from the witness. After this direct examination, the prosecution rests, and the defense is permitted to *cross-examine* the witness.

In this defense cross-examination, most states apply what is referred to as the restrictive rule. Under this rule, the defense counsel must restrict questions to those facts brought out by the prosecutor in the direct examination. After the cross-examination, the defense rests, and the prosecutor is given the opportunity to conduct a *redirect examination* of the witness. Often the prosecutor may question the witness on only those new facts brought out in the defense cross-examination. After the redirect examination, the defense is then given the opportunity to conduct a *recross-examination* of new facts that were brought out in the redirect examination. After the state has concluded its case, it rests.

The *defense case* is the next stage of the trial. Sometimes the defense at this stage will make a motion for dismissal on the grounds that the state did not prove the defendant guilty "beyond a reasonable doubt." If the judge concurs, the case is dismissed, and the accused is released. If the judge does not accept the motion, the defense then begins its case, following the steps outlined above. After the defense has concluded its case, it rests.

The next phase of the trial is called the *prosecutor's rebuttal*. The prosecutor may elect to introduce new witnesses or evidence in an effort to rebut the defendant's evidence. The same format of direct examination, cross-examination, redirect, and recross-examination is followed. At the conclusion of the prosecutor's rebuttal, the defense can again make a motion for dismissal of the charges, which is usually referred to as requesting a directed verdict or verdict of acquittal. If the motion is denied, the defense is entitled to the *defense surrebuttal*, and alternating examinations by both sides are again conducted.

Finally, both sides present their *closing arguments* to the jury. In most states, the prosecutor makes the state's closing argument first. Both the state and the defense usually have broad latitude in their range of discussion, the use of illustration, and the employment of persuasions, so long as they confine themselves to the discussion of the evidence presented and to normal deductions that might be made from the evidence.[25]

Instructions to the Jury

At the conclusion of the closing arguments to the jury, the judge charges the jury to retire to the jury room and consider the facts of the case and the testimony presented, and from their deliberations to return a just verdict. The judge's charge to the jury includes instructions as to the possible verdicts. The jurors are given a written form for each verdict. The foreman is instructed to sign the appropriate verdict and return it to the court after the jury has reached agreement. The typical forms of verdict in a criminal case are "guilty" or "not guilty." The jury in certain types of cases, however, may have the option of determining the particular degree of the offense, for example, murder in the first degree, murder in the second degree, and manslaughter. In certain cases, the verdict of "not guilty by reason of insanity" may also be a possible verdict.

After the jurors have been charged by the judge, they are placed in the custody of the court bailiff, who sees that they are sequestered (isolated from nonmembers of the jury) during their period of deliberation. Normally, they retire to a jury room to deliberate the verdict. The jurors take with them the pleadings in the case, the judge's instructions, and sometimes any evidence that has been introduced at the trial. Some states, however, do not permit the jurors to take anything with them to the jury room. No juror is permitted to leave the jury room until a verdict has been returned or unless the jurors have to be accommodated for the night, if the jury's deliberation lasts that long. The bailiff, who has the responsibility of maintaining complete security over the jury deliberations, must ensure that the jurors are not approached by any person who is not a juror, and that they do not receive any communications that might influence their vote.

If during the course of their deliberations, the jurors want to refresh their memories about the testimony of a witness or want further explanation of the instructions given by the court, they contact the bailiff. If necessary, the court clerk provides them with the transcript of the testimony, and the judge and the attorneys send new instructions to them by way of the bailiff. However, a great deal of caution exists in some jurisdictions over this practice. In some states, the court may not emphasize any testimony or instruction by rereading it.

Jury Deliberations and Return of the Verdict

The foreman of the jury, who is usually chosen by the jury itself, often begins the deliberations by taking a vote of the jury. Although the first vote can result in a unanimous verdict, usually, the first vote indicates a divided jury. The jurors then further discuss the case in an attempt to resolve their differences and reach unanimity.

If after a prolonged period they cannot reach a unanimous verdict, they report this fact to the court. A jury that cannot reach a verdict is called a "hung jury" and is dismissed by the judge in open court. A hung jury does not automatically result in the acquittal of the defendant. The accused can be retried with a new jury. but the fact that a jury cannot reach a unanimous verdict sometimes results in the state deciding not to conduct another trial. The state may reason that since it could not convict the defendant in the first trial, there is little reason to believe that it could do so in a second trial.

In recent years, some states have passed laws that permit defendants to be convicted with less than unanimous verdicts. Oregon, for example, requires a minimum requisite vote of ten to two. When this law was challenged by a convicted defendant, the U.S. Supreme Court upheld it. The Court ruled that a verdict that is less than unanimous does not violate the Sixth Amendment right to a trial by jury.[26]

Once the jury has reached a verdict, the jury is brought back into the courtroom where the defendant, the judge, and the attorneys for the prosecution and defense are present. The judge inquires whether the jurors have reached a verdict. When they reply that they have, the bailiff takes the written verdict that the foreman has signed and attested to and hands it to the judge. The judge then reads it and hands it back to the bailiff to read aloud in court. The verdict is usually phrased in the following language: "We, the jury, duly empaneled and sworn, find the defendant guilty (or not guilty) as charged."

The prosecutor or defense counsel may request that the jurors be *polled*. When a jury is polled, the judge or perhaps the bailiff asks each juror individually if the verdict announced is his or her individual verdict. This is done to determine whether each juror is in accord with the verdict rendered and has not been pressured into voting a particular way by the other jurors.

POST-TRIAL MOTIONS

If the verdict is not guilty, the defendant is immediately released from custody. If a guilty verdict is returned by the jury, most jurisdictions permit the accused the right to file for a motion for a new trial or to set the judgment of the jury aside. Usually, the defense has ten days or so to file this motion. The grounds are usually one of the following: (1) that the state failed to charge an offense in the indictment or the court lacked proper jurisdiction in the case;[27] (2) that the jury was guilty of misconduct in its deliberation (e.g., a juror was in contact with an outsider who influenced her or him); (3) that the court made a mistake in judgment in permitting some evidence to be introduced or in overruling an objection, etc.; or (4) that the instructions that the judge gave to the jury were improper.

The trial judge may grant or deny any of these post-trial motions. Again, a hearing on the motion is held, and the judge, after listening to the arguments, issues a ruling. Most motions are denied. In some instances, these motions permit the judge to review the case before the accused files for an appeal by the appellate courts. In this way, an error can often be corrected at this level without having to go to the higher courts.

THE PRESENTENCE INVESTIGATION

After the conclusion of the hearing on post-trial motions that do not change the guilty verdict of the jury, the judge in most jurisdictions has a presentence investigation conducted. About half the states now make a presentence report mandatory in all felony cases. These reports are usually conducted by the probation officers assigned to the court. The purposes of a presentence investigation are fivefold:

1. To aid the court in determining the appropriate sentence.
2. To aid the probation officer in the rehabilitative efforts during probation and parole supervision where probation, and later parole, are warranted.
3. To assist the Department of Corrections in their classification and treatment programs and in their release planning.
4. To furnish the parole board with information pertinent to its consideration of parole.
5. To serve as a source of information for systematic research.[28]

The United States Probation Office has developed a model presentence investigation report which is employed by federal probation officers in the U.S. district courts. Figure 9-4 shows the face sheet of this report, while Figure 9-5 indicates the narrative summary that accompanies it.

THE SENTENCE

Once the presentence investigation is completed and reviewed by the trial court judge, the accused is brought back into court for the imposition of sentence. The state legislatures and the U.S. Congress provide by statute the sentences that state and federal judges can impose for various crimes. However, many state legislatures prescribe that in capital cases the determination of the sentence rests with the jury rather than the judge. This practice is widely disavowed by reformers who would abolish the authority of the jury to render sentence. In recent years, there has been a trend in a few states to turn the sentencing authority over to an administrative body. One such administrative body was the California Adult Authority. Under this system, a defendant was merely sentenced by the court to be imprisoned in a state penitentiary. The individual was then turned over to the director of corrections, and the department of corrections fixes the particular term of imprisonment.

One form of sentence is the *definite sentence,* which is for a stated number of years. An *indeterminate sentence,* which most states employ, has a minimum and a maximum length. Thus, an individual may be sentenced to imprisonment for two to five years.[29] A *truly indeterminate sentence* is one that theoretically has no maximum and no minimum. Thus, the individual could be incarcerated from one day to life.

Many states also have *habitual-offender statutes.* These statutes call for an increased period of incarceration for someone who has previously been convicted of two or more felonies or two or more felonies of a certain type. Under certain circumstances, then, someone could be sentenced to life imprisonment upon the conviction of a third felony. However, habitual offenders statutes are rarely invoked by the courts.

In the last few years, a number of states have passed *mandatory sentencing acts.* These acts impose an *additional* mandatory penalty for certain circumstances that pertain to the crime. For example, if the convicted offender

PROBATION
FORM 2
FEB 65

UNITED STATES DISTRICT COURT
Central District of New York

PRESENTENCE REPORT

NAME	DATE
John Jones	January 4, 1974
ADDRESS	DOCKET NO.
1234 Astoria Blvd. New York City	74-103
LEGAL RESIDENCE	OFFENSE
Same	Theft of Mail by Postal Employee (18 U.S.C. Sec. 1709) 2 counts
AGE DATE OF BIRTH 2-8-40	
33 New York City	PENALTY
SEX RACE	Count 2: 5 years and/or $2,000 fine
Male Caucasian	PLEA
CITIZENSHIP	Guilty on 12-16-73 to Count 2 Count 1 pending
U.S. (Birth)	
EDUCATION	VERDICT
10th grade	
MARITAL STATUS	CUSTODY
Married	Released on own recognizance. No time in custody.
DEPENDENTS	
Three (wife and 2 children)	ASST. U.S. ATTY
SOC. SEC. NO.	Samuel Hayman
112-03-9559	DEFENSE COUNSEL
FBI NO.	Thomas Lincoln Federal Public Defender
256 1126	
DETAINERS OR CHARGES PENDING:	
None	Drug/Alcohol Involvement: Attributes offense to need for drinking money
CODEFENDANTS (Disposition)	
None	

DISPOSITION

DATE

SENTENCING JUDGE

Source: "The Selective Presentence Investigation Report," *Federal Probation*, December 1974, 53. Reprinted by permission.

FIGURE 9-4   Face Sheet for Model Selective Presentence Investigation Report

used a dangerous weapon in the commission of the crime, he or she would be sentenced to a period of incarceration in excess of that received for committing the crime itself.

Another characteristic of sentences is that they may be imposed on either a *concurrent* or a *consecutive* basis. An offender may be tried for more than one offense at the same time or may be tried for more than one count. For

Offense: Official Version.—Official sources reveal that during the course of routine observations on December 4, 1973, within the Postal Office Center, Long Island, New York, postal inspectors observed the defendant paying particular attention to various packages. Since the defendant was seen to mishandle and tamper with several parcels, test parcels were prepared for his handling on December 5, 1973. The defendant was observed to mishandle one of the test parcels by tossing it to one side into a canvas tub. He then placed his jacket into the tub and leaned over the tub for a period of time. At this time the defendant left the area and went to the men's room. While he was gone the inspectors examined the mail tub and found that the test parcel had been rifled and that the contents, a watch, was missing.

The defendant returned to his work and picked up his jacket. He then left the building. The defendant was stopped by the inspectors across the street from the post office. He was questioned about his activities and on his person he had the wristwatch from the test parcel. He was taken to the postal inspector's office where he admitted the offense.

Defendant's Version of Offense.—The defendant admits that he rifled the package in question and took the watch. He states that he intended to sell the watch at a later date. He admits that he has been drinking too much lately and needed extra cash for "drinking money." He exhibits remorse and is concerned about the possibility of incarceration and the effect that it would have on his family.

PRIOR RECORD

Date	Offense	Place	Disposition
5-7-66 (age 26)	Possession of Policy Slips	Manhattan CR. CT. N.Y., N.Y.	$25.00 Fine 7-11-66
3-21-72 (age 32)	Intoxication	Manhattan CR. CT. N.Y., N.Y.	4-17-72 Nolle

Personal History.—The defendant was born in New York City on February 8, 1940, the oldest of three children. He attended the public school, completed the 10th grade and left school and was active in sports, especially basketball and baseball.

The defendant's father, John, died of a heart attack in 1968, at the age of 53 years. He had an elementary school education and worked as a construction laborer most of his life.

The defendant's mother, Mary Smith Jones, is 55 years of age and is employed as a seamstress. She had an elementary school education and married defendant's father when she was 20 years of age. Three sons were issue of the marriage. She presently resides in New York City, and is in good health.

Defendant's brother, Paul, age 32 years, completed 2½ years of high school. He is employed as a bus driver and resides with his wife and two children in New York City.

Defendant's brother, Lawrence, age 30 years, completed three semesters of college. He is employed as a New York City firefighter. He resides with his wife and one child in Dutch Point, Long Island.

The defendant after leaving high school worked as a delivery boy for a retail supermarket chain then served 2 years in the U.S. Army as an infantryman (ASN 123 456 78). He received an honorable discharge and attained the rank of corporal serving from 2-10-58 to 2-1-60. After service he held a number of jobs of the laboring type.

The defendant was employed as a truck driver for the City of New York when he married Ann Sweeny on 6-15-63. Two children were issue of this marriage, John, age 8, and Mary, age 6. The family has resided at the same address (which is a four-room apartment) since their marriage.

The defendant has been in good health all of his life but he admits he has been drinking to excess the past 18 months which has resulted in some domestic strife. The wife stated that she loved her husband and will stand by him. She is amenable to a referral for family counseling.

Defendant has worked for the Postal Service since 12-1-65 and resigned on 12-5-73 as a result of the present arrest. His work ratings by his supervisors were always "excellent."

Evaluative Summary.—The defendant is a 33-year-old male who entered a plea of guilty to mail theft. While an employee of the U.S. Postal Service he rifled and stole a watch from a test package. He admitted that he planned on selling the watch to finance his drinking which has become a problem resulting in domestic strife.

Defendant is a married man with two children with no prior serious record. He completed 10 years of schooling, had an honorable military record, and has a good work history. He expresses remorse for his present offense and is concerned over the loss of his job and the shame to his family.

Recommendation.—It is respectfully recommended that the defendant be admitted to probation. If placed on probation the defendant expresses willingness to seek counseling for his domestic problems. He will require increased motivation if there is to be a significant change in his drinking pattern.

Respectfully submitted,

Donald M. Fredericks
U.S. Probation Officer

Source: "The Selective Presentence Investigation Report," *Federal Probation,* December 1974, 54. Reprinted by permission.

FIGURE 9-5 Narrative Section of a Model Selective Presentence Investigation Report

example, an individual who is apprehended and charged with the commission of three robberies could be tried separately for each offense or charged in one trial on three counts. If found guilty, most states permit the judge to run the sentences concurrently or consecutively. If the sentences run concurrently, they run simultaneously; if they run consecutively, the individual must serve one after the other.

APPEALS AND POSTCONVICTION REVIEWS

The right of appeal, as prescribed by modern American statutes, is not found in the common law.[30] The early English courts began to permit very limited rights of appeal around the fifteenth century. Most of the rights of appeal, as we know them today, began to develop in the nineteenth century.

Since then, there have developed extensive procedural rights for an accused to obtain a review of his or her case.

Rights of review from the decisions of state trial courts of general jurisdiction are made to either the state supreme court or the state court of appeals if the state has adopted an intermediate-level appellate court. In an appeal, the defendant alleges that the trial court erred in some manner interpreting or applying the law in the specific case.

Appeals are based on the written record of what transpired in the trial at the lower court level. Thus, the appellate court concerns itself only with the particular errors alleged by the defendant. The appellate court does not conduct a new trial but merely examines the transcript of the case and any supporting briefs by the attorneys for both sides, hears oral arguments that are presented, and rules accordingly. However, if a defendant is appealing a case from a court of limited or special jurisdiction (e.g., magistrate's or municipal court) to a general trial court for review, the general trial court usually holds a completely new trial.

Before the higher courts accept an appeal from a lower court ruling, they usually require that the party who is appealing show that the particular point upon which the appeal is based had been appropriately objected to during the course of the trial. The higher court must be convinced that the rights of the defendant were so violated as to adversely affect the course of the trial and its results.

In most cases, appeal is not automatic—that is, the aggrieved party must apply for appellate review. However, some states provide for an automatic appellate review of a trial court's decision if the defendant has been sentenced to death and in a few cases if the defendant has received life imprisonment. The individual who appeals the case must show the higher court that he or she has exhausted all remedies such as writs, motions, etc., with the lower trial court.

In most cases, the rights of appeal of the state are very limited and, therefore, the prosecutor can rarely appeal an adverse ruling. Such a practice would constitute a form of double jeopardy and would also put a burden upon the defendant in having to defend himself again.

Most appeals from state trial courts of general jurisdiction never get past the state intermediate court of appeals or the state supreme court. The number of cases heard in state trial courts that eventually get to the U.S. Supreme Court is almost infinitesimal. In most cases, the state appellate courts refuse to grant a review. In a few instances, if the defendant alleges that his or her constitutional rights have been violated, the defendant may file a petition for a writ of certiorari with the U.S. Supreme Court for review.

The petition for a writ of certiorari indicates the particular nature of the case, the errors alleged, and the previous court dispositions of the case.[31] The writ is granted by the Supreme Court when four justices feel that the issues raised are of sufficient public importance to merit consideration. Petitions for writs of certiorari are filed in accordance with prescribed forms, the petitioner stating why the Court should grant the writ. The opposing party also may file a brief, outlining why the case should not be reviewed by the Court on certiorari. According to the revised rules of the Supreme Court, "a review on writ of certiorari is not a matter of right, but of sound judicial discretion, and will be granted only where there are special important reasons therefore."

If the writ of certiorari is not granted, the defendant may resort to a collateral attack upon the judgment. Although various post-appeal remedies are available in different states, the most universal method of collateral attack is by petition for a writ of habeas corpus.[32] This writ, which has its origin in the ancient common law, has been incorporated as a right in state constitutions and in Article I, Section 9, of the U.S. Constitution. A petition for a writ of habeas corpus questions the legality of the detention of the petitioner and requests that the court issue an order that directs the state or the person who has custody of the petitioner to bring the individual before the court to see whether the person is being held illegally.

If, upon hearing, the court determines that there is no legal authority to detain the petitioner, the court must order his discharge, and the individual holding the petitioner must release him. The petition for habeas corpus can be granted even after the final judgment by the highest court of competent jurisdiction.[33] Generally, the petition may be filed with the trial court, but in some states the state supreme court has original jurisdiction in such matters. These petitions may also be filed in a federal court and in the U.S. Supreme Court from an individual incarcerated in a state. Federal judges may grant writs of habeas corpus whenever it appears that a petitioner is being detained in violation of his or her constitutional rights by either federal or state authorities.

Review by the Chief Executive

The President of the United States and the governors of each state have the power to pardon an individual convicted of a crime, to commute the sentence to a less severe one, or to grant a reprieve in some cases. A *pardon* is a forgiveness for the crime committed and bars subsequent prosecution for the crime. It has the effect of legally erasing the conviction. A *commutation* does not remove the defendant's guilt, but does mitigate the punishment imposed. It has usually been used to reduce the penalty from death to life imprisonment without requiring any demonstration or condition of future behavior. A *reprieve* is a delay in the execution of a sentence and has no effect on the defendant's guilt or punishment. It is most likely to be used in postponing execution of the death sentence so that the accused may have additional time to file a motion for relief in judgment.

Most of these powers are usually vested exclusively in the chief executive and may be exercised at his or her discretion. A few states, however, require that petitions for executive clemency be first filed with a clemency board or committee for review. This board or committee reviews the petition, in some cases holds public hearings on the matter, and makes its recommendations to the governor accordingly. In a couple of states, the clemency board may only have to agree in the affirmative before the governor can exercise executive prerogative in this area.

SUMMARY

The judicial process in misdemeanor cases is very simple compared with the procedure in felony cases. In a felony case, the arrestee is first brought before a court of limited or special jurisdiction for a preliminary hearing. If there are reasonable grounds to believe that a felony has been committed and that the accused committed it, the defendant's case may be bound over to a grand jury, which issues an indictment if it believes a trial is warranted. More commonly, the case is brought to trial by the prosecutor's filing an information.

Once the accused is bound over to a court of general jurisdiction for trial, the next step is an arraignment. At this stage of the judicial process, the accused is asked to enter a plea to the charge(s). If he or she pleads not guilty and wishes a jury trial, the selection of the jury will take place. Once the jury has been chosen and empaneled, the trial begins. Evidence is presented in a very formalized manner.

After receiving its instructions from the judge, the jury retires and deliberates. If the jury returns a verdict of guilty, most jurisdictions require that a presentence investigation be conducted before the judge imposes sentence. Following the imposition of sentence, the offender can employ a number of postconviction remedies and appeals.

REVIEW QUESTIONS

1. What are the steps in the judicial process in a misdemeanor case?
2. What are the steps in the judicial process in a felony case?
3. Is the use of the grand jury mentioned in the Constitution? In what way?
4. Name two important functions of the grand jury.
5. What is an *information?* What purpose does it serve?
6. What is a "true bill" of indictment? What must the indictment state?
7. What pleas can a defendant enter at the arraignment? How will the court react to each of these pleas?
8. List and briefly explain the pretrial motions that a defendant can file before arraignment or the trial.
9. Define the following:
   a. Jury panel or venire
   b. Voir dire examination
   c. Challenge for cause
   d. Peremptory challenge
   e. Prosecutor's rebuttal
   f. Defense surrebuttal
   g. Closing arguments
10. Define the following:
   a. Definite sentence
   b. Indeterminate sentence
   c. Truly indeterminate sentence

    d. Habitual-offender statutes
    e. Mandatory sentencing acts
    f. Concurrent sentence
    g. Consecutive sentence

DISCUSSION QUESTIONS

1. Are there too many due process procedures in processing a felony case? Discuss.

2. Do you agree with the Supreme Court's ruling in *Williams* v. *Florida* that a 12-member jury is not specifically required in trying a criminal case? Why or why not?

SUGGESTED ADDITIONAL READINGS

American Bar Association. *Law and Courts.* Chicago: American Bar Association, 1960.

Deming, R. *Man and Society: Criminal Law at Work.* New York: Hawthorn, 1970.

Felkenes, George. *The Criminal Justice System: Its Functions and Personnel.* Englewood Cliffs, N.J.: Prentice-Hall, 1973.

Graham, Kenneth, and Leon Letwin. "The Preliminary Hearing in Los Angeles." *UCLA Law Review* 18 (1971):635–757.

Inbau, Fred E., and James R. Thompson. *Administration of Criminal Justice.* New York: Foundation Press, 1970.

Lewis, Peter W., and Kenneth D. Peoples. *The Supreme Court and the Criminal Process.* Philadelphia: Saunders, 1978.

Newman, Edwin S. *Police, the Law and Personal Freedom.* Dobbs Ferry, N.Y.: Oceana Publications, 1964.

Uviller, H. Richard. *Adjudication.* St. Paul, Minn.: West, 1975.

Vetter, Harold J., and Clifford E. Simonsen. *Criminal Justice in America.* Philadelphia: Saunders, 1976.

NOTES

    1. Some minor courts have no provision for a jury trial. In these instances, if the accused demands a jury trial, the case will usually be transferred to another court which is set up to routinely empanel juries for cases.

    2. See *Gideon* v. *Wainwright,* 372 U.S. 335 (1963), and *Argersinger* v. *Hamlin.* 407 U.S. 25 (1972).

    3. See *McNabb* v. *United States.* 318 U.S. 332, 63 S. Ct. 608 (1943); *Mallory* v. *United States,* 354 U.S. 499, 77 S. Ct. 1356 (1957); *Upshaw* v. *United States,* 355 U.S. 410, 69 S. Ct. 170 (1948).

    4. Pub. L. 93–619, (1975).

    5. See U.S.C. Chap. 28, 3161–3174.

    6. Actually, the Court ruled that a "probable cause" hearing must be held. The preliminary hearing is such a determination. See *Gerstein* v. *Pugh,* 420 U.S. 103 (1975).

7. President's Commission on Law Enforcement and Administration of Justice, *Task Force Report: The Courts* (Washington, D.C.: U.S. Government Printing Office, 1967), pp. 43–44.

8. National Advisory Commission on Criminal Justice Standards and Goals, *Courts* (Washington, D.C.: U.S. Government Printing Office, 1978), p. 89.

9. American Bar Association Project on Minimum Standards for Criminal Justice, *Standards Relating to Discovery and Procedure before Trial,* approved draft (Chicago: American Bar Association, 1970).

10. National Advisory Commission, *Courts,* pp. 89–91.

11. In criminal cases, the accused cannot be compelled to take the stand and testify.

12. National Advisory Commission, *Courts,* p. 91.

13. See Marvin E. Frankel and Gary P. Naftalis, *The Grand Jury—An Institution on Trial* (New York: Hill and Wang, 1977).

14. Ibid., pp. 6–7.

15. James L. LeGrande, *The Basic Processes of Criminal Justice* (Encino, Calif.: Glencoe, 1973), p. 98.

16. M. Cherif Bassiouni, *Criminal Law and Its Processes* (Springfield, Ill.: Thomas, 1969), p. 454.

17. This immunity is often granted by the court and bars the use against the witness of any statements or evidence derived from these statements in any legal proceedings against him.

18. LeGrande, *The Basic Processes of Criminal Justice,* p. 102.

19. *Kercheval* v. *United States,* 274 U.S. 220, S. Ct. 348 (1927).

20. The statute of limitations normally begins when the crime is committed, not when it is discovered. The statute of limitations can be "tolled," or stopped from running, when a formal complaint is issued, an indictment returned, or an arrest warrant issued.

21. R. Van Sickle, "The Omnibus Pretrial Conference," *North Dakota Law Review* 50 (1976): 178–189.

22. National District Attorneys Association, *National Prosecution Standards* (Chicago: National District Attorneys Association, 1977), p. 162.

23. 390 U.S. 145, 88 S. Ct. 1444 (1968).

24. See Paul B. Weston and Kenneth M. Wells, *The Administration of Justice* (Englewood Cliffs, N.J.: Prentice-Hall, 1967), pp. 193–196.

25. LeGrande, *The Basic Processes of Criminal Justice,* p. 132.

26. *Apodaca* v. *Oregon,* 406 U.S. 404, 92 S. Ct. 1628, 32 L. Ed. 2d 184 (1972).

27. These grounds may serve the same purpose as a pretrial motion to dismiss the indictment. However, there are some distinguishing differences. A reason sufficient to sustain dismissal of an indictment may be insufficient to sustain a motion in arrest of judgment. It must be shown that the defect in the indictment or information was such that it affected the legal basis of the offense charged and the proof of guilt. See Bassiouni, *Criminal Law and Its Process,* pp. 506–507.

28. Administrative Office of the United States Courts, "The Selective Presentence Investigation Report," *Federal Probation* 38 (December 1974): 48.

29. Although this example seems to imply that the individual must serve a minimum of two years, this is often not what happens. For example, states and the federal government employ "good time" to reduce the period of imprisonment. This "good time" might be computed on the basis of three months for every year served. Thus, the inmate serving a two- to five-year sentence could be released on parole after only eighteen months. The time might even be less than eighteen months if the state credits the inmate with the time served in jail before trial.

30. J. O'Halloran. "Development of the Right of Appeal in England in Criminal Cases," *Canadian Bar Review* 27 (1949): 153.

31. LeGrande, *The Basic Processes of Criminal Justice,* p. 152.

32. Ibid.

33. See Hazel B. Kerper and Janeen Kerper, *Legal Rights of the Convicted* (St. Paul, Minn.: West, 1974), pp. 207–238.

10

Courtesy of Los Angeles Superior Court (a simulation)

1. Who are the principal actors in the judicial process?
2. What constraints are placed upon judges in their decision-making capacity?
3. What is the role of the prosecutor in a criminal case?
4. What is the role of the defense attorney?
5. How are juries selected and how do they deliberate to reach a decision in a case?

These are some of the questions this chapter will answer.

Although it is beyond the scope of this text to examine the social and psychological factors that influence human behavior, it is nonetheless important for the student to be aware of the impact that the perceptions and values of the individual participants in the justice system have upon the administration of justice in the American courts. Each courtroom actor is vulnerable to the same weaknesses as the rest of society—a fact that, at times, may color the criminal justice system, but one that we must live with and accept. In addition to examining the respective roles of the actors in the judicial process, the chapter looks at other important considerations in how justice is administered in our criminal courts.

THE JUDGE

To most people, the judge is the final and most visible dispenser of criminal justice. Although the police may, in fact, be more visible agents of criminal justice, they serve as the initiators in the process rather than as the final arbiters of justice. Because of this final decision-making responsibility, judges (other than those at the lowest level of the judiciary) are generally accorded the highest status among all the personnel involved in the criminal justice process.

The role (and usually the prestige) of judges is often *institutional in nature*— that is, the status of the court in the judicial hierarchy as well as the level of government in which the court is located are important. For example, justices of the peace and judges in local courts are usually accorded less status than judges who preside over state courts of general jurisdiction. By the same token, federal judges are accorded greater prestige than state judges on comparable judicial levels.

The role that judges play in the administration of justice is a very broad and meaningful one. The judges of our criminal courts are advisers and guardians of the accused's legal rights. Every person who is arrested is brought before a judge to be advised of his or her rights. The judge inquires into the circumstances of the arrest to ensure that the police have not infringed upon the individual's rights. Judges also have discretion over whether or not the individual may be released either by posting bail or on his or her own recognizance. The judge hears and rules on pretrial motions of the accused and the state. At the arraignment, a judge hears the defendant's plea, and if the accused pleads guilty, the judge is responsible for examining the understanding and basis for the plea. In a jury trial, the judge interprets the law and determines the admissibility of evidence. In a nonjury trial, the judge rules not only on issues of law, but on issues of fact and determines the defendant's guilt or innocence. When guilt has been determined after the trial or when the defendant voluntarily enters a guilty plea, the judge is responsible for deciding the proper sentence.

Another important but less visible role that judges perform is that of a manager. The judge is often responsible for the management of the court and courtroom. Among these managerial duties are the selection and training of court clerks, the supervision of court records, and the recruitment and supervision of probation officers. The scheduling of cases is often at least indirectly the responsibility of the judge, as is the appointment and supervision of the court bailiff in many jurisdictions. In larger jurisdictions, these administrative tasks are the responsibility of the senior presiding judge. In recent years, professionally trained court administrators have been employed by a growing number of the larger state court systems so that the judges can concentrate strictly on their judicial responsibilities.

Constraints on Judges

Although judges apparently have a great many opportunities to exert a decisive influence on the administration of justice, they are, in fact, constrained by a number of factors. The process of setting bail, for example, is governed by the criminal code of the state; both the state codes and the Eighth Amendment prohibit excessive bail. The criminal codes also limit the discretion of the judge in rendering sentence for an offense by prescribing, in most cases, the statutory maximum and minimum sentence that can be imposed. Judges are also constrained by their relationship with other actors in the administration of criminal justice. Since the judiciary must rely on the police and the prosecutor to bring cases before them, these individuals can significantly determine the workload of the court. Judges may also be hampered by a lack of knowledge of the facts that have been developed through prearrest and pretrial investigation. In many instances, the judge is completely unfamiliar with the case until the testimony begins to unfold during the trial.

Plea Bargaining   The absence of independent and complete information is probably most visible in the area of plea bargaining. This practice, sometimes referred to as plea negotiation or "copping a plea," is quite common in the administration of justice. Although a prosecutor plays a more significant role than the judge in these negotiations, the judge does become involved in a number of ways. The judge must decide whether the court will accept the recommendation of the prosecutor. This recommendation itself is often the result of a negotiation that has taken place between the prosecutor and the defendant (or more likely, the defendant's counsel) in the judge's absence. In many instances, the judge accepts the recommendation which, in effect, is a vote of confidence in the prosecutor's judgment. In plea bargaining, the judge's only responsibility is to ensure that the defendant *voluntarily* and *intelligently* entered into the negotiated plea according to the guidelines imposed by the U.S. Supreme Court.[1] For instance, if the defendant agrees to plead "guilty" for some negotiated consideration, the defendant waives certain fundamental rights such as the right to jury trial, the right to confront witnesses, and the privilege against self-incrimination. The judge must then determine whether such justice by guilty plea is voluntarily and intelligently given by the accused.

The extent of plea bargaining inducements, together with the tendency of some judges to accept almost unquestionably the recommendation of the prosecutor, can significantly reduce the importance of the role of the judge in criminal proceedings. In this way, judicial behavior is significantly constrained.

Probation Officer's Recommendations   The judge is also constrained by the suggestions made by probation officers in their presentence investigation reports.[2] Usually the judge requests that these reports contain the dispositional recommendations of the officer who investigated the accused's background. If the judge trusts the probation officer's wisdom, these recommendations will probably be adopted. How much this approach constrains the judge we do not know, for a second set of factors may be operating. The probation officer may often accommodate his or her recommendation to the judge, rather than vice versa. For example, through experience with a particular judge, the probation officer may recommend a disposition that he or she thinks the judge wants or will accept.

Backlog of Cases   The backlog of cases in the lower criminal courts in many urban areas severely limits the role of judges. Although the judge is supposed to serve as an adviser and guardian of the legal rights of the accused, this important function often cannot receive the attention it should because of time restrictions. Preliminary and bail hearings and hearings on motions and arraignments are typically conducted on an assembly-line basis, lasting no more than several minutes or so per case in these trial courts.[3] In bail hearings, for instance, judges typically do not consider the facts that surround the commission of the crime or the characteristics of the accused. They must concentrate instead on the particular offense charged and the prior record of the defendant. Using these factors as guidelines, the judges often must rely on a bail bond schedule or accept the suggestion of the prosecutor or arresting police officers.

 These constraints on judges and the gulf that separates the ideal from the actual vary from city to city and court to court. In courts that have lighter workloads, the judge may have adequate time to exercise the proper judicial role. In smaller communities the judge may develop closer relationships with the local prosecutor and defense attorneys that will provide better insight into the cases that come before the bench. In larger cities, where the judge must deal with hundreds of attorneys from the prosecutor's office, private law firms, and public defender's offices, the situation is typically much different.

THE PROSECUTOR

The office of the prosecutor is known by various names in different states. In some states, the office is referred to as the district attorney, the county solicitor, or the state's attorney. At the federal level, the prosecutor is known as the U.S. attorney. The prosecutor plays perhaps the most crucial role in the administration of criminal justice because the office occupies a central and very important position between the police and the courts. In fact, the prosecutor is the "traffic cop" of the criminal justice process. The decisions that the prosecutor makes determine how cases that are brought by the police will be disposed of. For example, the prosecutor may decide to "nolle pros" *(nolle prosequi)* a case—that is to decline prosecution, or he or she may decide to reduce the charge through plea bargaining or for some other consideration. In a number of jurisdictions, warrants of arrest must be approved by the prosecutor before the court issues the warrant. In many of these instances, the screening by the prosecutor results in the court merely rubber stamping the petition for a warrant that the prosecutor brings before the court.

Role in the Plea-Bargaining Process

As mentioned in the preceding section, although the judge is involved in varying degrees, it is the prosecutor who plays the most direct role in the plea-bargaining process. The prosecutor is in a position to offer a number of important inducements to the defendant to plead guilty, although the ultimate acceptability of these inducements usually rests with the judge. Further, if the prosecutor has a good "track record" of influencing the court to accept these plea-bargained recommendations, additional pressure is imposed on the defendant to accept some form of negotiated plea, particularly if the state has a good case against the accused.

The inducements to plea bargain that the prosecutor can use are numerous.[4] For example, the "benefit" most frequently offered a defendant by the prosecutor is a *reduction in the charges,* which in most cases automatically reduces the possible maximum sentence. The prosecutor, for instance, might offer the accused who is charged with the offense of robbery or burglary a reduction to the less serious crime of larceny in return for a guilty plea to a larceny charge. Aggravated assault might likewise be reduced to a simple assault.

The *charge dismissal* is the second most commonly offered inducement. By obtaining dismissal of one or more related charges, the accused avoids the possibility of multiple convictions and longer sentences. Sometimes the prosecutor will agree not to press additional criminal charges that could subject the defendant to more severe punishment under a habitual offender statute.

The third most common proposal is that the prosecutor agrees to recommend a particular sentence—such as probation or a fine—to the sentencing judge. Again, although judges are not required to accept a prosecutor's recommendation following plea negotiations, they often will acquiesce to the prosecutor's proposals.

Other prosecutorial plea bargaining inducements include: (1) a promise not to oppose probation or a suspended sentence; (2) a promise not to prosecute the defendant's accomplices; (3) a stipulation that the defendant enlist in the armed forces; (4) a promise to recommend that the defendant serve his sentence in a particular rehabilitation program; and (5) a promise that the defendant will be adjudicated in a juvenile court.[5]

In exchange for this, the defendant may also be required to promise, for example, that he or she will forego any appeal, cooperate with the police, supply additional information to the prosecutor, or testify as a witness in a subsequent trial.

Plea bargaining seems to be an important ingredient of the criminal process to both the prosecution and the defense. It is an important "tool" for the prosecutor because it helps to reduce the system's workload so that every arrest and prosecution can be handled without having to resort to a full trial on the issues. Prosecutors are also aware that they are often judged by the number of successful convictions they obtain, and getting the accused to plead "guilty" to a reduced charge through plea bargaining does result in this objective.

For the defendant there is some benefit in plea bargaining in that it is generally known that defendants who plead guilty receive lighter sentences than they would have had they exercised their constitutional rights to a trial and had been convicted.[6]

On the basis of research into the plea bargaining process in the Connecticut courts, Heumann paints a very interesting picture in the following observation:

> Typically, in the circuit court a line forms outside the prosecutor's office the morning before court is convened. Defense attorneys shuffle into the prosecutor's office and in a matter of two or three minutes, dispose of the one or more cases "set down" that day. Generally, only a few words have to be exchanged before agreement is reached.[7]

The need for the prosecutor to thoroughly prepare his or her case is well represented in an article written by a prosecutor which was published in a newsletter that was subsequently sent to all the prosecutors in the state. It provides us with an insight into the thinking of most prosecutors about the relative merits of plea bargaining:

> The obvious reason for thoroughly preparing for the trial of a criminal case, of course, is to insure a conviction should the case go to trial. There are, however, several other reasons that complete and early trial preparation is important. If a case is thoroughly prepared long before trial time, the prosecutor, in his dealings with the defense attorney, is able to show in a concise manner that he is able to obtain a conviction should the subject case go to trial. *That, in turn, will aid the prosecuting attorney in persuading the defense to accept a negotiated plea* (emphasis added).[8]

Extensive plea bargaining reflects the heavy workload of the prosecutor's office and of the court itself. But there is a certain amount of "gamesmanship" involved as well. If the prosecutor feels that the evidence is sufficient to convict the accused for the crime charged, there is little incentive for the prosecutor to negotiate. If, on the other hand, there is a probable chance that the accused will be acquitted, the situation changes. The prosecutor, in order to obtain a conviction, may be predisposed to bargain with the defendant. Defense attorneys can often use this set of circumstances to their advantage.

Also, experienced criminal defense lawyers and defendants often feel, perhaps rightly, that a defendant who is found guilty will receive a harsher sentence than one who has plea bargained. Many defendants with records of arrest and conviction ask their defense lawyers to try to "cop a plea." They know that there is a good chance that the prosecution will win if the case goes to trial and that their past record will have an important influence on the sentence they receive.

How prevalent is plea bargaining in our criminal courts? Nobody really knows. We can, however, get some idea of its extent from the number of criminal court cases that are settled by pleas of guilty and, therefore, never go to trial. Newman found, in his examination of criminal court cases in Wisconsin, that 93.8 percent of all cases in that state during the period studied were

TABLE 10-1
Guilty Plea Convictions in Ten Jurisdictions[a]

JURISDICTION	TOTAL CONVICTIONS	GUILTY PLEAS	
		NUMBER	PERCENTAGE
California (1965)	30,840	22,817	74.0
Connecticut	1,596	1,494	93.9
Hawaii	393	360	91.5
Illinois	5,591	4,768	85.2
Kansas	3,025	2,727	90.2
Massachusetts (1963)	7,790	6,642	85.2
Minnesota (1965)	1,567	1,437	91.7
New York	17,249	16,464	95.5
Washington, D.C.	1,515	817	73.5
U.S. district courts	29,170	26,273	90.2
Average			87.0

[a]1964 date unless otherwise indicated.
Source: President's Commission on Law Enforcement and Administration of Justice, *Task Force Report: The Courts* (Washington, D.C.: U.S. Government Printing Office, 1967), p 9.

disposed of by a guilty plea without trial.[9] The President's Commission on Law Enforcement and Administration of Justice examined the number of criminal cases that were disposed of by guilty pleas in the federal courts and the courts of eight states and the District of Columbia and found that an average of 87 percent of all defendants in those areas entered pleas of guilty. Table 10-1 shows the results of the study.

Of course, the extent that plea bargaining is engaged in depends in part on the willingness of the prosecutor and the judges to engage in this tactic. Locale also seems to be a factor. Cole points out that the courts of the primarily rural state of Maine, without the backlog of cases of our major metropolitan areas, infrequently engage in plea bargaining.[10] On the other hand, he notes that major metropolitan cities such as Philadelphia and Pittsburgh use the negotiated settlement in less than one-third of the cases.[11] In these cities, a system of expedited trials has reduced the administrative pressures for bargaining, and, as a result, the police and prosecutor more carefully screen the cases.[12]

It would seem that plea bargaining has become institutionalized in some of our major urban areas. Neumann found such a system existing in Connecticut's urban courts in his recent study.[13] Until recently, Detroit had a highly developed system in that city's Recorder's Court. In that city there was a special "bargaining prosecutor" who was available to consult with the defense attorneys who would queue up for consultation and plea negotiation. Near the prosecutor's office there was a "bullpen" where prisoners awaited trial or arraignment. A steady stream of lawyers flowed back and forth between these holding cells and the prosecutor's office, trying to negotiate a plea when the defendant appeared for trial.[14]

Role in the Grand Jury Process

The prosecutor also controls the grand jury. In states where cases must first be presented to the grand jury, the prosecutor plays a crucial role in determining whether the accused will be indicted. Since the grand jury hearing is an ex-parte proceeding, the prosecutor has almost unlimited discretion in producing evidence, interviewing witnesses, and so forth. Since the prosecutor is the only attorney present during the grand jury hearings, his or her legal opinions and judgments obviously carry considerable weight with the members of the grand jury. The prosecutor also has the authority to control and direct the investigative powers of the grand jury and often selects the particular activities that the grand jury will examine. An excellent example of this can be seen in the attempt of a New Orleans prosecutor, Jim Garrison, to use the grand jury of that parish (county) to overturn the findings of the Warren Commission in the assassination of John F. Kennedy. Garrison single-handedly convinced the grand jury that a leading businessman in that city conspired to kill Kennedy. The accused was eventually exonerated at the trial, but his business and reputation were destroyed in the process. Such is the awesome power of the prosecutor.

Role as Supervisor and Investigator

Prosecutors are also investigators and initiators of the criminal process in other ways. As the chief law enforcement official of the jurisdiction, the prosecutor often works closely with the police on important investigations; in many cases that deal with complex and technical matters such as fraud, organized crime, homicide, and the corruption of public officials, the prosecutor even supervises the police investigation. In larger cities, the office is usually assigned a special staff of investigators; in many instances, they are police detectives temporarily detailed to this office, but, in some instances, they may be an independent group of investigative personnel.

Of course, since the prosecutor has the responsibility of presenting the government's case in court, he or she needs to fulfill the role of a skillful trial attorney. In fact, the role of the prosecutor is a very broad one that is sometimes very difficult to grasp. For example, one noted legal expert offers this observation about the role of the prosecutor:

> Appraisal of the role of the prosecutor is made difficult because that role is inevitably more ambiguous than that of the police or the trial court. It is clear that the police are concerned with the detection of crime and the identification and apprehension of offenders; it is likewise apparent that courts must decide the issue of guilt or innocence. A prosecutor, however, may conceive of his principal responsibility in a number of different ways. He may serve primarily as trial counsel for the police department, reflecting the views of the department in his court representation. Or, he may serve as a sort of "house counsel" for the police, giving legal advice to the department on how to develop enforcement practices which will withstand challenge in court. On the other hand, the prosecutor may consider himself primarily a representative of the court, with the responsibility of enforcing rules designed to control police practices and perhaps otherwise acting for the benefit of persons who are proceeded against. Another possibility is that the prosecutor, as an elected official . . . will try primarily to reflect community opinion in the making of decisions as to whether to prosecute. The uncertainty as to whether the prosecutor is responsible for all these tasks and as to which is his primary responsibility creates difficult problems in current administration.[15]

Selection and Jurisdiction

Because of the immense power that this office has, it is very attractive to some attorneys who have political ambitions. With the possible exception of the mayor's office, no one local official has such opportunities for public exposure through the media. The important trials they prosecute, the investigations they conduct, and their public statements are often given widespread publicity. The important political value of this publicity can be seen in the fact that with the exception of Delaware and Rhode Island in which the attorney general handles criminal prosecutions for the state, the prosecutor is a local official. In 45 states, the office is an *elective* one with all but one state using a partisan ballot. In the remaining five states, the prosecutor is an appointed official. The prosecutor is elected on a county basis in 29 states, by judicial district in 12 states, and from both county and judicial district in four states.[16] In 38 states, the prosecutor has both criminal and civil responsibilities; in only 12 states does the prosecutor handle criminal cases solely.[17] The Advisory Commission on Intergovernmental Relations classified the prosecutor systems of the states into the following nine categories:

1. State prosecutor systems: Alaska, Delaware, and Rhode Island.
2. State-appointed local prosecutors: Connecticut and New Jersey.
3. Local (judicial district) prosecutors with criminal and appeals responsibilities: Georgia and Massachusetts.
4. Local (judicial district) prosecutors with solely criminal responsibilities: Arkansas, Colorado, Indiana, New Mexico, North Carolina, and Tennessee.
5. Local (judicial district) prosecutors with civil and criminal responsibilities, but no appeals duties: Alabama, Louisiana, Oklahoma and South Carolina.
6. Local (county) prosecutor with criminal and appellate responsibilities: Hawaii, Illinois, Kansas, Michigan, Minnesota, New York, North Dakota, Ohio, Oregon, Pennsylvania, Vermont, and Washington.
7. Local (county) prosecutors with solely criminal responsibilities: Missouri and Texas.
8. Local (county) prosecutors with criminal and civil, but not appellate responsibilities: Arizona, California, Idaho, Iowa, Maine, Maryland, Montana, Nevada, Nebraska, New Hampshire, South Dakota, Virginia, West Virginia, Wisconsin, and Wyoming.
9. Overlapping county-judicial district prosecutors: Florida, Kentucky, Mississippi, and Utah.[18]

Most of the more than 2,900 state prosecutors serve in very small offices with just one or two assistants. Although in the largest cities this office may consist of several hundred personnel made up of assistant prosecutors and various staff assistants, most prosecutors lack the assistance and facilities that they need. Many prosecutors serve only part-time and rely upon their outside private law practices to support them. In 1966, the National District Attorneys Association conducted a survey of all state and local prosecutors in the nation and found that the median annual salary for a prosecutor was less than $4,000.[19] By 1973 this figure had increased to a median salary of $12,500, but the post still remains a less than lucrative one.[20]

Characteristics

The prosecutor's office generally attracts two kinds of individuals. In the smaller communities, where the salary of the prosecutor is low, young attorneys who are financially struggling and relatively inexperienced are most likely to be attracted to the office. They often seek the position of prosecutor because the public exposure of the office will provide them with the opportunity to build up a clientele for their private practice and to acquire trial experience. The second type often comes from the lower or middle ranks of the legal profession and is someone who has become interested in politics to further his or her career. Such individuals are most likely to be found in larger cities and are often more experienced attorneys of middle age who hope that the office and the publicity that surrounds it can propel them into a judgeship or some higher state political office. They are aware that the office of the prosecuting attorney is an excellent stepping-stone for such political ambitions.

Consequently, the turnover in most prosecutor's offices is quite high, with the average tenure rarely exceeding two 4-year terms.[21] Some studies have put the turnover rate even higher. Gelber, for instance, contends that the turnover rate in prosecutor's offices across the country runs as high as 33-percent annually.[22] In most cities, prosecutors also select a high proportion of their assistants primarily on the basis of party affiliation and the recommendations of ward leaders and elected officials.[23] These factors create many foreseeable conflicts of interest. As the attorney for the state, the prosecutor is supposed to vigorously and impartially prosecute the crimes that come to the attention of this office. Yet, because the prosecutor is usually very politically sensitive and must rely on informal accommodations with other attorneys and with private clients, it is very questionable whether he or she can, in fact, be impartial.

This lack of impartiality may be expressed in other ways that endanger the proper administration of justice. One such concern is that prosecutors as legal representatives of the people do not zealously prosecute corruption or illegal actions by the police or members of the judiciary. For example, because prosecutors must work closely with law enforcement authorities they may not find it in their best interests to bring charges against the police. In support of this reluctance to prosecute is the fact that in the state of Arkansas there have been a number of very questionable killings of suspects by the police in the last few years. Not once did a local prosecutor in that state call for an investigatory grand jury nor were charges of any type filed. Any action taken was initiated by the federal courts by way of their rather limited jurisdiction under the Civil Rights Act.

Another major characteristic of state prosecutors is the absence of supervision by the states. The prosecutor is virtually unrestrained in his or her conduct or in the management of the office and the cases handled. Even the state attorney general's office has virtually no control over prosecutors. A few states have attempted to remedy this by giving the attorney general's office the right to inquire into the operations of local prosecutors, but this legislation has had little supervisory effect.

U.S. Prosecutors This set of circumstances does not exist at the federal level. The term of office for U.S. attorneys is 4 years. Although U.S. attorneys are politically appointed by the President, the Department of Justice screens the nominees for the position and maintains continuous contact and supervision over the U.S. attorneys situated throughout the country. All U.S. attorneys are provided with specific guidelines from the Department of Justice which they are expected to follow. In the event that the U.S. attorney is dealing with a particularly important or sensitive criminal case, the case must often be referred to Washington for review and instructions on how it should be handled. In recent years, the Department of Justice has taken a special interest in the handling of organized crime investigations and prosecutorial action by the U.S. attorneys in the field. In many of these cases, Washington delegates a special strike force of attorneys and investigators to assist, coordinate, and supervise the efforts of the particular U.S. attorney in the field.

Training

Many attorneys become prosecutors without any meaningful experience in the criminal justice process and only a rudimentary knowledge of criminal law. Part of this problem stems from the lack of preparation that law schools provide in the area of criminal law. Most law schools require only one course in criminal law during the entire 3-year course of study. The National District Attorneys Association survey mentioned earlier found that the typical assistant prosecutor is hired after very limited experience in practice and that most of that experience was in civil law. Even the prosecutor who is elected to office often lacks substantial criminal law experience.[24]

This lack of experience and knowledge of criminal law has some strange consequences. More often than is generally known, the fledgling prosecutor relies upon veteran police detectives for assistance in coping with the intricate nature of criminal law and the criminal law process. Since almost no jurisdictions provide any form of training for new prosecutors, they have to learn through experience. In larger offices that employ assistant prosecutors, a young assistant is often assigned to the traffic court or the complaint bureau. The idea is to give him or her experience in handling minor cases so that if errors are made they will not be important ones. Then, after gaining experience and demonstrating ability, the assistant can progress to handling more important cases. Although there certainly may be advantages to such on-the-job training, there are some less visible problems as well. Many times, young and inexperienced prosecutors who are assigned to the complaint bureau become advocates of the police. They may tend to become overly reliant upon the police officer's judgment in determining what complaints should be filed rather than acting as impartial legal experts who screen complaints based upon their merit.[25]

Even our largest cities sometimes offer no formal training. In some cases, the new assistant is provided with a written manual of policy guidelines, but these directives do not explain *how* to handle the many situations that confront a prosecutor. Occasionally, the new assistant is exposed to staff meetings and discussions about certain policies or cases with which the office must deal, but for the most part, staff meetings deal with office procedures and details. Recognizing this serious deficiency, the National District Attorneys Association is pressing states to develop programs for certifying attorneys and aspiring prosecutors in the specialties of criminal trial advocacy.[26]

THE CRIMINAL DEFENSE ATTORNEY

Most people have a very distorted view of the practice of criminal law. Television would have us believe that the private practice of criminal law is a stimulating challenge in which the skillful art of criminal trial advocacy is pitted against the legal adversary of the state in the cause of triumphant justice. Thus the defense counsel is depicted as a tireless and thorough investigator, a skillful legal adversary, and the champion of justice. The fact of the matter is that the practice of criminal law is often not nearly so stimulating or intellectually challenging, and criminal defense lawyers are certainly not the superhuman heroes popularized in fictional accounts.

The defense counsel plays an important role in our system of law and justice. Theoretically at least, our legal system is an adversarial one—that is, circumstances, and indeed the truth or falsity of legal issues, can be made known by submitting them to the test of advocacy in which one side is pitted against the other. Since the law is complex and the accused is unskilled in its intricacies, that individual needs assistance in preparing a defense. Thus, the defendant almost by necessity must obtain legal counsel in cases where the penalty could be severe.

The primary responsibility of the defense attorney is to *represent* the client. The defense attorney is responsible for preparing the case and for selecting the strategy of defense. To do this, mutual confidence and cooperation must exist between attorney and client. Without a good relationship, the lawyer (and indeed the client) cannot effectively function under our system of trial advocacy.

Many people wonder why a defense lawyer consents to defend a guilty client. They feel that this is a perversion of justice and that under the circumstances the accused should not be entitled to legal assistance. Similarly, many law-abiding citizens are upset when they hear of a defendant who by the lawyer's skillful manueverings is able to "beat a rap" on a legal technicality. Again, they feel that this certainly is a perversion of justice.

Admittedly, this is very difficult for many of us to accept. However, you must understand the theory of law in America and the responsibilities the adversary system of criminal justice entails. Since it is an adversary system, our laws recognize that those accused of crime have every right to use the skill and resources at their disposal to gain the ultimate goal of winning. In fact, the code of the legal profession demands that the attorney represent the client with all the resources and legal skills at his or her command. This is true in spite of the defendant's guilt or innocence. To do otherwise would violate the principles of American jurisprudence. The doctrine of fairness also plays a role here. The resources of the state are quite formidable, and the defendant must be entitled to use whatever resources he has at his disposal. If this means that a case is dismissed because of a technical error on the part of the police, this is the price that we must pay to ensure that the scales of justice remain in balance between the power of the state on the one hand and the rights of the individual on the other. In this way, we also maintain that delicate system of governmental checks and balances between the executive branch (in this case the police) and the judiciary. Without such checks and balances we could not enjoy those fundamental liberties that are uniquely ours in the United States.

Characteristics

How then does the practice of criminal law square with the popular image, and how far does it depart from the ideal? First, the practice of criminal law and the professional competence of many of its practitioners leave a great deal to be desired. Many criminal attorneys who practice regularly in our criminal courts are members of what has been called "the courthouse gang." In the District of Columbia, they are called the "Fifth Streeters," and in Detroit they are referred to as the "Clinton Street Bar Group." In most large cities, certain criminal attorneys have their offices conveniently situated near the building that houses the criminal courts and are often found prowling the courts searching for clients who can pay a modest fee.[27] As Blumberg so well describes them, these criminal defense lawyers, whom he refers to as "regulars," are:

> highly visible in the major urban centers of the nation; their offices—at times shared with bail bondsmen—line the back streets near courthouses. They are also visible politically, with clubhouse ties reaching into judicial chambers and the prosecutor's office. The regulars make no effort to conceal their dependence upon the police, bondsmen, jail personnel, as well as bailiffs, stenographers, prosecutors and judges.[28]

The average criminal trial lawyer is certainly no F. Lee Bailey or Melvin Belli, who enjoy national reputations as criminal defense lawyers. These individuals are at the pinnacle of their profession and usually accept only the most sensational and dramatic cases or those that assure them sizable fees. Many criminal legal specialists just manage to eke out a modest living. Defending criminals, except in a few celebrated cases, is certainly not a financially rewarding undertaking. Many defendants are not well off and they can scarcely afford to pay high fees to their legal counsel. Attorneys who practice this type of law soon realize this fact. Oftentimes, criminal trial attorneys have contacts with pawnbrokers, used-car and used-furniture outlets, or similar places of business that will dispose of the property of the defendant so that the attorney can be assured of receiving something in the way of a fee. In other cases, the attorney makes every effort to either obtain money in advance or somehow work out a financial obligation that will bind the family of the accused to paying the fee.

"The lawyer goes out and tries to squeeze money from the defendant's mother or an aunt," explains Judge Charles W. Halleck, of the local trial court in Washington, D.C. "Sometimes, he asks a jailed defendant, 'You got $15 or $25? Here let me hold it for you,' and, later, that becomes part of the fee."[29]

This situation is very different from that found in civil trial practice, where the attorney may take part of the settlement as the legal fee or may work on a contingency basis. As a consequence, criminal trial attorneys are most likely to be the strongest advocates of plea bargaining. They thus avoid the expense and work of a trial for a client who cannot pay.

Much of their success depends upon their sociability and contacts rather than their legal skills. For example, many criminal attorneys spend a great deal of their time trying to develop contacts with the police for possible referral of clients, with bailbondsmen for leads, and with the prosecutor's office and the judges for plea-bargaining considerations. If they get the reputation for too zealously defending their clients, particularly in more serious crimes, they run the risk of alienating the judges, prosecutors, and the police. This is especially true if the attorney is able to gain acquittals based on legal technicalities. Judges, prosecutors, and the police do not like to look foolish when their cases are overturned by the higher courts or when their investigative and arrest procedures are brought into question or receive publicity.

Because of these characteristics of criminal trial practice, the legal profession holds the average criminal trial lawyer in lower regard than most other specialists in the profession. Cole describes the status of the criminal trial attorney within the legal profession as follows:

> The membership of the urban bar appears to be divided into three parts. First, there is an inner circle which handles the work of banks, utilities and commercial concerns; another circle includes lawyers representing interests opposed to those of the inner circle; and finally, an outer group scrapes out an existence by "haunting" the courts in the hope of picking up crumbs from the judicial table. With the exception of a highly proficient few who have made a reputation by winning acquittals in difficult, highly publicized cases, most of the lawyers dealing with criminal justice belong to this periphery.[30]

Consequently, many attorneys either avoid the practice of criminal law altogether or, even worse, do not prepare themselves adequately for the cases they do defend. In a study of the criminal courts of Virginia, over 40 percent of the criminal appeals that were heard by the Virginia Supreme Court of Appeals during the 1970 term affirmed the decision of the lower court without consideration of the constitutional issues involved because during the trial the defense attorneys failed to make proper and timely objections.[31]

This picture of criminal trial practice is more typical of large urban areas; in smaller cities and communities, the practice of criminal law is usually more respectable, and there are, of course, conscientious, dedicated, and honest criminal trial lawyers who practice their specialties throughout the criminal courts of our nation. However, it does remain an unfortunate fact of our society that criminal law practice is generally held in low esteem. The tragedy of this situation is that the practice of criminal law has the potential for being one of the most challenging undertakings of the entire legal system. However, until there is a significant overhaul of the machinery of criminal justice, the practice of criminal law will still be relegated to the making of deals in the back rooms of police stations, the recesses of the criminal court corridors, or the prosecutor's office.

Defense of Indigents

Studies have indicated that in some of our major cities as many as 75-percent of all defendants in criminal cases are unable to afford the cost of hiring an attorney to defend them.[32] The Supreme Court, in the 1963 case of *Gideon* v. *Wainwright,* ruled that defendants in felony trials are constitutionally entitled to be represented by publicly provided attorneys if they are unable to afford to retain counsel.[33] In 1972, the Supreme Court extended this right by holding that no person could be imprisoned as the result of a criminal prosecution in which he or she was not accorded the right to public representation, thus, effectively expanding the right to almost all criminal cases.[34] Although the Court required the appointment of counsel in these cases, it did not set standards for indigency. As a consequence, jurisdictions throughout the country have established different standards.

Throughout the United States, there are basically three systems by which indigent defendants are provided defense counsel: (1) *the assigned-counsel system;* (2) *the voluntary defender program;* and (3) *the public defender system.* Each of these programs features different characteristics that are worth examination.

GIDEON v. WAINWRIGHT (1963)

Whether the indigent defendant in a criminal felony trial has the right to court-appointed counsel.

FACTS:
Clarence Gideon was tried and convicted in a Florida state court of the felony of breaking and entering with intent to commit a misdemeanor. Gideon was too poor to hire his own defense attorney, so he requested that the trial court appoint counsel to represent him. The request was denied because, under Florida law, appointed counsel was available to indigents only in capital cases. Gideon represented himself, but was convicted by a jury and sentenced to five years' imprisonment. The Florida Supreme Court upheld the trial court. He then appealed to the Supreme Court.

DECISION:
In its decision the Supreme Court cited the Sixth Amendment which says, "In all criminal prosecutions, the accused shall enjoy the right . . . to have the assistance of counsel for his defense." The Court ruled that access to counsel was a fundamental right of an accused person. This right was to be observed by the states through the equal protection guaranty of the Fourteenth Amendment. The judgment of the trial court and the Florida Supreme Court was overturned.

SIGNIFICANCE OF THE CASE:
Indigent defendants have the right to court-appointed attorneys in criminal cases. (Note: This was later clarified and extended to indigent defendants in misdemeanor cases. See *Argersinger* v. *Hamlin,* 1972.)

The Assigned-Counsel System   In this system, the judge after determining that the accused cannot afford to retain private counsel will provide a court-assigned attorney. Attorneys are usually assigned from a list that the court maintains of attorneys who have registered with the court and indicated their willingness to defend indigents. The vast majority of states use this method but it has drawbacks. In the first place, lawyers who voluntarily place their names on this list are most likely to be young and inexperienced. They are seeking the experience they require. Obviously, an established criminal trial lawyer who is successful and has clients need not resort to this approach.[35]

Another problem is that in many instances the attorney is appointed so late in the proceedings that he or she does not have the chance to really study the facts of the case, conduct the required investigations, and prepare the defense. As a result, the attorney often has to ask for a postponement of the case, which can be a particular hardship for the accused, particularly if he is in jail and cannot make bond. Even when a defendant is free on bond, the mental anguish from the postponement of the trial date can be severe for many defendants and families.

A further disadvantage is that many jurisdictions pay for the services of a court-appointed attorney on a sliding-fee basis, and the fees are too low for the attorney to spend a great deal of time in preparing the case or taking it to trial, for that matter. Instead, the attorney is likely to persuade the indigent client to plea bargain. However, since so many inexperienced attorneys are represented by this system, they are perhaps more prone to take the case to trial simply for the sake of the trial experience that it will provide. Furthermore, since they do not have a long list of clients awaiting their services, they can prolong their services through a trial proceeding and thus obtain additional remuneration.

The Voluntary Defender Program   This program is offered by private law offices usually affiliated with a Legal Aid Society, which specializes in providing legal assistance to the poor, and by legal aid bureaus associated with various charitable organizations. Until the 1960s, these programs existed in only a few metropolitan areas. Since the mid-1960s, however, the federal government has provided a great deal of additional funding, and today such programs have assumed a major role in providing legal services to the poor. Originally funded by the Office of Economic Opportunity, they are now largely funded by the Legal Services Corporation, which came into existence in 1974 after OEO was disbanded and the federal government passed the Legal Services Act. In addition, Legal Aid societies receive portions of their budgets from local charities such as the United Way, various grants-in-aid such as federal revenue sharing, and local bar associations. Although current figures are not available, a study done in 1968 indicated that the federal government in that year funded 299 such programs at a cost of $30.4 million and that approximately 1,800 full-time attorneys handled nearly 900,000 cases and served 300,000 clients.[36]

These programs suffer from a number of weaknesses. The major weakness is the uncertainty of continued financial support, especially if the agency must rely on charitable contributions to sustain itself. There is also some evidence that private agencies are less willing than government-financed agencies to bring their cases to court.[37] Such agencies also receive varying degrees of resistance from local bar associations and judges who view these organizations as competitors for fees that they or members of their profession might otherwise obtain.[38] Although this is a very questionable basis for rejection since many of the clients they serve could hardly pay for private legal counsel, this problem does exist. Finally, there is the very simple yet real problem of trying to cover all the courts in a metropolitan area or servicing the numbers of poor who could use their legal assistance.

The Public Defender System   The first public defender office was created in Los Angeles County in 1914. Since that time, public defender offices have been established throughout the country. Although there are some who criticize public defender programs for not going "all out" for their clients, this cannot be taken as an across-the-board condemnation.[39] All factors considered, the public defender system is probably the best method that exists for providing legal assistance to indigent defendants. It operates on public funds, and thus the attorney's staff and office have a relatively stable base of financial support. Many public defenders are experienced trial attorneys and are often given civil service status at fairly decent salaries. Moreover, defender offices, particularly in larger communities, often have funds available for investigative purposes and some even have their own investigative staff. Studies have shown that the public defender system is no more expensive to operate than are assigned-counsel systems when you consider how many cases they can handle.[40] Since the income of the public defender continues regardless of whether or not a case goes to trial, there is less likelihood that the attorney will plea bargain an otherwise meritorious case away or engage in delaying tactics so as to frustrate the prosecution into a bargaining position.

One of the problems this office has always faced is a lack of adequate public support. Many citizens are hostile to this agency because they feel that criminals do not deserve to be defended by their tax dollars. Although the same argument could be raised for the assigned-counsel system and the voluntary defender program, which in part often rely on public tax support, the operations of these systems and agencies are not quite so visible to the public, nor does the public understand as fully their method of financing. Some people criticize the public defender system because it does not really provide the indigent defendant with a choice of attorneys since, in most instances, the accused is assigned an attorney. However, most public defender offices do have provisions for reassigning staff members if there is an obvious conflict between an attorney and a client.

JURIES

The role that juries serve today is far different from their originally intended purpose. The original jury system, which developed in England during the Middle Ages, was designed to compel testimony in trials. Early jurors were not unbiased members of the community or a representative sample of peers, but rather witnesses who were brought before the courts of the crown and commanded to relate what they knew about the crime and the accused. The present use of the jury originated from a major concession forced upon King John in the Magna Carta that henceforth noblemen were granted the right to a trial by their peers.[41]

Trial juries play a crucial role in the administration of criminal justice. Usually, the decision rendered by a jury terminates the trial process in criminal cases—that is, in most states a verdict of not guilty cannot be overturned by subsequent appeals and a verdict of guilty is rarely overturned through the appellate process.

Composition

It is well recognized that the decision a jury renders depends a great deal on the makeup of the jury and how the jurors were chosen. It is true that most juries are composed of ordinary citizens, but they are often not representative of a true cross-section of the community. For the most part, they operate without any guidelines from their fellow citizens. In fact, the entire deliberative process of the jury is so designed by its secretiveness and its seclusion to eliminate the impact of community attitudes upon the members' judgment. As Jacob puts it: "They are selected by chance to *serve* their community rather than *represent* it."[42]

Let us explore this question of community representation further. Although in theory every citizen should have an equal chance to be selected for jury duty, this does not occur. Statutes usually prescribe that jurors be chosen from voter registration lists, which is discriminatory. Those citizens who are not qualified to vote, such as convicted felons and citizens who have not been in the community long enough to satisfy residency requirements, are automatically excluded. In studying voting behavior, political scientists have often found that the poor and members of minority groups, which are often synonymous, are not registered voters and, therefore, automatically excluded.

In many instances, certain professionals such as doctors and lawyers are excluded from jury service, in addition to working people who would experience substantial financial hardship by serving as members of a jury. This bar to jury service is slowly disappearing in areas where union contracts provide for some compensation during jury service, and many firms encourage jury participation by making up the difference in pay that a person would lose by jury service.[43]

Studies conducted in Baltimore, Los Angeles, and Milwaukee indicated that housewives, retirees, professionals, managers, and proprietors are overrepresented on juries, while working-class citizens are underrepresented.[44] In Baltimore, for example, people in the occupational classifications of manager, professional, or proprietor made up 40.2 percent of the jurors, but constituted only 18.7 percent of the general population. On the other hand, although 41.3 percent of the population consisted of working-class people, only 13.4 percent of blue-collar workers were found on the juries studied.[45]

Similarly, many studies have documented the fact that discrimination seems to run along racial lines. A study in Virginia indicated that adult blacks, although constituting an average of 14 percent of the population of the jurisdictions studied, constituted only slightly less than 2 percent of the jurors empaneled in those particular districts.[46]

Deliberations

Research conducted using simulated and real juries has provided some interesting insights into this normally secret process. The research suggests that juries are far less deliberative in criminal cases than might be imagined. A University of Chicago research group, after conducting extensive interviews of criminal trial jurors in New York and Chicago, found that almost all juries voted as soon as they retired to their chambers. In 30 percent of the cases, it took only one vote to return a unanimous verdict. In those cases where subsequent votes were taken, the eventual vote was unanimous 90 percent of the time. The striking fact was that in this 90 percent, if the original vote was a majority one, that was the way the final vote ended up. It would seem that peer pressure was enough to change the minds of the dissenters. The instance of an individual holding out and not voting in accord with the majority and causing a hung jury is very rare indeed.[47]

In a later study by this same research group, additional interesting facts were uncovered. As might be imagined, the juror's occupation and biases seemed to play an important role. Jurors let the defendant's vocation influence their estimate of his or her worth. In criminal cases, racial prejudice by jurors from a variety of occupational backgrounds seemed to influence their decisions concerning defendants who were members of minority groups.[48]

Videotape simulations of jury deliberations have indicated that there are some obvious decision-making dynamics that occur in jury deliberations. Women play a far more passive role than men in these deliberations.[49] The more formal education a juror had, the more likely that individual was to participate openly and frequently in the discussions and deliberations.[50] Most of the discussion in the jury room centered on how to conduct the deliberations and on an exchange of personal experiences that the jurors felt would aid them in making an appropriate decision. There was far less discussion of the testimony offered during the trial or of the instructions that they had received from the judge than might be imagined.[51]

The nationality of the jury members seemed to play an important role in determining whether the accused would be found guilty or not. Jurors of German, Scandinavian, and English ancestry were much more likely to vote for the state, while jurors of Negro or East European background were much more likely to side with the defense.[52]

An extensive study of juries by Kalvern and Zeisel found that judges agreed with the decision of juries in about two-thirds of all cases. In those cases in which the judge disagreed with the jury, it was usually because the jury was perceived as being too lenient. Many of the disagreements between the judge and the jury also centered on such factors as the jury's belief that the punishment for the crime was too severe since the defendant had already suffered as a result of having committed the crime and need not be punished further. Juries were also more sensitive to improper police methods and to defendants who were charged with crimes that occurred among subcultures where norms differed from those of the jury members themselves. Finally, juries tended to weigh more heavily than the judges the contributory fault of the victim in rape and assault cases.[53]

Although there are certain reform groups who would abolish the jury system, history and the lack of a viable substitute would seem to indicate that juries will continue to play an important role in the administration of criminal justice. If the future should indicate any changes in the traditional jury system, it is likely to occur only in the manner of selection and composition and the number of jurors used.

WITNESSES

Witnesses in criminal trials are classified into two categories: (1) the lay or ordinary witness; and (2) the expert witness.

The lay or ordinary witness is a person who has some personal knowledge of the facts of the case and who has been called upon to relate this information in court. Police officers usually fall within this category. The lay witness is permitted to testify only about facts and generally may not state an opinion unless this is permitted by the judge.[54] Lay witnesses are allowed to testify only to what they perceived through their five senses that is relevant to the case.

With the great advance of science and with the wide variety of skilled occupations, juries are often called upon to pass judgment on many matters about which the jurors have no personal knowledge. The services of the expert witness have been developed to assist them. The function of the expert witness is to give the jury the benefit of his or her knowledge of a particular science or skill. Expert witnesses are permitted to express their opinions concerning a particular set of facts or circumstances or about some examination of evidence made by them. Of course, the jury may or may not accept their opinions.

An expert witness must satisfy two fundamental rules: (1) the subject matter to which the expert witness will testify must be a field in which the average person has little or no knowledge; and (2) the witness must have the qualifications that are necessary to make him or her an expert in the field. A voir dire examination is conducted by both the prosecutor and defense counsel to establish the expertise of the witness. However, the final decision as to whether someone qualifies as an expert witness is made by the trial judge. Even though the trial judge rules that the individual is indeed an expert witness, the opposing counsel can cross-examine the expert in an effort to destroy his or her credibility to the jury.

THE BAILIFF

The bailiff is an officer of the court. This office evolved from the Statute of Winchester in 1285, by which King Edward I tried to establish a uniform system of law enforcement in England. The original responsibility of this official was to keep persons under surveillance who were traveling about town streets after dark, and to periodically check on all known and observed strangers. Today the bailiff is responsible for keeping order in the court and protecting the security of jury deliberations and court property. At the county level, the bailiff is often a member of the sheriff's department who, as a uniformed officer, is assigned to the court. Many municipal courts rely on a form of political patronage to fill this position, and the bailiff is appointed by the judge to serve in a particular court.

THE COURT CLERK

The office of court clerk is normally attached to the main trial court of the county or municipality. In most states, the court clerk is a popularly elected official. In some states, this position is considered a patronage appointment for the party represented by the senior judge on the bench or by the party that is represented by the majority of judges in the court. The court clerk collects fines, forfeitures, penalties, and court costs in criminal cases, is usually responsible for keeping the records of the court proceedings and actions, and may be empowered to prepare formal writs and process papers issued by the court. Court clerks usually are salaried officials, but in some states they are still paid on a fee basis. In several states, the position of court clerk is combined with that of the elected county clerk, who records legal papers in the county as well as handling the administrative and clerical responsibilities of the court.

THE COURT REPORTER

Court reporters are employed to record and transcribe trial or other court proceedings. In the past, the court reporter normally used shorthand, but most now use stenotype machines. In the last few years, courts, in an effort to become more cost effective, are increasingly turning to tape recorders. One of the problems of using tape recorders is the difficulty of editing the tape to remove objectionable comments. In most cases, the court reporter is salaried and is also paid an additional sum, usually by the page, for the transcribing and preparation of the court record in cases of appeal. In some instances, the court reporter is responsible for the care and security of the physical evidence introduced during the trial if it is not the express responsibility of the bailiff to do so. However, this responsibility extends only to the time that the evidence is in the courtroom; permanent responsibility for the maintenance of the evidence during the trial is usually the task of the court clerk or, in the case of the state's evidence, the police in certain circumstances.

THE CORONER

The office of coroner, although not a judicial office in the strictest sense, does perform quasi-judicial functions. The first mention of this official is recorded in 1194 during the reign of King Richard I of England. Unfortunately, little is known of his specific responsibilities other than that he was a representative of the crown assigned to perform ministerial tasks at the county level.

The present-day function of the coroner seems to date from 1275, when under Edward I his responsibilities were expanded to include the specific task of conducting investigations into unnatural and sudden deaths. He was also charged with the duties of overseeing criminal prosecutions that involved the forfeiture of the accused's property to the crown, the collection of taxes, and the levying and collection of fines.

Today, the coroner in the majority of states is an elected county official whose chief function is to investigate the cause of death that occurs in the absence of witnesses, under suspicious circumstances, or where there is evidence of possible violence. The coroner is authorized to conduct *inquests* concerning suspicious deaths. These are quasi-judicial hearings that have some of the same characteristics as a trial. The coroner usually has the authority to subpoena witnesses and documents, cross-examine witnesses under oath, introduce evidence, and receive testimony. Most states do not require that the inquest follow the exacting rules of criminal procedure that govern trials. If the hearing suggests just cause, the coroner is authorized to issue warrants of arrest or at least require the prosecutor to initiate the obtaining of such a warrant.

One of the major criticisms of this office has been the lack of qualifications required of the coroner. Since, in many cases, coroners have no background in medicine or law, they cannot perform their obligations satisfactorily. As a result of this, a number of states have abolished the office of coroner and substituted the office of *medical examiner* in its place. The medical examiner must be a licensed physician and in some instances must also be a qualified specialist in pathology. Many states, such as Massachusetts, which was the first to adopt this idea in 1877, have vested the legal responsibilities in the office of the county prosecutor and the medical responsibilities in the appointed medical examiner. A few states have appointed medical examiners who operate out of a central state agency.

SUMMARY

The judge, prosecuting attorney, defense counsel, and jury play extremely important roles in the administration of justice—roles that are often very different from those commonly portrayed through the media. For example, judges are much more constrained in their actions by other members of the court and criminal justice system than most people imagine.

By the same token, the power and discretion of the prosecuting attorney is much broader than most people realize. In fact, the prosecutor is probably the most important actor in the judicial process—and perhaps, in the entire criminal justice system. This official's power to decline to prosecute a case; to play a central role in plea bargaining, and to exert authority over grand jury inquiries and police investigations makes the prosecutor a very formidable instrument of justice.

The role of the defense attorney is also often perceived far differently than the role that he or she actually plays. The Perry Mason image of the defense lawyer as a crusading searcher for justice and trial advocacy is more than a little far-fetched. In fact, the defense attorney's role is more likely to be one of accommodation and expediency in many criminal cases.

Finally, the role of the jury was examined. In addition to these major roles, this chapter explored the characteristics of indigent defense arrangements, and various secondary officials such as witnesses, the court bailiff, the court clerk, the court reporter, and the coroner's office.

REVIEW QUESTIONS

1. Name the principal actors involved in a criminal court proceedings.
2. What is the role of the judge in court?
3. Briefly describe common constraints placed on judges in the hearing of a case.
4. Why is the prosecutor called the "traffic cop" of the criminal justice system?
5. What are three inducements that a prosecutor might use in plea bargaining?
6. What are the extraordinary powers the prosecutor has over the proceedings of a grand jury?
7. Is the office of prosecutor politically important? Why?
8. What is the primary responsibility of the defense attorney? Explain your answer.
9. In the text, the role of the defense attorney is described as adversarial. What does that mean in relation to the other actors in the judicial process?
10. What purpose does the jury serve in the criminal justice system?

DISCUSSION QUESTIONS

1. Plea bargaining undermines and destroys the purpose of the judicial process. Is this statement true? Discuss.
2. Politics plays too important a role in the selection of prosecutors and district attorneys. Thus prosecutors should be appointed, not elected to their office. Discuss.
3. A defense attorney should do everything possible to win a favorable verdict for his or her client. Discuss.

SUGGESTED ADDITIONAL READINGS

Advisory Commission on Intergovernmental Relations. *Court Reform.* Washington, D.C.: U.S. Government Printing Office, 1971.

American Bar Association Project on Standards for Criminal Justice. *Standards Relating to the Prosecution Function: Approved Draft.* Chicago: American Bar Association, 1970.

Frank, Jerome. *Courts on Trial.* New York: Atheneum, 1969.

Mileski, Maureen. "Courtroom Encounters: An Observation Study of a Lower Criminal Court," *Law and Society Review* 5 (1971): 473–538.

Nagel, Stuart. *Improving the Legal Process: Effects of Alternatives.* Lexington, Mass.: Heath, 1975.

Nagel, Stuart, and M. Neff. "The Impact of Plea Bargaining on Judicial Process Changes," *American Bar Association Journal* 62 (1976): 1020–1023.

Oaks, D., and W. Lehman. *Criminal Justice System and the Indigent.* Chicago: University of Chicago Press, 1968.

Watson, Richard A., and Ronald G. Dowling. *The Politics of Bench and Bar: Judicial Selection Under the Missouri Nonpartisan Court Plan.* New York: Wiley, 1969.

NOTES

1. *Boykin* v. *Alabama,* 395 U.S. 238, 89 S. Ct. (1969).

2. For example, see Marvin E. Frankel, *Criminal Sentences: Law Without Order* (New York: Hill & Wang, 1973).

3. Maureen Mileski, "Courtroom Encounters: An Observation Study of a Lower Criminal Court," *Law and Society Review* 5 (1971): 473–538.

4. This section was adopted from Peter W. Lewis and Kenneth D. Peoples, *The Supreme Court and the Criminal Process* (Philadelphia: Saunders, 1978), pp. 974–975.

5. Ibid., p. 975.

6. For example, see Milton Heumann, *Plea Bargaining—The Experiences of Prosecutors, Judges and Defense Attorneys* (Chicago: University of Chicago Press, 1978); J. Ferguson, "The Role of the Judge in Plea Bargaining," *Criminal Law Quarterly* 15 (1972): 50–51; and *Dewey* v. *United States,* 268 F. 2d 124, 128 (8th Cir. 1959)

7. Heumann, *Plea Bargaining,* p. 35.

8. Henry A. Allen, "Trial Preparation," *Informant* 3 (March 1978): 6.

9. Donald J. Newman, "Pleading Guilty for Considerations: A Study of Bargain Justice," *Journal of Criminal Law, Criminology and Police Science* 46 (March-April 1956): 780–790.

10. George F. Cole, *The American System of Criminal Justice* (North Scituate, Mass.: Duxbury Press, 1975), p. 297.

11. Albert N. Alschuler, "The Prosecutor's Role in Plea Bargaining," *University of Chicago Law Review* 61 (1968).

12. Cole, *The American System of Criminal Justice,* p. 297.

13. Heumann, *Plea Bargaining,* p. 35.

14. Ibid.

15. Wayne R. LaFave, *Arrest: The Decision to Take a Suspect into Custody* (Boston: Little, Brown, 1965), p. 515.

16. Advisory Commission on Intergovernmental Relations, *State-Local Relations in the Criminal Justice System* (Washington, D.C.: U.S. Government Printing Office, 1971), pp. 113–114.

17. Yong Hyo Cho, *Public Policy and Urban Crime* (Cambridge, Mass.: Ballinger, 1974), p. 57.

18. Advisory Commission, *State Local Relations,* p. 113.

19. National District Attorneys Association, *The Prosecuting Attorneys of the United States* (Chicago: NDAA, 1966), pp. 193–195.

20. National District Attorneys Association, *National Prosecution Standards* (Chicago: NDAA, 1977), p. 15.

21. Richard L. Enstrom, "Political Ambitions and the Prosecutorial Office," *Journal of Politics* 33 (1971): 190–194.

22. W. Gelber, "Who Defends the Prosecutor?" *Crime and Delinquency* 14 (1968): 315–323.

23. President's Commission on Law Enforcement and Administration of Justice, *Task Force Report: The Courts* (Washington, D.C.: U.S. Government Printing Office, 1967), p. 73.

24. National District Attorneys Association, *The Prosecuting Attorneys of the United States*, p. 194.

25. H. R. Wildermann, "The Process of Socialization in the Role of the Prosecutor," *Journal of Social Interaction* 2 (Spring 1965): 26–35.

26. National District Attorneys Association, *National Prosecution Standards*, p. 51.

27. Cole, *The American System of Criminal Justice*, p. 257.

28. Abraham S. Blumberg, "Lawyers with Convictions," *Transaction* 4 (July 1967): 18.

29. As quoted in Leonard Downie, Jr., *Justice Denied* (New York: Praeger, 1971), p. 173; and Cole, *The American System of Criminal Justice*, p. 263.

30. Cole, *The American System of Criminal Justice*, p. 260.

31. Board of Governors, Criminal Law Section, Virginia State Bar, *Report to the Governor and the General Assembly of Virginia: A Study of the Defense of Indigents in Virginia* (Annapolis, Va., 1971).

32. J. Edward Lumbard, "Better Lawyers for Our Criminal Courts," *Atlantic Monthly*, June 1964, p. 86.

33. 372 U.S. 335 (1963).

34. *Argersinger* v. *Hamlin*, 407 U.S. 25 (1972).

35. Bertram F. Wilcox and Edward J. Bloustein, "Account of a Field Study in a Rural Area of the Representation of Indigents Accused of a Crime," *Columbia Law Review* 59 (April 1959): 551–583.

36. Harry P. Stumpf and Robert J. Janowitz, "Judges and the Poor: Bench Response to Federally Financed Legal Services," *Stanford Law Review* 221 (1969): 1059.

37. Harry P. Stumpf, "Law and Poverty: A Political Perspective," *Wisconsin Law Review* (1968): 698–699.

38. Ibid., p. 699.

39. For example, see Dallin H. Oaks and Warren Lehman, *Criminal Justice System and the Indigent* (Chicago: University of Chicago Press, 1968); and Michael Moore, "The Right to Counsel for Indigents in Oregon," *Oregon Law Review* 44 (Spring 1965).

40. For example, see "Representation of Indigents in California: A Field Study of the Public Defender and Assigned-Counsel Systems," *Stanford Law Review* 13 (1961): 522–565.

41. Herbert Jacob, *Justice in America* (Boston: Little, Brown, 1972), p. 121.

42. Ibid., p. 122.

43. Ibid., p. 123.

44. Edwin S. Mills, "Statistical Study of Occupation of Jurors in a U.S. District Court," *Maryland Law Review* 22 (1962): 205–216; W. S. Robinson, "Bias, Probability and Trial by Jury," *American Sociological Review* 15 (1950): 73–78; and Marvin R. Summer, "Comparative Study of Qualifications of State and Federal Jurors," *Wisconsin Bar Bulletin* 34 (1961): 35–39.

45. ——— "Statistical Study . . ." p. 208.

46. S. W. Tucker, "Racial Discrimination in Jury Selection in Virginia," *Virginia Law Review* 52 (1966): 749.

47. Dale W. Broeder, "University of Chicago Jury Project," *Nebraska Law Review* 38 (1959): 746–747.

48. ———— "Occupational Expertise and Bias as Affecting Juror Behavior: A Preliminary Look," *New York University Law Review* 40 (1965): 1079–1100.

49. Fred L. Strodtbeck et al., "Social Status in Jury Deliberations," *American Sociological Review* 22 (1957): 713–719.

50. Rita M. James, "Status and Competence of Jurors," *American Journal of Sociology*, 64 (1959): 563–570.

51. Ibid.

52. Broeder, "University of Chicago Jury Project," pp. 748–749.

53. Harry Kalvern, Jr., and Hans Zeisel, *The American Jury* (Boston: Little Brown, 1966).

54. Gilbert B. Stuckey, *Evidence for the Law Enforcement Officer* (New York: McGraw-Hill, 1968), p. 61.

11
CURRENT ISSUES
AND TRENDS

Michael D. Sullivan

1. What changes in pretrial processes could relieve the congestion in the courts?
2. Should plea bargaining and grand juries be abolished?
3. How can the jury system be reformed to speed up the trial process?
4. How can the caliber of prosecutors be improved?
5. What might be done to obtain better cooperation of witnesses in trials?
6. Is reform of bail methods desirable?

These are some of the questions this chapter will answer.

This chapter looks at some reform suggestions and new developments to improve the judicial process. However, whereas the preceding chapter examined role reform, this chapter will examine ideas and suggestions for the reform of the structure and process of the judicial system.

MAJOR HISTORICAL MILESTONES IN COURT REFORM

In recent years, our judicial system has been receiving increased criticism. A *New York Times* poll conducted in 1977 indicated that the public felt that the courts were in need of more drastic reform than any other component of the criminal justice system.[1] There is probably a great deal of justification for this criticism. Whereas law enforcement and corrections have adopted some important reform strategies and programs, the courts continue to lag behind. However, it should also be recognized that the courts, because of their unique role in the administration of justice, have many built-in constraints that make reform more difficult than with other agencies.

The recognized need for court reform is not new. In 1906, Roscoe Pound, who later became dean of the Harvard Law School, delivered his famous plea to the America Bar Association in which he claimed that the judicial system was archaic in three respects.[2] First, he maintained that there were simply too many courts which created duplication, waste, and inefficiency. Second, he argued that concurrent jurisdiction in cases was unnecessary and out of place in modern society. Finally, he pointed out that because of jurisdictional boundaries, unequal workloads existed that often resulted in considerable judicial waste because some jurisdictions would have too much work and others too little. Pound's comments led to the creation of an American Bar Association committee that was given the responsibility to propose reform legislation for the judiciary. In 1913, the American Judicature Society was founded to promote the efficient administration of justice.

During the 1930s, another important figure in the history of court reform emerged. While president of the American Bar Association, Arthur T. Vanderbilt emphasized the need to reform state courts. Of particular concern were such issues as improving pretrial procedure, methods of selecting juries, improving trial practice, improving the law of evidence, simplifying appellate procedure, controlling state administrative agencies, and improving judicial organization and administration.[3] Reform efforts were curtailed during the war years. In 1952, the Institute of Judicial Administration was founded under the leadership of Arthur Vanderbilt. Associated closely with the New York University School of Law, it conducted numerous studies of state court systems.[4]

In 1963, the National College of the State Judiciary was established through the efforts of former Justice Tom C. Clark and the American Bar Association. During the 1960s and 1970s reform efforts were continued through the efforts of former Chief Justice Earl Warren, the current Chief Justice, Warren Burger, and such associations as the American Judicature Society, the American Bar Association, and other interest groups.[5] Through these efforts such notable court reform institutions as the Institute for Court Management, the National Center for State Courts, and the Federal Judicial Center have been established to improve the overall judicial process. Although it is not possible to review all the current suggestions for court reform, some of the more popular are highlighted in the remainder of this chapter.

RECOMMENDED REFORMS OF THE JUDICIAL PROCESS

There are numerous possible reforms of the judicial process. Some of these reforms could be easily implemented; others would prove more difficult. Among the suggested reforms are changes in the pretrial process, redirecting misdemeanor cases out of the courts, abolishing plea bargaining, changing jury size, and reforming bail procedures.

CHANGES IN THE PRETRIAL PROCESS

In the pretrial process, more emphasis should be placed on screening and diversion. If more attention were placed on these alternatives, fewer cases would come to trial.

The rationale behind screening and diversion from the judicial process is twofold: (1) the number of cases that burden the courts must be reduced; and (2) there may be more appropriate ways to deal with offenders than through the trial process. This is not a call for leniency. Rather, it merely recognizes that in terms of both financial and less tangible costs to society, it may be more practicable to consider alternatives. The purpose of pretrial screening is to reduce the number of cases, so that the criminal courts can concentrate on those cases that deserve the time and expense of adjudication.

The pivotal figure in the pretrial screening and diversion process is the prosecutor. In a pretrial process, prosecutors would examine the case much more closely than they now routinely do. They would create certain decisional guidelines on whether a trial is in the best interests of society, the courts, and the accused. Some considerations might be the sufficiency of the evidence against the defendant, which would indicate whether a conviction was likely and whether the conviction, once obtained, could be sustained on appeal. The more difficult questions that the prosecutor would have to consider if the trial process is invoked concern the potential of preventing future criminal behavior by the accused (and by others). Furthermore, the prosecutor would have to weigh whether the safety of society would be endangered if a diversionary method were used in dealing with the accused. The prosecutor would also have to consider the possibility that a trial and incarceration might seriously disrupt family ties, create severe financial hardship, and expose the accused to an experience that would produce an individual who was even more embittered and prone to criminal tendencies than when he or she entered the criminal justice system.

RELIEVING THE LOWER COURTS OF CERTAIN MISDEMEANOR CASES

In 1976, the National Conference on the Causes of Popular Dissatisfaction with the Administration of Justice was held. One of the conference's main recommendations was to find alternatives to the lower courts to process the many minor matters that now glut these courts and detract from their more important judicial role. The conference supported establishing alternative dispute resolution machinery other than our lower courts. It was felt that in addition to unburdening the lower courts, such arrangements might expedite justice by avoiding the encumbrances of the legal system. For instance, minor disputes could be resolved directly by the parties rather than having to hire the services of an attorney to guide the disputants through the formalized legal machinery.

Generally it was recognized that formal litigation was not necessarily the best way to resolve differences. For example, mediation and fact-finding procedures and hearings could be used as informal methods where community members could be employed as hearing officers. Instead of the limited options of the court to settle problems through the imposition of fines, probation, or incarceration, disputants could be referred to social service agencies, to small claims courts, be required to perform community service, or engage in victim restitution programs.[6] Any combination of these dispositions might be jointly used in resolving a case.

Such informal hearings could also serve as a screening device. If it became apparent that the circumstances warranted the intervention of more formal trial court proceedings, the case could be referred to the proper criminal or civil court.[7]

Such a system is known as a Neighborhood Justice Center. As a result of the recommendations of the 1976 conference, the Law Enforcement Assistance Administration has sponsored the development of several of these models throughout the United States.[8] At the present time, there is no one recommended model on how they should be established, what specific jurisdiction they should have, or how cases should be adjudicated. Because the concept is so new, the idea and its application is still in the developmental stage. In some localities, these justice centers have been established by the prosecutor's office; others have placed the center under court sponsorship. In San Francisco, it was decided that the Neighborhood Justice Center would operate by referrals from the police.[9]

There are a great many problems still to be ironed-out in the concept. For instance, questions of jurisdiction and authority, format for resolving differences, what types of personnel are needed to operate such a system, and whether it is to operate solely by court, police, or prosecutor's referral or some combination of these. Also, the question of self-initiated referral by a crime victim or civil disputant has been discussed.

Developments in this area deserve watching in the years ahead. In particular, it will be important to evaluate whether, in fact, these diversionary and screening methods do relieve the lower courts of their minor criminal and civil caseload.

ABOLITION OF PLEA BARGAINING

As mentioned earlier, in many courts the majority of criminal convictions are obtained because the defendant enters a guilty plea, often as a result of plea bargaining arrangements between the prosecutor and the defense counsel. To many this is a particularly pernicious practice that destroys the basic concept of justice.[10] Some see it as harmful to society because it reduces the deterrent impact of the law, and it can be harmful to the accused who by engaging in plea bargaining forfeits those rights that have been incorporated into the trial process for his or her protection. Invariably, in any discussion of court reform, one of the major recommendations that arises is to abolish plea bargaining. Prosecutors and judges justify its existence on the grounds that if it did not exist, the entire judicial system would break under the strain of the workload.

Let us look at this problem more carefully. There is no question that such practices lead to injustices. However, perhaps the alternative of abolishing such practices might be just as bad. In the United States today there is an attempt by legislative bodies to eliminate, or at least drastically curtail, discretionary decision making in imposing punishment for the commission of crimes. Discretionary decision making includes the practice of plea bargaining. Thus although there seems to be a quest for "efficiency," this approach may well overlook the fact that mechanical law enforcement is both undesirable and impossible.[11] The problem with trying to eliminate discretion by abolishing plea bargaining also presents the danger of not being able to consider the mitigating circumstances in individual cases. This may be the real crux of the illusive concept of justice. If prosecutors and judges must treat every case of burglary the same without consideration for these factors, is it any better than the so-called nonjustice system brought about by bargaining and negotiation? In attempting to bring about uniformity, we might in fact be creating a system that results in greater injustice. Such changes and their possible effects must be considered thoroughly before changes are implemented.

For these and other reasons it probably is not advisable or practical to abolish plea bargaining completely. What is needed immediately, however, is meaningful reform in the plea bargaining process. The first move is for the court to assume a larger role. In too many cases, judges merely acquiesce to the bargain arrived at by the prosecutor and the defense counsel. Judges should examine all the facts of the case and require of prosecutors written explanations for their decisions. Judges should also make certain that the accused fully understands the consequences of the bargain and the guilty plea and that the accused understands that he or she is forfeiting all rights to a trial. All too often, the accused is at the mercy of the defense counsel and must rely upon the counsel for the appropriate legal advice. If judges would take a larger role in the plea bargaining process and refuse to accept settlements unquestioningly, there would probably be less criticism of this practice.

ABOLITION OF THE GRAND JURY

The grand jury has by and large outlived its usefulness in the majority of criminal proceedings. This would seem to be particularly true now that the Supreme Court has required states to adopt a "probable cause" hearing (preliminary examination). The functions of this preliminary hearing and the grand jury certainly duplicate each other. Great Britain abolished the use of grand juries in 1933, although the right to be indicted by a grand jury had existed in that country since the fourteenth century. Willoughby puts the entire issue of the grand jury into perspective when he says:

> A grand jury is in the nature of a fifth wheel; that real responsibility for the bringing of criminal charges is, in fact, exercised by the prosecuting attorney, the grand jury doing little or nothing more than following his suggestions; that it entails delay . . . ; that it renders prosecution more difficult through important witnesses getting beyond the jurisdiction . . . or through memory of facts becoming weakened by lapse of time; that it entails unneccessary expense to the government; and that it imposes a great burden on the citizen called upon to render jury service.[12]

Grand juries are extremely costly to select, service, and maintain. Although the grand jury was originally conceived as a screening device to protect the accused from false accusations, it no longer serves this objective. For example, a study of the operations of the grand jury in Baltimore indicated that this grand jury returned indictments in 98.18 percent of those cases it heard, only to have 42 percent of these indictments later dismissed before trial because of insufficient evidence or some technicality that made prosecution impossible.[13]

The use of grand juries also has another dysfunctional consequence for the administration of justice. In some cases, their legal intricacies of empaneling, conduct, and deliberations have actually thwarted justice. Individuals who may have been guilty have been able to have charges against them dismissed because of legal irregularities in the grand jury process which a skilled defense attorney has been able to use advantageously.

However, the continued use of the investigatory grand jury is recommended by most legal reform groups. The grand jury that is routinely used in the processing of criminal cases is the hearing grand jury. The investigatory grand jury is a special type of grand jury that is convened to inquire into particular areas such as organized crime or official corruption in the community. In some politically sensitive areas, where the police or the prosecutor are reluctant to conduct the necessary investigations, these special grand juries can perform an important role in the investigation and accusation that leads to the prosecution of crime.[14]

It should be pointed out, however, that investigatory grand juries also pose some serious problems for the administration of justice. History is replete with examples of the unscrupulous use of such an instrument for personal and political interests. For example, during Lincoln's administration they were used against those who did not support the Union's cause. During Roosevelt and Truman's administration they were used to silence Bolshevik and Nazi sympathizers. Later they were used by Senator Joseph McCarthy and Representative Richard Nixon during the red-baiting scare of the 1950s.[15]

Although the investigatory grand jury can be used effectively to weed out local corruption and organized crime, they must be controlled very carefully if they are to serve as effective instruments of justice and not tools of oppression against certain minority interests. In fact, this concern for the almost tyrannical power of both hearing and investigatory grand juries is coming under a great deal more scrutiny today. Congress has recently introduced some far-reaching reforms to reshape federal grand juries. Among other stipulations, this proposed legislation, for the first time, would allow witnesses, including persons under investigation, to bring their attorneys into the grand jury rooms. Currently, witnesses must leave the room to consult with their attorneys, a process that can be time consuming and potentially prejudicial. The legislation would also limit to 6 months the time that a recalcitrant witness could be jailed for contempt, and stiff penalties would be provided for anyone who violates the rules of secrecy.

Another provision would provide for full so-called transactional immunity for witnesses—that is, that witnesses who appear before the grand jury could not be prosecuted later for any offense discussed in their testimony. As it is now, federal grand jury witnesses now receive only "use" immunity, which applies only to their actual testimony and allows charges to be brought that are based on independent evidence.

The reform proposal has been referred to the Senate Judiciary Committee which is also working on the proposed revision of the federal criminal code.

TIMELY PROCESSING OF CRIMINAL CASES

One of the immediate goals of court reform is to shorten the time between arrest and the beginning of trial. Every state should require that, at least in felony cases, an arrestee be brought before a magistrate within 6 hours of arrest for an initial appearance. This initial appearance would be used to advise the individual of his constitutional rights and to inquire into the police conduct in this area. In addition, the accused should be advised of the charges against him, and the appropriate bail should be determined.

Once this has occurred, states should require that in cases when the individual is jailed and cannot make bond, a preliminary hearing should be conducted within at least 10 days. Individuals who are incarcerated should receive priority in scheduling preliminary hearings. In those cases where the individual is out on bond, provisions should be made to conduct the preliminary hearing within 2 weeks of the arrest.

According to the recommendations of the National Advisory Commission, the entire process from arrest to trial should take no longer than 60 days. The realization of this proposal would require a number of changes. First, pretrial motions and conferences would have to be conducted within certain time frames—for example within 10 days after the preliminary hearing. Defense attorneys would have to file their motions. Prosecutors would have to file their countermotions within 7 days of the filing of the motion by the defense attorney, and the judge would have to rule on the motion within the following 5 days. Similar time frames would have to be adopted for the scheduling of the arraignment and the grand jury where it is used.

Reforms in scheduling court trials should deal with the problems associated with continuances. In many jurisdictions, the granting of continuances often unnecessarily prolongs the time required to get the case to trial. Defense counsels are particularly notorious for using delaying tactics. Many times, they ask a judge for a continuance on the grounds that they need additional time to prepare the defense. In some cases, this may be a meritorious request; other times it is used to frustrate the prosecution, the state's witnesses, or the complaining victim, or to cover up the fact that they have as yet made no effort to prepare the defense case. Judges should be more careful in granting such continuances and insist upon a definite showing of need.

JURY SIZE AND UNANIMITY

Requiring less than 12 jurors is often recommended as a reform proposal. About 20 states have enacted statutes to the effect that there can be 6 jurors in certain courts of limited jurisdiction, and other states are considering such legislation. In the 1970 case of *Williams* v. *Florida* (see pages 283–284), the U.S. Supreme Court held that Florida's use of a 6-person jury did not violate the defendant's Sixth and Fourteenth Amendment rights to trial by jury. The Court held that the important factor was not the size of the jury, but whether the group was "large enough to promote group deliberation, free from outside attempts at intimidation and to provide a fair possibility for obtaining a representative cross-section of the community."[16]

In light of the ruling of the Supreme Court, the National Advisory Commission recommends that "juries in criminal prosecutions for offenses not punishable by life imprisonment should be composed of less than 12, but at least 6 persons."[17] A jury of less than 12 persons can still provide the required group deliberation and resistance to outside influences and can reflect a representative cross-section of the community. The 6-person jury would be far less costly to empanel and maintain, particularly in cases that involve sensational crimes, where it becomes exceedingly difficult to empanel 12 persons acceptable to the prosecution and the defense. Recently, a number of researchers have demonstrated through the use of elaborate statistical models that a 6-member jury is more than 50 percent likely to convict an innocent person or acquit a guilty defendant.[18] Another researcher has purportly found that a 6-member jury has an average hung-jury rate of 2.4 percent, compared with the approximately 5.5 percent rate for the 12-member jury. He concludes that smaller juries reduce the chances that minority positions among jurors will be maintained.[19]

Another question relevant to juries concerns the fact that a unanimous verdict of guilty beyond a reasonable doubt must generally be found before a jury can convict. It has been argued, for example, that "the unanimity of a verdict in a criminal case is inextricably interwoven with the required measure of proof."[20] Most state constitutions require that there can be no conviction except by unanimous verdict; few states permit conviction by less than a unanimous verdict for crimes.[21] As mentioned earlier, Oregon, for example, provides that 10 votes can convict except in first-degree murder cases.

However, there are those who adamantly maintain that unanimity must be required. Probably the most succinct argument for the retention of the unanimous requirement has been expressed by Holtzoff, who says:

> Unanimity is important and vital for two reasons: first, it leads to a more thorough consideration of the questions at issue and a more careful deliberation in the jury room than might otherwise be the case, since debate and discussion must continue until a unanimous verdict is reached; and second, the fact that the verdict is unanimous is in itself strong assurance of its fairness and justice. The only possible drawback to the requirement of unanimity is that occasionally it leads to a deadlock and,

thereby, requires re-trial before another jury. The percentage of cases in which this happens in jurisdictions in which the common law system still prevails is, however, not sufficiently large to constitute an important factor.[22]

In spite of this, the American Bar Association, in examining the research on the question of jury deliberations as well as the legal considerations involved, concluded that the requirement for unanimity serves no useful purpose. Its Advisory Committee stated that "the minimum standards should recognize the propriety of less than unanimous verdicts as now permitted in six states."[23]

JUDICIAL SELECTION AND REMOVAL

Many students of the American judiciary have been concerned about the methods that are used to select judges because selection processes can impede the appointment of the most qualified to judgeships. These concerned groups, which include the American Bar Association, the American Judicature Society, state and local bar associations, and numerous civic organizations, have been instrumental in producing needed reforms in a number of states.

The states employ a variety of methods to select state court judges. Nearly half of the states still rely on partisan elections. In these states, a disproportionate number of which are in the South, individuals are popularly elected after receiving their party's nomination at a political convention or after winning a primary election. The next most frequent method is the nonpartisan election, in which the individual is popularly elected on a ballot that does not specify any affiliation with a political party. In 14 states, mostly in the Northeast, some judges are selected by the chief executive of the jurisdiction. This method is similar to the procedure used in the federal system, where judges are appointed by the President with the advice and consent of the Senate. A few states still retain the system that was popular in the early years of our nation's history in which the legislative body selects judges. For the most part, however, this form of selection is only for judgeships in the courts of limited and special jurisdiction.

In recent years, there have been increasing efforts to reform the traditional methods of selecting judges. The best-known reform idea has been the Missouri Plan of merit selection. Since it was first adopted for certain courts in that state in 1940, six other states have adopted similar systems. Under the Missouri Plan, a nonpartisan nominating commission—which consists of three attorneys selected by the Missouri Bar Association, three lay persons appointed by the governor, and the chief justice of the state supreme court— sends to the governor the names of three qualified individuals for the vacant judgeship. From this nominating list, the governor appoints one person. The newly appointed judge serves for a 1-year probationary period, and then must win approval of the voters by running unopposed on a separate nonpartisan judicial ballot. The only question appearing on the ballot is: "Shall ——— be elected to the office for the term prescribed by law?" If there is a majority of affirmative votes, the individual is elected to the full term of office. A few other states have adopted the idea of separate nominating commissions or, as they are sometimes called, merit commissions or judicial qualifications commissions. For the most part, however, they nominate judges only for certain state or city courts.[24]

The President's Commission on Law Enforcement and Administration of Justice has expressed concerns over the fact that politics plays such an important role in the selection of judges in most states, and that political selection in no way ensures that top-notch people will be elected or even consent to run because of the politicization of the office. Regarding the role of politics in the selection of judges, the commission says:

> In our largely urban society where only a small portion of the electorate knows anything about the operation of the courts, it is usually impossible to make an intelligent choice among relatively unknown candidates for the bench. The inevitable result is that in partisan elections the voters tend to follow their party's nominations without any serious attempt to evaluate the relative merits of the candidates. In normally Democratic or Republican districts, designation as the majority party's nominee ordinarily assumes election.[25]

Under this system, the leaders of the dominant party select the judges. This selection process takes place in closed meetings in which compromises and bargaining strategies are carried on in an effort to reward party supporters; under these circumstances, too little attention is given to the abilities of the party's nominees. In an effort to avoid such situations, many people advocate nonpartisan elections of judges. Although this method may appeal to those who would like to diminish the impact of partisan politics, it also has some evils associated with it. Winters and Allard question this method on the following grounds:

> It nullifies whatever responsibility political parties feel to the voters to provide competent candidates and thereby closes one of the avenues which may be open to voter pressure for good judicial candidates. Indeed, experience indicates that where appeal to the voters on political grounds is made impossible . . . other considerations equally irrelevant to a candidate's qualifications for judicial office are injected into the election. . . .[26]

The President's Commission on Law Enforcement and Administration of Justice is a strong advocate of the merit selection plan. The commission recommends that nonpartisan nominating boards be supplied with professional staffs and be made permanent agencies. It further recommends that the states direct intensive efforts toward developing standards that the nonpartisan nominating committee can employ in the selection of qualified potential jurists. Some states are now moving in that direction.

Another proposed reform to improve the judicial process is the recommendation that states establish an effective means to remove incompetent or corrupt judges. Traditionally judges in most states can be removed only by: (1) being voted out of office; (2) an impeachment process which normally requires a two-thirds vote of the legislature or the state senate; (3) the use of citizen-initiated recall which requires a substantial number of qualified voters to sign the recall petition; or (4) by the Governor after an address by both houses of legislature. In a number of states, removal of an incumbent judge occurs only after several of these steps have been taken.[27]

As a result of these formidable processes, very few judges are ever removed from office unless they lose an election. A few states that have recognized the dangers of such systems have adopted various reform measures to make the removal of corrupt or incompetent judges easier. States like California, North Carolina, Georgia, and Minnesota have established special commissions on judicial qualifications or tenure which are given the responsibility to receive and investigate complaints and make recommendations to the state supreme court for appropriate action. It would seem that the establishment of such bodies are not only more effective than more traditional ways of removing unqualified judges, but they can also serve as a watchdog agency to better ensure that judges "clean up their acts."

Probably the most notable plan is found in California which, in 1960, established the Commission on Judicial Qualifications. The commission is composed of five members of the judiciary, two members of the bar, and two laypeople. The function of the commission is to receive and investigate complaints on five specific grounds: (1) willful misconduct in office; (2) willful and persistent failure to perform judicial duties; (3) habitual intemperance; (4) conduct prejudicial to the administration of justice that brings the judicial office into disrepute; and (5) disability that interferes with the performance of duty.[28]

The commission receives complaints from any interested source. If the information contained in the complaint appears to merit further consideration, an informal inquiry is made to see if there is any substance to the complaint. The next stage is the conduct of a preliminary hearing in which the judge is asked to respond to the complaint. If the commission still is not satisfied, it arranges for a formal hearing in which the judge has the right to counsel, the right to introduce evidence in his or her own behalf, and to examine and cross-examine witnesses.

Following the hearing, the commission either dismisses the complaint or recommends censure, removal, or retirement of the delinquent judge to the Supreme Court, which enters its order. Those who advocate the plan feel it has made a substantial improvement in the California judiciary. In its first 6 years of operation, 44 judges became motivated to voluntarily leave the bench during commission investigation. It is also said that the commission serves an educational function; practices that have developed through carelessness or as a result of lack of insight can be discreetly brought to the judge's attention. Finally, the commission serves as a deterrent to judicial misconduct simply by being "visible and viable."[29]

UPGRADING THE PROSECUTOR

Among those who desire to improve the judicial process, changes in the present methods of selecting, retaining, and training of prosecutors and their legal assistants are absolutely essential. There is a recognized need to improve the caliber of persons attracted to this office and to retain them as careerists. It has been suggested that selection of prosecutors be based upon their qualifications similar to the selection of judges under the Missouri Plan. In addition, there is a need to drastically increase their salaries and those of their assistants to retain them in this very important position. The National Advisory Commission recommends that prosecutors receive the same remuneration as the presiding judge of the trial court of general jurisdiction.[30] Once this has been accomplished, it would be possible to prohibit them from engaging in the private practice of law, which quite frequently leads to conflicts of interest.

Likewise, the salaries for assistant prosecutors should be commensurate with salaries paid to attorney associates in private law firms in the area. In addition, there is the real need to provide prosecutors and assistant prosecutors with extensive training in the criminal law and trial practice and with an adequate legal research capability. In medium-sized cities, the prosecutor's staff should have at least one researcher to help research the necessary case and statutory laws. In smaller jurisdictions where this may not be practicable, the prosecutor should at least have access to an adequate legal library.

IMPROVING DEFENSE SERVICES FOR THE INDIGENT DEFENDANT

States need to improve the system of defense counsel to indigent defendants. This would require, as a minimum, the appointment of a full-time public defender at a salary commensurate with the job's responsibilities plus provision of the necessary facilities and staff. Applicants for this position should be nominated and approved by a select body of responsible citizens, who would send a list of three qualified nominees to the governor, who would then appoint the individual. The public defender would be a salaried employee of the state, appointed for at least a 4-year term and removed from office by a special judicial commission which would also have the authority to investigate and remove judges for cause.

Like the prosecutor, the public defender should be provided with legal research capabilities and funds for investigative facilities needed to prepare the client's defense as well as funds to employ such experts as psychiatrists, forensic pathologists, and criminal investigators when necessary.

WITNESS COOPERATION

Increasing concern is developing over problems with witnesses. Two recent comprehensive studies of the prosecution of criminal cases in Washington, D.C., and New York City indicate that the most frequent reasons cases are rejected at the initial screening or lost in court are due to problems with witnesses.[31] For example, prosecutors in the Washington study gave "witness problem" as the most significant factor in dismissing robbery and other violent crimes, and second only to "insufficiency of evidence" as a reason for rejection in nonviolent property crime cases.[32]

Another recent study in our nation's capital indicated that witnesses in criminal cases in that city voiced several complaints that directly or indirectly resulted in less or no cooperation on their part. The most significant complaint was that there was a need for better protection against reprisals by the accused. The next most frequently mentioned complaint was that the courts needed to speed-up trials and to display better attitudes toward the witnesses themselves. Finally, they recommended better pay for witnesses, and lastly, better facilities and other conveniences.[33]

It would seem that the problem of witness cooperation in the courtroom is just one aspect of the overall problem in this area. Lack of witness cooperation spills over into such other areas as not reporting crimes to the police, or not cooperating with the police in their investigation. As can be seen by the various witness complaints, some are more difficult to deal with than others. For example, the concern about reprisals is more properly a function of police protection. However, it should come as no surprise that police personnel resources are so limited that little can be expected in this area. Even the federal government with its special "Witness Security Protection Program" is extremely limited in the types of cases and resources they have to deal with the problem. However, because these are concerns that are outside the immediate discussion of judicial improvements, they need not be dealt with here.

What can be done? One of the major problems seems to be that the police do not correctly obtain the names and addresses of witnesses. Later subpoenas are returned as "addressee unknown." Another study in Washington, D.C., indicated that the police did not verify witnesses' names and addresses from identification documents such as driver's licenses, etc. Some of the police were observed asking for the name and address of the witness in the presence of the arrestee.[34] Many of the witnesses indicated that they were confused about the entire process, what specifically they were supposed to do, and what they could expect. This points out a very serious problem in failing to communicate with the witness by the prosecutor's office. Some cities now have the police provide witnesses with a pamphlet that explains the process to them. Washington is also considering the development of a program to protect witnesses from possible reprisals. Under this program, as soon as the prosecutor receives the names of witnesses, he or she contacts them to inform the witnesses that any threats or acts of intimidation should be reported and that protection will be provided. Suggestions are being made that communities with such problems establish and widely publicize a special investigative unit that would conduct the necessary investigation, and if threats have been made, to notify the prosecutor to seek bail revocation or have the police provide protection.

Among some of the other suggestions relative to solving the witness problems are better management of court schedules so that trial delays would be prevented and the development of special career-criminal case reporting systems in which witnesses would be provided with closer monitoring and protection if necessary. Another suggestion is to use paralegals to assist in the interviewing of witnesses, obtaining statements, coordinating witness conferences, staffing a witness notification unit, coordinating requests for continuances, answering inquiries, monitoring cases for witness problems, and supervising issuance and processing of subpoenas.

Although the problem with witnesses is not new to the administration of criminal justice, it seems to be only in the last few years that it is receiving the attention it deserves. Like the earlier mentioned concept of the Neighborhood Justice Center, developments in witness management and programs are an important area to watch in the next few years.

BAIL REFORM

The issue of bail reform always centers around the three traditional arguments in this area: (1) that bail is discriminatory because it works against the poor defendant; (2) that bail is a form of assuring the court that the accused will appear for trial; and (3) that bail is a way of ensuring that certain dangerous offenders will not be put back on the streets before their trial. In this latter instance, it is assumed that by keeping the required bail as high as possible, the accused will be kept incarcerated until his or her trial and disposition.

Those who advocate bail reform usually point to the first argument; those who feel that traditional bail measures should be employed justify their position by citing the last two arguments. Although it is not possible to discuss all of the issues that surround bail and bail reform in any depth, certain facts about bail, its administration, and suggested reforms should be understood.

There are several methods of obtaining pretrial release. The first method is *cash bail*. This is the most widely used form. The defendant raises the required bond either through direct payment of the full amount to the court or with the help of a bondsman. The amount of the bail is set in one of three ways: (1) by reference to a fixed bail schedule which lists the amount according to a specific crime; (2) by the judge who may have complete discretion to set bail at any amount he or she desires as long as it is not "excessive or unreasonable"; (3) by a judge who may use the bail schedule as a guideline although he or she maintains the authority to select the exact amount within these limits.[35]

If the defendant obtains the bond from a bondsman, the defendant is normally required to pay as a deposit 10 percent of the bond's value. The bondsman is a private businessman and does not have to post bond for the accused if for some reason he doesn't want to. In 1964, the state of Illinois in an attempt to improve the defendant's chances for pretrial release, adopted a Ten Percent Bail Deposit Provision. According to this provision, the defendant must post only 10 percent of the bond, and all but 1 percent which is used for administrative handling is returned to the defendant after the judicial process is completed.

Other forms of obtaining pretrial release are the posting of a *property bond* in which property is put up as a pledge; the use of *conditions of release* in which the judge, where authorized, can require in addition to some form of cash or property bond that the accused abide by certain conditions (e.g., to return to work); and the *personal bond* (or recognizance bond) in which the individual is released on his or her own signature without having to raise any financial security.

The subject of bail reform has been hotly debated in recent years. There are those who advocate a "get tough" with bail position. Such an attitude was reflected in the passage of the District of Columbia Court Reform and Criminal Procedure Act of 1970. Under the provisions of this act, the courts were directed not only to set bail at an amount that would assure that the defendant would appear for the court date, but they were also instructed to determine and obtain without bail any defendant who would endanger "the safety of any other person in the community."[36]

During the time that the Washington act was developed and passed, a number of jurisdictions throughout the country were experimenting with various other reform projects that would substitute for traditional practices and the usual money bail system. By far the most popular response has been the development of what is generally called the bail reform project. This is a program that systematically investigates an arrested defendant, usually through the use of a standardized fact-finding mechanism, in order to determine the defendant's reliability for release on a personal recognizance bond. Such a system attempts to predict the defendant's likelihood for appearing in court by examining the defendant's community ties, past criminal record, and the seriousness of the current charge.[37] Often such programs are conducted by law and graduate students, VISTA volunteers, or former police officers or probation officers. Upon the completion of the investigation, a written report is submitted to the judge which suggests whether or not the defendant should be released on his or her own recognizance.

In the years ahead, there will probably be increased adoptions of variations of both systems. Attention will be focused on the career or dangerous criminal who will then face preventive detention guidelines. On the other hand, increasing use will also be made of investigative examinations and recognizance programs for those who qualify. Perhaps in this way society can be better assured that the career criminal or dangerous offender is not released on bail, and, on the other hand, that those who present little danger will not be penalized by their inability to raise the required bail or to purchase the services of a bailbondsman.

SYSTEMS ANALYSIS IN THE MANAGEMENT OF CRIMINAL CASES

An innovation that promises to bring badly needed reform to the judicial process is the introduction of new technological advances in the prosecution of criminal cases. Such a systems model, known as the Prosecutors Management Information System (PROMIS), has been operating in Washington, D.C., since 1971.[38]

Essentially, PROMIS makes available to the prosecutor's office a wealth of computerized information on each case, as well as reports and analyses of all case data so that priority areas can be identified and the prosecutor's legal staff can more meaningfully control their workload. This is accomplished by computerizing a great deal of information about persons who have been arrested and who are scheduled to appear for trial; also included is extensive information concerning the circumstances that surround the crimes. For example, the PROMIS system provides the prosecuting attorney's office with the following information:

> Information about the defendant, including name, alias, sex, race, date of birth, address, facts about prior arrests and convictions, employment status, and alcohol or drug abuse.
>
> Information about the crime, including the date, time, and place of the crime, the number of persons involved, and information about the gravity of the crime in terms of the amount and degree of personal injury, property loss, or damage.

Information about the time, date, and place of arrest; the type of arrest; and the identity of the arresting officer.

Information about criminal charges including the charges originally placed by the police, and the charges actually filed in court, and the reasons for changes in the charges by the prosecutor.

The dates of every court event in a case from preliminary hearing through arraignment, motion hearing, continuance hearing, and final disposition to sentencing; the names of the principals involved in each event, including the defense and prosecution attorneys and the judge; the outcomes of the events; and the reasons for these outcomes.

The names and addresses of all witnesses and victims, the prosecutor's assessment of whether each witness is essential to the case or not, any indications or reluctance to testify on the part of the witness, and other witness characteristics, such as whether he or she is related to the victim or defendant.[39]

As might be imagined, this PROMIS-generated information is of major assistance in helping the prosecutor prepare and manage his or her caseload. For example, since the establishment of this system, prosecutors have been able to concentrate their attention on the more serious cases, which can be identified by means of the information provided. Also, potential problem areas can be identified and handled prior to the trial date. The system automatically prepares a list of witnesses and their addresses so that subpoena lists can be compiled. In addition, the system compiles a workload report so that the court can monitor the progress of cases and pinpoint any unusual delays.

At this time, PROMIS applications are being used in several jurisdictions throughout the country. With improvement, the system should find widespread application in other congested urban courts throughout the country.

THE COURT ADMINISTRATOR

States are realizing that the responsibility for the management of the courts can no longer properly rest with the judiciary. If the court process is to be speeded up and judges are to devote their time to adjudicating cases, reviewing plea bargaining agreements, and generally improving the legal process, they must be relieved of the responsibilities of court management.

Although Connecticut is credited with the first state use of a court administrator in 1932, the model that has served as an impetus to develop the concept at the state level has been the Federal Judicial Center. This center, created in 1967, has been given the responsibility to develop and apply relevant management techniques to the administration of the federal courts. Among its important accomplishments are the application of the systems analysis and design to reorder the case calendaring systems in metropolitan district courts, a feasibility study of the use of circuit law clerks, an examination of the impact of specific types of litigation on the resources and workload of the courts, the use of computers for case scheduling, and the conduct of training sessions for judges and other court personnel.[40]

At the state level, the court administrator is often appointed by the chief justice or presiding judge of the state's highest appellate court. The responsibilities of this office are to establish across-the-board policies and guidelines for the management and operations of all state courts. This includes: (1) the development of a general budget for the operation of all state courts for submission to the state legislature; (2) the establishing of uniform personnel practices in recruitment, hiring, removal, compensation, and training of all nonjudicial employees of the courts; (3) the compilation of statistical summaries on court operations; (4) complete fiscal management responsibilities such as purchasing, disbursement, accounting, and auditing for the entire state court system; (5) training programs for judicial and nonjudicial personnel assigned to the courts; and (6) judicial assignment under the auspices of the presiding or chief justice in order to ensure that judges will be assigned to those jurisdictions where they are needed.[41]

Because of this recent interest in court administration, new career opportunities and programs are developing for individuals interested in court management as a vocation. One such program, the Institute for Court Management at the University of Denver, has been duplicated by other universities that have begun to develop special graduate degree programs in court management. Usually these programs apply public and business management to court operations and include courses in the legal process, budgeting and fiscal management, personnel, and computer applications. From all indications, this career field will grow substantially in the years ahead.

SUMMARY

Court reform is a major issue today. However, it is not a new issue as efforts at court reform have been of interest for many years. Much of the criticism centers around how court systems are structured and how they process cases.

One of the major areas of interest is the growing examination of ways to screen-out and divert cases from the judicial process that might be better handled in alternative ways. One such recommendation is the newly created idea of the Neighborhood Justice Center.

Another common recommendation is for the abolition of plea bargaining. Although many reform groups have been calling for the curtailment of this practice for years, it is unlikely—and probably undesirable—that it be abolished.

Another common reform recommendation is to abolish the use of grand juries. There are growing numbers of scholars and practitioners who feel that this ancient institution no longer serves a useful purpose. However, there may be some merit in still retaining the investigatory grand jury.

Other proposed judicial reforms involve the more timely prosecution of criminal cases, the issue of jury size and unanimity of verdicts, upgrading the office of prosecutor, improving defense services for the indigent defendant, needed improvements in the area of witness cooperation, systems analysis in the management of criminal cases, bail reform, and the growing use of court administrators.

REVIEW QUESTIONS

1. How would screening and diversion reduce the court's burdensome caseload?
2. If misdemeanor cases were taken out of hands of the lower courts, who would hear and settle these cases?
3. What advantages might be realized by abolishing plea bargaining? What disadvantages?
4. Has the grand jury outlived its usefulness? Why or why not?
5. Why is it important to shorten the time between the arrest of a defendant and the beginning of the trial?
6. Are a defendant's rights placed in jeopardy by reducing the number of jurors that hear a case?
7. Must a jury deliver a unanimous opinion to convict someone of a crime?
8. Should judges be elected or appointed to office? What safeguards are needed in either method of selection?
9. How can witness cooperation be improved?
10. What are the arguments for and against bail reform? Which do you agree with and why?

DISCUSSION QUESTIONS

1. Of the court-related issues and trends discussed in this chapter, which do you feel are the most important? Why?
2. Discuss some of the reasons why the courts as a component of the criminal justice system have been so slow to adopt change.
3. Explain the importance of and the problems related to witness cooperation. What might be done by the criminal courts in your community to improve such situations?
4. Discuss bail reform and its implications. Do you approve or disapprove of the way bail is handled today by most courts? What alternatives and implications do reform measures pose?

SUGGESTED ADDITIONAL READINGS

Aaronson, David et al. *The New Justice: Alternatives to Conventional Criminal Adjudication.* Washington, D.C.: U.S. Government Printing Office, November 1977.

Advisory Commission on Intergovernmental Relations. *Court Reform.* Washington, D.C.: U.S. Government Printing Office, 1971.

Carlson, Kenneth. *One Day/One Trial Jury System.* Washington, D.C.: National Institute of Law Enforcement and Criminal Justice, July 1977.

Friesen, Ernest, Edward C. Gallas, and Nesta M. Gallas. *Managing the Courts.* Indianapolis: Bobbs-Merril, 1971.

Hays, Steven W. *Court Reform.* Lexington, Mass.: Heath, 1978.

James, Howard. *Crisis in the Courts.* New York: McKay, 1971.

Jones, Harry, ed. *The Courts, the Public, and the Law Explosion.* Englewood Cliffs, N.J.: Prentice-Hall, 1965.

Mileski, Maureen. "Courtroom Encounters: An Observation Study of a Lower Criminal Court." *Law and Society Review* 5 (1971):473–538.

Skolnick, Jerome. "Guilty Plea Bargaining: Compromises by Prosecutors to Secure Guilty Pleas." *University of Pennsylvania Law Review* 112 (1964): 865–885.

Suffet, Fredric. "Bail Setting: A Study of Courtroom Interaction." *Crime and Delinquency* 12 (1966):318–331.

Vera Institute of Justice. *Programs in Criminal Justice Reform.* New York: Vera Institute of Justice, 1972.

Watson, Richard A., and Rondal G. Downing. *The Politics of the Bench and Bar: Judicial Selection Under the Missouri Nonpartisan Court Plan.* New York: Wiley, 1969.

NOTES

1. "A Growing Dissatisfaction with Our Courts," *New York Times,* August 17, 1977, p. 14.

2. Roscoe Pound, "The Causes of Popular Dissatisfaction with the Administration of Justice," *Journal of the American Judicature Society* 20 (February 1937):178–187.

3. See Arthur Vanderbilt, "Section of Judicial Administration Launches Program on Wide Front," *American Bar Association Journal* 24 (January 1938):5–6.

4. Larry C. Berkson, Steven W. Hays, and Susan J. Carbon, *Managing the State Courts* (St. Paul, Minn.: West, 1977), p. 11.

5. For example, see William F. Swindler, ed., *Addresses and Papers on the National Conference of the Judiciary, Williamsburg, Virginia,* March 11–14, 1971 (Washington, D.C.: U.S. Government Printing Office, 1971).

6. American Bar Association, *Report of the Pound Conference Follow-up Task Force* (Chicago: American Bar Association, August 1976), p. 1.

7. See Daniel McGillis and Joan Mullen, *Neighborhood Justice Centers: An Analysis of Potential Models* (Washington, D.C.: U.S. Government Printing Office, October 1977), p. 30.

8. Ibid.

9. See E. Johnson, V. Cantor, and E. Schwartz, *Outside the Courts: A Survey of Diversion Alternatives in Civil Cases* (Denver: National Center for the State Courts, 1977); and R. Shonholtz, *Proposal for Neighborhood Justice Centers,* San Francisco Community Board Program, unpublished manuscript, 1977.

10. It should be pointed out that some observers feel that plea bargaining is absolutely indispensable to true justice. See Arthur Rosett and Donald R. Cressey, *Justice by Consent* (Philadelphia: Lippincott, 1976).

11. Donald R. Cressey, "Doing Justice," *The Center Magazine* 10 (January-February 1977):21–28.

12. W. F. Willoughby, "Principles of Judicial Administration," in James M. Burns and Jack W. Peltason, eds., *Government by the People* (Englewood Cliffs, N.J.: Prentice-Hall, 1963), p. 202.

13. National Advisory Commission on Intergovernmental Relations, *State-Local Relations in the Criminal Justice System* (Washington, D.C.: U.S. Government Printing Office, 1971), p. 75.

14. For example, see the recommendations in Committee for Economic Development, *Reducing Crime and Assuring Justice* (New York: CED, June 1972), Chap. 3.

15. See Richard Harris, "Annals of Law, Taking the Fifth—Part III," *New Yorker,* April 19, 1976, pp. 42–97.

16. 399 U.S. 78, 100 (1970).

17. National Advisory Commission, *State-Local Relations in the Criminal Justice Systems,* p. 101.

18. See Alan E. Glefand, "A Statistical Case for the 12-Member Jury," *Trial* 13 (February 1977): 41–42.

19. See Hans Zeisel, "And Then There Were None: The Diminution of the Federal Jury," *Chicago Law Review* 38 (1971): 710–724.

20. *Hidbon v. United States* 204 F. 2d 834 (6th Cir. 1953).

21. For example, Montana requires two-thirds; Oklahoma and Texas require three-fourths; and Idaho requires five-sixths.

22. R. Holtzoff, "Modern Trends in Trial by Jury," *Washington and Lee Review* 27 (1959): 27–28.

23. American Bar Association Project on Standards for Criminal Justice, *Standards Relating to Trial by Jury* (New York: Institute of Judicial Administration, 1968), p. 28.

24. For example, see Glenn R. Winters, "The Merit Plan for Judicial Selection and Tenure: Its Historical Development," in Glenn Winters, ed., *Judicial Selection and Tenure,* pp. 29–44.

25. President's Commission on Law Enforcement and Administration of Justice, *Task Force Report: The Courts* (Washington, D.C.: U.S. Government Printing Office, 1967), p. 66.

26. Glenn R. Winters and Raymond Allard, "Judicial Selection and Tenure in the United States in American Assembly," *The Courts, the Public and the Law Explosion* (Englewood Cliffs, N.J.: Prentice-Hall, 1965), pp. 142–144.

27. See the Council of State Government, *State Court Systems—1967* (Lexington, Ky.: The Council of State Governments, 1976).

28. Richard S. Buckley, "The Commission on Judicial Qualifications: An Attempt to Deal with Judicial Misconduct," in Glenn Winters, ed., *Selected Readings: Judicial Discipline and Removal* (Chicago: American Judicature Society, 1973), pp. 60–74.

29. Jack E. Frankel, "Judicial Discipline and Removal," *Texas Law Review* 44 (1966): 1117–1131.

30. National Advisory Commission, *State-Local Relations in the Criminal Justice System,* p. 229.

31. Brian Forst et al., *What Happens After Arrest?* (Washington, D.C.: Institute of Law and Social Research, August 1977); and Vera Institute of Justice, *Processing Felony Cases Through New York City Courts* (New York: Vera Institute of Justice, 1976).

32. Forst, *What Happens After Arrest?,* p. 67.

33. Frank J. Cannavale and William D. Falcon, *Witness Cooperation* (Lexington, Mass.: Heath, 1976), especially Chap. 5.

34. Ibid., p. 28.

35. Paul B. Wice, *Freedom for Sale* (Lexington, Mass.: Heath, 1974), p. 8.

36. District of Columbia Court Reform Act of 1970, Public Law 91-358, sec. 23-1321.

37. Wice, *Freedom for Sale,* p. 99.

38. See Sidney Brounstein and William Hamilton, "Analysis of the Criminal Justice System with the Prosecutors Management Information System (PROMIS)," in Leonard Oberlander, ed. *Quantitative Tools for Criminal Justice Planning* (Washington, D.C.: U.S. Government Printing Office, 1975), pp. 91–111.

39. Ibid., p. 97.

40. Joseph D. Tydings, "The Courts and Congress," *Public Administration Review* 31 (March-April 1971): 116–117.

41. See National Advisory Commission, *State-Local Relations in the Criminal Justice System,* Chap. 9.

PART 5

Corrections

The workday for the correctional officer begins with a security check similar to the type used at airports.

During the day, routine office chores such as telephone calls and paperwork are part of the job.

Some time is usually spent talking with the prisoners and getting to know them better.

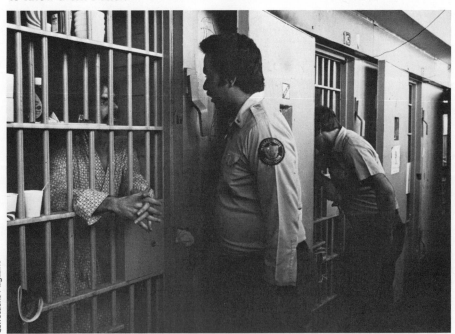

Vocational educational classes are a major part of the rehabilitative function of correctional institutions.

At this prison, meals are prepared in the prison kitchen and distributed to the inmates in their cells.

At day's end, the correctional officers are the lucky ones because they can freely walk out the gates.

12
CORRECTIONS: HISTORICAL PERSPECTIVE

Courtesy of New York Public Library

1. What purposes has corrections served in past history and modern societies?
2. How has the British penal system influenced American correctional reform?
3. What were the early American prison systems and where were they started?
4. Why was the reformatory movement significant in American correction?
5. What was the industrial prison model?
6. How is the federal prison system organized?

These are some of the questions this chapter will answer.

The evolution of corrections mirrors our changing attitudes toward the proper response of society to the deviant behavior of the offender and the growth and change of the criminal law. Imprisonment is a very recent societal response to deviancy. Although history tells us very little of how societies dealt with criminal behavior, particularly cultures outside Western Europe, we do know that as people began to form groups for collective safety certain customs and habits became established mores. In primitive times, individuals sought redress from those who wronged them by any means they saw fit. Later, when group customs and mores developed, individual retribution was somewhat supplanted by group retribution. Even later, as political states were formed and custom began to develop into law, the state became the instrument of punishment in place of the individual, the tribe, or kinfolk. Table 12-1 shows the general transformation of punishment, social relationships, and sanctions throughout Western history.

SOCIETY AND CORRECTIONS

The student must realize that correctional systems do not exist outside of the influence of society. Society determines how the correctional process is to be defined and develops the broad policy guidelines it expects corrections to adhere to. In the heterogeneous and pluralistic societies of the Western world—particularly that of the United States—guidelines on the proper disposition and handling of the offender have undergone profound change as those societies evolved and changed. An excellent example is the issue of capital punishment. In homogeneous societies, where there is a greater uniformity of attitudes based upon common culture and mores, it is possible to define more clearly and with greater social consensus both the seriousness of different acts of criminal behavior and the proper disposition of those who offend the defined legal code.

PURPOSES OF CORRECTIONS

Throughout history corrections has served such purposes as punishment, deterrence, isolation of the criminal, rehabilitation, and reintegration.

Punishment

Over the centuries, corrections and punishment have been synonymous. Even today, this attitude is held by a sizable segment of the American public, particularly in cases that involve serious crimes. Although basic attitudes toward punishment have not significantly changed, at least the means of exacting the punishment have. Today, through more "humane" techniques, society acts as the agent of punishment on behalf of the victim rather than permitting the private settling of feuds. In some views, punishment has been defended as permitting the offender the feeling of having atoned for his or her antisocial actions while reaffirming the appropriateness of noncriminal behavior among the law-abiding members of society.

TABLE 12-1
Historical Development of Law and Punishment

PERIOD	500,000–200,000 B.C.: Appearance of genus homo	200,000–25,000 B.C.: Appearance of early modern man	25,000–3500 B.C.: Development of rudimentary religion	3500–400 B.C.: Development of first criminal codes	400 B.C.–A.D. 500: Development of roman law	500–1750: Medieval and feudal justice	1750 to present
NATURE OF SOCIAL RELATIONSHIP	Pretribal	Incipient group and tribal	Intermediate group and tribal	Intermediate group and tribal	Advanced group and tribal; incipient state	Feudal and intermediate organized state	Advanced organized state
SANCTIONS	?	Incipient customs and mores	Intermediate customs and mores	Customs and mores; incipient laws	Customs and rudimentary laws	Customs and common law	Statutory laws
FORM OF PUNISHMENT	Personal retribution	Personal retribution; group and tribal retribution	Personal retribution; group and tribal retribution	Personal retribution; group and tribal retribution; state retribution	State retribution; group and tribal retribution; personal retribution	State and ecclesiastical retribution	State retribution, reformation, rehabilitation, and reintegration
	Injury, torture, death		Torture, injury, death, banishment, forfeiture			Torture, forfeiture, injury, death, excommunication, banishment	Fine, supervision, incarceration, death

Deterrence

Next in importance as a meaningful principle of corrections is deterrence—that is, the concept that punishing the criminal will reduce the incidence of criminal behavior in a society. This idea of deterrence arose in Italy and England during the latter part of the eighteenth century. Judges at that time had very broad discretion to render retributive punishments to offenders, and sentences and forms of punishment were often completely out of proportion to the seriousness of crimes.[1] The proponents of what is now referred to as the classical school of criminology were outraged by these excessive punishments. It was their belief that the ultimate objective of punishment was to deter criminal behavior, and therefore penalties should be no greater than needed to prevent the commission of crime. In this vein, Jeremy Bentham (1748–1832), an English judge, philosopher, and prolific writer, introduced the concept of the "hedonistic calculus," whereby punishment would be rendered in proportion to the seriousness of the crime. He believed that criminal behavior would be effectively deterred by punishing an offender to the point where the pain of punishment was slightly greater than the pleasure received from committing the offense. The same pleasure–pain principle would also deter potential offenders.

Isolation

Society has also subscribed to the idea that offenders should be isolated from lawful members of the community in order not to contaminate the law-abiding, and to protect the public from those who by their criminal acts would prey upon others. This principle of isolation was the major impetus behind the exile-and-transportation method of dealing with the offender. Even after the curtailment of exile and transportation, this purpose of corrections remained and was expressed in the fortresslike structure and security precautions characteristic of many early prisons. Today, this desire to isolate the offender is often expressed in a community's hostility toward the establishment in their area of correctional institutions and treatment programs for offenders.

Rehabilitation

Yet another philosophical goal of corrections that has received major emphasis in recent years because of the "new penology" is rehabilitation. This goal links criminal behavior with abnormality or some form of deficiency in the criminal. It assumes that human behavior is the product of antecedent causes and that in order to effectively deal with any deviant behavior, these various causes must be identified—be they physical, moral, mental, social, vocational, or academic. Once the offender's problems are diagnosed and classified for treatment, the offender can be corrected by the right psychological or physical therapy, counseling, education, or vocational training. Unfortunately, it is now being recognized that regardless of how laudable it may sound and how it appeals to our more humane instincts, the goal of rehabilitation suffers from a number of weaknesses that make it very elusive.

First, in many cases, it is impossible to identify these antecedent conditions and how they interact in causing criminal behavior. For example, how can it be said with any assurance that poverty and the lack of education are the causes for criminal behavior when there are many wealthy, well-educated people who also commit crimes. Furthermore, the vast majority of poor people with little formal education are not criminals. How, then, can treatment programs be measured in any meaningful way in determining their effectiveness in correcting a problem? Second, the rehabilitative philosophy assumes the characteristic of a medical model implying that the offender is somehow "sick" because he or she cannot adjust to society. This is fallacious reasoning. Offenders may well be aware of their actions and completely rational in deciding that their involvement in crime has a higher personal payoff than legitimate behavior. The rehabilitative model also assumes that the one being treated must accept or learn to accept the values of those conducting the treatment even though their backgrounds, perceptions, and attitudes may be completely different. This is a particularly questionable assumption in prisons today where increasingly larger percentages of inmates are expressing open hostility to the assumptions of the rehabilitative model. They perceive themselves as de facto political prisoners or as victims of society's capricious system of laws and justice which operates under a dual standard for the poor and well-to-do.[2] In these instances, rehabilitative personnel are seen as agents of the establishment who are trying to brainwash them into accepting their view of society.[3]

Many critics of this model also claim that the rehabilitative ideal, which is supposedly therapeutic in nature, takes on a punitive harshness in application. They point to the rehabilitative ideals that underlie the founding of the juvenile courts and sexual psychopath laws as examples of rehabilitative ideals gone awry.[4] The report on the experiences of the Attica prison rebellion pointed out that rehabilitation and reform are often no more than a facade. In the words of the official commission's report:

> Prison administrators throughout the country have continued pledging their dedication to the concept of rehabilitation while continuing to run prisons constructed in the style and operated in the manner of the 19th century walled fortresses. "Security" has continued to be the dominant theme: The fantasy of reform legitimatized, but the functionalism of custody has perpetuated them.[5]

Reintegration

The newest philosophical basis for corrections is reintegration of the offender into the free community. This model is a practical and realistic extension of the rehabilitative philosophy and tries to compensate for the weaknesses of that approach while adopting some more acceptable ideas. It sees the cause of crime and the functions of corrective efforts along two dimensions. Like the rehabilitative model, it views the offender as needing help—but at the same time it recognizes that criminal behavior is often a result of disjunction between the offender and society. It is this characteristic that separates it from the rehabilitative model. In the rehabilitation model, emphasis is focused on treating the offender as an isolated entity and looking for the cause of behavior as emanating from within the individual. The reintegrative model realizes that society and the individual are inseparable, and therefore the offender's environment is also emphasized. If offenders are to be helped, then they must be assisted in coping with the forces of the everyday environment to which they will return upon release from prison. This environment is a very different world from the highly controlled and artificial world of the penitentiary or other similar institution.

In reintegration, contact and interaction with positive elements of the free society are an important part of the overall treatment program. This appears to be the direction that corrections has been moving in the past few years and probably will continue to increasingly emphasize in the future.

EARLY BRITISH REFORMERS AND REFORMS

With few exceptions, the history of English penology tells us very little about an enlightened response in dealing with convicted offenders. However, some British penologists did have a lasting influence on the reform movements in the United States.

In the seventeenth and eighteenth centuries, England transported prisoners to the New World colonies where they worked as penal labor. After losing the American colonies in the Revolution, Britain discontinued transportation and began to quarter prisoners in ships on the Thames River and, later, at Gibraltar off the coast of Spain. These hulks were squalid and disease-ridden, and reformers demanded that something be done to help prisoners. In 1779, Parliament, fearing the spread of contagious diseases from the ships, called for the construction of two permanent long-term penitentiaries. However, these prisons were never built, for the discovery of the vast land area of Australia in 1770 brought back transportation as the preferred method of removing criminals from society.

At this time, changes in groups emerged in England that called for reform of the harsh criminal code and of the existing means of handling offenders. One of the most influential reformers was John Howard. After his appointment as the high sheriff of Bedfordshire in 1773, he witnessed firsthand the terrible abuses of prisoners. In 1777 he published his famous *State of Prisons*. He also traveled across the European continent inspecting jails and prisons and documenting the terrible conditions he found. Through these efforts he became the leading spokesman in the reform of English penal methods.

He proposed a number of "correct principles" for handling prisoners. Some of these principles were:

1. Women offenders should be segregated from males and young offenders from old and hardened criminals.
2. Jailers should be honest, active, and humane . . . and should have salaries proportioned to the trust and trouble.
3. No prisoner should be subject to any demand for fees. The jailer should have a salary in lieu of having to rely on fees.
4. There should be provisions for an infirmary, a chaplain, and a proper diet of wholesome food.
5. Separate cells for each prisoner should be provided as well as linen and bedding and stoves to warm the day-room in winter.[6]

A second notable penal reformer was Sir Robert Peel. In 1821, Peel was appointed as home secretary and he immediately set about reforming the criminal code and applying Howard's principles to local prisons. Through his efforts capital offenses were reduced from 200 to 14. He pushed through Parliament a law requiring prison facilities to meet certain minimum requirements for proper health and sanitation facilities.

Alexander Maconochie was the third reform figure. In his capacity as commander of the Norfolk Island Prison Colony off the coast of Australia, he learned that any prison system that debases prisoners could never expect to reform them. Thus, he developed an administrative system in the Colony with the following provisions:

1. Sentences should not be for a period of time, but for the performance of a specified and determined quantity of labor; in brief, time sentences should be abolished and task sentences substituted;

2. The quantity of labor a prisoner must perform should be expressed in a number of "marks" which he must earn by improvement of conduct, frugality of living, and habits of industry before he can be released;

3. While in prison, he should earn everything he receives; all sustenance and indulgences should be added to his debt of marks;

4. When qualified by discipline to do so, he should work in association with a small number of other prisoners, forming a group of six or seven, and the whole group should be answerable for the conduct and labor of each member of it;

5. In the final stage, a prisoner while still obligated to earn his daily tally of marks, should be financially compensated for his labor and be subject to a less rigorous discipline in order to prepare him for his release and return to society.[7]

He also abolished flogging and use of chains as disciplinary measures except in extreme cases. And he instituted the first form of inmate participation in running a penal colony.

Unfortunately, Maconochie's ideas were too revolutionary for his staff and the Board of Overseers to whom he reported. The guards particularly resented his curtailment of their use of corporal punishment on the prisoners. In 1844 he was relieved of command under the charge that discipline had disappeared without any improvements in the moral character of the prisoners. The real reason was that his system had increased operational expenses.[8]

The last notable reformer was Sir Walter Crofton and his so-called Irish System. Like England, Ireland's prisons were not reforming prisoners. In 1854, Crofton was appointed chairman of the board of directors of the Irish prisons. He became convinced that reform did not come through corporal punishment and prisoners had to be treated as humans and not as convicts.

When England passed legislation permitting the use of tickets of leave (see next section), Crofton developed a classification program that would be tied to the eventual rewarding of the prisoners with earned tickets of leave. When the prisoner entered prison he was placed under close discipline and supervision for four months. After this period of time, he was transferred to the second stage. In this stage he could work in his trades or in the maintenance of the prison. The inmates in this stage were given elementary schooling if they wanted it.

If the prisoner warranted consideration, he was transferred after eight months to another prison where he labored on military and penal fortifications in the area. The prisoner earned marks for his satisfactory behavior, and each step required the accumulation of a certain number of marks. In addition, small wages were paid according to the conduct class the inmate was in.

Crofton employed a moral instructor who counselled the prisoners in stressing the advantages of leading a law-abiding life, maintaining regular employment, and avoiding evil companions.[9] The moral instructor also worked with the inmates to obtain their tickets of leave and in seeking employment for those who were released. He even continued to visit the released offender and supervise his conduct after he returned to free society.[10]

Tickets of Leave

In 1857, Parliament passed an act that ended the transportation of offenders. Now a way had to be found to handle offenders who in the past were shipped off to a penal colony and forgotten. Since Parliament did not want to spend money to build prisons to house offenders for long periods of time, it passed legislation authorizing tickets of leave. Under this system, prisoners who had served a year of congregate labor could earn, by hard work and good conduct, a conditional release and thus be permitted to return to their homes before the completion of their sentence. Their freedom was contingent on two conditions: they had to abstain from crime and be legitimately employed.

EARLY AMERICAN INSTITUTIONS

The colonies of Massachusetts and Pennsylvania share the credit for the first colonial attempts to develop an alternative to the corporal and capital punishments that were dispensed under the king's justice as the only means to deal with offenders. The idea began to form that long-term incarceration might be an effective and more enlightened substitute. In 1632, Boston became the site of a small wooden building that could be considered the first prison in the colonies. It served for 6 years as the only such institution in the Massachusetts Bay Colony. In 1638, a second and even smaller institution was established in New Plymouth. By 1655, the general court of the Massachusetts Bay Colony felt that there was a growing need for institutions to house petty offenders, drunkards, and debtors. It was proposed that such institutions should be established in each county, and the counties were authorized to build such facilities. Although it took many years before such an institutional arrangement would become a reality, a few counties did establish such institutions at that time.

In 1784, Massachusetts established the first known centralized institution in North America for housing offenders who were sentenced to long-term incarceration. Unlike its predecessors in Boston and New Plymouth, it accepted prisoners from throughout the colony rather than just local offenders. The facility was located on Castle Island in Boston Harbor and received prisoners who were sentenced to long terms or for life at hard labor. However, the state felt that the Boston Harbor facility was not secure enough to house long-term desperate offenders, and it was abandoned in 1800 in favor of a maximum-security prison which had just been built at Charlestown.[11]

The Pennsylvania System

The early colonists in Pennsylvania were members of the Society of Friends or, as they came to be known, the Quakers. On religious and humanitarian grounds, they were opposed to what they perceived as a harsh and barbaric code of criminal justice that was embodied in the English law that had prevailed in the colony since its founding. In 1682, William Penn's first assembly passed "The Great Law," which incorporated the Quaker criminal code and was much more humane than the English criminal law. However, the king of England did not look favorably upon this attempt to repeal the English law. He saw it as another attempt by the colonists to question his country's right of sovereignty over the colonies. Threatening direct military intervention, he forced the Quakers to repeal their newly enacted criminal code.

Historical Background Up to the outbreak of the American Revolution, the Quakers continued to protest the harshness of the English code and constantly sought to reform it. By 1762, they had succeeded in having the list of capital offenses reduced to first-degree murder and had instituted fines and imprisonment in lieu of death or torture for many offenses. After the American Revolution, the Quakers turned their attention to prison reform and began to formulate ideas on better ways to handle and reform criminals. In May 1787, a group of Quakers formed the Philadelphia Society for Alleviating the Miseries of Public Prisons and set about immediately to redress the shocking conditions found in Philadelphia's Walnut Street Jail. This society, consisting of many of the leading citizens of the city, sought legislative approval for transforming the Walnut Street Jail into a prison. Approval for the conversion was granted, and this facility is recognized by penal historians as the first true prison in America.

The members of the Philadelphia Society were committed to the following ideas: First, prisons should be controlled by a group of citizens who would voluntarily serve as members of an unpaid board of inspectors. This was viewed as a way in which more efficient, less costly, and more humane treatment could be given the prisoners. Second, public labor by prisoners would be abolished and "more private or even solitary labor" would be substituted.[12] Third, reformation would occur through an individual offender's being subject to solitude, where he or she could "reflect" on his past offenses and atone for his actions.

Physical Setup of the Prison The Pennsylvania legislature passed a law authorizing all county courts, at their discretion, to send to the Walnut Street Jail convicts sentenced to hard labor for terms of more than one year.[13] For the more hardened offenders, there were 16 solitary cells in a specially constructed "penitentiary house" adjacent to the Walnut Street Jail. These cells each measured 6 feet wide, 8 feet long, and 9 feet high. In addition, six similar cells were constructed on the ground floor of one of the workshops where convicts could labor in total solitude.

Offenders convicted of more serious crimes were confined to the solitary cells. These prisoners were not permitted to have visitors or any contact with the outside world except for an occasional visit by a clergyman. They performed no labor, but were to spend their solitary existence contemplating their sins and atoning for their crime. Each of the cells had double doors and a small hatch that covered the single tiny window which was locked from the outside. In this way, the convict was exposed to almost total darkness even during the day. The prisoner was fed a daily diet of maize and molasses. For a primitive toilet, a large uncovered leaden pipe in the floor of each cell led to an outside sewer in the prison courtyard. The only heat was provided by a totally inadequate, small stove in the common corridor of the cell block.

Offenders who were considered more tractable or who had been sentenced for less serious crimes lived together in eight rooms where they worked together at carpentry, shoemaking, weaving, and nail making. The unskilled prisoners were given more menial tasks to perform. The few women sent to the Walnut Street Jail lived together in other quarters and were employed spinning cotton, carding wool, preparing flax and hemp, washing, and mending. Unlike the male prisoners, the women were permitted to engage in conversation in the shops and during meals. The men were forced to work in total silence, but some conversation was permitted prior to retiring at night. Each of the male prisoners was credited with roughly the prevailing wage for the particular work he performed. Out of this was deducted the cost of his maintenance, his trial, and his fine. If he still owed money for his maintenance when his sentence expired, he was held in confinement until the debt was fully paid. If, on the other hand, he was owed money for his labors, he was given it in full. During the period of confinement, special emphasis was placed upon the value of religious services and the development of Christian ideals.[14]

Under such leadership and organization, the Walnut Street Jail became, in the words of its founders, "the happy reformation of the penal system. The prison is no longer a scene of debauchery, idleness and profanity; an epitome of human wretchedness; a seminary of crimes destructive to society; but a school of reformation and a place of public labor."[15] However, this success was short-lived. Increasingly, larger numbers of more serious offenders were sent to the Walnut Street Jail for longer sentences, and it soon was so crowded that it became a mere warehouse of humanity. The original unpaid, supervisory board of citizen-inspectors was supplanted by Philadelphia politicians, who took over the operation and management of the institution. As a result, after 1800 the Philadelphia Society became a force of opposition and campaigned bitterly for the reenactment of their form of penal system.

The Principles of the System The principles governing the Pennsylvania system advocated by the Quakers were well expressed by Robert Vaux in his *Letter on the Penitentiary System of Pennsylvania* in 1827:

1. Prisoners should not be treated with revenge; but rather in a manner to convince them that the way of the transgressor is hard and by selective forms of suffering they can be made to amend their lives.

2. To prevent the experience of imprisonment becoming a corrupting experience, prisoners should be kept in solitary confinement.

3. Solitary confinement and the seclusion it affords will give the offender the opportunity for deep reflection and moral guidance so that he may repent for his transgressions.

4. Solitary confinement offers the same variety of discipline as any other mode affords. It is particularly punishing to man, who by his very nature is a social animal.

5. Solitary confinement is more economical since prisoners will: a) not have to be sentenced for such long periods of time for the required penitential experience, b) fewer keepers will be required, c) expenditures for clothing will be diminished.[16]

Based on the principles of the Pennsylvania system, in 1818 the Commonwealth of Pennsylvania began construction of the Western Penitentiary at Pittsburg. One hundred ninety solitary cells, measuring 7 by 9 feet each, were constructed in a semicircle around the central prison yard. However, this arrangement quickly proved unworkable. Solitary isolation was not provided and the cells were too small to permit solitary labor. As a result, by 1833 the board of managers recommended the demolition of the prison because it was unsuitable for the purposes for which it was originally designed.[17]

The Auburn Plan

Thomas Eddy, a Quaker philanthropist from New York, became impressed with the work of the Philadelphia Society and how it had transformed the Walnut Street Jail into a prison. He also fell under the spell of Cesare Beccaria, who in 1764 published his very influential *Essay on Crimes and Punishment.* The purpose of this monumental essay was to call attention to the need to make punishment less arbitrary and severe than it had been, and it argued quite eloquently for the need to eliminate the excessive reliance on capital punishment.[18] Under Eddy's guidance, Newgate Prison opened near New York City in 1797, and he became the first warden. Newgate consisted of 54 rooms and was constructed as a *congregate prison* — that is, convicts were lodged together in large rooms with eight prisoners to a room. The inmates were employed in a rather extensive system of prison industries, and as in the early days of the Walnut Street Jail, the prisoners were paid the prevailing wage for their work less the cost of their maintenance and trial. Immediate problems arose with the system of congregate lodging, and politicians began to meddle in the operation of the institution and eventually took over the management and control of the prison itself. In a short time, overcrowding aggravated moral contamination and created disorder. Mass pardons favored non-obedient prisoners over penitent and reformed criminals, and as a result, Eddy resigned in 1803.[19]

This "failure" of the Newgate Prison led to what has been called the Auburn plan of prison program and design. It was recognized that there was a certain value to permitting prisoners to work together at congregate labor as Newgate had done and which the Pennsylvania system with its emphasis on solitary confinement did not effectively provide for. However, the experiences at Newgate also indicated the disadvantages of congregate work and housing facilities in terms of the potential for disorder. Somehow, the best features of both Newgate and the Pennsylvania system would have to be incorporated.

In 1816, New York began the construction of a new prison at Auburn. In 1819, the prison opened with a master carpenter as the warden and a hatter as his assistant. Originally, the prison was to have been constructed after the model provided by the Pennsylvania system, with its emphasis on solitary confinement. However, it was felt that the cost of constructing separate solitary cells would be prohibitive, and so only a few such cells were built to meet the requirements of the law as to solitary confinement and to provide a solitary cellblock for disciplinary cases. As a result, most of the prisoners were housed in large, congregate night rooms.

Physical Setup of the Prison   In the first few years of operation, an experiment was conducted in which a classification or grading system was devised. The most incorrigible offenders were placed in solitary cells without labor in order to test the relative merits of the Pennsylvania system over the congregate system in terms of reformative effects. In the second category, less recalcitrant prisoners were also placed in solitary confinement with labor being provided as a form of recreation and reward. In the third category were the most tractable offenders and those who appeared to have the best chance of reforming. In this grade, the prisoners worked together as a group during the day and were secluded at night.[20] The experiment was abandoned in 1823 as a failure. Particularly obvious was the terrible impact of idleness and solitary confinement on the minds of inmates. A large number of those confined to solitary went insane and horribly mutilated themselves or committed suicide. In addition, solitary confinement without labor had deleterious effects on the inmates' physical health, and most of them were severely impaired for life. As a result, the governor in 1823 pardoned most of the inmates who had been confined to solitary cells.

The Principles of the System   However, in the open-congregate system, problems of control, discipline, contraband smuggling, and inmate corruption similar to the experience of Newgate began to develop. As a result, a compromise plan was adopted which became known as the Auburn system. Under this system, instead of mingling freely in the yard, workrooms, and congregate sleeping quarters, prisoners were permitted to associate with each other only during the day in order to permit maximum industrial production. This association, however, was conducted in strict silence, and the rule of total and perpetual silence was harshly enforced. Nor was the prisoner permitted to communicate with anyone on the outside except under the most unusual circumstances. At night, the prisoners were separated totally. This was felt to be necessary in order to eliminate the corruption of prisoners by their fellow inmates and to reduce the opportunity for inmates to develop plans that would be disruptive to the administration of the institution. Another characteristic of the Auburn system was the emphasis placed on hard manual labor as a reformative tool and as a means of economic self-sufficiency for the prison. Warden Elam Lynds believed that adult convicts were hopelessly incorrigible and that industrial efficiency was the overriding purpose of the prison.[21] Finally, a great deal of emphasis was placed on the use of corporal punishment to maintain absolute discipline and obedience. Warden Lynds is reported to have said:

> I consider the chastisement by the whip the most efficient and at the same time the most humane which exists; it never injures health and obliges the prisoners to lead a life essentially healthy. Solitary confinement, on the contrary, is often insufficient and always dangerous. I have seen many prisoners in my life whom it was impossible to subdue in this manner and who only left the solitary cell to go to the hospital. I consider it impossible to govern a large prison without a whip. Those who know human nature from books only may say the contrary.[22]

THE CONTROVERSY OVER THE PENNSYLVANIA AND AUBURN SYSTEMS

A hot controversy arose over the relative merits of the Pennsylvania and Auburn plans. The Philadelphia Society pushed for the adoption of the Pennsylvania system, while the Boston Society for the Improvement of Prison Discipline and the Reformation of Juvenile Offenders supported the Auburn plan.[23] Both societies were convinced of the merits of their plans, and both groups were zealous crusaders for reform as well as completely unscrupulous in their use of statistics to prove their arguments. The controversy even spilled over into other nations that were developing prisons modeled after America's system. In addition, famous international figures became involved in the controversy. Charles Dickens, after a visit to America, extensively criticized the Pennsylvania system in his *American Notes*. However, Beaumont and de Tocqueville praised it quite highly.[24] In fact, most European countries were in favor of the Pennsylvania system and adopted it in a modified form.

The single, most instrumental spokesman for the Auburn system was Reverend Louis Dwight, who, as secretary of the Boston Society, traveled extensively to proselytize the merits of the Auburn system. He became the best-known American prison expert during the first half of the nineteenth century and was particularly influential in convincing the states to adopt the Auburn system. His arguments focused attention on the economics of each system. Under the Auburn system, prison construction costs were lower because of the reduced emphasis on total solitary confinement. Also, the use of congregate inmate labor had definite revenue-producing advantages. As a result, the Auburn system was adopted by all the states except Pennsylvania and New Jersey. In a short time, even these two states abandoned the Pennsylvania solitary system because overcrowding forced the placing of two inmates in a cell. All this controversy and the attention it focused on prisons was responsible, however, for the creation in America, by 1835, of the first genuine penal system in the world. The development of this system is summarized in Table 12-2.

TABLE 12-2

Early American Prisons, 1790–1835

STATE	NAME AND LOCATION OF PRISON	YEARS OF RECEIVING FIRST PRISONER
Pennsylvania	Walnut Street Jail, Philadelphia	1790
New York	Newgate Prison, New York City	1797
New Jersey	State Penitentiary, Lamberton	1798
Kentucky	State Penitentiary, Frankfort	1800
Virginia	State Penitentiary, Richmond	1800
Massachusetts	State Prison, Charlestown	1805
Vermont	State Prison, Windsor	1809
Maryland	State Penitentiary, Baltimore	1812
New Hampshire	State Prison, Concord	1812
Ohio	State Penitentiary, Columbus	1816
Georgia	State Penitentiary, Milledgeville	1817
New York	Auburn Prison, Auburn	1819
Tennessee	State Prison, Nashville	1831
Illinois	State Penitentiary, Alton	1833
Louisiana	State Penitentiary, Baton Rouge	1835

Source: Wayne Morse, ed., *The Attorney General's Survey of Release Procedures* (Washington, D.C.: U.S. Government Printing Office, 1940).

THE REFORMATORY MOVEMENT

The next major development in the history of corrections was the so-called reformatory movement. This period, which lasted until 1910, began with the opening of New York's Elmira Reformatory in 1877. Originally designed for adult felons, the Elmira Reformatory took, instead, offenders between the ages of sixteen to thirty who were serving their first term in prison. The inmates were classified according to conduct grades and could earn higher classification through good conduct in the institution's education and shop programs.

The emphasis of the movement was on rehabilitation, and towards that end an extensive educational program was provided for the inmates. In addition, programs in plumbing, tailoring, telegraphy, and printing were established to provide the prisoners with trade skills. Those sentenced to Elmira were given indeterminate sentences which permitted their release at a time corresponding to their demonstrated rehabilitation. Parole services were also extended to those released under the indeterminate sentence.

The reformatory and rehabilitation programs established at Elmira soon spread to other states, but the movement died out after 1910 because it failed to meet the high expectations of its advocates. Among the major reasons for its failure were: (1) the "old grand" prison employees were too conditioned to a punitive ideology and did not support the new concepts; the educational staff was too overworked to develop the academic program; and the practice of sentencing of the hard-core offenders to the reformatory who turned the system into a junior prison.

Although it was not a success, the reformatory movement left an important legacy in some of its contributions—notably, the indeterminate sentence and parole; the idea of educational programs and vocational training; and efforts to develop rehabilitation programs. These reforms gained increasing emphasis in correctional systems in the years ahead.[25]

THE INDUSTRIAL PRISON MODEL AND BEYOND

The twentieth century ushered in the industrial prison. As inmate populations rose, many large Auburn-type institutions built by the states as new facilities were required to handle the increasing prison population. Such massive institutions as the large maximum security prisons represented by the California State Prison at San Quentin, Illinois State Penitentiary at Stateville, the State Prison of Southern Michigan, and the Ohio State Prison at Columbus were built very early in the twentieth century.

These fortress-like structures operated on the principle of mass congregate incarceration. The use of inmate labor to produce industrial goods for sale in the open market, thereby creating a self-sustaining prison system, was widely encouraged. However, restrictions on the use of prison-made industries backed by organized labor's efforts soon made its impact felt and the industrial production of prisons shifted to the production of items that could be used by the state such as the manufacture of license plates.

The years from 1935 to 1960 have been called the "period of transition" for American prisons.[26] These were the years when notable reformers and the Federal Bureau of Prisons began to introduce new reforms that focused more on the rehabilitation of the individual. For example, the Federal Bureau of Prisons introduced such procedures as diagnosis and classification of inmates and the use of psychiatrists and psychologists in their rehabilitative efforts. The state systems soon followed the reforms introduced in the federal prisons.[27]

Since the 1960s there has been something of a conflict in prison philosophy. On the one hand, society continues to subscribe to the rehabilitative goals of prison ideology. This can be witnessed in the increased efforts to develop community-based programs that have rehabilitative potential. On the other hand, the past several years have seen a growing support for viewing prisons simply as places to incarcerate offenders. What the future holds for our penal efforts seems to be unclear at this time. One thing is certain from the study of the history of corrections—these same issues have been with us for as long as we have had organized corrections in the United States.

In the chapters that follow, we examine some of the traditional methods of dealing with offenders, prison systems as they exist today, and some of the more innovative ways to deal with offenders.

THE FEDERAL PRISON SYSTEM

In addition to the corrections systems of the states, there is a federal prison system. Most people are familiar with at least two of its facilities—Alcatraz (now closed) and Lexington. In 1776, the Continental Congress provided that persons convicted of violating federal laws be confined in colonial and local institutions. These institutions would be paid a fee on the basis of the cost for housing each prisoner. During the late eighteenth and most of the nineteenth centuries, there were relatively few federal prisoners because the law enforcement authority of the federal government was limited to the offenses of counterfeiting, piracy, and other felonies committed on the high seas. As Congress began to extend the enforcement powers of the federal government, federal prisoners began to populate local and state prisons. The states did not object to boarding federal prisoners as long as they were permitted to sell their labor to private individuals. Many abuses resulted from this practice, and in 1887, Congress prohibited the employment of federal prisoners by contract or lease. As a result, the states began to charge the federal government the then exorbitant rate of 25 to 35 cents a day per prisoner for board. Some states refused to accept any federal prisoners because they could no longer sell their services for profit.

As the numbers of federal offenders increased, the problem of their custody became more acute. In 1891, federal commitments to penitentiaries numbered 1,600, and it was recognized that something had to be done.

The First Federal Prisons

At the urging of the Department of Justice in 1889, Congress authorized the purchase of three sites for federal penitentiaries. It was decided to construct one in the South, one in the North, and one in the far West; however, no money was appropriated for their construction. In 1895, Congress transferred the military prison at Fort Leavenworth, Kansas, to the Department of Justice for the confinement of federal civilian prisoners. In a few short years, this facility proved to be much too small, and the Department of Justice finally convinced Congress that it was completely inadequate. Congress then appropriated funds for a federal penitentiary to be built on an 800-acre site adjacent to Fort Leavenworth. Using prison labor, the 1,200-capacity institution was first occupied in 1906, but it was not completely finished until 1927. After the prisoners were transferred to the new institution, the old Fort Leavenworth facility was returned to the War Department for the use of military prisoners.

The number of federal prisoners grew rapidly. In June 1895, there were 2,500 prisoners; a year later, 3,000. In 1899, Congress appropriated funds for a federal penitentiary at Atlanta, Georgia. Construction began in 1900, and in 1902 a group of 350 prisoners first occupied the institution.

The penitentiary slated for the West was eventually located at McNeil Island, Washington, a 7-mile stretch of territory lying in Puget Sound. The federal government first established a small territorial jail at this site in 1875. It offered to donate this jail to the new state of Washington in 1889, but the offer was declined. Although the Department of Justice urged that this territorial jail and its site be abandoned on a number of occasions, it remained federal property. In 1903, Congress voted funds to convert the jail into a penitentiary.

The Development of Additional Federal Institutions

Women prisoners continued to board in institutions operated by the states. By the early 1920s, the number of female prisoners had increased to the point where a special facility for women became a necessity. The assistant attorney general of the United States at this time was a woman, and with the aid of a number of women's organizations, Congress was persuaded to construct an independent reformatory for women. In 1924, Congress appropriated the necessary funds, and in 1927 a 500-inmate institution was opened at Alderson, West Virginia.

In 1925, Congress authorized the purchase of an institution for male offenders between the ages of seventeen and thirty, and as a result, the federal reformatory at Chillicothe, Ohio, was opened in 1926 at the site of an old World War I training facility. In 1929, the federal government purchased a garage near the Hudson River docks in New York City and converted it into a jail facility for federal prisoners awaiting trial.

The Creation of the U.S. Bureau of Prisons

On May 14, 1930, President Hoover signed an act of Congress that created the Bureau of Prisons. The original authorization stated:

> That there is hereby established in the Department of Justice a Bureau of Prisons responsible for the safekeeping, care, protection, instruction, and discipline of all persons charged with or convicted of offenses against the United States. The control and management of said institution shall be vested in the Attorney General, the said institutions to be so planned and limited in size as to facilitate the development of an integrated Federal penal and correctional system which will assure the proper classification and segregation of Federal prisoners according to their character, the nature of their crime, their mental condition and such factors as should be taken into consideration in providing an individualized system of discipline, care, and treatment.[28]

To relieve overcrowding in federal prisons, the bureau was authorized to transfer prisoners to open camps, a move that set the stage for similar programs by the states. Congress approved additional construction of another penitentiary, a reformatory, a medical center, and several institutions for short-term offenders. It directed the U.S. Public Health Service to furnish medical personnel and services to all the institutions. It placed the small U.S. Probation Service within the bureau's organization and established an independent three-man Board of Parole to replace the old system of separate boards at each institution. New legislation authorized diversified industrial employment within the institutions of the federal system.

In the years since its inception, the Federal Bureau of Prisons has grown rapidly, adding new institutions and programs to the point where it now is the acknowledged leader in American correctional systems. By 1979 the Bureau of Prisons had evolved to the point that it operated an integrated system of 38 facilities for men and women covering five correctional categories:

Penitentiaries (maximum security)

Correctional institutions (medium security)

Camps (minimum security)

Detention centers

Community treatment centers and halfway houses[29]

SUMMARY

The historical quest for philosophical goals in corrections has been elusive. Over the years, we have subscribed to such goals as punishment, deterrence, isolation, rehabilitation, and reintegration. The newest concept of reintegration is based on the rehabilitative model which recognizes that society and the individual are inseparable considerations, and that the two must be incorporated into an integrated program.

Rather than adopting a European model to develop our prison systems, the United States was a world leader in prison reform. The two models—the Pennsylvania system and the Auburn plan—were widely studied by European nations for adoption. The Pennsylvania system founded by the Quakers emphasized solitary confinement, whereas the Auburn plan operated on the principle of the congregate system.

The British also made some important advances in penology in the late eighteenth and nineteenth centuries. Under the farsighted leadership of such noted reformers as John Howard and Alexander Maconochie, more humanitarian measures for handling prisoners were advanced.

Another noted reformer was Sir Walter Crofton who developed the Irish system of prison reform. In this system convicts were categorized by stages of reform, depending upon their behavior. Through their behavior they earned additional privileges leading up to their eventual conditional release.

These reformers strongly influenced American prison systems. The Reformatory Movement developed in Elmira, New York, and spread to other states. However, the reformatory did not meet the expectations of the reformers for several reasons. During the early twentieth century America then developed the Industrial Prison Model.

In the past several decades, we have seen many reforms instituted by our prisons. At this point in time there is growing disagreement over the purpose of prison. The years ahead should be interesting as to the path prison philosophy will take.

REVIEW QUESTIONS

1. Corrections has served many purposes throughout history. Briefly describe the reason behind each of the following:
   a. Punishment
   b. Deterrence
   c. Isolation
   d. Rehabilitation
   e. Reintegration

2. What correctional reforms did John Howard call for in his book *State of Prisons?* Why are these reforms noteworthy?

3. What were tickets of leave? Why were they important in the history of corrections?

4. List the principles that governed the Pennsylvania system.

5. What was the Auburn plan?

6. The reformatory movement, though short-lived, had a lasting effect on corrections in the United States. What reforms grew out of this movement?

7. What was the industrial prison? Why did it fail as a correctional method?

8. What different kinds of correctional facilities are run by the Federal Bureau of Prisons?

DISCUSSION QUESTIONS

1. In your opinion, what is the primary purpose of corrections? Why?

2. What were the differences between the Pennsylvania system and the Auburn plan? How did each system contribute to modern penology?

3. Should the federal government run its own prison facilities or should it contract with state institutions to house prisoners in state institutions?

SUGGESTED ADDITIONAL READINGS

Barnes, Harry Elmer. *The Story of Punishment.* Boston: Stratford, 1930.

Burns, Henry, Jr. *Corrections: Organization and Administration.* St. Paul, Minn.: West, 1975.

Conrad, John. *Crime and Its Correction.* Berkeley: University of California Press, 1965.

Heath, James. *Eighteenth-Century Penal Theory.* London: Oxford University Press, 1963.

Honderich, Ted. *Punishment: The Supposed Justifications.* Middlesex, England: Penguin, 1969.

Huff, C. R. *Contemporary Corrections—Social Control and Conflict.* Beverly Hills, Ca.: Sage, 1977.

Ives, George. *A History of Penal Methods.* London: Stanley Paul, 1914.

Jarvis, D. C. *Institutional Treatment of the Offender.* New York: McGraw-Hill, 1978.

Jones, Howard. "Punishment and Social Values." In Grygier Tadeusz, Howard Jones, and John C. Spencer, eds., *Criminology in Transition.* London: Tavistock, 1965, pp. 1–23.

Lewis, Orlando F. *The Development of American Prisons and Prison Customs, 1776–1845.* Albany, N.Y.: Prison Association of New York, 1922.

Menninger, Karl. *The Crime of Punishment.* New York: Viking, 1968.

Rusche, George, and O. Kirchheimer. *Punishment and Social Structure.* New York: Columbia University Press, 1939.

Sellin, Thorsten. "A Look at Prison History." *Federal Probation* 18 (September 1967).

Sutherland, Edwin. *Criminology.* Philadelphia: Lippincott, 1924.

Teeters, Negley K. *They Were in Prison.* Philadelphia: Winston, 1937 ——— and John D. Shearer. *The Prison at Philadelphia: Cherry Hill.* New York: Columbia University Press, 1957.

NOTES

1. Paul W. Tappan, *Crime, Justice and Correction* (New York: McGraw-Hill, 1960), p. 243.

2. James W. L. Park, "What Is a Political Prisoner?" *American Journal of Corrections* (November-December 1972): 22–23.

3. Notes from a discussion with inmates of Southern Michigan Prison, Jackson, Mich., during a series of meetings in 1975.

4. Francis A. Allen, "Criminal Justice, Legal Values and the Rehabilitative Ideal," *The Journal of Criminal Law, Criminology and Police Science* 50 (September-October 1959): 226–232.

5. New York State Special Commission on Attica, *Attica* (New York: Bantam, 1972), p. 2.

6. John Howard, *State of Prisons,* in George G. Killinger and Paul F. Cromwell, Jr., eds., *Penology* (St. Paul, Minn.: West, 1973), pp. 5–11.

7. Quoted by John V. Barry in "Captain Alexander Maconochie," *The Victorian Historical Magazine* 27, no. 2 (June 1957):5.

8. Ibid., p. 147.

9. Robert A. Terrell, *History of the Irish Prisons* (London: Trafalger, 1929), p. 49.

10. Ibid.

11. American Correctional Association, *Manual of Correctional Standards* (Washington, D.C.: American Correctional Association, 1966), p. 3.

12. Thorsten Sellin, "The Origin of the Pennsylvania System of Prison Discipline," *Prison Journal* 50 (Spring-Summer 1970): 14.

13. Ibid.

14. Orlando F. Lewis, *The Development of American Prisons and Prison Customs, 1776–1845* (Albany: Prison Association of New York, 1922) pp. 26–28.

15. Francis C. Gray, *Prison Discipline in America* (London: Murray, 1848), p. 22.

16. Sellin, "The Origin of the Pennsylvania System of Prison Discipline," pp. 15–17.

17. Lewis, *The Development of American Prisons,* pp. 43–57.

18. Cesare Beccaria, *An Essay on Crimes and Punishment* (London: Almon, 1967).

19. Elmer H. Johnson, *Crime, Correction and Society,* rev. ed. (Homewood, Ill.: Dorsey, 1968), p. 485.

20. Lewis, *The Development of American Prisons,* p. 80.

21. Ibid., pp. 86–95.

22. Gustave de Beaumont and Alexis de Tocqueville, *On the Penitentiary Ssystem in the United States and Its Application in France* (Carbondale: Southern Illinois University Press, 1964), p. 201.

23. See Steward H. Holbrook, *Dreamers of the American Dream* (New York: Doubleday, 1957), pp. 240–244.

24. Beaumont and de Tocqueville, *On the Penitentiary System,* pp. 57–58.

25. Harry E. Allen and Clifford Simonsen, *Corrections in America,* 2nd ed. (Encino, Ca: Glencoe, 1978), p. 53.

26. Ibid., p. 57.

27. Ibid., p. 58.

28. Federal Bureau of Prisons, *Thirty Years of Prison Progress* (Washington, D.C.: U.S. Government Printing Office).

29. U.S. Department of Justice, *Federal Prison System, 1978* (Washington, D.C.: U.S. Government Printing Office, 1979).

13
TEMPORARY DETENTION FACILITIES

1. What are the origins of the American jail systems?

2. What is the purpose of a jail?

3. How do the police, the courts, and corrections in general interact with the jail system?

4. In what ways is the jail system failing to meet its responsibilities?

5. What measures are being taken to improve conditions in the jail system?

These are some of the questions this chapter will answer.

Jails are local facilities usually used to house misdemeanants after they have been convicted and persons accused of crimes who have not yet appeared in court. Jails are also used for other purposes. A person found guilty of a felony is often remanded to the custody of the local jail while the court decides the appropriate sentence. Many jurisdictions authorize the courts to remand a material witness to a crime to jail if it appears that the individual's safety is jeopardized and he or she needs custodial protection or if there is reason to believe that the witness will flee the jurisdiction and therefore not be available to testify in court. In most cases, however, material witnesses are placed under protective custody in their own homes, with relatives in another city, or in a hotel rather than being confined in jail.

Jails are usually operated on a county basis under the authority of the county sheriff. In some larger cities, jails are operated at the municipal level and are under the administration of the local police. Although many smaller police departments have a few cells to temporarily hold arrested persons, strictly speaking, these are not jails, but lockups. Those arrested for certain minor offenses, such as public drunkenness or driving under the influence, are detained in lockups until the next day or so, when they appear before the city magistrate to stand trial.

The latest and most comprehensive survey of jails throughout the nation was conducted in 1972. At that time, the *National Jail Census* reported that there were 3,921 locally administered jails with the authority to detain prisoners for 48 hours or longer.[1] What is interesting from the viewpoint of the problems associated with improving these jails is that nearly three-fourths of these facilities had fewer than 21 inmates at the time of the national survey. This points out the broad decentralization and proliferation of these institutions at the local level through the United States. The sheer numbers of these jails and the fact that for the most part they are under the control of local authorities does not offer much promise for major reforms in our existing so-called jail system.

At the time of the survey, these jails held 141,588 inmates, including nearly 8,000 juveniles. More than half (53 percent) of the adults were awaiting trial, and nearly two-thirds (64.8 percent) of the juveniles were awaiting a formal hearing.[2] Thus, it would seem that the jails are used more for pretrial detention than they are for post-trial incarceration. The implication of this is that under our system of law, these prisoners are still technically innocent of the charges brought against them.

HISTORY OF JAILS: A SHAMEFUL LEGACY

The jail is the oldest institution for incarcerating offenders. American jails trace their ancestry to England, where jails developed in the tenth century.[3] At that time, the shire or county was a very important locus of government authority. County governments were independent and powerful, and jails became a part of that powerful machinery. As towns and cities grew and formed their own governments, they created separate penal institutions. Thus, county and municipal jails developed side by side.

By the late sixteenth and seventeenth centuries there existed 200 "common jails" in England.[4] They were provided, owned, and administered by several different authorities. Responsibility for maintaining the county jail rested with the sheriff. Towns had their own jails under the jurisdiction of their own officials. Indeed, nearly every municipality during this time, however small, had its own jail.[5] Private jails were also established by various ecclesiastical orders, members of the church hierarchy, and high-ranking noblemen, who operated them on a profit basis.[6] In theory, each of these jails was the property of the crown, and those who operated them were responsible to the monarch as keepers of common jails.

As mentioned in the previous chapter, these early jails had little resemblance to today's jails. The sheriff was authorized to repair or rebuild with county funds any county jail that was "presented" by the grand jury to be insufficient or inconvenient.[7] (Even today, grand juries in a number of states are responsible for investigating conditions in county jails.) By law, the grand jury could levy a sum known as the "county bread" that was used to buy food for poor prisoners. Although the sheriff was considered the caretaker of the jail, he seldom exercised direct custodial control over its operations. His position was one of importance and influence, and he contracted a keeper to perform the actual duties of caring for the jail and its occupants.[8]

Usually the keeper did not receive a salary. He was paid by a system of fees that made jail keeping a very lucrative occupation. In fact, the job of keeper was usually sold by the sheriff to the highest bidder. Under the supervision of the keeper were turnkeys, who were paid from the fees collected by the keeper. He had no obligation to the prisoners themselves, other than to see that they did not escape.[9]

Inmates had to support themselves. To do so, they were allowed to beg. Sometimes relatives and friends helped them when they could or charitable persons donated food and clothing. Some limited work was also available. In some jails, inmates were permitted to work at producing nets, laces, and purses, which were sold outside the jail. Frequently the inmates could be seen in jail tied to a chain that was fixed to the front wall of the jail from which they pleaded with passersby to purchase their wares.[10]

Not until the beginning of the nineteenth century did England's jails begin to assume functions more characteristic of modern jail administration. Up to this time the jails were not special institutions designed to house prisoners for short-term periods of incarceration. Instead, they were temporary holding or security facilities to which convicted offenders were sent for very brief periods of incarceration prior to being placed in the stocks, executed, subjected to branding or some form of mutilation for their misdeeds, or, in the seventeenth and eighteenth centuries, transported to penal colonies. Only in the case of debtors, who were kept imprisoned until they paid their creditors, were these early jails used for any form of long-term imprisonment. By the nineteenth century, some parts of the criminal code had been modified and jails began to house those who had been convicted of minor offenses. About this time jail imprisonment for debt began to disappear and the jails began to receive both accused and convicted criminals on a regular basis.[11]

Jail Development in the United States

The English jail tradition came with the colonists to the New World. The oldest jail system in America was established in Virginia at the time of the founding of the Jamestown colony. In 1626, Virginia prescribed that the marshal's fee for admission and discharge of prisoners was 2 pounds of tobacco.[12] Five years later, the Virginia general assembly raised and restructured the fee schedule so that the marshal would receive 10 pounds of tobacco for arresting an individual, 10 pounds for admitting him to jail, and another 10 pounds for his discharge.[13]

In 1634, the Virginia colony was divided into eight shires, each run by a sheriff. In 1642, the general assembly of that colony passed the first laws dealing with the erection and maintenance of jails. It stipulated that jails were to be built in each county by the county commissioners and were to house those arrested and waiting trial. The sheriff was to maintain custody of the jail and its prisoners. Payment for food and lodging was to be provided by the prisoners themselves. The cost was to be determined by mutual agreement between the sheriff and the inmates.[14]

The counties were slow to comply with these laws and continued to use the back rooms of taverns as jails. It was not until the general assembly enacted a penalty against the counties for noncompliance in the form of a fine of 5,000 pounds of tobacco and liability for the escape of any prisoners that the counties started to build the required jails.

During this time, Pennsylvania was also developing a jail system, a process that passed through three stages. The typical English jail system was established under the laws of the Duke of York in 1676.[15] By 1682 this system was replaced by the adoption of the Quaker workhouse or house of correction, which became the basis of the colony's jail system for about 30 years.[16] When the criminal code was modified in 1718, corporal punishment was substituted for imprisonment and in most cases, this led to less emphasis on the workhouse as a place of confinement. Instead, whippings, branding, and other forms of physical punishment were meted out. In other cases, fines were established as substitutes for imprisonment.

The first law that created a county jail in Pennsylvania was passed on March 20, 1725.[17] This legislation later became a model for other states in establishing a county jail system. The law provided for the appointment of a board of five special county commissioners or trustees, who were authorized to purchase the land for the jail site and to estimate its cost. Each county was to follow this procedure and was required to establish a county jail. The administrative control of each county jail was to rest with the sheriff. The five commissioners were responsible for maintaining the facility and were authorized to assess taxes for its support. The sheriff had the authority to appoint an undersheriff or keeper to run the day-to-day operations of the facility.

The customary extortion and other forms of abuse associated with the English jail system were present in the early jails of Pennsylvania.[18] The sheriff was able to demand exorbitant fees from those confined. Sometimes for the proper price prisoners were able to live in taverns or even the sheriff's own house. Wealthy prisoners could altogether escape from the degradation of jail confinement by simply bribing the sheriff to permit them to live in private homes with little or no control or surveillance.[19] Normally, no attempt was made to feed or cloth the inmates, who were compelled to provide for their own needs. Whereas wealthy inmates might live quite comfortably, it was not unknown for prisoners who had no resources to die of starvation.[20]

Beginning about 1730, attempts were made to eliminate some of these abuses. The sheriff was prohibited from selling intoxicating spirits to the prisoners. However, all this accomplished was to provide a middle-man's profit to the sheriff, who now would merely send out for liquor or food at the request of the prisoner and charge him a "handling fee" for this service. Laws were also passed that prohibited a sheriff from holding office for more than 3 successive years, after which time he would not be able to hold the office again until 3 years had passed. This resulted in attempts to gouge the prisoners even more during the time that the sheriff was in office. In many instances, this law was circumvented by having the sheriff and the undersheriff "trade off" official positions. When the incumbent sheriff's 3 years were up, his undersheriff would be appointed as sheriff and he in turn would be appointed as the undersheriff. In this manner, they traded the office back and forth.[21]

This then was the heritage that was passed on from Virginia and Pennsylvania to other colonies and later states. The idea of the jail was adopted by Massachusetts in 1699, New Jersey in 1754, South Carolina in 1770, and Georgia in 1791.[22]

THE JAIL IN THE CRIMINAL JUSTICE SYSTEM

The jail is an integral part of the criminal justice system. Although it might be considered a subsystem of the corrections component, it plays a far more important role than this classification would suggest. Since it is a subsystem of a larger system, it must coordinate its efforts with other parts of the criminal justice process. Like the human body, the criminal justice system does not function well if any of its parts are operating below acceptable standards. As we shall see, the jail has traditionally operated below standard.

The jail serves as the portal to the criminal justice system. It is important as an indicator of the interest and concern with justice, punishment, and rehabilitation expressed by society and the local community. The person who is awaiting trial or serving a sentence experiences first-hand and with varying degrees of intensity what it is like to be exposed to the values of society as they relate to crime and punishment.

A stay in jail is the most widely experienced form of incarceration. Only the police and the courts represent the justice system more directly as determined by numbers of citizen contacts. There are no exact figures on the number of people arrested and detained in jails throughout the nation on an annual basis. The earlier figure cited of 141,588 by the *1972 National Jail Census* reflected the confinement *at the time the survey was undertaken.* Thus, these data reflect the jail population at only one time. Since jail populations turn over frequently within a year, this is a significant underestimate of the total number of persons handled by our jails in any one given year.

The best estimate of the numbers of inmates handled by our nation's jails on an annual basis was compiled by the President's Crime Commission. The Commission found that in 1965, of the 2 million persons committed to institutions, two-thirds were confined in jails and workhouses. However, even these figures drastically understate the numbers handled by our jails. In the first place, they represent only those sentenced to jails and workhouses *and not those confined in jail awaiting trial.* On the basis of the *1972 National Jail Census* data, this represents less than one-half of the inmates. Second, it can be assumed that these numbers are even higher today because of the increase in our national population and the increasing numbers of arrests made by the police. It is apparent, then, that the influence of the jail in terms of the number of persons who experience some form of confinement is considerable.

The Jail and the Police

The jail is important not only in terms of the number of persons who come in contact with it and the influence it has on them, it also performs a service function for the other agencies within the system. The relationship of the jail to the police is one of accommodation and necessary cooperation. The jail has the responsibility to accept any prisoner who is legally arrested and can be legally received and detained by the jail. Not all persons arrested by the police can be legally received and detained. For example, in some jurisdictions juvenile arrestees have to be detained in special juvenile facilities.[23] Initially, the jail plays a passive role in the justice system, and to some extent the jail population reflects this. If the community and therefore the police are particularly concerned with enforcing laws against drunks or vagrants, the jail will probably contain a large number of such people. If it is the policy of police department personnel to "rough up" certain individuals they arrest, those arrested are likely to become more recalcitrant and provide further problems for the jail personnel. The important point is that community and police policy affects the jail. By the same token, the way the jail operates will also affect the community and the criminal justice system.

Since the jail holds the accused until the formal machinery of criminal justice begins to move, jail personnel and the police have to work together. For example, if accomplices must be kept separated, the police will request jail personnel to do this. When a long-term investigation is required, the police and the jail may need to coordinate their efforts in scheduling investigative interviews or in making the accused available to the police, the prosecuting attorney, and defense counsel. This need for coordination and information exchange is also necessary and important when the jail is holding a material witness for the police or the prosecutor.

The Jail and the Courts

The jail and the courts must also work in close cooperation. The court both influences the jail's activity and in turn is dependent on the jail's successful handling of the court-imposed workload. Unlike the passive role it plays in its relationship with the police, the jail takes a much more active role in scheduling and coordination in its relationship with the court—so much so in fact, that it almost seems that the jail in many instances is a department of the courts.

The extent of this interdependence between the court and the jail can be demonstrated by examining the sentencing decision rendered by the court. The courts can sentence an individual to jail, modify his sentence before completion, place an offender on probation, and in some instances sentence him to a work release program. These decisions affect the jail population, its composition, and the extent to which the jail must be involved in alternative programs. For example, the court in some jurisdictions may authorize work release and order the jail to provide such a program. The jail must then make the necessary arrangements for handling such a program. If misdemeanants are sentenced to the jail rather than to workhouses or work farms, this increases the number of prisoners that the jail must deal with. Similarly, setting aside arrests for public drunkenness clearly has an impact on jail populations. In other cases, the courts may decide that the jail should serve only as a temporary detention facility before trial and that all sentenced offenders should be sent to a county correctional institution, which would reduce the jail population.

The jail functions as the distributor in the criminal justice system. It serves as the transfer point for prisoners who have been sentenced to the workhouse, county farm, or a penal institution. In some cases, it also transfers individuals to the federal corrections system.

Until recently, the jail served a passive role in bail proceedings, which are court-supervised even though in some cases the matter is routine. The accused either made bail and was released or was unable to make it and was held for trial. Some new bail projects have now expanded the roles of the jail. In a few jurisdictions today, jail authorities are now involved in selecting persons for release on their own recognizance. In some cases this may be done by jail personnel themselves, although in most cases it is handled by the probation department or by joint agreement and consultation among the courts, probation personnel, and jail officials.

Because of the need for close coordination between the court and jail, jail facilities have been built in close proximity to the court. This has been done to make it easier to transport offenders to the court and limit the problems of security when prisoners are transferred. In recent years, jail consultants and progressive jail administrators have increasingly recommended that jails be built on the outskirts of cities, particularly in larger cities that must house a sizable number of prisoners.[24] Admittedly, this has created some problems because the courts and police headquarters are situated downtown. However, the advantages of situating the jail on the outskirts of the city would seem to far outweigh the disadvantages. The use of downtown jails limits jail programming. With no facilities available for recreational and similar programs, prisoners are confined to the internal recesses of the jail and their activities are quite limited. In these situations, pent-up frustrations and crowding can lead to serious jail disruptions and rioting, as witnessed in jail facilities in New York, Washington, D.C., and other cities. It would seem that the inconvenience of locating such facilities away from the central city would be more than compensated for by the increased opportunities this presents for the development of a wider range of programs for prisoners.

The Jail and Corrections

Many view the jail as having primarily a law enforcement function because of the nature of many of its operations and because the chief administrator of the jail is usually a law enforcement officer. However, the jail does not have specific law enforcement functions. It does not serve as a base of operations for criminal detention or apprehension although it may be in a department where these activities go on. Jail personnel may be sheriff's deputies or police officers; however, their specific duties while working in the jail are not in the area of law enforcement.

Jails are part of the overall corrections program. They are, in fact, penal institutions. Like other correctional institutions, they hold many prisoners who are serving sentences, and they have a responsibility for their care. In the past, the emphasis of most jails was on detention. In recent years this traditional role has been redefined and now the courts and the community in some locales are demanding that their jails develop correctional and rehabilitative programs.

The jail, in many cases, has a particular advantage over other correctional institutions in that it is located in the community and can coordinate community resources to develop effective programs. Additionally, it deals mainly with misdemeanants, who may be more tractable and amenable to various programs than are felons. It is particularly important that rehabilitative efforts are developed for the misdemeanant before the offender reaches the point where his or her actions or attitudes require long-term incarceration. The argument for the role of the jail in the overall correctional process has been well stated by the President's Commission on Law Enforcement and Administration of Justice:

> On the correctional continuum, jails are the beginning of the penal or institutional segment. They are, in fact, the reception units for a greater variety and number of offenders than will be found in any other segment of the correctional process, and it is at this point that the greatest opportunity is offered to make sound decisions on the offender's next step in the correctional process. Indeed, the availability of qualified services at this point could result in promptly removing many from the correctional process who have been swept in unnoticed and undetected and who are more in need of protective, medical and dental care from welfare and health agencies than they are in need of custodial care in penal and correctional institutions. In a broad sense, the jails and local institutions are reception centers for the major institutions.[25]

In addition to its own correctional function, the jail must develop close and effective coordination with the state correctional program so that both can learn from the experiences of the other. Since the jail typically has too few personnel and resources to develop a training program, the state department of corrections can be an important assistance in providing training opportunities. The state can also share its acquired knowledge with jail personnel, particularly in terms of program implementation and rehabilitative techniques that have proved successful and can be adopted by local jails. The jail system is also important as a focus of research efforts and data gathering that can aid state correctional efforts in program evaluation, particularly as states move into the area of developing community-based treatment alternatives.

THE JAIL TODAY: MAJOR PROBLEMS AND AREAS OF NEGLECT

The harsh reality is that most jails remain a serious problem in the system of American justice. For years, criminologists, study commissions, interested citizen groups, and some governmental officials have deplored the conditions of our nation's jails. The ill and the healthy, the old and the young, petty offender and the hardened criminals, the mentally defective, the psychotic and sociopathic, the vagrant and the alcoholic, the habitual offender who is serving a life sentence in short installments—all continue to populate our jails in an indiscriminate mass of human neglect. Since there are some 4,000 local jails in the United States, they are shaped by characteristics as varied as the social fabric of the communities in which they are found.

Certain negative characteristics associated with our jails almost defy improvement. Often, one or more of these characteristics affect the other characteristics, so that any overall solution is that much more difficult to attain. These negative characteristics are:

1. The heterogeneity of the offenders in our jails
2. The problems of local control and politics
3. Demeaning physical facilities
4. Inadequate personnel
5. Inept administration
6. Failure to adopt alternative programs and dispositions

Heterogeneity of Offenders

The heterogeneous nature of our jail population presents problems in terms of program development and rehabilitative strategies. At any time, our jails are likely to be populated by women, juveniles, the first offender, the habitual criminal, the dangerous and assaultive individual, and the down and out "wino." When jails must deal with such a broad range of offenders, their individual needs, and security considerations, it is not really possible to develop specific programs to deal with each situation. Lack of available resources further complicates the problem.

Jail inmates do, however, share certain socioeconomic characteristics. Inmates are typically poor, have low levels of educational attainment, and have histories of chronic unemployment. A relatively high percentage of them are members of minority races. Unfortunately, these characteristics are most likely the reasons they languish in jail to begin with. This is particularly true among pretrial detainees. Those who are employed or have the means to post bond escape incarceration.

Although inmates might be similar in financial status, race, and other characteristics, they are completely dissimilar in needs. The petty thief, the alcoholic, the juvenile or female prisoner, the narcotics user, the child beater, the assaultive armed robber, and the wife deserter are, to one degree or the other, all in need of different programs of treatment and require different security concerns.

Local Control and Politics

The fact that jails are local institutions is another of the major problems. Many communities are without the leadership, insight, or resources to bring about change. Having to rely primarily on property taxes for a financial base, local communities facing higher operating costs and demands for educational support, roads and streets, capital improvement, and a host of other considerations cannot give priority to jail services without foregoing needs in other areas. Since jail improvement has a low priority for most citizens, money to finance a jail or to provide the most rudimentary correctional program is usually absent.

Local politics have also played an important role. Of all the jails in the United States, 73.3 percent are administered by the sheriff.[26] In many states, the sheriff is an elected officer whose responsibilities for maintaining the local jail are clearly spelled out in the state constitution. Thus, the sheriff is free to operate with almost no control by the state. Even in fiscal appropriations, this officer is relatively unsupervised. Monies are usually appropriated by the county legislative authority in accordance with constitutional or statutory declarations that the county government must provide monies for the maintenance of the jail. In many cases where the states have tried to extend some supervisory control over the jail, individual sheriffs and their state political associations have been able to rebuff these attempts.

Another problem that makes it more difficult to wrestle control of jails away from the county sheriff is the encroachment of municipal and separate county police forces into the enforcement responsibilities of the sheriff's departments. As these functions are reduced, the county jails become a larger share of each sheriff's vested interest and, thus, a function that sheriffs are less willing to relinquish.

Strangely enough, studies have shown that the population of a jail is not directly related to the size of the population in the jurisdiction it serves. The Nebraska Commission on Law Enforcement and Criminal Justice in 1970 did a study of its jails and the counties they serve. It found that the jail populations, in this state at least, reflect the particular sentencing policies of the local courts and the policies of law enforcement practices more than the absolute population of the county itself.[27] Much of this is, of course, due to the existence or nonexistence of alternative dispositions and institutions, such as detoxification centers and state misdemeanant institutions. Since it is usually the larger urban centers which have alternative programs and institutions, relative numbers of prisoners in urban jails are reduced.

Although many inmates are in jail only temporarily until they come to trial, the "temporariness" of this period of incarceration can be quite lengthy. An Illinois survey found that pretrial detention, in some cases, can run into years, depending upon the legal maneuvers in the courts brought about by the prosecution and defense postponing or continuing cases, unavailability of witnesses, etc.[28] Although such lengthy delays are very unusual, since court decisions and statutory pronouncements are designed to avoid such occurrences, this problem does exist to various degrees in many jurisdictions.

In fact, for different reasons the problem has grown worse in recent years. With the state prisons filled to capacity, the jails are forced to take serious offenders who have been found guilty by the courts and are being held in jails because the prison system cannot admit them. This is bad for a number of reasons. First, nearly 75 percent of the jails in the national survey did not separate first offenders from repeater offenders and over two-thirds of the jails did not separate pretrial detainees from sentenced offenders.[29] This is a potentially serious situation that leads to many documented cases of exploitation and contamination of inmates by other inmates. The crowding of prisoners into these institutions in forced idleness as they await delayed trials or transportation to other institutions also creates potentially explosive situations that are dangerous to both inmates as well as the jail staff.

Demeaning Physical Facilities

A recent study of the old District of Columbia jail points out the terrible state of affairs in many of America's jails today. One wonders if even the best programs available would make any difference in such squalor. The report provides an insight into the jail conditions that until recently existed in the capital of the nation that prides itself on its humanitarian concerns and position of leadership in the Western world. In the words of the report:

> The District of Columbia jail is a filthy example of man's inhumanity to man. It is a case study in cruel and unusual punishment, in the denial of due process, in the failure of justice.
>
> The jail is a century old and crumbling. It is overcrowded. It offers inferior medical attention to its inmates, when it offers any at all. It chains sick men to beds. It allows—forces—men to live in crowded cells with rodents and roaches, vomit and excreta. It is the scene of arbitrary and capricious punishment and discipline. While there is little evidence of racial discrimination (the jail "serves" the male population of the District of Columbia and, is therefore, virtually an all-Black institution), there are some categories of prisoners who receive better treatment than others.
>
> The eating and living conditions would not be tolerated anywhere else. The staff seems, at best, indifferent to the horror over which it presides. This, they say, is the job society wants them to do. The facilities and amounts of time available for recreation and exercise are limited, sometimes by a guard's whim. Except for a few privileged prisoners on various details, there are no means by which an inmate may combat idleness—certainly nothing that could be called education, counseling or self-help.[30]

The President's Commission on Law Enforcement and Administration of Justice reports that 35 percent of the jail cells that are in use across the country are at least 50 years old and that some of them were built in the nineteenth century.[31] The commission reported that one New England state had four jails that had a total of 899 cells without any sanitary facilities. Since the construction of many of these institutions predates inside plumbing and electricity, the sanitary and safety conditions are often deplorable. Inmates are kept in large unsegregated bullpens rather than in individual cells. One New England state was reported to have three jails that were over 160 years old. A 1978 survey taken of jails in Arkansas disclosed that nearly two-thirds of the jails in the state did not meet even minimum sanitary and security standards.[32]

The National Advisory Commission on Criminal Justice Standards and Goals points out that the general upkeep of the jail facility is often related to its use. Jails that hold few prisoners tend to be neglected, and those that are constantly overcrowded are forced to push their equipment and fixtures beyond the breaking point.[33] Under either set of circumstances, the jail's physical plant is soon badly in need of repairs.

The *1972 National Jail Census* also found that 9 percent of the jails included in its study were significantly overcrowded. Ironically, the larger the jail and its capacity to house prisoners, the more likely it was to be overcrowded.[34] At the same time, studies in some areas report that a large percentage of available jail space is unoccupied. For example, surveys of Idaho's jail population at different times showed that the jails in that state were operating at only 55 to 65 percent of their design capacity.[35] This indicates first that little thought or consideration goes into the planning or renovation of existing jail facilities, and second, that the problem will not be solved by building new and more appropriately sized jail facilities—the entire system of detention and delivery must be examined more closely if past mistakes are to be avoided.

One of the major problems associated with the demeaning nature of jails, even in new facilities, is the traditional way jails are constructed. In order to provide maximum security at minimum cost, certain standard construction characteristics have been developed. Glaser provides a picture of the typical jail:

> In nearly all jails, the available space is divided into inflexible cells or cage-like day rooms. Rows of cells compose self-contained cell-blocks that face a large cage or "bullpen." The arrangement is designed so that a relatively small number of staff can insure the secure confinement of a comparatively large number of inmates. Items are passed into the bullpens through slotted doors, largely preventing contact between staff and inmates.
>
> Many jail cells have neither toilets nor wash basins. The majority of inmates have access to shower facilities less than once a day. These inadequacies, combined with the short supply or complete lack of such items as soap, towels, toothbrushes, safety razors, clean bedding and toilet paper, create a clear health problem, not to mention the depressing psychological effects on inmates.[36]

Given the fact that even basic sanitary facilities are often missing, it should come as no surprise that other facilities such as a dining room, recreation area, chapel, classrooms, or a place for inmates to enjoy some solitude other than the dreariness of their cells are also absent in many jails.

Inadequate Personnel

The neglect of local jails is as obvious in the caliber of staff personnel as it is in dismal physical facilities. Jail employees almost invariably are untrained, too few in number, and underpaid. They are second-level victims of the societal arrangements that perpetuate the jail.[37]

In its 1972 survey of local jails, the Law Enforcement Assistance Administration found that less than 4 percent of the jails had professional staff in such areas as social work, psychology, psychiatry, and other treatment specialties.[38] This is not much of an improvement over earlier findings. For example, in 1966 the National Council on Crime and Delinquency conducted a similar survey of jails throughout the country and found that approximately 3 percent of the nation's jail facilities had such personnel.[39] Even though the federal government substantially increased expenditures for local criminal justice programs between 1966 and 1972, when these surveys were taken, it appears that little was done to add treatment personnel to the staffs of local jail facilities. Table 13–1 indicates by size of jail population, the types and numbers of professional employees on the staff. As expected, the larger jails more typically had these professional employees. Even in the case of these larger jails, however, the percentage having such employees is still quite small.

The National Council on Crime and Delinquency and the President's Commission also examined the types and qualifications of personnel who supervise local jail facilities. The majority of personnel (78 percent) were custodial guards. For the position of superintendent, warden, or head jailer, 53 percent of the institutions called for no specific minimum educational requirement, 39 percent required a high school education, and only 8 percent required the jail administrator to have a college degree. As might be imagined, the requirements for a custodial officer or jail guard were even less. In over one-half of the institutions surveyed, there was no educational requirement whatsoever.[40] Table 13–2 indicates the minimum educational requirements for some categories of jail personnel. Although the data reflect 1966 figures, there probably has been little overall improvement during the intervening years, with the possible exception that a few social workers on jail staffs must now have college degrees.

As for preservice training of jail personnel, only 8 percent of local jails required any form of training. Only 38 percent of the institutions surveyed offered any kind of in-service or formal on-the-job training for their staff. Where the jail did require some in-service training, it usually consisted of the

TABLE 13-1
U.S. Jails by Size of Population and Type of Professional Employee (1972)

TYPE OF PROFESSIONAL EMPLOYEE[a]	ALL JAILS (N = 3921)		JAILS WITH FEWER THAN 21 INMATES (N = 2901)		JAILS WITH 21 TO 249 INMATES (N = 907)		JAILS WITH 250 OR MORE INMATES (N = 113)	
	NO.	%	NO.	%	NO.	%	NO.	%
Nurse	229	(5.8)	51	(1.8)	101	(11.1)	77	(68.1)
Psychiatrist	114	(2.9)	32	(1.1)	52	(5.7)	30	(26.5)
Psychologist	95	(2.4)	21	(0.7)	43	(4.7)	30	(26.5)
Social Worker	182	(4.6)	55	(1.9)	79	(8.7)	47	(41.6)
Teacher (academic)	136	(3.4)	14	(0.5)	82	(9.0)	40	(35.4)
Teacher (vocational)	78	(2.0)	11	(0.4)	40	(4.4)	26	(23.0)
Total percentage		3.5		1.07		7.3		36.8

[a] Detail may not add to total shown because of rounding.
Source: Law Enforcement Assistance Administration, Sourcebook of Criminal Justice Statistics, 1977 (Washington, D.C.: U.S. Government Printing Office, February 1978), p. 198.

TABLE 13-2
Minimum Educational Requirements by Percentage of Local and State Institutions (1966)

| | MINIMUM EDUCATIONAL REQUIREMENT, PERCENT | | | |
POSITION	NONE	HIGH SCHOOL OR EQUIVALENT	COLLEGE	GRADUATE STUDY
Superintendent, head jailer, etc.	53	39	8	
Custodial officer	53	46	1	
Social worker	9	41	44	6

Source: President's Commission on Law Enforcement and Administration of Justice, *Task Force Report: Corrections* (Washington, D.C.: U.S. Government Printing Office, 1967), p. 165

handling of firearms, techniques of physical restraint, training in riots and disorders, and the supervision of correspondence.[41] Most of the local jails surveyed provided no merit system or merit incentive programs for jail employees, which indicates that sophisticated systems of personnel management and development were practically nonexistent.[42]

The President's Commission also examined existing salary ranges for jail personnel. Unfortunately, these data are for 1966 and have not been updated; nevertheless we can get some idea of the relatively meager salaries we pay jail personnel. For example, the average salary of the chief administrator of a jail facility was less than $7,000 per year ($14,000 in 1979 dollars), and custodial personnel received an average annual salary of less than $4,000 ($8,000 in 1979 dollars).

In local jails, law enforcement personnel are traditionally used as custodial officers. Even in California, which has one of the more advanced and professional jail management systems, a large percentage of sworn law enforcement personnel are engaged in custodial tasks. A 1970 jail survey in that state found that over 25 percent of the deputies in 58 county sheriff's offices were engaged in custodial activities.[43] In other states, the figure would probably be even higher. Because law enforcement personnel have a difficult enough task enforcing the law and keeping the peace, under the circumstances it is not realistic to expect them to be either expert or very much interested in managing local jails. In addition, the psychological role-set of a law enforcement officer is to arrest offenders and to see to it that they are jailed; the role of a correctional worker should be more rehabilitative and should prepare an inmate to leave jail and return to the community as a law-abiding citizen. However, the use of low-paid custodians to relieve law enforcement personnel is no solution to this problem. In many cases, such individuals are even less qualified and competent to perform the responsibilities than are the law enforcement officers they replace.

Nationally, there were 3.2 inmates for each custodial officer in our nation's jails in 1972. This number varied from state to state and ranged from 1.3 to 11.4[44] On the surface, this might appear adequate. However, this figure includes part-time custodial personnel, and the typical custodial person is also involved in administrative tasks, such as records keeping, booking, and other forms of paperwork. In addition, jails must be manned 24 hours a day every day of the year. Thus, the effective ratio of jail personnel to inmates shrinks to

1:23. Given the conditions that exist in many jails, this does not even permit the custodial officer to effectively supervise the inmates in terms of security, let alone become a participating member in alternative programs that might be developed. The Nebraska study indicated that staff personnel could not observe all prisoners from their assigned stations.[45] The Idaho research pointed out the seriousness of this problem, particularly at night, when it noted that only 32 percent of the jails in that state had a full-time staff member present during the night.[46]

Administrative Problems

One of the major impediments to change in our jails is the quality of administrative leadership. There is adequate documentation attesting to the fact that many sheriffs and police chiefs are not even effective administrators of law enforcement let alone having the managerial abilities associated with maintaining a jail facility. Many sheriffs are particularly poor administrators. For the most part, they are politicians who are primarily interested in developing and maintaining the necessary political connections to ensure their tenure in office.

If they have to demonstrate any managerial competency, it is in the law enforcement function since citizens are much more likely to demand high levels of police service than they are to concern themselves with jail operations. The only time most citizens are apt to question the managerial competence of the jail operation is when disorders or escapes occur.

Furthermore, since most of the citizens who are politically powerful in a community are those least likely to find themselves incarcerated in jail, they have no firsthand knowledge of the conditions that exist. Even if arrested, they are most likely to make bond and thereby avoid an actual experience with the physical jail facility and its operations.

Given these circumstances, most sheriffs or police chiefs with responsibility for maintaining detention facilities are concerned first with security and next with ensuring that riots and disorders do not occur. They wish to avoid the negative publicity that is often associated with escapes and disorders. Third, jail administrators want to appear to be servicing the courts properly. This generally means developing operating policies that ensure that inmates will be present before the court on their trial date and that court orders are carried out. Finally, jail administrators are concerned with keeping operating costs for the jail at a minimum to avoid inquiries and citizen concern. This is not meant to imply that these should not be important concerns; however, in too many instances these are the *only* concerns.

All in all, the emphasis seems to be on maintaining a high degree of anonymity in terms of the operation of the jail. The objective appears to be to keep the entire operation removed as far as possible from contact with the public, and in those instances when public contact is unavoidable, to make that exposure as brief as possible, and to make it appear at least superficially that the agency and its chief administrator are competent.

The overriding concern for security has manifested itself in some strange accommodations in the operating policies of many jails. Given limited manpower, custodial personnel have often knowingly or unwittingly turned over the internal maintenance of the jail to the inmates themselves. In this way, they rely on the inmates (or at least the inmate leaders) to maintain order. The ramifications of this policy are far-reaching. Inmate leaders become exploiters, not only of other prisoners, but even of the jailers themselves. They begin to make innocent demands upon the custodial staff for certain concessions. As they win concessions, they strengthen their power base and become more demanding.[47] As the power cliques develop, disastrous consequences can ensue. A study of the Philadelphia jail pointed out that development of certain leadership cliques in that facility led to "mass intimidation" and sexual assaults upon other inmates. Even the jail administrators themselves were forced to acknowledge that virtually every young man of slight build committed by the courts is sexually approached within a day or so after he is admitted. Many of the young men were repeatedly raped by gangs of prisoners.[48]

Lack of Alternative Programs and Dispositions

The *1970 National Jail Census* indicated that 86 percent of all jails had no recreational facilities and 89 percent had no educational programs.[49] The follow-up survey conducted in 1972 showed that only 12 percent of all jails had any vocational program or programs that in some way would help prisoners obtain employment or employment-related counseling.[50] In fact, the 1972 survey indicated that over two-thirds of all the jails had no general rehabilitative programs whatsoever, not even group counseling, remedial education, or alcoholic or drug-related programs.[51]

As a consequence, most inmates face a daily routine of boredom and idleness. Card playing, conversation, and occasional television viewing are the only pastimes available. Even though community resources in both programs and personnel are usually available, they are seldom used or even solicited. The problems associated with this type of idleness are well stated by Glaser, who says of this condition:

> The major costs to society from jail conditions probably stem not from the clear violations of moral norms that the inmates suffer there, but rather from the prolonged idleness of the inmates in highly diverse groups cut off from much communication with outsiders. In this inactivity and crowdedness, day after day, those inmates most committed to crime "brainwash" the inexperienced to convert initial feelings of guilt or shame into smug rationalizations for crime. Also, jail prisoners become extremely habituated to "killing time," especially during pretrial confinement. Thus, deficiencies of ability to support themselves in legitimate employment, which may have contributed to their criminality, are enhanced at their release. While reformatories and prisons are often called "schools for crime," it is a far more fitting label for the typical urban jail.[52]

These then are some of the negative features that have come to be associated with American jails, and they are, indeed, formidable obstacles to change. The next section examines some of the changes in the traditional methods of dealing with misdemeanants that either are occurring or have been recommended. Although a great deal remains to be done, it is encouraging to see that at least in a few instances improvements are being sought.

NEW MEANS OF DEALING WITH MISDEMEANANTS AND RESTRUCTURING JAILS

With the courts burdened by impossible case loads and the jails overpopulated with misdemeanants, new means are being sought to alleviate these problems. In addition, several practical solutions have been voiced concerning reforms of the jail system.

Diversionary Measures

One of the major recommendations for reform is to divert those accused of misdemeanor crimes and many adjudicated offenders from the process of incarceration. The development of diversionary programs has been recommended by the President's Commission on Law Enforcement and Administration of Justice, the American Bar Association Commission on Correctional Facilities and Services, several federal agencies that have studied the problem, and a variety of individuals, including judges, legislators, correctional workers, police, prosecuting attorneys, and defense lawyers.[53]

It needs to be pointed out that although diversion is increasingly being described as a proved, successful reform policy, many basic questions about it remain unanswered and, in fact, may never have been raised or debated. What programs qualify as diversion programs? What reforms are encompassed by diversion? How do diversion programs function? What are their objectives? How successful have they been?

Since alternative diversionary programs are, for the most part, new ventures, little evaluation has been attempted to determine their impact, and programs that have been evaluated have often been evaluated improperly.[54] As a consequence, most of our knowledge about their success or failure must be impressionistic. Fortunately, more rigorous evaluative techniques are being applied to these programs which will give us a better insight into their relative merits in the near future.

Some of the more notable diversionary techniques are reviewed here:

Citation in Lieu of Arrest Any strategy for minimizing the detention of persons not yet convicted of a criminal offense should be directed at the point of first contact with the criminal justice system—that is, at the point of arrest. Just as the police are authorized to issue citations for traffic violations, it has been recommended that they also have the authority to issue citations for certain categories of offenses under prescribed conditions. The citation would indicate the time and place that the accused was to appear in court to answer the charges. No physical arrest would be made.

Statutory and administrative guidelines would be needed first to authorize the police to deal with offenders in this manner, and secondly to prescribe the criteria that must be met before this could be done. Usually, the issuance of the citation in lieu of an arrest would be warranted in the following instances:

1. The offense is a misdemeanor where there is no danger of physical harm involved. This could also be applied to some felonies in certain situations.

2. The accused is identified and a member of the local community.

3. The police officer has reason to believe that the continued liberty of the accused does not constitute an unreasonable risk of bodily injury to himself or others.

4. There is no reason to believe that the accused will flee from the jurisdiction or not appear at his trial at the appointed place or time.

The implementation of such a program would require that police departments develop certain administrative procedures. For example, it would be necessary to give police officers on the street the necessary discretionary authority to do this. This, in turn, would require special training and the availability of certain departmental resources, such as access to a communications and records system that could verify the identity of the accused in order to satisfy the above criteria. A number of police agencies are now experimenting with this approach. Oakland, California, implemented its Police Citation Program in 1970. Under this program, police officers are authorized to issue summonses rather than making formal arrests for misdemeanors. The accused is instructed where to appear for booking and charging. If the officer in the field decides to take the individual into custody, the desk supervisor on duty can authorize a release on a citation if he or she feels it is warranted. When the program was first initiated, there was a high rate of failure to appear for booking or trial, but a year later the rate was appreciably less.

A number of other cities are using a station house release procedure. An individual who is arrested is taken to the police station, booked, and then released with a citation to appear for trial. In New York, this has developed into the Manhattan Summons Project, and the citation program of the Sunnyvale, California, police department also operates in this manner. In the Sunnyvale program, almost 50 percent of those arrested are released under this program without having to post bond or be incarcerated in the jail. The failure-to-appear rate, under this program, has been approximately 7 percent.[55]

In the Manhattan project, 36,917 summonses were issued in the first 2 years of the program's existence. The failure-to-appear rate was only 5.3 percent, and a number of these "no-shows" resulted from such factors as hospitalization or the fact that the defendant was being held in detention by another jurisdiction. Estimates are that in the first 2 years of the program's existence, the New York City police department saved over 368,000 police work-hours, which saved the taxpayers of that city an estimated $2.5 million in police services alone.[56]

Jail Regionalization

Another recommendation for the improvement of the jail system in America calls for transferring control and responsibility for maintaining them to the state and for developing jails and lockups on a regional basis under the control of correctional authorities who can develop the needed program services.[57]

In terms of cost-benefit analysis, particularly when the "costs" of not being able to provide the necessary services to inmates housed in local detention facilities are included, the arguments for jail consolidation are impressive. What now exists is an ugly tapestry of small, local jails scattered about. Regionalization would consolidate existing facilities by means of cooperative agreements between governmental jurisdictions. For example, designating one county as the site of a jail to serve the adjacent two to three counties is one proposal. The county that served as the jail site would maintain the facility under its jurisdictional control and the other counties would send their arrestees to it under a contractual agreement that stipulates that the host county receive so much money per inmate. Such an arrangement exists in Liberty County, Georgia.

Another proposal that combines the advantages of the regional jail concept with better programming is for the states to enact legislation that would turn these facilities over to the state department of corrections. Since the states have more highly developed correctional systems, including more highly trained correctional and treatment specialists, and more sound fiscal bases, they could incorporate the existing jail systems into statewide systems of misdemeanant institutions. In this manner, reception and classification programs could be developed, alternative community-based programs implemented, and more effective research and evaluative data gathered. Although only a couple of states have adopted this proposal, a number of states are presently looking into the feasibility of such an approach.

It should be pointed out, however, that regionalizing jail systems has some drawbacks. It may not be practicable to house pretrial detainees in these facilities, particularly if the various courts that the facility serves are widely dispersed. Such an arrangement may make it difficult to transport defendants back and forth from the courts as well as making it difficult for attorneys to consult with their clients. It may be better under the circumstances to detain prisoners *temporarily* in local detention facilities *for no longer than twenty-four hours.* Local courts would have to be administered to ensure that the accused is brought before the court within that period. Such provisions already apply at the federal level in felony cases.[58] The states, however, have usually not adhered to this requirement.

A second problem with the regionalization of jails is that this removes the accused from his family. Often, an indigent defendant's family cannot afford the expense of traveling to visit him. This maintenance of family ties is considered by all penologists to be an important factor in any meaningful program of rehabilitation. In addition, the site of a regional jail facility may be such that it does not provide opportunities for work or academic release. All these factors must be carefully considered in determining the feasibility of adopting such a concept.

State Supervision of Local Jail Facilities

When the President's Commission released its report in 1967, only about 40 percent of the states had set any standards for the operations of jails or local institutions, and what standards they did set focused almost exclusively on construction and health standards. Even the U.S. Bureau of Prisons, which for a number of years has had its own jail inspection teams that travel to local jails to certify them as temporary detention facilities for federal prisoners, is usually only concerned with the jail's construction and security characteristics and health-related matters.

In the last few years, however, the states have taken a more meaningful role in supervising local jail facilities. As of 1974, only 16 states had not enacted special statutory authority to some agency of state government to prescribe standards.[59] In most instances, the supervisory agency is the state's Department of Corrections. Michigan, as an example, passed legislation in 1973 which authorized the creation of the Office of Jail Services within the Michigan Department of Corrections. This agency is empowered to make inspections of all local jail facilities in the state. All jails are required to provide adequate security; mail and visitation privileges; special programs for inmates; and the segregation of offenders by age and crimes committed; as well as the usual concerns for facilities and health. Failure to comply as noted by the Office of Jail Services results in the matter going to the state attorney general, who can then seek court-ordered compliance.

In addition, the Michigan Office of Jail Services provides training and programming assistance to the local jails, utilizing the experienced personnel available within the Michigan Department of Corrections. At first, there was a great deal of concern from the sheriffs and police officials in that state that the passage of such legislation and the creation of this special unit would result in a state takeover of local jails. However, these fears did not materialize, and now most of the law enforcement officials in that state who are responsible for maintaining the jails welcome the assistance provided.

On the other hand, a few states have prescribed that the supervisory authority over jail facilities be vested in a special independent body. This does not seem to be an effective solution. Arkansas, which probably has the worst record of penal operations in the country, created a Criminal Detention Facilities Board in 1973. Unlike the more progressive steps taken in other states, Arkansas law provides that the board is empowered to inspect *only adult* criminal detention facilities in the state to see if they meet certain standards of construction, maintenance and operation.

Instead of using a professional group of correctional personnel as Michigan does, Arkansas vested the authority in an eight-member board consisting of the director of the state's Department of Corrections, two politically prominent judges, a sheriff, a police chief, a prosecuting attorney and two appointed layman. The board conducts an annual inspection of each detention facility in the state. If the facility "fails," the local officials are notified and are given 6 months in which to correct or close the facility. If the official in charge of the facility is unhappy with the order of the board, he applies for a hearing in a local court which can set aside the board's order. As mentioned earlier, although nearly two-thirds of the Arkansas facilities have failed to meet these standards, as of 1978 they still continue to operate in a makeshift manner.

As mentioned in the Michigan example, these supervisory authorities usually enforce certain prescribed standards on the operation of jails within the state. Typically, these would include the following requirements:

1. Female matrons to supervise female prisoners and the separation of female from male prisoners.
2. The total separation of juveniles from adults.
3. The isolation of inmates suspected of having contagious disease.
4. Documented plans of medical and emergency medical attention.
5. Compliance with the rights of inmates (visitation privileges, censorship guidelines, standards and procedures to protect prisoners from injury by fellow prisoners, protection of prisoners from negligent or intentional harm by sheriffs, jailers and deputies, and provision of adequate treatment, food, clothing and shelter.)
6. Maintenance of minimum exercise or recreation facilities.
7. Maintenance of established security standards, fire protection and escapes, and 24-hour availability of jail supervision.[60]

The Use of Jail Volunteers

Recently, there has been interest in using volunteers in rehabilitative programs in jails. However, few jails have tried to establish such programs. The use of volunteers inside the jail has several advantages, one being that it reduces the public's ignorance of how bad the situation is. Conditions considered to be tolerable by the jail administration may seem completely intolerable to the volunteer. For example, few if any volunteers would accept a total lack of medical service as a condition of incarceration in even the smallest jail. In addition to their usefulness as providers of supplementary services in the jail, volunteers are thus a source of public information and of public demands for improved jail conditions.[61]

One of the leading jail volunteer programs in the country has been established at the Ingham County Jail outside of Lansing, Michigan. This institution has a broad rehabilitative program, offering services designed to meet the vocational, academic, social, and personal needs of inmates. An outstanding component of the rehabilitation plan at the jail is its volunteer involvement. In the first 2 years of the program, volunteers were instrumental in establishing programs in auto mechanics, blueprint reading, math, physics, arts and crafts, and accounting.

Work Release, Educational Programs, and Counseling Services

A number of jails and misdemeanant institutions have established work-release programs for their inmates. Such programs exist in Birmingham, Alabama; Cincinnati, Ohio; Denver, Colorado; Honolulu, Hawaii; Phoenix, Arizona; Multnomah County, Oregon; and Seattle, Washington.[62] Santa Clara, California, has administered a work-release program since 1957. All inmates in that county's Elmwood Rehabilitation Center, which houses 600 sentenced felons and misdemeanants, are eligible for the program. Approximately one-third of the population is out on work release on any one day. A follow-up study, comparing a sample of inmates who participated in the program with a sample that did not, indicated that participants remained free in the community following work release longer than did nonparticipants.[63]

These work-release programs are of two types. In the more typical program, the inmate works at a place of employment during the day and returns to the jail facility after working hours. The second type permits the offender to work and live at home during the week and to serve out the jail sentence on the weekends.

This type of work release program—which some refer to as weekend jail—seems to be increasing quietly among many local jails and detention facilities throughout the United States. For example, in Chicago's Cook County Jail weekend sentencing began in 1969 with only a handful of offenders; in 1977, nearly 500 were sentenced to weekends. It is likely that in Los Angeles more men and women report for Saturday and Sunday lockup than in any other county in the United States. A survey taken on one weekend in 1977 indicated that 450 were in the county's Hall of Justice jail, a third more than during a similar period a year earlier.[64]

Like shock probation which is discussed in Chapter 15, the weekend work release program provides the court with a sentencing alternative between probation and full-time incarceration. Surveys conducted of such programs indicate that the number of weekends an inmate serves will vary as widely as the entire brief periods of incarceration for as short a span as two weekends, while others have been ordered to do as much as two years of consecutive weekends.[65] In most cases, those sentenced to this type of a program are sentenced for alcohol and motor vehicle related misdemeanors; the next highest category of offenders are those convicted of property crimes. Felons are rarely sentenced to such programs although there have been a number of exceptions.[66]

Some jails are also beginning to establish educational programs. At the Cook County Jail, a nonprofit organization provided an educational program for inmates. In order to assess the program's effectiveness, a group of inmates exposed to the educational program was compared with a group that was not. It was found that the inmates who had participated in the educational program encountered less difficulty in seeking and obtaining employment after their release, had higher employment aspirations, worked longer, and experienced fewer arrests. With an average of 5.4 months spent in the educational program, the average gain was 1.1 academic grade levels. As the amount of time spent in the program increased, so did the level of overall academic achievement. There was a significant relationship between overall academic achievement and success upon release.[67]

The last programming area to be discussed is the development of counseling services within jail systems. One of the most unfortunate consequences of our misdemeanant justice system is that inmates tend to pass through the system repeatedly, often returning for the same kind of offense. Generally they receive little or no help with the very personal problems that may be the major contributor to their behavior. It is imperative that these persons receive counseling in order to redirect their lives.

Every institution for misdemeanants should have sufficient counseling services, staffed by competent, trained personnel. Unfortunately, jails do not provide these services. The National Council on Crime and Delinquency survey indicated that jails have trained counselors or social workers in the ratio of 1 for every 846 inmates.[68] In addition, group interaction programs with trained discussion leaders are also notably absent. Although some jails do provide these services, they are still few and far between.[69] In their place, the inmates often develop their own "group interaction programs," where the counseling emphasis is often on how to commit crimes and escape justice. It is time that such dialogues were supplanted by more appropriate and positive counseling services.

The road to jail reform has often been a slow, tortuous path of deep resistance and frustration. Even today, with the exception of the few isolated examples presented in this chapter, the picture is dismal. It has taken over three centuries to progress this far and it is uncertain whether in our lifetimes jails will accept the principles of penology.

SUMMARY

The jail serves as the gateway to the criminal justice process. The history of jails in both England and later America is a story of neglect, brutality, and debasement. Although jails have improved substantially in the twentieth century, they still are operated in a manner that we as a nation cannot be proud of.

The major problems that confront our jails are interrelated and complex. In the first place, the sheer numbers and variety of offenders create difficult problems for devising meaningful rehabilitative programs. The problem is made more difficult by the fact that jails are under local control, and jail administrators are often local politicians with law enforcement interests. Many jails are totally inadequate in terms of physical facilities and personnel and are hampered by having inept administrators. As a result of these factors, we have failed to adopt meaningful alternative programs to deal with the hundreds of thousands of individuals who each year serve some period of time in jail.

In the past few years, a number of changes have been proposed and adopted in some jurisdictions throughout the country. For example, an increasing emphasis is being placed on diverting the offender through such programs as citations in lieu of arrest and reforms in the bail bond system. Other suggested reforms are jail regionalization, state supervisory authority over local jails, and the increased use of volunteers and support programs in jails.

REVIEW QUESTIONS

1. What kinds of offenders are held in jails?
2. Why is the jail called the "portal" to the criminal justice system?

3. Approximately how many offenders are held in U.S. jails in any one year?

4. In what ways do jails serve the courts?

5. Is the purpose of the jail primarily to detain or to rehabilitate?

6. What is meant by the heterogeneity of offenders?

7. What are six negative characteristics of most jails in the United States? Briefly state why each is a problem.

8. Name the prescribed conditions under which a police officer would issue a citation to someone for a noncriminal offense rather than arrest the person.

9. Is there regional control of your local jail system? How does the regional control work?

10. What are the two types of work-release programs? Explain how each works.

DISCUSSION QUESTIONS

1. Do modern-day jails still reflect some of the characteristics of their predecessors? Discuss.

2. What should be the function of the jail in the criminal justice system?

3. What are the major problems facing America's jails today?

4. Will the new proposals for handling misdemeanants, such as citations instead of jail sentences, be effective? Why or why not?

SUGGESTED ADDITIONAL READINGS

Alexander, Myrl. *Jail Administration.* Springfield, Ill.: Thomas, 1957.

Allen, Harry E., and Clifford E. Simonsen. *Corrections in America.* 2nd ed. Encino, Calif.: Glencoe, 1978.

Amir, Menachem. "Sociological Study of the House of Correction," *American Journal of Corrections* 29, no. 2 (March–April 1967): 36–41.

Fishman, Joseph F. *Crucibles of Crime: A Shocking Story of American Jails.* New York: Cosmopolitan Press, 1923.

Flynn, Edith E. *Prisoners in America.* Englewood Cliffs, N.J.: Prentice-Hall, 1973.

Glaser, Daniel. "Some Notes on Urban Jails," in Daniel Glaser, ed., *Crime in the City.* New York: Harper & Row, 1970.

Goldfarb, Ronald. *Jails: The Ultimate Ghetto.* Garden City, N.Y.: Anchor, 1975.

Law Enforcement Assistance Administration. *1970 National Jail Census.* Washington, D.C.: U.S. Government Printing Office, 1971.

Mattick, Hans. "The Contemporary Jails of the United States." in Daniel Glaser, ed., *Handbook on Criminology.* Chicago: Rand McNally, 1974.

——— and Ronald P. Sweet. *Illinois Jails: Challenge and Opportunity for the 1970s.* Washington, D.C.: U.S. Government Printing Office, 1970.

McGee, Richard A. "Our Sick Jails," *Federal Probation* 35 (March 1971): 3–8.

National Sheriff's Association. *Manual of Jail Administration.* Washington, D.C.: National Sheriff's Association, 1970.

Wayson, Billy L., et al. *Local Jails.* Lexington, Mass.: Lexington Books, 1977.

Webb, Sidney, and Beatrice Webb. *English Prisons Under Local Government.* Hamden, Conn.: Archon, 1963. (Originally published in 1906.)

NOTES

1. Law Enforcement Assistance Administration, *Sourcebook of Criminal Justice Statistics–1977* (Washington, D.C.: U.S. Government Printing Office, February 1978), p. 195.

2. —— *The Nation's Jails: A Report on the Census of Jails from the 1972 Survey of Inmates of Local Jails* (Washington, D.C.: U.S. Government Printing Office, 1975) pp. 21–33.

3. Frederick Pollack and Frederick W. Maitland, *History of the English Law* (Cambridge: Cambridge University Press, 1952), p. 516.

4. Sidney Webb and Beatrice Webb, *English Prisons under Local Government* (Hamden, Conn.: Shoe String, 1963), p. 3.

5. Henry Burns, Jr., *Origin and Development of Jails in America* (monograph) (Carbondale: Southern Illinois University Press), p. 2.

6. See John Howard, *The State of the Prisons* (London: Dent, 1929).

7. E. M. Leonard, *History of English Poor Relief* (Cambridge: Cambridge University Press, 1900), pp. 220–221.

8. H. E. Barnes and N. K. Teeters, *New Horizons in Criminology* (Englewood Cliffs, N.J.: Prentice-Hall, 1949), p. 389.

9. Burns, *Origin and Development of Jails in America,* p. 4.

10. Ibid.

11. Ibid., p. 6.

12. Ibid., p. 8.

13. Ibid.

14. Oliver P. Chitwood, *Justice in Colonial Virginia,* vol. XXIII (Baltimore: Johns Hopkins, 1905), pp. 111–112.

15. Louis N. Robinson, *Penology in the United States* (Philadelphia: Winston, 1922). p. 37.

16. Burns, *Origin and Development of Jails in America,* p. 11.

17. Harry E. Barnes, *The Evolution of Penology in Pennsylvania* (Indianapolis: Bobbs-Merrill. 1927), pp. 58–63.

18. Ibid., pp. 63–65.

19. Burns, *Origin and Development of Jails in America,* p. 13.

20. Harry E. Barnes, *The Story of Punishment* (Boston: Stratford, 1930), p. 192.

21. Robert T. Treymine, *Early Colonial Jails* (New York: Meinster, 1899), pp. 111–113.

22. Robinson, *Penology in the United States,* pp. 36–37.

23. A number of federal courts are now ruling that the confinement of a juvenile in a county jail for adults is in violation of the provision against "cruel and unusual punishment" of the Eighth Amendment; see Bureau of National Affairs, Inc., *The Criminal Law Reporter* 16 (Dec. 18, 1974): 1045.

24. Public Management Consultants, *Recommended Changes for Jail Management in Atlanta, Georgia* (Atlanta, Ga.: 1969).

25. President's Commission on Law Enforcement and Administration of Justice, *Task Force Report: Corrections* (Washington, D.C.: U.S. Government Printing Office, 1967), pp. 162–163.

26. Richard A. McGee, "Our Sick Jails," *Federal Probation* 35 (March 1971): 5.

27. Nebraska Commission on Law Enforcement and Criminal Justice, *For Better or for Worse? Nebraska's Misdemeanant Correctional System* (Lincoln: 1970), pp. 97–105.

28. Hans W. Mattick and Ronald Sweet, *Illinois Jails: Challenge and Opportunity for the 1970s* (Washington, D.C.: U.S. Government Printing Office, 1970), p. 49.

29. LEAA, *The Nation's Jails,* p. 28.

30. American Civil Liberties Union, *The Seeds of Anguish: An ACLU Study of the D.C. Jail* (Washington, D.C.: ACLU, 1973), pp. 3, 5.

31. President's Commission, *Corrections,* p. 166.

32. Ibid.

33. National Advisory Commission on Criminal Justice Standards and Goals, *Corrections* (Washington, D.C.: U.S. Government Printing Office, 1973), p. 275.

34. Law Enforcement Assistance Administration, *Local Jails,* pp. 5–6.

35. Idaho Law Enforcement Planning Commission, *State of Idaho Jail Survey of City and County Law Enforcement Agencies* (Boise: 1969), pp. 12–13.

36. Daniel Glaser, *Crime in the City* (Harper & Row, 1971), p. 238.

37. Mattick and Sweet, *Illinois Jails,* p. 368.

38. Law Enforcement Assistance Administration, *The Nation's Jails* (Washington, D.C.: U.S. Government Printing Office, May 1975).

39. National Council on Crime and Delinquency, *Corrections in the United States* (New York: National Council on Crime and Delinquency, 1967).

40. Henry Burns, Jr., "American Jail in Perspective," *Crime and Delinquency* 17 (October 1971): 451–452.

41. President's Commission, *Corrections,* p. 165.

42. Ibid., p. 455.

43. California Board of Corrections, *A Study of California County Jails* (California Council on Criminal Justice, 1970), p. 102.

44. Law Enforcement Assistance Administration, *The Nation's Jails,* p. 9.

45. Nebraska Commission on Law Enforcement, *For Better or for Worse?* p. 27.

46. Idaho Law Enforcement Planning Commission, *State of Idaho Jail Survey,* p. 9.

47. For an excellent portrayal of how this occurs and the results of such power shifts, see Greshan M. Sykes, *A Society of Captives* (New York: Antheneum, 1970), especially Chap. 3.

48. Allen J. Davis, "Sexual Assaults in the Philadelphia Prison Systems and Sheriff's Vans," *Trans-Action* 6 (1968): 9.

49. Law Enforcement Assistance Administration, *1970 National Jail Census,* p. 191.

50. Law Enforcement Assistance Administration, *The Nation's Jails,* p. 39.

51. Ibid., p. 41.

52. Glaser, *Crime in the City,* p. 241.

53. Raymond T. Nimmer, *Diversion: The Search for Alternative Forms of Prosecution* (Chicago: American Bar Foundation, 1974), p. 3.

54. Nancy Goldberg, "Pre-Trial Diversion: Bilk or Bargain?" *NLADA Briefcase,* 31 (1974): 490.

55. *Handbook for Expansion of Pretrial Release in the San Francisco Bay Area* (Berkeley, Calif.: Association of Bay Area Governments, 1971).

56. *The Manhattan Summons Project* (New York: Criminal Justice Coordinating Council of New York City, 1970), p. 2.

57. President's Commission, *Corrections*, p. 79.

58. See 18 U.S.C. 3501, and *United States* v. *Keeble*, 495 F.2d 757 (8th Cir. 1972).

59. See American Bar Association, *Survey and Handbook on State Standards and Inspection Legislation for Jails and Juvenile Detention Facilities* (Washington, D.C.: American Bar Association, 1974), pp. 10–16.

60. U.S. Bureau of Prisons, *Jail Management–Legal Problems* (Washington, D.C.: U.S. Government Printing Office, 1973).

61. Tully L. McCrea and Don F. Gottfredson, *A Guide to Improved Handling of Misdemeanant Offenders* (Washington, D.C.: U.S. Government Printing Office, 1974), pp. 28–29.

62. Sharron Lee, "Comparisons and Considerations for Social Services in Local Jails" (Seattle, Wash.: Seattle-King County Corrections Development Project, 1972), pp. 15–18.

63. A. Rudoff, T. C. Esselstyn, and George L. Kirkham, "Evaluating Work Furlough," *Federal Probation* 35 (March 1971): 34–39.

64. Edgar May, "Weekend Jail: Doing Time on the Installment Plan," *Correction Magazine* 4 (March 1978): 28–36.

65. Ibid., p. 29.

66. Ibid.

67. Paul S. Venezia and Stephen D. Gottfredson, "The PACE Institute: A Limited Assessment of Its Effectiveness" (Davis, Calif.: National Council on Crime and Delinquency Research Center, 1972).

68. National Council on Crime and Delinquency, *Corrections in the United States*, p. 142.

69. See Edith E. Flynn, "Jails and Criminal Justice," in Lloyd Ohlin, ed., *Prisoners in America* (Englewood Cliffs, N.J.: Prentice-Hall, 1973), p. 75.

14
PRISON SYSTEMS

1. What are the five most common types of institutions?
2. How are state correctional institutions administered?
3. What type of organizational structure is found in most prisons?
4. Who are the key personnel in a large institution?
5. What inmate programs are available in most adult prisons today?
6. In prison administration, what is the traditional model and what is the collaborative model?
7. What does the composite profile of the typical male and female prisoner reveal about the prison populations?
8. What are the six problem areas in correctional reform?

These are some of the questions this chapter will answer.

The correctional system in the United States is extremely diverse. It includes a broad range of institutions, theories, programs, and operating strategies. The problems associated with institutional and program diversity are compounded by the diversity of offenders with which the system must deal. A number of offenders are hardened recidivists who are irrevocably committed to criminal careers; others subscribe to more conventional values; still others are aimless individuals who are committed to neither socially appropriate nor socially inappropriate behavior. Each offender must be handled by appropriate casework techniques as well as security considerations.

TYPES OF INSTITUTIONS

There are several types of institutions among prison systems today. These institutions are usually designated by the type of security they afford which, in turn, is determined by the characteristics of the offenders in them.

Maximum-Security Institutions

The more hardened and dangerous offenders are found in maximum-security prisons. A typical maximum-security prison is usually enclosed by massive concrete or stone walls from 18 to 25 feet high or by a series of double or triple perimeter fences topped with barbed wire and spaced 15 to 20 feet apart. Located on the outer-perimeter walls are well-protected towers strategically placed so that the guards have an open field of fire and can observe the external and internal sections of all the surrounding walls and the prison yard. Today, more and more institutions use electronic sensing devices to monitor the prison's perimeters.

The internal security considerations are just as formidable. The inmates are housed in interior cell blocks, each of which has its own self-contained security enclosure. The cell blocks are partitioned off from each other by a series of enclosures that limit internal movement. The idea behind this construction is to create a series of miniature prisons within a prison so that in the event of riots or escapes, each section can be sealed off from the others. Thus, any prisoner seeking to break out would first have to penetrate the internal security system before he could challenge the external wall and perimeter security devices.

In recent years, the trend has been away from the construction of these types of institutions, particularly ones surrounded by massive stone walls, because of their prohibitive cost. New maximum-security institutions often use technological intrusion and security devices, such as infrared sensors and closed-circuit TV for security, which permits the facility to have a more campus-like appearance.

Medium-Security Institutions

Medium-security institutions house inmates who, although not as dangerous to society and their fellow inmates as those confined in maximum-security prisons, do pose a threat of escape and often have served prior sentences.

Normally, medium security prisons are not fortress-like structures, although, in most instances, a series of fences or enclosures surround the perimeter. Many of these institutions are constructed on a block arrangement in which inmates live together in designated units. Less emphasis is placed upon controlling the internal movement of prisoners. These facilities often have dormitories, honor units, or some similar form of housing for inmates that have earned the privilege of living in such quarters. There is usually a special maximum-security unit for inmates who pose a threat to the security of the institution or to other inmates. Often such inmates will be transferred to a maximum-security prison until they demonstrate the appropriate conduct or are released at the expiration of their sentence.

Minimum-Security Institutions

Minimum-security prisons do not utilize fixed observation posts for armed guards on the perimeter. In fact, depending upon where they are situated and the type of offenders they contain, there may be no perimeter fence. Inmates in minimum-security institutions are generally housed in private or semiprivate rooms or in dormitories. Although housing inmates in individual rooms has certain advantages, such facilities are often too costly to construct, and thus most inmates live in small dormitories accommodating from 10 to 20 inmates. Recent years have seen a large growth in the number of minimum-security facilities. The President's Commission found that of the 350 state institutions surveyed, 55 were maximum-security, 124 were medium-security facilities, 103 were classified as minimum-security, and the remaining 68 were mixed-security institutions.[1]

The minimum-security institution, of course, houses less dangerous offenders. In many instances, offenders with relatively short sentences and/or without extensive criminal records are housed in these facilities. Since these institutions offer greater freedom to the inmate, many correctional departments transfer inmates to them from medium-security institutions when they have demonstrated by their conduct that they have earned this privilege. Often, the minimum-security institution provides an adjustment stage prior to release. For example, inmates of more closely guarded institutions who have a year or so left to serve may be transferred to one of these facilities to help them adjust to less controlled discipline so that they are better prepared for their ultimate release.

Prison Camps

Prison camps are a form of minimum-security institution that started in the Midwest, the West, and the South. In the Midwest and the West, they usually are farming and forestry camps. Pennsylvania, Maryland, California, Oregon, Ohio, Wisconsin, and Washington have all used prison camps extensively. These institutions provide instructive work for inmates within a more favorable environment than can be created within traditional institutions. They also enable prisoners of various types to be separated, thus reducing the possibility of contamination of attitudes. Work camps relieve the problem of overcrowding in other correctional institutions and are less costly then maintaining traditional prisons.

Until recent years, Southern prison camps had a very poor reputation. First begun during the period of reconstruction following the Civil War, they were operated under a lease system. Private bidders contracted with the state for the use of inmate labor, the bidders then leased the inmates to private individuals who used them in lumbering, quarrying, and turpentine operations. When the federal courts began to prohibit the leasing of prisoners, this practice disappeared and the Southern states turned to using their inmate labor on road crews and chain gangs, which labored under brutal conditions. In recent years, however, the Southern states have abolished their road gangs and have developed various camp institutions devoted to farming and forestry. In some cases, these camps are among the best such programs in the nation.

Special Institutions

Some specialized institutions have been developed for handling certain categories of offenders. For example, the California camp or ranch system, which operates under county authority but is partially subsidized by the state, provides special facilities for the rehabilitation of juvenile offenders. The California Youth Authority also has a number of camps for youthful offenders, which permits the state to separate young offenders by age, crime, and individual needs so that younger, first-time offenders do not associate with more criminally sophisticated and intractable youths.

A few states and the federal government have developed special facilities for inmates who need intensive medical and psychiatric help that is not normally available in other institutions. Among these are the California Medical Facility at Vacaville and the United States Medical Center at Springfield, Missouri. States have also developed special institutions and programs for the criminally insane; Michigan constructed the first such facility in 1885. Special institutions and programs are also available for women offenders—for example, the state institute at Clinton, New Jersey, and the federal one at Alderson, West Virginia. Today, the various types of special institutions and programs offer a wide choice of alternatives for meeting the particular needs of offenders.

ADMINISTRATION OF STATE CORRECTIONAL SYSTEMS

Until the beginning of the twentieth century, prisons in the various states operated almost as independent fiefdoms. The wardens and superintendents of these institutions reported directly to the governor or the legislature. This was a period of political patronage, and prison administrators and custodial staff held their jobs by virtue of political connections. It was not unusual for newly appointed governors to engage in large-scale dismissal of prison personnel, replacing them with their own political followers. During this period, the governor or the legislature did the hiring, the purchasing, and the budget-making for the prisons within the state. After the Civil War, some of the states attempted to bring their prisons under some sort of administrative control by appointing boards of charities or corrections, which were the forerunners of present state departments of correction.

Today, every state has a centralized department of corrections. It may be an autonomous agency or a unit within a department of human resources or similar body. The corrections department supervises all state-run correctional institutions, and is also responsible for all state-sponsored community-based correctional institutions and programs. In many states, parole services including all parole officers and, in some instances, the parole board, are also under the department of corrections. In recent years, additional responsibilities have been given to various state departments of correction. For example, some are now responsible for inspecting local jails, lockups, and other misdemeanant institutions. Michigan and Ohio are also beginning to incorporate probation services within the department of correction.

The head of the state department of corrections is usually referred to as the director of corrections. In most states, this officer is appointed by the governor with approval of the legislature. In recent years, more and more states are filling these directorships with qualified penologists as political considerations become less important. In states where the department of corrections is an autonomous state agency, the director is responsible for the administration of the entire state penal system, which includes the presentation of the budget to the chief executive and its defense before the state legislature. Besides being a knowledgeable penologist and administrator, the director must be skilled in the art of politics so as to represent the agency effectively before the legislature and obtain the required program authorizations and appropriations.

PRISON ADMINISTRATION

The head of the prison is known by various titles, usually warden, superintendent, or director. The responsibilities of this individual are to manage the institution and to present the institution's budget to the director of corrections or some fiscal agent of the executive department. In some instances, the warden may also be required to defend budget requests before the executive fiscal agency or even the state legislature or one of its committees.

In larger institutions, the warden is usually assisted by one or more associate wardens. Many states and the Federal Bureau of Prisons have adopted the organizational recommendations developed by the American Correctional Association which call for two associate wardens in medium to large prisons. One associate warden is directly responsible for custody, which includes the custodial guard force, and the other is responsible for the classification and treatment maintained by the institution. Custody and treatment are the major operating units within most prisons. Directly under the associate warden for custody is the captain of the guard force, who is the commanding officer of the custodial line personnel. This custody section also consists of a number of watch lieutenants and sergeants and a large number of correctional officers or guards. Contrary to popular belief, the custodial officer's main job is not preventing escape from the prison; perimeter security devices such as high walls and guard towers generally perform this function. The main responsibility of the custodial officer is to maintain control within the prison to assure the safety of both inmates and prison employees. The custodial line personnel are in daily contact with the inmates and can make an important contribution to the efforts of the treatment personnel.[2]

Depending upon the institution, its budget, and the prevailing philosophy, the treatment unit may consist of such professional personnel as psychiatrists, psychologists, social workers, medical personnel, chaplains, counselors, and teachers of academic and vocational programs. In addition, there may be a prison industries manager who is responsible for the industrial production enterprises of the prison; a business manager who is responsible for accounting, procurement, payroll, and supplies; and a medical services manager who is responsible for the medical, dental, and other health-related facilities within the prison. Figure 14-1 shows an organizational chart for a medium-sized prison for men.

The management of a prison is no small task, rivaling that of many large industries in its complexity of administrative functions. The large inmate population with the special problems associated with the prison environment makes it even more difficult to manage. Under these circumstances, the management of prisons may indeed be one of the most complex and demanding tasks facing any public administrator. It certainly requires the most capable managers to be found anywhere in the public service today.

THE INSTITUTIONAL STAFF

Larger prisons are typically divided into two major operating units: custody and treatment. Within each of these, there are certain key personnel. Some of the more common and important members of the prison staff are correctional officers, staff psychiatrists or psychologists, and prison counselors or social workers.

Correctional Officer

The correctional officer is primarily responsible for fulfilling the custody role of the prison. In this role, he or she is responsible for such diverse activities as maintaining discipline among the inmates, preventing the smuggling of contraband, controlling inmate movement within the institution, protecting inmates from other inmates, and preventing escapes.

In spite of these important responsibilities, recruitment and hiring standards and procedures have not established sufficiently high educational or personality standards for the position of correctional officer.[3] As a result, many correctional officers are underpaid, undereducated, and ill-trained for any role but security.

The role of the correctional officer depends on the orientation of the prison. For instance, Johnson comments:

> When custody is the only factor, the "good jail man" takes a group of prisoners out and brings them all back; he has a forceful personality and is courageous in dangerous situations. In an industrial program, the correctional officer–work supervisor, when there is such a hybrid role, must be informed in trades and capable of motivating workers. He must maintain production on security concurrently. When rehabilitation of prisoners is given high priority, the (correctional officer) is expected to maintain security with minimum coercion and greater reliance on understanding of factors shaping behavior.[4]

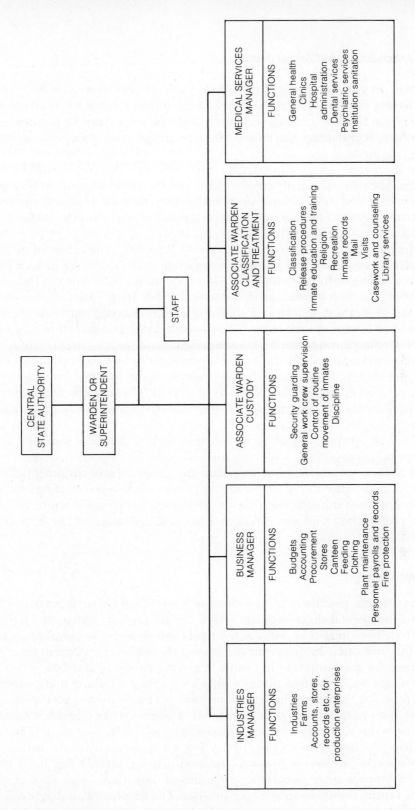

Reprinted (with change in title) with permission of The American Correctional Association from the *Manual of Correctional Standards*, 1966 ed., p. 319.

FIGURE 14-1 Organizational Arrangement for an Adult Male Institution of Less Than 2,000 Inmates

There is a growing recognition of the key role that correctional officers play in affecting the attitudes and behavior of the inmates. Since the correctional officers are in close contact with the prisoners on a daily basis, they can contribute to or damage the efforts of the treatment staff. As a result, efforts are being made to train custody personnel in counseling techniques. There are some problems associated with such efforts. The major problem is whether the correctional officer-counselor can overcome the conflict between the policing and authoritative elements of the custodial role and the free communication and mutual understanding required of the role as counselor.[5]

Donald Clemmer describes such an experiment. Employees were prepared for the innovation by an in-service training program, publication of an administrative order, and an article on counseling in the employer publication. The counseling technique employed was rather simple, "the type in which one neighbor talks with another neighbor over the back fence." Clemmer claimed that the program demonstrated that neither the custodial staff nor the inmates tried to exploit each other. The custodial personnel gained insight and understanding through the training experience and study of the classification documents that described the inmates' personalities and backgrounds. Correctional officers demonstrated more interest in the inmates and the emotional atmosphere of the institution was improved. The program also reduced the tendency for the custodial and treatment staffs to remain aloof from each other.[6]

Of course, the success of programs that seek to combine custodial and treatment responsibilities under the correctional officer's position depends on many factors. Among the most important are: the general environment of the institution; the attitudes of high-ranking prison officials; the existing level of conflict between inmates and custody personnel; the composition of the inmate population; and the characteristics and attitudes of the custodial personnel.

Psychiatrist

The role that psychiatry plays within the correctional system is burdened by some fundamental disagreements within the profession. Although psychiatrists have been long-time critics of the rigid controls and restrictions of prison life, they are often in disagreement among themselves concerning the role and need for psychotherapy in prisons. Psychiatrists also tend to be abstract in their diagnoses. This often makes it difficult for the action-oriented custodial staff to accept them into the treatment team as readily as, say, psychologists.

The few psychiatrists who are employed in prisons make diagnostic examinations, write reports for parole boards, and advise on the disposition of problem prisoners. They serve as referring agents when psychotic prisoners are transferred to mental hospitals. In most prisons, psychiatrists have little time or hospital space to conduct programs of individual or group therapy, which, ideally, should be their major function. Once a prisoner is diagnosed as requiring psychiatric treatment, the absence or shortage of therapeutic resources frequently requires the assignment of the psychiatrist to routine classification and counseling duties.[7] Under these conditions, psychiatry is reduced to lip-service support of a custodial regime. The psychiatrist can also be useful in training prison personnel, especially custodial staff, to recognize and handle mental disturbances and emotional reactions to confinement.[8]

Psychologist

Like psychiatrists, the qualified Ph.D. psychologist is too infrequently found in correctional systems. The psychologist performs any number of responsibilities. Two of the most important are psychological testing and diagnosis which serve as the foundation for any treatment program suggested for the prisoner. Psychologists are most typically used at the time of classification when the inmate first arrives at the institution. In addition to administering the various psychological tests, the psychologist can conduct intensive interviews of inmates on a selected basis. These interviews are used to supplement personality and projective tests, intelligence scores, and other devices that can be used in determining appropriate treatment programs.

Psychologists also assist the counseling staff in their efforts and help to develop in-service training programs for custodial people who work as counselors. They also provide input for discipline and classification committee decisions.[9]

Counselors

Counselors fill the major roles in the wide-ranging treatment programs in most prison systems. Today, one of the most common forms of treatment can generally be referred to as group methods—for example, group therapy, group counseling, guided group interaction, and psychodrama. Prison counselors play an important role in developing and operating such programs on a daily basis. One of the more promising approaches is to make the inmates themselves part of the overall group process. The idea of using peer pressure to promote improvement is a product of the 1960s. In this process, the inmates themselves participate in groups and provide the leadership that helps individuals improve themselves.[10] The prison counselor plays an important role in the development, supervision, and maintenance of such efforts.

A number of institutions have developed a therapeutic community approach. This is a system whereby the entire institutional program is geared toward treatment. In this setting, a treatment-oriented staff and custodial personnel work as a team in the treatment effort. As members of the treatment team, prison counselors are often given the primary responsibility to develop the treatment approach and to maintain it among the custodial staff and the inmates.

PRISON PROGRAMS

Penal institutions have varied programs, depending upon the age, sex, prior criminal record, education, and medical and psychiatric needs of inmates. Since it is not possible to review all specialized programs existing, emphasis is placed on those programs that typically are found in most adult prisons today.

Classification

Classification attempts to match the needs of the offender with the appropriate program. In the not too distant past, judges had the authority to sentence convicted offenders to any institution within the state. Usually this provided no means to match the needs of the offender with the various treatment programs that existed in different institutions. Beginning in the 1930s, a few correctional systems in the United States began to adopt the classification concept, and other states have now followed suit. Under this system, the department of corrections has the authority to assign inmates to institutions where they can receive the treatment they need. The only exception to this is that in some instances in the case of less serious crimes, the judge can sentence someone on a short-term basis to a local facility or workhouse.

Out of the classification concept have arisen reception and diagnostic programs and facilities. The first of these was the diagnostic depot at the Joliet, Illinois, prison. Where such programs exist, all inmates sentenced to a state correctional system are first sent to a special centralized facility for extensive testing and evaluation. The objectives of these facilities are typically:

1. Diagnosis of case problems
2. Prescription of classification to specific programs to meet diagnosed problems
3. Induction and orientation of inmates to the correctional system
4. Medical examination, quarantine, and treatment of new inmates.[11]

At the reception and diagnostic center, the new inmate is interviewed by specialized clinical personnel, such as psychologists, psychiatrists, physicians, dentists, and a chaplain. Often, a presentence report (see Chapter 9) gathered by probation or parole authorities accompanies the individual to the center and provides background information which guides the clinical personnel in their evaluation. Frequently, letters of inquiry are also sent to the inmate's immediate family and to previous employers and schools in an effort to obtain better information on the individual's background. Many times, the center questions social welfare agencies in the prisoner's former locale that may have had prior contact with him or her.

After all this information has been gathered, a social history is prepared. The staff of the center then classifies the inmate in terms of his or her particular needs and potential security risk. For example, the individual might be found to be in need of intensive psychiatric help, alcoholic or drug-related rehabilitation, group therapy, educational programs, or some combination of these. Once these needs are determined, the inmate is sent to the particular institution that has the necessary programs. Although these centers perform a very important function, knowledgeable observers point out that they tend to drain the institutions themselves of professional personnel, thus placing a premium on diagnosis rather than on treatment.[12]

In states without a centralized reception and diagnostic facility, individual institutions have developed their own classification committees. The committees vary somewhat in composition, but usually consist of the associate warden for classification and treatment or the associate warden's immediate subordinate, a high-ranking custodial officer, and the counselor, psychologist, or social worker who prepared the social history. This classification committee meets with the inmate and makes an appropriate program assignment on the basis of the social history report and the interview with the inmate.

A more recent development in classification is the treatment-team concept developed at the federal correctional institution in Ashland, Kentucky, and the Air Force Retraining Facility at Amarillo, Texas. In the team approach, a counselor, a custodial officer, and a teacher from the institution's academic program are jointly assigned to individual inmates. The same team may be assigned all the prisoners in a particular dormitory or cell block. In addition to being responsible for the original classification, the team also handles all disciplinary problems among its assignees. This approach relieves the classification committee of its very time-consuming disciplinary function and provides some continuity in supervision. It also makes custodial and academic staff more treatment-oriented by virtue of their involvement in the correctional treatment process.

Health

Most prisons of any size have a health and medical program. In states without centralized reception and diagnostic facilities, the prison medical facility quarantines all inmates for a week or 10 days. The medical services unit is responsible for maintaining proper sanitary conditions in the physical plant and in the food service area. Hospitals are usually maintained in most of the larger prisons and are staffed by physicians, nurses, and other health-related personnel. All but the largest prisons contract the services of an optician and dentist, who make periodic visits to the institution. In some of the largest institutions, prison hospitals are reasonably well-equipped, even for major surgery. When necessary, nearby hospitals are used. Psychiatric services are very limited. A 1974 survey of prisons in the United States indicated that slightly more than 1 percent of all adult institutions provided psychiatric services.[13]

Academic Programs

Academic programs in prisons range from courses for illiterates to college extension courses. Most prisons have some sort of prison school that is usually administered by a director of education. Unfortunately, in some adult institutions, academic instruction is provided mainly by inmate teachers. Many of them lack a college education, and some have not even completed high school. Invariably, these inmate teachers are pressured by their students to make the classes effortless and to complete false reports on student progress. Inmate teachers are also susceptible to bribes from their students for good grades and reports. Prisons are also typically short on classroom facilities and teaching aids.

In too many instances, civilian teachers at correctional institutions tend to be rejects from public school systems. Like many of the inmates, the instructors are primarily interested in putting in their time with a minimum of work.

Little effort is exerted to make the classroom sessions more meaningful or to employ teaching techniques that could be of more benefit to the inmates.

Vocational Training

Many American prisons have developed a variety of vocational training programs. With the passage of the 1965 amendments to the Vocational Rehabilitation Act, significant vocational training opportunities became available to inmates because correctional institutions were able to acquire the necessary equipment and trained instructors. Such shops as automobile repair and maintenance, radio and television repair, welding, sheet metal work, and woodworking are now rather common. The well-organized shops have civilian vocational instructors, a place to do the shop work, and space to conduct the necessary instruction. This situation has greatly improved from the time, just a few short years ago, when the usual vocational activity consisted of making license plates, doing laundry, or producing brooms and twine.

One of the recurring problems that prisons face in developing meaningful vocational training programs is finding appropriate jobs for former offenders who have acquired a skill while in prison. It is often difficult for a released offender to acquire a job as a mason, carpenter, or other skilled worker because of the reluctance of unions to permit them to join. Often, regardless of the person's skill, the ex-offender is usually relegated to an apprenticeship, since the unions do not consider prison-sponsored vocational training programs as sufficient qualification for a journeyman's level.

Libraries

Most prisons have some kind of library which usually range from very bad to mediocre in terms of the available reading materials. Cost is the major problem in trying to develop adequate libraries. Since very few institutions have specific money set aside in their operating budget to purchase up-to-date library materials, they must rely on books donated from outside sources, which are often out-dated and not of general interest to the inmates.

Of special concern to some inmates is access to legal books. Many inmates spend a great deal of their time filing legal petitions with the courts for relief by way of habeas corpus writs. In California, the question of whether prison administrators are required to furnish law libraries to inmates has been answered in the affirmative. In the case of *Gilmore* v. *Lynch,* a statewide regulation that had severely restricted titles of law books that could be placed in a prison library was held unconstitutional. The court noted that the adequate filing of petitions for habeas corpus writs by inmates required prisons to maintain sufficient legal resources so that inmates could obtain the information they needed.[14]

A number of good libraries are maintained by the Federal Bureau of Prisons. Some have professional librarians to operate the libraries and to supervise the prisoners who act as attendants or helpers in the library. An excellent example of an institutional library can be found in the federal government's

Kennedy Youth Center in Morgantown, West Virginia. The library at this facility is impressively large, with an excellent collection as well as audiovisual and other learning aids. In this institution, a special committee with inmate representatives selects the materials that the library acquires.

Prison Industries

The subject of prison industries has an interesting history. Prison industries have been based on the so-called sheltered and open-market systems. Today, prison industries are based on the state-use system and the public-works-and-ways system, both considered sheltered-market systems.[15] The state-use system produces goods and renders services for agencies of the state or its political subdivisions. Thus, prison industries manufacture goods that are not sold on the open market, but only to other state or local governmental jurisdictions. Public-works-and-ways systems involve road construction and repair, reforestation, soil-erosion control activities, and the like on public property only.[16]

This was not always the case. During the nineteenth century, prison industries sold their goods and services in competition with private industry. Labor unions and employers' associations applied a great deal of pressure on Congress and state legislatures to prohibit the sale of inmate-produced goods or inmate services on the open market. In 1929, Congress passed the Hawes-Cooper Act, which deprived prison-made goods of their interstate character and made them subject to state law. The Ashurst-Summers Act of 1953 prohibited transportation of prison-made goods into states forbidding their entry and required the labeling of prison-made goods shipped in interstate commerce. By 1940, every state had passed legislation that prohibited the sale of inmate-produced goods on the open market.[17]

In any institution there is usually only a small percentage of the prison's total inmate population engaged in prison industries. Many inmates are assigned to kitchen or mess duties, the laundry, maintenance work, and unskilled tasks such as pushing a broom or cleaning windows.

Prison wages are very nominal in American prisons. In the mid-1960s, a married prisoner might earn 8 cents an hour for working a 40-hour week; half of this would be sent to his family and half would be deposited in his account (one-quarter for use in the prison commissary and one-quarter for going-home money).[18] Even today, the average prevailing pay in almost all state institutions is still probably less than 50 cents an hour. Some federal institutions are paying their inmate labor more, based upon the skill involved in performing the specified job.

Several renowned penologists have suggested that prisons pay their inmate labor the prevailing wage for the particular work they perform and then charge them for their maintenance and care after taking out an appropriate share of the individual's earnings for his family's support. However, this scheme has very little chance of becoming a reality in view of the prevailing attitude which demands that as part of the inmate's punishment, the prisoner be legally, socially, and economically disabled.[19]

Recreation Programs

Almost all prisons have developed a recreation and leisure-time program. The major sports of football, basketball, and baseball are participated in by intramural teams, and some prisons even have extramural teams that compete with teams from the outside community. Some prisons that have adequate funds to hire a director of recreation and purchase equipment have developed fairly broad recreation programs. Some institutions even have gymnasiums, weight-training programs, and a host of other athletic sports. For inmates who do not engage in the very active sports, most prisons provide alternative forms of recreation. Arts and crafts are often available, as are organized chess matches, debating teams, music groups. Even dramatic groups have been formed in some places. Movies are provided on a routine basis, as are TV-viewing rooms, and many institutions permit radios in individual cells or dormitories. Some institutions permit outside entertainers to perform in the institution periodically as well as permitting inmates with special entertainment skills to perform on the outside.

CLASSIFYING INSTITUTIONS BY PROGRAM EMPHASIS

In addition to classifying penal institutions by the degree of security they offer or by the age and type of offenders they contain, they must be further defined, according to their administrative characteristics. Administratively, prisons may follow either the *traditional* model or the *collaborative* model.

HOLT v. SARVER (1971)

Prison Conditions That Violate Prisoner's Constitutional Rights

FACTS:

A group of prisoners in the Arkansas prison system brought suit in the U.S. District Court for the Eastern District of Arkansas alleging that their rights, privileges, and immunities secured to them by the due process and equal protection clauses of the Fourteenth Amendment were being violated by that state's prison system. They contended that they had the following rights: (1) the right not to be imprisoned without meaningful rehabilitative opportunities; (2) the right to be free from cruel and unusual punishment; (3) the right to be free from arbitrary and capricious denial of rehabilitation opportunities; (4) the right to minimal due process safeguards in decisions that determined fundamental liberties; (5) the right to be fed, housed, and clothed so as not to be subjected to loss of health or life; (6) the right to unhampered access to counsel and the courts; (7) the right to be free from the abuses of fellow prisoners in all aspects of daily life; (8) the right to be free from racial segregation; (9) the right to be free from forced labor; and (10) the right to be free from the brutality of being guarded by fellow "trusty" inmates.

The court upheld most of the prisoners allegations and held that because of the existing conditions, confinement in the Arkansas penitentiary system amounted to cruel and unusual punishment which is prohibited by the Eighth Amendment. Prison officials then appealed this decision to the U.S. Eighth Circuit Court of Appeals.

DECISION:

The Eighth Circuit Court of Appeals upheld the lower court decision. This court found, among other things, that: (1) the prison was largely run by inmate trusty guards who breeded hatred and mistrust; (2) the open barracks within the prison invited widespread physical and sexual assaults; (3) the isolation cells were overcrowded, filthy, and unsanitary; and (4) there was a total absence of any rehabilitation or training program. Like the lower court, it then concluded that these conditions, as a whole, constituted cruel and unusual punishment. The court also upheld the lower court's order that these deficiencies must be corrected and also upheld the lower court order that placed the supervision of the Arkansas penitentiary system under the scrutiny of the federal courts to ensure compliance with these findings.

SIGNIFICANCE OF THE CASE:

This was a landmark decision which found that conditions within penal institutions could be such that they constitute cruel and unusual punishment. It also placed an entire state's prison system under the direction of the federal courts which would supervise the required remedial action to bring the prison system up to an acceptable standard.

The Traditional Model

The traditional institution is administered with the idea that security is of paramount importance in order to protect the institutional staff as well as the community. To accomplish this, high walls are constructed, mechanical security devices and armed guards are employed, and inmate searches and body counts are made frequently. However, it is not necessary that all the physical aspects of gun towers, fences, and other obvious displays of security be present for an institution to be traditional. Administratively contrived security precautions, such as frequent searches and "shake-downs," head counts, disciplinary segregation, and other forms of control less visible to the outside world can prevail even in institutions that are not bounded by high walls or fences.

Traditional institutions adhere to the idea that deterrence requires strict discipline, regimentation, and punishment, all in an atmosphere of impersonality and quasi-military rigidity. Mail is censored, visitation privileges are closely controlled, privacy is virtually nonexistent, and inmates march in groups and are identified by number.

Certain operational policies characterize such institutions. Particular emphasis is placed upon maintaining staff and inmate "distance." The inmates are required to defer to the status of custodial and staff personnel by addressing them as "mister" or by their appropriate rank. Disciplinary infractions are dealt with summarily—for example, guards are required to "write up" any offensive conduct by an inmate; failure to do so brings an immediate reprimand from the guard's superior.

This impersonality and social distance is maintained by mass handling of prisoners. Inmates, for example, are often marched in groups to meals, to work, and to recreation. As a consequence, inmates and staff have very little opportunity for personal interaction. This massive impersonality of the traditional institutions can be seen in Sykes's study of a maximum-security institution in New Jersey. Each inmate who came to the institution was issued a *Handbook for Inmates* which stated, among other things, the following:

> Form by twos when passing through the Center. Keep your place in line unless you are ordered to step out.
>
> When walking in a line, maintain a good posture. Face forward and keep your hands out of your pockets.
>
> When the bell rings for meals, work, or other assignment, turn out your light, see that your water is turned off, and step out of your cell promptly.
>
> On returning to your Wing, go directly to your cell, open the door, step in, and close the door without slamming it.
>
> Gambling in any form is not allowed.
>
> Do not speak or make gestures to persons who are visiting the institution.[20]

Although prison systems typically no longer demand such tight regimentation, it still exists in less obvious and visible ways in some institutions.

A number of observers who have studied the patterns of interaction in a traditional prison have pointed out that this distance does break down. It is not possible for custodial people to maintain their authority over inmates because prisoners do not perceive the authority of the guards as legitimate and thus they do not feel compelled to obey. Also, the guards cannot distribute meaningful rewards or sanctions that might provide them with control over the inmates. Increasingly, the courts are forbidding the use of many of the usual forms of discipline that correctional officials relied upon in their attempts to control prisoners. This has greatly eroded the false control and distancing mechanism that the guards of traditional institutions had functioned under in the past. Also, what may be intended by officials as a punishment, such as solitary or segregated confinement, may actually be viewed as a "reward." The individual receives greater prestige in the eyes of the inmates for ignoring the rules and being punished.

BAXTER v. PALMIGIANO (1976)

Prison Disciplinary Hearings and Due Process

FACTS:

The U.S. Supreme Court was asked to review the decisions of lower courts in two separate cases.

Palmigiano, an inmate at the Rhode Island Adult Correctional Institution who was serving a life sentence for murder, was charged by prison officials with "inciting a disturbance." He was told by prison officials that he might be prosecuted under state law, that he should consult an attorney (although his attorney could not be present during the prison disciplinary hearing), and that he had a right to remain silent at the hearing, but his silence could be used against him. At the hearing, Palmigiano remained silent and was placed in "punitive segregation" for 30 days. He filed on an action under federal law, alleging that the procedures utilized at the disciplinary hearing violated the due process clause of the Fourteenth Amendment. The U.S. Court of Appeals heard the case and held that: (1) an inmate of a prison disciplinary hearing must be informed of his right to remain silent; (2) he must not be questioned further once he exercises that right; (3) such silence may not be used against him at that time or in future proceedings; and (4) when criminal charges are a realistic possibility, prison officials should consider whether defense counsel, if requested, should be permitted at the disciplinary hearing.

John Clutchette and other inmates at San Quentin filed an action seeking relief under federal law alleging that the procedures used in disciplinary proceedings at San Quentin violated their rights to due process and equal protection of the laws under the Fourteenth Amendment. Both the U.S. District Court and the U.S. Court of Appeals held that: (1) minimum notice and a right to respond are due an inmate faced with even a temporary suspension of privileges; (2) an inmate of a disciplinary hearing who is denied the privilege of confronting and cross-examining witnesses must receive written reasons therefor or the denial will be deemed prima facie evidence of abuse of discretion; and (3) an inmate facing prison discipline for a violation that might also be punishable in state criminal proceedings has a right to counsel, not merely a counsel substitute, at a prison hearing.

DECISION:

Upon review of these two lower court decisions, the United States Supreme Court held that: (1) inmates do not have a right to either retained or appointed counsel in disciplinary hearings and prison authorities do not have to advise the inmate of this right; (2) prison disciplinary hearings are not criminal proceedings; but if inmates are compelled in these proceedings to furnish testimony that might incriminate them in a later criminal trial, they cannot be compelled to testify; (3) permitting an adverse inference to be drawn from an inmate's silence at his disciplinary is not in and of itself an invalid practice; (4) prison officials can decide in terms of the interests of the prison whether inmates in a disciplinary proceeding should have the right to confront and cross-examine adverse witnesses; and (5) the Court did not find it necessary to hold that minimum due process—such as notice, opportunity for response, and statement of reasons for action by prison officials—was necessary where inmates were deprived of privileges.

SIGNIFICANCE OF THE CASE:

The Supreme Court refused to apply the broad standards of due process available to a defendant in a criminal trial, to an inmate in a penitentiary facing disciplinary proceedings.

Within most traditional prisons, the pressures that prison officials apply have been shown to increase the rapid growth and development of an inmate subculture. Such prison subcultures present an interesting view of human behavior under conditions of enforced control and confinement.

The most obvious manifestation of these subcultures is the formation of *inmate groups*. These groups are fostered by the stresses and deprivations associated with imprisonment. Since inmates spend extensive time together under the circumscribed environment of regimentation and confinement, they are drawn together on the basis of similar experiences which develop into common perceptions and interests. These prisoner groups provide meaningful rewards to their members since they offer protection from the actions of the prison officials and other inmates. The group, in turn, exerts influence over its members as well as restraining nonmembers. The leader's knowledge of prison life is used to manipulate official policies and custodial personnel so that they can be used for the benefit of the group. The "old con" instructs the new inmate. Through membership, the individual inmate gains access to special privileges and "grapevine" communication, which is particularly important when officials restrict communication. In return for conforming to the demands of the inmate group, the inmate gains satisfaction from membership among persons who understand him, and he enjoys the greater physical security which the group provides.

Certain mechanisms maintain the inmate groups. Newcomers are screened for membership qualifications, and once accepted, they are taught certain values and attitudes which have been transmitted through generations of prisoners. In addition, a novice is taught certain argot or slang expressions which are part of the inmate subculture. This argot permits the inmate to classify his perceptions of others into some sort of role framework. In the free world, we speak of Mr. Smith, the attorney, or of Mr. White, the engineer. Thus, some role-sets develop, according to the occupation of the individual. In prison, almost everybody is just another "con"; in order to differentiate and identify individuals by role-sets, such expressions as a "real man," "fag," "wolf," or "ball buster" are applied. Thus, the newcomer learns that his fellow inmates are as varied as people in the outside world. Some are okay; others are dangerous and should be avoided. Group ties are supported by sanctions ranging from gossip and ostracism to violence. Inmate commitment to these groups is encouraged by the basic split between officials and inmates, the emphasis on custody, and the inmate's hostility against officials.[21]

In order for an individual to become a member of an inmate group, the novice must first be accepted for membership and then must be willing to accommodate himself to the values and customs of the inmate group. Clemmer calls this the process of "prisonization," which is the taking on by the inmate "in a greater or less degree, the folkways, mores, customs, and general culture of the penitentiary." The newcomer adapts to the life of the prison, accepting the humble role of prisoner, new habits of eating and sleeping, and a new language. He makes the values of the inmate group his own.[22]

Sykes and Messinger have examined the values and general culture that prisoners within custodial-oriented institutions adopt as a part of the inmate society. They refer to these values as the "inmate social code," which is similar to Clemmer's idea of prisonization. This social code admonishes inmates to:

1. Not interfere with other inmate's interests

2. Never rat on another con to the prison officials

3. Don't be nosy; don't have a loose lip; keep off a man's back

4. Be loyal to your class—the cons

5. Don't exploit other inmates. This means breaking your word, selling favors, being a racketeer or welshing on debts

6. Play it cool—do your own time

7. Don't be a sucker—guards are hacks or screws and aren't to be trusted

8. Be tough—don't suck around; don't whine or cop out.[23]

A number of researchers have examined how inmates become socialized to the values of the inmate subculture over time. Wheeler set about to see the degree to which prisoners identified with the values of the institutional staff as compared with the values of the inmate code. He found that the period of time a prisoner spends inside the institution affects the way he identifies with the values of the staff or the values of other inmates. For the first six months of incarceration, the attitudes and values of the inmates are more similar to those of the prison staff. After six months of imprisonment, the inmate begins to identify more and more with the other inmates and the prison social code. When it comes near the time for his release from prison (less than six months to serve), the inmate becomes more accepting once again of staff values and influence.[24]

Another study of prisoners in a maximum-security institution, conducted by Garabedian, confirmed Wheeler's findings and found that inmates in the early phases are twice as likely to conform to staff norms as inmates in the middle period. This trend suggests that there may be a steady absorption of the prison culture similar to the process of prisonization, but that this process is reversed as the inmate comes to the end of his prison career.[25]

The Collaborative Model

In recent years, prison administration has undergone some significant changes. Increased emphasis is being placed upon the development of a collaborative model that offsets the negative consequences of the authoritarian programming that exists in the traditional model. The collaborative model maintains that inmate rehabilitation and reintegration can be better accomplished through closer interpersonal relationships between inmates and the institutional staff and through the use of the full range of community resources.

This model stresses the need to reduce mass treatment and depersonalization. A number of prisons have implemented certain policies in this regard. Under certain circumstances, inmates are allowed to express their individuality by wearing civilian attire rather than the traditional prison garb. Some freedom is also permitted in hair styles or the growth of a beard, sideburns, or mustache. The old policy of requiring inmates to march to the dining hall and to sit in silence on one side of long, narrow tables has given way to the use of small, scattered, informal dining rooms, where the inmates sit around a conventional table and are able to converse with each other.

Greater emphasis is placed on decreasing the size of residential units. In medium- and minimum-security institutions, many states are constructing small dormitories or individual rooms. In fact, in spite of the cost, some institutions are being constructed so that it is physically impossible to house a second person in the room. Hygiene facilities, such as toilets, washrooms, and showers, are being partitioned for greater privacy.

One of the most important and imaginative features of the collaborative model is its emphasis upon a coordinative endeavor to achieve inmate rehabilitation.[26] One such promising program is the *integrated treatment team concept*. This arrangement may prove to be the single most meaningful contribution of the collaborative approach. In the traditional model, custodial personnel were often suspicious of treatment personnel and vice versa; inmates were often distrustful of both and would play one off against the other.

Although line personnel were in much more frequent contact with inmates than were members of the treatment staff, they were often downgraded by the treatment personnel for their preoccupation with security rather than treatment. By the same token, the treatment staff was often criticized by custodial people for not understanding the necessity for security and for being "bleeding hearts."

The integrated treatment team approach recognizes that for purposes of rehabilitation, certain conditions and attitudes must prevail. It is based on the belief that:

1. Effective communications must exist between treatment and custodial personnel and between these groups and the inmates.

2. Custodial personnel have a very important role to play in treatment and rehabilitation because of their daily contact with inmates.

3. The experience of custodial people can be of importance to the rehabilitative objectives of the treatment staff.

4. Treatment personnel can be of assistance to the custodial force in helping them to recognize certain behavioral manifestations of inmates and to diagnose and deal with inmate problems.

5. Any program of meaningful change must involve the inmate in the program.

This development is in sharp contrast with the classification and counseling practices that usually prevail in traditional institutions. In these, a single classification committee, presided over by senior custodial personnel, is concerned primarily with security classification of inmates and their work assignments. Caseworkers present information regarding an inmate to this committee and make recommendations for educational and vocational training and work assignments. Rarely are members of the custodial force consulted, nor is the inmate significantly involved. Consequently, the custodial staff feel no obligation to participate in the inmate's program and to oversee his or her progress. The social workers usually have so many prisoners to counsel that counseling sessions are nothing more than a few minutes' discussion with the inmate. The social workers have no idea of how well inmates are doing because they lack contact with the custodial personnel assigned to the cell block or work area. Only in serious disciplinary cases is the caseworker even aware of any problems that the inmate might be having; by the time the case becomes serious, what might have been prevented has already occurred. By the same token, the inmate, who is unable to receive help from the infrequent counseling sessions with the caseworker and is ignored by custodial personnel, turns to fellow inmates for support.

The collaborative model and communications. As might be imagined, the collaborative model has contributed to the growth of communication among treatment staff, custodial personnel, and the inmates themselves. Custodial personnel, in most instances, have found that inmate morale and cooperation are more directly related to the manner in which inmates are treated than to how strictly discipline, security, and other control measures are imposed. This should come as no surprise. Inmates who have provided some meaningful input into the decisions made about them are more likely to react favorably to their particular programs and be more interested in proving that their ideas are correct than are inmates who are given little or no opportunity to express themselves.

Inmate expression is very important to the concept of the collaborative model, and therefore group counseling is used extensively to foster communication. Group counseling sessions, involving treatment and custodial people and inmates, are held periodically. Although most of these sessions center on the concerns of the inmate, they provide the treatment and custodial personnel the opportunity to understand the range of problems and attitudes associated with prison life and to express themselves and explain their actions to the inmates as well.

In these counseling sessions, a primarily nondirective method is employed by both treatment and custodial staff. The custodial staff is trained by counseling specialists in how best to develop their own counseling techniques. Many of these sessions are quite frank and open. Although a number of the inmates often use these sessions to blame the police, the correctional personnel, or others for their problems, they do provide the custodial and treatment personnel some insight into who might be potential troublemakers and they give inmates a chance to express their feelings. Without these sessions, the institutional personnel might never know who these individuals are and how to deal with their negative attitudes. Further, without the opportunities for mutual discussion, an inmate is likely to express his negative attitudes in disruptive behavior within the institution, which heightens tension and could conceivably lead to serious problems of disorder within the prison.

The collaborative model and participatory decision making. Another significant feature of the collaborative model is the utilization of inmate representatives in the institutional policy-making process. This inmate representation has two purposes:

1. To enable inmates to have some advisory input into the management policies and decisions of the institution.
2. To assist the administration in the actual day-to-day management of the institution by offering alternative mechanisms to solve inmate grievances and to improve discipline.[27]

The idea of inmate councils or a form of inmate self-government is not new. In the 1860s, the Detroit House of Correction, under the leadership of its director, Zebulon Brockway, established a policy whereby selected prisoners were assigned to custodial and monotorial duties.[28] In 1888, the warden of the Michigan State Prison in Jackson formed the Mutual Aid League of Michigan in which he appointed nine prisoners to serve as an advisory board for the purpose of preserving "good order."[29] The individual most responsible for the development of inmate governance was Thomas M. Osborne, who, beginning in the first quarter of the present century, established inmate governments at the Auburn and Sing Sing prisons in New York and at the naval prison at Portsmouth, New Hampshire. Inmate governance councils based on the system developed by Osborne, were then adopted by a number of other prisons in the eastern United States.

Inmate governance councils generally have certain features in common. Inmate representatives are chosen by the inmates themselves. These representatives then meet at periodic intervals with institutional representatives to discuss rules and regulations that guide the policies of the institutional staff in their handling of the prison population. This affords the inmates some input into the regulatory process. In some cases, these inmate councils serve as adjudicatory boards to handle inmate grievances and discipline. For example, an inmate court can be established to determine appropriate disciplinary measures for the violation of certain regulations by inmates. Instead of the prison administration unilaterally deciding what disciplinary action to impose, the matter is turned over to the inmate council for disposition.

Inmate governance councils can also keep the prison administration aware of certain grievance areas that threaten the stability of the institution. The problems associated with racism are a particularly sensitive area within many prisons today. One of the major difficulties in combating this phenomenon is the absence of dialogue between prison staff and inmate groups. Without this dialogue, attitudes are often expressed in aggression and violence, inmate strikes, and a further polarization between inmate groups as well as between inmates and prison officials. The importance of opening up channels of communication through inmate participation in decision making can be seen by the following report of the South Carolina Department of Corrections:

> One way in which to head off confrontation is the use of the concept of maximum feasible participation. This term means little more than the notion that those who are allowed a voice in the rule-making process are more likely to obey such rules. It does not mean that the prisons would be run by a town meeting of the cell blocks or even that there would be any real power given to inmates to control the prisons. All that is implied by the notion is that at some point along the line, the inmate (either individually or through a representative) is allowed to make a meaningful input into the decision-making process that surrounds him with rules. One means of accomplishing this goal would be the establishment of an inmate council with elected representatives. Such a council should be able to present questions to the administration concerning various rules and practices of the institution and receive a straightforward answer. The inmate council would then be able to accept the explanation or suggest alternatives for the consideration of the administrators. Through a series of long-range dialogues between inmates and administrators, many of the problems which plague our prisons could be worked out.[30]

It must be pointed out that shared decision making through the development of inmate councils has not enjoyed a great deal of success in the past. Typically, a number of problems have arisen. First, correctional officials have been very reluctant to share any of their prerogatives with inmates. This has led to situations where inmate councils have little legitimacy with the prison officials and, as a result, even less legitimacy with the inmate population. Thus, rather than advising on problems that are meaningfully connected with the actual management of the institution, the inmates are often given less sensitive tasks, such as organizing inmate recreation and cultural activities, athletic contests, talent shows, and arts and crafts projects.

Much of the opposition that prison officials have towards these shared decision-making programs stem from past negative experiences. Sometimes, inmate cliques have controlled elections to councils or have put pressures on those elected to reduce their orientation to staff objectives. Often these advisory groups are oriented primarily to articulating and exaggerating inmate complaints and presenting the prison officials with their demands without addressing the merits of the complaints objectively. In some instances, inmate council members have used their position on the council to extort special considerations from other inmates. In a few institutions where these councils do exist in any meaningful way, the trend in recent years has been to actively engage them in important areas of mutual concern such as food service, housekeeping, and safety, but retain key management decision making by prison officials.

MEN IN PRISON

In 1974 the U.S. Bureau of the Census conducted a national survey of inmates in state correctional institutions for LEAA. Although now several years old, the survey still provides the most recent and comprehensive data on adult and youthful (but not juvenile) male offenders. Data in the survey were gathered from a cross-section of inmates in state institutions, and the complete survey contains extensive facts on the social and economic characteristics, criminal and correctional background, adjudication and prison experience of the interviewed prisoners.

Figure 14-2 is based on the findings of the survey. It represents only a small percentage of the total amount of information contained in the survey, however.

Age: Young; 60% were under 30; 23% between the ages 30 to 39.

Ethnic: 51% were white; 47% were black; 2% of other ethnic groups.

Education: 26% had finished eight years or less of grade school; 35% completed 1 to 3 years of high school; 28% finished high school; 8% has been in college 1 to 3 years; and 1% had finished 4 or more years of college.

Marital Status: At time of incarceration, 48% were single; 24% were married; 8% were separated; 17% were divorced.

Juvenile Sentence Record: 67% had no record of sentence for offenses as juveniles.

Work: 68% were employed in the month prior to arrest.

Offense: 23% for robbery; 18% for homicide; 18% for burglary; 6% for larceny; 6% for minor drug offense; 5% for forcible rape; 4% for major drug offenses; 4% for forgery, fraud, embezzlement; 3% for aggravated assault; 2% for motor vehicle theft.

Length of Sentence (Maximum): 2% for less than 1 year; 24% for 1 to 5 years; 25% for 5 to 10 years; 29% for 10 to 21 years; 8% for 21 or more years; 12% for life.

Source: Law Enforcement Assistance Administration, *Survey of Inmates of State Correctional Facilities, 1974* (Washington, D.C.: U.S. Government Printing Office, 1975).

FIGURE 14-2 A Composite Profile of the Typical Incarcerated Adult Male Offender

WOMEN IN PRISON

Until recently, the problems of female offenders have been largely ignored because women comprised a very small percentage of the total adult offender population. As the crime rate among women grew substantially during the past decade, the housing and treatment of female adult offenders has assumed greater importance. In order to understand the full extent of the problem, the federal government launched a large-scale national study of women's correctional programs and released its report, *National Study of Women's Correctional Programs,* in 1977.[31] Much of the following discussion is based on that research effort.

Although women in prison have always presented special problems, such problems were generally ignored both in terms of the women inmates themselves and the institutions that housed them. Prison research invariably focused on the male inmate population and male institutions. In recent years a change is noticeable, largely because of a growing public awareness of the changing role of women in society. The women's movement has helped to

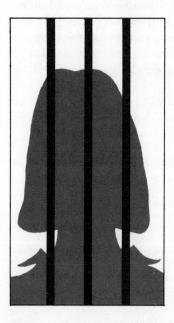

Age: Young; two-thirds were under 30 and the median age of sentenced felons was 27.

Ethnic: 50% of the incarcerated women were black; Indians were also overrepresented.

Education: Generally less educated than other women. Educational level was significantly related to ethnic group. Whites and Indians were better educated, followed by blacks, with Hispanics notably behind the other groups.

Marital Status: At time of incarceration, 27% were single, 19% were nonmarried but living with a man, 20% were married, 28% were separated or divorced, and 7% were widowed.

Children: 73% had borne children; and 56% of the women had dependent children living at home prior to incarceration. The average number of children per inmate mother was 2.48.

Childhood: 50% came from two-parent homes; 31% lived with mother only; 3% with father only; and 4% lived with nonrelatives.

Work: Almost all of the women had worked at some time in their lives; 40% had worked in the two months prior to incarceration.

Offense: Misdemeanants: 41% for property crimes (shoplifting, forgery, fraud); 20% for drug offenses; and 11% for violent crimes (usually assault, battery, or armed robbery). Felons: 43% for violent crimes (murder, armed robbery); 29% for property crimes (forgery, fraud, larceny); 22% for drug offenses.

Offense History: Nearly one-third of the women had been arrested for the first time at age 17 or younger. Another 49% were first arrested between ages 18 and 24. Almost one-third of the women had spent time in juvenile institutions.

Property offenders were most often recidivists; murderers were most likely to be first offenders. The women with the most extensive involvement with criminal justice systems were the habitual offenders—prostitutes, drug offenders, and petty thieves.

Source: Law Enforcement Assistance Administration, *National Study of Women's Correctional Programs* (Washington, D.C.: U.S. Government Printing Office, June 1977), pp. xvii–xx.

FIGURE 14-3 A Composite Profile of the Typical Incarcerated Adult Female Offender

focus attention on the way women are treated by the criminal justice system, and most certainly by the correctional component of that system.[32]

The same problems that have traditionally plagued male inmates and prisons have been even more of a problem with the female offenders. Many of the problems that deal with female offenders are a result of our traditional view of women and their roles in society. For example, the history of women's programs shows an early shift from punishment to treatment, when in the late nineteenth century, social reformers urged the establishment of separate institutions for women. These new prisons were called reformatories and were intended to help women learn to accept appropriate female role behavior.[33]

Research into the characteristics of women prisoners indicate that severe pathological problems are often present. In many cases, their lives have been based on rejection and exploitation by men and the inability to form lasting positive relationships. Unlike the male role of the exploiter, they are exploited.[34] Typically, the female prisoner has a very negative self-image which is often reinforced by incarceration and being labeled as an ex-con. If they are mothers, the problem of self-image is further compounded by the feeling of having failed in this role. Under such circumstances, the problems of rehabilitation are often much more difficult to deal with than for male prisoners.[35] Burkhardt claims that the life experiences of the female inmate population tend to produce so much hostile behavior that up to 80 percent of women in prisons receive Thorazine, Librium, or other drugs on a daily basis to keep them "manageable."[36]

Traditionally, effective rehabilitative programs in women's prisons have been nonexistent. If resources for such rehabilitation as vocational training, education, and related programs have been conspicuously absent in men's institutions, women's institutions have fared even worse. About one-third of the women in institutions are enrolled in some type of vocational or academic program. However, these vocational "rehabilitative" programs are often geared to the stereotyped female tasks such as sewing, food service, and laundry. Burkhardt reports that only a handful of women prisoners throughout the country are trained to be such things as dental assistants, although none receive official credentials. Similarly, although a few learn cosmetology, as convicted felons they cannot obtain licenses in many states.[37]

In the 1977 federal survey, administrators of women's institutions were asked their views concerning the special needs of women prisoners. Their comments indicate the range and the depth of the problem:

- The inmate's social role in society is homemaking; she needs a homelike setting, even in prison (this is why women inmates turn to homosexuality); she needs stronger ties to family and better relationships with her children; she needs to learn how to care for her children.

- Being "head of a household" is a big problem for many women inmates.

- Women inmates are unmotivated; they need more counseling and positive social involvement; they need to acquire problem-solving skills; women inmates have low self-esteem because of societal stigmas.

- Women have difficulty dealing with institutionalization.

- Women inmates need to learn to be self-sufficient.

- They seek more medical help more often.
- The women have few skills; they have employability problems.[38]

Perhaps, like so many other aspects of the criminal justice system, we will witness some long needed improvements in the years ahead. Along with adult male and juvenile institutions in general, a great many efforts must be devoted to dealing with the institutionalized female offender.

CORRECTIONAL REFORM

The National Advisory Commission on Criminal Justice Standards and Goals identifies six problems that make correctional reform difficult to achieve:

1. Fragmentation of corrections
2. Overuse of corrections
3. Overemphasis on custody
4. Ambivalence of the community
5. Lack of financial support
6. Lack of knowledge base for planning.[39]

Fragmentation of Corrections

Corrections, like all other agencies of criminal justice, is structured and administered on the concept of political federalism in which the maintenance of correctional institutions and programs is divided among jurisdictions at the federal, state, county, and municipal levels of government. This fragmentation has produced semiautonomous responsibility for dealing with convicted offenders among a multiplicity of programs and jurisdictions. The result has been the poor utilization of resources, inequities in financial support for program improvement, lack of effective supervisory control, duplication and waste in institutional construction and program implementation, and the influence of local politics in the administration of these programs and facilities.

In the past, there may have been a need to maintain local correctional facilities because of the problems associated with inadequate transportation and communication networks, but this is certainly no longer the case. Today, the trend in modern penological thinking is toward the consolidated administrative control of all correctional programs and institutions in the state.

There are a number of sound arguments for consolidation. In the first place, the taxing resources of states have a number of advantages not available to local or county governments. Thus, program support for the purchase of required resources for a statewide correctional system would be better. Consolidation would also provide for a more equitable distribution of taxes required to support correctional institutions. Statewide systems could also develop standardized policies and procedures that would ensure higher standards of program performance and efficiency.

A centralized administrative authority would also have other positive benefits. For example, a large agency would have the political leverage to compete better for scarce appropriations. Career opportunities, training, salaries, and a host of other personnel considerations would conceivably also improve.

Last, with the present trend of corrections toward community-based programs and specialized institutions tailored to the particular needs of offenders, it is almost mandatory that the states assume responsibility, for local and county governments are not capable of providing such facilities and programs.

Whether consolidation can ever become a reality is open to some doubt. The political partisanship and desire for local autonomy that has always characterized American political institutions and interests must be overcome. It has been a major obstacle to correctional reform in the past, and a significant contributor to the failure of our correctional programs to be more effective. Until this impediment to change can be overcome, we will continue to be frustrated in our attempts at more meaningful correctional strategies.

Overuse of Corrections

Society's response to criminal behavior has been based on the concepts of punishment as a deterrent and punishment for retribution. From the inception of American corrections, we have increasingly turned to the law and the use of penal institutions as a means of controling our urban society. Since the beginning of the 1970s, an ever-growing number of offenders are being imprisoned. Table 14-1 shows the growth in numbers of prisoners in state and federal institutions from 1971–1975, and these figures are not simply a reflection of population increases. In 1971, the incarceration rate was 96.4 per 100,000 population; by 1975, the number had increased to 113.[40] What seems to underlie this growth in incarceration is an increasingly "get tough" attitude that is being expressed by a sizable segment of the American population. Such attitudes are then carried over into laws enacted by our legislative bodies and sentences imposed by our judges.

Yet, punishment by means of incarceration, both as a deterrent and as a form of retribution, does not appear to have been very effective. The criminal laws still are violated with impunity. Institutionalization of offenders seems generally to have failed in terms of deterrence as indicated by the high percentage of offenders who, upon release, commit new crimes and are returned to prison.

Perhaps in the past when there were no alternatives available for dealing with the offender, there was some justification for incarcerating law breakers,

TABLE 14-1

Prisoners in State and Federal Institutions for the Years 1971, 1973, and 1975

YEAR	MALE	FEMALE	TOTAL
1971	191,732	6,329	198,061
1973	197,527	6,684	204,211
1975	233,900	8,850	242,750
Increase (%) 1971–1975	+22	+40	+23

Source: Law Enforcement Assistance Administration, *Sourcebook on Criminal Justice Statistics–1977* (Washington, D.C.: U.S. Government Printing Office, February 1978).

at least on the grounds of protecting society. Although some classes of offenders do pose a real threat to society if they are allowed their freedom, a great many inmates could be handled much more meaningfully outside the walls of our traditional prisons in such institutions as community-based facilities. Many progressive prison administrators are now saying that our correctional systems should exist primarily to deal with those offenders who can be helped only by intensive institutional care and supervision and with those individuals whose freedom is a clear threat to the safety of society.[41] This argument calls for greater consideration of alternative methods of dealing with offenders. As long as we continue to invoke laws that are made to be broken and indiscriminately sentence offenders to our penal institutions, we saddle our correctional systems with an impossible task.

Overemphasis on Custody

The security of any facility is determined by the most dangerous inmate in the prison population. Although an institution may have only a few such individuals, security precautions must be guided by the possible actions of these few. Because of the public concern with prison escapes, wardens and other administrators risk their careers if they manage institutions where such occurrences are frequent. Under these circumstances, the primary concern expressed by prison administrators for maintaining tight security is quite understandable.

However, this emphasis on security works against the development of effective treatment programs within institutions. For example, the massive structures that for years dominated prison design were completely unsuitable for vocational programs, recreational facilities, and more diversified prison industries programs. Security in an institution that has treatment programs is more difficult to maintain because of the movement of inmates within the institution as they attend classes, counseling sessions, and vocational training programs.

This overemphasis on custody can also be seen in the proliferation of jails, juvenile detention homes, and large institutions for adult and juvenile offenders. The National Advisory Commission commented on the results of years of emphasis on custody in prison design and programming:

> The mega-institution, holding more than a thousand adult inmates, has been built in larger number and variety in this country than anywhere else in the world. Large institutions for young offenders have also proliferated here. In such surroundings, inmates become faceless people, living out routine and meaningless lives. And, where institutions are racially skewed and filled with a disproportionate number of ill-educated and vocationally inept persons, they magnify tensions already existing in our society.[42]

Lack of Financial Support

Considering the number of inmates who must be supervised and the facilities that must be maintained, the corrections component, including probation and parole, does not receive a large share of the revenues that support the operations of the criminal justice system. Table 14-2 indicates the percentages of total criminal justice expenditure by function and level of government for 1974.

Although the courts and legal services receive less money for their functions than do corrections, these agencies are not responsible for the maintenance of facilities and for the care of the nearly 1.9 million individuals who were under some form of correctional control in 1974.[43] In an effort to provide more funds for correctional activities, laws passed in 1973 require that at least 20 percent of the federal funds disbursed by the Law Enforcement Assistance Administration to the states to aid crime control be allocated specifically to corrections. This seems to have had some effect. Whereas in 1969 corrections received only 19.9 percent of all criminal justice expenditures, by 1974 this percentage had increased to 22.2 percent.

Attitude of the Community

Because large correctional institutions often provide substantial numbers of jobs for local residents, nearby communities often tolerate the presence of penal institutions. However, this tolerance is usually a conditional one. It exists as long as the inmates are locked up and out of sight; the surrounding communities feel reasonably safe, provided the convicts are maintained behind massive walls and elaborate security precautions exist to prevent escapes. When these conditions don't exist, the neighboring communities are far less likely to accept a penal institution on their doorstep. In the past few years, as correctional institutions and programs have tried to start alternative community-based programs, strong opposition has come from neighborhood citizen groups who feel that such programs-without-walls jeopardize their security.

Part of the blame for such attitudes must rest with prison administrators of the past, who were only too quick to isolate corrections from the general public by high walls and locked doors. Unfortunately, they failed to realize that the antidote to intolerance of convicted offenders is the active involvement of wide segments of the community in support of correctional processes.

TABLE 14-2
Percentage of Total Criminal Justice Expenditure by Function and Level of Government (1974)

LEVEL OF GOVERNMENT[a]	POLICE	JUDICIAL	LEGAL SERVICES, PROSECUTION, AND INDIGENT DEFENSE	CORRECTIONAL	TOTAL
Federal	8.4	0.9	1.4	1.4	12.1
State	8.9	3.0	1.6	12.4	25.9
Local	21.2	8.4	4.0	8.4	62.0
Total percentage	58.5	12.3	7.0	22.2	100.0

[a]Includes direct expenditure only and does not include the small miscellaneous category of "other criminal justice expenditure."
Source: Law Enforcement Assistance Administration, *Sourcebook of Criminal Justice Statistics, 1976* (Washington, D.C.: U.S. Government Printing Office, February 1977), p. 44.

Lack of Knowledge Base for Planning

One of the major obstacles to correctional reform lies in our failure to develop sound knowledge of the problem based on thorough research activities. Such data would give us the ability to determine which correctional practices are effective with which types of offenders.

We need to know much more about crime, how to prevent it, and how to treat individuals who engage in criminal behavior. Without such information, the whole policy formulation process breaks down. Consequently, administrators rely on experience or intuitive hunches as a basis for planning. When we consider the possible consequences of such seat-of-the-pants decision making, it becomes very apparent why traditional correctional programs can boast of very little success.

CURRENT STATUS OF CORRECTIONS

Although corrections have made definite progress in recent years, hard questions are being raised as to how meaningful this progress has really been. A great deal of concern is being expressed over whether prisons, even with the employment of innovative programs, will ever succeed in reforming a significant number of inmates. Many knowledgeable penologists feel that because of the very nature of the environment within prisons, even the best devised programs can, at best, achieve only a limited success by almost any standard.

Today the situation is somewhat paradoxical. On the one hand, we are developing more and better programs and personnel to operate them; on the other hand, problems within prisons are also accelerating. In the face of mounting fiscal problems, states are unable to allocate the necessary resources to operate correctional systems; at the same time, more and more offenders are being sentenced to institutions that are often unable to accommodate them. With greater use of probation and other diversionary measures, our prison populations are increasingly becoming populated with the more hardened and intractable offender. Racial problems, drugs, violence, and a multitude of other concerns face prison managers. Society continues to subsidize this failure in ever more costly ways. It has been estimated that it costs the taxpayers between $6,000 and $7,000 annually to keep an unmarried man in prison and approximately $11,000 to imprison a married man when we include the cost of public welfare support which goes to his family during his absence.[44] When we measure our "product" by theses cost factors, it is obvious that we should seriously examine some possible alternative solutions.

One final comment should be made. This need for more meaningful alternatives is not meant to imply, as some would recommend, that we abolish prisons completely—such suggestions are ludicrous. A certain percentage of offenders pose a threat to the safety of society and must be imprisoned. However, there are many prisoners in our penal institutions today who would be more effectively dealt with by means other than imprisonment. Assuming these prisoners can be identified, the question then becomes: Are we, as a society, more interested in punishment or do we really want to improve the chances of having an offender lead a noncriminal life? The next chapter examines some new correctional programs that are attempting to accomplish that goal.

SUMMARY

The corrections component of the criminal justice system in the United States is a checkerboard affair of various programs, philosophies, and institutions. Overall, it suffers from a number of weaknesses: It is overly fragmented; it has been overused; it has traditionally emphasized custody; and it suffers from citizen apathy, lack of financial support and lack of an effective means to evaluate its work.

Prison programming generally includes vocational and academic training, health programs, libraries, recreational programs, prison industries, and some form of classification procedure. Prisons may be classified by the degree of security they provide and by their program emphasis. While the traditional model emphasizes an authoritarian environment, the collaborative model emphasizes integrating treatment and custodial personnel in a team approach that includes the inmate in the operations of the institution and in his own program.

In recent years, there has been a sharp increase in the number of female inmates. With the lack of resources, program efforts, and the particularly difficult task of dealing effectively with the unique problems of female offenders, corrections has another burden added to its already troublesome task.

REVIEW QUESTIONS

1. What are the chief characteristics of the following types of institutions and what kinds of inmates are housed in each?
   a. Maximum security
   b. Medium security
   c. Minimum security
   d. Prison camps
   e. Special institutions

2. What is the primary purpose of the state department of corrections?

3. Draw an organization chart for an adult male institution of less than 2,000 inmates.

4. Describe the duties of each of the following key prison personnel.
   a. Correctional officer
   b. Psychiatrist
   c. Psychologist
   d. Counselor

5. What is the purpose of a diagnostic center in a state correctional system?

6. Briefly explain the characteristics of the traditional model in administering a prison facility.

7. Briefly explain the characteristics of the collaborative model in administering an institution.

8. Identify and briefly describe six problem areas that are hindering correctional reform.

DISCUSSION QUESTIONS

1. Are there valid reasons for having five separate categories of prison institutions? Why or why not?

2. Compare and contrast the traditional and collaborative models of prison administration. Why is the collaborative model more appropriate from the viewpoint of rehabilitation?

3. What similarities and dissimilarities are evident in the composite profiles of male and female prisoners?

SUGGESTED ADDITIONAL READINGS

Clark, Ramsey. "Prisons: Factories of Crime." In David M. Petersen and Charles W. Thomas, ed. *Corrections: Problems and Prospects.* Englewood Cliffs, N.J.: Prentice-Hall, 1975.

Cohn, Alvin W. "Contemporary Correctional Practice: Science or Art?" *Federal Probation* 34 (September 1970).

Dinitz, Simon, and Walter C. Reckless, ed. *Critical Issues in the Study of Crime.* Boston: Little, Brown, 1968.

Geis, Golbety. "Recruitment and Rentention of Correctional Personnel." *Crime and Delinquency* 12 (July 1966).

Gill, Howard B. "A New Prison Discipline." *Federal Probation* 34 (June 1970).

Glaser, Daniel. "Politicization of Prisoners: A New Challenge to American Penology." *American Journal of Correction* 33 (November–December, 1971): 6–9.

Goldfarb, Ronald, and Linda Singer. "Disaster Road: The American Prison System." *Intellectual Digest* 2 (December 1971).

Jarvis, D.C. *Institutional Treatment of the Offender.* New York: McGraw-Hill, 1978.

Martlin, M., ed. "Corrections in the United States." *Crime and Delinquency* (January 1967).

Megathlin, William L., and Sherman R. Day. "The Line Staff as Agents of Control and Change." *American Journal of Corrections* 34 (May–June, 1972).

National Council on Crime and Delinquency. *Coordinating California Corrections: Institutions.* Sacramento, Calif.: NCCD, July 1971.

Piven, Herman, and Abraham Alcabes. *The Crises of Qualified Manpower for Criminal Justice: An Analytic Assessment with Guidelines for New Policy.* Vol. 1. Washington, D.C.: U.S. Government Printing Office, 1969.

Teeters, Negley K. "State of Prisons in the United States: 1870–1970." *Federal Probation* 33 (December 1969).

Toch, Hans. *Living in Prisons—The Ecology of Survival.* New York: Free Press, 1977.

NOTES

1. President's Commission on Law Enforcement and Administration of Justice, *Task Force Report: Correction* (Washington, D.C.: U.S. Government Printing Office, 1967), p. 51.

2. Louis P. Carney, *Introduction to Correctional Science* (New York: McGraw-Hill, 1974), p. 128.

3. Harry E. Allen and Clifford E. Simonsen, *Corrections in America,* 2nd ed. (Encino, Calif.: Glencoe, 1978), p. 419.

4. Elmer H. Johnson, *Crime, Correction and Society,* 3rd ed. (Homewood, Ill.: Dorsey, 1974), p. 440.

5. Ibid., pp. 442–443.

6. Donald Clemmer, "Use of Supervisory Custodial Personnel as Counselors: An Expedient," *Federal Probation* 20 (December 1956): 36–42.

7. Johnson, *Crime, Correction and Society,* p. 504.

8. Ibid.

9. Henry Burns, Jr., *Corrections: Organization and Administration* (St. Paul, Minn.: West, 1975), p. 417.

10. Vernon Fox, *Introduction to Corrections* (Englewood Cliffs, N.J.: Prentice-Hall, 1972), p. 188.

11. Michigan Governor's Committee on Corrections, *Committee on Corrections Report* (Lansing, Mich.: 1972), p. 12.

12. Fox, *Introduction to Corrections,* p. 174.

13. Law Enforcement Assistance Administration, Health Related Services in Adult Institutions (Washington, D.C.: U.S. Government Printing Office, June 1976), p. 3.

14. *Gilmore v. Lynch,* 400 F.2d 228 (9th Cir. 1968) aff'd *Younger v. Gilmore,* 404 U.S. 15, 92 S. Ct. 250, 30 L. Ed. 2d 142 (1971).

15. Johnson, *Crime, Correction and Society,* p. 560.

16. Ibid.

17. Ibid., p. 562.

18. Walter C. Reckless, *The Crime Problem* (New York: Appleton-Century-Crofts, 1967), p. 705.

19. Ibid., p. 706.

20. Gresham M. Sykes, *A Society of Captives* (New York: Atheneum, 1970), p. 23.

21. George H. Grosser, "The Role of Informal Inmate Groups in Change of Values," *Children* 5 (January–February 1958): 26.

22. Donald Clemmer, *The Prison Community* (New York: Holt, Rinehart & Winston, 1958), pp. 298–300.

23. Gresham Sykes and Sheldon I. Messinger, "The Inmate Social Code," in Norman Johnston et al., eds., *The Sociology of Punishment and Correction* (New York: Wiley, 1970), pp. 401–408.

24. Stanton Wheeler, "Socialization in Correctional Communities," *American Sociological Review* 26 (October 1961): 699–700.

25. Peter G. Garabedian, "Social Roles and Processes of Socialization in the Prison Community," *Social Problems* 11 (Fall 1963): 145.

26. For example, see Robert B. Levinson and Roy E. Gerard, "Functional Units: A Different Correctional Approach," *Federal Probation* 37 (December 1973): 8–15.

27. Stanley Vroman, "Models of Inmate Goverance," *Corrections Digest* 2 (June 1975): 12.

28. Zebulon R. Brockway, *Fifty Years of Prison Service* (New York: Charities Publication Committee, 1912), pp. 96–97.

29. Harold M. Helfman, "Antecedents of Thomas Mott Osborne's 'Mutual Welfare League' in Michigan," *Journal of Criminal Law, Criminology and Police Science* 40 (January–February 1950): 597–600.

30. South Carolina Department of Corrections, *The Emerging Rights of the Confined* (Columbia, S.C.: 1972), p. 94.

31. Law Enforcement Assistance Administration, *National Study of Women's Correctional Programs* (Washington, D.C.: U.S. Government Printing Office, June 1977).

32. Ibid., pp. xxi–xxii; and Ann Grogan, "Women Locked Up: Feminist Perspectives and Alternatives," text of keynote address of Conference of Women in Prison, Denver, Colo., January 18, 1975.

33. See Rose Giallombardo, *The Seasonless World: A Study of a Women's Prison*, University Microfilms, Ann Arbor, Mich., Ph.D. dissertation, 1965, p. 103.

34. See Kathryn W. Burkhardt, *Women in Prison* (New York: Doubleday, 1973).

35. For example, see Dorie Klien, "The Etiology of Female Crime: A Review of the Literature," *Issues in Criminology* 8, no. 2 (Fall 1973): 3–30; Margery Velimesis, "Report on the Survey of 41 Pennsylvania County Court and Correctional Services for Women and Girl Offenders," 1969; and Helen Gibson, "Women's Prisons: Laboratories for Penal Reform," *Wisconsin Law Review* (1973).

36. Burkhardt, *Women in Prison.*

37. Ibid.

38. Law Enforcement Assistance Administration, *National Study of Women's Correctional Programs*, pp. 38–39.

39. National Advisory Commission on Criminal Justice Standards and Goals, *Corrections* (Washington, D.C.: U.S. Government Prinitng Office, 1973), pp. 10–14.

40. U.S. Department of Justice, *Prisoners in State and Federal Institutions, National Prisoner Statistics Bulletin* (Washington, D.C.: U.S. Government Printing Office, 1977), pp. 16–17.

41. See Michael S. Serrill, "Profile—Minnesota," *Corrections Magazine* 1, no. 3 (January–February 1975): 3–28.

42. National Advisory Commission, *Corrections,* p. 1.

43. Law Enforcement Assistance Administration, *Sourcebook of Criminal Justice Statistics —1976* (Washington, D.C.: U.S. Government Printing Office, February 1977).

44. N. C. Chamelin, V. B. Fox, and P. M. Whisenand, *Introduction to Criminal Justice* (Englewood, Cliffs, N.J.: Prentice-Hall, 1975), p. 396.

15
PAROLE AND
PROBATION

1. From what historical precedents has modern parole originated?
2. What are the objectives of parole?
3. Is there more than one set of guidelines in granting parole?
4. What factors does a parole board examine before granting parole to a prisoner?
5. How is the U.S. Parole Commission's salient-factor score used in determining eligibility for parole?
6. What are the roles that a parole officer plays?
7. What landmark legal cases have affected parole procedures?
8. Is probation different from parole? In what ways?
9. What are the duties of a probation officer and how does a person qualify for the job?

These are some of the questions this chapter will answer.

As auxiliary components of the criminal justice system, parole and probation authorities are responsible for the supervision of offenders who have been found guilty of a crime. In 1976 while there were only slightly over 450,000 adults and juveniles confined in state and local institutions, the number of state and local parolees and probationers under supervision was nearly 1.5 million.[1] Thus parole and probation services play an important role in the overall administration of criminal justice.

PAROLE

Parole is the conditional release of an individual from a correctional institution back to the community. The offender must abide by rules of conduct that are specified by the paroling authority and enforced by a parole officer. These rules are in effect until the expiration of the parolee's sentence. If the parolee breaks a rule, parole may be revoked and the offender will be returned to a correctional facility.

It is important to note that parole operates *after* the offender has served a period of post-trial incarceration.

Historical Background

The history of parole, like the history of corrections, reflects the changing philosophy of how society deals with the offender. The reader will recall that in the late eighteenth and early nineteenth centuries, the philosophy that guided the development of corrections shifted from punishment to reform. The idea became that if prisons were to be institutions that were to reform the offender, then there had to be a continuation of the reform efforts of the prison in the lives of those released. In this way parole developed as a means to assist in the reform and rehabilitation efforts that were begun in the prison and to help the inmate adjust to the conditions of the "free world" upon release.

There have been several precursors to modern parole. The first was called a *conditional pardon.* Under this system the English courts would recommend to the king a list of prisoners who would be transported to the English colonies under stays of execution. A stay of execution was granted if the offender agreed to go to the colonies in the service of the king for a prescribed period of years. Upon completion of this service the offender would be granted a conditional pardon.

Another forerunner of parole was the practice of *indentured service.* The Crown would give "property in the service" to the shipmaster who transported the prisoner to an English colony. Upon arriving at the colony, the shipmaster would then sell the prisoner's service to the highest bidder. At that moment the prisoner ceased technically to be a criminal and became an indentured servant to his or her new master for the period of the original sentence.

A third precursor was transportation to Australia and the *ticket-of-leave system.* Initially, prisoners transported to Australia were given conditional pardons by the Australian governor after satisfactorily serving their sentence.

These pardons were at first granted quite freely, but problems arose. The Crown then authorized that the governor could use tickets of leave with conditional pardons. In this situation the prisoner was given a conditional pardon and released on a ticket-of-leave license. The offender was required to refrain from further criminal acts, find legitimate employment, and avoid the company of notoriously bad characters. If he or she violated the conditions of the ticket of leave, the person was apprehended and recommitted to prison under the original sentence.[2]

A later extension of the ticket-of-leave system was developed by Sir Walter Crofton in Ireland. Under Crofton's system, a *supervised ticket-of-leave program* developed. Crofton created the position of inspector of released prisoners. The inspector found employment for prisoners and saw that they lived up to the conditions of their release. In addition, he required that they report to him at regular intervals, visit their homes every two weeks, and verify their employment. Because of the success of this system, England later abandoned its unsupervised ticket-of-leave system and adopted Crofton's program. Crofton's program would also influence American corrections.

Prison Reform in America and the Indeterminate Sentence

In addition to the direct influence of the Irish ticket-of-leave system, the development of parole in the United States was based on three basic concepts: (1) shortened imprisonment as a reward for good conduct; (2) the indeterminate sentence; and (3) supervision.[3] The idea of shortening the term of sentence gained statutory recognition in 1817 when New York passed the first good-time law. In 1869, Michigan adopted the first indeterminate-sentence law. However, it was in New York that the indeterminate sentence became a reality. Zebulon Brockway, first warden of New York's Elmira Reformatory, was familiar with ticket-of-leave policies (particularly Ireland's). He convinced New York officials that the length of an inmate's sentence should be flexible, depending on his conduct. He campaigned for the use of the indeterminate sentence for inmates sentenced to Elmira, and in 1876 New York passed the necessary authorizing legislation. Under the provisions of the indeterminate sentence, the offender was to be released at a time when his conduct demonstrated that he was ready to be returned to society. Since the offender was released before the expiration of his sentence, special provisions were made to provide him with community supervision, and parole became a reality. In this way, parole became an indispensable partner of the indeterminate sentence. Brockway's reforms, as practiced at Elmira, are credited with establishing the concept of parole in the United States.

At first, responsibility for supervising the paroled offender was assumed primarily by private reform groups. Later, a few states appointed agents to help released offenders obtain employment. But only in the first two decades of the twentieth century did the states finally adopt the idea of professionally trained public employees—parole officers—to carry out the task of supervision.

The Functions of Parole

Parole can be considered as an extension of the *rehabilitative (and now, rein-tegrative) program of the prison.* Although parole is often considered as a form of leniency by its critics, it is an extension of the rehabilitation begun in the prison that seeks to release the inmate at a time when he or she is most able to benefit by release and return to society to lead a law-abiding life. If prisons are, in fact, to be concerned with modifying criminal behavior so that the offender can eventually be reintegrated into society, parole is also supposed to provide the supervision and assistance that makes successful reintegration possible. Finally, parole is a means to protect society. By careful selection and community supervision, parole should afford an element of protection not available if the offender were simply released at the expiration of his or her sentence.

The Organization of State Paroling Authorities

The states vary somewhat in the way they organize their parole authority and the responsibilities the parole authority has. Most states also separate adult and juvenile parole authorities. Although many people believe that the adult paroling authority is responsible only for reviewing applications and granting or denying parole, this is not necessarily the case. In addition to these typical responsibilities, parole authorities often perform other functions as well. A study conducted by the National Council on Crime and Delinquency of adult parole authorities throughout the country discovered that some state parole boards were involved in other responsibilities such as:

Conducting clemency hearings

Commuting sentences

Appointment of parole supervisors

Administration of parole services

Granting of parole from local institutions

Granting or revoking "good time"

Supervision of probation services

Determining standards for "good time"

Granting of pardons[4]

Three Types of Adult Parole Authorities   Although states employ a variety of organizational arrangements for their adult paroling authorities, the National Advisory Commission on Criminal Justice Standards and Goals developed three classifications into which most adult paroling authorities can be grouped—the *institutional, independent,* and *consolidated* models.[5]

The institutional model is based on the idea that parole should be carefully linked with the correctional institution in which the offender is incarcerated. Behind this model is the theory that institutional staff members are in the best position to carefully judge the suitability of the inmate for parole and that the parole decision itself can be more appropriately coordinated with the overall institutional program devised for the particular offender.

Those who argue against this arrangement contend that institutional factors may play a major role in deciding whether or not the inmate should be paroled. For example, an institution faced with problems of overcrowding may tend to release individuals prematurely. Prison officials may also use the threat of not granting parole as a means to keep inmates in line and to enforce strict rules and regulations. Because of such abuses, some years ago reformers sought to remove decision-making authority from institutional officials. This reform movement was so effective that today the purely institutional model (for dealing with adult offenders) does not exist in any state.

The independent model arose when reformers advocated that independent parole boards should make the ultimate decision on granting parole. Although it may be argued that this model is more objective than the institutional model, it too suffers from a number of weaknesses. First, independent parole boards often do not understand the programs carried on by the correctional institution and the role parole plans play in the overall treatment plan once an individual is released. Independent boards are also criticized for relying too heavily on subjective and inappropriate considerations such as the feelings of the local police chief. Occasionally, these independent boards are tainted with scandals of political corruption, such as those that occurred a few years ago in Georgia in which it was alleged that members of the parole board were paid to award parole to certain inmates. Another frequent criticism is that members of independent parole boards are often appointed for strictly political reasons and lack the necessary training or experience in corrections.

This lack of knowledge about the correctional process and correctional programming may be the single most important argument against this type of organizational arrangement. With the increased use of release programs, half-way houses, and other community-based alternatives, overall programs must be linked very closely with institutional efforts for parole considerations. This requires that parole board members have a broad knowledge of corrections and develop a close working relationship with correctional institutions.

The third type is the consolidated model, which more and more states are now adopting. It combines the best features of the institutional and independent models while diminishing the negative features of both. This arrangement consolidates all state correctional programs within a state under a department of correctional services which is divided into institutional and field programs (parole services). For example, in 1974, Kansas established a department of corrections with one division responsible for facility and jail standards and another for parole. About 40 percent of the states have now adopted similar programs.[6] A few of these states provide that the director of corrections or a designated staff officer has the authority to sit on the parole board as a decision-making member.

Advocates of the consolidated model maintain that because the parole authority is actually a part of the correctional services system, there is a greater understanding of the overall correctional process. They claim that sensitivity to institutional programs seems more pronounced in consolidated systems than in autonomous ones. They also contend that the removal of parole decision making from the control of the correctional institution gives greater weight to a broader set of considerations, a number of which are outside direct institutional concerns.[7]

The primary organizational concerns of parole require that states support close coordination between parole decision makers and the increasingly complex set of programs now being developed in many correctional systems, while at the same time preserving the autonomy that permits parole boards to serve as checks on the overall system. At present, the consolidated authority seems to be the best means to accomplish this task.

The United States Parole Commission

In 1976, Congress passed the Parole Commission and Reorganization Act which created an independent agency within the Department of Justice called the United States Parole Commission. This new agency replaced the former U.S. Board of Parole that had existed since 1930. The commission is headed by a chairperson and eight commission members who are appointed by the president for 6-year terms. An examination of the federal system will provide us with an understanding of how a parole board system can work.

Responsibilities of the Commission Generally, the commission is responsible for making decisions in regards to release on parole; conditions of parole; termination of supervision; and revocation of parole.[8] Since federal penal institutions and federal parolees are scattered throughout the United States, the operations of the commission are conducted on a regional basis. In addition to the regional offices, there is a National Appeals Board, which is located in Washington, D.C. This board was established to permit federal prisoners to appeal a decision of any of the five regional commissioners. Unlike most state parole boards, the commissioners do not sit *en banc* to consider requests from federal prisoners for parole. Since federal institutions are scattered, parole requests are conducted by two hearing examiners who periodically visit federal institutions and hold parole hearings. During the hearing, the examiners discuss with the prisoner the prisoner's offense-severity rating and salient-factor score (to be described later), the offender's institutional conduct record, and any other matter that the panel may deem relevant. After the hearings, the examiners then submit their recommendation which is reviewed by the regional office.

Commission Proceedings The federal system permits the prisoner to be represented at this hearing by a person of his or her choice. The function of the prisoner's representative is to provide a statement at the conclusion of the interview and to provide such additional information as the examiner panel requests. Interested parties who oppose parole may select a representative to appear and speak in opposition to the granting of parole.

At the conclusion of the hearing, the panel informs the prisoner of its recommendation and, if the recommendation is for denial of parole, the reasons for such a recommendation. Later these reasons are provided in writing. Like all parole boards, the commission provides for what are called interim proceedings. If a prisoner is refused parole, he or she is scheduled for an automatic future hearing date to be reconsidered. In the case of the federal government, it is generally either 18 or 24 months depending upon the length of time remaining to be served on the offender's sentence.

Like state prisoners, federal prisoners have parole eligibility dates that designate the earliest date a prisoner can be considered for parole. For instance, federal prisoners are usually eligible for consideration after serving one-third of their sentence or after completing the court-imposed designated minimum sentence. In the case of a life sentence or a sentence of over 30 years, the inmate becomes eligible after serving a minimum of 10 years. The commission, however, is given greater latitude in the case of certain types of offenders. For instance, inmates who are sentenced as juvenile delinquents or youthful offenders, may be released at any time at the discretion of the commission. Similarly, prisoners who have been sentenced under the Narcotic Addict Rehabilitation Act may be released on parole at the discretion of the commission after completion of at least 6 months in treatment.

The right to a parole hearing is not automatic. Like state parole hearings, inmates must apply for a hearing when they become eligible. Although under no obligation to apply, if a prisoner does not want to apply for parole, he or she must knowingly and intelligently waive this right. If the prisoner waives this right, he or she may later apply for parole and have a hearing during the next visit that the hearing examiners make to the institution.

Normally, a prisoner who has been granted parole remains under community supervision until the sentence has expired. For instance, if a parolee is released after serving 4 years of a 10-year sentence, the offender remains in parole status for 6 years. However, many states and the federal government have special provisions for early termination of parole. For example, the state parole authority can request that the parole board terminate parole supervision before the individual's maximum sentence has expired. If the parole board approves this request, the parolee is discharged from supervision.

Detainer　　In some cases, a *detainer* may be associated with an offender's parole picture. A detainer is a claim by another jurisdiction that they have charges pending against someone incarcerated in another state. Assume that a prisoner in Oregon is wanted in New Hampshire for a crime he committed before he was imprisoned for his present crime. New Hampshire officials could apply for a detainer writ and notify the Oregon officials. The prisoner could then be released on parole (or upon the expiration of the sentence) and be immediately turned over to New Hampshire to answer the charges in that state.

U.S. Probation Officers　　Federal parolees are supervised by U.S. Probation officers who handle both probation and parole cases. Appointments to these posts are made by the chief federal judge of the particular U.S. District Court with ultimate approval of the appointment required by the Administrative Office of the United States Courts. Although these probation officers supervise both probationers and parolees, this is often not the case in the states. Usually states have separate probation and parole officers. In recent years, a growing number of states have created statewide probation and parole departments as an executive agency of state government.

Decisions Upon Which Parole Is Based

Most parole boards base their decisions on whether or not an inmate should be granted parole on a number of factors.

Prior Record   Since an extensive criminal record is one of the better predictors of further criminality, this factor weighs very heavily. Since first offenders have the best prospects for parole success, most paroling authorities give special consideration to such offenders. Also often considered for early parole are situational offenders—that is, individuals who acted under impulse and the situation of the moment in committing the crime and do not have a past history of law violations.

The habitual offenders, particularly if they are chronic sex offenders or armed robbers, show a history of assaultive crimes, or have previously demonstrated little or no response to incarceration and to institutional programs, must usually show significant change before parole boards favorably consider their parole requests. Generally, parole boards consider professional criminals to be bad risks. Many such offenders consider the risk of imprisonment as a cost of doing business and almost invariably return to their former life styles upon release.

Seriousness and Nature of Current Offense   A second very important consideration is the offense for which the individual is currently incarcerated. Normally, the criminal code and the sentencing judge set the prison term so that it is relative to the seriousness of the offense. However, since the type of offense has predictive value with respect to the commission of further crimes, parole boards consider this factor, especially where the current offense is part of an established behavior pattern that is likely to continue. Studies have shown that larceny, burglary, forgery, and auto theft seem to be the most likely to be repeated.[9] Similarly, persons who are serving sentences for escapes have proven to be poor parole risks.[10] Parole boards must also carefully consider paroling the individual whose offense, if repeated, would be a serious threat to the safety of the public.

Circumstances of the Offense   The personal and social circumstances that the sentencing court took into consideration may also be relevant to the parole decision, since the board must consider the likelihood of recurrence of such circumstances or situations. For example, an individual whose crimes are related to alcoholism or drug abuse may be a higher risk for parole than an individual who committed the same offense but who does not have these aggravating factors. The knowledge of circumstances that either extenuate or aggravate the offense can be useful in predicting whether a repetition will occur.

The Parole Plan The board also carefully reviews and considers the situation into which the individual will go if paroled. This includes where the offender will live, in what sort of housing and with whom; what employment is assured or expected and at what rate of pay; any special conditions of parole recommended by the prison staff (participation in an alcoholism clinic, staying away from former partners in crime); and any indications of possible adverse community reaction to the inmate's release. In some states, the prosecutor and judge who were responsible for the conviction are given an opportunity to comment on the desirability of paroling this person.[11]

Institutional Record The board reviews the individual's record while incarcerated. Prisoners who do not behave responsibly in the prison are usually poor risks for a successful return to the community. The individual who is assaultive, who cannot get along with people, or who cannot work responsibly will probably have similar problems on the outside. On the other hand, a prisoner who has made a sincere effort toward rehabilitation is more likely to be a prospect for reintegration into society. In attempting to determine the prisoner's efforts, the board reviews such matters as the type and quality of work; the prisoner's performance in any academic or vocational training courses; any disciplinary charges made against the prisoner and the subsequent action taken on each; the prisoner's socialization within the prison community; his or her health record; and reports by psychiatrists, caseworkers, instructors, and other staff.[12]

The Development and Use of Prediction Methods

In the last two decades, there has been a great deal of interest among researchers in developing prediction criteria that could aid parole boards in making their decisions.[13] Researchers have gathered data on successful and unsuccessful parolees in an effort to identify the specific characteristics that are associated with success and failure. With the increasing adoption of better research designs and computer technology with its storage and retrieval capabilities, the future would seem to hold some promise for more "scientifically" enlightened decisions by parole boards. However, current prediction methods still suffer from a number of weaknesses. First, researchers have not been able to identify all the factors that may lead an individual to commit a crime nor all the factors that may cause the commission of further offenses once the prisoner is released. The second problem is one of reliability. For example, a parole board may be provided with prediction tables suggesting that offenders with certain characteristics have a 75 percent chance of success on parole. Assume that the offender before them has these characteristics. The problem then becomes to determine whether the prisoner falls into the 75 percent who will be successful or the 25 percent who will fail. Although this may be an improvement over having no predictive statistics, it tells the board very little about the particular individual's chances for parole success.

OFFENSE CHARACTERISTICS: Severity of Offense Behavior (Examples)	OFFENDER CHARACTERISTICS: Parole Prognosis (Salient Factor Score)			
	Very Good (11 to 9)	Good (8 to 6)	Fair (5 to 4)	Poor (3 to 0)
LOW Escape [open institution or program (e.g., CTC, work release)—absent less than 7 days] Marihuana or soft drugs, simple possession (small quantity for own use) Property offenses [theft or simple possession of stolen property] less than $1,000	6-10 months	8-12 months	10-14 months	12-18 months
LOW MODERATE Alcohol law violations Counterfeit currency (passing/possession less than $1,000) Immigration law violations Income tax evasion (less than $10,000) Property offenses [forgery/fraud/theft from mail/embezzlement/interstate transportation of stolen or forged securities/receiving stolen property with intent to resell] less than $1,000 Selective Service Act violations	8-12 months	12-16 months	16-20 months	20-28 months

MODERATE
Bribery of a public official (offering or accepting)
Counterfeit currency (passing/possession $1,000 to $19,999)
Drugs:
    Marihuana, possession with intent to distribute/sale [small scale (e.g., less than 50 lbs.)]
    "Soft drugs", possession with intent to distribute/sale (less than $500)
Escape [secure program or institution, or absent 7 days or more—no fear or threat used]
Firearms Act, possession/purchase/sale (single weapon: not sawed-off shotgun or machine gun)
Income tax evasion ($10,000 to $50,000)
Mailing threatening communication(s)
Misprison of felony
Property offenses (theft/forgery/fraud/embezzlement/interstate transportation of stolen or forged securities/receiving stolen property) $1,000 to $19,999
Smuggling/transportation of alien(s)
Theft of motor vehicle (not multiple theft or for resale)
	12-16 months	16-20 months	20-24 months	24-32 months

HIGH
Counterfeit currency (passing/possession $20,000 to $100,000)
Counterfeiting (manufacturing)
Drugs:
    Marihuana possession with intent to distribute/sale [medium scale (e.g., 50 to 1,999 lbs)]
    "Soft drugs", possession with intent to distribute/sale ($500 to $5,000)
Explosives, possession/transportation
Firearms Act, possession/purchase/sale (sawed-off shotgun(s), machine gun(s), or multiple weapons)
Mann Act (no force—commercial purposes)
Theft of motor vehicle for resale
Property offenses [theft/forgery/fraud/embezzlement/interstate transportation of stolen or forged securities/receiving stolen property] $20,000 to $100,000
	16-20 months	20-26 months	26-34 months	34-44 months

FIGURE 15-1 Guidelines in Approving Parole for Offender

U.S. Parole Commission's Salient-Factor Score

In an effort to structure its broad discretion and provide greater consistency in parole release decision making, the U.S. Parole Commission has adopted and implemented explicit decision-making guidelines.[14] These guidelines are contained in what is called a salient-factor score guide as shown

OFFENSE CHARACTERISTICS: Severity of Offense Behavior (Examples)	OFFENDER CHARACTERISTICS: Parole Prognosis (Salient Factor Score)			
	Very Good (11 to 9)	Good (8 to 6)	Fair (5 to 4)	Poor (3 to 0)

VERY HIGH
Robbery (weapon or threat)
Breaking and entering [bank or post office-entry or attempted entry to vault]
Drugs:
    Marihuana, possession with intent to distribute/sale [large scale (e.g., 2,000 lbs. or more)]
    "Soft drugs", possession with intent to distribute/sale (over $5,000)
    "Hard drugs", possession with intent to distribute/sale (not exceeding $100,000)
Extortion
Mann Act (force)
Property offenses [theft/forgery/fraud/embezzlement/interstate transportation of stolen or forged securities/receiving stolen property] over $100,000 but not exceeding $500,000
	26-36 months	36-48 months	48-60 months	60-72 months

GREATEST I Aggravated felony (e.g., robbery: Weapon fired—no serious injury) Explosive detonation (involving potential risk of physical injury to person(s)—no serious injury occurred) Robbery [multiple instances (2-3)] Hard drugs [possession with intent to distribute/sale-large scale (e.g., over $100,000)] Sexual act-force (e.g., forcible rape).	40-55 months	55-70 months	70-85 months	85-110 months
GREATEST II Aggravated felony-serious injury (e.g., injury involving substantial risk of death, or protracted disability, or disfigurement) Aircraft hijacking Espionage Kidnapping Homicide (intentional or committed during other crime)	Greater than above—however, specific ranges are not given due to the limited number of cases and the extreme variation possible within the category.			

NOTES:
1. These guidelines are predicated upon good institutional conduct and program performance.
2. If an offense behavior is not listed above, the proper category may be obtained by comparing the severity of the offense behavior with those of similar offense behaviors listed.
3. If an offense behavior can be classified under more than one category, the most serious applicable category is to be used.
4. If an offense behavior involved multiple separate offenses, the severity level may be increased.
5. If a continuance is to be given, allow 30 days (1 month) for release program provision.
6. "Hard drugs" include heroin, cocaine, morphine, or opiate derivatives, and synthetic opiate substitutes. "Soft drugs" include, but are not limited to, barbiturates, amphetamines, LSD, and hashish.
7. Conspiracy shall be rated for guideline purposes according to the underlying offense behavior if such behavior was consummated. If the offense is unconsummated, the conspiracy will be rated one step below the consummated crime.

in Figures 15-1 and 15-2 which depict the factors and guidelines currently in use for adult cases.

The development of these guidelines came from a 2-year follow-up study of 2500 inmates released from federal prisons in 1970. The salient factor score guide was first implemented as part of a pilot project in 1972 and was expanded to all federal parole release decisions in 1974. When the Parole Commission and Reorganization Act was passed in 1976, the legislation specifically

NOTICE OF ACTION—PART II—SALIENT FACTORS

Register Number .... Name ....

ITEM A .... ☐ *1*

    No prior convictions (adult or juvenile) = 3
    One prior conviction = 2
    Two or three prior convictions = 1
    Four or more prior convictions = 0

ITEM B .... ☐ *0*

    No prior incarcerations (adult or juvenile) = 2
    One or two prior incarcerations = 1
    Three or more prior incarcerations = 0

ITEM C .... ☐ *1*

    Age at first commitment (adult or juvenile):
        26 or older = 2
        18-25 = 1
        17 or younger = 0

*ITEM D .... ☐ *1* ___

    Commitment offense did not involve auto theft or
        check(s) (forgery/larceny) = 1
    Commitment offense involved auto theft [X], or
        check(s) [Y], or both [Z] = 0

*ITEM E .... ☐ *1* ___

    Never had parole revoked or been committed for a
        new offense while on parole, and not a probation
        violator this time = 1
    Has had parole revoked or been committed for a
        new offense while on parole [X], or is a probation
        violator this time [Y], or both [Z] = 0

ITEM F .... ☐ *1*

    No history of heroin or opiate dependence = 1
    Otherwise = 0

ITEM G .... ☐ *1*

    Verified employment (or full-time school attendance)
        for a total of at least 6 months during the last 2
        years in the community = 1
    Otherwise = 0

TOTAL SCORE .... ☐ *6*

* NOTE TO EXAMINERS:
If item D or E is scored 0, place the appropriate letter (X, Y or Z) on the line
to the right of the box.

FIGURE 15-2 Salient Factor Worksheet

required that this guideline model be used for all parole decisions. Although
the commission is required to use the salient-factor score, decisions outside
the guidelines—either above or below—are authorized after showing of
"good cause" and upon the provision of specific written reasons.[15]

The seriousness of the prisoner's present offense is rated on one axis of the two-dimensional guideline. On the other axis is the "parole prognosis" which is defined as the likelihood of new criminal conduct or parole violation. To understand how the process operates imagine yourself as a Hearing Examiner; and begin filling out a salient-factor worksheet as shown in Figure 15-2 for an individual who was convicted of burglarizing a post office:

Item	Points
A. Two or three prior convictions	1
B. Three or more prior incarcerations	0
C. Nineteen years old when first committed to prison	1
D. Commitment did not include auto theft, checks, forgery, or larceny	1
E. No parole revocation or offense committed while on parole	1
F. No history of heroin or opiate dependence	1
G. Did have a job for 10 months	1
Total salient-factor score	6 = good prognosis for parole

Taking the factors contained in the salient factor worksheet and looking at Figure 15-1 we consider the following: offense severity: "very high" (i.e., breaking and entering bank or post office) jail time served, 3 months; prison time, 10 months—total 13 months, Guidelines used: adult

Looking at Figure 15-1, the guidelines point to 36 to 48 months for very high severity and good prognosis. Our burglar has served 13 months of combined jail and prison time, so the Examiner could recommend anywhere from 23 to 35 more months in prison before parole.

The commission's competent research staff continuously monitors the predictive validity of the salient-factor formula. Such continued research holds the promise for important refinements and improvements in parole decision making in the years ahead.

Resistance by State Parole Boards   Although the federal government uses prediction methods rather extensively, the states generally do not. Hayner has examined why state parole boards are reluctant to use such devices, and he believes there are several reasons:[16] First, parole board members are extremely sensitive to public opinion and therefore are reluctant to parole individuals that the public would object to even though these individuals might possess all the predictive characteristics of being able to successfully return to society, as many murderers do. In the last few years, parole decisions have become highly politicized. Many actual or aspiring politicians have sensed the "get tough" attitudes many Americans are expressing toward crime and criminals. Such "law-and-order" candidates are quick to blame the parole board for what they perceive as policies of leniency. In this type of political environment, boards are pressured to become increasingly conservative and when there is any doubt, to refuse to grant parole. Under such situations, parole boards are not likely to open themselves up to further criticism by the use or encouraged development of some possibly misunderstood prediction device. Second, parole boards want to encourage constructive use of prison time. As progress is made in the administration of correctional institutions, increasing opportunities for self-improvement are available to inmates. Boards want to facilitate the work of prison staffs by rewarding prisoners who take advantage of their opportunities. The majority of prediction instruments give little weight to the institutional factors that many parole boards rely on in making their determinations. The reason researchers do not include institutional behavior and adjustment factors is that these factors are recognized as having little validity. An individual's adjustment in the institution is very often not meaningfully related to that person's behavior outside of prison. Many inmates soon learn to "play the game" and engage in activities that the parole board will look upon favorably. Third, parole board members share the conviction that each case is unique. Although they may act on the basis of hunches about uniformities in prisoner backgrounds, they hesitate to admit the hunches. The idea is strongly entrenched that there is no substitute for careful study of the individual case.

Another problem is that many states have imposed legal restrictions that make it impossible for a parole board to release a prisoner when it appears that the offender will be able to avoid involvement in further offenses. For example, a number of states have adopted deadly weapon statutes that make certain sentences mandatory when the offender has been convicted of using a firearm in the commission of the crime. These statutes usually prohibit parole until a fixed proportion of the sentence has been served. Finally, there is the problem of overcoming traditional ways of thinking. Many parole board members simply refuse to accept that prediction studies have any merit and would rather rely on intuition and common sense to guide their decisions.

Characteristics Associated with Parole Success or Failure

Probably the most comprehensive research on the post-release success of inmates is the encyclopedic work of Glaser.[17] In a 5½-year study of the rehabilitative effects of parole and prison agencies of the Bureau of Prisons, Glaser followed the post-release successes and failures of inmates and was able to develop a number of important associations between certain characteristics and success or failure. Some of the conclusions he reached were:

- The older a man is when released from prison, the less likely he is to return to crime.
- The younger a person is when first arrested, convicted, or confined for any crime, the more likely he is to continue in crime.
- Drug offenders and individuals committed for economic-related offenses such as auto theft, burglary, larceny, and check forgery are most likely to recidivate. Those convicted of robbery, kidnapping, and violation of liquor laws have intermediate levels of recidivism. The best chances for parole success are for persons convicted of homicide, rape, embezzlement, and income tax fraud.

- Race is not related in any meaningful way to parole success or failure.
- The more prior felony sentences an individual has, the more likely he is to continue in crime.
- Most parolees seek noncriminal careers. When they fail, it is because of a complex set of social, economic, and personal relationships.

Although Glaser and other researchers have made some headway in examining factors related to success or failure on parole, these scholars would be the first to admit that, like other predictive criteria, much more extensive and intensive examination is needed. There is an immediate need for more extensive *cohort analysis,* in which a large selected group of offenders are tracked from the time they are arrested until perhaps 5 years after their release from prison or until they recidivate. An important component of this analysis would be an examination of prearrest factors, such as the individual's environment, psychological characteristics, and other factors that might have some relationship to his or her criminal behavior. Associated with this is the need to study the effects of processing the individual through the criminal justice system, the impact of institutionalization, and finally the factors that are instrumental in bringing about criminal or noncriminal behavior after the prisoner's release. Whether these factors can ever be identified and related with any predictive validity to parole success or failure is questionable.

Parole Officer

The functions of the parole officer normally entail several important responsibilities. The relative importance of each of these roles is often determined by the needs of the parolee and the parole officer's perception of his own role.

In a *helper* role, the parole officer may assist the parolee in finding and keeping a job, dealing with family or marital problems, budgeting money, or in assisting the parolee to contend with problems such as alcohol or drug abuse. In general, the officer provides assistance in helping the parolee adjust to free society and to avoid reverting to antisocial or criminal behavior.

The second role of the parole officer is that of an *investigator.* For instance, the officer investigates the situation of release and advises the parole board of the conditions so that they can determine the probable success of paroling the individual. This investigation normally involves such factors as the attitude of the parolee's family about his or her release, attitudes in the community toward the prisoner, and the attitudes of local law enforcement officials toward the individual's return to the community. The parole officer also investigates whether the parolee is living up to the conditions of parole.

The third major role is that of a *police officer.* The parole officer uses the threat of coercive power through the ability to at least initiate the parole revocation process.

These various roles and responsibilities receive different emphasis according to the individual parole officer's style. For example, many parole officers subscribe more to their helping and investigative roles than they do to their roles as police. On the other hand, there are those parole officers who take the attitude that "my job is to keep them in line." Of course, the parolee's behavior

STATE OF NEW JERSEY
CONDITIONS OF PAROLE

1. From the date of your release on parole and until the expiration of the maximum of your sentence(s), unless sooner discharged from parole, you shall continue to be in the legal custody of the Chief Executive Officer of the Institution from which you are released and under the supervision of the Bureau of Parole of the Department of Institutions and Agencies.
2. You shall be required to abide by the rules and regulations formulated by the State Parole Board for the supervision of persons on parole.
3. As a condition of your being on parole, you are required to:
   a. Conduct yourself in society in compliance with all laws and ordinances;
   b. Conduct yourself with due regard to moral standards.
   c. Demonstrate that your conduct on parole has been good at all times;
   d. Demonstrate that you are a fit person to be at liberty;
   e. Make restitution for your crime, when required;
   f. Contribute to the support of your dependents;
   g. Abstain from the use or sale of narcotics and the excessive use of intoxicating beverages;
   h. Refrain from association with persons of bad character or those who are considered by the Parole District Supervisor or his designated representative to be undesirable companions;
   i. Refrain from conduct while on parole which shall give reasonable cause to believe that you have resumed, or are about to resume, criminal conduct or associations;
   j. Reside in a place approved by the Bureau of Parole;
   k. Seek employment diligently and render to your employer the best service of which you are capable;
   l. Report to or notify your Parole District Supervisor or his designated representative:
      (1) As soon as possible but in any event within forty-eight hours after your release on parole from the institution;
      (2) Whenever you are in any kind of trouble or in need of advice;
      (3) As soon as possible after an arrest on any new charge;
      (4) Whenever you are instructed to report by the Parole District Supervisor, his designated representative, or other competent authority;
      (5) Before paying any fine or attempting to obtain bail;
   m. Obtain permission from your Parole District Supervisor or his designated representative;

FIGURE 15-3 State of New Jersey Conditions of Parole

to a great extent may also determine the role that the parole officer will assume in dealing with a particular client.

Parolee's Rights

In the past 50 years, states have developed certain procedures for returning a parole violator to prison. Because of Supreme Court decisions that pertain to parole revocation, states must provide a parole revocation hearing (unless this is waived by the parolee) before a parolee can have parole revoked. In

(1) Before marrying or applying for a divorce;

(2) Before purchasing a motor vehicle, obtaining a learner's permit, a driver's license, or applying for a motor vehicle registration;

(3) Before entering any form of conditional sales agreement or borrowing money or articles of substantial value;

(4) Before entering any business, changing your place of residence, or changing your employment;

(5) Before leaving the State of your approved residence;

(6) Before applying for a permit to carry a firearm, securing a hunting license, or carrying a firearm for any purpose.

4. This parole may be revoked without notice:

a. If you violate any of the conditions of your parole, other than by subsequent conviction of crime, you shall be required to serve the time remaining on your sentence(s), to be computed from the date you are declared delinquent, unless said revocation is rescinded or unless reparoled.

b. If you are convicted of a crime while on parole, or commit an offense on parole which subsequently results in a conviction of a crime, you shall be required to serve the time remaining on your sentence(s) to be computed from the date of your release on parole, unless said revocation is rescinded or unless reparoled.

NOTE: In cases where the prisoner is paroled from a county penitentiary, the term "Chief Probation Officer" shall be substituted for the term "District Parole Supervisor" in the above conditions of parole.

SPECIAL CONDITION(S)

In consideration of the action of the State Parole Board in paroling me, I hereby accept this parole and such State Parole Board action and I hereby agree to be bound by the foregoing conditions which shall constitute my parole contract with the State of New Jersey. Any violation of any condition hereof shall be sufficient cause for revocation of my parole.

Dated _____ 19_____

Witness:

_____   _____
                                              Signature

order to understand this development, we must examine the parole process more closely.

When a parolee is released, he or she must abide by the general conditions of parole that are applicable to all parolees released in the particular jurisdiction. In addition, the parole board may require that the parolee abide by special conditions. These special conditions of parole will also be contained in the conditions of parole. General parole conditions are illustrated in the "Conditions of Parole for the State of New Jersey." Note that space has been provided for any special conditions that the parole board thinks should be imposed on a particular parolee.

How parole is actually revoked varies somewhat from state to state. Assume that there is a "technical violation" of a parolee's general or special conditions of parole. In some states, upon evidence that the parolee has violated the conditions of parole, the parole officer can arrest the alleged parole violator without warrant, pending a revocation hearing. In other states, the parole officer does not have the power to arrest, and instead, must apply to a parole supervisor or the parole board to issue a holding warrant before the individual can be taken into custody for a parole violation.

In the federal system, parole revocation operates in another way. If there is evidence that the federal parolee has violated the conditions of parole, the federal probation officer first investigates the alleged violation and then reports the findings through the chain of command to the U.S. Parole Commission itself. If the commission considers the parolee's violation to be serious enough to warrant revocation of parole, the commission then issues a revocation warrant. The Probation Service, the U.S. Marshal's Service, or the FBI is then empowered to make the actual arrest.

Once an individual is arrested for parole violation, he or she must have a parole revocation hearing. Until the late 1960s, however, the "hearing" was often nothing more than a request by the parole agent or the parole supervisor that the parole board revoke an individual's parole, a request that usually was automatically complied with. In too many instances, parolees were sent back to prison for such ambiguous and undefined reasons as "poor attitude" or allegations of "failure to cooperate." It was generally felt that since the parolee was on parole by grant of this privilege, there was little need for parole boards to concern themselves with questions of the parolee's right of due process, the right to a hearing and review, and matters of proof.

A study of parole board revocations in 1964 indicated that there was no hearing at all in at least seven states. Even in those states that did provide for a revocation hearing, the individual was immediately returned to prison, and often it would be weeks before any type of hearing was held.[18] When the parole board did get around to conducting a revocation hearing, it was usually so superficial and one-sided as to render it meaningless.

In only a few cases did the parole board conduct meaningful hearings, and in even fewer cases was the warrant canceled and the inmate again released to parole. Even if the warrant was withdrawn, the parolee had already suffered a disruptive experience, and family relationships and employment were already disturbed. During these revocation hearings, it was almost unheard of to permit the parolee to be represented by counsel, to cross-examine the witnesses against him, to demand proof, or to introduce witnesses in his own behalf. In those rare instances when counsel was permitted, the states would not assign an attorney to indigent parolees, which was the category many fell into.

Court Rulings Beginning in the 1960s, the appellate courts have become increasingly concerned with parole practices. Although the entire parole process has come under a great deal of scrutiny in recent years, parole revocation practices have come under the closest examination. The courts have developed a distinctive theme in the law that states if a privilege such as parole is to be denied, it can be done more readily before rather than after it is granted.

The courts have taken a rather zigzag approach in dealing with the legal questions that surround parole revocation. At first, the courts held that parole revocations were entirely within the discretion of parole boards and that as a consequence, there was no justification for making the hearing an adversarial process in which the parolee had the right to counsel, to be confronted by his accusers, and to cross-examination of witnesses. However, in the last decade, the courts have been chipping away at the idea that the parolee has no right to invoke certain requirements from the parole board. In 1967, in *Mempa v. Rhay,* the Supreme Court addressed itself to this question in the case of a probationer who had his probation revoked and was sentenced to an institution.[19] The Supreme Court held that a state probationer had the right to a hearing and to counsel when it was alleged that a probationer had violated probation and was to be sentenced to an institution. As a result of this decision, many states began adopting this rule not only for probationers, but for parolees as well.[20]

MEMPA v, RHAY (1967)

Revocation of Probation When Sentence Not Previously Imposed—I

FACTS:

Seventeen-year-old Jerry Mempa was convicted in the Spokane County Superior Court of "joy-riding." He was then placed on probation for 2 years on the condition that among other things, he first spend 30 days in the county jail; the imposition of sentence was then deferred.

About 4 months later, the county prosecutor moved to have Mempa's probation revoked on the ground that he had been involved in a burglary while on probation. A hearing was held in the Spokane County Superior Court at which Mempa was accompanied by his stepfather. He was not represented by counsel and was not asked whether he wished to have counsel appointed for him. Nor was any inquiry made concerning the appointed counsel who had previously represented him. At the hearing, Mempa responded in the affirmative when asked if he had been involved in the alleged burglary. A probation officer testified without cross-examination that according to his information, Mempa had been involved in the burglary and had previously denied participation in it. Without asking Mempa if he had anything to say or any evidence to supply, the court immediately entered an order revoking Mempa's probation and then sentenced him to 10 years in the penitentiary. Six years later, Mempa appealed to the Washington State Supreme Court, claiming that he had been deprived of his right to counsel at the proceeding at which his probation was revoked and sentence imposed. The Washington Supreme Court denied the petition. The case was then appealed to the United States Supreme Court.

DECISION:

The accused must be afforded an attorney at a probation revocation or deferred sentencing hearing. Otherwise the accused may lose important legal rights since the probation revocation hearing is also a "critical stage" of a criminal proceeding.

SIGNIFICANCE OF THE CASE:

This was the first application of due process rights in relation to probation revocation hearings.

GAGNON v. SCARPELLI (1973)

Revocation of Probation When Sentence Not Previously Imposed—II

FACTS:

Gerald Scarpelli pleaded guilty in 1965 to a charge of armed robbery in Wisconsin. The trial judge sentenced him to 15 years imprisonment, but suspended the sentence and placed him on probation for 7 years in the custody of the Wisconsin Department of Public Welfare. At that time, he signed an agreement specifying the terms of his probation and a "Travel Permit and Agreement to Return" which allowed him to reside in Illinois with probation supervision under an interstate compact. He was then accepted for supervision by the Cook County, Illinois Adult Probation Department.

Scarpelli was apprehended by Illinois police who had surprised him and a confederate in the course of burglarizing a house. After being advised of his constitutional rights, Scarpelli admitted that he and the other arrestee had broken into the house to steal merchandise or money. He later asserted that his statement was false because it was given under duress. After he was arrested, the Wisconsin Department of Welfare revoked his probation without a hearing. The grounds for the revocation were: (1) that he associated with criminals in direct violation of his probation regulations; (2) he was involved in and arrested for the burglary in Illinois. He was then sentenced to the Wisconsin State Reformatory to begin serving the 15 years to which he had been sentenced by the trial judge. At no time was he afforded a hearing.

Some 3 years later, while still in prison, he petitioned the U.S. District Court to hear his case on the grounds that he had the right to a revocation hearing and a right to appointed legal counsel at the hearing because he was an indigent. Both the U.S. District and the Court of Appeals agreed. The U.S. Supreme Court was asked to review these lower court decisions.

DECISION:

The U.S. Supreme Court ruled that Scarpelli had a right to a revocation hearing(s). However, the Court would not hold that there must be a per se rule requiring the appointment of counsel at probation revocation hearings when a sentence had previously been imposed, and, instead, left the decision as to the need for counsel to be made on a case-by-case basis.

SIGNIFICANCE OF THE CASE:

This finding modified the earlier *Mempa* v. *Rhay* decision and it also indicated some of the changes in thinking from the time of the Warren Court (Mempa) to the Burger Court (Gagnon).

In 1973, the Burger court modified the Court's holding somewhat in the case of *Gagnon* v. *Scarpelli*. In this case, the Court held that providing counsel to indigent probationers in a revocation hearing was to be decided on a case-by-case basis. Nonetheless, the earlier holding of the *Mempa* case meant that drastic changes were called for, not only in long-standing legal positions, but also in the procedures required to revoke the parolee's or probationer's privilege. For example, the New York Court of Appeals, basing its decision on the *Mempa* case, reversed its former position and required the state parole board to permit parolees to be represented by counsel at revocation hearings. The changing philosophy of the courts in their concern for procedural due process is quite well expressed in *Murray* v. *Page* [429 F.2d 1359 (10th Cir. 1970)]:

> Therefore, while a prisoner does not have a constitutional right to parole, once paroled he cannot be deprived of his freedom to be informed of the charges and the nature of the evidence against him, and the right to appear and be heard at the revocation hearing is inviolate. Statutory deprivation of this right is manifestly inconsistent with due process and is unconstitutional: nor can such right be lost by the subjective determination of the executive that the case for revocation is "clear."[21]

Generally, parole boards have resisted these court orders, regarding them as an arbitrary encroachment by the courts into their area of authority. Many parole board members feel that the adoption of an adversarial format will cause the fact-finding mission of the hearing to be lost in legal argument and maneuvering.

On June 29, 1972, the U.S. Supreme Court rendered a landmark decision which is having a significant impact upon parole boards throughout the nation. In the case of *Morrissey* v. *Brewer*[22] two parolees petitioned the Supreme Court on the grounds that their paroles had been revoked without a hearing, which was in violation of their rights to due process. The Court stated that the question was not whether parole was a "right" or a "privilege" but whether by the actions of a governmental agency (parole board), the individual can be made to suffer a "grievous loss." Although the Court admitted that the parolee is not entitled to the full range of rights due a defendant in a criminal proceeding, it did rule that due process requires that a parolee be given a two-stage hearing. First, a preliminary examination must be conducted promptly by a hearing officer soon after the arrest or alleged violation. The purpose of this hearing is to determine if there is probable cause to believe that the parolee has committed a parole violation. At this preliminary hearing, the parolee may appear and speak in his own behalf and may bring whatever documents and witnesses are necessary to support his case. The parolee is further entitled to receive advance notice of the hearing, its purpose, and the alleged violation.

Then if the parolee desires a subsequent hearing prior to the final decision, he must be afforded this right. In this hearing, he has certain fundamental rights, among which are: (1) the right to receive written notice of the conditions of parole he allegedly violated; (2) the right to be informed of all evidence against him; (3) the opportunity to be heard in person and to present evidence in his behalf; (4) the right to confront and cross-examine adverse witnesses unless the hearing examiner or parole board considers it in the best interests of the witness not to have his identity disclosed; and (5) the right to receive a written statement by the board or the fact finders as to the specific evidence relied upon to revoke parole.

Generally, if the parole revocation hearing concludes that the parole should be revoked, the individual is sent back to prison. If the revocation is made on the basis of a "technical violation," the parolee will usually be credited with his good "street-time." For instance, if an individual was originally sentenced to 10 years, served 6 years before being paroled, and violated the conditions of parole in the seventh year, he would only have a maximum of 3 more years to serve because he is credited with his 1 good year on parole. However, if his parole is violated by the commission of another crime, he generally will not be credited with any good "street-time." In this case, he would have to serve the remaining 4 years on his first sentence in addition to the sentence he receives for the commission of the new crime.

Developing Trends in Parole

Development of Parole Teams In most instances, a parolee is arbitrarily assigned to a parole officer who has a vacancy in his or her case load. This traditional pairing up is being modified in a number of parole offices throughout the United States today. In its place, a team approach is being employed in which a team of parole officers assumes collective responsibility for a parolee group as large as their combined former case loads. Under this system, parolees are assigned to parole officers who are best able to relate to and supervise them. For example, if certain parole officers seem to have better success with drug-related offenders, then parolees with this type of history are assigned to them.

This team approach is a much more prudent use of human resources available in parole agencies. It also facilitates the use of paraprofessionals and volunteers, which is becoming increasingly popular as a means to assist parole officers and parolees. Often the use of carefully selected volunteers has proved to be very beneficial, as it provides a means to match parolees with individuals who can understand their particular problems of adjustment and, as a consequence, relate in more meaningful ways.

In some parts of the country, volunteer groups have developed to help prisoners even before their release. In the state of Washington, concerned citizens developed a volunteer sponsors group to visit men in prison, particularly those who had infrequent contacts from the outside. The group's goal was to establish a human contact in which there is real commitment and to follow it up with specific help when the inmate is paroled. This program now numbers over 500 volunteers.[23] In California, a program that uses volunteer parole aides, some of whom are exconvicts, has begun. One of the most interesting developments is the National Parole Aid Program begun by the American Bar Association. This program was started as a result of the feeling that the citizen volunteer movement, although very popular in probation, was not being utilized to its fullest potential in parole. The program operates by enlisting attorney volunteers to act as parole officers for a single offender under the general supervision of an experienced parole officer.[24]

Parole Contract Plan A few states, such as Florida, Georgia, Michigan, North Carolina, and Minnesota, have implemented parole contract plans as an innovative means to make institutional programs more effective. Under the parole contract plan, an inmate meets with counseling specialists when he or she first arrives at the prison. Together, these counseling specialists and the inmate devise a mutually satisfactory plan that the individual will engage in during the period of incarceration. For example, the inmate may be in need of further education and express a willingness to obtain a high school diploma and then go on to complete a vocational trade program. The counseling staff will then draw up a contract agreement with the inmate. The contract specifies that the department of corrections agrees to provide the inmate with the opportunity to obtain a high school diploma and to participate in a vocational training program; the inmate agrees to fulfill these goals by a certain date; and the parole board agrees to parole the inmate upon fulfillment of the contractual obligation.

The basic elements of the parole contract plan are the following:

A written, legally enforceable contract between the inmate, his institution, and the parole authority;

A target date, which becomes the parole date if all contract provisions are met by the inmate;

Face-to-face negotiations between the inmate (often helped by an advocate), the institution, and the parole authority;

The involvement of an outside party who independently determines whether the contract has been fulfilled;

Contract provisions spelling out measurable goals for inmates in the areas of education, training, counseling, and institutional behavior, and a guarantee from the correctional system that programs and services to fulfill these goals will be available as needed.[25]

Inmates enter into the contracts voluntarily. If they withdraw from the program or fail to meet the contract terms, they revert to the regular parole process. Some states permit inmates to renegotiate their contracts if they cannot live up to the agreement. In some states, as many as half of all inmates with parole contracts fail to complete them.[26] In Michigan, a study done by that state's department of corrections indicated that in the first year of the parole contract program, 20 percent of the 202 inmates participating in the program had their contracts terminated.[27] No doubt more would have their contracts revoked as the program continued.

The advocates of the plan cite a number of advantages for such programs. First, the correctional authorities are forced to examine the programs within the system and in the community that can be developed and used and to account for their availability and effectiveness. The contract also forces a parole board to define its criteria for release. The contract plan should also result in reduced tension in prison, increased inmate motivation, lower costs resulting from less time served in institutions, better program coordination, fewer parole hearings, and immediate input from the parole board regarding an offender's program during the period of incarceration.[28]

Another major advantage is that the program places the responsibility on the inmate. Rather than fostering dependency as prison life usually does because all meaningful decisions are made by prison officials, it encourages the inmates to set their own goals. These attitudes, if properly channeled, increase the inmate's ability to cope with the problems of the free world upon release. Figure 15-4 shows the parole contract agreement used by Michigan. This plan is for the most part being used for first-time offenders and those sentenced for less serious crimes. States using this agreement are already studying its impact to see if it can be expanded.

SAMPLE #3

MICHIGAN DEPARTMENT OF CORRECTIONS

CONTRACT SERVICE PROGRAM AGREEMENT

CSO-250A REV.10/74

This agreement made this day between __John Q. Resident__, no. __A-222111__, the Bureau of Correctional Facilities, the Bureau of Field Services and the Michigan Parole Board, upon all parties hereto being fully and completely informed in the particulars, the parties do hereby contract and agree as follows:

PART I — RESIDENT

I, __John Q. Resident__, no. __A-222111__, understand and agree to successfully complete* the objectives as they are specifically outlined in Part IV below in consideration for a specific date of parole. I understand that programs offered at Bureau of Correctional Facilities institutions outlined in Part IV must be completed before I may take part in programming offered by the Bureau of Field Services. I understand that, at any time, I may submit a request to my assigned counselor for renegotiation of this contract. I will to the best of my ability carry out the objectives of this contract, and realize that failure to do so will cancel and negate the contract.

PART II — BUREAU OF CORRECTIONAL FACILITIES/BUREAU OF FIELD SERVICES

I, __Wayne Monroe__, representing the Bureau of Correctional Facilities, agree to provide the necessary programs and services at institutions within the Bureau of Correctional Facilities as specified in Part IV below in sufficient time to enable __John Q. Resident__, no. __A-222111__, to successfully perform and complete the objectives of this contract.

I, __Leslie Mason__, representing the Bureau of Field Services, agree to provide the necessary programs and services associated with work release, work study and/or community residential placement as specified in Part IV below in sufficient time to enable __John Q. Resident__, no. __A-222111__, to perform and successfully complete the objectives of this contract.

PART III — PAROLE BOARD

We, __Alger Kent__, __Emmet St. Clair__ and __Crawford Calhoun__, of the Michigan Parole Board agree to order a parole for the above named resident on or before __August 22, 1977__, contingent upon his successful completion of the objectives mentioned in Part IV below.

PART IV — OBJECTIVES (List and number each separately.)

1. By August 1975, I will enroll in the high school program on a full-time basis so that I graduate from high school by January 1976.

2. By January 1976, I will enroll in college programming so that I complete a minimum of one college class per semester until my release.

3. By September 1975, I will begin regular participation in group counseling attending a minimum of 80% of the meetings so that I earn average or better reports regarding progress in group counseling for at least six months.

4. By May 1977, I will be screened for transfer to a corrections center; if eligible, I will be placed in a corrections center until my release.

5. While at the corrections center I will secure home placement and employment for my release.

FIGURE 15-4 Parole Contract Agreement

One interesting variation of the parole contract plan is being tried in Massachusetts where a Victim Restitution Parole Project has been established. Participation in the program is restricted to property offenders who are serving a minimum 1-year sentence; offenders who are convicted of assault, drug or sex offenses, or white-collar crimes are not eligible. Eligible inmates negotiate a parole contract with the parole board, a correctional representative, and a parole officer. The contract specifies institutional programming, a parole release date and a restitution agreement. For restitution contracts, the parole

S A M P L E # 3

MICHIGAN DEPARTMENT OF CORRECTIONS
CONTRACT SERVICE PROGRAM AGREEMENT — Page 2

CSO-250B

PART IV - CONTINUED   John Q. Resident, A-222111

6. Upon completion of my high school programming outlined above I will participate on a routine institutional work assignment and earn average or better reports regarding adjustment and performance on the assignment until my release.

7. While on the work assignment I will maintain a savings in my resident account equal to a minimum of 10% of my wages earned for my release.

8. Prior to my release I will secure dental treatment.

PART V — CONDITIONS UNDER WHICH THE CONTRACT MAY BE VOIDED

1. I understand that, during the course of this agreement, should I commit an act which, if dealt with in a court of law, could result in conviction for a criminal offense (felony or misdemeanor), this agreement is subject to renegotiation or termination.

2. I understand that if I commit more than one infraction of rules and regulations promulgated by the Department of Corrections regarding resident behavior in any thirty day period or any act of serious insubordination, attempt to escape or escape this contract is subject to review. The terms may be renegotiated or the agreement terminated.

3. I understand that it is my responsibility to protect that level of custody to which I am assigned after transfer from the Reception and Guidance Center. Should this agreement call for a reduction in custody, (for example, a transfer to a community residential placement), it is my responsibility to assure that I continue to be eligible for a transfer to that reduced custody status. I further understand that should I fail to progress to reduced custody status, or should I transfer to an increased custody status, this agreement is subject to review. The terms may be renegotiated or the agreement can be terminated.

4. I understand that should I commit an act which may be considered a breach of contract under paragraphs 1 thru 3 above, before the effective date of parole in Part III, the Parole Board may suspend the order of parole pending the outcome of an administrative hearing regarding the possible breach of contract.

5. If previously unknown information regarding pending felony prosecution or detainers from other jurisdictions become available, this agreement is subject to review and the terms may be renegotiated or the agreement may be declared null and void. I understand that should a detainer be lodged against me by another jurisdiction, the commitment to parole in Part III above shall be subject to that detainer.

SIGNATURE RESIDENT *John Q. Resident*	DATE	MEMBER — PAROLE BOARD Alger Kent	DATE
John Q. Resident	6/19/75	MEMBER — PAROLE BOARD Emmet St. Clair	DATE
CORR. FAC. REPRESENTATIVE Wayne Monroe	DATE	MEMBER — PAROLE BOARD Crawford Calhoun	DATE
FIELD SERVICES REPRESENTATIVE Leslie Mason	DATE		

*Successfully completed for the purpose of this contract means completed with a passing grade or evaluation of satisfactory within the reasonable capabilities of the resident, for the specific program or service objective being evaluated by the responsible staff member assigned to the individual program or service objective.

officer contacts the victim to determine the financial loss. Generally, the offender reimburses the victim from salary earned on work release. If financial restitution is not feasible, the inmate may perform alternative community service.

The Need to Attract Qualified Parole Board Members   A few states have begun to realize the need to attract qualified individuals to serve on parole boards. Very few states require any specific qualifications for appointment to the boards—nor does the federal government. Table 15-1 indicates the methods by which adult parole board members were appointed in 1976.

TABLE 15-1
Method of Selection of Parole Board Members (1976)

APPOINTING OFFICER OR AGENCY	NUMBER OF STATES
Governor	40
State Official	4
Special boards	3
Civil service	3

Source: Law Enforcement Assistance Administration, *State and Local Probation and Parole Systems* (Washington, D.C.: U.S. Government Printing Office, February 1978).

In some jurisdictions, highly competent individuals have been appointed to parole boards and some have gained experience through years of service as board members. However, in 1976, parole board members in 46 states were serving terms of 6 years or less.

Another problem is that in over 40 percent of the states, parole board members serve only part time[29] although there is a trend toward full-time boards The National Advisory Commission on Criminal Justice Standards and Goals has recommended that all boards be full time.[30] Experience has shown that it is not unusual for new parole board members to be appointed whenever there is a change in the governor's office. Under these circumstances, the politics of a patronage system often become more important than the appointee's qualifications.

In an effort to curb this practice, states such as Michigan and Ohio have placed their parole board members under the state civil service system with indeterminate periods of tenure. Michigan and Wisconsin require appropriate college degrees and experience in corrections or closely related areas. Many of the parole board members in these states have extensive experience in responsible positions in corrections before joining the parole board. Florida requires that appointees pass a special examination in penology and criminal justice which is administered by a special examining board of specialists in these areas. It would seem that as more complex and diverse institutional programs develop, states must begin to realize that parole board members must be trained professionals in the field of corrections.

Abolition of the Indeterminate Sentence and Parole

A topic of growing interest throughout the country has been for a reform in sentencing structures. The basis for this is a growing dissatisfaction with the indeterminate sentence.[31] Since 1869 when Michigan enacted the first indeterminate sentence law, it was widely believed that an indeterminate sentence was the best mechanism to rehabilitate inmates. By providing for some degree of indeterminancy in sentencing—for example, from 2 to 10 years for a specific offense—an inmate would be motivated to take advantage of the rehabilitative aspects of prison in an effort to be paroled near the minimum sentence. The indeterminate sentence also shifted the responsibility from imposing the actual length of sentence from the judge to the parole board. The judge merely sentenced the individual according to the range provided for the particular crime. The parole board then decided when, within that range, the individual had been "rehabilitated" and could be released.

Today, the indeterminate sentence is under attack, and with it, parole. Since the justification for parole was to provide community supervision for someone who was released from an institution before serving the statutory maximum, the abolition of the indeterminate sentence is also bringing about the clamor that there is no need for parole.

What some reformers are suggesting is that the "flat" or determinate sentence be used instead of the indeterminate sentence. The combination of the use of the determinate sentence and the abolition of parole has already been accomplished in Maine, and several other states are considering doing the same.[32]

Under Maine's new criminal code, judges must sentence offenders to determinate sentences. The code assigns crimes to one of several categories and the sentencing judge must set a definite term of incarceration within the limits of the category. The maximum term for a class A crime (e.g., armed robbery) is 20 years; for a B crime (e.g., arson), 10 years; a C crime (e.g., burglary), 5 years; a D crime (e.g., possession of LSD), less than 1 year; and a class E crime (e.g., public indecency), 6 months. Criminal homicide in the first degree carries a mandatory life sentence, while criminal homicide in the second degree requires a minimum sentence of 20 years. In order to permit some flexibility in the new determinate sentences, good-time provisions remain.

In addition to instituting the determinate sentence, Maine has abolished parole. The individual is sentenced to a fixed number of years permitted to accrue "good time" and is then released without parole supervision when that time is up.

A number of factors led Maine to these reforms. Correctional administrators recognized that use of the indeterminate sentence and parole forced many inmates to volunteer for rehabilitative programs in which they had no interest in order to "look good" to the parole board. It was also generally felt that correctional rehabilitative programs (particularly under such situations) were a sham; that parole served no useful rehabilitative purpose; and that the parole board was releasing inmates from prison too soon. (In the past, the board had granted parole to 97 percent of those who came up for first hearings.)

California is another state that has restructured its sentencing laws.[33] Judges now have a narrow range of penalties from which to choose when sentencing a convicted offender to prison. For example, in the case of robbery, the range is 2, 3, or 4 years. The judge is required to choose the middle term (i.e., 3 years) unless specific mitigating or aggravating circumstances are proven at a separate hearing. In this case, if aggravating circumstances were present, the accused would receive the flat sentence of 4 years. The penalty can also be increased if other factors are present—for example, 1 additional year is provided for carrying a weapon during the crime, and 3 years are added for seriously injuring a victim or for prior conviction for a violent felony. This is far different than under an indeterminate sentencing structure where the offender might get 2 to 10 years for the offense.

Although California still retains parole, there is some discussion of abolishing it under the new sentencing legislation. Indiana has also gone to the determinate sentencing with years added on or subtracted for aggravating or mitigating factors. Along with these changes, Indiana has established that the parole period cannot exceed 1 year after release.[34]

This movement toward the reform of our sentencing laws and the growing disenchantment with attempts to rehabilitate prisoners, sentencing disparities, misuse of parole, and the seeming lack of success of parole supervision to make much of a difference in whether an individual goes straight or reverts to crime, may portend some significant changes in the overall administration of justice. Not the least of which may be the effect of all this on parole.[35]

PROBATION

Whereas parole is the conditional release of an offender who has served a period of incarceration in prison, probation is the conditional release of an individual by the court after the offender has been found guilty of the crime charged. In the case of probation then, the individual has not been sentenced to prison, although he or she may, in fact, have been incarcerated in jail following arrest and while awaiting trial. In the case of parole, the decision is made by a parole board; in probation, the decision is made by the sentencing judge. At the judge's discretion an individual may be placed on probation where he or she is supervised by a probation officer and is subject to court-imposed guidelines of behavior. Probation violations may cause the judge to revoke the probation, and the individual may then be sentenced to a period of incarceration as prescribed by the statute that was originally violated.

The decision to place an offender on probation is generally a combination of factors: the recommendation of the prosecuting attorney (if made); the presentence investigation report prepared by the probation officer that would include a host of considerations concerning the commission of the crime and the offender's characteristics; the attitudes of the community and perhaps the attendant publicity of the crime; and in some cases, the attitude of the police. The judge normally considers many of these factors including the complete social history of the accused in trying to reach a decision whether the interests of justice would be served by probation and whether it would also be in the best interests of the defendant.[36]

Like parole, many critics of probation consider it a form of leniency. Compared with the alternative of incarceration, it might be. Nonetheless, probation is, in fact, a sentence and not a dismissal of the charges. The court specifies the conditions of this form of sentence, which might be to obtain or remain in gainful employment, to make restitution to the victim, to abstain from the use of alcoholic beverages, to remain in the jurisdiction of the court, or other conditions. The probationer agrees to these conditions for the duration of the probationary period after which he or she is discharged from the sentence.

A sentence of probation is imposed by a judge in one of two ways: the judge may impose a prison sentence as determined by the statute violated and then suspend its execution and place the offender on probation; or the judge may defer sentencing and place the individual directly on probation. If the offender should violate the conditions of probation in the first instance, the period of incarceration has already been determined. If in the second instance, the

PROBATION FORM NO. 7
(March 1973)

UNITED STATES DISTRICT COURT

FOR THE

Eastern District of Arkansas

SAMPLE FORM

To ___James Lee Creedmore___   Docket No.   178--3744

Address___1267 E. 5th St., Little Rock, AR 72202___

In accordance with authority conferred by the United States Probation Law, you have been placed on probation this date, November 18, 1980   , for a period of three (3) years   by the Hon. Peter A. O'Brien   United States District Judge, sitting in and for this District Court at Little Rock, Arkansas

CONDITIONS OF PROBATION

It is the order of the Court that you shall comply with the following conditions of probation:

(1) You shall refrain from violation of any law (federal, state, and local). You shall get in touch immediately with your probation officer if arrested or questioned by a law-enforcement officer.

(2) You shall associate only with law-abiding persons and maintain reasonable hours.

(3) You shall work regularly at a lawful occupation and support your legal dependents, if any, to the best of your ability. When out of work you shall notify your probation officer at once. You shall consult him prior to job changes.

(4) You shall not leave the judicial district without permission of the probation officer.

(5) You shall notify your probation officer immediately of any change in your place of residence.

(6) You shall follow the probation officer's instructions.

(7) You shall report to the probation officer as directed.

The special conditions ordered by the Court are as follows:

  1. To abstain from the consumption of any and all intoxicating
      beverages.

I understand that the Court may change the conditions of probation, reduce or extend the period of probation, and at any time during the probation period or within the maximum probation period of 5 years permitted by law, may issue a warrant and revoke probation for a violation occurring during the probation period.

I have read or had read to me the above conditions of probation. I fully understand them and I will abide by them.

(Signed) _James Lee Creedmore_   _11/18/80_
                              Probationer   Date

You will report as follows:

On the first and third Saturdays of each month at 9:00 A.M. in Room 507 of the Federal Building at 200 Spring Street in the city of Little Rock, Arkansas.

James T. Hargrove   _11/18/80_
                   U. S. Probation Officer   Date

FPI-MI—9-1-76-60M-6087

FIGURE 15-5 An Example of Federal Probation Conditions

conditions of probation are violated, the probationer is brought back to the court to have sentence imposed.

In most jurisdictions, the judge's discretion in granting the time an offender serves on probation is limited by the period of time that the sentence specifies. For example, if the statute calls for a possible period of incarceration of 1 to 3 years, the judge cannot sentence the offender to probation for more than the 3-year maximum. However, in some states, the length of the probated term may exceed the term that the defendant would be required to serve if incarcerated.[37] Many states also specify that in the case of more serious crimes, probation is not an alternative. In a few jurisdictions, a jury may recommend probation and the judge must follow the recommendation; in most jurisdictions, however, the decision rests solely with the judge.

Origins of Probation

Modern probation stems from early common law practices that developed as methods of avoiding the severity of criminal laws. During the period of its widespread temporal power, the Roman Catholic Church demanded the right of immunity from secular law for clericals.[38] This immunity was known as *benefit of clergy*. Later, *rights of sanctuary* developed by which those accused of crimes were granted immunity from the civil authorities by seeking the protection of the Church.

Probation, as we know it today, is primarily an American development. In 1841, while a spectator in the Boston Police Court, John Augustus requested that the judge permit him to be the sponsor for an offender about to be sentenced. The court agreed to his request, and the convicted offender was sentenced to his custody. Augustus, who is considered the father of probation, continued his efforts and developed several features that often characterize probation today. First, he selected offenders who were charged with their first offense and appeared amenable. Second, he assumed responsibility for an offender only after a careful examination of the facts of the case and of the history and character of the defendant. Third, he agreed to send the offender to school or to see that he obtained employment and housing. Finally, he developed a system of making impartial reports to the court on the status of those committed to his supervision and of maintaining a careful register of his probationers.

In 1878, the Massachusetts legislature approved the idea that the mayor of Boston should appoint a probation officer as part of the police force. From Boston, the idea spread slowly across the United States. At first, most probation officers handled only juvenile cases, but as the years passed, courts were increasingly inclined to extend this service to adult offenders. The idea of using probation as an alternative to incarceration spread to other countries as well. The first countries to adopt it outside of the United States were Australia and New Zealand. When England adopted the Probation of Offenders' Act in 1907, the idea soon spread to European countries where it was eventually adopted.

The Growth and Use of Probation

Probation is the largest community-based program for handling offenders and is being increasingly used for individuals who are not considered persistent professional or dangerous offenders. Of the approximately 1.5 million persons on parole or probation in 1976, over 1.2 million of these were on probation—of which over one-third were juveniles.[39] A study of sentencing practices in the courts of Indiana during 1972 indicated that of those persons convicted of an offense for which imprisonment was an alternative, 56 percent received probation.[40] Generally, the success of probation is quite high. For instance, the Michigan Department of Corrections studied 2,411 cases of adults placed on probation in 1968. The success rates of these probationers were studied for 3 years, and it was found that 79.1 percent of the offenders were successful under probation. Of the 20.9 percent that failed, 15.3 percent had their probation revoked for technical violations, while only 5.6 percent committed new offenses.[41]

The Organization of State Probation Agencies

State probation departments are organized in diverse ways. They may be a part of the executive or the judicial branch, and they are administered by both state and local governments. For example, in Michigan, certain probation departments are administered by local courts whereas others are under the control of the state department of corrections, which is an agency of the executive branch. In Ohio, juvenile probation is a local function of the Ohio courts that deal with juvenile matters, whereas adult probation is handled in some cases under the administrative authority of the local courts and in other cases by the Probation Development and Supervision Section of the Adult Parole Authority which is an agency located in the executive branch of state government. In Texas, adult and juvenile probation services come under the appointive power and supervision of the local and juvenile courts.

There has been a great deal of argument over which administrative arrangement is best. Although the National Advisory Commission on Criminal Justice Standards and Goals advocates placing all state probation services under a unified state correctional system, many argue that this function should be retained by the local courts. The arguments for both sides have been summed up as follows:

Arguments for Having Probation Services Administered by Local Courts
Under this arrangement, probation would be more responsive to court direction. Throughout the probation process, the court could provide guidance to probation workers and take corrective action when policies were not followed or proved ineffective.

This arrangement would provide the judiciary with an automatic feedback mechanism on effectiveness of dispositions through reports filed by probation staff. Judges would place more trust in reports from their own staff than in those compiled by an outside agency.

Courts have a greater awareness of needed resources and may become advocates for their staffs in obtaining better services.

Increased use of pretrial diversion may be furthered by placing probation services under the auspices of the courts. Since courts have not been inclined to delegate their authority to persons not connected with the judiciary or its staff, it is likely that probation services which are not under the court will have less discretion in employing diversionary measures.[42]

Arguments for Having Probation Services Administered by a Central State Executive Agency
When probation services are attached to the courts, judges frequently become the administrators of probation in their jurisdictions—a role for which they are usually

ill-equipped. Judges cannot effectively divide their time between administering probation services and yet perform their judicial functions.

When probation is within the judicial system, the probation staff is likely to give priority to services for the courts such as issuing summonses, serving subpoenas, etc., rather than providing services to probationers.

Since the criminal courts in particular are adjudicatory and regulatory rather than service-oriented organizations, probation services that are attached to courts will not develop a professional identity of [their] own.

The executive branch contains the allied human service agencies, including social and rehabilitative services, medical services, employment services, and housing, which can be used to develop more coordinated cooperative and comprehensive program efforts with probation agencies.[43]

Shock Probation

One of the suggested methods of handling offenders is to incarcerate them for a brief part of the sentence, suspend the remainder, and place them on probation. This approach, called *shock probation,* attempts to avoid the long-term prison commitment and its effects on the offender. Those who advocate the use of shock probation contend: (1) that short-term institutionalization may be to the inmate's advantage since the period of incarceration can provide probation agencies the opportunity to evaluate the needs of the offender in more detail so that they are in a better position to help; (2) it will jolt the individual into a realization of the realities of prison life and thereby serve as a more meaningful deterrent to future criminal behavior than probation alone; and (3) that it provides a way to combine probation with short jail terms as a compromise between immediate release and a regular prison sentence.[44]

Ohio was the first state to pass such an act in 1965. Since 1970, several other states have passed laws that give judges the option of applying shock probation as an alternative. Under the Ohio law as amended in 1967 and 1976, offenders can apply for shock probation between their thirtieth and sixtieth day in prison. Under the statute, the offender may be sentenced to prison and then released by a judge after serving between 30 and 130 days. In response to public complaints that serious offenders were being released too soon under the law, a 1976 amendment excluded from shock probation all "dangerous" offenders and all those convicted of violent crimes or crimes that involve a weapon.[45]

During its first year of operation, only 85 cases were released on shock probation. As of 1977, over 11,000 cases were handled by this technique. Partly because of the Ohio Department of Correction's inadequate research facilities, and partly because of the difficulty in gathering data from all the courts in Ohio's 88 counties, statistics on the success or failure of the program are sparse. The only figures made available by the department are the number of shock cases per year and the number of recommitments to state prison. There are no figures on types of crimes committed by shock probationers or on those who committed new crimes out-of-state, committed new crimes without being incarcerated, or absconded from supervision.[46]

The department claims that only slightly over 10 percent of shock probationers are recommitted. A research study of probationers under the program during its first 4 years of operation came up with a similar success rate.[47] However, these rates have been challenged by a 5-year study of the program, completed in 1975, by Harry R. Angelino of the Behavioral Sciences Laboratory of the Ohio State University. Dr. Angelino's study of 554 men and women released on shock probation between 1966 and 1970 showed that, over a 5-year period, 31.3 percent were convicted of subsequent felonies. However, the study also showed that most of the crimes committed by shock probationers after release were nonassaultive and less serious than those for which they were originally imprisoned.[48]

Probation Subsidy Programs

A few states, notably Michigan and California, recently developed a probation subsidy program in which the state pays counties that administer probation services to *keep juvenile offenders out of state institutions*. The concept of the subsidy program is in keeping with modern correctional philosophy that strives to keep delinquents out of institutions that often further educate them in crime and at the same time stigmatize them. The most highly developed program is in California, where the program was inaugurated on a trial basis in 1965. By 1973, 45 of California's 58 counties were participating.

Juveniles in California, who without the provisions of the program would be sentenced to one of the California Youth Authority institutions, are eligible for the program which the authority manages. Under the subsidy plan, the participating counties are paid as much as $4,000 per year for each probation case that they retain. Most of the cases come from the juvenile courts; however, a few serious cases of youthful offenders found guilty by the general criminal courts have also been involved in the program. As of 1971, a fraction over 20 percent were removed from the program because they had in some way violated the conditions of probation.[49]

Los Angeles County, the most populous county in the state, received over $5 million in subsidies during the 1968-1969 fiscal year. By 1971, subsidies to the participating counties amounted to nearly $20 million. Although this is a large sum of money, it is far less than the state would have to pay for the institutionalization of these offenders. The program has helped California cut back drastically on its costs of institutionalization and the need to expand institutional facilities and programs during a period of critical budget cuts. The program has also enabled the counties to develop outstanding probation departments and to expand their staffs and attract many qualified professionals. Although some claim that overall it has been a demonstrated success and others claim that the program is too lenient and does not serve as a deterrent to crime, it is still too early for any conclusive argument to be made concerning its success or failure.

Use of Indigenous Paraprofessionals or Volunteers

In the past 10 years, there has been a growing trend among probation departments to recruit auxiliary personnel from the same social class as the probationers. Such persons are referred to as *indigenous paraprofessionals*.

Many probation officers agree that their clientele are often alienated from the mainstream of society by virtue of their norms, values, and life styles. Frequently, these probationers are referred to as hard to reach, unmotivated, mistrustful, and resentful of authority. As Beless and others have said: "There exists a marked *social distance* between many middle-class professional corrections workers and a large segment of their lower-class clientele."[50]

As a consequence, a number of probation departments are experimenting with the use of indigenous paraprofessionals to assist probation officers. Grosser sees the local resident worker as a bridge between the lower class client and the middle-class professional worker.[51]

In addition to the indigenous paraprofessional, a number of probation agencies are now using former offenders in their assistance programs. This idea draws upon the experience of such groups as Alcoholics Anonymous and Delancey Street, which operates on the idea that those who have experienced and overcome a problem have a unique capacity to help others with similar problems. Riesman characterized this phenomenon as the helper therapy principle and concluded:

> Perhaps, then, social work's strategy ought to be to devise ways of creating more helpers! Or, to be more exact, to find ways to transform *recipients* of help into *dispensers* of help, thus reversing their roles, and to structure the situation so that recipients of help will be placed in roles requiring the giving of assistance.[52]

One such program is the Chicago-based Probation Officer Case Aide (POCA). This program uses indigenous paraprofessionals for federal probation and parole, with some being former offenders. Applicants for probation officer assistant (POA) are recruited primarily from neighborhoods that have a high proportion of offender clients. Applicants come to the project by way of recommendations of probation staff officers, referrals from local social service agencies, and self-referrals. In establishing the program, the crucial issue was the selection criteria. It was decided that applicants would be chosen by a selection committee of the project staff. Once selected, the POA attends orientation and training sessions and is then assigned to a probation officer who supervises ten POAs.

It has been found that these indigenous paraprofessionals are interested, available, and able to work well under professional supervision. It also has been demonstrated that they provide a productive and effective service to professional probation officers. They are frequently able to intervene in cases where probation staff officers might encounter problems.[53]

Another interesting variation of this idea has been proposed by the National Council on Crime and Delinquency, which not only recommends the use of former offenders to assist in probation work, but even suggests using carefully selected probationers to work with other probationers. In this way, an individual, while helping others, would be contributing to his or her own self-help and improvement and would be developing skills that might help the probationer become a probation officer or other social service employee.[54]

Something similar has already occurred in the Chicago POCA project. One former offender in the program joined the POCA project and began attending classes at a local junior college. He was later admitted to the criminal justice program in a major university and was hired by the Illinois Department of Corrections as an adult parole officer. Another man, after serving as a POA, obtained employment with the Illinois Department of Social Services as a youth supervisor.

A last program worthy of mention is a special LEAA sponsored project in Lincoln, Nebraska, called the Volunteer Probation Counselor Program. It is considered by LEAA to be an "exemplary" project which is a special distinction that has been given to only 13 outstanding criminal justice programs throughout the nation. The program's primary goal is to help rehabilitate high-risk misdemeanants between the ages of 16 and 25. A probationer is assigned to a volunteer for supervision and assistance, matched on the basis of mutual interests and the probationer's interpersonal needs. Volunteer counselors, all of whom have been carefully screened and trained in counseling skills, are each responsible for a single probationer.

In addition to one-to-one counseling, citizens from the community provide services in a variety of different roles, serving as instructors and group leaders for court-conducted educational classes, performing clerical and public relations work for the probation office, tutoring offenders with reading deficiencies, and similar projects. The program is coordinated by a member of the court's probation office, and volunteers serve without remuneration.

The volunteers are recruited in a number of ways. Two volunteer bureaus, one in the city of Lincoln and the other at the University of Nebraska, publicize the program and seek recruits. The media also creates public awareness of the program, and probation officers appear before community and university groups to discuss volunteer activities. The screening of volunteers is quite thorough. Applicants are judged on the basis of information provided on the application form, interviews with the volunteer coordinator, psychological testing, and performance during training. The volunteer's occupation, education, organizational affiliations and activities, hobbies and special interests, tutoring or counseling experience, and family background are taken into consideration. Likewise, the candidate's motives for wanting to become a counselor are closely scrutinized.

The training program is quite interesting. After applicants are introduced to the purposes of the program, they receive a description of relevant community resources, and participate in small group discussions of study questions provided in a fictitious presentence investigation report. Another session focuses on counseling skills, the nature of high-risk offenders, and techniques for handling crisis situations. A judge briefly describes the legal system and the role of probation. Role playing exercises are conducted and comments and feedback are provided by other volunteers and the probation office staff. Volunteers who are accepted into the program are formally sworn in by the judge during a court ceremony and are given identification cards.

The results of the program have been subjected to evaluation. Whereas 70.5 percent of the high-risk offenders who received regular probation committed additional offenses, only 55.5 percent of those in the volunteer program were recidivists. Table 15-2 shows that the group in the volunteer program has also had far less involvement with the criminal justice system during the probation year.

TABLE 15-2

Recidivism Comparisons During the Probationary Year for Volunteer Program Probationers and Regular Probationers

	VOLUNTEER PROGRAM (N = 40)	REGULAR PROBATION (N = 44)
Additional offense	55.5%	70.5%
Additional nontraffic offense	15.0%	63.7%
More than one additional offense	10.0%	52.5%

Source: U.S. Department of Justice, *The Volunteer Probation Counselor Program* (Washington, D.C.: LEAA n.d.), p. 15.

Probation Work as a Career

Like the other agencies of criminal justice, probation suffers from a lack of qualified personnel and financial resources. In 1976, there were nearly 42,000 officers and administrative (nonclerical) personnel engaged in federal, state, and local probation and parole services in the United States.[55] It is not possible to break these figures down in order to provide a more accurate picture of the number of probation officers because some jurisdictions combine the functions of parole officer and probation officer. In addition, some probation officers handle only juveniles, and some supervise only adults. Data are not available that would differentiate these categories. Only a few states, such as Wisconsin, have combined all adult and juvenile probation cases, whether felon or misdemeanant, in a single bureau of probation and parole in an attempt to centralize services at the state level.[56]

Probation services and departments range from small, rural offices in which the chief probation officer is the entire staff to highly complex and specialized organizations, such as the Los Angeles County Probation Department, which employs over 4,000 staff members, about 2,200 of which perform professional probation services as deputy probation officers and supervisors.

Qualifications The American Correctional Association, in its *Manual of Correctional Standards,* suggests that individuals preparing to become probation officers complete earning either a master's degree in social work, or do 2 years of work in a comparable behavioral science with at least 1 year of graduate study. In addition, probation officers should possess highly developed skills in casework, counseling, interpersonal communications, and leadership.[57] Carney believes that these criteria are unrealistic because of the critical shortage of probation officers across the nation and because higher education offered in corrections is inadequate.[58] He bases his argument on the fact that most schools of social work offer very few courses in the field of corrections. Consequently, students in traditional social work programs are not being adequately prepared for the unique problems that they will face in working with offenders. Many young probation officers indicate that they would be more successful if they had acquired more knowledge of the system of criminal justice before beginning their careers.

Most academic programs are also woefully inadequate in training social work students in the process of decision making, although probation officers must make countless decisions—not to take action, to delay action, or to take one form of action in lieu of another. Cohen has said that the only "legally relevant" issue in probation and parole is that which "involves authoritative decision makers exercising a vast discretion."[59] Immediate work needs to be done to understand how best to reach appropriate probational decisions. This will be a difficult task because the majority of probation officers' decisions are unrecorded—indeed, most of them are not normally thought of as decisions. Furthermore, these decisions are not simply a function of an offender's behavior, but rather reflect the interrelationship of many factors, some of which are explicit, such as the operating procedures of the probation office, and some of which are considerably more complex and subtle and include the probation officer and the social and political system in which he or she operates.[60]

Functions Probation officers are responsible for the management and supervision of the offenders who make up their case loads. For a number of years, the recommended case load has been established at 50 units. The American Correctional Association and the President's Commission on Law Enforcement and Administration of Justice recommend 50-unit and 35-unit case loads, respectively, with the provision that each presentence investigation and report that the probation officer is required to compile should count as five supervised cases. Both of these arbitrary figures seem to be without any meaningful justification. The usual rationale for smaller case loads is that the fewer individuals the probation or parole officer has to supervise, the more effective the supervision will be. However, research has indicated that there appears to be no relationship between size of case load and success or failure of a probationer or parolee. Adams conducted detailed reviews of case-load size research in which he summarized the findings of a dozen case-load studies conducted in the federal system and in California in which case loads ranged from only 12 offenders to 210. He could find no evidence to indicate that offenders in the smaller case loads did any better than offenders who were part of much larger case loads.[61]

A probation officer does far more than merely supervise a case load of probationers. In addition to providing counseling, employment assistance, and other related services, a probation officer must be an investigator and a diagnostician of the needs of the probationer and must be able to develop, coordinate, and implement the special casework services needed. Probation officers also perform another important role in that they often serve in a quasi-judicial function, especially where judges more or less automatically impose the sentence recommended in the probation officer's presentence report. Various studies have shown a very high relationship between probation officers' recommendations and dispositions made by judges. Carter and Wilkins have pointed out that judges follow probation officers' recommendations in better than 95 percent of the cases.[62] Part of this might be attributable to the probation officer anticipating what sentence the judge is predisposed to give and then recommending it, but there are probably many instances where the judge goes along with the recommended sentence on the assumption that the probation officer, having conducted the presentence investigation, has the most complete facts.

Unless prevented by statute, the court has the power to set the specific conditions of probation for adult offenders. Often the judge imposes the specific requirements on the probationer that the probation department recommends. The probation officer is also responsible for initiating revocation of probation, although it is the judge who actually revokes probation. Most probation revocation statutes are so vague that it is not difficult for the probation officer who wishes to do so to find cause to invoke the revocation process, usually on the basis of some technical violation. Finally, the probation officer has the ability to render punishment under the guise of rehabilitation—for example, by demanding that the probationer not live in or frequent certain areas, not engage in certain employment, and not associate with certain people.[63]

Probation will probably continue to be used extensively as a means to divert offenders from institutions, and use of probation volunteers and indigenous paraprofessionals will probably increase. The future of parole seems to be somewhat uncertain, particularly as states establish definite periods of imprisonment after which the offender is released without community supervision. At this time, however, it is too early to tell whether such trends will develop extensively in the future.

SUMMARY

Parole is the conditional release of an offender who has served a period of time in prison, while probation is the conditional release of an individual who has been found guilty in court. Parole has its roots in such practices as conditional pardons, indenture, tickets of leave, and indeterminate sentences. Modern parole originated at the Elmira Reformatory. Parole is not a form of leniency but rather an extension of the rehabilitative and reintegrative program begun in the institution. States have traditionally organized adult paroling authority around three models—the institutional, the independent, and the consolidated. In recent years, the consolidated model has been adopted by most states. Just as each state has its own parole authority, so does the federal government. Decisions of parole boards are usually based upon the seriousness and nature of the current offense, the circumstances of the crime, the placement situation, and the offender's institutional record. In recent years, some states and the federal government have been developing prediction methods to assist parole boards in making their decisions.

Among some of the recent changes in parole are increased legal rights of the parolee, the development of parole teams, the parole contract plan, and improvements in the selection of parole board members. In spite of the advances in parole, there is some indication that in the years ahead parole, along with the indeterminate sentence, may cease to exist. Both are being closely examined by some states.

Probation services are also undergoing changes. One is the movement toward providing adult probation services through a centralized state authority rather than on a strictly local basis. Other innovations are probation subsidy programs, shock probations, and use of volunteers, indigenous paraprofessionals, and former offenders as probation aides. Probation will probably continue to be used extensively as a diversionary practice.

REVIEW QUESTIONS

1. What is parole and at what stage in the criminal justice process is an offender granted parole?
2. Name four historical precedents of parole. Briefly explain each of them.
3. Identify three basic concepts underlying parole in the United States.
4. Briefly describe the three classifications of adult paroling authorities recommended by the National Advisory Commission on Criminal Justice Standards and Goals.
5. What factors are considered in deciding whether or not to grant parole to an offender?
6. What is the salient-factor score? How much more additional time might an offender spend in prison if he has committed a high-severity offense, has a good prognosis, and has already served 7 months in prison?
7. List the conclusions reached by Daniel Glaser in his research on the post-release success of inmates.
8. What are the major roles played the parole officer?
9. What does the term *indeterminate sentence* mean? Why is the indeterminate being criticized?
10. What is probation? What are the two ways a judge can impose a sentence of probation?
11. What are the responsibilities of the probation officers?
12. Summarize the importance of the following two cases:
    a. *Mempa* v. *Rhay*
    b. *Gagnon* v. *Scarpelli*

DISCUSSION QUESTIONS

1. Discuss the various alternative ways that states administer their parole services. What are the relative advantages and disadvantages of each?
2. How does the U.S. Parole Commission operate? How does this agency employ its Salient Factor Score?
3. Discuss the decisions upon which parole is typically based. Can you think of any other consideration which might be important?
4. Discuss the issue of parolee's rights. Do you agree or disagree with court-imposed guidelines in this area?
5. Should states institute "flat" sentences and abolish parole? Why?
6. How do courts normally impose probation?
7. Discuss some of the reforms suggested for probation services.

SUGGESTED ADDITIONAL READINGS

Abadinsky, Howard. *Probation and Parole: Theory and Practice.* Englewood Cliffs, N.J.: Prentice-Hall, 1977.

American Bar Association Project on Minimum Standards for Criminal Justice. *Standards Relating to Pretrial Release*. New York: Institute of Judical Administration, 1968.

————. *Standards Relating to Probation*. New York: Institute of Judicial Administration, 1970.

Bates, Sanford. "When Is Probation Not Probation?" *Federal Probation* 24: 13–20.

Blair, Louis H. *Monitoring the Impacts of Prison and Parole Services*. Washington, D.C.: The Urban Institute, 1977.

Campbell, W. J. *Probation and Parole: Selected Readings*. New York: Wiley, 1960.

Dressler, D. *Practice and Theory of Probation and Parole*. New York: Columbia University Press, 1960.

Empey, Lamar T. *Alternatives to Incarceration*. Washington, D.C.: U.S. Government Printing Office, 1967.

England, R. "What Is Responsible for Satisfactory Probation and Post-Probation Outcome?" *Journal of Criminal Law, Criminology and Police Science* 47 (1957):667–676.

Friday, Paul C., David M. Peterson, and Harry E. Allen. "Shock Probation: A New Approach to Crime Control." *Georgia Journal of Corrections* 1 (July 1973):1–13.

Glaser, Daniel, and V. O'Leary. *Personal Characteristics of Parole Outcome*. Washington, D.C.: U.S. Government Printing Office, 1966.

Meiners, R.C. "A Halfway House for Parolees." *Federal Probation* 29 (June 1965):47–52.

Pigeon, Helen D. *Probation and Parole in Theory and Practice*. New York: National Probation and Parole Association, 1942.

Smith, Alexander B. *Introduction to Probation and Parole*. St. Paul, Minn.: West, 1976.

Smith, Robert L. *A Quiet Revolution—Probation Subsidy*. Washington, D.C.: U.S. Department of Health, Education, and Welfare, 1972.

Stanley, David T. *Prisoners Among Us—The Problem of Parole*. Washington, D.C.: The Brookings Institution, 1976.

NOTES

1. Law Enforcement Assistance Administration, *State and Local Probation and Parole Systems* (Washington, D.C.: U.S. Government Printing Office, February 1978), p. 1.

2. Charles L. Newman, *Sourcebook on Probation, Paroles and Pardons* (Springfield, Ill.: Thomas, 1970), p. 26.

3. William Parker, *Parole: Origins, Development, Current Practices and Statutes* (College Park, Md.: American Correctional Association, May 1972), p. 10.

4. National Council on Crime and Delinquency, *Corrections in the United States* (New York: NCCD, 1967), p. 217.

5. National Advisory Commission on Criminal Justice Standards and Goals, *Corrections* (Washington, D.C.: U.S. Government Printing Office, 1973), pp. 395–397.

6. David T. Stanley, *Prisoners Among Us: The Problem of Parole* (Washington, D.C.: The Brookings Institution, 1977), p. 27.

7. National Advisory Commission, *Corrections*, pp. 396–397.

8. The operations of the commission are fully explained in *Federal Register*, 42, no. 151 (August 5, 1977): 39808–39822.

9. Daniel Glaser, *Effectiveness of a Prison and Parole System* (Indianapolis: Bobbs-Merrill, 1959), p. 23.

10. Michigan Department of Corrections, "Operation and Philosophy of the Michigan Parole Board" (mimeo), February 10, 1975, p. 3.

11. Stanley, *Prisoners Among Us*, p. 49.

12. Ibid., p. 49.

13. For example, see Don F. Gottfredson, "A Shorthand Formula for Base Expectancies," California Department of Corrections, Research Division, *Research Report No. 5* (Sacramento, July 1962); P. G. Ward, "Validating Prediction Scales," *British Journal of Criminology* 7 (1967): 36–44; Peter B. Hoffman and James L. Beck, "Parole Decision-Making: A Salient Factor Score," *Journal of Criminal Justice* (Winter 1974): 195–206.

14. 28C.F.R. § 2.52, 38 Federal Register 222 (November 19, 1973) as amended. Also see D. M. Gottfredson, P. B. Hoffman, M. H. Sigler, and L. T. Wilkons, "Making Paroling Policy Explicit," *Crime and Delinquency* 21 (1975).

15. 28C.F.R. § 2.20 (c), p. 37322. See also 18 U.S.C. 7206 as revised (1976).

16. Norman S. Hayner, "Parole Boards' Attitudes Toward Predictive Devices," in Norman Johnson et al., eds., *The Sociology of Punishment and Correction* (New York: Wiley, 1970), pp. 839–843.

17. Daniel Glaser, *Effectiveness of a Prison and Parole System* (Indianapolis: Bobbs-Merrill, 1959).

18. Robert Sklar, "Law and Practice in Probation and Parole Revocation Hearings," *Journal of Criminal Law, Criminology and Police Science* 55 (1964): 75.

19. 389 U.S. 128 (1967).

20. National Advisory Commission, *Corrections*, p. 405.

21. Quoted in ibid., pp. 405–406.

22. 408 U.S. 471 (1972).

23. "A New Helping Hand for Prison Inmates," *Reader's Digest* 97 (August 1970): 147–150.

24. Louis P. Carney, *Introduction to Correctional Science* (New York: McGraw-Hill, 1974), p. 327.

25. Steve Gettinger, "Parole Contracts: A New Way Out," *Corrections Magazine* 2, no. 1. (September–October, 1975): 4.

26. Ibid.

27. Michigan Department of Corrections, "Contract Service Program Pilot Phase," mimeo (1975), p. 4.

28. Gettinger, "Parole Contracts," p. 5.

29. Law Enforcement Assistance Administration, *State and Local Probation and Parole Systems*, pp. 107–178.

30. National Advisory Commission, *Corrections*, p. 420.

31. For example, see American Friends Service Committee, *Struggle for Justice: A Report of Crime and Punishment in America* (New York: Hill & Wang, 1971); Jessica Mitford, *Kind and Unusual Punishment: The Prison Business* (New York: Knopf, 1973).

32. The following discussion of the new provisions in Maine is based on Steve Gettinger, "Profile: Maine," *Corrections Magazine* 1, no. 6 (July–August, 1975): 13–26.

33. See Richard A. McGee, "California's New Determinate Sentencing Act," *Federal Probation* 42 (March 1978): 3–7.

34. Stephen Gettinger, "Fixed Sentencing Becomes Law in Three States," *Corrections Magazine* 3 (September 1977): 16–42.

35. Of course, it should be expected that there are those who would defend the need for continued parole supervision. See Robert Martinson and Judith Wilks, "Save Parole," *Federal Probation* 41 (September 1977): 23–26; and Maurice H. Sigler, "Abolish Parole?" *Federal Probation* 39 (June 1975): 42–47.

36. For a more thorough discussion of how such decisions are made, see Alexander B. Smith and Louis Berlin, *Introduction to Probation and Parole* (St. Paul, Minn.: West, 1975), especially Chap. 3.

37. Hazel B. Kerper and Janeen Kerper, *Legal Rights of the Convicted* (St. Paul, Minn.: West, 1974), p. 251.

38. Elmer H. Johnson, *Crime, Correction and Society* (Homewood, Ill.: Dorsey, 1968), p. 666.

39. Specifically, there were 923,064 adults on probation and 328,854 juveniles. LEAA, *State and Local Probation,* p. 1.

40. State of Indiana, *Report to the Citizens Council on Probation* (1973), p. 2.

41. State of Michigan, Department of Correction, *Criminal Statistics* (Lansing, 1972).

42. National Advisory Commission, *Corrections,* p. 313.

43. Ibid., p. 314.

44. See I. R. Kaufman, "Enlightened Sentences Through Improved Techniques," *Federal Probation* 26 (1962): 3–10; Irving W. Jayne, "The Purpose of the Sentence," *National Probation and Parole Association Journal* 2 (1956): 315–319; and Joan Potter, "Shock Probation: A Little Taste of Prison," *Corrections Magazines* 3 (December 1977): 49–55.

45. Potter, "Shock Probation," p. 50.

46. Ibid., pp. 51–52.

47. See Paul C. Friday, David H. Petersen, and Harry E. Allen, "Shock Probation: A New Approach to Crime Control," in David H. Petersen and Charles W. Thomas, *Corrections* (Englewood Cliffs, N.J.: Prentice-Hall, 1975), p. 251.

48. Potter, "Shock Probation," p. 52.

49. California Youth Authority, *Probation Subsidy Evaluation* (Sacramento, Calif.: May 1972).

50. Donald W. Beless, William S. Pilcher, and Ellen Jo Ryan, "Use of Indigenous Nonprofessionals in Probation and Parole," *Federal Probation* 36 (March 1972): 11.

51. C. F. Grosser, "Local Residents as Mediators between Middle-Class Professional Workers and Lower-Class Clients," *Social Service Review* 40, no. 1 (March 1966): 56–63.

52. F. Riesman, "The 'Helper' Therapy Principle," *Social Work* 10 (April 1965): 28.

53. Beless et al., "Use of Indigenous Nonprofessionals in Probation and Parole," p. 15.

54. See National Council on Crime and Delinquency, *Team Management in Probation and Parole* (Paramus, N.J.: NCCD, 1972).

55. See Law Enforcement Assistance Administration, *Sourcebook of Criminal Justice Statistics—1976* (Washington, D.C.: U.S. Government Printing Office, February 1977) and LEAA, *State and Local Probation.*

56. However, the supervision of juvenile probationers by the Wisconsin state authority is only in cases where the committing court asks for their help or where counties have not established their own juvenile probation office.

57. American Correctional Association. *Manual of Correctional Standards* (College Park, Md.: American Correctional Association, 1971), p. 98.

58. Louis P. Carney, *Introduction to Correctional Science* (New York: McGraw-Hill, 1974), p. 303.

59. Fred Cohen, "The Legal Challenge to Corrections," *Joint Commission on Correctional Manpower and Training*, Washington, D.C., March 1969, pp. 26–27.

60. Robert M. Carter et al., *Corrections in America* (Philadelphia: Lippincott, 1975), p. 194.

61. See Stuart Adams, "Some Findings from Correctional Caseload Research," *Federal Probation* 31 (December 1967): 55.

62. Robert M. Carter and Leslie T. Wilkins, "Some Factors in Sentencing Policy," *Journal of Criminal Law, Criminology and Police Science* 58, no. 4 (1967): 503–504.

63. Eugene H. Czajkoski, "Exposing the Quasi-Judicial Role of the Probation Officer," *Federal Probation* 37 (September 1973): 9–13.

16
CURRENT ISSUES
AND TRENDS

1. Why are community-based programs gaining favor within corrections?
2. What rationale is used to justify community-based corrections?
3. What are the major community-based programs?
4. What facilities serve the parolee after returning to the community?
5. What will be the issues and trends within corrections in the near future?

These are some of the questions this chapter will answer.

In the preceding chapters on corrections, we have discussed developments in traditional jails and detention facilities and in parole and probation. In this chapter, we explore the growing popularity of community-based correctional programs such as work-release and home furlough programs and examine general issues and trends in the broad areas of corrections, such as inmate rights and the improving quality of correctional staffs.

COMMUNITY-BASED CORRECTIONS

The term *community-based corrections* applies not only to changes in the traditional location and use of prisons but also to the inclusion of specific programs of rehabilitation within this new design of institutional programming.

Community-based programs are becoming increasingly popular as an alternative to traditional forms of imprisonment for several reasons. First, prison administrators are realizing that massive and isolated prisons do not provide the best setting for rehabilitative programs. In order to better achieve the rehabilitative goals of imprisonment, institutional programs and inmates must interact more with society. Rehabilitation behind prison walls is often centered around artificial environments and pressures that are not conducive to a meaningful adjustment to society when the inmate is released. Such rehabilitative programs effectively remove the offender from the positive influences of society and also prevent rehabilitative personnel from observing an inmate's ability to interact with society and to cope with the pressures of the nonprison environment. After all, it is these pressures and adjustments that the offender must contend with upon leaving prison.

Second, community-based programs permit a broader range of programs and rehabilitative strategies than would be possible under traditional forms of imprisonment. By utilizing existing community resources, these correctional programs can provide a wide range of treatment specialists, who otherwise would not be available to the prisoners.

Because the benefits of community-based programs are now being recognized, several changes are occurring in prison systems throughout the country. Offenders who require institutionalization are increasingly being involved in these programs. To accommodate the gradual movement of an increasing number of inmates into these programs, structural changes are now taking place within the prison system. For instance, the massive institutions built in rural areas for purposes of isolation and security are giving way to the development and construction of smaller facilities located near population centers.

Also, community resources and personnel are being used more in the rehabilitative effort. A number of specialized programs have been developed such as work and study release, restitution programs, and furloughs to help the inmate bridge the gap between life inside and outside prison. Some of the more widely adopted and popular programs based on the community-based model are discussed in the pages that follow.

BASIS FOR COMMUNITY-BASED CORRECTIONS: DIVERSION

The basic rationale behind community-based corrections is diversion; that is, directing offenders away from the traditional process of the criminal justice system. Diversion, which is a commonly used term among criminal justice specialists, has any number of meanings. Used in connection with *preventive strategies*, it means that offenders are diverted from criminal behavior so that they will not come in contact with the justice system to begin with. This approach, most commonly used in juvenile corrections, relies on parents, police, schools, agencies, and peers to address social problems in such a way that the individual does not become involved in antisocial behavior.

Diversion also means diverting offenders to alternative assistance programs rather than referring them to the adjudicatory process of the courts. It can mean, finally, diverting convicted offenders to a form of community supervision such as probation rather than imprisonment. In this chapter, *the term is used to indicate diverting incarcerated offenders to special programs and institutions instead of warehousing them in a conventional prison.* The use of diversion in this context was brought about by three important factors.

Failure of Traditional Methods

The usual means of handling offenders has been an abysmal failure. In fact, it could be argued that it has contributed to the incidence of crime rather than deterring or preventing it. For example, even the U.S. Bureau of Prisons, which is probably our most progressive penal system, was encouraged by a recent study which showed that 2 years following release from that system only one-third of the released offenders were recidivists.[1] Many penologists would put the actual rate of recidivism much higher, around 50 to 60 percent. Since it is likely that many released offenders commit additional crimes but are never caught, the picture is even bleaker.

Impact of the Community on Behavior

The idea that social forces in the community have a favorable or unfavorable impact upon the individual is by no means new. Studies conducted in the late 1920s and the early 1930s by a group of sociologists at the University of Chicago pointed out that community disorganization contributed significantly to criminal behavior. Out of this research developed the famous Chicago Area Projects, which focused on providing casework assistance to gangs and neighborhood youths to prevent crime and to interest the youths in noncriminal activities.[2] These early projects provide the theoretical basis for community-based corrections. Since that time, other cities have developed similar programs.[3]

Although the community can have both negative and positive effects, placing an offender in a prison often strengthens the negative influences. Separated from the positive influence of noncriminal elements of the community, the offender falls back on the influences of follow inmates. Through the process of socialization, the prisoner is often likely to become even more procriminal and less willing and able to identify with more appropriate non-criminal references in the outside world upon release. Under these circumstances, the inmate is likely to seek out associations in the community that hold similar attitudes to those he or she became accustomed to while in prison. The community-based correctional concept realizes that offenders must be encouraged to identify and maintain whatever ties they have with law-abiding members of society which incarceration usually severs; at the same time, these programs recognize the need to provide offenders with the appropriate supervision and help in order to limit their exposure to those who encourage continued criminal behavior.

Growing Demands of Interest Groups

Interested citizens both within and outside the criminal justice system are becoming increasingly alarmed at the failure of our traditional correctional institutions to "correct" and are waging an effective campaign to encourage the adoption of alternative means for dealing with offenders. A corollary development in the long run may be even more effective than the particular influence of these groups. In the past decade, many Americans have become disenchanted with government. They have come to see themselves as being acted upon, rather than actors in the process of government. This displeasure with governmental functions has certainly affected the public's attitude toward corrections, for a recent survey found that 69 percent of Americans had lost confidence in the ability of prisons to rehabilitate offenders.[4]

These three factors—the failure of the criminal justice system to deter crime or prevent its recurrence, recognition that the community has a significant impact upon behavior, and the growing involvement of interest groups in penal reform—are modifying our traditional responses to crime and channeling our efforts in the direction of diversion with its emphasis on movement away from the justice system.[5] In the years ahead, we will probably see more community-based programs in which established agencies of justice relinquish their traditionally unilateral handling and responses to deviant behavior in favor of joint programs that involve the total community.[6]

The Relationship of Diversion to Reintegration

Both the immediate and long-range goals of diversion as a correctional technique are to offer the means for the successful reintegration of the offender into community life as a law-abiding citizen. To achieve this, the concept of community-based corrections is guided by three considerations:

1. *More realistic adaptation of institutional life to realities of life in the community.* Prisons, jails, and juvenile institutions need to introduce changes which will make conditions in them more similar to conditions in a free society. This does not mean that inmates should be provided with a host of creature amenities. It does mean that within the context of necessary security and requirements for discipline, inmates be confined under conditions conducive to developing more self-generated control rather than induced and forced control through exacting discipline and regimentation. This

will permit the observations of behavior under conditions more similar to the natural environment to which almost all inmates will someday return.

It also recognizes that supportive ties of a positive nature may be very critical to successful treatment and readjustment. For example, maintenance of such positive ties as family need to be encouraged and sustained.

2. *Link to other community assistance agencies.* Correctional efforts and resources are limited. There are a wide variety of organizations, public and private, offering services to people who need help. Many inmates need these same types of service and assistance. Examples are vocational rehabilitation, mental health, family counseling, and drug and alcohol abuse programs. There must be a bridging by corrections to utilize these services to help corrections achieve its own goals.

3. *Civic engagement and participation.* Both by means of formal organizations and through the assistance of individuals, there is increasing recognition that volunteer citizen participation offers tremendous potential for working with offender reintegration programs. Traditionally, this civic participation has come from established religious, social service, and employer groups. The correctional field needs to learn more effective methods of engaging these resources and applying their help.[7]

COMMUNITY-BASED PROGRAMS

At present, there are four notable types of community-based programs. They are known as work-release, academic-pass, conjugal and family visit, and home furlough programs.

Work-Release Programs

Under work-release programs, selected inmates are released from the institution during the day to continue their regular jobs in the community while spending daily after-work hours and weekends in confinement. Vermont started the first work-release program in 1906. Its legislature enacted a law providing for civilian employment and authorized county sheriffs to set their prisoners to work outside the jail. Sheriff Frank H. Tracey, of Montpelier, rebuffed in his efforts to find employers, hired some of his prisoners to work on his own farm at prevailing rates paid civilian laborers. Part of the prisoner's earnings were paid to the state, and the remainder was retained by Sheriff Tracey and given to the prisoners when they finished their jail sentence. This early form of work release had most, if not all, of the basic elements found in todays' work-release programs.[8]

Although Vermont is credited with the original idea, the Huber Act passed by Wisconsin in 1913 is the model upon which modern work-release programs are based. The act provided that county jail inmates, with the permission of the court, could be enrolled in work-release programs under the supervision of the sheriff. In 1957, a North Carolina statute extended work release to offenders in state institutions, but only certain misdemeanants recommended for work release by sentencing judges were eligible. In 1959, North Carolina passed new provisions that extended eligibility to certain classes of felony offenders. By 1971, 41 states and the District of Columbia had adopted work-release programs. Today, all states have such programs.

The Prisoner Rehabilitation Act passed by Congress in 1965, authorized the U.S. Bureau of Prisons to use work-release programs.[9] In Europe, Sweden passed similar legislation in 1945, followed by Scotland in 1947. During the 1950s, Norway, Great Britain, and France also authorized similar programs.[10]

States that have implemented work-release programs usually follow one of two established approaches or a combination of the two. In the older approach, prisoners work in the community while living in the penal institution. This arrangement has caused some problems for both prison officials and inmates who participate in the program. The work releasees are often harassed and intimidated by nonparticipating inmates, who accuse them of being "privileged characters." This has sometimes led to situations where qualified inmates have refused to participate in such programs. Another problem is controlling the flow of contraband smuggled back into the prison by work releasees either voluntarily or because of inmate intimidation and threats. A third problem is that many prisons are situated in relatively remote areas where job opportunities in neighboring communities are very limited.

The second approach, which is gaining in popularity, is to use a special small facility situated near an urban center as a residential unit for inmates on work release. This arrangement seems to have overcome many of the problems associated with trying to administer a program from the prison institution itself.

Advantages and Limitations of Work Release Work-release programs have advantages for the inmate and for the state. These programs permit the inmate to develop contacts and work experience not usually available within the prison. In this way, the individual becomes better prepared for eventual release. By establishing himself or herself in a job while still in prison, the offender has immediate employment upon release and does not face the problem of trying to find legitimate work with the associated stigma of being an exconvict. Work experiences can also be beneficial to many inmates who have failed to develop appropriate work habits throughout their lives. Prison industries have not been shown to be very effective in developing appropriate work habits, but work-release programs can help overcome some of these problems.[11]

The second major advantage is economic. As pointed out in the previous chapter, it is very costly to keep an offender in prison, especially an inmate who supports a family. In work release, inmates are required to pay for their own room and board and to provide support for their families. A prescribed portion of their earnings is taken out by prison officials for these purposes. A small sum is retained by the inmates to purchase necessities and any remainder is put into a special fund which the offenders receive upon release.

A number of studies have been conducted to determine the effectiveness of work-release programs. One of the largest and most intensive studies was made of work releasees in Santa Clara County, California, from 1967 to 1971. Data were gathered from the postinstitutional adjustment records of 991 inmates who had been on work release and compared with those of 1,369 prisoners who had not. The inmates in the sample had been released from the institution during the period from 1957 to 1967.[12] Among other things, the study indicated that inmates who had participated in work-release programs felt closer ties to their families and that their families were more predisposed to accept them, whereas families of nonparticipating inmates were more likely to reject them. Work releasees displayed slightly greater hostility toward the criminal justice system. The researchers felt that the reason for this was that individuals in the work-release program were less likely to perceive themselves as criminals and thus, were more resentful toward the police, courts, and corrections for their incarceration. The work releasees also were more successful in maintaining jobs during the period following their release. Finally, the work releasees were less likely to be rearrested and convicted for the commission of additional crimes after their release.[13]

Work release also has some problems associated with it. One of the major problems is the psychological consequences that result from prohibiting an individual to participate in certain conduct. For example, he cannot stop on the way home after work for a drink with his fellow workers, regardless of how they might implore him to "have a beer" with them. By the same token, he must refrain from the use of any narcotic. Although a well-adjusted member of society could ignore these temptations, many offenders show a psychological predisposition toward lack of self-control. As a result, these temptations may be too much for the individual to handle. Many administrators of work-release programs go to great lengths to control such behavior, such as requiring that all individuals participating in the program take Antabuse, a substance that induces nausea if one drinks alcoholic beverages. Likewise, periodic urine specimens are taken to determine if the work releasee has taken narcotics.

Another negative consequence of work release is that these programs often compete directly with prison industries. If a prison system uses the work-release plan intensively, many well-motivated and skilled workers are diverted from prison industry programs. Also, unscrupulous private employers may exploit the individual on work release because of his vulnerability. Program administrators must constantly be alert to these consequences.

Academic-Pass Programs

Academic-pass or study-release programs are similar to work-release programs in that inmates are permitted to leave the institution to attend school and return to the prison or community facility after class. Most academic-pass programs utilize nearby educational institutions, such as vocational-trade institutes, junior and community colleges, and universities. In a few instances, correctional authorities also use nearby high schools, but generally high-school classes are taught within the institution. Inmate attendance at high schools presents certain problems with inmate and student peer interactions that are not normally found at the college level. The Michigan Department of Corrections contracts with that state's regional network of community colleges to provide degree programs both inside the penal facility and at the community college. All costs for tuition, books, and other supplies are paid for by the state. One of the most extensive study programs is the cooperative program between Jackson Community College and Southern Michigan Penitentiary. It is not unusual in that program to find correctional employees and inmates sitting in the same classroom with regular students, exchanging and sharing viewpoints, and gaining new perspectives through dialogue.

One interesting program, which had its beginnings in Oregon, is the New Gate Project. This project is now being sponsored by the National Council on Crime and Delinquency. This program is designed to offer inmates the opportunity to obtain an on-campus university education. In conjunction with cooperating universities, inmates are enrolled in academic programs and live like other students in university residence halls or dormitories. They must refrain from use of alcoholic beverages or narcotics and must report to supervising counselors in their dormitories at least once a week. The cost of this program is about the same as maintaining an unmarried prisoner in the traditional penitentiary.[14]

The purpose of academic-pass programs is, of course, to enable deserving, interested inmates to obtain the education and job skills necessary to lead legitimate and productive lives upon their return to society. Through education, it is hoped that they can assimilate more appropriate values and become contributing members of society.

Conjugal and Family Visitation Programs

Conjugal visitation is a program by which the spouse and in some cases the children of an inmate are permitted to visit in a special private facility of the prison. Usually, a separate section of the prison or small cottages are made available. Here, the inmate may have privacy and engage in the physical phase of the conjugal relationship. Advocates of conjugal visitation programs contend that these programs help inmates maintain meaningful ties with their families, and that it reduces the incidence of homosexuality among inmates. Those opposed to such programs argue that: (1) conjugal visits are incompatible with existing mores since they emphasize the physical satisfaction of sex; (2) married inmates who participate in these programs are those individuals who can best adjust to prison life anyway; (3) those inmates who present the greatest sexual problems—that is, homosexuals and other sex deviates—won't benefit from the program; (4) such programs offer no solution to the sexual tensions of single male or female prisoners; (5) wives may become pregnant, creating further problems for the state and the inmates; and (6) the maintenance of these separate, private facilities is too costly.[15]

Conjugal visits were first established in the United States at the Parchman Prison farm in Mississippi in 1918. At this institution, a "little red house" was set aside for the use of inmates and their wives. More recently, the California State Prison at Tehachapi instituted a somewhat similar program. At Tehachapi, housing which was previously occupied by staff has been set up to accommodate family visits. Eligible inmates are permitted to use this facility for a 2- or 3-day period, during the prerelease phase of their sentence. This situation more closely resembles the full family setting. Facilities for cooking and recreation are provided, and the children are included.

The Latin American countries and a number of West European nations have for many years sanctioned conjugal visits. Many Latin American countries do not restrict their programs to male inmates as American institutions with such programs do; in certain cases, female inmates are permitted conjugal visits with their husbands. Some Latin American nations even permit male prisoners to engage the service of prostitutes, who are brought into the penitentiary for the men.[16]

The value of conjugal or family visiting programs is unclear. There is some evidence that the fears of those who argue against them have not been realized. On the other hand, there also exists no well-documented evidence that such programs have been very successful in meeting the objectives of their proponents.

Michael Serill, writing for *Corrections Magazine,* describes the operation of the family visiting program at California's San Quentin Penitentiary in the article quoted below.[17]

Family Visiting at San Quentin

Richard Schwerdtfeger pulled his station wagon up to the gate of San Quentin prison and began unloading box after box of groceries. The boxes, along with several pieces of luggage, were searched by a guard and transferred to an electric cart inside the prison gate. Schwerdtfeger, his wife, and his daughter, Joanna, piled into the cart themselves and chugged off to the main prison several hundred yards away. The cart passed through an electric gate leading to a triangular patch of grass enclosed by a high fence topped with barbed wire. Forming two sides of the triangle were the walls of two of San Quentin's giant cellblocks. The third side was a cliff leading down to San Francisco Bay.

Within the enclosure were three 2-bedroom house trailers, each twelve by sixty feet. They were recently purchased by the California Department of Corrections for $6,000 each. The Schwerdtfegers, very excited, began moving their luggage and boxes of groceries into one of the trailers. Suddenly, a young man appeared—their son, Michael. Michael, twenty-nine, has been a resident of San Quentin for six and a half years. His crimes: murder, kidnapping, and robbery. His sentence: death, commuted four years ago for life without possibility of parole.

The Schwerdtfegers had been a very tightly knit family, they said, and had come to visit Michael frequently. But this was their first opportunity to see him privately, thanks to the Department of Corrections' "family visiting program." The program was "outstanding," according to the elder Schwerdtfeger, a heavy-set, jolly man with a bushy gray mustache. Just to be able to sit down and eat a meal with his son, to sit comfortably and talk, to watch television—it would be so much more "normal," he said, than the crowded atmosphere in the San Quentin visiting room. The family had been granted a nineteen-hour visit.

California's family visiting program has been in operation seven years now and Department of Corrections officials are as enthusiastic about it as they ever were. Twelve of the department's thirteen institutions permitted 9,000 private visits with wives, parents, and other relatives through the program last year and the department has plans to expand it to perhaps double that size.

The visits last either nineteen or forty-three hours, and take place in the privacy of prison outbuildings and furnished trailers purchased for that purpose. New trailers, like those at San Quentin, have been installed within the security areas of several institutions so that all inmates except those in maximum security will have a chance to participate.

At San Quentin the man in charge of the program is Sergeant Hal Brown, a sixteen-year veteran of the prison. In June, about 150 of the prison's 2,400 inmates were enrolled in the program, Brown said, and many more qualify. Medium-security inmates, like Michael Schwerdtfeger, have their visits in the trailers inside the walls, while minimum-security men occupy seven apartments in two houses outside the walls.

Though inmates' wives are the most frequent visitors, Brown said, to call the program "conjugal visiting" would be a misnomer. To prove his point, Brown noted that in April there were 114 visits and 267 visitors; in May there were 87 visits and 174 visitors—meaning that many children and other relatives also come.

To qualify for the program, inmates must have twelve months "clean time," must never have been caught introducing contraband into the prison, and cannot be designated as a "mentally disordered sex offender." Wives must bring their marriage licenses with them to be admitted. The program operates six days a week, and visitors must supply all the food for the visits.

Correction officers are not permitted inside the apartments and trailers while a visit is going on; inmates are instructed to appear outside at certain hours of the day for the regular count.

Inmates can generally get a nineteen-hour visit about every twenty days, Brown said, and a forty-three-hour visit about every forty days. In mid-June, the forty-three-hour visits were booked until September 29. "A nucleus of people get twice as many visits as anyone else," Brown said, because when there is a last minute cancellation there are a few wives who live near the prison and can be there within thirty minutes.

Brown, who handles the entire program alone, is well liked by both the visitors and inmates. The visitors greet him by his first name and give him kisses. He is the only staff member ever to have gotten a "certificate of appreciation" from the Black Muslims inside the prison for his "courtesy, fairness and helpful manner." Brown explained his popularity by saying that he is "flexible" in running the program. "It's not a normal thing to go to a state prison for a family visit, so you've got to give a little bit."

Despite the fact that he is heavily overworked, spending up to five hours a day of his own time on the program, Brown says that "Not one inmate is going to suffer. No visitor is going to suffer. . . . I'm going to do it [alone] to the best of my ability because I believe in it."

The sergeant says the family visiting program has been a "tremendous boost to morale in this institution. . . . The thing that really impresses me is that we're saving families. If we're saving families we're saving inmates, and we're saving kids." Brown contends that the initial opposition to the program by the line staff has largely dissipated.

Officials in other states largely oppose conjugal or family visiting within institutions, partly on the grounds that the same objective could be better accomplished through home furloughs. But Sergeant Brown pointed out that the great majority of inmates at San Quentin and other California institutions will never have a chance for furloughs, and said that the family visiting program is a viable alternative.

It has also been charged that conjugal visiting is degrading to both the inmate and his wife. But all Brown sees is "tremendous joy, happiness. People have the desire to be together and they don't [care] where. . . . [Furthermore] I don't think these guys are hunting for sex alone. The drive is to be with the people they love, to be with their families."

While the Schwerdtfegers were moving into their trailer in the medium-security visiting area, another group of people, and a swarm of children, were unpacking their groceries and making coffee in the two family visiting houses outside the walls.

George 2X Jackson and his wife Cynthia 2X, sat down in the living room of the "pink house" to talk to a visitor, while their two-year-old son George, Jr. romped happily on the rug. Jackson, doing one-to-fourteen years for forgery, said the family visiting program is "the best thing that ever happened" to California prisoners.

Jackson said he has been receiving visits since November 1973, when he was classified minimum custody, and has had two or three a month ever since.

Jackson said he was married once before when he started another term in prison in 1968. He snapped his fingers, indicating that the marriage immediately broke up. "No contact," he said. "Across the table [in the visiting room] it's not real. There is no contact. You've got to be able to touch to maintain romantic love."

Asked whether he thought the program was degrading, Jackson bristled and escorted his visitor to his family's living quarters, which consisted of one large room with a bed, other furniture, and a private bath. "Is this degrading?" he asked. "We are Muslims. We respect our women. If I thought this degraded her, I would never do it."

To those who say that the family visiting program is more than any criminal deserves, Jackson replies: "Though we have broken the rules, we're still human. We still breathe and eat and love."

Home Furlough Programs

In place of the conjugal visit, more and more states are trying home furlough programs. These programs should be distinguished from emergency release programs in which an inmate is allowed to return home temporarily because of a serious situation in the immediate family, such as a death or grave illness, and is often accompanied by a supervising custodial officer. In home furlough programs, the inmate returns home for a few days without supervision.

In 1918, Mississippi was the first state to introduce furlough programs; these were 10-day holiday leaves for minimum-custody inmates. Arkansas followed in 1922; Louisiana was next in 1964. The U.S. Bureau of Prisons, North Carolina, Utah, and the District of Columbia introduced these programs into their systems in 1965. By 1972, 29 states had home furlough programs for adult offenders.[18] Most had similar basic criteria for determining an inmate's eligibility for home furlough: (1) the security risk which was based on the adjustment the individual had made while in prison and the type of crime for which he or she was sentenced; and (2) the time remaining to serve, which, in many instances, had to be served under minimum-security conditions. Sex offenders were almost always excluded.[19]

A survey conducted in 1974 indicated that all but 11 states had adopted home furlough programs for adult offenders, and that all but five states authorized home furloughs for juvenile offenders.

Today, more than 350,000 furloughs are now granted annually to adult inmates in America's prisons. Once adult furlough programs were initiated, they grew with incredible speed. In Oregon, the first such program was approved in 1967 and nine furloughs were granted the following year; during 1974, a total of 27,000 such leaves were granted. Florida alone granted over 42,000 furloughs between July 1974 and April 1975; however, all but 12,000 of these went to residents of Florida's network of community correctional centers. By the same token, the vast majority of furloughs in Oregon were to residents in work-release centers.

The corrections directors in Connecticut, Illinois, Michigan, and other states with large furlough programs contend that furloughs are only one part of an overall program designed to build a solid base of community and family support *before* the inmate walks out the front gate of the prison. Another benefit of furloughs, they say, is that they improve morale in institutions and give parole boards something tangible to look at when deciding whether an offender should be released.

One of the most controversial furlough programs is in Massachusetts. This state has a program by which inmates serving life sentences for murder can ultimately participate in furlough programs. Massachusetts, like other states, has had to overcome tremendous public and political hostility to the adoption of such programs. The most typical criticism is that furlough releasees will commit new crimes during their period of freedom from institutional surveillance. Unfortunately, in a few instances, this has happened and has heightened the controversy. Another frequently expressed fear is that releasees will flee. Finally, there are those who contend that such programs increase the risk that additional children will be born to "problem families."[20] Society faces similar hazards from inmates released on parole and in many respects, furlough releasees are less likely to get into trouble than parolees. In the first place, since fewer individuals are released on furlough, correction officials can examine all the factors and be much more selective of the inmates who are chosen to participate in these programs. Second, the criteria for participation in such a program are much more stringent than those for parole eligibility. Since correctional officials will be blamed if an individual on furlough does get into trouble, they are very careful in their selection of home furlough releasees.

There are some sound arguments in favor of home furlough programs. An inmate's behavior and adjustment during temporary release gives correctional officers an opportunity to gauge the suitability of the individual for eventual release to parole. Home furlough allows outside facilities and resources to be utilized more fully, thus reducing the need to build, staff, equip, and supply certain institutional programs. For example, certain prerelease activities, such as mock job interviews could be replaced by direct "real" experience, and the family's home could be used rather than special facilities constructed within the institution for family visits. Such programs would also militate against the general trend of family dissolution, which is often a result of extended incarceration.[21] Prison officials also point out that experience with home furlough programs makes the inmates more cooperative, more willing to obey orders from correctional guards, and more willing to participate in prison programs.[22]

Like other community-based institutional programs, home furlough programs will undoubtedly continue to be increasingly used as an alternative to long-standing correctional practices. The immediate need is to develop extensive research capabilities and analysis of its successes and failures so that guidelines can be developed for the future use of such programs.

TYPES OF COMMUNITY-BASED FACILITIES

To assist the parolee in returning to community life, there are several programs and facilities at his or her disposal. They are prerelease guidance centers, halfway houses, victim restitution, and community corrections centers.

The Prerelease Guidance Center

Prerelease guidance centers are facilities where inmates are sent usually 3 to 12 months before their release on parole.[23] They are usually located near urban areas. Their purpose is to facilitate the adjustment of inmates from institutional life to free society by gradually exposing them to fewer controls. To offset the dependency syndrome that often accompanies extended incarceration, inmates in these settings are encouraged to be more independent in a positive sense.

The U.S. Bureau of Prisons began in 1961 to gradually establish a network of these centers in major urban areas throughout the United States. When a deserving inmate is within a few months of release, he or she is sent to one of these centers, ideally, in his home city. Each center closely supervises about 20 federal prisoners.

Inmates wear civilian clothes at the center. Following orientation sessions, they are encouraged to go out into the community and obtain employment. Gradually, as time passes and they begin to show that they are adjusting, they are given more freedom. As their parole date approaches, some may even be permitted to move out of the center, although they are still required to return for counseling sessions and conferences several times a week.[24]

These centers are often staffed by specialists in counseling therapy who are rotated from regular institutional staff. Several of these programs utilize carefully screened college students in the behavioral sciences who work with youthful offenders as paraprofessional counselors. They often also assist the regular staff by providing coverage during the late night hours and weekends.[25] An important feature of this concept is the active involvement of federal parole officers in the counseling sessions. Thus, the parole officer who will assume the individual counseling responsibility when the inmate is placed upon parole has the opportunity to interact with the inmate before his release. Killinger and Cromwell give us some insight into how the program functions:

> When an individual returns from a temporary release to home, work or school, his experience can be discussed with him by staff, to try to assess his probable adjustment and to note incipient problems. Many difficulties can be anticipated in this way. The inmate's anxieties can be relieved by discussion, and discussion may also help him develop realistic plans for coping with prospective problems. When persistent or serious misbehavior occurs, sanctions are available to staff, ranging from restriction of further leaves or temporary incarceration to renewed institutionalization, with recommendation to the parole board that the date of parole be deferred.[26]

In recent years, a number of states have developed similar prerelease centers, and cooperative arrangements have been made between the U.S. Bureau of Prisons and some states in the development and utilization of such programs. For example, federal prerelease guidance centers in Detroit and Kansas City receive state inmates, and in a number of states the federal prison system sends its prisoners to state centers prior to their release. In this manner, duplication of facilities is avoided through cooperative correctional programming.

Halfway Houses

A recent trend in community-based corrections is the halfway house. Indeed, the prerelease guidance center is a form of halfway house since it can be considered a "halfway-out" facility. Other programs are considered "halfway-in." The concept of the halfway house is not new. A special study commission in 1820 recommended that Massachusetts establish such programs.[27] In 1864, Boston opened a halfway house for women released from that state's prison system. In a few years, religious and volunteer groups opened similar facilities in Philadelphia, New York, Chicago, and New Orleans. All these operations were privately supported and managed. One well-intentioned group opened a halfway house for exconvicts in New York in 1896. This facility, known as Hope Hall, was run by a husband-and-wife team who, because of their action, suffered such police intimidation and harassment that they appealed to the president of the United States to intercede in their behalf and to restrain the police.[28]

The purpose of these early halfway houses was similar to their use today. They were founded to provide exconvicts a temporary place of shelter, food, clothing, advice, and aid in obtaining gainful employment.[29] The founders of these early halfway houses were the pioneers of community-based treatment centers. Unfortunately, they were often scorned and held in contempt by professional correctional workers. They also often met with a great deal of hostility and resentment from the communities where they were located as well as from public officials and law enforcement officers.

In the 1950s, interest in the halfway-house concept was renewed. Like their earlier counterparts, these modern halfway houses were also privately sponsored by interested citizens or religious organizations. In the last few years, there has been increasing interest in halfway houses supported by public monies and managed by professional correctional personnel. Recently, federal legislation was passed authorizing the use of halfway houses for federal parolees who are having difficulty adjusting to their lives in free society and appear to be running the risk of parole revocation. Rather than waiting for failure and having to recommit the individual to prison, the alternative is to send the exoffender to a community treatment center for additional intensive treatment, counseling, and supervision.

The federal government has also been developing what can be referred to as "halfway-in" programs. In October 1971, Congress authorized the federal courts to direct a probationer to reside or participate in the program of a community treatment center as a condition of probation and as an alternative to prison incarceration. In 1978, the U.S. Bureau of Prisons operated such institutions throughout the United States and had contracts with 425 halfway houses run by state, local, or private agencies.[30]

A similar program, known as Probationed Offenders Rehabilitation and Training (PORT), has been established on a multicounty basis in Minnesota. This program provides an alternative for male offenders who require a greater change in their life-style than probation can accomplish and yet do not belong in prison. The program provides for a live-in residence facility on the grounds of a state hospital. Both felons and misdemeanants are sentenced to this institution by the courts in the sponsoring three-county area. The program is supervised by a corporate board of directors, which consists of citizens in the area as well as local and county law enforcement and probation officials. Special efforts are made to enroll the offenders in educational institutions in the community, to find work for them, and to expose them to professional treatment and interaction with lay volunteers made up of interested citizens and students in nearby colleges.[31]

It would appear that the use of halfway houses will continue to grow in the years ahead and that these facilities will play new and important roles. For example, they probably will be used increasingly for individuals with special difficulties, such as drug abuse, alcoholism, and psychiatric problems. In an effort to serve these target groups, halfway houses will require a larger share of the correctional manpower and resources now being applied to the maintenance of traditional prisons. It has also been recommended that halfway houses serve still another important function. With the advent of bail reform, individuals who can meet certain criteria are being released on their own recognizance. One of the usual requirements is that the individual have roots in the community. Many accused individuals, however, have poor family ties and poor work histories, which are often the result of educational and cultural deprivation. Not meeting some of the basic criteria, they are excluded from the use of recognizance bond and must await final disposition in jail. The halfway house could enable such inmates to become eligible for recognizance bond. At a minimum, this would include providing shelter and supervision prior to final disposition. Whether the accused is found guilty or not, he or she is usually in need of a range of services that the halfway house is often in a position to provide, directly or indirectly, such as medical, dental, psychological, and psychiatric services, individual and group counseling, and employment placement services. The delays that occur between the time of arrest and final disposition are often lengthy, in some cases 6 months or more. Even if the process is speeded up and the time from arrest to final disposition is reduced to 2 or 3 months, much can still be accomplished during this time.[32]

Victim Restitution

Another alternative to incarceration or probation is victim restitution. Generally, it is used in one of two ways: (1) as a condition of probation whereby the court will grant probation to an offender if he or she agrees to make restitution to the victim during the period of probation; or (2) in conjunction with incarceration. For example, as a condition of work release (and generally early parole), the incarcerated inmate agrees to repay the victim from his or her earnings. It also is frequently employed as a condition of weekend incarceration. For instance, in the handling of more serious misdemeanor cases, the offender may serve jail time on the weekends and be free to work at a job during the week, or alternatively to return to the jail at night after working at a job during the day. In either way, the court may demand that the offender make restitution to the victim out of earned wages.

Victim restitution programs are different in several ways from the victim compensation programs discussed in Chapter 3. First, restitution is a form of payment directly from the offender to the victim. In victim compensation programs, the state compensates the victim from a public fund set aside for such a purpose. Second, the states administer these programs through commissions or boards, and the victim files a claim with these agencies in much the same way as an insurance claim is filed. On the other hand, victim restitution programs are administered directly by criminal justice agencies—usually the courts or corrections.

There are many issues involved in the concept of victim restitution such as determining the amount of restitution; the hardship that payment might impose on indigent offenders; the prospects that restitution, if used as the sole correctional program, might allow certain offenders to purchase their freedom with relative ease; and the weight that should be given to the views of the victim. Because these issues cannot be thoroughly discussed in an introductory text, the interested reader is encouraged to read the developing literature in this area.[33]

The following section concentrates on corrections-based programs of victim restitution rather than on court-based programs. Several states have developed programs of victim restitution which will serve as our point of analysis.

The Minnesota Restitution Center In 1972, Minnesota corrections officials started the Minnesota Restitution Center. This pioneering corrections project operates under the theory that offenders should pay for their crimes by working and paying back their victims, not by sitting in a prison cell. As the first program of its kind in the country, the center has attracted considerable attention among corrections professionals and the national media.

Most of the funding for the program has come from the LEAA. This agency was so impressed with the concept that it has funded five other restitution centers, four in Georgia and one in Iowa. Several other states are considering similar programs. After visiting the Minnesota Restitution Center, a group of Canadian correctional officials began developing similar programs in that country. One of the advantages of the restitution center is that it has demonstrated itself to be a politically acceptable program, which would tend to encourage its establishment in other states.

Minnesota corrections administrators feel that the primary advantage of the program is that it finally focuses attention on the victim, who has long been neglected by the criminal justice system. It also significantly reduces costs to the taxpayers. On the average, it costs Minnesota between $16 and $25 a day to keep an inmate in a state prison, while the estimated daily cost of offender maintenance in a restitution center is only $14.50. At the same time, the inmates in the center are working, paying taxes, supporting families who might otherwise be on welfare, and of course, paying back their victims.

To be eligible for the program, an offender must meet certain conditions. For example, he or she must reside in the seven-county Twin Cities metropolitan region (which contains about two-thirds of the state's population); the crime that the offender was sentenced for must not have involved the use of violence or weapons; the offender must not have been arrested for a violent or weapons offense for the preceding 5 years; the offender's earning ability has to be compatible with the amount of restitution and the time remaining on his or her parole; and the individual must not be a professional criminal.

Those chosen to participate in the program serve approximately 4 months in prison. Before they are released, they must sign a contract with the parole board and the department of corrections by which they agree to abide by the rules of the restitution center and the conditions of the special parole that they are receiving. The conditions are that they obtain and hold a job and use a part of their earnings to make regular payments to their victims. They must also agree to pay for their room and board while staying at the center and to participate in both center and outside therapy programs if they have psychiatric, alcohol, or drug problems. If an offender fails to abide by these conditions, the center can petition the parole board to revoke his parole, and he will be returned to prison.

One feature of the program is that the potential candidate for the restitution center must meet with his victim. This is a unique experience for most offenders and often seems to make a strong impression on them.

The Georgia Restitution Program Georgia, with the help of LEAA funds, has opened four restitution centers. Although the centers handle both probationers and parolees, only parolees are examined here.

The target population for the program is made up of male offenders who the parole board consider to be "marginal risks but nonviolent offenders" who would normally be incarcerated and for whom restitution would be appropriate. Referrals to the program come from the parole board.

In general, parolees are required by the parole board to live at one of the centers for a specified period of time, to remain regularly employed while there, and to make restitution. Each of the centers develops specific programs based upon the needs of its client group. While in residence, the inmate's behavior and activities are closely supervised. Offenders receive individual and group counseling from center staff and referrals are made to community resources when medical, vocational, legal, or educational services are needed. All of the offender's paycheck goes to an official at the center who then disburses the money into special budget accounts such as restitution payment, family support, room and board, incidental living expenses, etc.[34]

Under the Georgia program, restitution can either be monetary or symbolic. Symbolic restitution usually involves performing work for the community, a charitable organization, or some other group rather than money paid directly to the victim. In the Georgia program, probationers are generally involved in the monetary restitution program whereas parolees have primarily made up the symbolic group. In Georgia, unlike Minnesota, victim involvement has generally been kept to a minimum. Apparently, Georgia has experienced many cases where victims merely want to recover their losses without further contact with the offender. However, where warranted, face-to-face contact and restitution between the offender and the victim can be arranged.

Generally, criminal justice officials in Georgia have reacted in a very positive manner to the program. The judges in the case of probationer restitution seem to favor the program because it gives them a sentencing alternative between probation and incarceration. Likewise, the parole board is given an option beyond parole or keeping the offender incarcerated for an additional period of time. It is also reported that community reaction is strongly positive because the public likes to feel that the offender is working constructively, paying taxes, and partially defraying the cost of institutionalization.[35]

In fact, the plan has been so successful in Georgia that the Department of Corrections and Offender Rehabilitation is now in the process of opening additional centers throughout the state. The long-range goal of the department is to locate one restitution center in each of the state's 42-judicial districts.

The Community Corrections Center

A number of states are developing community-based correctional institutions in selected city neighborhoods in an effort to reduce the isolation of offenders from community services and other resources. Most of these centers require that the individual live in. He or she may be released for short periods to work or visit with family, but must return to the center at night. Others are centers for released offenders, such as individuals on parole. Special services and programs are available to help the released offenders. If they are having a difficult time adjusting to release, they are encouraged to come to the center for assistance and counseling. As an extension of parole or post-release services, such a center can draw upon the medical, social work, psychiatric, educational, and employment resources of the entire community and can involve community, neighborhood residents, and family members in offender rehabilitation and reintegration.

At the present time, there appears to be no single model for the facilities or program design of a community corrections center. However, one of the most promising proposals has resulted from a recent project undertaken by the Institute for the Study of Crime and Delinquency. This project was designed to develop conceptual, operating, and architectural designs for correctional practice, and it resulted in the proposal for a community-based program for young adult offenders.[36] This so-called youth correctional center calls for three residential units located in the high-delinquency areas from which the young adult felon population is drawn. In phase I, offenders are housed in a medium-security residential unit, where they are strictly confined at all times under close security. This phase usually lasts for a month. In phase II, offenders live in a less custody-oriented unit and are given limited access to the outside community for work, school, or other activities. This period would last approximately 3 months. In phase III, offenders reside in the community and return to the unit once a week or more often for group meetings and special services. This phase would last about 20 months.[37]

FUTURE CORRECTIONAL ISSUES AND TRENDS

Although it is dangerous to try to predict the changes that may occur in corrections in the last two decades of the twentieth century, some observations can be offered. Definite trends seem to be developing today that might be useful for predicting the future issues, programs, and focus of corrections. Some of the more important trends are examined in this section.

Judicial Expansion of Inmate Rights

In recent years, the courts, particularly those at the federal level, have been applying broad constitutional standards to the operations of penal institutions. The courts are beginning to insist that prisoners have certain rights that are no different from the rights of a free citizen. This trend is nothing less than a fundamental reinterpretation of the law. In the past, an offender, as a matter of law, was considered to have forfeited virtually all rights upon conviction and to have retained only those rights which were expressly granted by statute or the correctional authority.[38] The offender was considered a noncitizen and excluded from the constitutional protections afforded free members of society.

The National Advisory Commission on Criminal Justice Standards and Goals succinctly points out the former status of convicted offenders and the attitudes of the courts:

> The courts refused for the most part to intervene. Judges felt that correctional administration was a technical matter to be left to experts rather than to courts, which were deemed ill-equipped to make appropriate evaluations. And, to the extent that courts believed the offenders' complaints involved privileges rather than rights, there was no special necessity to confront correctional practices, even when they infringed on basic notions of human rights and dignity protected for other groups by constitutional doctrine.[39]

This attitude existed because society cared very little about corrections and even less about convicts themselves. The changes have occurred because society itself has become more concerned. The closer scrutiny of correctional practices was just one result of society's more sweeping concern for individual rights and governmental accountability, particularly of the executive branch, of which corrections is a part. This concern had its beginnings with the civil rights movement and was reflected in such areas as juvenile justice, public welfare, mental institutions, and military justice. Part of the growth of reform in correctional institutions and policies arose from the fact that corrections for the first time was being scrutinized and experienced by large segments of society who formerly had no contact with the system of justice and corrections in particular. The correctional experiences of dissenting groups, many of whom came from middle-class backgrounds, acted as a catalyst for change upon the entire justice process.

Finally, the questionable effectiveness of correctional systems as rehabilitative instruments, combined with the unbelievable conditions existing in many penal institutions, could no longer be ignored by the courts. As the courts began to examine the operations of correctional institutions and systems more carefully, they began to redefine the legal framework of corrections. They placed binding legal restrictions on correctional administrators and required that correctional systems measure up to externally imposed criteria rather than permitting them to police themselves, which had usually been the policy before.

As the courts started exerting more supervisory control over correctional operations, many aggrieved inmates saw that the courts were now for the first time being receptive to their claims. As a consequence, offenders flooded the courts with petitions for judicial relief, and the courts addressed themselves to the petitions. For example, in its 1971–1972 term the U.S. Supreme Court decided no less than eight cases that dealt with convicted offenders, in addition to a few other related cases. In each case, the Supreme Court ruled in favor of the offender, and in five of the eight cases the decision was unanimous.

Some of the more significant Supreme Court rulings in the area of corrections have been: (1) that a formal procedure must be held in order to revoke one's parole[40]; (2) that institutionalized offenders are entitled to access to legal materials[41]; (3) that a sentencing judge cannot use unconstitutionally obtained convictions as a basis for sentencing an offender.[42]; and (4) that indefinite commitment of one who is not mentally competent to stand trial for a criminal offense violates due process of law.[43]

The National Advisory Commission on Criminal Justice Standards and Goals has proposed that states take the following immediate steps to insure that their correctional systems comply with the changes occurring in the adjudicated rights of prisoners:

1. Each correctional agency should immediately develop and implement policies and procedures to ensure that those in custody have the right to immediate access to the courts (a) to challenge the legality of their confinement or conviction; (b) to seek redress for illegal conditions of treatment while in custody; (c) to pursue remedies in existing civil legal problems; and (d) to assert their constitutional rights when violated by correctional or governmental authority.

2. Each correctional agency should immediately develop and implement policies and procedures to ensure that offenders have access to legal assistance through counsel or a chosen substitute with problems or proceedings relating to their custody control management or legal affairs while under correctional authority. This would include counsel at: (1) post conviction proceedings testing the legality of conviction or confinement; (2) proceedings challenging conditions or treatment under confinement or other correctional supervision; (3) probation revocation and parole grant and revocation proceedings; (4) disciplinary proceedings in a correctional facility that impose major penalties and deprivations.

3. Each correctional agency should establish immediately policies and procedures to fulfill the right of offenders to be free from personal abuse by correctional staff

or other offenders. The following should be prohibited: (1) corporal punishment; (2) the use of physical force by correctional staff except in extreme cases for self-defense, etc.; (3) any deprivation of clothing, bed and bedding, light, ventilation, heat, exercise, balanced diet or hygienic necessities; (4) infliction of mental distress, degradation or humiliation.[44]

The effects of these changes are being felt throughout correctional systems in the United States. The expansion of offenders' rights is the most recent indication that corrections is moving from a punitive strategy to a strategy of reintegration which requires that we acknowledge that 99 percent of all prisoners will someday return to free society. Without doubt, these judicial pronouncements have created difficulties for correctional administrators, as the suddenness of these changes found many prison officials unable to cope with them. In the long run, however, just as the pronouncements of the Supreme Court in the 1960s contributed significantly to increased professionalism among the police, they can serve a similar role in corrections.

Improving the Caliber of Corrections Administration

As corrections moves ahead, one of the first concerns must be improving the professionalism of correctional administrators. In the past, corrections has shown a virtual absence of professionally trained managers. Just as in the police service, advancement was often made through the ranks with little thought given to the more difficult demands placed upon those in higher levels of management. When corrections viewed itself merely as the custodial arm of the criminal justice system, the demands upon correctional administrators were fewer. Today, the problems of administration have grown tremendously as corrections is becoming increasingly involved in a wide range of programs, types of institutions, and policy decisions that are being imposed by the courts, legislative directives, and important reform groups.

Correctional systems are beginning to realize that a modern-day correctional administrator must be able to cope with such concerns as inmates' rights, employee-management relations, treatment programs, fiscal management, and the administration of the physical plant. New programs and approaches are demanding expert managerial skills.

A number of state correctional systems are implementing programs of career development for middle- and upper-level management personnel. Young, college-educated men and women are being brought in and given experience in the various phases of the correctional system. As they mature and indicate their potential, they are encouraged to obtain advanced degrees in the area of management, such as public or business administration, or in their specialist areas, such as psychology, social work, or sociology.

Manpower skills are also being developed among personnel in the lower levels of correctional institutions. This is being brought about by some major organizational changes in a number of correctional institutions. In the past, most large correctional institutions were organized on the basis of two major operating units—custodial and treatment. As we have seen, custody personnel are primarily concerned with maintaining discipline and security within the institutions, and the treatment staff consists of such personnel as psychiatrists, psychologists, educators, social workers, and correctional counselors. Today, more and more institutions are being organized into small, relatively self-contained units of those that employ the correctional team concept.[45] For example, 50 to 100 inmates are housed together as a unit and work in a close, intensive treatment relationship with a multidisciplinary, relatively permanent team of staff members whose offices are located in the unit. Inmates assigned to one unit may have a history of narcotics abuse, another unit may be for inmates involved in academic or vocational programs, and another unit may be for inmates who present special security problems or have emotional problems that need intensive scrutiny.

As we saw in Chapter 14, the team approach, in which custodial and treatment personnel work together, recognizes that custodial personnel play a very important role in the programs the institution has established, and they are given additional training in order to carry out their responsibilities.

The Development of Correctional Alternatives

Diversion and community-based programs will almost certainly continue to grow as alternatives to the traditional methods of handling offenders, and greater emphasis will be placed on the development and testing of these alternatives. A number of pilot programs are now being developed under the sponsorship of the federal government, and there are indications that the number of such programs is growing rapidly. Such programs as detoxification centers for alcoholics and offenders with related problems are being established in many parts of the country. Community programs for youth who are drifting away from parental control, community psychiatric programs, and services for those with chronic problems of unemployment are examples of the types of programs that are needed and are beginning to appear.[46]

The emphasis is on preventive services rather than on waiting until the problems of crime and delinquency have manifested themselves and then reacting through the very expensive process of incarceration. Increasingly, it would seem that incarceration will be used only when other alternatives have failed and for those individuals who demonstrate that because of their danger to society they must be locked up. In order to implement such preventive and diversionary strategy, however, we must develop better predictive or early warning systems that will indicate that certain individuals are moving toward the correctional system. This strategy should reduce the workload of corrections and focus its attention more sharply upon those whose problems cannot be met more appropriately by other agencies.[47]

Changes in the Organization and Delivery of Correctional Services

The reader will recall that one of the obstacles to correctional reform is the fragmentation of correctional systems among various levels of government. Although the immediate future will not see all correctional programs and institutions centralized at the federal level or even at the state level, there will be less correctional fragmentation among political units than exists today. New programs and the associated involvement of the courts, law enforcement, and mental health and social welfare agencies will facilitate greater communication, resource exchange, and information sharing, and will conceivably reduce the multiplicity of correctional agencies among these levels of government.

Although the autonomous governmental control of correctional programs will be less, many more types of programs will be available. The Joint Commission on Correctional Manpower and Training sees the relationship between centralized administrative control and decentralized programming in the following way:

> The correctional system of the future will have a configuration of numerous, quite autonomous subsystems operating to maximize cooperation and interchange . . . [and] we ought not to expect a monolithic correctional apparatus for the United States in the future. But remedies must and will be found for the present problems of fragmentation. They will take the form, we predict, of a large repertoire of reciprocal arrangements between the parts of the total system. These new arrangements will be used flexibly and with much less reverence for the sanctity of organizational and governmental boundaries than is evident today.
>
> Offenders with special requirements will be sent to specialized facilities capable of meeting their needs, regardless of the jurisdictional niceties involved. Offenders whose primary requirement is to reestablish themselves in their home communities will be routed there and supervised by local authorities. The federal and state governments will facilitate the efforts of local governments to develop strong community-based programs and will backstop them with resources they cannot provide; for example, a fully staffed center for screening and diagnosis of offenders or an institution for mentally ill offenders.
>
> The administrators of a cooperative correctional system would need to understand the national network of services of which their particular program would be an integral part. They would need to be aware of the laws, policies, and procedures through which cross-jurisdictional cooperation could be implemented. They would need to participate in those public and private organizations which address the problems of coordinating correctional efforts across the country and carry out planning and information-gathering activities. In sum, they would need to be outwardly directed, rather than concerned only with local activities. They would need to work with the totality of corrections-related activities rather than with the happenings of their own organizational enclave.[48]

Changes in Crime and the Offender Population

Many of the so-called victimless crimes will probably receive less emphasis than they have in the past. These "crimes," which often indicate some form of personal maladjustment rather than constituting a direct threat to the well-being of society, will probably either be decriminalized through less strict enforcement or will be handled outside the formal process of criminal justice by diversionary programs or the use of civil penalties in lieu of criminal charges.

We may well see some changes in the types of offenders who come under correctional supervision in the years ahead. The noted criminologist Daniel Glaser, in a very insightful paper on the future of corrections, sees some meaningful changes occurring in the types of offenders dealt with by corrections in the years ahead.[49] He contends that offenders as a group will tend to take on characteristics similar to those of the general population, with the exception that correctional clients will probably be increasingly younger in age if greater correctional effort is directed at prevention rather than acting after the crime has occurred.

Today, the typical prison population includes disproportionate numbers of males, young offenders, racial and ethnic minorities, and the poor, under-employed, and uneducated residents of large central city neighborhoods. Glaser feels that those committed to corrections will come to include more affluent, more white, and more female offenders. A larger proportion will not suffer the social disadvantages of many of those in our correctional systems today. He believes that these changes will occur because poverty among certain disadvantaged segments of our population will be lessened, and they will enjoy greater economic and social opportunities than they have in the past.[50]

Although Glaser does not address this possibility, we may see increasing enforcement of white-collar crime in the United States in the years ahead. Such offenses as tax fraud, corporate price fixing and other white-collar crimes may, under pressure for equal enforcement of the criminal law and through the urgings of consumer advocate and reform groups, become more important concerns of the criminal justice system. If this occurs, the composition of offender groups will change accordingly.

Glaser believes that the increase of females in the offender group will come about from the same dynamics that have produced the women's liberation movement. With the emancipation of the female from sex-segregated roles, women may become increasingly involved in traditional masculine roles, including various forms of criminal behavior. This would mean a change from the more passive crime-related behavior of the female in the past (e.g., prostitution, check passing, and shoplifting) to more aggressive acts, such as robbery, burglary, confidence games, and more violent types of crime.

It would seem that some of the trends Glaser discusses are now occurring. For example, women are increasingly making up a larger percentage of offenders who are convicted and sentenced in the criminal courts. If correctional statistics were available on offenders in *all* existing correctional programs, we probably would see some slight changes in the composition of the offender population. However, within institutions a disproportionate number of offenders are still the disadvantaged, and in future years those less-advantaged than others will still probably make up more of the correctional population.

Research Efforts

Although a great deal of meaningful and important research remains to be done on the corrections process, more work has probably been done in the past 10 years than in all preceding years. During the 1960s, a number of university research centers were established to conduct research directly applicable to corrections. In addition, such agencies as the Ford Foundation, the Law Enforcement Assistance Administration, the National Probation and

Parole Institutes, the Joint Commission on Correctional Manpower and Training, and the National Institute of Mental Health have initiated research into correctional programs and the broad areas of crime and delinquency.

The efforts of these groups and others have helped corrections develop better programs and gain insights in dealing with offenders. An information base is being created and will certainly grow in the future as research efforts are expanded. Regarding this expanding base of correctional research, Carter, McGee, and Nelson say:

> We predict by the year 2000 that there will be an on-going and reasonably effective informational network which will tie practitioners together with correctional researchers and facilitate their communications with each other. It seems probable that the Federal government will play a leading role in funding and maintaining this network.[51]

The National Institute of Corrections   Since the preceding statement was written, the federal government has taken major steps to encourage research and information dissemination in corrections. In 1974, Congress approved the creation of the National Institute of Corrections within the U.S. Bureau of Prisons. This new agency was authorized by Congress to make a significant effort to improve the administration of corrections in the United States. Among its specific responsibilities were:

- To receive and make grants that would improve corrections;
- Serve as a clearinghouse and information center for corrections;
- Provide consultant services to Federal, State, and local criminal justice agencies;
- Assist Federal, State, and local agencies, and private organizations in developing and implementing improved corrections programs;
- Conduct seminars, workshops, and training programs for all types of criminal justice personnel associated with the rehabilitation of offenders;
- Conduct, encourage, and coordinate correctional research;
- Formulate and disseminate correctional policy, goals, and standards;
- Conduct programs evaluating the effectiveness of new correctional approaches, techniques, systems, programs, and devices.[52]

This agency views its role as bringing organization, direction, and leadership to the corrections community. In the first year of its operation, it focused primarily on the development of more effective personnel in corrections, including correctional administrators, researchers, criminal justice educators in colleges and universities, general correctional personnel, and volunteers in corrections.

In the years ahead, it sees its responsibilities in three areas. The first responsibility of the institute is *research and evaluation.* It plans to conduct, encourage, and coordinate research relating to corrections, including the causes, prevention, diagnoses, and treatment of criminal offenders. It also plans to conduct evaluation programs to study the effectiveness of new approaches, techniques, systems, programs, and devices employed to improve the corrections systems. The second area of major effort will be *policy formulation and implementation.* This includes formulating and disseminating correctional policy, goals, standards, and recommendations for federal, state, and local correctional agencies, organizations, institutions, and personnel. Third, the agency will serve as a *clearinghouse and information center* for the collection, preparation, and dissemination of information on corrections, including such areas of concern as programs for prevention of crime and recidivism, training of correction personnel, and rehabilitation and treatment of criminal and juvenile offenders.

These, then, are some of the developing ideas, trends, and programs that corrections seem to have charted out for itself during the last quarter of the twentieth century. In spite of a deep skepticism many seem to hold about the general efficacy of reform efforts in corrections, we must remember that we have progressed a great deal in the last 200 years when we look at the total history of how we have dealt with offenders. Although a great deal remains to be accomplished, the pace of change seems to be accelerating rapidly. Certainly, the troubled enterprise of corrections in America warrants our continued concern and efforts.

THE IMPENDING DANGER

An ironic situation faces correctional efforts today. When the first edition of this book was completed in 1976, reintegration coupled with rehabilitation was the guiding philosophy of our correctional efforts. Thus, major emphasis in the literature of reform emphasized reintegrative-rehabilitative programming in the form of community-based and other efforts to make the institutional experience a truly "corrective" one. This is still a major goal of corrections today, but in the past several years there has been some rethinking of this as a guiding concept. Today, while corrections still tries to accomplish this, it also must deal with a competing philosophy that seems to be growing—that is, that corrections should redirect its efforts back to incapacitation and deterrence as a primary goal. This feeling arises from the widely recognized (and now general public knowledge) that our correctional systems are not rehabilitating. The logic then becomes: "If we are not rehabilitating, prisons serve no other purpose than to merely incapacitate. If this is the case, we should use incapacitation as a means to deter the offender and others from committing crimes. This latter response seems to underlie the growing public insistance that prisons be places of punishment and confinement. So now, as we have seen so often before, the pendulum of how to deal with the offender begins to swing back. Such has been the history of public attitudes and correctional efforts. We saw this earlier in England, and our nation's own experiences with how to deal with the offender have followed a similar ebb and flow of public opinion.

There is much truth in the belief that corrections does not "correct." Corrections has unquestionably made mistakes and those interested in correctional improvement need to learn a great deal more about how to best deal with offenders if they are to "correct." However, this observation should not only be viewed as a criticism of corrections, but rather should also focus on the criticism of the state-of-the-art today in terms of what we know about methods of rehabilitation. The subject of effective rehabilitation is so complex, and so little is known about it, that we cannot fault correctional efforts in this area without bringing in a host of other considerations that are also important for understanding the problem.

However, we can fault corrections in one important way. Out of self-interest, correctional officials often gave the false impression that in spite of the inherent limitations of traditional prisons and programs for rehabilitation success, they could still bring "correction" about. Thus, the rehabilitative model was used to justify expansion of program efforts, new facilities, specialized staffs, higher salaries, and professional stature for those associated with such "rehabilitation" efforts. Yet while correction leaders praised rehabilitation programs, there is little evidence that they really believed that correction could be achieved via this avenue; more importantly, correction officials must be faulted for their lack of commitment to accomplish such goals.

However, to say that rehabilitation cannot be accomplished and to revert to punishment as the sole correctional role is just as irresponsible. The purpose of corrections is still to correct *by whatever means*. If rehabilitation programs have not been very successful in "correcting," punishment and more incarceration have been repeatedly demonstrated to be *even less effective* as correctional means. Does this imply that nothing short of imposing capital punishment on offenders will solve the problem? Of course not.

It would seem that two things must be done. First, offenders who will not "correct" either through punishment or rehabilitative measures must be locked-up (even permanently), for the protection of society. The problem comes in determining when and on what basis is an offender considered intractable. But to warehouse all offenders during their period of imprisonment is simply not a responsible alternative.

The second course of action must be to focus more resources on the examination of factors that can help us answer such pressing questions as: What rehabilitative methods work? Under what conditions do they work? With whom do they work? We must continue to develop rehabilitative programs for those who can be helped, and to do this successfully, we must be able to evaluate them.

SUMMARY

Community-based correctional programs provide an alternative to traditional methods of handling offenders. The idea behind community-based program efforts is the *reintegration* of the offender back into society upon release by the means of *diversion* from the demonstrated negative influences of traditional imprisonment.

Such efforts are generally associated with the rehabilitative model of corrections in its attempt to provide an environment similar to the one that the inmate will encounter in the free world. In this way, rehabilitation can operate more effectively than in the artificial environment of a traditional prison and its programs of rehabilitation.

Some of the more popular community-based institutions and program efforts are work release, community corrections centers, academic pass, pre-release guidance centers, halfway houses, conjugal and family visitations, home furloughs, restitution centers, and victim restitution programs.

Current trends that will shape the future of corrections include the judicial expansion of inmate rights, improvements in correctional personnel, the development of correctional alternatives based upon preventive strategies, changes in the organization and delivery of correctional services, changes in the nature of crime and offender population, and increased research efforts.

One major concern threatens the progress of present correction efforts—that society has begun, again, to view prisons solely as places of punishment. This reflects an increasingly retributive philosophy among Americans who have become disenchanted with the inability of corrections to correct. In large part, blame for this change in attitude must be borne by corrections itself for misleading the public on their ability to "correct" when, in fact, little real understanding or effort went into such efforts. Instead, the rehabilitative model was too often used for the self-interest of corrections itself.

REVIEW QUESTIONS

1. Give reasons explaining the increasing popularity of community-based programs over traditional correctional methods.
2. What is the basic rationale of community-based corrections? Why has this correctional method a better chance of effectively coping with the usual problems of the offender in returning to society?
3. Name and briefly explain the four major types of community-based programs.
4. Describe the purpose of the following:
   a. Prerelease guidance center
   b. Halfway house
   c. Victim restitution
   d. Community corrections center
5. What fundamental changes have resulted from recent court rulings regarding the rights of prison inmates? What are some of these rulings?
6. How is the caliber of correctional managers and administrators being improved?
7. To some criminologists, there will be definite changes in the types of offenders and the crimes they commit in the future. What are these foreseeable changes?
8. If rehabilitation and reintegration don't work, what will be the most likely reaction within the corrections field?

DISCUSSION QUESTIONS

1. What are the possible drawbacks to community-based programs?
2. Are prison inmates entitled to the civil rights guaranteed to American citizens by the Constitution? Why or why not? On what issues might civil rights be legitimately denied them?
3. If punitive correctional methods are restored, how might the correctional system of the United States be affected?

SUGGESTED ADDITIONAL READINGS

Allen, Harry E., and Clifford E. Simonsen. *Corrections in America: An Introduction.* 2nd ed. Encino, Calif.: Glencoe, 1978.

Frank, Benjamin. *Contemporary Corrections: A Concept in Search of Content.* Reston, Va.: Reston Publishing, 1973.

Griggs, Bertram S., and Gary R. McCune. "Community-Based Correctional Programs: A Survey and Analysis." *Federal Probation,* June 1972.

Harlow, Eleanor, Robert J. Webber, and Leslie T. Wilkins. *Community-Based Correctional Programs: Models and Practices.* Washington, D.C.: U.S. Government Printing Office, 1971.

Hickey, William L. "Strategies for Decreasing Jail Populations," *Crime and Delinquency Literature* 3 (1971):76–94.

Hood, Roger, and Richard Sparks. *Key Issues in Criminology.* New York: McGraw-Hill, 1970.

Keller, Oliver J., and Benedict S. Alper. *Halfway Houses: Community Centered Corrections and Treatment.* Lexington, Mass.: Raytheon/Heath, 1970.

McCartt, John M., and Thomas Mangogna. *Guidelines and Standards for Halfway Houses and Community Treatment Centers.* Washington, D.C.: Law Enforcement Assistance Administration, May 1973.

Milton, Luger. "Utilizing the Ex-Offender as a Staff Member: Community Attitudes and Acceptance." In *Offenders as a Correctional Manpower Resource.* Washington, D.C.: Joint Commission on Correctional Manpower and Training, 1968.

Moyer, Frederic D. *Guidelines for the Planning and Design of Regional and Community Correctional Centers for Adults.* Urbana: University of Illinois, 1971.

Schafer, Stephen. *Victimology—The Victim and his Criminal.* Reston, Va.: Reston Publishing Co., 1977.

Schwartz, Richard D., and Jerome H. Skolnick. "The Stigma of 'Ex-Con' and the Problem of Reintegration." *Social Problems* 10 (Fall 1962):133–42.

Turner, Merfyn. "The Lessons of Norman House." *Annals of the American Academy of Political and Social Science* (January 1969).

NOTES

1. U.S. Department of Justice, Bureau of Prisons, "Success and Failure of Federal Offenders Released in 1970," mimeo (April 11, 1974), p. 1.

2. Solomon Kobrin, "The Chicago Area Project—A 25-Year Assessment," *The Annals of the American Academy of Political and Social Science* 322 (March 1959): 19–29.

3. Walter B. Miller, "Preventive Work with Street Corner Groups," *The Annals of the American Academy of Political and Social Science* 322 (March 1959):97–106.

4. *The New York Times,* November 30, 1973, sec. II, p. 2, col. 1.

5. It should be pointed out, however, that an opposite trend toward a "get tough" policy with offenders may be developing. Popular sentiment is calling for stricter laws and their enforcement. At this time, it is too early to gauge the effect of such attitudes on corrections.

6. For example, see George Killinger and Paul F. Cromwell, *Corrections in the Community* (St. Paul, Minn.: West, 1974).

7. Law Enforcement Assistance Administration, National Institute of Law Enforcement and Criminal Justice, *Reintegration of the Offender into the Community* (Washington, D.C.: U.S. Government Printing Office, 1973), p. 5.

8. Walter H. Busher, *Ordering Time to Serve Prisoner* (Washington, D.C.: U.S. Government Printing Office, June 1973), p. 3.

9. Ibid., pp. 3–4.

10. Stanley E. Grupp, "Work Release and Misdemeanants," *Federal Probation* 29 (June 1965): 7.

11. See Daniel Glaser, *The Effectiveness of a Prison and Parole System* (Indianapolis: Bobbs-Merrill, 1969), especially Chap. 10.

12. Alvin Rudoff and T. C. Esselstyn, "Evaluating Work Furlough: A Follow-Up," *Federal Probation* 37 (June 1973): 48–53.

13. Ibid., pp. 50–53.

14. N. C. Chamelin, V. B. Fox, and P. M. Whisenand, *Introduction to the Criminal Justice System* (Englewood Cliffs, N.J.: Prentice-Hall, 1975), p. 397.

15. Columbus B. Hopper, "The Conjugal Visit," *Journal of Criminal Law, Criminology and Police Science* 53 (September 1962): 340–343.

16. For example, see Norman E. Hayner, "Attitudes toward Conjugal Visits for Prisoners," *Federal Probation* 36 (March 1972): 43–49.

17. Source: Michael S. Serill, "Family Visiting at San Quentin." Reprinted with permission from the July-August 1975 issue of *Corrections Magazine,* published by the Correctional Information Service, Inc., 801 Second Avenue, New York, NY 10017.

18. Carson W. Markley, "Furlough Programs and Conjugal Visiting in Adult Correctional Institutions," *Federal Probation* 37 (March 1973): 19–26.

19. Ibid., pp. 22–24.

20. Donald R. Johns, "Alternatives to Conjugal Visiting," *Federal Probation* 35 (March 1971): 48–51.

21. Ibid.

22. Serill, "Family Visiting at San Quentin," p. 12.

23. Chamelin et al., *Introduction to the Criminal Justice System,* p. 397.

24. Killinger and Cromwell, *Corrections in the Community,* p. 68.

25. Ibid.

26. Ibid., p. 69.

27. Oliver J. Keller and Benedict S. Alper, *Halfway Houses* (Boston: Heath, 1963), p. 7.

28. Ibid.

29. Killinger and Cromwell, *Corrections in the Community,* p. 78.

30. U.S. Department of Justice, *Federal Prison System-1978* (Washington, U.S. Government Printing Office, 1979), p. 4.

31. Kenneth F. Schoen, "PORT: A New Concept of Community-Based Correction," *Federal Probation* 36 (September 1972): 35–40.

32. John M. McCartt and Thomas Mangogna, *Guidelines and Standards for Halfway Houses and Community Treatment Centers* (Washington, D.C.: U.S. Government Printing Office, June 1973), pp. 17–18.

33. For example, see Stephen Schafer, *Compensation and Restitution to Victims of Crime* (Montclair, N.J.: Patterson-Smith, 1970); and Stephen Schafer, "The Proper Role of a Victim Compensation System," *Crime and Delinquency.* 21 (January 1975).

34. Anne Newton, "Aid to the Victim Part II: Victim Aid Program," *Crime and Delinquency Literature* 8 (December 1976), p. 287.

35. Ibid.

36. H. B. Bradley, "Community-based Treatment for Young Adult Offenders," *Crime and Delinquency* 15 (1969): 359–370.

37. E. Harlow, R. Weber, and L. T. Wilkins, "Community-based Correctional Programs," in E. Eldefonso, ed., *Issues in Corrections* (Encino, Calif.: Glencoe, 1974), p. 367.

38. National Advisory Commission on Criminal Justice Standards and Goals, *Corrections* (Washington, D.C.: U.S. Government Printing Office, 1973), p. 18.

39. Ibid.

40. *Morrissey* v. *Brewer,* 408 U.S. 471 (1972).

41. *Younger* v. *Gilmore,* 404 U.S. 15 (1971).

42. *United States* v. *Tucker,* 404 U.S. 443 (1972).

43. *Jackson* v. *Indiana,* 406 U.S. 715 (1972).

44. National Advisory Commission, *Corrections,* pp. 23–31.

45. See Robert B. Levinson and Roy E. Gerard, "Functional Units: A Different Correctional Approach," *Federal Probation* 37 (December 1973): 8–15.

46. Robert M. Carter, Richard A. McGee, and E. Kim Nelson, *Corrections in America* (Philadelphia: Lippincott, 1975), p. 375.

47. Ibid., p. 376.

48. Elmer K. Nelson, Jr., and Catherine H. Lovell, *Developing Correctional Administrators* (Washington, D.C.: Joint Commission on Correctional Manpower and Training, November 1969), p. 15.

49. Daniel Glaser, "Changes in Corrections during the Next 20 Years," paper presented before the American Justice Institute, March 2, 1972.

50. For another interesting viewpoint, see Edward C. Banfield, *The Unheavenly City* (Boston: Little, Brown, 1970).

51. Carter et al., *Corrections in America,* p. 395.

52. National Institute of Corrections, *Status Report* (Washington, D.C.: U.S. Government Printing Office, October 1975), pp. 2–3.

PART 6

Juvenile
Justice System

Many juveniles are said to be delinquent because they have committed status offenses. Status offenses are acts that are considered unlawful if committed by a juvenile but not so if committed by adults. Running away from home, truancy, and ungovernable behavior are status offenses.

Juvenile delinquents are sent to various types of institutions, depending on the crime they committed, their attitude and personality, and the available resources. Most institutions fall into the following categories: (1) training (reform) schools, (2) camps and ranches, (3) halfway (group) homes, and (4) foster homes.

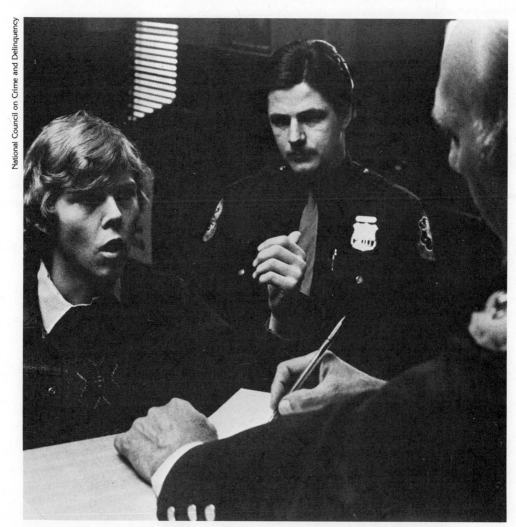

When a juvenile is arrested for a crime, an intake interview is conducted by a probation officer. The purpose of the interview is to investigate the case, to protect the interest of the youth, and to dispose of cases that do not warrant court procedure.

17
THE JUVENILE
JUSTICE SYSTEM

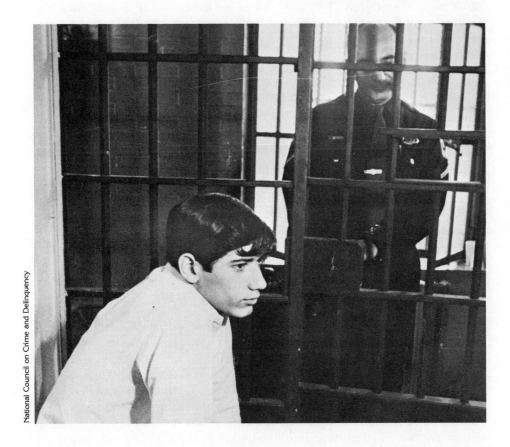

1. Why is delinquency considered to be a serious problem for our society?
2. What are the origins of the juvenile justice system?
3. What is the role of the juvenile court in the juvenile justice system and what problems does the court face in fulfilling its role?
4. What are the steps in processing a delinquency case in the juvenile justice system?
5. How have Supreme Court decisions influenced juvenile court proceedings?
6. What are the major types of juvenile institutions?
7. What are the most common types of diversion programs?

These are some of the questions this chapter will answer.

Although the proportion of youth in the U.S. population has declined from the all-time high of the late 1950s and 1960s, the growing number of juvenile arrests continues to be a subject of widespread alarm—particularly since this trend is most pronounced in the area of violent crimes. Between 1968 and 1977, arrests for violent crimes among those under 18 throughout the United States increased by 60 percent. As might be expected, the greatest incidence of juvenile-involved violent crimes is the most serious in our larger cities. In San Francisco, children of 17 and under are arrested for 57 percent of all felonies against people (homicide, rape, assault, etc.) In 1976 in Chicago, one-third of all arrests for homicide were committed by persons aged 20 or younger. This represented nearly a one-third increase from the previous year.[1] In Detroit, the youth crime problem became so serious that the police were hesitant to patrol certain areas without a substantial back-up force to provide help if they needed it. Officials in the city became so alarmed with the situation that they passed a special 10 P.M. curfew to be rigorously enforced against anyone under the age of 16.

TRENDS IN DELINQUENCY

In the nearly two decades between 1957 and 1977, the number of delinquency cases increased by nearly 200 percent, while the relative growth of the juvenile population between ages 10 to 17 increased by about 10 million or slightly over 40 percent.[2] Figure 17-1 shows this trend for the years 1957 to 1976. In the past few years, however, the percentage of arrests of juveniles under 18 for these serious crimes seems to have declined slightly. This trend probably more accurately reflects the fact that this age group represents an increasingly smaller percentage of the nation's population, rather than the conclusion that children are becoming more law abiding. Our society on the average is becoming older as the "baby boom" of the post-World War II years pass and women are having fewer children. In all likelihood, this phenomenon explains one of the reasons for the recent decline in the overall crime rate.

However, as shown in the discussion of crime statistics in Chapter 3, we must be very cautious in interpreting crime rates from these kinds of data. Among other facts, the statistics do not reveal the number of juvenile crimes that do not come to the attention of the police, and as a consequence are never shown in the statistical compilations of the *Uniform Crime Reports*. In addition, the police handle many juvenile cases informally without referring them to the juvenile justice system. In 1977, over 38 percent of juvenile offenders taken into custody were handled informally within the police department and released.[3]

Delinquency Among Girls

Most of the talk about delinquency is focused on male juveniles. Yet there is a growing concern over increased delinquency among young girls. Although delinquency is primarily a problem of male youth, official statistics indicate that the historical disparity between the number of boys' and girls' delinquency court cases is narrowing. This has some meaningful implications for

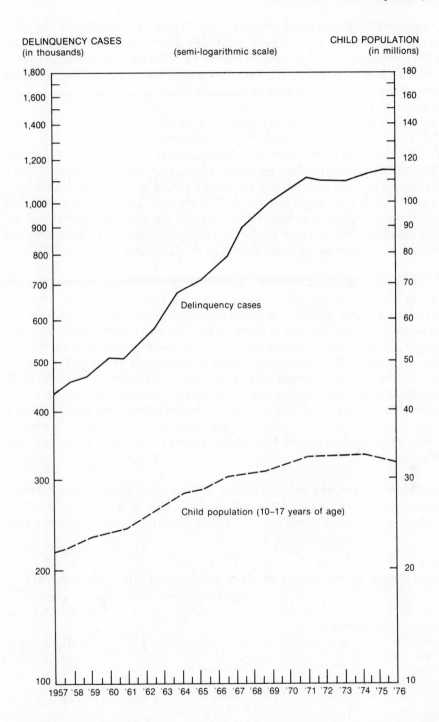

DELINQUENCY CASES
(in thousands)

(semi-logarithmic scale)

CHILD POPULATION
(in millions)

Delinquency cases

Child population (10–17 years of age)

Source: Department of Health, Education, and Welfare, *Juvenile Court Statistics* — 1973 and 1976 (Washington, D.C.: U.S. Government Printing Office, 1975 and 1978)

FIGURE 17-1 Trends in Juvenile Court Delinquency Cases and Child Population for Ages 10–17, 1957–1976

the juvenile justice process. For many years, boys were referred to court for delinquency about four times as often as girls. In the past few years the ratio has been reduced to about three to one and is still slowly declining.

Not only are girls being referred to the juvenile court in ever-growing numbers, but the juvenile courts are also adjudicating them as delinquents at a rate faster than for boys. Between 1965 and 1975, the number of girls formally adjudicated as delinquent increased by nearly 120 percent, whereas the number of boys' cases increased by about 50 percent.

Police arrest rates also show disturbing trends. Compare the figures in Table 17-1 for males and females under 18 arrested for the years 1968–1977. Particularly thought provoking is the total increase in crimes of violence for which female youth are being arrested. Although it should be noted that because there is a smaller initial base rate for the girls, the percentage increases in their arrests appear larger as compared to the boys' arrest rate, still the absolute magnitude of these changes are disturbing.

The Impact of Status Offenses　Another important current issue that affects the juvenile crime rate—particularly the rate for girls—is what are referred to as *status offenses*. These are acts that are considered delinquent if committed by a child, but are not considered crimes if committed by an adult. Examples of such offenses are runaways, ungovernable behavior, curfew violation, truancy, promiscuity, and a minor in possession of alcohol. Although boys are infrequently charged with these crimes, estimates are that 50 to 75 percent of females are arrested and confined to a juvenile institution for such crimes.[4] What compounds the problem is that in spite of the nature of these offenses, research indicates that girls are often held in detention for longer periods of time and placed less frequently in community programs than are boys.[5]

Inadequate Resources and Institutions　States often do not have effective programming in institutions for delinquents. This is particularly true for female youth. The state training schools for youthful female offenders offer

TABLE 17-1
Percent Change in Arrest Rates for Males and Females Under 18, 1968–1977

OFFENSE CHARGED	PERCENT CHANGE IN MALE ARRESTS	PERCENT CHANGE IN FEMALE ARRESTS
Murder and nonnegligent homicide	+36.4	+ 61.5
Forcible rape	+32.9	——
Robbery	+46.7	+112.5
Aggravated assault	+67.2	+158.7
Burglary	+25.5	+ 88.2
Larceny-theft	+23.7	+ 87.4
Motor vehicle theft	−27.1	+ 29.2
Total violent crime	+53.5	+138.8
Total property crime	+15.5	+ 83.8

Source: FBI, *Crime in America—1977* (Washington, D.C.: U.S. Government Printing Office, 1978), p. 175.

even fewer institutional services, such as educational and vocational programs, than are available for the boys. As a result, young female offenders have less access to the range of community programs that can make the after-release transition from a troubled adolescence to well-adjusted adulthood possible.[6]

The lack of programs and facilities for female offenders is only one part of the problem. The total lack of available alternatives for juvenile court judges in many of our states is yet another concern. The following case history points out vividly some of the problems that the juvenile justice system has in dealing with female delinquents.

> Susie, a 12-year-old who had run away from home to escape her stepfather's sexual advances, was sent by the juvenile court to a juvenile correctional facility as a "person in need of supervision" (a status offender). Once there, she became the victim of sexual assaults by other girls as well as the counselors. Then she was put into solitary confinement in a strip cell for several weeks. She was fed on a meager ration of bread and water, given nothing to read, and only thin pajamas to wear. As her anger increased, so did her custodian's assessment of her unmanageability. She was eventually transferred to a state mental institution, where she is still in custody.[7]

The problems in our juvenile justice system are so severe that some critics have suggested that it should be dismantled. The problem, however, is establishing an acceptable alternative. The remainder of this chapter examines the operations of the juvenile court together with certain other considerations that bear upon the juvenile justice system.

ORIGINS OF THE JUVENILE JUSTICE SYSTEM

Scholars and historians are unable to agree on the legal foundation for the present-day juvenile court. Some argue that its beginnings can be traced to the English feudal courts of high chancery. Under the English laws of equity, the courts of high chancery were given the responsibility by the crown to serve as *parens patriae* (in place of the parent) to protect the interest of the child whose property was in jeopardy. Later, these courts extended their protection to other areas of general child welfare and incorporated the neglected and dependent child within their jurisdiction. There is no indication, however, that these courts exercised any jurisdiction over the delinquent child.

The other view suggests that juvenile courts sprang from the common law of crimes. Under the common law, a child under 7 years of age was considered incapable of developing the required criminal intent, and a child between the ages of 7 and 14 was also deemed incapable of developing the required intent unless it could be shown by his maturity and understanding that he was aware of the consequences of his actions. Because of this and because adult criminal courts were unable to deal effectively with youthful offenders, special quasi-judicial tribunals began to develop to deal with children. Eventually the administrative and procedural guidelines that grew out of these tribunals became commonly accepted policies which were then institutionalized into practice as a way to deal with delinquent youth.

Until about 1825 there were no special provisions for handling delinquents in America. The common law and customary practice of dealing with youthful offenders was to assume that children accused of misbehavior and crimes were guilty as charged. Possible innocence was not considered: the jury's responsibility was to determine whether children understood their offenses. Juries were often reluctant to sentence children to jail and often acquitted them after a brief trial, finding "lack of knowledge" the reason for the crime.[8]

By the early nineteenth century this method of handling delinquents had become unsatisfactory for two major reasons. First, despite courtroom partiality toward youths, increasing numbers were being convicted and sent to jails, where it was commonly believed that they were schooled in crime by adult offenders. Second, and more important, some children gained acquittal by appealing to the jury's sympathy—an equally unsatisfactory disposition because it allowed them to escape the consequences of their actions.[9]

Early Juvenile Reformatories

These shortcomings in the criminal justice system prompted concerned reform groups in Boston, New York, and Philadelphia to create special institutions for juveniles. The first refuge was founded in New York in 1824 by members of the Society for the Reformation of Juvenile Delinquents. In 1826, following the recommendation of Boston's mayor, the Boston City Council founded the House of Reformation for juvenile offenders. At the same time, a group of Philadelphia's leading citizens received a charter to form a house of refuge, which opened in 1828. The New York and Philadelphia refuges were privately managed although they did receive public sanction and financial aid; the Boston House of Reformation was a municipal institution. These three institutions were the only organized efforts to reform juvenile delinquents until 1847, when state institutions were opened in Massachusetts and New York.[10]

The guiding premise of these early reformatories was that children should be punished not cruelly, but correctly. Thus a regimen of work, study, and imposed discipline was adopted in which they would be taught the habits of piety, honesty, sobriety, and hard work.[11] These early reformatories were required by their charters to receive destitute and orphaned children as well as those convicted of crimes—crimes sometimes no greater than vagrancy, idleness, or stubbornness.[12]

Although their initial purpose of reform must be admired, the refuges did not live up to the glowing expectations of their founders. These institutions were soon criticized for their inability to halt juvenile delinquency or to prevent the spread of violent activities by gangs of youth who roamed the streets of our major cities after the Civil War. Although one cannot blame these reformatories completely for the growing upsurge in delinquency since they were not equipped to handle all the children who came before the courts, they can be directly blamed for failing to deal effectively with those under their care.

These early institutions were immediately faced with the problem of overcrowding and having to deal with large numbers of children without adequate financial support. To make ends meet, they began entering into contractual agreements with private business to provide child labor. This soon led to scandalous instances of brutality and neglect by private entrepreneurs who exploited the children. Although education was an initial goal of these refuges, it was quickly replaced by economic opportunism. The children were soon seen as laborers who could produce both a profit for the private business as well as ensuring the financial stability of the institution. Thus time devoted to schooling could no longer be justified on economic grounds.

Another problem that contributed to the failure of the refuges was the indiscriminate grouping of serious offenders with children who were not delinquents or who had committed only minor offenses. Inevitably, the recalcitrant and youthful serious offenders began exerting their influence, and the refuges became miniature schools of crime.[13]

The Development of Juvenile Courts

Developing along with the idea that juveniles and adults should be institutionalized separately was the concept that children should be separated from adults before and during the trial. In 1861, the mayor of Chicago was authorized to appoint a special commission to hear and decide cases that involved boys from ages 6 to 17 who were charged with committing minor offenses. In 1867, this commission was empowered to place the delinquents who came before it on probation or to sentence them to a special institution for delinquent children. In 1869, a Massachusetts law permitted the employment of a state agent who would be available for counsel and guidance to the court and would locate and report on foster homes that the court might use in placing of the children who came before it.[14] Boston passed a law in 1870 which required that children's cases should be heard separately and that an authorized state agent should be appointed to investigate cases, attend trials, and protect children's interest.[15] A few years later, Massachusetts passed additional legislation which specified that in juvenile cases, the courts were to hold separate sessions, schedule juvenile cases by a special docket, and maintain a separate records system.

Chicago is credited with the first true juvenile court in the United States. In the last decade of the nineteenth century, a group of reformers that consisted of some local jurists, the Illinois Bar Association, civic groups, and social scientists and social workers worked to persuade the Illinois state legislature to enact laws dealing with children and to vest the authority for applying these laws in a court that would be designated specifically for this purpose. In April 1899, the legislature passed the Act to Regulate Treatment and Control of Dependent, Neglected and Delinquent Children, and on July 1, 1899, the Juvenile Court of Cook County was established in Chicago. It marked the first time that a specific court had the responsibility for dependent, neglected, and delinquent children. The philosophy that guided the original legislation, and which is still important in present-day thinking, was that the juvenile should be protected and that this protection was a responsibility of the court. The delinquent child was not to be treated as a criminal, but as a person in need of help and reform.[16] To accomplish this, some changes were made in juvenile courts. In place of the adversarial proceedings which typify the adult criminal trial, informal hearings were conducted in an atmosphere more conducive to treatment than to adjudicating guilt or fixing blame. In this informal atmosphere, the judge assumed the role of a fatherly and sympathetic figure while remaining a symbol of authority. Special emphasis was placed on investigating, diagnosing, and prescribing treatment. The individual's background was more important than the facts of a given incident; specific conduct was regarded more as symptomatic of the need for the court to apply its resources and to help rather than as a prerequisite for jurisdiction.

Because the ostensible purpose of the juvenile court was to treat and help rather than adjudicate guilt or innocence, the court was empowered to act in ways inconsistent with many of the procedural safeguards available to adults in the regular courts. For example, since the hearing was not an adversarial process, there was no need for defense lawyers or a prosecutor to be present. Trials by juries were dispensed with for the same reason. Other basic rights, such as the right to cross-examine and to be confronted with the witnesses against the accused, were seldom practiced in these courts. By the same token, the child who was found guilty of a delinquent act had no right to appeal to a higher state court for review.

In place of these legal guarantees and rights, the courts employed behavioral scientists, particularly social workers, psychologists, and psychiatrists, because delinquency was considered a disease that needed expert diagnosis and treatment. This use of treatment personnel had been a unique characteristic of the entire juvenile justice process since its inception. Along with this emphasis, a new legal vocabulary developed that was adopted by the juvenile court. Instead of a complaint, a petition was substituted; a summons was used in place of a warrant; instead of a preliminary hearing, there was an intake interview; in place of an arraignment, there was a hearing or inquiry; finding of involvement replaced a conviction; and there was a disposition instead of a sentence.

Another characteristic of juvenile courts that has developed over the years is the extension of their authority over forms of behavior which if committed by an adult would not be a crime, but under the provisions of state juvenile codes places the child under the authority of the court. From our earlier discussion, we now know that these are called *status offenses*. For example, the Michigan Probate Code vests jurisdiction in the juvenile division of that state's probate court over a child:

1. Who has violated any municipal ordinance or law of the state or of the United States
2. Who has deserted his home without sufficient cause or who is repeatedly disobedient to the reasonable and lawful commands of his parents, guardian, or other custodian
3. Who repeatedly associates with immoral persons or who is leading an immoral life; or is found on premises occupied or used for illegal purposes
4. Who being required by law to attend school, willfully and repeatedly absents himself therefrom, or repeatedly violates rules and regulations thereof.
5. Who habitually idles away his or her time
6. Who repeatedly patronizes or frequents any tavern or place where the principal purpose of the business conducted is the sale of alcoholic liquors.[17]

By 1911, a dozen states had followed the example set by Illinois, and by 1925 all but two states had instituted juvenile courts. Today there is a juvenile court act in all 50 states and the District of Columbia, with approximately 2,700 courts responsible for hearing cases involving children.[18] Although juvenile courts vary greatly in their organization and staffing, generally the states adopted the basic philosophy and principles of the Chicago court and the Illinois act as well as many of the legal features associated with these pioneer efforts.

THE JUVENILE COURT TODAY

Over the years, the court has evolved from an institution that was established to help reform delinquents to an institution that some contend is nearly as bad as the social ill it is supposed to correct. As a result, the juvenile court has increasingly been the subject of reform efforts. Underlying the growing criticism of the court is the harsh observation that it often functions as a sieve through which most troubled children come and go with neither punishment, rehabilitation, nor help. To properly evaluate these criticisms, we must first understand what the court actually is and how it operates.

Role

The juvenile court today has the responsibility and authority to adjudicate matters that involve young people. It has original jurisdiction over all children under a specific age, usually 17. In some states juvenile courts share jurisdiction with the general trial courts under youthful offender statutes which raise the age limit to 21 or 23 for offenders with no prior criminal record. In addition to delinquency cases, juvenile courts in most jurisdictions handle cases that involve neglected and dependent children as well as children who are considered in the law to be "wayward." A "wayward child" is typically defined as "a child between 7 and 17 years of age who habitually associates with vicious or immoral persons, or who is growing up in circumstances exposing him to lead an immoral, vicious, or criminal life."[19]

Juvenile courts sometimes adjudicate offenses committed by an adult upon a child, such as child abuse or contribution to the delinquency of a minor. In large urban areas, juvenile courts also are often responsible for the maintenance of detention facilities. Usually these detention facilities are for the temporary housing of children who come to the attention of the court either as delinquents or as neglected or dependent children. A child charged with a serious criminal offense is usually transferred to a state juvenile institution after adjudication by the court. The court usually tries to have neglected or dependent children transferred to special foster homes or child welfare facilities.

In about 40 states, the juvenile courts have some flexibility in exercising their original jurisdiction and thus can waive jurisdiction over a minor, who will then be transferred to the adult criminal court for trial. These waiver laws vary greatly. In about half of the states that permit this practice, the juvenile court alone decides whether the child should be transferred to the adult court.

In about one-third of these states, waiver is authorized for any offense but usually only when the child is above the age of 15 or 16. Some states permit waiver when the child commits another crime while under court supervision. In other states, the authority for the juvenile court to transfer a minor to the general trial courts is determined by both the offender's age and the type of crime committed.[20] For example, the juvenile code of Michigan provides that:

> In any case where a child over the age of 15 years is accused of any act the nature of which constitutes a felony, the judge of probate of the county wherein the offense is alleged to have been committed may after investigation and examination, including notice to parents if address is known, and upon motion of the prosecuting attorney, waive jurisdiction; whereupon it shall be lawful to try such child in the court having general criminal jurisdiction of such offense.[21]

Although many states have this type of authorizing legislation, juveniles are rarely turned over to the adult criminal courts for trial. The few exceptions are usually in cases that involve crimes such as homicide and rape, where the offender is at least 16 or 17 years old and has a long history of serious criminal offenses.

Organization

Typically, juvenile courts follow two patterns of organization. In most areas, they are a specialized function of a probate court, court of domestic relations, or family court. As such they are merely appendages of courts whose main responsibility is to deal with wills and estates, divorces, and similar legal proceedings, and there may or may not be a specially designated judge who handles juvenile cases. For example, it is not unusual for a judge on a probate court to view juvenile matters as an irritating sideline. In densely populated areas, a practice is to rotate the job of juvenile court judge among the several jurists serving the court. Sometimes a particular judge who has indicated a preference or expertise in juvenile matters is assigned to concentrate on these cases.

In large metropolitan areas, the juvenile court may be an entirely separate court of general jurisdiction. This type of arrangement establishes the juvenile court as a respected judicial entity on a par with courts of similar importance in the state.

Problems

Overall, juvenile courts suffer from a number of weaknesses. First, the diversity of the juvenile court's role often creates problems. Although it is expected to help wayward children, it is also expected to protect the community from offenders who are often as dangerous as adult criminals.

Another source of difficulty is the inferior position that the juvenile court usually has in the court hierarchy. Because few jurisdictions have made it a separate court on a level with other courts of general jurisdiction, it is held in low regard by lawyers, judges, and the police. The court by virtue of its organization must rely greatly on local government, organizations, and often the local voters for funds and support. Thus, juvenile courts are vulnerable to external factors because they require more court-related resources such as social services, detention facilities, foster and group homes, and so forth. Adult courts do not require these additional services. Its dependent state makes the court very vulnerable to criticism and further complicates its already intricate relationships with other criminal justice agencies. Increasingly, the juvenile court has been looked upon as a provider of the social services to which local government has become more and more committed. To carry out even a portion of these obligations, it must not only curtail its own activities, particularly its judicial responsibilities, but also rely heavily on the goodwill and assistance of many local groups, such as the police, schools, and welfare agencies. This reliance often creates cross-pressures, such as the police demanding that the court deal more strictly with delinquents while another agency urges greater leniency. Consequently, the juvenile court has often found itself embroiled in local conflicts between the police and school officials over the handling of arrests made during school hours and on school property for marijuana use and other offenses.

Underlying and intensifying these difficulties is the court's lack of resources. Procedures for gathering and recording information and other essential tasks are cumbersome and antiquated. The struggle to carry out service functions without adequate staff and facilities undermines judicial responsibilities. In the final analysis neither the delinquency prevention functions nor the general service functions are properly performed.

THE JUVENILE JUSTICE PROCESS

The vast majority of juveniles who appear in juvenile court are referred there by the police who have arrested them. In some cases, private citizens or the child's parents can refer the child to the jurisdiction of the court. Just as the arrest of an adult must be accompanied by an arrest warrant, a legal instrument called a *petition* must be filed with the juvenile court to give the court the authority to intervene in the matter. Like an arrest warrant, a petition must specify the particular statutory violation, and it usually includes such additional information as the name, age, and residence of the child; the names and residences of the child's parents or guardians; and a brief description of the circumstances surrounding the commission of the offense.

The Intake Interview

The next step is the intake interview. If the child is in custody, most states require that an *intake interview* be held within a specified time after arrest. The intake interview is a preliminary examination of the facts conducted by the court. Usually, the intake process is presided over by a referee. Although not a judge, the referee usually has a background in social work or the behavioral sciences and in a few instances may also be an attorney. Frequently, the referee is a probation officer assigned to the juvenile court. The functions of the intake interview are to protect the interests of the child and to dispose of those cases that do not warrant the time and expense of court adjudication. This preliminary inquiry may vary from a brief examination of the facts to an in-depth investigation of the juvenile's case, including a background investigation of the child's family, interviews with school officials, psychological or psychiatric testing, and health examination. Most states also provide that relevant witnesses can be summoned by the court at the intake interview and be forced to appear and give testimony under penalty of law. If the interview is a formal one, the child, the child's parents, and an attorney can be present. Depending upon the referee's judgment as to the sufficiency of evidence, the need for court intervention, and the basis for legal jurisdiction of the court, the referee can: (1) dismiss the case; (2) authorize a hearing before the juvenile court judge; or (3) make an informal adjustment. If the referee chooses the latter course, he or she can exercise some limited discretion in properly disposing of the case. In many juvenile courts, approximately half of the cases are informally adjusted by referral to another agency, by continuation on informal probation, or in some other way. For example, in the 1973 survey of juvenile courts in the United States conducted by the Office of Youth Development of the Department of Health, Education, and Welfare, 54 percent of delinquency cases received nonjudicial dispositions.[22]

The referee or intake officer also determines whether a child should be detained pending court action. In some jurisdictions, the child does not have the statutory right to bail as do most adults accused of crimes. In most jurisdictions that do not extend the right of bail to the juvenile, there are provisions for the child to be released to his parents unless it can be demonstrated that the release of the child poses a threat to the safety and well-being of the community or himself. When detention is warranted, the referee usually has the right to place the child into detention but only limited authority to hold him there. If more extended detention pending the formal appearance of the child before the court is warranted, this must be authorized by the juvenile court judge.

The Adjudication Inquiry and Adjudication Hearing

If the referee or intake officer determines that the court should formally intervene in the case, the juvenile then appears before the judge for the arraignment. This step is usually called an *adjudication inquiry*, a *judicial hearing*, or, in some courts, a *formal appearance*. At this stage, the juvenile court judge determines if the facts and the nature of the child's behavior warrant an adjudication hearing by the court. In recent years, provisions have been made to notify the juvenile at this stage of the charges against him and to advise him of his constitutional rights and his right to an attorney.

At the adjudication inquiry, the judge can dispose of the case or order a formal adjudication hearing, depending upon the seriousness of the case. If it is a case of serious misbehavior or if the child indicates that he or she wants a hearing or wants to hire an attorney, the judge schedules an adjudication hearing.

The adjudication hearing in the juvenile process is considerably different from the adult trial process. In order to keep the process more informal and less adversarial, rules of evidence are often not strictly adhered to, and unsworn and hearsay testimony are often received and considered. The standard of proof is supposed to be guilt beyond a reasonable doubt, but this requirement is not always adhered to. Most juvenile courts have no provisions for jury trials, and the state is not usually represented by the prosecutor. Instead, the prosecution of the case may fall upon a probation officer who acts less like a legal inquisitor, such as a prosecutor would, and more like an investigator giving testimony on the alleged offense and the investigation of the case.

Since their objective is to protect and help the child, juvenile courts usually attempt to exclude from these proceedings all persons except those who have relevant and material testimony to present. In determining its disposition of the juvenile, the court places a great deal of reliance on the clinical and social report prepared by the probation officer and the diagnostic staff. This report is very similar to the presentence investigation which is conducted in the adult criminal court, with the possible exception of its greater emphasis on diagnostic testing.

Disposition

Most states give juvenile court judges very broad discretion to dispose of cases. At these *disposition hearings,* the judge has the power to dismiss the case, give the juvenile a warning, fine him, place him on probation, arrange for restitution, refer him to an agency or treatment facility, or commit him to an institution. A child sentenced to an institution usually receives an indeterminate sentence not to exceed his twenty-first birthday. If the child's crime or the community's protection warrants a longer period of incarceration, at age 21 he will be transferred to an institution that handles adult offenders. Under these circumstances, a juvenile might be committed to an extended period of incarceration in both juvenile and adult institutions. The Children's Bureau of the Department of Health, Education, and Welfare is very critical of this practice and recommends that in most cases the child not be committed for more than 3 years unless the threat to the community or the possibility for harm to the child necessitates that he remain in protective custody.[23] Figure 17-2 indicates the basic juvenile justice process.

There is as much variation in the structure and organization of agencies that administer services and facilities for delinquent children as there is in the structure of the courts. As a result, the responsibility for the child often shifts back and forth among courts and a variety of public and private agencies, both state and local. A number of states are now trying to incorporate all public agencies that deal with the child into a single unified state agency. In Michigan, a proposed department of children and youth services would have the following responsibilities:

1. To provide all State institutional, probation, and aftercare services to children committed to the Department by the juvenile court.

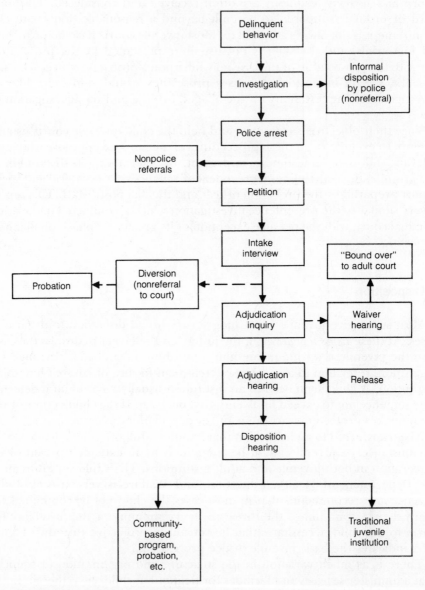

*Note: In a number of states the filing of the petition follows the intake interviews. In those states, if the referee or similar official concludes that the facts of the case warrant the formal intervention of the court, a petition is issued that binds the child over to the jurisdiction of the court. In other states, a petition must be signed before the formal process (beginning with intake) can be initiated.

FIGURE 17-2 Basic Juvenile Justice Process

2. To set minimum standards for all State, local, private, and public institutions including probation and aftercare programs for neglected, dependent, and delinquent juveniles.

3. The operation of any public institutional program, probation, and aftercare services that do not meet the minimum standards as set forth by the Department.[24]

Role of the Probation Officer

One of the most important members of the juvenile court team is the juvenile probation officer. The function of the juvenile probation officer is to match individualized, rehabilitative diagnosis and treatment with effective community supervision. Probation officers investigate the juvenile's social history and serve as a link between the court and the behavioral scientists, such as psychologists or psychiatrists, who diagnose the treatment required by the child. The probation officer is required to make factual and objective reports to the court as well as recommendations and suggestions for the proper treatment and disposition of the juvenile.

As a legal representative of the court, the probation officer is also responsible for developing the probation plan. The probation plan is both a study of the child and a recommended course of action for the court in dealing with the child. It is based on a social study of the child which comes from such sources as the delinquent himself, his parents or relatives, school officials, the police, social agencies, and the diagnostic services of behavioral scientists who have examined the child. The plan specifies whether the child needs the services of the court, whether it is more feasible to treat him in the community under a supervising probation officer, or whether institutionalization is warranted. If the investigation indicates that the child can better use the services of community agencies other than the court, the probation officer must see that the delinquent is willing to accept the referral and must provide the agency with the information needed to work effectively with the child. If the probation plan does not call for institutionalization and if the child is placed under supervision in the community, the probation officer is also responsible for seeing that the child adheres to the probation plan.

It is generally agreed that the most appropriate role for the juvenile probation officer is that of a correctional social worker rather than that of a law enforcement officer. Thus the probation officer is expected to provide treatment consistent with the philosophy of social work as practiced today. To accomplish this, the juvenile probation officer must know how to use and interpret findings from psychological testing and psychiatric examinations. The probation officer also guides and counsels the child about problems that may have played an important role in his past delinquencies.

THE JUVENILE COURT AND PROCEDURAL SAFEGUARDS

Throughout its history, the juvenile court in America has maintained that since its function was to protect the child, it was not appropriate for that tribunal to engage in the adversarial tactics that mark the adult criminal trial. This philosophy has had a tremendous impact on how the juvenile court has operated. From its inception, wide differences have been tolerated—indeed insisted upon—between the procedural rights accorded to adults and those of juveniles. As a consequence, almost all jurisdictions until recently did not grant juveniles the basic constitutional rights that are afforded adults charged with a crime. Although the U.S. Supreme Court has extended a number of constitutional rights to juveniles being handled by the juvenile courts, the child still does not have the right to bail, to indictment by grand jury, to a public trial, or to trial by jury. Rules governing the arrest and interrogation of adults by the police are frequently not observed in the case of juveniles.[25]

According to Shears, since the child should be made "to feel that he is the object of the state's care and solicitude" and not that he is under arrest or on trial, the rules that govern our criminal trials are considered by many to be inappropriate to juvenile court proceedings. The right of the state to deny to the child procedural rights is based on the assertion that a child, unlike an adult, has a right "not to liberty, but to custody." He can be made to obey his parents, to go to school, etc. If the parents do not provide the proper supervision and care of the child—that is, if the child is delinquent—the state may intervene. When the court intervenes, it does not deprive the child of any rights, because the child has none. The court merely provides the custody to which the child is entitled.[26]

Attitudes such as these and the absence of basic constitutional rights in juvenile court proceedings prompted Roscoe Pound, a former dean of the Harvard Law School, to say of the juvenile court:

> The powers of the Star Chamber [medieval site of torture used to extract a confession from an accused] were a trifle in comparison with those of our juvenile courts. . . . The absence of substantive standards has not necessarily meant the child receives compassionate and individualized treatment. The absence of procedural rules based upon constitutional principles have not always produced fair, efficient and effective procedures. Departures from established principles of due process have frequently resulted not in enlightened procedure, but in arbitrariness.[27]

Supreme Court Decisions

Beginning in the late 1960s, the Supreme Court began to examine the question of whether the juvenile offender was entitled to the same constitutional guarantees as an adult has in our criminal court system. The first major case of importance was *Kent* v. *United States,* which was decided in 1966.[28]

Morris A. Kent, Jr., age 16, was arrested by the Washington, D.C., police in 1961 and charged with housebreaking, robbery, and rape. Kent had a rather extensive juvenile record for housebreaking and purse snatching dating back to 1959 and was on probation for earlier offenses at the time of his arrest. Upon being apprehended, Kent was taken to police headquarters and interrogated for seven hours, during which time he confessed to other acts of housebreaking, robbery, and rape. After making the confession, Kent was detained at the juvenile receiving home for almost a week without any examination by a judicial officer as to the legality of the arrest and detention.

The juvenile court then waived jurisdiction over Kent, and he was turned over to the adult criminal court to stand trial. The District of Columbia juvenile court was permitted to turn a juvenile over to the adult courts after completing a "full investigation" of the facts in a case. In the Kent case, this "full investigation" consisted of the judge's reviewing the probation report and the social service file that the court's probation staff maintained on Kent. The Supreme Court did not determine the propriety of the waiver or consider the other questionable issues of the validity of the confession or detention without an appropriate judicial hearing. Instead, the Court sent the case back to the juvenile court to determine whether review of a probation file, maintained in regard to the defendant for a prior offense, satisfied the requisite of a full investigation.

The significance of this case lay not so much in the decision as in the indication it gave of the general attitude of the Supreme Court. The Court was putting the juvenile justice system on notice that these courts could not be afforded the luxury of procedural arbitrariness, and it questioned the efficacy of the *parens patriae* philosophy. In the words of the Court:

> There is evidence, in fact, that there may be grounds for concern that the child receives the worst of both worlds; that he gets neither the protection accorded to adults nor the solicitous care and regenerative treatment postulated for children.[29]

The warning of the Court in the Kent case exploded like a bombshell in 1967, when the U.S. Supreme Court proclaimed in the landmark decision of *In re Gault* that children handled by the juvenile courts were entitled to many of the due process guarantees afforded adults.[30] Gerald Gault was a fifteen-year-old who had been committed to the state industrial school by the juvenile court of Gila County, Arizona. Like Kent, Gault was already subject to an earlier juvenile court probation order, based on his having been along with another boy when a woman's purse was taken. In the case that the Court reviewed, a neighbor had charged that Gault and another boy had made an obscene telephone call to her. The police arrested Gault. Gault's parents were at work at the time, and apparently no efforts were made to contact them after their son was taken into custody; they seem to have first learned of their son's detention that evening through the parents of the other boy about whom the neighbor had complained. After hearing of his arrest, Gerald's parents went to the detention home, where they were told why their son was being detained and that a hearing would be held the following day.

The next day the police officer in charge of the case filed a petition for the hearing to be held that day. No copy of the petition was given to the boy's parents. The petition contained only legal allegations and recited no facts. The hearing was conducted in the judge's chambers without the complainant being present, and no sworn testimony was given. The court made no effort to make any record of the proceedings so that the only information concerning the hearing was in the record of a habeas corpus proceeding brought after the juvenile court hearings had been concluded.

Gerald was released from custody two days after the initial hearing, and on that day the police left a note for Mrs. Gault to inform her that there would be another hearing three days later. At the second hearing, the judge apparently relied on admissions that the police had obtained from Gerald after he had been arrested. The arresting officer indicated that Gerald had admitted to making the phone call in question. At the beginning of the second hearing, Mrs. Gault asked the court to compel the complainant to attend. The judge ruled that her attendance was not necessary; her version was reported in court on the basis of a telephone conversation that the investigating officer had conducted with her. Although the judge had a probation "referral report," it was not shown to Gerald or his parents. At the conclusion of the hearing, the judge committed the boy to the state industrial training school "for the period of his minority, unless sooner discharged by due process of law." Since Gerald was 15 at the time, he would have been subject to custodial control until his twenty-first birthday. Interestingly, the same offense if committed by an adult would have constituted only a misdemeanor under Arizona law.

Arizona did not have a law that provided for a juvenile to appeal from a juvenile court to a higher state appellate court. Under the circumstances, the Gaults could only file a habeas corpus writ with the Arizona Supreme Court, which was done a few months later. The Arizona Supreme Court ordered a hearing to be held on the writ in the superior court; the latter court denied the writ on the ground that there was no denial of either constitutional or statutory rights in the juvenile court hearing, and the Arizona Supreme Court concurred. On review, the U.S. Supreme Court reversed the decision of the Arizona Supreme Court, finding that Gault had been denied his fundamental rights to due process. In doing so, it imposed a far-reaching set of standards upon the thousands of juvenile courts throughout the nation. Specifically, the Court imposed the following procedural safeguards in delinquency cases and thus decreed a new direction in the juvenile court practice.

1. Under the due process clause it is constitutionally mandated that there be notice of charges given to the juvenile himself and to his parents. This notice must be in writing and must contain the specific charge or allegations of fact on which the proceeding is to be based. The notice must be given as early as possible and "in any event sufficiently in advance of the hearing to permit preparation."[31]

2. In delinquency proceedings which may result in commitment to an institution, the child and his parent must be notified of the child's right to be represented by counsel. If they are indigent, the court must appoint defense counsel.[32]

3. The juvenile has the right to be confronted with the witnesses against him.

4. The juvenile must be advised on his right against self-incrimination.

The U.S. Supreme Court did not specifically decide in the Gault case whether there is a right to appellate review or whether juvenile courts are required to provide a transcript of the hearings for review. Nor did it answer the question of whether the juvenile offender is entitled to trial by jury or what should be the burden of the state in proving its case against a youth accused of a crime. These issues have been addressed by the Supreme Court in more recent cases. *In re Winship* [397 U.S. 358 (1970)], the Court reversed the conviction of a twelve-year-old boy who had been declared delinquent after having been accused of stealing $112. The burden of proof used in the delinquency proceeding was a "preponderance of the evidence." The Court held that the correct standard is "proof beyond a reasonable doubt" and that anything less is a violation of the due process requirements of the Fourteenth Amendment.

In the case of *McKeiver* v. *Pennsylvania* [403 U.S. 528 (1971)] the Supreme Court declined to rule that a juvenile facing delinquency proceedings has a constitutional right to a jury trial. The Court felt:

> If the jury trial were to be injected into the juvenile court system as a matter of right, it would bring with it into that system the traditional delay, the formality, and the clamor of the adversary system and, possibly, the public trial.[33]

Although many students of the juvenile justice process believed that the mandates of the Court would spell the end of the traditional philosophy of the juvenile court, this has not happened. Research on the impact of the Court's pronouncements indicates that a number of things have occurred. First the requirements issued by the Court have not been uniformly adopted by the states. Some researchers believe that the juvenile courts have made only minimal procedural changes in reaction to these decisions.[34] Certainly there was no overnight rush to comply, and the courts have been able to retain their basic philosophy while slowly phasing in the adjustments that the Supreme Court ordered.

Undoubtedly, the overall impact of the Gault case has been to increase legal fact finding. Probably the greatest change has occurred from the growing use of defense lawyers; this procedure seems to have decreased the number of cases that reach adjudication and disposition.[35] From 1957 to 1973, there was a steady decline in the number of cases handled judicially and a steady increase in the number of cases disposed of by nonjudicial means.[36] This may very well indicate that because of more legalistic screening more cases are being diverted from the formal process of the adjudication hearing.

In the final analysis, it would seem that procedural due process for juveniles does not conflict with the benevolent philosophy of the court as many juvenile court advocates thought it would as a result of the changes brought about by the Gault case.

TYPES OF JUVENILE INSTITUTIONS

Federal, state, and local governments have developed a wide range of juvenile institutions based upon such factors as the type of crime committed, the need to provide security in the case of dangerous youth, the needs of juveniles, the programs and resources available, and similar considerations. Generally, however, the majority of these institutions can be classified into one of four types: (1) the training (reform) school; (2) camps and ranches; (3) halfway (group) homes; and (4) foster homes. Each of these institutions is generally distinguished by the type of offender it handles, the kind of treatment it offers, its size, and the problems that it was designed to deal with.

Training (Reform) School

The training school, which is often known by its older name, the reform school, handles the more serious delinquent. In the training school, the child is generally maintained under close custody. Most of these institutions have various programs of psychotherapy, education, and vocational training. Because of overpopulation, budgetary and staff limitations, poor facilities, and the housing of the more hardened delinquent, they generally are not very successful corrective mechanisms. As Coffey says:

> Of those juveniles who finish their detention period in a typical training school, 25 to 50 percent return for other offenses. If the role of the training school is to "correct" and "rehabilitate," this percentage of returnees indicates how poorly these goals are being met.[37]

The failure of these training schools is universally acknowledged. Several years ago, Massachusetts did a study of its training schools and found that more than 70 percent of the graduates were returned for the commission of new crimes. For many children, the so-called treatment became the first step in criminal careers. As a result, sweeping changes were instituted and all such training schools were closed in that state.[38] As an alternative, Massachusetts developed a system of smaller community-based treatment centers.

Camps and Ranches

Camps and ranches are normally run by the state or the county. Their programs vary but their general purpose is to avoid the crime-producing atmosphere of the training school and to maintain the delinquent child as part of the community during the treatment process. For instance, these programs typically provide for frequent contact with the community and the development of a program of counseling that involves the child and his parents. The emphasis of the program is to modify delinquent attitudes and behavior and to substitute constructive behavior patterns.

Such programs are generally not structured to deal with the delinquent who has serious behavioral patterns. In some states, however, the opposite is true. Special camps or ranch programs have been established in California, Florida, and New York specifically to deal with the seriously disturbed delinquent.

Halfway Houses and Day-Care Centers

The juvenile halfway house or group home is becoming an increasingly popular way of dealing with delinquency prevention and treatment. Like its adult counterpart, the juvenile halfway house attempts to bridge the gap between confinement in an institution and the total freedom of the community. In many instances, states sign contracts with private group homes and do not run the homes directly. A few states, such as Washington, run homes owned, staffed, and operated by the state.[39]

The state of Michigan, one of the leaders in this area, has established halfway houses that are staffed by a caseworker and five childcare workers who work on an 8-hour-shift basis. Each home has a capacity to house 12-delinquents, and the program consists of both work and school experience. This dual program allows the child to continue his education, obtain some work experience, and achieve some financial independence. If the delinquent is not capable of, or not interested in further formal education, he is given the opportunity to work full time.[40]

The day-care facility, which is operated in a number of jurisdictions today, is similar in purpose to the halfway house. The idea behind the day-care facility is the recognition that there are many juveniles who will not do well on probation but who do not need to be institutionalized. In day-care programs, the delinquent reports to the facility on a daily basis for schooling or counseling.

Foster Home

The last institution that needs to be mentioned is the foster home. These are generally private homes run by foster parents.[41] Most juvenile courts have direct access to such foster homes in which dependent children can be placed if they are likely to experience continued neglect or abuse in their own home. Unfortunately, there are not enough good foster homes to supply the need.

Through the care, control, and guidance that qualified foster parents can provide, rehabilitation is often insured. In these homes, the probation officer and foster parents often form what amounts to a treatment team. Viewed in this team context, the foster home is certainly correctional and, in many cases, provides perhaps the best elements of any treatment program—close personal attention, understanding, and sympathetic firmness about the necessity of following "family" rules.[42]

Future Juvenile Institutions

Future types and characteristics of juvenile institutions will most likely reflect some of the same concerns that we are now facing in adult institutions. On the one hand, there will probably be an increased use of such community-based treatment-services as halfway homes, agency-operated residential treatment centers, day-care programs, regional detention facilities, foster homes, and youth service bureaus (which will be discussed later). Although all these institutions exist now, it is likely that more program alternatives and a larger share of the total criminal justice expenditures will be devoted to youth services. Already, the emphasis of the federal government's programs are shifting to the juvenile justice system in an effort to intercede early in a delinquent's life.

However, the juvenile justice system, like its adult counterpart, is being buffeted by an increasing "hardline" approach to offenders who commit serious offenses or who have a history of committing such crimes. Although such legislation as New York State's 1978 Act is specifically intended to apply to the adjudicatory handling of juveniles who commit serious felony offenses, this increasing law-and-order approach may be expressed through growing treatment of juveniles as adults. Under these circumstances, the combination of longer sentences for juveniles convicted of such crimes and the increased authority of youth services departments of state governments to transfer institutionalized juveniles to the adult correctional institutions may have some implications for the institutional handling of certain classes of delinquents.

Finally, several other issues will affect the future of juvenile institutions and their programs. As of 1977, 12 states and the District of Columbia have recognized that juveniles have a statutory right to treatment.[43] Other states will undoubtedly enact similar legislation. As a part of its stated purpose of providing resources and leadership in preventing and reducing juvenile delinquency, the Juvenile Justice and Delinquency Prevention Act of 1974 (which will be discussed later), mandates that states participating in the act should no longer hold status offenders in detention and correction facilities.[44]

JUVENILE PAROLE (AFTERCARE)

When a juvenile is released from an institution, he or she typically has a period of community supervision somewhat similar to parole for adult offenders. This period is generally referred to as *aftercare* service or supervision.

As the chapter on adult parole pointed out, the staff of the institution influences the parole board in determining when the offender should be released.

In juvenile institutions, the staff plays an even greater role in determining when a delinquent should be released, even though it does not have the authority to actually parole. For example, if a juvenile stay in an institution depends on his or her "progress toward rehabilitation" under a juvenile indeterminate sentencing law, then the institutional staff is primarily responsible in judging "progress."

Like adult parole, certain factors enter into the decision whether the child should be released to aftercare. Simonsen and Gordon point out the 10 most common considerations:

1. Whether the juvenile has profited by his or her stay in the institution.
2. Whether reform has taken place so that it is unlikely that another offense will be committed.
3. Behavior in the institution.
4. Whether suitable employment, training or treatment is available on release.
5. Whether the juvenile has a home or other place, such as a group home, to which to go.
6. The youth's perception of his ability to handle reintegration into the community.
7. Seriousness of past offenses and the circumstances in which they were committed.
8. Appearance and attitude prior to release.
9. Behavior on probation and/or former parole, if applicable.
10. The institutional staff worker's perception for the youth's successful return to the community.[45]

Once placed on parole, the child is supervised by an aftercare supervisor or the staff member of a halfway house if sent to one of these programs. Like adult parole supervision, the child is provided with conditions of aftercare that must be adhered to, although these conditions are not usually as extensive as those of parole. And like parole, aftercare can be revoked.

Whereas most aftercare services were once operated on an institutional basis, this has changed somewhat in recent years. Since states have centralized their systems of juvenile institutions, it follows that they would also consolidate aftercare services. This has generally been done in one of three ways. The first method incorporates all juvenile services under a special state agency that deals with a broad range of social services. Louisiana, for example, has created a Division of Youth Services under that state's Department of Health and Human Resources. Another model calls for the creation of a special division under the state's Department of Corrections. Indiana, for instance, has both an adult and youth authority under their Department of Corrections. The third method, such as in Massachusetts, is to create an entirely separate agency at the state level.

DELINQUENCY DIVERSION PROGRAMS

In recent years, the juvenile justice system has begun to concentrate its attention and resources on alternatives for dealing with delinquent youth. The major emphasis today is on diverting youth before they are adjudicated and labeled "deviant" or "undesirable."

Evidence cited by the President's Commission in 1967 suggests that a child's chances of becoming a chronic and serious delinquent are increased once he or she enters the criminal justice system and is officially labeled "delinquent."[46] In spite of the supposedly benevolent intent of juvenile statutes and the juvenile court, the fact that the child is processed under them imposes a stigma that is difficult for the child to overcome. Models of delinquency diversion seek to avoid this detrimental social-psychological phenomenon.

This problem of labeling a child as a criminal takes on greater importance when one realizes that many children are referred to juvenile court for acts that although symptomatic of behavioral problems do not really constitute a crime in the strictest sense. Such acts as running away from home, frequenting an undesirable place, associating with undesirable companions, truancy, ungovernability, and curfew violations bring juveniles to the attention of the juvenile courts in most jurisdictions. Once in court, they are defined as "delinquent" with all of the undesirable connotations that such labeling attaches. Because all categories of juvenile crime are given equal dispositions, children who have not engaged in real criminal conduct find themselves drawn into the correctional system.

The idea that legal systems may themselves contribute to the very problems that they were established to correct is given detailed examination by Sheridan. He says:

> The label of "delinquent" sets a youngster apart from his peers—in his own estimation and by the community in general. Through forced association with others similarly labeled, this feeling is reinforced. He begins to think of himself as a delinquent and acts accordingly.
>
> Placing of such children in correctional institutions exposes them to association

with more sophisticated delinquents who have committed serious offenses and developed a pattern of delinquent conduct. . . . Despite all measures, statutory or otherwise, to protect from stigma the youngster who is a product of the correction system, it is well known that such stigma exists to almost as great a degree as in the adult field.[47]

Upon examining how juvenile courts typically handle their referrals, one finds that a large percentage—54 percent in 1973—are "adjusted" short of appearance before a judge.[48] This does not mean that the child was not in fact guilty of the particular delinquent act; it merely means that the court intake officer for any number of reasons felt that the behavior did not necessitate an appearance before the judge, and as a consequence the statutorily sanctioned authority of the judge was not invoked. In a large court, one-half to three-fourths of all complaints received may be handled in this way. It is certainly not unusual for a young offender to have his case "adjusted" two, three, four, or more times before being taken before the judge.

If such a large number of delinquency complaints can be handled in this way, it is conceivable that many of them could have been diverted without ever being referred to court at all. As a consequence, advocates of diversionary measures argue that delinquency rates could become more realistic, courts could be freed to concentrate on more difficult chronic offenders, and children could in many cases avoid the stigma of official labeling.

Although it is not practicable to review all the diversion models that have been developed, the beginning student in criminal justice should be aware of some of the more notable programs. These programs can be classified into four types: (1) school-related; (2) court-related; (3) police-related; and (4) community-related models.[49]

School-Related Diversion Programs

The school-related programs recognize that the school plays an important role in delinquency prevention. It is often in the school that the first indications of delinquency-prone conduct are observable. It is also recognized that youth who drop out of school prematurely commit more crimes than those who finish their education. In an effort to combat this problem, a number of school-related delinquency diversion programs have been implemented in recent years.

The Collegefields Group Educational Center Collegefields Group Educational Center in Newark, New Jersey, provided a specialized educationally based rehabilitation program for delinquent and predelinquent boys ages 14 and 15 who were perceived by school and juvenile court authorities as potential dropouts and having delinquency-prone attitudes. The boys were exposed to intensive guided group interaction techniques to rehabilitate toward more prosocial attitudes and better school performance. They were also given the opportunity to gain work experience along with their usual academic studies. The Family Service Bureau of Newark provided casework services to the families of the boys in the program to minimize the impact of negative family influences.[50]

Providence Educational Center Funded by the Law Enforcement Assistance Administration, the Providence Educational Center is a program that focuses on and identifies outstanding criminal justice projects with the hope that through careful program analysis and research these projects can be adopted by other communities throughout the nation. This program is being developed in St. Louis among inner-city youth. After adjudicating a child as either neglected or delinquent, the juvenile court has the alternative of sending the child to the Providence Educational Center, a nonresidential school and resocialization center for boys 12 to 16 years of age who have learning problems. Over 62 percent of the referrals have committed serious crimes, such as stealing, armed robbery, destruction of property, attempted rape, and attempted homicide.

By improving classroom performance and reversing negative attitudes, the program aims to help the juveniles hold down jobs or successfully reenter high school after leaving the program. The approach of the program is to combine an emphasis on counseling and treatment with individualized instruction and supported learning. A special counseling office charts each student's progress on an individualized treatment plan. The classes are geared to help the child through remedial education and consist of no more than 12 students who are supervised by two master teachers and a full-time social worker. Individual counseling, "rap" sessions, and regular lessons proceed side by side so that the emotional problems that often underlie learning problems can be treated as they arise.

The child remains in the project until he has attained an eighth-grade reading level, and his social skills and behavior have shown similar progress. Continual monitoring and evaluation help school officials decide whether the child is capable of making it on the outside without resorting to criminal behavior. The average length of stay is nine months.

To ensure that the growth and improvement continues after the child returns to the community, the center has initiated an aftercare program that offers essentially the same counseling services provided to the individual while he was in the school. The aftercare staff begins working with a student several months prior to his anticipated release. Together with the boy's classroom teachers, the staff reading specialist, and juvenile court officers, the aftercare staff discusses the student's options and outside goals. The child may choose to return to public school for a high school diploma, to work, or to enter a work program or vocational school. The aftercare staff maintains liaison with his teachers in the public schools, his employer, or the youth's supervisors in a vocational program until a successful transition is made.

A preliminary analysis of the program seems to indicate a much higher degree of success than that of traditional programs for dealing with delinquents. In standardized tests administered to students who have been at the school from 2 to 7 months, the average reading achievement score increased from 4.4 to 4.8 and the average math score from 3.6 to 4.5. These are important increases in view of the fact that the center's students are "problem learners."

Similarly, while 28.1 percent of the school's students committed offenses while enrolled in the school or during the 6-month aftercare period, some

70 percent of the youths released on conventional probation in St. Louis and 50 percent of those assigned to conventional residential institutions committed further offenses.[51]

Court-Related Diversion Programs

The emphasis of court-related diversionary programs is on diverting youthful offenders before adjudication. After a preliminary examination of the facts indicates guilt, the courts may postpone finding the child delinquent until he or she has completed a designated program or committed another offense while in the program.

Maryland's Intake Services Law   Under a statutory revision of Maryland's juvenile code, a child who comes before the juvenile courts may, at the option of the court, undergo informal disposition. As part of this informal disposition, "adjustment services" may be provided for up to 45 days. These services include counseling with the child or his family or referral to appropriate community agencies. This action can be taken only after all conditions are explained to the parties concerned and there is voluntary agreement to accept the conditions of the service. Once the decision has been made to follow the informal procedure, the court agrees not to file the petition unless a new complaint has been received. On a statewide basis, approximately 50 percent of all complaints are disposed of in this manner.[52]

Project Crossroads   A federally funded project, Project Crossroads, is designed to test the feasibility of using extensive professional and volunteer sources to develop remedial education programs, job placement opportunities, and counseling for delinquent offenders. The program enlists the support of the juvenile courts and the police for a pretrial diversion program in which the child receives 90 days of rehabilitative services prior to the court hearing. The court can extend this period up to 16 months. At the conclusion of the service period, the child's case is reviewed and the court decides whether the child warrants its further attention.[53]

Other court-related services include probation volunteers; court-sponsored group homes for children who are not yet delinquent but who have prodelinquent attitudes or behavioral problems; volunteer interpreters to explain to non-English-speaking families the process of the juvenile court and availability of services; employment aides to help the court obtain employment for youth; and educational aides to help the child obtain remedial education or entry into appropriate vocational training programs.

Police-Related Diversion Programs

Many police agencies also recognize that they have an important role to play in diverting potential delinquents from the juvenile justice system. For many years police agencies have been involved in varying degrees with prevention activities such as sponsoring athletic teams, maintaining day-camp programs, and other activities. In recent years, however, some police agencies have become much more involved in delinquency prevention programs.

Police-School Liaison Programs   A sizable number of police agencies have police-school programs. Generally the programs are little more than periodic visits by the police to the schools in the community where the latest police gadgetry is displayed and the children are allowed to turn on the siren of the police automobile. Other police agencies, however, have initiated much more meaningful programs. Los Angeles, for example, has a program in which officers are permanently assigned to schools. The officers in this program have college degrees, often in education, and conduct courses in the social sciences and help students familiarize themselves with the system of criminal justice. These police officers also perform counseling functions and thus are in frequent contact with students.

Police Department Social Service Unit   The city of Wheaton, Illinois, participated in a 3-year action research project with the University of Illinois Graduate School of Social Work to demonstrate that the combined efforts of law enforcement and social work would be more effective than separate and independent efforts. Social workers worked with the police to provide direct treatment and crisis-intervention service 24 hours a day. In addition, they handled nonviolent clients who were referred by the police department and sent individuals to appropriate community agencies. Although not directed specifically at juveniles, the project dealt extensively with problems of youth that bring them into contact with the police, such as drug abuse, running away, and other offenses. The primary purpose of the project was to reduce the number of cases referred to the criminal justice system for disposition. Of course, one of the important priorities of the project was to develop interprofessional relationships built around a police-social worker team, which may become a more acceptable organizational model for some police agencies of the future.[54]

Many other recommendations have been made that the police increase their diversionary efforts in dealing with potential delinquents. One of these recommendations is that the police develop and encourage the creation of *neighborhood citizen action programs* in which groups of citizens who have a greater understanding of the area's crime and delinquency problems bring them to the attention of the police. Another proposal is for the establishment of volunteer *block mothers programs,* in which the police with the help of social workers train a group of responsible women to care for and supervise children and to interview and work with adolescents and older youth. The establishment of *police youth councils* is another recommendation. Since the police and youth often interact only in negative circumstances, there is a need to involve both groups in less conflict-laden situations. The average teenager has little understanding of the problems and responsibilities of the police, but police youth councils with broad representation from all types of youth could meet periodically with police representatives to discuss student and police attitudes and activities. Such a council might also explore alternatives to existing police methods for dealing with youth and delinquents.[55]

Community-Related Diversion Programs

Community-related diversion programs often overlap with schools and court-related diversion programs. Community-related programs may take numerous forms, including group homes, halfway houses, day-care centers, youth treatment centers, citizen volunteer programs, youth service bureaus, community health and recreation programs, church projects, and others.

Criswell House: An Alternative to Institutionalization Criswell House in Tallahassee, Florida, is a demonstration project designed to serve as an alternative to the training school. The program, operated by the Florida Division of Youth Services, helps youngsters who need something less than incarceration but more than remaining at home. The boys referred to Criswell House live in residence and attend local public schools during the day. The program is designed around a somewhat unstructured setting in which decisions by staff members are kept at a minimum so that the child develops the responsibility for making decisions that affect his own life and those with whom he lives. This is not meant to imply that the youth has free rein; although staff members consciously try to avoid making the child dependent upon them for decisions, they are readily available for counsel and guidance.[56]

Homeward Bound Program The homeward bound program has received a great deal of publicity because of its unusual approach to treating delinquents. It utilizes the lure of adventure and challenge and recognizes that delinquent boys often have a strong need to express manliness. The program entails a strenuous physical regimen conducted along the rugged terrain of the Appalachian Trail in Massachusetts. Long overland hikes of 90 to 100 miles, rappelling exercises down cliffs, and other challenges seem to particularly appeal to many of the delinquent youth participating in the program. The emphasis of the program is on challenging youth and altering many of their personal characteristics. The following description of the program indicates how this might be accomplished:

> The need to pace oneself, and the requirements of persistence in the morning run and dip, the circuit training, and the 90- to 100-mile overland expeditions challenge the delinquent's impulsivity and endurance.
>
> The necessity of safety rules and climbing regulations in rappelling, sea expeditions, and search and rescue operations, causes him to question his previous concept that laws and regulations are to be ignored or treated lightly.
>
> The placing of larger measures of responsibility on him as he holds the safety line of a peer who is rappelling, or assumes leadership of his brigade in stressful situations, forces him to re-evaluate his worth in relationship to his peers.
>
> His dependence on his brigade leader and peers for success, safety and well-being cause him not only to re-examine his attitude towards authority, but also to understand and attempt the strength and weaknesses of himself and others.

Lastly, the sobering experience of the solo causes him to think deeply and long about his accomplishments, and consider what brought him to Homeward Bound, and where and how he is going from here.[57]

Youth Service Bureau (YSB) One of the most promising community-based programs is the Youth Service Bureau. A youth service bureau is basically an independent public delinquency-prevention agency established to divert children and youth from the juvenile justice system by: (1) mobilizing community resources to solve youth problems; (2) strengthening existing youth resources and developing new ones; and (3) promoting positive programs to remedy delinquency-breeding conditions.

The primary target of the youth service bureau is children between the ages of 7 and 18 who have been referred to the justice system but for whom the authority of the court is not necessary. The bureau also seeks to help children with problems that might eventually bring them into conflict with the law, and it works to improve and strengthen other agencies and resources that may unwittingly be contributing to delinquency-producing conditions.

The bureau can be organized on a town, city, or county basis, and it operates independently of other agencies or systems. Its organization is structured around a policy-making board of citizen leaders drawn from the power structure of the community and from high-delinquency neighborhoods. The bureau may have branches, each with its own neighborhood board, professional advisory council, working citizen committees, and youth service workers.

Sources of referral to the youth service bureau are quite broad and include parents, schools, social agencies, and youth themselves. The National Council on Crime and Delinquency recommends that the bureau accept referrals from the juvenile justice system only on the condition that these authoritative agencies close such cases and that the bureau not refer a juvenile to these agencies if service is refused or if the child or his family is uncooperative. An "open-door" policy is always maintained so that the youth can refer himself back to the bureau.

The entire thrust of the program can be seen in the principles by which the bureaus operate. These are:

1. Involves citizens, youth, and professionals in the neighborhood as well as persons in a position of social, economic, and political power to perform YSB functions through active volunteer working committees, giving them a decision-making voice on the YSB citizen board.

2. Promotes relationship of confidence and trust between the YSB and its clients as a cornerstone of all the activities and operations of the bureau; strives to avoid any trace of stigma to children referred to the bureau on the part of staff, citizen aides, or the community.

3. Involves the client in identifying problems underlying behavior and draws on a variety of resources in solving them.

4. Does not intervene in the lives of children and their families if its services are not wanted but always leaves the door open.

5. Documents gaps in community services for youth and seeks to have them filled

through citizen action but resists the temptation to fill service gaps with its own staff in long term direct service programs.

6. Seeks to strengthen existing agencies by assisting them with problems of hard-to-reach youth; demonstrates innovative programs.

7. From its inception, builds in evaluation under the supervision of a qualified research agency to keep operation in line with goals.[58]

These then are some of the delinquency diversion programs being developed to handle youth outside the juvenile justice system.

THE JUVENILE JUSTICE AND DELINQUENCY PREVENTION ACT OF 1974

The process and institutions of the juvenile justice system are in need of reexamination. The system cannot continue its policy of acting in isolation from the other agencies of justice, from public and private social agencies, and from meaningful programs of research. A major legislative attempt to curtail this isolationism and the "shotgun" approach to delinquency prevention was made by Congress in 1974. The Juvenile Justice and Delinquency Prevention Act established the Office of Juvenile Justice and Delinquency Prevention within the Law Enforcement Assistance Administration of the U.S. Department of Justice. This new office was given legislative authority over a wide range of programs involving the juvenile justice system, such as prevention, diversion, training of juvenile justice personnel, treatment, rehabilitation, evaluation and research, and other areas which might improve the juvenile justice system of the United States. Specifically, the purposes of the act were as follows:

1. To develop an agency which would provide for the thorough and prompt evaluation of all federally assisted juvenile delinquency programs.

2. To provide technical assistance to public and private agencies, institutions and individuals in developing and implementing juvenile delinquency programs.

3. To establish training programs for persons including professionals, paraprofessionals, and volunteers who work with delinquents.

4. To establish a centralized research effort on the problems of juvenile delinquency including an information clearinghouse to disseminate research findings.

5. To develop and encourage the implementation of national standards for the administration of juvenile justice, including recommendations for administrative, budgetary, and legislative actions at the federal, state, and local levels to facilitate the adoption of such standards.

6. To assist states and local communities with resources to develop and implement programs to keep students in elementary and secondary schools and to prevent unwarranted and arbitrary suspensions and expulsions.

7. To establish a federal assistance program to deal with the problems of runaway youth.[59]

To help this office accomplish its important coordinative undertaking at the federal level, a special Coordinating Council was established consisting of heads of federal departments whose agencies are involved in delinquency-related programs. Such officials as the attorney general, the secretary of labor, the secretary of health, education, and welfare, and the director of the Special

Action Office for Drug Abuse and Prevention serve on this council. To give professional advice to the council, a special National Advisory Committee for Juvenile Justice and Delinquency Prevention was also created. This committee, appointed by the president, consists of 21 advisers who represent juvenile or family court judges, juvenile probation and correctional personnel, law enforcement agencies, private and voluntary organizations, and community-based programs.

The Office of Juvenile Justice and Delinquency Prevention is authorized to provide grants and contracts to agencies of state and local government as well as private institutions and individuals to assist in the development of delinquency-related programs. The major emphasis of these programs, however, must be on the development of advanced programming techniques. In fact, 75 percent of all monies spent by this office must be specifically earmarked to develop and maintain advanced programs. The following categories are to receive special emphasis:

1. Community-based programs to work with youth (development of foster care and shelter care, group homes, halfway houses, home health services, etc.)

2. Community-based programs to work with parents in order to strengthen the family unit

3. Youth service bureaus

4. Comprehensive programs of drug and alcohol abuse

5. Educational programs or supportive services designed to keep delinquents and other youth in schools

6. Expanded use of probation; recruitment and training of probation officers and other professionals and volunteers

7. Youth-initiated programs such as Outreach, which tries to involve those juveniles most alienated or removed from the positive influences of society

8. Probation subsidy programs

9. Research and evaluation

10. Monitoring of jails and detention facilities to ensure that proper procedures and facilities are available and that juveniles are not incarcerated along with adults

For the first time we are organizing our human and physical resources to investigate the national problem of delinquency in a concerted and coordinative manner. Although this is a significant step, it will be many years before any significant and wide-ranging solutions are uncovered. In the meantime, we will continue to experience frustration and disappointment with the limited success of many of our programs.

SUMMARY

Although the juvenile crime rate has declined somewhat in recent years, it still continues to be a serious problem. Delinquency is no longer a male-related phenomenon as witnessed by the rapid rise in female delinquency. Of particular concern is the sharp increase in the number of female youth who are involved in violent crimes. However, the majority of female offenders are still involved in status offenses.

The juvenile court is a twentieth-century response to the problems of dealing with children who are law violators or who need society's protection. Juvenile court procedure differs from the procedure in adult courts because juvenile courts were founded on the philosophy that the function of the court was to treat and to help. In recent years, the operations of the juvenile court have received a great deal of criticism and a number of important Supreme Court decisions changed the way the courts must approach the rights of children.

The range of institutions for children that come under the authority of our juvenile courts can generally be classified into four major types: the training school, camps and ranches, halfway or group homes, and foster homes. Each of these specific institutions is generally distinguished by the type of offender it handles, the kind of treatment it offers, and the problems it was designed to deal with.

Juvenile parole is available to the delinquent child. Such a service is generally referred to as aftercare. Although somewhat similar to adult parole, it differs in several important ways.

The major emphasis of the juvenile justice system still remains one of diversion and treatment rather than adjudication and incarceration, although this may be changing somewhat in the cases of more serious juvenile offenders. Such diversion programs can be classified into school-related, court-related, police-related, and community-related models. In 1974, Congress established a special federal office to coordinate the efforts of the juvenile justice system of the federal, state, and local levels.

REVIEW QUESTIONS

1. What are some recent trends in juvenile delinquency?

2. What is a status offense? Name four kinds of status offenses.

3. Where and when was the first true juvenile court founded? What was its guiding philosophy concerning juveniles?

4. Identify the jurisdiction of the juvenile court and specify the types of cases it is authorized to hear.

5. Define and briefly describe the following:
   a. Intake interview
   b. Adjudication inquiry
   c. Adjudication hearing
   d. Disposition
   e. Probation officer

6. Explain the significance of the following judicial decisions for the juvenile justice system:
   a. *Kent* v. *United States*
   b. *In re Gault*
   c. *In re Winship*
   d. *McKiever* v. *Pennsylvania*

7. What are the major types of juvenile institutions and how do they differ?
8. Briefly describe the four types of delinquency diversions programs.

DISCUSSION QUESTIONS

1. In what ways will the juvenile justice system be affected by the present trends in delinquency?
2. Discuss the major differences between the processing of an adult defendant through the criminal courts and processing of a juvenile through a juvenile court.
3. Are juveniles entitled to the same due process protections of the Constitution as adults? Why or why not?
4. Among the many juvenile diversion programs, which is the most likely to succeed? Why?

SUGGESTED ADDITIONAL READINGS

Amos, William E., and R. L. Manella. *Delinquent Children in Juvenile Correctional Institutions.* Springfield, Ill.: Thomas, 1966.

Finkelstein, M. Marvin. *Prosecution in the Juvenile Courts: Guidelines for the Future.* Washington, D.C.: U.S. Government Printing Office, December 1973.

Garabedian, Peter C., and Don C. Gibbons. *Becoming Delinquent: Young Offenders and the Correctional System.* Chicago: Aldine, 1970.

Griffin, B. S., and C. T. Griffin. *Juvenile Delinquency in Perspective.* New York: Harper & Row, 1978.

The Institute of Criminal Justice and Criminology, University of Maryland. *New Approaches to Diversion and Treatment of Juvenile Offenders.* Washington, D.C.: U.S. Government Printing Office, June 1973.

Mack, Julian. "The Juvenile Court." *Harvard Law Review* 23 (1909). Management and Behavioral Sciences Center, Wharton School, University of Pennsylvania. *Planning and Designing for Juvenile Justice.* Washington, D.C.: LEAA, 1972.

McNeil, F. "A Halfway-House Program for Delinquents." *Crime and Delinquency* 13 (October 1967):538–544.

Platt, A. M. *Child Savers—The Invention of Delinquency,* 2nd ed. Chicago: University of Chicago Press, 1977.

Rubin, Ted, and Jack F. Smith. *The Future of the Juvenile Court: Implication for Correctional Manpower and Training.* Washington, D.C.: U.S. Government Printing Office, 1968.

Schlossman, S. L. *Love and the American Delinquent—The Theory and Practice of "Progressive" Juvenile Justice, 1825–1920.* Chicago: University of Chicago Press, 1977.

U.S. Department of Health, Education, and Welfare, Youth Development and Delinquency Prevention Administration. *State Responsibility for Juvenile Detention Care.* Washington, D.C.: U.S. Government Printing Office, 1970.

NOTES

1. See "The Youth Crime Plague," *Time,* July 11, 1977, pp. 18–28; and FBI, *Uniform Crime Reports—1977* (Washington, D.C.: U.S. Government Printing Office, 1978).

2. See U.S. Department of Health, Education, and Welfare, *Juvenile Court Statistics—1973* (Washington, D.C.: U.S. Government Printing Office, 1975), p. 1; and U.S. Department of Justice, *Crime in the United States—1976* (Washington, D.C.: U.S. Government Printing Office, 1977).

3. FBI, *Uniform Crime Reports,* p. 219.

4. Law Enforcement Assistance Administration, *Little Sisters and the Law* (Washington, D.C.: U.S. Government Printing Office, August 1977), p. 1. Also see Robert D. Vinter, ed., *Time Out: A National Study of Juvenile Correctional Programs* (Ann Arbor, Mich.: Institute of Continuing Legal Education, June 1976).

5. Law Enforcement Assistance Administration, *Little Sisters and the Law,* p. 1.

6. Ibid., p. 13.

7. Kenneth Wooden, *Weeping in the Playtime of Others* (New York: McGraw-Hill, 1976), p. 128.

8. Anthony Platt, *The Child Savers* (Chicago: University of Chicago Press, 1969), p. 202.

9. Robert M. Mennel, "Origins of the Juvenile Court," *Crime and Delinquency* (January 1972): 70.

10. Ibid., pp. 70–71.

11. New York Society for the Reformation of Juvenile Delinquents, *Annual Report* (New York: 1927), pp. 3–4.

12. Mennel, "Origins of the Juvenile Court," p. 71.

13. James Lieby, *Charities and Corrections in New Jersey* (New Brunswick, N.J.: Rutgers University Press, 1967), p. 82.

14. President's Commission on Law Enforcement and Administration of Justice, *Task Force Report: Juvenile Delinquency and Youth Crime* (Washington, D.C.: U.S. Government Printing Office, 1967), p. 3.

15. Ibid.

16. See *Commonwealth* v. *Fisher,* 213 Pa. St. 48, 62 A. 198 (1905).

17. Michigan Probate Code, chap. XII-A, § 712A.2.

18. President's Commission, *Juvenile Delinquency and Youth Crime,* p. 3.

19. Mass. Gen. Laws Ann., Chap. 119 52 (1969).

20. President's Commission, *Juvenile Delinquency and Youth Crime,* p. 4.

21. Michigan Probate Code, § 712A.4 (1968).

22. U.S. Department of Health, Education, and Welfare, *Juvenile Court Statistics—1973* (Washington, D.C.: U.S. Government Printing Office, March 1975), p. 11.

23. U.S. Department of Health, Education, and Welfare, *Standards for Juvenile and Family Courts* (Washington, D.C.: U.S. Government Printing Office, 1966), p. 84.

24. Michigan Advisory Council on Criminal Justice, *Criminal Justice Goals and Standards for the State of Michigan* (Lansing, Mich.: MACCJ, 1975), p. 46.

25. F. W. Miller, R. O. Dawson, G. E. Dix, and R. I. Parnas, *The Juvenile Justice Process* (Mineola, N.Y.: Foundation Press, 1971), p. 1162.

26. Robert Shears, "Legal Problems Peculiar to Children's Courts," *American Bar Association Journal* 48 (1962): 720.

27. Foreword to Pauline V. Young, *Social Treatment in Probation and Delinquency* (New York: McGraw-Hill, 1973), p. xxvii.

28. 383 U.S. 541 (1966).

29. 383 U.S. at 556.

30. 387 U.S. 1 (1967).

31. 387 U.S. at 33.

32. 387 U.S. at 41.

33. Frederick L. Faust and Paul J. Brantingham, *Juvenile Justice Philosophy* (St. Paul, Minn.: West, 1974), p. 537.

34. See Norman Lefstein, Vaughan Stapelton, and Lee Teitlebaum. "In Search of Juvenile Justice: Gault and Its Implementation," *Law and Society Review* 491 (1969).

35. Charles E. Reasons, "Gault: Procedural Change and Substantive Effect," *Crime and Delinquency* 16 (April 1970): 163–171.

36. See U.S. Department of Health, Education, and Welfare, *Juvenile Court Statistics—1973*, p. 11.

37. Alan R. Coffey, *Juvenile Justice as a System* (Englewood Cliffs, N.J.: Prentice-Hall, 1974), p. 128.

38. Y. Bakal, "The Massachusetts Experience," *Delinquency Prevention Reporter*, April 1973, pp. 1–3.

39. Clifford E. Simonsen and Marshall S. Gordon, *Juvenile Justice in America* (Encino, Calif.: Glencoe, 1979), p. 221.

40. For an excellent discussion of such halfway-house programs, see Robert C. Trojanowitz, *Juvenile Delinquency Concepts and Control* (Englewood Cliffs, N.J.: Prentice-Hall, 1973), especially Chap. 10.

41. For some good materials on the use of volunteers in delinquency treatment and prevention programs, see Ira M. Schwartz, Donald R. Jensen, and Michael J. Mahoney, *Volunteers in Juvenile Justice* (Washington, D.C.: U.S. Government Printing Office, October 1977); and Dane County Volunteers in Probation, *Citizen Participation in the Juvenile and Adult Criminal Justice System* (Madison, Wis.: Volunteers in Probation, May 1975).

42. Coffey, *Juvenile Justice as a System*, p. 131.

43. National Institute for Juvenile Justice and Delinquency Prevention, *Juvenile Dispositions and Corrections*, vol. 9 (Washington, D.C.: U.S. Government Printing Office, 1977), p. 57.

44. See Office of Juvenile Justice and Delinquency Prevention, *Cost and Service Impacts of Deinstitutionalization of Status Offenders in Ten States* (Washington, D.C.: U.S. Government Printing Office, October 1977).

45. Simonsen and Gordon, *Juvenile Justice in America*, pp. 288–289.

46. President's Commission, *Juvenile Delinquency and Youth Crime*, p. 417.

47. William H. Sheridan, "Juveniles Who Commit Non-Criminal Acts: Why Treat in a Correctional System?" *Federal Probation* (March 1967): 26–27.

48. U.S. Department of Health, Education, and Welfare, *Juvenile Court Statistics—1973*, p. 11.

49. This typology of delinquency diversion models is taken from Institute of Government, Corrections Division, *Models for Delinquency Diversion* (Athens, Ga.: University of Georgia, October 1971).

50. Saul Pilnich, "Collegefields Group Educational Center," United Community Fund and Council of Essex and West Hudson Counties, New Jersey (Grant No. 65015).

51. Law Enforcement Assistance Administration, *Providence Educational Center: A Program for Juvenile Delinquents* (Washington, D.C.: U.S. Government Printing Office, 1975).

52. Institute of Government, *Models for Delinquency Diversion*, p. 33.

53. The National Committee for Children and Youth, *Project Crossroads: Final Report, Phase I* (Washington, D.C.: U.S. Department of Health, Education, and Welfare, 1970).

54. See Institute of Judicial Administration, *Criminal Justice Newsletter* 2 (August 9, 1971).

55. See National Council on Crime and Delinquency, *Citizen-Action to Crime and Delinquency* (Paramus, N.J.: NCCD, 1968), p. 18.

56. John M. Flackett, "Criswell House: An Alternative to Institutional Commitment for Juvenile Offenders," *Federal Probation* 34 (December 1970): 30–37.

57. Herb C. Willman, Jr., and Ron Y. F. Chun, "Homeward Bound: An Alternative to the Institutionalization of Adjudicated Juvenile Offenders," *Federal Probation* 37 (September 1973): 56.

58. National Council on Crime and Delinquency, "What Is a Youth Service Bureau?" mimeo (1971), p. 3.

59. "The Juvenile Justice and Delinquency Prevention Act of 1974," *The Criminal Law Reporter* 15 (September 11, 1974).

Appendices

APPENDIX A

THE CONSTITUTION OF THE UNITED STATES

We the people of the United States, in order to form a more perfect union, establish justice, insure domestic tranquility, provide for the common defense, promote the general welfare, and secure the blessings of liberty to ourselves and our posterity, do ordain and establish this Constitution for the United States of America.

ARTICLE I

Section 1.

1. All legislative powers herein granted shall be vested in a Congress of the United States, which shall consist of a Senate and House of Representatives.

Section 2.

1. The House of Representatives shall be composed of members chosen every second year by the people of the several States, and the electors in each State shall have the qualifications requisite for electors of the most numerous branch of the State legislature.

2. No person shall be a Representative who shall not have attained to the age of twenty-five years, and been seven years a citizen of the United States, and who shall not, when elected, be an inhabitant of that State in which he shall be chosen.

3. Representatives and direct taxes shall be apportioned among the several States which may be included within this Union, according to their respective numbers, *which shall be determined by adding to the whole number of free persons, including those bound to service for a term of years, and excluding Indians not taxed, three fifths of all other persons.* * The actual enumeration shall be made within three years after the first meeting of the Congress of the United States, and within every subsequent term of ten years, in such manner as they shall by law direct. The number of Representatives shall not exceed one for every thirty thousand, but each State shall have at least one Representative; and until such enumeration shall be made, the State of New Hampshire shall be entitled to choose three, Massachusetts eight, Rhode Island and Providence Plantations one, Connecticut five, New York six, New Jersey four, Pennsylvania eight, Delaware one, Maryland six, Virginia ten, North Carolina five, South Carolina five, and Georgia three.

*Italics indicate passage has been affected by subsequent amendments to the Constitution.

4. When vacancies happen in the representation from any State, the executive authority thereof shall issue writs of election to fill such vacancies.

5. The House of Representatives shall choose their Speaker and other officers, and shall have the sole power of impeachment.

Section 3.

1. The Senate of the United States shall be composed of two Senators from each State, *chosen by the legislature thereof,* for six years; and each Senator shall have one vote.

2. Immediately after they shall be assembled in consequence of the first election, they shall be divided as equally as may be into three classes. The seats of the Senators of the first class shall be vacated at the expiration of the second year, of the second class at the expiration of the fourth year, and of the third class at the expiration of the sixth year, so that one third may be chosen every second year; *and if vacancies happen by resignation, or otherwise, during the recess of the legislature of any State, the executive thereof may make temporary appointments until the next meeting of the legislature, which shall then fill such vacancies.*

3. No person shall be a Senator who shall not have attained to the age of thirty years, and been nine years a citizen of the United States, and who shall not, when elected, be an inhabitant of that State for which he shall be chosen.

4. The Vice-President of the United States shall be President of the Senate, but shall have no vote, unless they be equally divided.

5. The Senate shall choose their other officers, and also a President *pro tempore,* in the absence of the Vice-President, or when he shall exercise the office of the President of the United States.

6. The Senate shall have the sole power to try all impeachments. When sitting for that purpose, they shall be on oath or affirmation. When the President of the United States is tried, the Chief Justice shall preside; and no person shall be convicted without the concurrence of two thirds of the members present.

7. Judgment in cases of impeachment shall not extend further than to removal from office, and disqualification to hold and enjoy any office of honor, trust, or profit under the United States; but the party convicted shall, nevertheless, be liable and subject to indictment, trial, judgment, and punishment, according to law.

Section 4.

1. The times, places, and manner of holding elections for Senators and Representatives shall be prescribed in each State by the legislature thereof; but the Congress may at any time by law make or alter such regulations, except as to the places of choosing Senators.

2. The Congress shall assemble at least once in every year, *and such meeting shall be on the first Monday in December, unless they shall by law appoint a different day.*

Section 5.

1. Each house shall be the judge of the elections, returns, and qualifications of its own members, and a majority of each shall constitute a quorum to do business; but a smaller number may adjourn from day to day, and may be authorized to compel the attendance of absent members, in such manner, and under such penalties, as each house may provide.

2. Each house may determine the rules of its proceedings, punish its members for disorderly behavior, and, with the concurrence of two thirds, expel a member.

3. Each house shall keep a journal of its proceedings, and from time to time publish the same, excepting such parts as may in their judgment require secrecy; and the yeas and nays of the members of either house on any question shall, at the desire of one fifth of those present, be entered on the journal.

4. Neither house, during the session of Congress, shall, without the consent of the other, adjourn for more than three days, nor to any other place than that in which the two houses shall be sitting.

Section 6.

1. The Senators and Representatives shall receive a compensation for their services, to be ascertained by law and paid out of the Treasury of the United States. They shall, in all cases except treason, felony, and breach of the peace, be privileged from arrest during their attendance at the session of their respective houses, and in going to and returning from the same; and for any speech or debate in either house they shall not be questioned in any other place.

2. No Senator or Representative shall, during the time for which he was elected, be appointed to any civil office under the authority of the United States, which shall have been created, or the emoluments whereof shall have been increased, during such time; and no person holding any office under the United States shall be a member of either house during his continuance in office.

Section 7.

1. All bills for raising revenue shall originate in the House of Representatives; but the Senate may propose or concur with amendments as on other bills.

2. Every bill which shall have passed the House of Representatives and the Senate shall, before it becomes a law, be presented to the President of the United States; if he approves he shall sign it, but if not he shall return it, with his objections, to that house in which it shall have originated, who shall enter the objections at large on their journal and proceed to reconsider it. If after such reconsideration two thirds of that house shall agree to pass the bill, it shall be sent, together with the objections, to the other house, by which it shall likewise be reconsidered, and if approved by two thirds of that house, it shall become a law. But in all such cases the votes of both houses shall be determined by yeas and nays, and the names of the persons voting for and against the bill shall be entered on the journal of each house respectively. If any bill shall not be returned by the President within ten days (Sundays excepted) after it shall have been presented to him, the same shall be a law, in like manner as if he had signed it, unless the Congress by their adjournment prevent its return, in which case it shall not be a law.

3. Every order, resolution, or vote to which the concurrence of the Senate and House of Representatives may be necessary (except on a question of adjournment) shall be presented to the President of the United States; and before the same shall take effect, shall be approved by him, or being disapproved by him, shall be repassed by two thirds of the Senate and House of Representatives, according to the rules and limitations prescribed in the case of a bill.

Section 8.

1. The Congress shall have power to lay and collect taxes, duties, imposts and excises, to pay the debts and provide for the common defense and general welfare of the United States; but all duties, imposts and excises shall be uniform throughout the United States;

2. To borrow money on the credit of the United States;

3. To regulate commerce with foreign nations, and among the several States, and with the Indian tribes;

4. To establish a uniform rule of naturalization and uniform laws on the subject of bankruptcies throughout the United States;

5. To coin money, regulate the value thereof, and of foreign coin, and fix the standard of weights and measures;

6. To provide for the punishment of counterfeiting the securities and current coin of the United States;

7. To establish the post-offices and post-roads;

8. To promote the progress of science and useful arts by securing for limited times to authors and inventors the exclusive right to their respective writings and discoveries;

9. To constitute tribunals inferior to the Supreme Court;

10. To define and punish piracies and felonies committed on the high seas, and offenses against the laws of nations;

11. To declare war, grant letters of marque and reprisal, and make rules concerning captures on land and water;

12. To raise and support armies, but no appropriation of money to that use shall be for a longer term than two years;

13. To provide and maintain a navy;

14. To make rules for the government and regulation of the land and naval forces;

15. To provide for calling forth the militia to execute the laws of the Union, suppress insurrections, and repel invasion;

16. To provide for organizing, arming, and disciplining the militia, and for governing such part of them as may be employed in the service of the United States, reserving to the States respectively the appointment of the officers, and the authority of training the militia according to the discipline prescribed by Congress;

17. To exercise exclusive legislation in all cases whatsoever over such district (not exceeding ten miles square) as may, by cession of particular States and the acceptance of Congress, become the seat of the Government of the United States, and to exercise like authority over all places purchased by the consent of the legislature of the State in which the same shall be, for the erection of forts, magazines, arsenals, dockyards, and other needful buildings; and

18. To make all laws which shall be necessary and proper for carrying into execution the foregoing powers, and all other powers vested by this constitution in the Government of the United States, or in any department or officer thereof.

Section 9.

1. The migration or importation of such persons as any of the States now existing shall think proper to admit shall not be prohibited by the Congress prior to the year one thousand eight hundred and eight, but a tax or duty may be imposed on such importation, not exceeding ten dollars for each person.

2. The privilege of the writ of *habeas corpus* shall not be suspended, unless when in cases of rebellion or invasion the public safety may require it.

3. No bill of attainder or *ex post facto* law shall be passed.

4. *No capitation or other direct tax shall be laid, unless in proportion to the census or enumeration hereinbefore directed to be taken.*

5. No tax or duty shall be laid on articles exported from any State.

6. No preference shall be given by any regulation of commerce or revenue to the ports of one State over those of another; nor shall vessels bound to or from one State be obliged to enter, clear, or pay duties in another.

7. No money shall be drawn from the Treasury but in consequence of appropriations made by law; and a regular statement and account of the receipts and expenditures of all public money shall be published from time to time.

8. No title of nobility shall be granted by the United States; and no person holding any office of profit or trust under them shall, without the consent of the Congress, accept of any present, emolument, office, or title, of any kind whatever, from any king, prince, or foreign State.

Section 10.

1. No State shall enter into any treaty, alliance, or confederation; grant letters of marque and reprisal; coin money; emit bill or credit, make anything but gold and silver coin a tender in payment of debts; pass any bill of attainder, *ex post facto* law, or law impairing the obligation of contracts, or grant any title of nobility.

2. No State shall, without the consent of Congress, lay any imposts or duties on imports or exports, except what may be absolutely necessary for executing its inspection laws; and the net produce of all duties and imposts, laid by any State on imports or exports, shall be for the use of the Treasury of the United States; and all such laws shall be subject to the revision and control of the Congress.

3. No State shall without the consent of Congress, lay any duty of tonnage, keep troops or ships of war in time of peace, enter into any agreement or compact with another State, or with a foreign power, or engage in war, unless actually invaded or in such imminent danger as will not admit of delay.

ARTICLE II

Section 1.

1. The executive power shall be vested in a President of the United States of America. He shall hold his office during the term of four years and, together with the Vice-President, chosen for the same term, be elected as follows:

2. Each State shall appoint, in such manner as the legislature thereof may direct, a number of electors, equal to the whole number of Senators and Representatives to which the State may be entitled in the Congress; but no Senator or Representative, or person holding an office of trust or profit under the United States, shall be appointed an elector.

3. *The electors shall meet in their respective States and vote by ballot for two persons, of whom one at least shall not be an inhabitant of the same State with themselves. And they shall make a list of all the persons voted for, and of the number of votes for each; which list they shall sign and certify, and transmit sealed to the seat of the government of the United States, directed to the President of the Senate. The President of the Senate shall, in the presence of the Senate and House of Representatives, open all the certificates, and the votes shall then be counted. The person having the greatest number of votes shall be the President, if such number be a majority of the whole number of electors appointed; and if there be more than one who have such majority, and have an equal number of votes, then the House of Representatives shall immediately choose by ballot one of them for President; and if no person have a majority, then from the five highest on the list the said House shall in like manner choose the President. But in choosing the President the votes shall be taken by States, the representation from each State having one vote; a quorum for this purpose shall consist of a member or members from two thirds of the States, and a majority of all the States shall be necessary to a choice. In every case, after the choice of the President, the person having the greatest number of votes of the electors shall be the Vice-President. But if there should remain two or more who have equal votes, the Senate shall choose from them by ballot the Vice-President.*

4. The Congress may determine the time of choosing the electors and the day on which they shall give their votes, which day shall be the same throughout the United States.

5. No person except a natural-born citizen or a citizen of the United States at the time of the adoption of this Constitution, shall be eligible to the office of President; neither shall any person be eligible to that office who shall not have attained to the age of thirty-five years, and been fourteen years a resident within the United States.

6. In case of the removal of the President from office, or of his death, resignation, or inability to discharge the powers and duties of the said office, the same shall devolve on the Vice-President, and the Congress may by law provide for the case of removal, death, resignation, or inability, both of the President and Vice-President, declaring what officer shall then act as President, and such officer shall act accordingly until the disability be removed or a President shall be elected.

7. The President shall, at stated times, receive for his services a compensation which shall neither be increased nor diminished during the period for which he shall have been elected, and he shall not receive within that period any other emolument from the United States or any of them.

8. Before he enter on the execution of his office he shall take the following oath or affirmation:

"I do solemnly swear (or affirm) that I will faithfully execute the office of President of the United States, and will to the best of my ability, preserve, protect, and defend the Constitution of the United States."

Section 2.

1. The President shall be commander-in-chief of the army and navy of the United States, and of the militia of the several States when called into actual service of the United States; he may require the opinion, in writing, of the principal officer in each of the executive departments, upon any subject relating to the duties of their respective offices, and he shall have power to grant reprieves and pardons for offenses against the United States, except in cases of impeachment.

2. He shall have power, by and with the advice and consent of the Senate, to make treaties, provided two thirds of the Senators present concur; and he shall nominate, and, by and with the advice and consent of the Senate, shall appoint ambassadors, other public ministers and consuls, judges of the Supreme Court, and all other officers of the United States, whose appointments are not herein otherwise provided for, and which shall be established by law; but the Congress may by law vest the appointment of such inferior officers, as they think proper, in the President alone, in the courts of law, or in the heads of departments.

3. The President shall have power to fill up all vacancies that may happen during the recess of the Senate, by granting commissions which shall expire at the end of their next session.

Section 3.

1. He shall from time to time give to the Congress information of the state of the Union, and recommend to their consideration such measures as he shall judge necessary and expedient; he may, on extraordinary occasions, convene both houses, or either of them, and in case of disagreement between them with respect to the time of adjournment, he may adjourn them to such time as he shall think proper; he shall receive ambassadors and other public ministers; he shall take care that the laws be faithfully executed, and shall commission all the officers of the United States.

Section 4.

1. The President, Vice-President, and all civil officers of the United States shall be removed from office on impeachment for and conviction of treason, bribery, or other high crimes and misdemeanors.

ARTICLE III

Section 1.

1. The judicial power of the United States shall be vested in one Supreme Court, and in such inferior courts as the Congress may from time to time ordain and establish. The judges, both of the supreme and inferior courts, shall hold their offices during good behavior, and shall, at stated times, receive for their services a compensation which shall not be diminished during their continuance in office.

Section 2.

1. The judicial power shall extend to all cases, in law and equity, arising under this Constitution, the laws of the United States, and treaties made, or which shall be made, under their authority; to all cases affecting ambassadors, other public ministers and consuls; to all cases of admiralty and maritime jurisdiction; to controversies to which the United States shall be a party; to controversies between two or more States; *between a State and citizens of another State;* between citizens of different States; between citizens of the same State claiming lands under grants of different States, and between a State, or the citizens thereof, and foreign States, citizens, or subjects.

2. In all cases affecting ambassadors, other public ministers and consuls, and those in which a State shall be party, the Supreme Court shall have original jurisdiction. In all the other cases before mentioned the Supreme Court shall have appellate jurisdiction, both as to law and fact, with such exceptions and under such regulations as the Congress shall make.

3. The trial of all crimes, except in cases of impeachment, shall be by jury; and such trial shall be held in the State where the said crimes shall have been committed; but when not committed within any State, the trial shall be at such place or places as the Congress may by law have directed.

Section 3.

1. Treason against the United States shall consist only in levying war against them, or in adhering to their enemies, giving them aid and comfort. No person shall be convicted of treason unless on the testimony of two witnesses to the same overt act, or on confession in open court.

2. The Congress shall have power to declare the punishment of treason, but no attainder of treason shall work corruption of blood or forfeiture except during the life of the person attained.

ARTICLE IV

Section 1.

1. Full faith and credit shall be given in each State to the public acts, records, and judicial proceedings of every other State. And the Congress may by general laws prescribe the manner in which such acts, records, and proceedings shall be proved, and the effect thereof.

Section 2.

1. The citizens of each State shall be entitled to all privileges and immunities of citizens in the several States.

2. A person charged in any State with treason, felony, or other crime, who shall flee from justice, and be found in another State, shall, on demand of the executive authority of the State from which he fled, be delivered up, to be removed to the State having jurisdiction of the crime.

3. *No person held to service or labor in one State, under the laws thereof, escaping into another, shall, in consequence of any law or regulation therein, be discharged from such service or labor, but shall be delivered up on claim of the party to whom such service or labor may be due.*

Section 3.

1. New States may be admitted by the Congress into this Union; but no new State shall be formed or erected within the jurisdiction of any other State; nor any State be formed by the junction of two or more States, or parts of States, without the consent of the legislatures of the States concerned as well as of the Congress.

2. The Congress shall have power to dispose of and make all needful rules and regulations respecting the territory or other property belonging to the United States; and nothing in this Constitution shall be so construed as to prejudice any claims of the United States or of any particular State.

Section 4.

1. The United States shall guarantee to every State in this Union a republican form of government, and shall protect each of them against invasion, and on application of the legislature, or of the executive (when the legislature cannot be convened), against domestic violence.

ARTICLE V

1. The Congress, whenever two thirds of both houses shall deem it necessary, shall propose amendments to this Constitution, or, on the application of the legislatures of two thirds of the several States, shall call a convention for proposing amendments, which in either case shall be valid to all intents and purposes as part of this Constitution, when ratified by the legislatures of three fourths of the several States, or by conventions in three fourths thereof, as the one or the other mode of ratification may be proposed by the Congress; provided that no amendment which may be made prior to the year one thousand eight hundred and eight shall in any manner affect the first and fourth clauses in the ninth section of the first article; and that no State, without its consent, shall be deprived of its equal suffrage in the Senate.

ARTICLE VI

1. All debts contracted and engagements entered into, before the adoption of this Constitution, shall be as valid against the United States under this Constitution, as under the Confederation.

2. This Constitution, and the laws of the United States which shall be made in pursuance thereof, and all treaties made, or which shall be made, under the authority of the United States, shall be the supreme law of the land; and the judges in every State shall be bound thereby, anything in the Constitution or laws of any State to the contrary notwithstanding.

3. The Senators and Representatives before mentioned, and the members of the several State legislatures, and all executive and judicial officers, both of the United States and of the several States, shall be bound by oath or affirmation to support this Constitution; but no religious test shall ever be required as a qualification to any office or public trust under the United States.

ARTICLE VII

1. The ratification of the conventions of nine States shall be sufficient for the establishment of this Constitution between the States so ratifying the same.

Done in convention by the unanimous consent of the States present, the seventeenth day of September, in the year of our Lord one thousand seven hundred and eighty-seven, and of the independence of the United States of America the twelfth. In witness whereof, we have hereunto subscribed our names.

G.º Washington —Presid. and deputy from Virginia

AMENDMENTS

The first ten amendments to the Constitution are known as the Bill of Rights and became effective on December 15, 1791.

I.

Congress shall make no law respecting an establishment of religion, or prohibiting the free exercise thereof; or abridging the freedom of speech or of the press; or the right of the people peaceably to assemble, and to petition the government for a redress of grievances.

II.

A well-regulated militia being necessary to the security of a free state, the right of the people to keep and bear arms shall not be infringed.

III.

No soldier shall, in time of peace, be quartered in any house without the consent of the owner, nor in time of war, but in a manner to be prescribed by law.

IV.

The right of the people to be secure in their persons, houses, papers, and effects, against unreasonable searches and seizures, shall not be violated, and no warrants shall issue but upon probable cause, supported by oath or affirmation, and particularly describing the place to be searched, and the persons or things to be seized.

V.

No person shall be held to answer for a capital or otherwise infamous crime, unless on a presentment or indictment of a grand jury, except in cases arising in the land or naval forces or in the militia when in actual service in time of war or public danger; nor shall any person be subject for the same offence to be twice put in jeopardy of life or limb; nor shall be compelled in any criminal case to be a witness against himself, nor be deprived of life, liberty, or property, without due process of law; nor shall private property be taken for public use without just compensation.

VI.

In all criminal prosecutions the accused shall enjoy the right to a speedy and public trial, by an impartial jury of the State and district wherein the crime shall have been committed, which district shall have been previously ascertained by law, and to be informed of the nature and cause of the accusation; to be confronted with the witnesses against him; to have compulsory process for obtaining witnesses in his favor, and to have the assistance of counsel for his defense.

VII.

In suits at common law, where the value in controversy shall exceed twenty dollars, the right of trial by jury shall be preserved, and no fact tried by a jury shall be otherwise re-examined in any court of the United States, than according to the rules of the common law.

VIII.

Excessive bail shall not be required, nor excessive fines imposed, nor cruel and unusual punishments inflicted.

IX.

The enumeration in the Constitution of certain rights shall not be construed to deny or disparage others retained by the people.

X.

The powers not delegated to the United States by the Constitution, nor prohibited by it to the States, are reserved to the States respectively, or to the people.

XI. *(Effective January 8, 1798.)*

The judicial power of the United States shall not be construed to extend to any suit in law or equity, commenced or prosecuted against one of the United States by citizens of another State, or by citizens or subjects of any foreign state.

XII. *(Effective September 25, 1804.)*

The electors shall meet in their respective States and vote by ballot for President and Vice-President, one of whom, at least, shall not be an inhabitant of the same State with themselves; they shall name in their ballots the person voted for as President, and in distinct ballots the person voted for as Vice-President, and they shall make distinct lists of all persons voted for as President and of all persons voted for as Vice-President, and of the number of votes for each, which lists they shall sign and certify, and transmit sealed to the seat of the government of the United States, directed to the President of the Senate. The President of the Senate shall, in the presence of the Senate and House of Representatives, open all the certificates and the votes shall then be counted. The person having the greatest number of votes for President shall be the President, if such number be a majority of the whole number of electors appointed; and if no person have such majority, then from the persons having the highest numbers not exceeding three on the list of those voted for as President, the House of Representatives shall choose immediately, by ballot, the President. But in choosing the President the votes shall be taken by States, the representation from each State having one vote; a quorum for this purpose shall consist of a member or members from two thirds of the States, and a majority of all the States shall be necessary to a choice. And if the House of Representatives shall not choose a President whenever the right of choice shall devolve upon them, before the *fourth day of March* next following, then the Vice-President shall act as President, as in the case of the death or other constitutional disability of the President.

The person having the greatest number of votes as Vice-President shall be the Vice-President, if such number be a majority of the whole number of electors appointed; and if no person have a majority, then from the two highest numbers on the list the Senate shall choose the Vice-President; a quorum for the purpose shall consist of two thirds of the whole number of Senators, and a majority of the whole number shall be necessary to a choice. But no person constitutionally ineligible to the office of President shall be eligible to that of Vice-President of the United States.

XIII. *(Effective December 18, 1865.)*

Section 1. Neither slavery nor involuntary servitude, except as a punishment for crime whereof the party shall have been duly convicted, shall exist within the United States or any place subject to their jurisdiction.

Section 2. Congress shall have power to enforce this article by appropriate legislation.

XIV. *(Effective July 28, 1868.)*

Section 1. All persons born or naturalized in the United States, and subject to the jurisdiction thereof, are citizens of the United States and of the State wherein they reside. No State shall make or enforce any law which shall abridge the privileges or immunities of citizens of the United States; nor shall any State deprive any person of life, liberty, or property, without due process of law; nor deny to any person within its jurisdiction the equal protection of the laws.

Section 2. Representatives shall be apportioned among the several States according to their respective numbers, counting the whole number of persons in each State, excluding Indians not taxed. But when the right to vote at any election for the choice of electors for President or Vice-President of the United States, Representatives in Congress, the executive and judicial officers of a State, or the members of the legislature thereof, is denied to any of the male inhabitants of such State, being twenty-one years of age, and citizens of the United States, or in any way abridged, except for participation in rebellion, or other crime, the basis of representation therein shall be reduced in the proportion which the number of such male citizens shall bear to the whole number of male citizens twenty-one years of age in such State.

Section 3. No person shall be a Senator or Representative in Congress, or elector of President and Vice-President, or hold any office, civil or military under the United States or under any State, who, having previously taken an oath as a member of Congress, or as an officer of the United States, or as a member of any State legislature, or as an executive or judicial officer of any State, to support the Constitution of the United States, shall have engaged in insurrection or rebellion against the same, or given aid or comfort to the enemies thereof. But Congress may, by a vote of two thirds of each house remove such disability.

Section 4. The validity of the public debt of the United States, authorized by law, including debts incurred for payment of pensions and bounties for services in suppressing insurrection or rebellion, shall not be questioned. But neither the United States nor any State shall assume or pay any debt or obligation incurred in aid of insurrection or rebellion against the United States, or any claim for the loss of emancipation of any slave; but all such debts, obligations and claims shall be held illegal and void.

Section 5. The Congress shall have power to enforce, by appropriate legislation, the provisions of this article.

XV. *(Effective March 30, 1870.)*

Section 1. The right of citizens of the United States to vote shall not be denied or abridged by the United States or by any State on account of race, color, or previous condition of servitude.

Section 2. The Congress shall have power to enforce this article by appropriate legislature.

XVI. *(Effective February 25, 1913.)*

The Congress shall have power to lay and collect taxes on incomes, from whatever source derived, without apportionment among the several States, and without regard to any census or enumeration.

XVII. *(Effective May 31, 1913.)*

The Senate of the United States shall be composed of two Senators from each State, elected by the people thereof, for six years; and each Senator shall have one vote. The electors in each State shall have the qualifications requisite for electors of the most numerous branch of the State legislature.

When vacancies happen in the representation of any State in the Senate, the executive authority of such State shall issue writs of election to fill such vacancies: *Provided,* That the legislature of any State may empower the executive thereof to make temporary appointments until the people fill the vacancies by election as the legislature may direct.

This amendment shall not be so construed as to affect the election or term of any Senator chosen before it becomes valid as part of the Constitution.

XVIII. *(Effective January 29, 1919.)*

Section 1. *After one year from the ratification of this article the manufacture, sale, or transportation of intoxicating liquors within, the importation thereof into, or the exportation thereof from the United States and all territory subject to the jurisdiction thereof for beverage purposes is hereby prohibited.*

Section 2. *The Congress and the several States shall have concurrent power to enforce this article by appropriate legislation.*

Section 3. *This article shall be inoperative unless it shall have been ratified as an amendment to the Constitution by the legislatures of the several States, as provided in the Constitution, within seven years from the date of the submission hereof to the States by Congress.*

XIX. *(Effective August 26, 1920.)*

The right of citizens of the United States to vote shall not be denied or abridged by the United States or by any State on account of sex.

Congress shall have power to enforce this article by appropriate legislation.

XX. *(Effective February 6, 1933.)*

Section 1. The terms of the President and Vice-President shall end at noon on the 20th day of January, and the terms of Senators and Representatives at noon on the 3rd day of January, of the years in which such terms would have ended if this article had not been ratified; and the terms of their successors shall then begin.

Section 2. The Congress shall assemble at least once in every year, and such meeting shall begin at noon on the 3rd day of January, unless they shall by law appoint a different day.

Section 3. If, at the time fixed for the beginning of the term of the President, the President-elect shall have died, the Vice-President-elect shall become President. If a President shall not have been chosen before the time fixed for the beginning of his term, or if the President-elect shall have failed to qualify, then the Vice-President-elect shall act as President until a President shall have qualified; and the Congress may by law provide for the case wherein neither a President-elect nor a Vice-President-elect shall have qualified, declaring who shall then act as President, or the manner in which one who is to act shall be selected, and such person shall act accordingly until a President or Vice-President shall have qualified.

Section 4. The Congress may by law provide for the case of the death of any of the persons from whom the House of Representatives may choose a President whenever the right of choice shall have devolved upon them, and for the case of the death of any of the persons from whom the Senate may choose a Vice-President whenever the right of choice shall have devolved upon them.

Section 5. Sections 1 and 2 shall take effect on the 15th day of October following the ratification of this article.

Section 6. This article shall be inoperative unless it shall have been ratified as an amendment to the Constitution by the legislatures of three-fourths of the several States within seven years from the date of its submission.

XXI. *(Effective December 5, 1933.)*

Section 1. The eighteenth article of amendment to the Constitution of the United States is hereby repealed.

Section 2. The transportation or importation into any State, territory, or possession of the United States for delivery or use therein of intoxicating liquors, in violation of the laws thereof, is hereby prohibited.

Section 3. This article shall be inoperative unless it shall have been ratified as an amendment to the Constitution by conventions in the several States, as provided in the Constitution, within seven years from the date of the submission hereof to the States by the Congress.

XXII. *(Effective February 26, 1951.)*

Section 1. No person shall be elected to the office of the President more than twice, and no person who has held the office of President, or acted as President, for more than two years of a term to which some other person was elected President shall be elected to the office of President more than once. But this Article shall not apply to any person holding the office of President when this article was proposed by the Congress, and shall not prevent any person who may be holding the office of President, or acting as President, during the term within which this Article becomes operative from holding the office of President or acting as President during the remainder of such term.

Section 2. This article shall be inoperative unless it shall have been ratified as an amendment to the Constitution by the legislatures of three-fourths of the several States within seven years from the date of its submission to the States by the Congress.

XXIII. *(Effective March 29, 1961.)*

Section 1. The District constituting the seat of Government of the United States shall appoint in such manner as the Congress may direct:

A number of electors of President and Vice-President equal to the whole number of Senators and Representatives in Congress to which the District would be entitled if it were a State, but in no event more than the least populous State; they shall be in addition to those appointed by the States, but they shall be considered, for the purposes of the election of President and Vice-President, to be electors appointed by a State; and they shall meet in the district and perform such duties as provided by the twelfth article of amendment.

Section 2. The Congress shall have power to enforce this article by appropriate legislation.

XXIV. *(Effective January 23, 1964.)*

Section 1. The right of citizens of the United States to vote in any primary or other election for President or Vice-President, or for Senators or Representatives in Congress, shall not be denied or abridged by the United States or any State by reason of failure to pay any poll tax or other tax.

Section 2. The Congress shall have power to enforce this article by appropriate legislation.

XXV. *(Effective February 23, 1967.)*

Section 1. In case of the removal of the President from office or of his death or resignation, the Vice-President shall become President.

Section 2. Whenever there is a vacancy in the office of the Vice-President, the President shall nominate a Vice-President who shall take office upon confirmation by a majority vote of both Houses of Congress.

Section 3. Whenever the President transmits to the President *pro tempore* of the Senate and the Speaker of the House of Representatives his written declaration that he is unable to discharge the powers and duties of his office, and until he transmits to them a written declaration to the contrary, such powers and duties shall be discharged by the Vice-President as Acting President.

Section 4. Whenever the Vice-President and a majority of either the principal officers of the executive departments or of such other body as Congress may by law provide, transmit to the President *pro tempore* of the Senate and the Speaker of the House of Representatives their written declaration that the President is unable to discharge the powers and duties of his office, the Vice-President shall immediately assume the powers and duties of the office as Acting President.

Thereafter, when the President transmits to the President *pro tempore* of the Senate and the Speaker of the House of Representatives his written declaration that no inability exists, he shall resume the powers and duties of his office unless the Vice-President and a majority of either the principal officers of the executive departments or of such other body as Congress may by law provide, transmit within four days to the President *pro tempore* of the Senate and the Speaker of the House of Representatives their written declaration that the President is unable to discharge the power and duties of his office. Thereupon Congress shall decide the issue, assembling within forty-eight hours for that purpose if not in session. If the Congress within twenty-one days after receipt of the latter written declaration, or, if Congress is not in session, within twenty-one days after Congress is required to assemble, determine by two-thirds vote of both Houses that the President is unable to discharge the powers and duties of his office, the Vice-President shall continue to discharge the same as Acting President; otherwise, the President shall resume the powers and duties of his office.

XXVI. *(Effective June 30, 1971.)*

Section 1. The right of citizens of the United States, who are eighteen years of age or older, to vote shall not be denied or abridged by the United States or any state on account of age.

Section 2. The Congress shall have power to enforce this article by appropriate legislation.

APPENDIX B
GLOSSARY OF TERMS

The following glossary of terms has been adopted from U.S. Department of Justice, Law Enforcement Assistance Administration, *Dictionary of Criminal Justice Data Terminology* (Washington, D.C.: U.S. Government Printing Office, 1976).

acquittal A judgment of a court, based either on the verdict of a jury or a judicial officer, that the defendant is not guilty of the offense(s) for which he has been tried.

adjudicated Having been the subject of completed criminal or juvenile proceedings, and convicted, or adjudicated a delinquent, status offender, or dependent.

adjudicatory hearing In juvenile proceedings, the fact-finding process wherein the juvenile court determines whether or not there is sufficient evidence to sustain the allegations in a petition.

alias Any name used for an official purpose that is different from a person's legal name.

appeal A request by either the defense or the prosecution that a case be removed from a lower court to a higher court in order for a completed trial to be reviewed by the higher court.

appearance, first or initial appearance The first appearance of a juvenile or adult in the court that has jurisdiction over his or her case.

appellant A person who initiates an appeal.

arraignment The appearance of a person before a court in order that the court may inform the individual of the accusation(s) against him or her, and to allow the accused to enter a plea.

arrest Taking a person into custody by authority of law, for the purpose of charging him or her with a criminal offense or for the purpose of initiating juvenile proceedings, which terminate with the recording of a specific offense.

arson The intentional destruction or attempted destruction, by fire or explosive, of the property of another or of one's own property with the intent to defraud.

assault   Unlawful intentional inflicting, or attempted or threatened inflicting, of injury upon another.

assault, aggravated   Unlawful intentional causing of serious bodily injury with or without a deadly weapon, or unlawful intentional attempting or threatening of serious bodily injury or death with a deadly weapon.

assault with a deadly weapon   Unlawful intentional inflicting, or attempted or threatened inflicting, or injury or death with the use of a deadly weapon.

assigned counsel   An attorney, not regularly employed by a government agency, assigned by the court to represent a particular person(s) in a particular criminal proceeding.

booking   A police administrative action officially recording an arrest and identifying the person, the place, the time, the arresting authority, and the reason for the arrest.

burglary   Unlawful entry of a structure, with or without force, with intent to commit a felony, or larceny.

caseload (corrections)   The total number of clients registered with a correctional agency or agent during a specified time period, often divided into active and inactive, or supervised and unsupervised, thus distinguishing between clients with whom the agency or agent maintains contact and those with whom it does not.

caseload (court)   The total number of cases filed in a given court or before a given judicial officer during a given period of time.

caseload, pending   The number of cases at any given time that have been filed in a given court, or are before a given judicial officer, but have not reached disposition.

charge   A formal allegation that a specific person(s) has committed a specific offense(s).

charging document   A formal written accusation, filed in a court, alleging that a specified person(s) has committed a specific offense(s).

child abuse   A willful action or actions by a person causing physical harm to a child.

child neglect   Willful failure by the person(s) responsible for a child's wellbeing to provide for adequate food, clothing, shelter, education, and supervision.

citation (appear)   A written order issued by a law enforcement officer directing an alleged offender to appear in a specific court at a specified time in order to answer a criminal charge.

commitment.   The action of a judicial officer ordering that an adjudicated and sentenced adult, or adjudicated delinquent or status offender who has been the subject of a juvenile court disposition hearing, be admitted into a correctional facility.

complaint   A formal written accusation made by any person, often a prosecutor, and filed in a court, alleging that a specified person(s) has committed a specific offense(s).

confinement facility A correctional facility from which the inmates are not regularly permitted to depart each day unaccompanied.

correctional agency A federal, state, or local criminal justice agency, under a single administrative authority, of which the principal functions are the investigation, intake screening, supervision, custody, confinement, or treatment of alleged or adjudicated adult offenders, delinquents, or status offenders.

correctional day program A publicly financed and operated nonresidential educational or treatment program for persons required by a judicial officer to participate.

correctional institution A generic name proposed in this terminology for those long-term adult confinement facilities often called "prisons," "federal or state correctional facilities," or "penitentiaries," and juvenile confinement facilities called "training schools," "reformatories," "boy's ranches," and the like.

correctional institution, adult A confinement facility having custodial authority over adults sentenced to confinement for more than a year.

correctional institution, juvenile A confinement facility having custodial authority over delinquents and status offenders committed to confinement after a juvenile disposition hearing.

corrections A generic term that includes all government agencies, facilities, programs, procedures, personnel, and techniques concerned with the investigation, intake, custody, confinement, supervision, or treatment of alleged or adjudicated adult offenders, delinquents, or status offenders.

court An agency of the judicial branch of government, authorized or established by statute or constitution, and consisting of one or more judicial officers, which has the authority to decide upon controversies in law and disputed matters of fact brought before it.

court of appellate jurisdiction A court that does not try criminal cases, but that hears appeals.

court of general jurisdiction Of criminal courts, a court that has jurisdiction to try all criminal offenses, including all felonies, and that may or may not hear appeals.

court of limited jurisdiction Of criminal courts, a court of which the trial jurisdiction includes no felonies, and that may or may not hear appeals.

crime or criminal offense An act committed or omitted in violation of a law forbidding or commanding it for which an adult can be punished, upon conviction, by incarceration and other penalties, or a corporation penalized, or for which a juvenile can be brought under the jurisdiction of a juvenile court and adjudicated a delinquent or transfer to adult court.

criminal history record information Information collected by criminal justice agencies on individuals, consisting of identifiable descriptions and notations of arrests, detentions, indictments, informations or other formal criminal charges, and any disposition(s) arising therefrom, sentencing, correctional supervision, and release.

Crime Index offenses or index crimes   A UCR classification that includes all Part I offenses with the exception of involuntary (negligent) manslaughter.

criminal justice agency   Any court with criminal jurisdiction and any other government agency or subunit, which defends indigents, or of which the principal functions or activities consist of the prevention, detection, and investigation of crime; the apprehension, detention, and prosecution of alleged offenders; the confinement or official correctional supervision of accused or convicted persons; or the administrative or technical support of the above functions.

criminal proceedings   Proceedings in a court of law, undertaken to determine the guilt or innocence of an adult accused of a crime.

defendant   A person against whom a criminal proceeding is pending.

defense attorney   An attorney who represents the defendant in a legal proceeding.

delinquency   Juvenile actions or conduct in violation of criminal law, and, in some contexts, status offenses.

delinquent   A juvenile who has been adjudicated by a judicial officer of a juvenile court, as having committed a delinquent act, which is an act for which an adult could be prosecuted in a criminal court.

delinquent act   An act committed by a juvenile for which an adult could be prosecuted in a criminal court, but for which a juvenile can be adjudicated in a juvenile court, or prosecuted in a criminal court if the juvenile court transfers jurisdiction.

de novo   Anew, afresh, as if there had been no earlier decision in a lower court.

detention   The legally authorized holding in confinement of a person subject to criminal or juvenile court proceedings, until the point of commitment to a correctional facility or release.

detention center   A government facility that provides temporary care in a physically restricting environment for juveniles in custody pending court disposition.

detention facility   A generic name proposed in this terminology as a cover term for those facilities that hold adults or juveniles in confinement pending adjudication, adults sentenced for a year or less of confinement, and in some instances post-adjudicated juveniles, including facilities called "jails," "county farms," "honor farms," "work camps," "road camps," "detention centers," "shelters," "juvenile halls," and the like.

detention hearing   In juvenile proceedings, a hearing by a judicial officer of a juvenile court to determine whether a juvenile is to be detained, continue to be detained, or released, while juvenile proceedings are pending.

diagnosis or classification center   A functional unit within a correctional institution, or a separate facility, that holds persons held in custody for the purpose of determining to which correctional facility or program they should be committed.

dismissal   A decision by a judicial officer to terminate a case without a determination of guilt or innocence.

disposition   The action by a criminal or juvenile justice agency which signifies that a portion of the justice process is complete and jurisdiction is relinquished or transferred to another agency; or which signifies that a decision has been reached on one aspect of a case and a different aspect comes under consideration, requiring a different kind of decision.

disposition hearing   A hearing in juvenile court, conducted after an adjudicatory hearing and subsequent receipt of the report or any predisposition investigation, to determine the most appropriate disposition of a juvenile who has been adjudicated a delinquent, a status offender, or a dependent.

disposition, juvenile court   The decision of a juvenile court, concluding a disposition hearing, that a juvenile be committed to a correctional facility, or placed in a care or treatment program, or required to meet certain standards of conduct, or released.

diversion   The official halting or suspension, at any legally prescribed processing point after a recorded justice system entry, of formal criminal or juvenile justice proceedings against an alleged offender, and referral of that person to a treatment or care program administered by a nonjustice agency, or a private agency, or no referral.

embezzlement   The misappropriation, misapplication, or illegal disposal of legally entrusted property with intent to defraud the legal owner or intended beneficiary.

ex-offender   An offender who is no longer under the jurisdiction of any criminal justice agency.

extortion   Unlawful obtaining or attempting to eventually obtain the property of another by the threat of eventual injury or harm to that person, a person's property, or another person.

felony   A criminal offense punishable by death or by incarceration in a state or federal confinement facility for a period of which the lower limit is prescribed by statute in a given jurisdiction, typically one year or more.

fugitive   A person who has concealed himself or herself, or fled a given jurisdiction in order to avoid prosecution or confinement.

halfway house   A nonconfining residential facility for adjudicated adults or juveniles, or those subject to criminal or juvenile proceedings, intended to provide an alternative to confinement for persons not suitable for probation, or needing a period of readjustment to the community after confinement.

hearing   A proceeding in which arguments, witnesses, or evidence are heard by a judicial officer or administrative body.

hearing, probable cause   A proceeding before a judicial officer in which arguments, witnesses, or evidence is presented and in which it is determined whether there is sufficient cause to hold the accused for trial or the case should be dismissed.

homicide   Any killing of one person by another.

homicide, criminal   The causing of the death of another person without justification or excuse.

homicide, excusable   The intentional but justifiable causing of the death of another or the unintentional causing of the death of another by accident or misadventure, without gross negligence. Not a crime.

homicide, justifiable   The intentional causing of the death of another in the legal performance of an official duty or in circumstances defined by law as constituting legal justification. Not a crime.

indictment   A formal written accusation made by a grand jury and filed in a court, alleging that a specified person(s) has committed a specific offense(s).

information   A formal written accusation made by a prosecutor and filed in a court, alleging that a specified person(s) has committed a specific offense(s).

inmate   A person in custody in a confinement facility.

intake   The process during which a juvenile referral is received and a decision is made by an intake unit either to file a petition in juvenile court, to release the juvenile, to place the juvenile under supervision, or to refer him or her elsewhere.

intake unit   A government agency or agency subunit that receives juvenile referrals from police, other government agencies, private agencies, or persons, and screens them, resulting in closing of the case, referral to care or supervision, or filing of a petition in juvenile court.

jail   A confinement facility usually administered by a local law enforcement agency, intended for adults but sometimes also containing juveniles, which holds persons detained pending adjudication and/or persons committed after adjudication for sentences of a year or less.

jail (sentence)   The penalty of commitment to the jurisdiction of a confinement facility system for adults, of which the custodial authority is limited to persons sentenced to a year or less of confinement.

judge   A judicial officer who has been elected or appointed to preside over a court of law, whose position has been created by statute or by constitution, and whose decision in criminal and juvenile cases may only be reviewed by a judge of a higher court and may not be reviewed de novo.

judicial officer   Any person exercising judicial powers in a court of law.

jurisdiction   The territory, subject matter, or person over which lawful authority may be exercised.

jurisdiction, original   The lawful authority of a court or an administrative agency to hear or act upon a case from its beginning and to pass judgment on it.

jury, grand   A body of persons who have been selected and sworn to investigate criminal activity and the conduct of public officials and to hear the evidence against an accused person(s) to determine whether there is sufficient evidence to bring that person(s) to trial.

jury, trial or jury, petit or jury   A statutorily defined number of persons selected according to law and sworn to determine certain matters of fact in a criminal action and to render a verdict of guilty or not guilty.

juvenile   A person subject to juvenile court proceedings because a statutorily defined event was alleged to have occurred while the person's age was below the statutorily specified limit or original jurisdiction of a juvenile court.

juvenile court   A cover term for courts that have original jurisdiction over persons statutorily defined as juveniles and alleged to be delinquents, status offenders, or dependents.

juvenile justice agency   A government agency, or subunit thereof, of which the functions are the investigation, supervision, adjudication, care, or confinement of juveniles whose conduct or condition has brought or could bring them within the jurisdiction of a juvenile court.

larceny or larceny-theft (UCR)   Unlawful taking or attempted taking of property, other than a motor vehicle, from the possession of another.

law enforcement agency   A federal, state, or local criminal justice agency of which the principal functions are the prevention, detection, investigation of crime, and the apprehension of alleged offenders.

law enforcement agency, federal   A law enforcement agency that is an organizational unit, or subunit, of the federal government.

law enforcement agency, local   A law enforcement agency that is an organizational unit, or subunit, of local government.

law enforcement agency, state   A law enforcement agency that is an organizational unit, or subunit, of state government.

manslaughter, involuntary or negligent manslaughter (UCR)   Causing the death of another by recklessness or gross negligence.

manslaughter, vehicular   Causing the death of another by grossly negligent operation of a motor vehicle.

misdemeanor   An offense usually punishable by incarceration in a local confinement facility, for a period of which the upper limit is prescribed by statute in a given jurisdiction typically limited to a year or less.

Model Penal Code   A generalized modern codification of that which is considered basic to criminal law, published by the American Law Institute in 1962.

motor vehicle theft   Unlawful taking, or attempted taking, of a motor vehicle owned by another, with the intent to deprive the owner of the vehicle permanently or temporarily.

National Crime Panel reports or National Crime Panel Survey Reports   Criminal victimization surveys conducted for the Law Enforcement Assistance Administration by the U.S. Bureau of the Census, which gauge the extent to which persons age 12 and over, households, and businesses have been victims of certain types of crime, and describe the nature of the criminal incidents and their victims.

nolo contendere   A defendant's formal answer in court, to the charges in a complaint, information, or indictment, in which the defendant does not contest the charges, and which, while not an admission of guilt, subjects the defendant to the same legal consequences as a plea of guilty.

offender or criminal   An adult who has been convicted of a criminal offense.

offense   An act committed or omitted in violation of a law forbidding or commanding it.

offenses, Part I   A class of offenses selected for use in UCR, consisting of crimes that are most likely to be reported, that occur with sufficient frequency to provide an adequate basis for comparison, and that are serious crimes by nature and/or volume.

offenses, Part II   A class of offenses selected for use in UCR, consisting of specific offenses and types of offenses that do not meet the criteria of frequency and/or seriousness necessary for Part I offenses.

parole   The status of an offender conditionally released from a confinement facility prior to the expiration of the offender's sentence, and placed under the supervision of a parole agency.

parole agency   A correctional agency, which may or may not include a parole authority, and of which the principal functions are the supervision of adults or juveniles placed on parole.

parole authority   A person or a correctional agency that has the authority to release on parole adults or juveniles committed to confinement facilities, to revoke parole, and to discharge from parole.

parolee   A person who has been conditionally released from a correctional institution prior to the expiration of his or her sentence, and placed under the supervision of a parole agency.

parole violation   An act or a failure to act by a parolee that does not conform to the conditions of parole.

penalty   The punishment annexed by law or judicial decision to the commission of a particular offense, which may be death, imprisonment, fine, or loss of civil privileges.

petition (juvenile)   A document filed in juvenile court alleging that a juvenile is a delinquent, a status offender, or a dependent, and asking that the court assume jurisdiction over the juvenile, or asking that the juvenile be transferred to a criminal court for prosecution as an adult.

plea   A defendant's formal answer in court to the charges brought against him or her in a complaint, information, or indictment.

plea bargaining   The exchange of prosecutorial and/or judicial concessions, commonly a lesser charge, the dismissal of other pending charges, a recommendation by the prosecutor for a reduced sentence, or a combination thereof, in return for a plea of guilty.

plea, guilty   A defendant's formal answer in court, to the charges in a complaint, information, or indictment, in which the defendant states that the charges are true and that he or she has committed the offense as charged, or that the defendant does not contest the charges.

plea, not guilty   A defendant's formal answer in court, to the charges in a complaint, information, or indictment, in which the defendant states that he or she is not guilty.

predisposition report The document resulting from an investigation undertaken by a probation agency or other designated authority, which has been requested by a juvenile court, into the past behavior, family background and personality of a juvenile who has been adjudicated a delinquent, a status offender, or a dependent, in order to assist the court in determining the most appropriate disposition.

pre-sentence report The document resulting from an investigation undertaken by a probation agency or other designated authority, at the request of a criminal court, into the past behavior, family circumstances, and personality of an adult who has been convicted of a crime, in order to assist the court in determining the most appropriate sentence.

prison A confinement facility having custodial authority over adults sentenced to confinement for more than a year.

probable cause A set of facts and circumstances that would induce a reasonably intelligent and prudent person to believe that an accused person had committed a specific crime.

probation The conditional freedom granted by a judicial officer to an alleged offender, or adjudicated adult or juvenile, as long as the person meets certain conditions of behavior.

probation agency or probation department A correctional agency of which the principal functions are juvenile intake, the supervision of adults and juveniles placed on probation status, and the investigation of adults or juveniles for the purpose of preparing pre-sentence or predisposition reports to assist the court in determining the proper sentence or juvenile court disposition.

probationer A person required by a court or probation agency to meet certain conditions of behavior who may or may not be placed under the supervision of a probation agency.

probation officer An employee of a probation agency whose primary duties include one or more of the probation agency functions.

probation (sentence) A court requirement that a person fulfill certain conditions of behavior and accept the supervision of a probation agency, usually in lieu of a sentence to confinement but sometimes including a jail sentence.

probation violation An act or a failure to act by a probationer which does not conform to the conditions of probation.

prosecuter An attorney employed by a government agency or subunit whose official duty is to initiate and maintain criminal proceedings on behalf of the government against persons accused of committing criminal offenses.

public defender An attorney employed by a government agency or subdivision, whose official duty is to represent defendants unable to hire private counsel.

public defender's office A federal, state, or local criminal justice agency or subunit of which the principal function is to represent defendants unable to hire private counsel.

rape   Unlawful sexual intercourse with a female, by force or without legal or factual consent.

rape, forcible   Sexual intercourse or attempted sexual intercourse with a female against her will, by force or threat of force.

rape, statutory   Sexual intercourse with a female who has consented in fact but is deemed, because of age, to be legally incapable of consent.

rape without force or consent   Sexual intercourse with a female legally of the age of consent, but who is unconscious, or whose ability to judge or control her conduct in inherently impaired by mental defect, or impaired by intoxicating substances.

recidivism   The repetition of criminal behavior; habitual criminality.

referral to intake   In juvenile proceedings, a request by the police, parents, or other agency or person, that a juvenile intake unit take appropriate action concerning a juvenile alleged to have committed a delinquent act, status offense, or to be dependent.

release from prison   A cover term for all lawful exits from federal or state confinement facilities primarily intended for adults serving sentences of more than a year, including all conditional and unconditional releases, deaths, and transfers to other jurisdictions, excluding escapes.

release on bail   The release by a judicial officer of an accused person who has been taken into custody, upon the promise to pay a certain sum of money or property if the accused fails to appear in court as required, which promise may or may not be secured by the deposit of an actual sum of money or property.

release on own recognizance   The release, by a judicial officer, of an accused person who has been taken into custody, upon the promise to appear in court as required for criminal proceedings.

release, pretrial   A procedure whereby an accused person who has been taken into custody is allowed to be free before and during his trial.

residential treatment center   A government facility that serves juveniles whose behavior does not necessitate the strict confinement of a training school, often allowing them greater contact with the community.

retained counsel   An attorney, not employed or compensated by a government agency or subunit, nor assigned by the court, who is privately hired to represent a person(s) in a criminal proceeding.

revocation   An administrative act performed by a parole authority removing a person from parole, or a judicial order by a court removing a person from parole or probation, in response to a violation on the part of the parolee or probationer.

revocation hearing   An administrative and/or judicial hearing on the question of whether or not a person's probation or parole status should be revoked.

rights of defendant   Those powers and privileges that are constitutionally guaranteed to every defendant.

robbery   The unlawful taking or attempted taking of property that is in the immediate possession of another, by force or the threat of force.

robbery, armed   The unlawful taking or attempted taking of property that is in the immediate possession of another, by the use or threatened use of a deadly or dangerous weapon.

security and privacy standards   A set of principles and procedures developed to ensure the security and confidentiality of criminal or juvenile record information in order to protect the privacy of the persons identified in such records.

sentence   The penalty imposed by a court upon a convicted person, or the court decision to suspend imposition or execution of the penalty.

sentence, indeterminate   A statutory provision for a type of sentence to imprisonment where, after the court has determined that the convicted person shall be imprisoned the exact length of imprisonment and parole supervision is afterwards fixed within statutory limits by a parole authority.

sentence, mandatory   A statutory requirement that a certain penalty shall be imposed and executed upon certain convicted offenders.

sentence, suspended   The court decision postponing the pronouncing of sentence upon a convicted person, or postponing the execution of a sentence that has been pronounced by the court.

sentence, suspended execution   The court decision setting a penalty but postponing its execution.

sentence, suspended imposition   The court decision postponing the setting of a penalty.

sheriff   The elected or appointed chief officer of a county law enforcement agency, usually responsible for law enforcement in unincorporated areas, and for the operation of the county jail.

speedy trial   The right of the defendant to have a prompt trial.

state highway patrol   A state law enforcement agency of which the principal functions consist of prevention, detection, and investigation of motor vehicle offenses, and the apprehension of traffic offenders.

state police   A state law enforcement agency whose principal functions may include maintaining statewide police communications, aiding local police in criminal investigation, police training, guarding state property, and highway patrol.

status offender   A juvenile who has been adjudicated by a judicial officer of a juvenile court, as having committed a status offense, which is an act or conduct which is an offense only when committed or engaged in by a juvenile.

status offense   An act or conduct that is declared by statute to be an offense, but only when committed or engaged in by a juvenile, and which can be adjudicated only by a juvenile court.

subpoena A written order issued by a judicial officer requiring a specified person to appear in a designated court at a specified time in order to serve as a witness in a case under the jurisdiction of that court, or to bring material to that court.

summons A written order issued by a judicial officer requiring a person accused of a criminal offense to appear in a designated court at a specified time to answer the charge(s).

theft Larceny, or in some legal classifications, the group of offenses including larceny, and robbery, burglary, extortion, fraudulent offenses, hijacking, and other offenses sharing the element of larceny.

training school A correctional institution for juveniles adjudicated to be delinquents or status offenders and committed to confinement by a judicial officer.

transfer hearing A preadjudicatory hearing in juvenile court for the purpose of determining whether juvenile court jurisdiction should be retained or waived over a juvenile alleged to have committed a delinquent act(s), and whether the juvenile should be transferred to criminal court for prosecution as an adult.

transfer to adult court The decision by a juvenile court, resulting from a transfer hearing, that jurisdiction over an alleged delinquent will be waived and that the juvenile should be prosecuted as an adult in a criminal court.

trial The examination of issues of fact and law in a case or controversy, beginning when the jury has been selected in a jury trial, or when the first witness is sworn, or the first evidence is introduced in a court trial, and concluding when a verdict is reached or the case is dismissed.

trial, court or trial, judge A trial in which there is no jury, and in which a judicial officer determines the issues of fact and law in a case.

trial, jury A trial in which a jury determines the issues of fact in a case.

UCR An abbreviation for the Federal Bureau of Investigation's uniform crime reporting program.

venue The geographical area from which the jury is drawn and in which trial is held in a criminal action.

verdict In criminal proceedings, the decision made by a jury in a jury trial, or by a judicial officer in a court trial, that a defendant is either guilty or not guilty of the offense(s) for which he or she has been tried.

verdict, guilty In criminal proceedings, the decision made by a jury in a jury trial, or by a judicial officer in a court trial, that the defendant is guilty of the offense(s) for which he or she has been tried.

verdict, not guilty In criminal proceedings, the decision made by a jury in a jury trial or by a judicial officer in a court trial, that the defendant is not guilty of the offense(s) for which he or she has been tried.

victim A person who has suffered death, physical or mental suffering, or loss of property, as the result of an actual or attempted criminal offense committed by another person.

warrant, arrest　A document issued by a judicial officer that directs a law enforcement officer to arrest a person who has been accused of an offense.

warrant, bench　A document issued by a judicial officer directing that a person who has failed to obey an order or notice to appear be brought before the court.

warrant, search　A document issued by a judicial officer that directs a law enforcement officer to conduct a search for specified property or persons at a specific location, to seize the property or persons, if found, and to account for the results of the search to the issuing judicial officer.

witness　A person who directly perceives an event or thing, or who has expert knowledge relevent to a case.

youthful offender　A person, adjudicated in criminal court, who may be above the statutory age limit for juveniles but is below a specified upper age limit, for whom special correctional commitments and special record sealing procedures are made available by statute.

APPENDIX C
MAJOR CONSTITUTIONAL CASES IN THE ADMINISTRATION OF CRIMINAL JUSTICE

I. GENERAL CONSTITUTIONAL CASES

The First Amendment in its Criminal Context: Freedom of the Press, Speech, Religion, and Assembly

Freedom of the Press: Obscenity and Pornography
Roth v. *United States,* 354 U.S. 476, 77 S. Ct. 1304 (1957).
Alberts v. *California,* 1 L. Ed. 2d 1498 (1957).
Stanley v. *Georgia,* 394 U.S. 557, 89 S. Ct. 1243 (1969).
Miller v. *California,* 413 U.S. 15, 93 S Ct. 2607 (1973).

Freedom of Speech
Cohen v. *California,* 403 U.S. 15, 91 S. Ct. 1780 (1971).
Spence v. *Washington,* 418 U.S. 405, 94 S. Ct. 2727 (1974).

Freedom of Religion: Compulsory Education
Wisconsin v. *Yoder,* 406 U.S. 205, 92 S. Ct. 1526 (1972).

Freedom of Assembly:
Healy v. *James,* 408 U.S. 169, 92 S. Ct. 2338 (1972).

The Fourth Amendment: Law of Arrest, Search, and Seizure

Protection of Persons
Katz v. *United States,* 389 U.S. 347, 88 S. Ct. 507 (1967).

Probable Cause: Arrest and Search Warrants
Draper v. *United States,* 358 U.S. 307, 70 S. Ct. 329 (1959).

Probable Cause and Warrantless Arrests
United States v. *Watson,* 423 U.S. 411, 96 S. Ct. 820 (1976).
Mincey v. *Arizona,* 434 U.S. 1343, 98 S. Ct. 23 (1978).

Probable Cause, Informants and Search Warrants
Spinelli v. *United States,* 393 U.S. 410, 89 S. Ct. 584 (1969).
United States v. *Harris,* 403 U.S. 573, 91 S. Ct. 2075 (1971).
Adams v. *Williams,* 407 U.S. 143, 92 S. Ct. 1921 (1972).
Zurcher v. *The Stanford Daily,* 436 U.S. 547, 98 S. Ct. 1970 (1978).
Marshall v. *Barlow's Inc.,* 436 U.S. 307 98 S. Ct. 1816 (1978).

Exclusionary Rule
Weeks v. *United States,* 232, U.S. 383 (1914).
Wolf v. *Colorado,* 388 U.S. 25, 69 S. Ct. 1359 (1949).
Mapp v. *Ohio,* 367 U.S. 643, 81 S. Ct. 1684 (1961).
Stone v. *Powell* and *Wolff* v. *Rice,* 428 U.S. 465, 96 S. Ct. 3037 (1976).

Search Incident to a Lawful Arrest and Related Concerns
>   *Chimel* v. *California,* 395 U.S. 752, 89 S. Ct. 2034 (1969).
>   *Cupp* v. *Murphy,* 412 U.S. 291, 93 S. Ct. 2000 (1973).
>   *United States* v. *Edwards,* 415 U.S. 800, 94 S. Ct. 467 (1973).
>   *United States* v. *Robinson,* 414 U.S. 218, 94 S. Ct. 467 (1973).
>   *Brown* v. *United States,* 411 U.S. 223, 93 S. Ct. 1565 (1973).
>   *Harris* v. *United States,* 390 U.S. 234, 88 S. Ct. 992 (1968).
>   *Colledge* v. *New Hampshire,* 403 U.S. 443, 91 S. Ct. 2022 (1971).
>   *Warden, Maryland Penitentiary* v. *Hayden,* 387 U.S. 294, 87 S. Ct. 1642 (1967).
>   *Schmerber* v. *California,* 384 U.S. 757, 86 S. Ct. 1826 (1966).
>   *United States* v. *Santana,* 427 U.S. 38, 96 S. Ct. 2406 (1976).
>   *Chambers* v. *Maroney,* 399 U.S. 42, 90 S. Ct. 1975 (1970).
>   *Cardwell* v. *Lewis,* 417 U.S. 583, 94 S. Ct. 2464 (1974).
>   *South Dakota* v. *Opperman,* 428 U.S. 364, 96 S. Ct. 3092 (1976).

Consent Searches
>   *Schneckloth* v. *Bustamonte,* 412 U.S. 218, 93 S. Ct. 2041 (1973).
>   *United States* v. *Matlock,* 415 U.S. 164, 94 S. Ct. 988 (1974).
>   *United States* v. *Watson,* 423 U.S. 411, 96 S. Ct. 820 (1976).

Border Searches
>   *Almeida-Sanchez* v. *United States,* 413 U.S. 266, 93 S. Ct. 2535 (1973).
>   *United States* v. *Martinez-Fuerte,* 428 U.S. 543, 96 S. Ct. 3070 (1976).
>   *United States* v. *Ramsey,* 431 U.S. 606, 96 S. Ct. 1972 (1977).

Stop and Frisk
>   *Terry* v. *Ohio,* 392 U.S. 1, 88 S. Ct., 1868 (1968).

Electronic Surveillance Issues
>   *Berger* v. *New York,* 388 U.S. 41, 87 S. Ct. 1873 (1967).
>   *OnLee* v. *United States,* 343 U.S. 747, 72 S. Ct. 967 (1952).
>   *United States* v. *White,* 401 U.S. 745, 91 S. Ct. 1122 (1971).

The Fifth Amendment: Double Jeopardy, Self-Incrimination, and the Grand Jury

Double Jeopardy
>   *United States* v. *Tateo,* 377 U.S. 463, 84 S. Ct. 1587 (1964).
>   *Waller* v. *Florida,* 397 U.S. 387, 90 S. Ct. 1184 (1970).
>   *Price* v. *Georgia,* 398 U.S. 323, 90 S. Ct. 1757 (1970).
>   *Ashe* v. *Swenson,* 397 U.S. 436, 90 S. Ct. 1189 (1970).
>   *Downum* v. *United States,* 372 U.S. 734, 83 S. Ct. 1033 (1963).
>   *Illinois* v. *Somerville,* 410 U.S. 458, 93 S. Ct. 1066 (1973).
>   *United States* v. *Dinitz,* 424 U.S. 600, 96 S. Ct. 1075 (1976).

Self-Incrimination
>   *Blackburn* v. *Alabama,* 361 U.S. 199, 80 S. Ct. 274 (1960).
>   *Malloy* v. *Hogan,* 378 U.S. 1, 84 S. Ct. 1489 (1964).
>   *Miranda* v. *Arizona,* 384 U.S. 436, 86 S. Ct. 1602 (1966).
>   *Michigan* v. *Mosley,* 423 U.S. 96, 96 S. Ct. 321 (1975).
>   *Harris* v. *New York,* 401 U.S. 222, 91 S. Ct. 643 (1971).
>   *Oregon* v. *Hass,* 420 U.S. 714, 95 S. Ct. 1215 (1975).

Doyle v. *Ohio*, 426 U.S. 610, 96 S. Ct. 2240 (1976).

Murphy v. *Waterfront Commission*, 378 U.S. 52, 84 S. Ct. 1594 (1964).

Kastigar v. *United States*, 406 U.S. 441, 92 S. Ct. 1653 (1972).

Lefkowitz v. *Cunningham*, 431 U.S. 801 97 S. Ct. 2132 (1977).

Hampton v. *United States*, 425 U.S. 484, 96 S. Ct. 1646 (1976).

Schmerber v. *California*, 384 U.S. 757, 86 S. Ct. 1826 (1966).

United States v. *Wade*, 388 U.S. 218, 87 S. Ct. 1926 (1967).

Stovall v. *Denno*, 388 U.S. 293, 87 S. Ct. 1967 (1967).

Foster v. *California*, 394 U.S. 440, 89 S. Ct. 1127 (1969).

Neil v. *Biggers*, 409 U.S. 188, 93 S. Ct. 375 (1972).

Manson v. *Brathwaite*, 432 U.S. 98, 97 S. Ct. 2243 (1977).

Lakeside v. *Oregon*, 435 U.S. 333, 98 S. Ct. 1091 (1978).

Grand Jury

Costello v. *United States*, 350 U.S. 359, 76 S. Ct. 406 (1953).

United States v. *Calandra*, 414 U.S. 338, 94 S. Ct. 613 (1974).

Branzburg v. *Hayes*, 408 U.S. 665, 92 S. Ct. 2646 (1972).

Alexander v. *Louisiana*, 405 U.S. 625, 92 S. Ct. 1221 (1972).

United States v. *Mandujano*, 425 U.S. 564, 96 S. Ct. 1768 (1976).

United States v. *Wong*, 431 U.S. 174, 97 S. Ct. 1823 (1977).

United States v. *Washington*, 431 U.S. 181 97 S. Ct. 1814 (1977).

The Sixth Amendment: The Right to Counsel, Trial by Jury, the Right to be Confronted with Adverse Witnesses, the Provision of Defense Witnesses and Public Trials

Right to Counsel

Powell v. *Alabama*, 287 U.S. 45, 53 S. Ct. 55 (1932).

Gideon v. *Wainwright*, 372 U.S. 335, 83 S. Ct. 792 (1963).

Argersinger v. *Hamlin*, 407 U.S. 25, 92 S. Ct. 2006 (1972).

Ross v. *Moffitt*, 417 U.S. 600, 94 S. Ct. 2437 (1974).

Faretta v. *California*, 422 U.S. 806, 95 S. Ct. 2525 (1975).

Brewer v. *Williams*, 430 U.S. 387, 97 S. Ct. 1232 (1977).

Holloway v. *Arkansas*, 435 U.S. 475, 98 S. Ct. 1173 (1978).

Trial by Jury

Williams v. *Florida*, 309 U.S. 78, 90 S. Ct. 1893 (1970).

Johnson v. *Louisiana*, 406 U.S. 356, 92 S. Ct. 1620 (1972).

North v. *Russell*, 427 U.S. 328, 96 S. Ct. 2709 (1976).

Ludwig v. *Massachusetts*, 427 U.S. 618, 96 S. Ct. 2781 (1976).

Swain v. *Alabama*, 380 U.S. 202, 85 S. Ct. 824 (1965).

Ristaino v. *Ross*, 424 U.S. 589, 96 S. Ct. 1017 (1976).

Murphy v. *Florida*, 421 U.S. 794, 95 S. Ct. 2031 (1975).

United States v. *Marion*, 404 U.S. 307, 92 S. Ct. 455 (1971).

Barker v. *Wingo*, 407 U.S. 514, 92 S. Ct. 2182 (1972).

Balleu v. *Georgia*, 435 U.S. 223, 98 S. Ct. 1029 (1978).

The Right to be Confronted with Adverse Witnesses

Pointer v. *Texas*, 308 U.S. 400, 85 S. Ct. 1065 (1965).

Illinois v. *Allen*, 397 U.S. 337, 90 S. Ct. 1057 (1970).

Bruton v. *United States*, 391 U.S. 123, 88 S. Ct. 1620 (1968).

Provision of Defense Witnesses
> *Washington* v. *Texas*, 388 U.S. 14, 87 S. Ct. 1920 (1967).
> *Webb* v. *Texas*, 409 U.S. 95, 93 S. Ct. 351 (1972).

Right to a Public Trial
> *In Re Oliver*, 330 U.S. 257, 68 S. Ct. 499 (1948).

II. SPECIAL AREAS

A. Juvenile Justice
> *In Re Gault*, 378 U.S. 187 S. Ct. 1428 (1967).
> *In Re Winship*, 397 U.S. 358, 90 S. Ct. 1068 (1970).
> *McKeiver* v. *Pennsylvania*, 403 U.S. 441. 91 S. Ct. 1976 (1971).
> *Breed* v. *Jones*, 421 U.S. 519, 95 S. Ct. 1779 (1975).
> *Ingraham* v. *Wright*, 430 U.S. 651, 97 S. Ct. 1401 (1977).

B. Excessive Bail and Fines
> *Stack* v. *Boyle*, 342 U.S. 1, 72 S. Ct. 1, 96 (1951).
> *Schlib* v. *Kuebel*, 404 U.S. 357, 92 S. Ct. 479 (1971).
> *Williams* v. *Illinois*, 399 U.S. 236, 90 S. Ct. 2018 (1970).
> Also see: The Federal Bail Reform Act of 1966, 18 U.S. CA. §§3146-3150

C. Cruel and Unusual Punishment
> *Robinson* v. *California*, 370 U.S. 660, 82 S. Ct. 1417 (1962).
> *Easter* v. *District of Columbia*, 361 F. 2d 50 (1966).
> *Powell* v. *Texas*, 392 U.S. 514, 88 S. Ct. 2145 (1968).
> *Furman* v. *Georgia*, 408 U.S. 238 (1972).
> *Gregg* v. *Georgia*, 428 U.S. 153 96 S. Ct. 2909 (1976).
> *Coker* v. *Georgia*, 433 U.S. 97 S. Ct. 2861 (1977).
> *Dobbert* v. *Florida*, 432 U.S. 97 S. Ct. 2290 (1977).
> *Woodson* v. *North Carolina*, 428 U.S. 280, 96 S. Ct. 2978 (1976).
> *Harry Roberts* v. *Louisiana*, 431 U.S. 633, 97 S. Ct. 1993 (1977).

D. Legal Rights of Convicted Offenders
> *Mempa* v. *Rhay*, 389 U.S. 128, 88 S. Ct. 254 (1967).
> *Morrissey* v. *Brewer*, 408 U.S. 471, 92 S. Ct. 2593 (1972).
> *Gagnon* v. *Scarpelli*, 411 U.S. 778, 93 S. Ct. 1756 (1973).
> *Procunier* v. *Martinez*, 416 U.S. 396, 94 S. Ct. 1800 (1974).
> *Baxter* v. *Palmigiano*, 425 U.S. 308, 96 S. Ct. 1551 (1976).
> *Meachum* v. *Fano*, 427 U.S. 215, 96 S. Ct. 2532 (1976).
> *Bounds* v. *Smith*, 430 U.S. 817, 97 S. Ct. 1491 (1977).
> *Jones* v. *North Carolina Prisoners' Labor Union, Inc.*, 433 U.S. 97 S. Ct. 2532 (1977).
> *Richardson* v. *Ramirez*, 418 U.S. 24, 94 S. Ct. 2655 (1974).

E. Guilty Pleas and Plea Bargaining
> *Boykin* v. *Alabama*, 395 U.S. 238, 89 S. Ct. 1709 (1969).
> *Brady* v. *United States*, 397 U.S. 742, 90 S. Ct. 1463 (1970).
> *North Carolina* v. *Alford*, 400 U.S. 25, 91 S. Ct. 160 (1970).
> *Santobello* v. *New York*, 404 U.S. 257, 29 S. Ct. 495 (1971).
> *Henderson* v. *Morgan*, 426 U.S. 637, 96 S. Ct. 2253 (1976).

F. Sentencing, Appeals, and Post-Conviction Remedies
   North Carolina v. *Pearce*, 395 U.S. 711, 89 S. Ct. 2072 (1969).
   Colten v. *Kentucky*, 407 U.S. 104, 92 S. Ct. 1953 (1972).
   McGinnis v. *Royster*, 410 U.S. 263, 93 S. Ct. 1055 (1973).
   Gardner v. *Florida*, 430 U.S. 349, 97 S. Ct. 1197 (1977).
   Wainwright v. *Sykes*, 433 U.S. 72, 97 S. Ct. 2497 (1977).

G. Due Process and the Fifth and Fourteenth Amendments
   Adamson v. *California*, 332 U.S. 46, 76 S. Ct. 1672 (1947).
   Duncan v. *Louisiana*, 391 U.S. 145, 88 S. Ct. 1444 (1968).
   Benton v. *Maryland*, 395 U.S. 784, 89 S. Ct. 2056 (1969).
   Drope v. *Missouri*, 420 U.S. 162, 95 S. Ct. 896 (1975).
   Bordenkircher v. *Hayes*, 434 U.S. 357, 98 S. Ct. 663 (1978).

H. Equal Protection of the Laws and the Criminal Process
   Griffin v. *Illinois*, 351 U.S. 12, 76 S. Ct. 585 (1956).
   Tate v. *Short*, 401 U.S. 396, 92 S. Ct. 410 (1971).
   Estelle v. *Dorrough*, 420 U.S. 534, 95 S. Ct. 1173 (1975).

I. The Civil Rights Act of 1964 and the Congressional Rights of Law Enforcement Officers
   42 U.S.C. § 1983
   Monroe v. *Pape*, 365 U.S. 167, 81 S. Ct. 473 (1961).
   Bivens v. *Six, Unknown Named Agents of the Federal Bureau of Narcotics*, 403 U.S. 388, 91 S. Ct. 1999 (1971).
   Paul v. *Davis*, 424 U.S. 693, 96 S. Ct. 1155 (1976).
   Dothard v. *Rawlinson*, 433 U.S. 321, 97 S. Ct. 2720 (1976).
   Garrity v. *New Jersey*, 385 U.S. 493, 87 S. Ct. 616 (1967).
   Kelley v. *Johnson*, 425, U.S. 238, 96 S. Ct. 1440 (1976).
   Bishop v. *Wood*, 426 U.S. 341, 96 S. Ct. 2074 (1976).

APPENDIX D
MAJOR CRIMINAL JUSTICE
JOURNALS AND
PERIODICALS

POLICE

Drug Enforcement. United States Department of Justice, Drug Enforcement Administration, 1705 I St., N.W., Washington, D.C. 20537.

Enforcement Journal. National Police Officers Association of America, Police Hall of Fame Bldg., Venice, Fla. 33595.

FBI Law Enforcement Bulletin. United States Department of Justice, Federal Bureau of Investigation, Washington, D.C. 20535.

Fingerprinting and Identification. CAREGRCO Institute of Applied Science, 1920 Sunnyside Avenue, Chicago, Ill. 60640.

From the State Capitals: Police Administration Trends in the States. Bethune Jones, Inc., 321 Sunset Avenue, Asbury Park, N.J. 07712.

IACP Law Enforcement Legal Review. International Association of Chiefs of Police, Inc., 11 Firstfield Road, Gaithersburg, Md. 20760.

IACP Law Enforcement Legislation and Litigation Report. International Association of Chiefs of Police, Inc., 11 Firstfield Road, Gaithersburg, Md. 20760.

IACP Legal Points. International Association of Chiefs of Police, Inc., 11 Firstfield Road, Gaithersburg, Md. 20760.

Journal of Police Science and Administration. International Association of Chiefs of Police, Inc., 11 Firstfield Road, Gaithersburg, Md. 20760.

Journal of Polygraph Science. National Training Center of Lie Detection Inc., 57 W. 57th St., N.Y., N.Y. 10019.

Law and Order. Copp Organization, Inc., 37 W. 38th St., N.Y., N.Y. 10018.

The Law Officer. Patrick Davies, International Conference of Police Associations, 2468 Louisiana Ave., No., Minneapolis, Minn. 55427.

Narcotics Control Digest. Washington Crime News Services, 7620 Little River Tpke., Annadale, Va. 22003.

Narcotics Law Bulletin. Quinlan Publishing Co., Inc., 88 Broad St., Boston, Mass. 02110.

The National Sheriff. National Sheriff's Association, 1250 Connecticut Ave., Washington, D.C. 20036.

The Police Chief. International Association of Chiefs of Police, Inc., 11 Firstfield Road, Gaithersburg, Md. 20760.

The Police Journal. Justice of the Peace (Holdings) Ltd., East Row, Little London, Chichester, Sussex, England.

Police Law Quarterly. Illinois Institute of Technology, Institute for Criminal Justice, 10 N. Franklin St., Chicago, Ill. 60606.

Police Research Bulletin. Home Office, Police Research Services Unit, Horseferry House, Dean Ryle St., London, 24W, England.

Police Times. American Federation of Police, 1100 N.E. 125th St., N. Miami, Fla. 33161.

Polygraph. American Polygraph Association, Box 74, Linthicom Heights, Md. 21090.

Search and Seizure Bulletin. Quinlan Publishing Co., Inc., 191 High St., Boston, Mass. 02210.

Traffic Safety. National Safety Council, 425 N. Michigan Ave., Chicago, Ill. 60611.

Training Key. International Association of Chiefs of Police, Inc., 11 Firstfield Road, Gaithersburg, Md. 20760.

LAW AND COURTS

AELE Legal Defense Manual. Americans for Effective Law Enforcement, 960 State National Bank Plaza, Evanston, Ill. 60201.

AELE Legal Liability Reporter. Americans for Effective Law Enforcement, 960 State National Bank Plaza, Evanston, Ill. 60201.

American Bar Association Journal. ABA, 1155 E. 60th St., Chicago, Ill. 60637.

American Criminal Law Review. ABA, 1155 E. 60th St., Chicago, Ill. 60637.

American Journal of Criminal Law. University of Texas School of Law, Austin, Tex. 78705.

Criminal Law Bulletin. Warren, Gorham & Lamont, Inc., 89 Beach St., Boston, Mass. 02111.

The Criminal Law Quarterly. Canada Law Book Limited, 80 Cowdray Ct., Agincourt, Ontario, Canada.

The Criminal Law Reporter. The Bureau of National Affairs, Inc., 1231 25th St., N.W., Washington, D.C. 20037.

The Criminal Law Review. Sweet and Maxwell Ltd., 11 New Fetter Ln., London EC4P 4EE, England.

From the State Capitals: Judicial Administration Modernization Progress. Bethune Jones Inc., 321 Sunset Avenue, Asbury Park, N.J. 07712.

Journal of Legal Studies. University of Chicago Law School, 1111 E. 60th St., Chicago, Ill. 60637.

Judicature. American Judicature Society, 1155 E. 60th St., Chicago, Ill. 60637.

The Justice System Journal. Institute for Court Management, 1612 Tremont Pl., Suite 210, Denver, Colo. 80202.

Trial. The Association of Trial Lawyers of America, 20 Garden St., Cambridge, Mass. 01238.

CORRECTIONS

American Journal of Corrections. American Correctional Association, World Publishing Co., 9 No. Fourth St., Minneapolis, Minn. 55401.

Corrections Digest. Washington Crime News Service, 7620 Little River Tpke., Annadale, Va. 22003.

Corrections Magazine. Correctional Information Service, Inc., 300 East 44th St., N.Y., N.Y. 10017.

Corrections Perspective. Minnesota Department of Corrections, 430 Metro Sq. Bldg., St. Paul, Minn. 55101.

International Journal of Offender Therapy and Comparative Criminology. Association for Psychiatric Treatment of Offenders, 199 Glouchester Place, London NW1, England.

Prison Journal. The Pennsylvania Prison Society, 311 S. Juniper St., Philadelphia, Pa. 19107.

PROBATION AND PAROLE

Federal Probation Quarterly. Administrative Offices of the United States Courts, Supreme Court Bldg., Washington, D.C. 20544.

Probation Journal. National Association of Probation Officers, Ambassador House, Brigstock Rd., Thornton Heath, Surrey CR4 7SG, England.

JUVENILE JUSTICE

Delinquency and Rehabilitation Report. Grafton Publications, Inc., 667 Madison Ave., N.Y.C., N.Y. 10021.

From the State Capitals: Juvenile Delinquency and Family Relations. Bethune Jones, Inc., 321 Sunset Avenue, Asbury Park, N.J. 07712.

Juvenile Justice. National Council of Juvenile Court Judges, Box 8000 University Sta., Reno, Nev. 89507.

Juvenile Justice Digest. Washington Crime News Services, 7620 Little River Tpke., Annadale, Va. 22003.

PRIVATE SECURITY

NBFAA Signal. National Burglar and Fire Alarm Association, 1730 Pennsylvania Ave., N.W., Washington, D.C. 20006.

Protection Management. Man and Manager, Inc., 700 Broadway, N.Y., N.Y. 10003.

Security Gazette. Security Gazette, Ltd., 326 St. John St., London ECIV 4QD, England.

Security Management. American Society for Industrial Security, 2000 K St., N.W. Suite 651, Washington, D.C. 20006.

Security Systems Digest. Washington Crime News Services, 7620 Little River Tpke., Annadale, Va. 22003.

Security World. Security World Publishing Company, 2639 S. LaCienega Blvd., Los Angeles, Calif. 90634.

GENERAL OR MISCELLANEOUS

The British Journal of Criminology. Stephens and Son Ltd., 11 New Fetter Lane, London, EC4 P4EE England.

Canadian Journal of Criminology and Corrections. Canadian Criminology and Corrections Association, 55 Parkdale, Ottawa KIY IE5 Ontario, Canada.

Crime and Delinquency. National Council on Crime and Delinquency, 411 Hackensack Ave., Hackensack, N.J. 07601.

Crime Control Digest. Washington Crime News Services, 7620 Little River Tpke., Annadale, Va. 22003.

Crimes and Punishment Encyclopedia. Symphonette Press, 6 Commercial St., Hicksville, N.Y. 11803.

Criminal Justice. American Bar Association, 1155 E. 60th St., Chicago, Ill. 60637.

Criminal Justice and Behavior. Sage Publications, Inc., 275 S. Beverly Dr., Beverly Hills, Calif. 90210.

Criminal Justice Digest. Washington Crime News Services, 7617 Little River Tpke., Annadale, Va. 22003.

Criminal Justice Review. Georgia State University, Atlanta, Ga. 30303.

Criminal Justice Newsletter. National Council on Crime and Delinquency, 411 Hackensack Ave., Hackensack, N.J. 07601.

Criminology: An Interdisciplinary Journal. Sage Publications, Inc., 275 S. Beverly Dr., Beverly Hills, Calif. 90210.

Howard Journal of Penology & Crime Prevention. Howard League for Penal Reform, 125 Kennington Park Rd., London, England.

International Journal of Criminology and Penology. Seminar Press, 111 Fifth Ave., N.Y., N.Y. 10003.

Issues in Criminology. University of California, 101 Haviland Hall, Berkeley, Calif. 94720.

Journal of Criminal Justice. Pergamon Press, Inc., Maxwell House, Fairview Pk., Elmsford, N.Y. 10523.

Journal of Criminal Law and Criminology. Williams and Wilkens Company, 428 E. Preston St., Baltimore, Md. 21202.

Journal of Research in Crime and Delinquency. National Council on Crime and Delinquency, 411 Hackensack Ave., Hackensack, N.J. 07601.

Law and Contemporary Problems. Duke University Law School, Durham, N.C. 27706.

Training Aids Digest. Washington Crime News Services, 7617 Little River Tpke., Annadale, Va. 22003.

Victimology: An International Journal. Visage Press, Inc., 3409 Wisconsin Ave., N.W., Washington, D.C. 20016.

INDEX